Deterrence in American Foreign Policy:
Theory and Practice

Deterrence in American Foreign Policy:
Theory and Practice

ALEXANDER L. GEORGE
RICHARD SMOKE

COLUMBIA UNIVERSITY PRESS
New York

Alexander L. George is Professor of Political Science at Stanford University and the author of several books, including *Woodrow Wilson and Colonel House* (with Juliette L. George, 1956), and *The Chinese Communist Army in Action* (1967). Richard Smoke is currently a Fellow at the Center for Advanced Study in the Behavioral Sciences in Stanford. He has been a postdoctoral fellow in psychology at the University of California at Berkeley, and a lecturer and assistant dean for research at the John F. Kennedy School of Government, Harvard University.

Library of Congress Cataloging in Publication Data

George, Alexander L
   Deterrence in American foreign policy: theory and practice

   Includes bibliographical references.
   1. United States—Foreign relations—1945– 2. United States—Military policy. 3. Deterrence
(Strategy)   I. Smoke, Richard, joint author.
II. Title.
E744.G46   1974   327.73   74-7120
ISBN 0-231-03837-2
ISBN 0-231-03838-0 (pbk.)

10 9

For my daughter Mary
                —A.L.G.

To the memory of my father
                —R.S.

Preface

ALMOST FROM THE BEGINNING of the Cold War, critics of American foreign policy have pointed to the dangers of overreliance by Washington on deterrence threats to prevent direct or indirect communist encroachments against other countries. This book provides the first comprehensive, in-depth assessment of both the theory and practice of deterrence in American foreign policy since World War II. Eleven historical cases are examined from this perspective, and the study concludes with a detailed and sobering analysis of the complex requirements of deterrence strategy and of the difficulties policy-makers can expect to encounter in attempting to use it.

This book is the latest in a series of publications to emerge from a research program on "Theory and Practice in International Relations," which is directed by Alexander George at Stanford University. One of the purposes of this program is to provide a clearer understanding and a critical evaluation of some of the major kinds of activities—such as deterrence, coercive diplomacy, crisis management, détente—that actors in world politics engage in from time to time in dealing with acute conflicts of interest with other countries.

To achieve this objective requires the development of a policy-relevant theory of international relations. The special kind of research approach needed for this purpose is outlined and applied in this book. (See especially chapters 4 and 16 and the Appendix.) Both authors have applied this research approach in earlier studies: Alexander George in *The Limits of Coercive Diplomacy* (1971, together with David K. Hall and William E. Simons); and Richard Smoke in his doctoral thesis at the Massachusetts Institute of Technology, *The Control of Escalation*, which was awarded the Helen Dwight Reid prize by the American Political Science Association for the best Ph.D. dissertation in international relations completed in 1971 or 1972.

While both authors share responsibility for the entire book, they divided the labor of preparing initial drafts of chapters. Richard Smoke is primarily responsible for chapters 1, 2, 3, 13, 14, and the Appendix. He is coauthor with Alexander George of chapters 4 and 21. Alexander George is responsible for the conception and design of the study, and is primarily responsible for chapters 5, 6, 7, 9, 12, 15, 16, 17, 18, 19, and 20. We received material assistance from Stephen J. Genco, a graduate student at Stanford University, who is primarily responsible for chapters 10 and 11, and is coauthor with Alexander George of chapter 8.

We take pleasure in expressing appreciation for the invaluable help and encouragement received from others. Exploratory work on deterrence was undertaken by the senior author in 1966–1968 while he was a member of the Social Science Department of The RAND Corporation. Useful comments and suggestions were received from colleagues. At that time Jane Howland provided invaluable research assistance and prepared preliminary versions of some of the cases presented in Part Two. Continuing the project after moving to Stanford University in 1968, the senior author benefited from the assistance of a number of students in graduate and undergraduate seminars: Pamela Ellis, Harry Harding, Raymond Morrow, John Oneal, Elye Pitts, Stanley Wells, and Frederik Wiant.

Richard Smoke joined the project as research colleague and coauthor in 1969; at that time he was engaged in research on the related topic of escalation control employing a similar research approach.

A number of scholars have read and commented on the entire manuscript or parts thereof: Ole Holsti, Burton Levin, Bruce Russett, Thomas Schelling, and Allen Whiting. Chapter

11 benefited from a careful reading by several specialists on American policy in the Middle East: John C. Campbell, Louis Gerson, and Malcolm Kerr; Fuad Jabber incorporated some of their suggestions and his own into the present version of this chapter.

For invariably cheerful and efficient secretarial and administrative support we are grateful to Lois Renner.

For financial support that enabled him and Richard Smoke to complete the study, the senior author expresses deep appreciation to the Committee on International Studies at Stanford University and to the National Science Foundation which awarded him a research grant for 1971–1972. The authors would also like to thank Doubleday & Company, Inc. for permission to use quotations from Roger Hilsman's *To Move a Nation* and Dwight D. Eisenhower's *The White House Years: Waging Peace, 1956–1961*, and the editors of *Policy Sciences* for permission to print, as the Appendix to this book, a much condensed version of the article that appeared under the title "Theory for Policy in International Relations" in *Policy Sciences*, December 1973.

The authors assume sole responsibility for the views expressed in this book.

Contents

Deterrence in American Foreign Policy:
Theory and Practice

Introduction

THIS BOOK PRESENTS a critical examination of deterrence
theory and deterrence strategy as they have been applied in
American foreign policy since the end of World War II. We
should make clear at the outset that the study is *not* concerned
with the problem of "strategic deterrence"—that is, the effort of
the United States and the Soviet Union to deter each other from
launching a general war. Strategic deterrence has a number of
special properties that make its problems relatively easy to conceptualize. After examining these particular properties early in
the book, in chapter 2, we leave aside this special kind of deterrence and give it no further attention.

Our study focuses, rather, on the effort of the United States
to deter *limited* conflicts that might start through encroachments by other countries on U.S. allies or neutral states. We
approach this problem of deterrence of limited warfare from the
standpoint of both theory and practice. This kind of deterrence
has played a major, even dominating role in United States
foreign policy since shortly after World War II. The onset of the
Cold War and its intensification generated strong pressure on
successive American administrations to find ways of using deterrence strategy as an instrument for containing the expansion
of Soviet influence and, more generally, the spread of international communism. This development stimulated efforts to understand deterrence processes in the international arena more
clearly and to conceptualize the requirements of deterrence in

the form of a general theory for possible policy applications.

The task of conceptualizing is appreciably more difficult in some ways for deterrence of limited conflicts than for strategic deterrence. Formulation of the former kind of deterrence theory has tended to follow, rather than leading or guiding, practice in employing deterrence strategy in U.S. Cold War policy. Part One of this study offers a critical assessment of deterrence theory as it relates to limited conflicts. We conclude that this theory has been markedly less useful to policy-makers than it might have been. But while its productive impact on American foreign policy was limited, it did have the negative effect of reinforcing the policy-makers' tendency to rely too heavily on deterrence strategy and deterrent threats in lieu of the more flexible instruments of inter-nation influence associated with classical diplomacy.

These conclusions are widely shared. But the causal factors underlying this critical assessment of deterrence theory have been ill understood. In attempting to explicate them, we find it necessary to emphasize the way in which deterrence theory was derived, largely deductively, from a priori premises. A major objective of this study is to demonstrate the questionable character of many of the premises and assumptions on which deterrence theory has been based. The oversimplified and often erroneous character of these theoretical assumptions is best demonstrated by comparing them with the more complex variables and processes associated with efforts to employ deterrence strategy in real-life historical cases. Accordingly, Part Two of the study presents eleven case histories in which the United States either applied deterrence strategy or considered applying it on behalf of weaker allies and neutral states between 1948 and 1963. (More recent events of this kind are discussed more briefly.) Remarkably few efforts have been made to weigh carefully the available historical experience in applying deterrence. The failure to do so has obscured the severe limitations of the guidance that deterrence theory has offered policy-makers.

We believe—and seek to demonstrate—that systematic study of relevant historical experience can assist in developing a better theory of deterrence. Further, we believe and attempt to show that such an *inductively* derived theory of deterrence will emphasize the limitations and risks of deterrence strategy, as well as its possible uses under certain circumstances. In Part Three of the study, we begin (although we certainly do not complete) this kind of reformulation of deterrence theory, deriving our conclusions explicitly from the empirical material of the case histories in Part Two. We give particular emphasis to developing a *differentiated* theory, one that discriminates among varieties and patterns of deterrence situations. This kind of theory offers policy-makers greater assistance in diagnosing new problems as they arise, in assessing what sort of deterrence strategy may be appropriate to them, and more importantly, in judging whether deterrence is indeed the proper kind of policy to apply to them.

While the study focuses on deterrence theory, our critical appraisal also extends to certain aspects of American foreign policy itself during the Cold War. We believe that a critical appraisal and reformulation of deterrence theory will benefit from, and indeed requires, a critical stance also toward the use of deterrence strategy in American foreign policy. Since deterrence is an instrument of foreign policy, the uses and limitations of deterrence strategy in any given context depend inescapably upon the nature of that foreign policy.

American foreign policy during these years must be kept in mind for another reason as well. As emphasized in Part One, deterrence theory per se does not define its own scope or relevance as an instrument of foreign policy. That is, the general theory of deterrence does not indicate when a state should attempt to apply deterrence strategy to protect weaker countries. The answer to this question can be determined only with reference to that state's foreign policy, not by deterrence theory per se. Deterrence is at times a necessary or useful instrument of foreign policy, but the correct and prudent use of deterrence strategy is by no means self-evident or easily determined in all circumstances.

While the American policy of "containment" of the Soviet

Union required some use of deterrence, the need for selective, discriminating use of deterrence and of alliance commitments gradually gave way to an overly rigid attempt to exclude loss of any territory (even the offshore islands lying a few miles off mainland China!). Our critical appraisal of American foreign policy since World War II, however, stops well short of the more extreme "revisionist" theses. Rather, we tend to agree with those who, like Senator William Fulbright,[1] in looking back upon the early postwar world find that something like containment in Europe was necessary and useful at the time, even while they deplore some of the ways in which it was justified and implemented—particularly in its extension to Asia and the Middle East.

Thus, it can be said on behalf of the American policy of containment and its handmaiden, deterrence, that they did at least establish some firm lines in the postwar world, when so much was fluid. The vacuum created in Central and Eastern Europe by the defeat of Nazi Germany was a source of dangerous conflict in the relations of the Western powers with the Soviet Union. In that historical situation something like the Cold War was probably inevitable, although its intensification and prolongation were another matter. Still, unless the United States was to abandon Western Europe to its fate, measures like the Marshall Plan and NATO were necessary for the strengthening of noncommunist societies in Western Europe in the coming division of Europe. Whether NATO and the U.S deterrence commitment were necessary cannot be judged solely with reference to whether the Soviet Union really intended, or would be tempted by the weakness of Western Europe, to engage in naked military aggression. Other maneuvers to extend Soviet control were also possible. And in any case, whether or not concern over Soviet intentions was fully justified, uncertainty on this score generated acute psychological

[1] J. William Fulbright, "In Thrall to Fear," *The New Yorker*, January 8, 1972, pp. 47–62. This article was incorporated with minor revisions in his later book, *The Crippled Giant: American Foreign Policy and Its Domestic Consequences* (New York, Random House, 1972).

anxieties and contributed to political instability within some of the Western European countries.

Deterrence is a policy which, if it succeeds, can only frustrate an opponent who aspires to changing the international status quo in his favor. The consequences of continued frustration, however, are not easily predictable and are not necessarily benign. The most reliable benefit successful deterrence can offer is more time—time in which some of the conflict-generating or conflict-exacerbating elements in a historical situation can abate, so that deterrence will no longer be necessary or, at any rate, so critical for the maintenance of peace. One possibility is that continued frustration under conditions that are imperfectly understood may indeed lead an opponent to abandon the objectives or modify the means of pursuing them that have contributed to conflict and tension. Thus, containment was applied to the Soviet Union in the hope that it would furnish time for developments in Soviet society and Soviet leadership to bring about a mellowing process, a lessening of the insecurities and strong ideological motives that gave Soviet foreign policy an expansionist thrust. Such a mellowing does appear to have occurred in the intervening years, though observers disagree on the dimensions, stability, and significance of the change and, indeed, on whether it is the Soviets who have changed or the Western leaders and public who have come to a more correct view of the nature of Soviet foreign policy.

Another possibility, of course, is that deterrence gives the opposing parties time to work out an accommodation of their conflicting interests, thereby reducing tensions and the potential for overt conflict in their relationship. But time is a precious commodity, and the failure or inability of the parties concerned to make use of it to reach an accommodation can easily transform deterrence into a more permanent way of life. We agree with those critics of American policy who view the Cold War as a tragedy of misperceptions and possibly missed opportunities. With the intensification and prolongation of the Cold War, both the United States and the Soviet Union came to rely too heavily on deterrence strategy and strategic power to achieve a broad range of conflicting foreign policy objectives. This contributed in an important and unforeseen way to bringing the two nuclear superpowers to the most dangerous of their confrontations in Cuba. Stepping back from the brink of thermonuclear war in the autumn of 1962, Kennedy and Khrushchev were finally able to break out of the straightjacket of the Cold War. The search for détente and accommodation through patient negotiation had finally begun.

But by this time the deformation of containment had led to a proliferation of American deterrence commitments throughout the world. Faced with complex and fluid situations in Asia and the Middle East that had arisen from the postwar shattering of empires, American policy-makers succumbed to the temptation to cope with them by applying containment on a global scale. In Asia, the United States attempted to apply containment to a situation which was not neatly structured, as was Europe, for a classical *defensive* application of deterrence strategy. The situation in Asia differed in important respects from the one in Europe. The task of applying containment and deterrence strategy against the Soviet Union was made easier by the fact that the Soviets had no unsatisfied irredentist claims; besides, the Soviet Union had enhanced its security by acquiring control over countries on its border in Eastern Europe. In contrast, Communist China was by no means a satisfied power. The Communist Chinese had yet to eliminate their rival in the civil war and to recover Taiwan. The threat which the Chinese Nationalist regime posed to Peking's security interests was much magnified as the United States drew closer to Chiang and gave him increased support. Because the Chinese civil war had not run its course, the American effort to employ deterrence strategy on behalf of the Nationalist regime on Taiwan resulted in a confusion of containment with "liberation," thereby greatly exacerbating tensions and inviting dangerous crises.

Similarly, following the Suez crisis of 1956, American policy-makers attempted to cope with still a different kind of complex and fluid situation in the Middle East by extending containment to that area as well. The unique situation in the Middle East, however, was probably even less suited to containment and deterrence than was the situation in Asia. Not only did the Soviet Union have no irredentist claims in this area of the world, but there were also no communist states in the region that could be seen as playing a role comparable to that of China, North Korea, or North Vietnam in Asia. But by 1956 the United States' reliance on deterrence threats and alliance commitments as the primary tools of its foreign policy vis-à-vis the Soviet Union had become a rigidified response to almost any perceived communist encroachment anywhere in the world. Thus, when U.S. leaders began to take notice of increased Soviet economic activities in the Middle East following the retraction of the American offer to assist Egypt in the building of the Aswan Dam, and when the sudden elimination of British influence in the area created what was perceived to be a "power vacuum" following the Suez crisis, the Eisenhower Administration responded with a deterrence-alliance policy that was completely inappropriate for the situation. The policy, aimed at deterring communist military thrusts into the region, proved powerless in counteracting the Soviet economic moves and, at the same time, alienated most Middle Eastern states because of its lack of relevance to what they considered to be the true problems of the region. The two main results of this ultimate extension of misapplied deterrence strategy under the Eisenhower Administration were severe damage to the Western position in the Middle East and at least the beginnings of a reevaluation of the efficacy of global containment as the backbone of United States foreign policy.

A postcontainment era now characterizes U.S. relations with Communist China as well as with the Soviet Union. But the problem of deterrence does not thereby vanish. Indeed, in some respects the problems of deterrence have become even more complicated. The final chapter of this study argues that in this new period United States policy-makers must resort to deterrence more selectively than in the past, and suggests a few guidelines for the admittedly difficult task of defining more careful and flexible deterrence policies within the framework of a new, as yet largely undefined foreign policy appropriate for the post–Cold War era.

Part One

The Nature of Contemporary Deterrence Theory

Chapter 1

Deterrence in History

IN ITS MOST GENERAL FORM, deterrence is simply the persuasion of one's opponent that the costs and/or risks of a given course of action he might take outweigh its benefits. But even within the context of deterrence as an aspect of international relations, the many kinds of situations in which this relationship between actors can occur and the historically changing international system within which such situations arise generate enormous complexity. Furthermore, the practitioners and theorists of deterrence approach these complexities from different perspectives, depending in part upon their own immediate purposes.[1]

[1] At least four general perspectives on the theory and practice of deterrence can usefully be distinguished. *Policy-makers* are interested in focusing upon operational concepts which can readily be translated into concrete action and declaratory policies. (We will discuss this in much greater detail subsequently.) *General theorists* of deterrence, by contrast, have focused upon its abstract theory, generally using strategic nuclear deterrence as their paradigm and later extending this paradigm to other applications. Efforts of this kind include the works of Schelling, Kaufmann, Snyder, Kahn, Pool's "Deterrence as an Influence Process," and Russett's "Calculus of Deterrence" and "Pearl Harbor: Deterrence Theory and Decision Theory." *International relations specialists* have tended to focus upon the relationships among "deterrence," the "balance of power," "collective security," and the nature of "the international system." In addition to the above, on deterrence and the balance of power see Claude, *Power and International Relations*, chapters 3 and 4, and Morgenthau, *Politics among Nations*. Finally there is a special group of theorists, sometimes called the *"spiral theorists,"* who focus upon the potential of deterrence policies for generating conflict and possible ways of supplementing deterrence with policies for con-

We begin our study, therefore, with an admittedly cursory review of the historical experience of deterrence to place the contemporary problem in context and to suggest a handful of ways in which technological and international-systemic changes can affect deterrence. If, as we suggest at the conclusion of this study, deterrence in the post–Cold War era may be taking on aspects reminiscent of earlier, especially "balance-of-power," eras, there may be an additional value in beginning from a historical perspective.

Deterrence before the Atomic Era

Theorizing about deterrence seems to be a rather new phenomenon, but its practice in a commonsensical, instinctive way must be as old as the military art. One of our earliest military writers, Thucydides, in his *Peloponnesian War* recounts many instances where one side or another maneuvered for allies or other advantages in such a way that its opponent would think that beginning a war, or expanding it, would not be worth the risks or costs. Among other early writers, Emperor Leo of Byzantium and Machiavelli both emphasized the "show of force" and similar devices as economical means of persuading an enemy that the costs and risks of aggressive action might be too high.

While the Thirty Years' War in northern Europe was causing devastation such as had not been seen since the depths of the Dark Ages,[2] the Italian *condotierri* were engaged in elegant

---

flict-reduction. Representative discussions include Boulding, "National Images and International Systems," and Etzioni, *The Hard Way to Peace;* also Milburn, "The Concept of Deterrence"; Charles Osgood, *An Alternative to War or Surrender;* Rapaport, *Strategy and Conscience;* Singer, "Threat-Perception and the Armament-Tension Dilemma," and *Deterrence, Arms Control, and Disarmament.* For a critical appraisal of "spiral theory" see the forthcoming study by Robert Jervis now tentatively entitled *Perception and International Relations.*

[2] Not only did millions—indeed, a significant fraction of the entire population of Europe—die in this war, but in many districts most of the towns and villages

battles of maneuver in which high casualties or costs were not acceptable, and a general faced with the prospect of them would sooner surrender.[3] Similarly, the absolute monarchies that arose in Europe after the exhaustion of the Thirty Years' War soon evolved a pattern of "limited warfare" in which the threat of inflicting high costs played at least as great a role as their actual infliction. Due to limitations in available manpower and wealth and the disputants' mutual desire not to ruin what they were contesting, the threat to go to war and, once at war, to endanger by maneuvers were an important part of the game: "The ultimate goal was the capture of a fortress or a town; but the game was often decided, almost bloodlessly, by a skillful maneuver into a superior position."[4] According to eighteenth-century conceptions of honor, a belligerent or potential belligerent faced with superior forces, or a potential belligerent faced with an apparently superior combination of probable foes, could surrender or abandon his objective without a fight and with no loss of esteem.[5]

The *levy en masse*, invented by the French Revolution and inherited by Napoleon, raised French capabilities to a point where the rest of Europe combined could not deter, and for a period could not defeat, Napoleon's expansionist adventures. In the period following the Congress of Vienna, however, the principal powers returned to a pattern of small military standing capabilities and limited commitments to warfare.

The balance-of-power system, adopted generally in the

---

were utterly destroyed. See, for instance, Fuller's *Military History;* or, for a longer treatment, Gindely's *History of the Thirty Years War.*

[3] Fuller, *Military History,* contains a treatment. For a brief description, see the same author's *Conduct of War.*

[4] R. E. Osgood, *Limited War,* p. 63.

[5] R. E. Osgood's *Limited War* contains a good brief treatment of this period, as does Fuller's *Conduct of War.* The latter quotes Ferrero as writing that "Restricted warfare was one of the loftiest achievements of the eighteenth century. It belongs to a class of hot-house plants which can only thrive in an aristocratic and qualitative civilization. We are no longer capable of it. It is one of the fine things we have lost as a result of the French Revolution" (p. 25). See also Speier, *Social Order and the Risks of War,* pp. 223–52.

eighteenth century and reaching its height in the nineteenth, had a number of features in common with what today would be called "deterrence" systems. In particular, the core concept of the balance-of-power system was that the military capabilities available to any combination of powers should be sufficiently balanced so that full-scale conflict would appear profitless. In effect a "mutual deterrent balance" remained stable for approximately a century after the close of the Napoleonic wars (though a few small wars were fought under its umbrella): "The typical limited war in Europe during the eighteenth and nineteenth centuries was fought in order to achieve marginal adjustments in the balance of power that diplomacy had failed to secure." [6] Indeed, a principal aim of diplomacy was to insure the stability of the deterrent balance, and reinforce it as required.

It is slightly surprising, in retrospect, how many of the concepts of contemporary deterrence theory—commitments, and how to reinforce or escape them, signaling, comparatively fine calculations of opposing forces, the fear of escalation and the use of that fear as a deterrent, the mutual assumption of rationality—were implicitly part of the diplomatic practice of the balance-of-power system, without being articulated in this kind of terminology.

Indeed, eighteenth- and nineteenth-century diplomatic and military history provides the politico-military analyst with a rich lode of empirical material for the expansion and refinement of contemporary concepts. This history has not been studied systematically from such a perspective, and cannot be here; but the mention of a few instances that include aspects of deterrence may be suggestive.[7]

---

[6] R. E. Osgood, *Limited War*, p. 62.

[7] The historical examples in the following passage are drawn from René Albrecht-Carrie, *Diplomatic History of Europe, passim.* The scope of this discussion does not permit detailed empirical or theoretical analysis of the differences and similarities between a "balance of power" system and a "deterrence" system. For a provocative, though now somewhat obsolescent, abstract discussion of these matters, see "From Balance to Deterrence," by Arthur Lee Burns. Two other deservedly classic analyses of the balance of power system are "Balance of Power in Theory and Practice," chapter 8 of Wolfers' *Discord and Collabo-*

Early in the Franco-Prussian War, for example, Bismarck carefully led Austria, then considering intervention on the French side, to believe that any such act would trigger Russian involvement on the Prussian side. Austrian decision-makers were reluctant to risk their then rather delicately poised empire in the fires of a general European war, and Bismarck's threat of escalation was successful in deterring Austrian entrance. Again, Britain and sometimes France demonstrated their commitment to oppose Russian intervention in the Ottoman Empire by periodically sending naval squadrons to the area in what today would be called a "signal." In 1854 such an action escalated into the Crimean War; in 1878 a similar action coerced Russia into agreeing to an early end to a Russo-Turkish War. Throughout the nineteenth century Britain regularly delivered deterrent threats against any intervention in the Low Countries (often contemplated by France); and these were as regularly successful. Napoleon III's abandonment of his "Belgian railways scheme" in 1869 after receiving a stern warning from Britain is one of many instances.

Though the measures that nineteenth-century powers took to demonstrate commitment and reinforce deterrence differ somewhat in details from those open to the Cold War superpowers, the earlier generations of statesmen were at least as imaginative, if often no more successful, in finding military and diplomatic tools to deter (and coerce) others. Mobilization of one's forces was, of course, the most serious of measures, but piecemeal mobilizations or other preparatory acts could serve as lesser warnings: in the summer of 1870 Austria decided against mobilization but in favor of purchasing horses and accelerating several key railroad construction projects—two "long lead time

---

ration, and "The International System," chapter 2 of Kaplan's *System and Process in International Politics*. Also important are "The Balance of Power in the Missile Age," by Glenn Snyder, "The Balance of Power: Prescription, Concept, or Propaganda," by Ernest Haas, and "An Analytic Study of the Balance of Power Theories," by Dina Zinnes. For more extended discussions, see "Theories of Balance and Imbalance," Part Four-A of *International Politics and Foreign Policy*, Rosenau, ed.; and *The Balance of Power and Nuclear Deterrence*, Gareau, ed.

items," as they would be called today—as a hedge and a demonstration of resolution. And in 1859, a partial mobilization by Prussia was instrumental in deterring Napoleon III from pursuing his war with Austria beyond its early, somewhat inconclusive stages; the Armistice of Villafranca, followed by a peace treaty, was a direct result.

Similarly, the dispatching of naval forces to trouble spots became during the nineteenth century a highly conventional, even slightly ritualized, codebook for the demonstration of a commitment—the size of the squadron or fleet dispatched often serving as an index of the power's commitment and perception of the seriousness of a crisis. So frequently was this technique resorted to—especially by Britain—that it apparently proved itself to be an ideal demonstrative device. It was effective in this role not only because it carried a threat of escalation—as in the Crimean case and in the accidental Navarino Bay episode of 1827 that was the proximate cause of Greek independence—but also because the limited forces involved often could effect a local military operation under the umbrella of the overall stable deterrent balance—as in the French capture of the city of Algiers in 1830.

The exchange of military observers was a technique designed both to bind an ally more tightly and to deter third parties: in 1869 and early in 1870, the French and Austrians exchanged military missions, leaving the French with the impression that they possessed a firm military ally. (As it happened, the Austrian observers were struck chiefly with the poor state of France's defenses, and the gambit failed, both as a means of guaranteeing Austrian intervention and as a deterrent to Prussia.) But the seeds of Franco-Russian alliance were sown in General Boisdeffre's military mission to Russia of 1891, which led to the signing of a military convention the following year on a return visit.

Since the rough balance required for stable deterrence was provided not by approximate technological parity, as in the mid-twentieth-century case, but by shifting diplomatic alliances, the usual object was to insure that one had as many great-power players on one's own side as were numbered among the likely opponents.[8] Accordingly, to be diplomatically "isolated"— without apparent allies—was to have one's deterrent capacities undermined, and to isolate one's opponent was the prerequisite to going to war against him. Russia was isolated in this way in 1853, partly by accident, prior to the Crimean War. And Bismarck, before launching his major wars, carefully isolated his intended victims with great deliberation: his Biarritz conference with Napoleon in October 1865 had (unknown to Napoleon) no other real purpose than to insure that France would not join Austria in the imminent war; in 1870, besides his escalation threat to Austria already alluded to, Bismarck employed a well-orchestrated series of moves to insure British neutrality.

Since the deterrent balance flowed from the number and weight of major players on each "side" at any moment, the principal instrument in constructing the deterrence system was the treaty of alliance. But since the system had to remain flexible, such treaties were generally of short term, and highly conditional. The result was a complicated web of diplomatic agreements of varying formality and duration. The fact that some of these were secret was not necessarily a hindrance to the system, for revelation could be a potent device for reinforcing deterrence. Thus Bismarck signed a secret, five-year alliance treaty with Austria in 1879 with the quite conscious intention of revealing it to the Tsar—against whom it was principally aimed— in the event of a crisis. On other occasions, the terms of Bismarck's treaty with one ally were used to help deter that ally from making any hostile moves against another ally. The passionate Italian *irredenta* movement against Austria was effectively stifled for a period when Bismarck drew Italy into the Triple Alliance of 1882. And the terms, as well as the negotiations, of the Reinsurance Treaty of 1887 between Germany and

---

[8] During much of the century, Britain employed a slight variation on this theme—to retain no allies, but to insure such divisions among the Continental powers that no general combination against Britain would be possible. It was the growing imbalance on the Continent in the early years of this century that forced Britain into an increasingly tight and permanent relationship with France, thus in part leading to World War I by generating increasing rigidities.

Russia very explicitly warned Russia against any attack on Austria, then Germany's ally.[9]

Several other features of the eighteenth- and nineteenth-century system merit brief mention. Deterrence was further undergirded by the perception of most of the powers that large-scale warfare might upset the domestic social order. Metternich's well-ordered Concert of Europe effectively maintained almost complete peace for some thirty years following the Congress of Vienna in 1815, in major part because all the powers, including monarchist France, had been frightened by the disruptions of the French Revolution. Later in the century, the great influence of the merchant and capitalist classes similarly worked against adventurism; in Britain, especially, these elements keenly appreciated the costs and risks of major warfare.

Finally, the deterrent system generated several devices designed to increase its flexibility. The doctrine of "compensation" allowed a power that for some reason had lost a possession, or found a rival gaining one, to receive an offsetting benefit, lest he otherwise accumulate motives for upsetting the balance. A different kind of flexibility was provided by two principles of international law, "retorsion" and "reprisal," that entitled an injured party to take limited, legally sanctioned diplomatic or military steps to regain its prerogatives—or to coercively threaten to do so—without the stability of the system being jeopardized. All these devices helped to drain tensions out of the system, thereby preventing accumulated grievances from motivating grave crises; and all of them provided recognized boundaries within which violence could be contained, thereby helping to minimize escalation.

As the end of the century drew nigh, two developments took place that were to foreshadow twentieth-century concepts of deterrence. One was the Anglo-German naval race, perhaps the closest analogue in history to the Cold War arms race. For a

[9] A clause in the treaty rendered it inoperative in the event of Russian attack on Austria, and in the course of negotiating it Bismarck made the rather dramatic move of briefly showing the Russian Ambassador the text of Germany's secret treaty with Austria, pledging military alliance if Austria were attacked.

period of approximately twenty years, England and Germany devoted very serious efforts to out-building each other in naval capital ships. The efforts were accompanied on both sides by novel doctrines—in Germany, the "risk theory," arguing that a sufficiently large German fleet would make the British one unusable due to fear of risking it in combat; in England, the dawning recognition that Britain, for the first time in history, needed naval allies. Japan and the United States were gradually approached.

But it was the coming of the airplane that truly set the stage for twentieth-century warfare and deterrence theory. A short aircraft-building race immediately preceded World War I, and that war was not many months old before both sides possessed a significant capability for dropping bombs hundreds of miles behind enemy lines. Beginning about 1915, military professionals, theorists, and the public in the technically advanced countries believed that their major cities were vulnerable to destruction from the air even while their air, sea, and land forces remained potent.[10] In 1917 the Germans subjected London to a serious bombing offensive, leading to panic and rioting by the city's inhabitants.[11] The war ended, however, before either side attained the capability of inflicting really widespread damage on the other's cities or civilian populace.

That limitation would not apply to the next war, it was widely realized; and the interwar period witnessed considerable theorization about the future role of air power. General Giulio Douhet, an Italian, was the most influential but by no means the only such theorist.[12] The great destructive effect on what today we would call "countervalue targets" which these theorists postulated was picked up and dramatized by popular writers. H. G. Wells's nightmare fantasy, *The Shape of Things to Come*, was the most widely known projection of a future world war, first as a book and later as a movie; and in prophesy-

[10] Quester, *Deterrence before Hiroshima*, chapters 3 and 4.

[11] *Ibid.*, pp. 32–38.

[12] The most widely influential work was Douhet's *Command of the Air*.

ing poison-gas attacks on cities it equaled in horror any recent
fantasy of atomic war.

Given this image of the technical possibilities, it is not surprising that the contemporary notion of a mutual deterrent balance eventually emerged. Jonathan Griffin wrote during the
1930s that "It would be a balance of terrors—for that is what the
balance of power, loaded with bombs, should truly be called. In
the end one group must strike." [13] The pessimism of the last
sentence, however, accurately reflects the failure of the interwar theorists to arrive at a concept of an indefinitely *stable*
balance of deterrence. Aside from the novelty of this concept,
there are several reasons for that failure. Many observers, especially in the thirties, accurately observed that the Versailles
Treaty was more of a truce than a peace, failing to resolve the
underlying power imbalance on the Continent that had
emerged from the Franco-Prussian War. Douhet and most other
theorists were themselves military men, professionally concerned with how to fight a war rather than how to prevent it; the
outbreak was assumed. The *concept* of indefinite stability may
be more easily arrived at in a bipolar universe containing only
two powers; this condition applied during much of the Cold
War but not before it. Finally, Douhet and others made it a
premise of their theories that what we would now call "secure
second-strike forces" were impossible; they assumed a "delicate balance of terror" with all the incentives for "preemption"
we now know that insecure, "first-strike" forces imply.[14]

The atomic bombs that ended World War II and the bipolar
world that emerged out of it set the stage for the emergence of
contemporary deterrence theory: the former made stable deterrence necessary, and the latter made it possible. Nuclear explo-
sives guaranteed that an entire nation could be shockingly

[13] Quoted in Michael Howard's review of Quester's *Deterrence before Hiroshima* in *Survival*, October 1966, p. 334.

[14] For a lucid review of Douhet's doctrines and their importance, see Brodie's
Strategy in the Missile Age, chapter 3. The explanations given in this paragraph
for the failure of the interwar theorists to arrive at a notion of stable deterrence
are not Brodie's but the authors'.

hurt—hurt far beyond the historical experience of modern societies—without its own military capabilities being able to prevent it. It could only be prevented by the threat of equal reprisal. Thus "deterrence" emerged out of the sideshow to seize
the center ring.

What deterrence as a concept had always lacked prior to at
least the interwar decades and did not clearly possess until the
coming of atomic weapons was a sharp, radical distinction between the power to hurt and the power to defeat military
forces—between punishment and victory (or, as some writers
have put it, between "punishment" and "denial"). For Thucydides, Machiavelli, and the "limited warriors" of the eighteenth
and nineteenth centuries, it was generally impossible to hurt an
enemy seriously—to burn his cities, rape his women, and seize
his property—until after one had defeated his military forces.
And since usually he would surrender and cede a portion of his
property first, the power to hurt was not employed, except idio-
syncratically. But with the advent of strategic bombing it became possible to hurt an enemy grievously before (or without)
destroying his military capability. With the opening up of this
possibility, the *threat* to hurt him could be separated—in fact
and therefore in theory—from the threat to engage and destroy
his forces. Deterrence was conceived in its modern sense when
it became possible to threaten vast damage and pain while leaving opposing military forces intact.

Deterrence 1945–1950

But in retrospect it is somewhat surprising not how quickly
but how slowly deterrence theory, and even clarity about the
concept, developed after World War II. Indeed, it is not a great
exaggeration to say that for about five years after the end of the
war, the United States and the West lacked any systematic strategy or theory linking military planning to foreign policy objectives. For several years after World War II, U.S. government

doctrine did not yet seriously consider the next war, its strategy, or its deterrence. The military was chiefly concerned with organizing the largest and most rapid demobilization in history, and with schemes for an imminent and drastic reorganization, consummated in 1947. In the realm of foreign affairs, policy-makers were of two minds about the existence of a serious Soviet threat, were reluctant to abandon their wartime goal of peaceful "collective security" under the United Nations, and were fashioning responses to specific Soviet intiatives on an ad hoc basis.[15]

What was to prove the hub concept of American Cold War foreign policy had its genesis in February of 1946 in a 16-page cable from George Kennan in the American Embassy in Moscow. It was circulated through the government, and expanded and published in July 1947 in *Foreign Affairs* by "Mr. X." As an analysis of "The Sources of Soviet Conduct" and a proof of a serious threat, Kennan's article was quickly accepted by many policy-makers and by important elements of the informed public. As a guide for action, however, it offered only a concept— "containment." Kennan argued the need to imprison communism, politically, economically, and socially, within its existing boundaries. Which among many possible foreign policies would

[15] The scope of this discussion allows only the most cursory and summarized history of the development of U.S. national security and foreign policies in the Cold War period. As a comprehensive treatment of this subject, to 1960, Huntington's *The Common Defense* is still unsurpassed. Somewhat less detailed but covering a longer period is Quester's *Nuclear Diplomacy*. Development of deterrence policy at the strategic level is lucidly reviewed in Kahan's forthcoming *Strategic Arms Policy*. Of many recent histories of the broader, foreign policy aspects of the Cold War, Halle's *Cold War as History* has proved the most influential. A few individuals, to be sure, were concerned with the nature and requirements of deterrence. A group of social scientists led by Bernard Brodie published a prescient but uninfluential book, in part discussing deterrence, as early as 1946: Brodie, ed., *The Absolute Weapon*, especially chapter 2, "The Implications for Military Policy," by Brodie. And even in late 1945 General H. H. ("Hap") Arnold, Chief of Staff of the Army Air Forces, was writing that prevention of future war rested on potential aggressors' knowing that U.S. retaliatory power was "in a state of constant readiness" and would be "devastating" and "immediate." Cited and quoted in Halle, *Cold War as History*, pp. 174–75.

best implement this concept was left unspecified, and it remained for the Truman Doctrine and the Marshall Plan to generate derivative policies in the political and economic realms.

Even less did "containment" represent a politico-military strategic theory. Though the concept had definite implications for policies in the military realm, the raw military threat posed by the communist powers was not considered in the "Mr. X" article—nor apparently in NSC-20, the basic government document (of the winter of 1947–1948) promulgating containment and its attendant policies as official doctrine. Nor, apparently, did any other general policy document prior to 1950 advance an analysis of deterrence, an analysis of the implications of containment for military policy, or any comprehensive strategic theory.[16] General politico-military theory was lacking. Narrower military planning within the services focused upon the contingency of another world war (conceived as total war), and comprehension of the value of forces-in-being for the deterrence of war dawned slowly:

> In the immediate postwar years the concept of deterrence by forces-in-being had little place in military planning. The Joint Chiefs did accord a deterrent role to the atomic bomb, but deterrence was seen as a peculiar function of the bomb and strategic airpower, not of the armed forces as a whole.[17]

Douhet's idea of deterrence still reigned. At the same time that the Truman Administration was dealing with actual

---

[16] Powers, "Who Fathered Containment?" See also Huntington, *The Common Defense*, pp. 39–47 for a review of this period. A classified State Department document dated June 23, 1948 stated or implied that "the maintenance of a permanent state of adequate military preparation" was necessary for "a deterrent"; Millis, *The Forrestal Diaries*, p. 508. Contrary to Huntington's assertion (p. 40), however, this does not amount to "most of the military requirements of a strategy of deterrence." Huntington believes that this paper "was, perhaps, a landmark in the evolution of American strategic thought . . . a new strategy of deterrence." The available record, however, suggests that this paper neither asked the fundamental strategic questions asked in 1950 by NSC-68, nor had any significant influence outside the State Department (if, indeed, inside it). If it was a landmark, it was not a very visible one.

[17] Huntington, *The Common Defense*, p. 45.

politico-military crises in Greece and Berlin, U.S. military doctrine was focusing almost exclusively on an image of an "all-out" World War III, employing essentially the concepts of World War II. Appropriate politico-military implications both of the "containment" concept and of its practice in Greece, Berlin, and elsewhere were not drawn.

This image of "the next war" as "all-out" had other implications. American intelligence estimated that the Soviet Union had been damaged so badly in World War II that it would need some years to recuperate enough to be able to fight another major war. By implicitly equating "warfare" with "all-out war," policy-makers therefore arrived at the conclusion that "warfare" with the communist bloc was unlikely for some time. Deterrence, being viewed only as a concept of warfare, thus was not generally perceived as relevant to crises such as Greece and Korea.

It was the function of the atomic bomb, of course, to deter all-out war. But here American strategists could comfort themselves that only the U.S. possessed "the ultimate weapon," which would have to be absolutely decisive in "the next war" as it had been in the past one. The Soviets were not expected to acquire the bomb for some years. The absence of any challenge to this specific capability seemed to imply little need to analyze that capability. The deterrent function of the bomb seemed almost automatic, and seemed to be more of a fact than a problem needing analysis.

In the postwar period up to 1950, therefore, the general foreign policy problem seemed to have two aspects which were thought to be rather sharply divided from each other. On the one hand was the possibility of "warfare," which meant another all-out war; this seemed unlikely because the Soviets had not yet recovered from World War II and because the American atomic monopoly would deter them. On the other hand was the fact of Soviet expansionism which was generating actual crises, but this was not seen as "warfare" and did not seem to involve "deterrence." In this period the U.S. possessed almost no intellectual awareness of the idea of "limited war" and very few

forces with which to fight one. The lack of any allies with significant military power and the presumedly enormous capabilities
of Soviet forces in Europe further restricted the range of options
available in crises. The result of this fairly sharp dichotomy was
that the Truman Administration did not try to apply deterrence
to the task of immediate containment, as in different ways later
administrations were to do.

The Truman Administration did make a tacit assumption, or
hope, that the U.S. atomic monopoly should somehow intimidate the Soviets from breaches of containment; to a degree it
was presumed that they could not risk local aggression unless
they were ready to risk World War III. But this assumption also
was based critically on the fact of the U.S. atomic monopoly,
which fact did not seem to require or permit analysis of the
application or reinforcement of deterrence.

There was one more factor discouraging the analysis of deterrence. The American atomic arsenal seemed inadequate.
Even as late as 1949, the actual stockpile of nuclear bombs was
quite small—perhaps around a hundred.[18] Given a militarily im-
potent and industrially prostrate Western Europe, an almost
wholly demobilized American army and navy, and gigantic Soviet ground forces in Europe, war planners assumed that every
atomic bomb would be desperately needed to cripple Soviet
war-making power. The American war plan at this time assumed easy Soviet seizure of all of Western Europe, followed
by United States Air Force atomic strikes to cripple Soviet war
industries, and a grand conventional remobilization by the U.S.
and reliberation of Europe on the World War II model.

In sum, during the period 1945–1950 the preconditions for
an articulate and analytical deterrence theory were still mostly
lacking. The elaboration of the requirements for strategic deterrence, which was to proceed so rapidly a decade later, did not
appear necessary while American atomic weapons were both
secure from surprise attack and held in monopoly. And the application of "deterrence" and related concepts to the task of dis-

[18] Quester, *Nuclear Diplomacy*, p. 5.

couraging smaller-scale aggression, to crisis-management, and
to diplomacy was greatly inhibited by an interlocking set of factors present during the immediate postwar scene: the scarcity of
atomic weapons, the extremely low levels to which U.S. conventional capability fell, the lack of militarily potent allies, the
threat to Western Europe of the Red Army, the slow growth of
comprehension that the U.S. faced an indefinite series of politico-military crises around the globe, and the American reluctance to use or threaten force except for objectives worthy of all-
out war.

Deterrence from NSC-68 to the Present

Events of the late 1940s began to alter these factors inhib-
iting the growth of deterrence theory. The Berlin crisis of
1948–1949, the fall of China, and the first Soviet atomic test
explosion years ahead of expectations shocked the American
government into a thorough-going reassessment. An inter-
departmental staff, headed by Paul Nitze, director of the State
Department's Policy Planning Office, generated early in 1950
"the first comprehensive statement of a national strategy" [19] for
the Cold War, a document labeled NSC-68. This analysis concluded that by 1954 the Soviets could make an atomic strike on
the U.S., and might therefore conclude at that time that SAC
was deterred from any strike on the USSR; they might even
hope to destroy most of SAC on the ground. The U.S. would
therefore have to greatly increase its strategic capabilities and
simultaneously increase NATO conventional forces in Europe
to deter the Red Army. Implicit in this analysis were most of the
strategic concepts that would be explicitly identified later—
"first-strike" and "second-strike" forces, different "types" of deterrence, "graduated" deterrence, etc. But before these ideas

[19] Senator Henry Jackson, "How Shall We Forge a Strategy for Survival?"
(address to the National War College, Washington, D.C., April 16, 1959); cited
in Huntington, *The Common Defense*, p. 51.

could be teased out, the Korean War intervened to alter the situation again. Major conventional forces were built up, but to meet the Asian challenge, not the demands of doctrine.

After two years of fighting, the Eisenhower Administration entered office committed to taking a "New Look" at the entire U.S. national security problem. By October 1953 a new planning document (NSC-162/2) [20] had been approved by the President, and three months later Secretary of State Dulles publicly announced the existence of a new policy which quickly became known as "Massive Retaliation." The United States would no longer constrain itself to meet communist military probes with local conventional counterforce, as it had in Korea. Instead, it would "depend primarily upon a great capacity to retaliate instantly" and massively against the major communist powers responsible. "Massive Retaliation" came to appear to be the strategic theory component of a new U.S. national security policy, the rationale for the force structure of the New Look, and indeed the guiding principle of American strategy for most of the decade of the fifties. It can also be viewed as the first systematic theory of deterrence in the Cold War era. For all these reasons it is worth glancing at in a little detail.[21]

Behind the emergence of Massive Retaliation lay three major interrelated factors. It was, in the first instance, a reaction against the experience of Korea. The United States, unaccustomed to the frustrations of "dirty little wars" (but quite accustomed to "total victories") had by 1953 become thoroughly sick of the costly but apparently indecisive stalemate in Korea; the virtual promise of a quick end to the war had been a major cause of the Republican landslide of the autumn of 1952. Within the military, but with considerable support from civilian opinion, an influential group of officers known as the "Never

[20] NSC-162/2 is reproduced in the *Pentagon Papers*, I, 412–29.

[21] The principal (secondary) sources for the historical development of the concept of Massive Retaliation are: Huntington, *The Common Defense*, pp. 64–88; Snyder, "The 'New Look' of 1953"; Brodie, *Strategy in the Missile Age*, pp. 248–55; Taylor, *The Uncertain Trumpet*, chapters 2 and 3; Gerson, *John Foster Dulles*; and Guhin, *John Foster Dulles*. The quotation is from Dulles's "Massive Retaliation Speech"; *New York Times*, January 12, 1954.

Again Club" was beginning to preach the doctrine of no further military involvements by U.S. ground forces on the Asian mainland. Yet if the concept of "containment" was to be maintained (at least without a major retreat in the frontier of the Free World), some means of projecting power into Eurasia was required. Massive Retaliation seemed to provide a neat alternative. Rather than again accepting the casualties, costs, and frustrations of directly defending the lands of the communist periphery, the United States would deter any attack upon them by threatening strategic nuclear strikes at the communist heartlands in reply.[22]

A second major factor behind Massive Retaliation was the question of economic costs during peacetime. The Eisenhower Administration was committed to maintaining both reasonably low tax rates and a balanced federal budget. This would be next to impossible if conventional forces were to be retained at Korean War levels. By comparison, nuclear weapons seemed very efficient: "more bang for the buck." Under Massive Retaliation, the threat to employ these weapons appeared to substitute for the far more expensive conventional forces. In addition, America's allies would be expected to provide the lion's share of the manpower for whatever conventional forces might still be needed.

The third factor was technological. A series of technical breakthroughs in the field of nuclear weapons and their delivery made it seem possible to avoid large conventional limited wars of the Korean type. By 1953, nuclear bombs were comparatively plentiful in the American inventory and were being packaged in a variety of yield sizes; an operational thermonuclear weapon, a thousand times more powerful than the Nagasaki bomb, was well on its way. Moreover, weapons designers were in the process of generating a rapidly growing family of small- to medium-yield "tactical nuclear weapons" that could

[22] The Eisenhower Administration applied this concept promptly by quietly communicating to Peking in the spring of 1953 a threat to broaden the Korean War, including the use of nuclear weapons, unless a prompt truce were agreed to. See chapter 8.

be delivered in very flexible ways by an increasing variety of delivery means.

These were the political, economic, and technological realities upon which the new policy was erected in late 1953. It offered as a basic decision the doctrine that the U.S. would fight no more sizable limited wars without using atomic weapons. Henceforward, while allies might provide manpower, nuclear weapons would be America's special contribution to the defense of the Free World. The strategic theoretical underpinnings for this policy were disclosed in Secretary Dulles' "Massive Retaliation Speech" of January 1954. In it, he discussed the painful Korean experience and the need to curtail military costs in order to sustain a "long haul," and he alluded to the growing nuclear armory. "Some basic policy decisions" therefore had been made by the National Security Council. "And the basic decision was . . . to depend primarily upon a great capacity to retaliate instantly by means and at places of our choosing." [23]

For the remainder of the 1950s, in fact, the New Look force structure of limited conventional forces and the Massive Retaliation doctrine reigned, with only relatively marginal adjustments—this in spite of the fact that in the many politico-military crises the administration faced, it never retaliated massively, seldom employed serious Massive Retaliation threats publicly, and never utilized the nuclear forces which it had focused upon acquiring.[24]

As the decade of the 1950s proceeded, Massive Retaliation came under increasingly serious and sophisticated attack from two directions. First, as the Soviet strategic armory grew steadily in size and sophistication, critics increasingly wondered whether American strategic nuclear forces, upon whose in-

[23] *New York Times*, January 13, 1954, p. 2.

[24] In estimating the utility of the Massive Retaliation policy, it is necessary however to consider what was not known to all its critics at the time, that the United States delivered private threats of "massive retaliation" on several occasions during the 1950s with arguable success. Besides the threat to Peking in early 1953 already alluded to, Dulles communicated such threats to the Chinese and Soviets in 1953 concerning Southeast Asia, and in 1955 to the Chinese concerning the Formosa Straits. For a more detailed account see chapters 8 and 9.

violability the doctrine rested, were not becoming vulnerable to surprise attack. (An apparent "bomber gap" was proved a mirage, only to be replaced by an even more troubling "missile gap"—also dispelled but only after the U.S. had committed itself to a huge strategic-missile-building program.) The problematical relationships of two thermonuclear forces *to each other* rapidly emerged as a new and separate deterrence question, one which for obvious reasons absorbed most of the attention. Rapid conceptual development in this special kind of deterrence problem quickly left Massive Retaliation behind; and from a welter of competing doctrines of the early 1960s there has gradually emerged a theoretical consensus embracing "sufficiency," stability in the strategic balance and in the strategic arms race, and an interest—of varying intensity in different quarters, to be sure—in strategic arms control.

But while the problem of vulnerability was being examined, critics of Massive Retaliation were also pointing out that, even if American strategic forces were to become completely safe, their use in anything but a general war was declining in *credibility*. As their own strategic forces grew, the Soviets would be less and less likely to believe that the United States would risk its cities by launching nuclear war in response to some relatively modest Soviet probe. Deliberately seeking a degree of ambiguity, the Eisenhower Administration had left it unclear just at what point a massive retaliation might become a real possibility, but the administration's small budget for conventional forces, and much of its rhetoric, suggested that violations of the containment line would be met relatively early by very explicit threats, quickly followed by the actuality, of nuclear strikes on the USSR. Such a policy, the critics argued, ran the growing risk that the Soviets would think us bluffing.

To meet this objection the Eisenhower Administration in the later 1950s gradually supplemented Massive Retaliation with the doctrine of "Graduated Deterrence." Small Soviet attacks across the containment line would be met by the threat, then early use of *tactical*, not strategic, nuclear weapons, restricted to the local theater. But the critics replied that this would be useful for a very few years only, because the Soviets soon would be acquiring their own tactical nuclear weapons. Thereafter, the tactical nuclear threat might be much the same as the strategic one, for nobody could see how a war with tactical nuclear weapons could be kept from spiraling into a general, strategic war.

When the Kennedy Administration came to office, it brought the critics' viewpoint with it. A policy of "Flexible Response" which these analysts had been urging was substituted for the previous doctrines; and in somewhat varying versions it has persisted to the present day. "Flexible Response" is not a single, unitary theory; it is more a grouping of ideas and attitudes that are capable of several interpretations.[25] Nonetheless, certain core ideas, implemented in the post-1961 period, can be readily identified. The force structure henceforward would be designed to give the President "multiple options" with which to deal with crises. A "sufficiency" of nuclear capabilities, both strategic and tactical, would be maintained for engagement either in local theaters or in a strategic exchange; but a major—perhaps the primary—function of these forces would be simply to deter the opponent's use of his own nuclear forces. (Additionally, though advocates of Flexible Response differed on this, the threat of initiating tactical use of nuclear weapons might serve to deter our major opponents from initiating large-scale conventional attacks that could overwhelm the defender's forces.) Below this hopefully stable deterrent balance, major fighting forces would be required to resist by active defense what could not be prevented with nuclear deterrence. This was a critical component and requirement of Flexible Response. Early in the Kennedy Administration, American conventional forces were very rapidly and greatly upgraded, both in quantity and in mobility, to give the President the ability to respond flexibly with any of a variety of options for the use or threat of force.

[25] Thus, for instance, at the time of the Cuban missile crisis, Paul Nitze and Robert McNamara, two ardent advocates of "Flexible Response," disagreed sharply about its operational significance for the crisis.

During the 1960s the logic of Flexible Response and "multiple options" focused analysts' attention more and more upon the relationships among different kinds of possible war. With the development early in the decade of secure, invulnerable, second-strike U.S. strategic forces, the possibility of World War III arising from an "attack out of the blue" came to be considered as highly improbable. A different image of World War III emerged: should it come, it would most likely be the result of the escalation of a lesser conflict, probably from conventional through tactical-nuclear to strategic warfare. Deterrence of thermonuclear war would therefore depend to an important extent upon the control of escalation. This image of World War III received powerful reinforcement from the events of the Cuban missile crisis, which impressed both theorists and practitioners with its risk of escalation. Deterrence theory in the 1960s therefore came to raise to visibility a kind of "intra-war" deterrence: the deterrence of escalation.[26]

At this point let us break off our examination of shifting doctrines of deterrence and step back to attain an overview of its development. A striking feature emerges: "deterrence" has been theoretically most developed, and practically best applied, to acute bipolar conflict where great values are at stake and where there is a potential for great violence. We observed earlier that deterrence as a concept became separated from the art of diplomacy when the capacity to inflict pain on the opponent became separable from the capacity to defeat his military forces or to defend one's territory. Somewhat coincidentally, this separation of the concept of deterrence also took place more or less simultaneously with the emergence of bipolar conflict for enormous stakes. In the postwar period the convergence of several new factors—the capability of vast destruction, the deterrent potential of the threat of such destruction, and the emergence of bipolarity—strongly encouraged the development of a theory

[26] Much of our awareness of this aspect of politico-military analysis is the result of the contributions of Schelling: *Strategy of Conflict* and *Arms and Influence.* See also Kahn, *On Escalation;* Holsti, *Crisis, Escalation and War;* Brodie, *Escalation and the Nuclear Option;* and Smoke, *Controlling Escalation.*

and practice of deterrence that focused upon extremely polarized situations and problems. The fact that the logic and requirements of deterrence proved to be simplest in such cases further enhanced this tendency.

Thus the Truman Administration assumed that the gravest threat, the atomic strike, could deter another world war, but did not seriously consider applying "deterrence" to the less simple and less polarized real-world crises of the period. The Eisenhower Administration attempted to apply the same threat to deter such lesser crises by making them as stark as possible, in order to simplify its politico-military and economic problems. And critics of that administration's policies, and successor administrations, again split nuclear deterrence off from the more general problems of deterrence and raised the special case of strategic interactions to a specialized art. Throughout it has been ·deterrence in its most polarized form, applied to the most violent and acute kind of conflict, that has enjoyed the most rapid development both in theory and in practice.

But the very recent history of deterrence has included a growing search for ways to extend theory and practice to less and less polarized applications, and to supplement deterrence theory with related theories for the reduction of polarization. These developments have paralleled the historical end of the acutely polarized Cold War, the collapse of the geopolitics of bipolarity, and increasing emphasis by the United States upon policies of détente and control of the arms race. As our image of world conflict has become less acute, less polarized, and much more complicated, efforts have grown to extend deterrence and related politico-military concepts to the much more complex foreign policy problems that have emerged.

In this process, we are experiencing a slow rediscovery of many of the variables that pre–World War II and especially nineteenth-century policy-makers were concerned with: the importance of context, the richness of the factors of situation and setting, the limited usefulness of threats, and so forth. When applied to the *prevention* of crises, and to the routine management of an international system characterized by serious but not stark conflict, deterrence takes on great richness and complexity. It is our major purpose in this study to emphasize and to clarify these complexities, which have often been ignored or inadequately appreciated in both the theory and the practice of deterrence in American foreign policy since World War II.

Bibliography

Albrecht-Carrie, René. *A Diplomatic History of Europe*. New York, Harper & Row, 1958.

Boulding, Kenneth. "National Images and International Systems." *Journal of Conflict Resolution*, 3, No. 4 (1959).

Brodie, Bernard. *The Absolute Weapon*. New York, Harcourt, Brace, 1946.

——. *Escalation and the Nuclear Option*. Princeton, Princeton University Press, 1966.

——. *Strategy in the Missile Age*. Princeton, Princeton University Press, 1959.

Burns, Arthur Lee. "From Balance to Deterrence: a Theoretical Analysis," *World Politics*, IX, No. 4 (July 1957), 494.

Claude, Inis. *Power and International Relations*. New York, Random House, 1962.

Deutsch, Karl. *The Analysis of International Relations*. Englewood Cliffs, N.J., Prentice-Hall, 1968.

De Weerd, H. A. "Concepts of Limited War: an Historical Approach." RAND P-2352. Santa Monica, California, The RAND Corporation, November 1961.

Douhet, Giulio. *Command of the Air*, trans. Dino Ferrari. New York, Coward-McCann, 1942.

Earle, Edward Mead, ed. *Makers of Modern Strategy*. Princeton, Princeton University Press, 1943.

Etzioni, Amitai. *The Hard Way to Peace*. New York, Collier, 1962.

Fuller, Maj. Gen. J. F. C. *A Military History of the Western World*. New York, Funk & Wagnalls, 1954.

——. *Conduct of War, 1789–1961*. New York, Funk & Wagnall's, 1961.

Gareau, Frederick, ed. *The Balance of Power and Nuclear Deterrence*. Boston, Houghton Mifflin, 1962.

Gerson, Louis. *John Foster Dulles*. New York, Cooper Square Publishers, 1967.

Gindely, Anton. *History of the Thirty Years War*. New York, Putnam, 1884.

Guhin, Michael. *John Foster Dulles: A Statesman and His Times*. New York, Columbia University Press, 1972.

Haas, Ernest. "The Balance of Power: Prescription, Concept, or Propaganda," *World Politics*, V, No. 4 (July 1953), 428–77

Halle, Louis. *The Cold War as History*. New York, Harper, 1967.

Holsti, Ole. *Crisis, Escalation and War*. Montreal, McGill–Queen's University Press, 1972.

Huntington, Samuel. *The Common Defense.* New York, Columbia University Press, 1961.

Jervis, Robert. *Perception and Mis-perception in International Politics.* Princeton, Princeton University Press, forthcoming.

Kahan, Jerome. *Strategic Arms Policy* (tentative title; forthcoming).

Kahn, Herman. *On Escalation: Metaphors and Scenarios.* New York, Praeger, 1965.

———. *On Thermonuclear War.* Princeton, Princeton University Press, 1961.

Kaplan, Morton. *System and Process in International Relations.* New York, Wiley, 1957.

Kaufmann, William W. *Military Policy and National Security.* Princeton, Princeton University Press, 1956.

Milburn, Thomas W. "The Concept of Deterrence; Some Logical and Psychological Considerations," *Journal of Social Issues,* 17, No. 3 (1961), 3.

Millis, Walter. *The Forrestal Diaries.* New York, Viking, 1951.

Montross, Lynn. *War through the Ages.* New York, Harper & Bros., 1944.

Morgenthau, Hans. *Politics among Nations.* 3d ed. New York, Knopf, 1960.

Oman, Charles W. C. *A History of the Art of War in the Middle Ages.* New York, Franklin, 1959.

———. *A History of the Art of War in the Sixteenth Century.* London, Methuen, 1937.

Osgood, Charles. *An Alternative to War or Surrender.* Urbana, Ill., University of Illinois Press, 1962.

Osgood, Robert E. *Limited War.* Chicago, University of Chicago Press, 1957.

Pentagon Papers, The. Senator Gravel edition. 5 vols. Boston, Beacon Press, n.d.

Petrie, Charles. *Diplomatic History, 1713–1933.* London, Hollis & Carter, 1947.

———. *Earlier Diplomatic History, 1492–1713.* London, Hollis & Carter, 1949.

Pool, Ithiel de Sola. "Deterrence as an Influence Process." China Lake, Calif., U.S. Naval Ordnance Test Station, November 1965.

Powers, Richard J. "Who Fathered Containment?" *International Studies Quarterly,* 15, No. 4 (1971), 526.

Quester, George. *Deterrence before Hiroshima.* New York, Wiley, 1966.

———. *Nuclear Diplomacy.* New York, Dunellen, 1970.

Rapaport, Anatol. *Strategy and Conscience.* New York, Harper & Row, 1964.

Ropp, Theodore. *War in the Modern World.* Durham, N.C. Duke University Press, 1959.

Rosenau, James, ed. *International Politics and Foreign Policy.* New York, Free Press of Glencoe, 1961.

Russett, Bruce. "The Calculus of Deterrence," *Journal of Conflict Resolution,* 7, No. 2 (June 1963), 97.

———. "Pearl Harbor: Deterrence Theory and Decision Theory," *Journal of Peace Research,* No. 2 (1967).

Schelling, Thomas C. *Arms and Influence.* New Haven, Yale University Press, 1966.

———. *The Strategy of Conflict.* Cambridge, Harvard University Press, 1960.

Singer, J. David. *Deterrence, Arms Control, and Disarmament.* Columbus, Ohio State University Press, 1962.

——. "Threat-Perception and the Armament-Tension Dilemma," *Journal of Conflict Resolution*, 2, No. 1 (March 1959).

Snyder, Glenn. "The Balance of Power in the Missile Age," *Journal of International Affairs*, XIV, No. 1 (1960), 21.

——. *Deterrence and Defense*. Princeton, Princeton University Press, 1961.

——. "The 'New Look' of 1953," in Warner Schilling, Paul Hammond, and Glenn Snyder, *Strategy, Politics and Defense Budgets*. New York, Columbia University Press, 1962.

Smoke, Richard. *Controlling Escalation*. Forthcoming.

Speier, Hans. *Social Order and the Risks of War*. New York, Stewart, 1953.

Taylor, Maxwell. *The Uncertain Trumpet*. New York, Harper & Bros., 1959.

Wells, Herbert George. *The Shape of Things to Come*. New York, Macmillan, 1933.

Wolfers, Arnold. *Discord and Collaboration*. Baltimore, Johns Hopkins Press, 1962.

Zinnes, Dina. "An Analytic Study of the Balance of Power Theories," *Journal of Peace Research*, IV, No. 3 (1962), 270.

Chapter 2

❦

Contemporary Deterrence Theory

WE HAVE SEEN that from the onset of the Cold War to the era of SALT negotiations, deterrence has grown into a relatively complex set of ideas and policies. Prior to NSC-68, there was very little analysis of the "requirements" of strategic deterrence, nor of the problems of applying deterrence to the complicated real crises and small conflicts of the emerging Cold War. The doctrine of Massive Retaliation tried in a simplistic way to use the threat of SAC to deter such crises and wars, but found itself increasingly open to criticism as Soviet capabilities grew. The Kennedy Administration and its successors, realizing the limited diplomatic and deterrence uses even of invulnerable strategic forces, for the most part split off the doctrine for such forces from the more general deterrence problem, made it a special case, and procured "multiple options" for "responding flexibly" to and hopefully deterring attack at *any* level of violence.

Against this chronological background we shall now attempt to place a more analytical examination of how contemporary deterrence theory has been structured.

Three Levels of Deterrence

By the late 1960s "deterrence" theory and practice were apparently proceeding on several levels. We can usefully distinguish three in particular. First, the deterrent relationship of the two superpowers' strategic thermonuclear forces to each other had been clearly differentiated from the more general questions and applications of deterrence and had become virtually a technical speciality all its own. Below the strategic level, the deterrence of "limited wars" had received some study, with particular attention going to the special case of the forces, nuclear and nonnuclear, facing each other across Central Europe. Finally, policies had been sought that could deter "sublimited" conflict at the low end of the spectrum of violence. Kennedy's policy of Flexible Response implied that forces and doctrine were needed to meet the requirements of deterrence—and, should deterrence fail, of defense—for *all* these levels. Of course, the various threats needing to be deterred are not completely distinct, but in reality merge together into a single spectrum. However they have been distinguished roughly in this threefold manner for analytical purposes, and in important respects in policy-making as well. Let us glance a little more closely at how these levels of deterrence theory and policy have been developed and how they vary in character.[1]

The deterrence of *strategic war* has received by far the greatest attention, particularly from the mid-1950s on. By the early 1960s it had become almost a separate discipline in itself, enjoying a rich literature, a panoply of specialized concepts, and its own technical vocabulary. It possessed particular methodologies—game theory, systems analysis, economic utility theory, and quantitative, computerized war-gaming—that were capable of achieving seemingly precise solutions to operational

---

[1] The three-way distinction under discussion here is not quite the same as Herman Kahn's three "types" of deterrence; see Kahn, *On Thermonuclear War*, pp. 126 ff. and pp. 282 f. Kahn's "Type I" deterrence, to be sure, concerns the balance of strategic forces. But his "Type II" deterrence concerns the use of strategic forces to deter major "provocations" which might be in the nature of limited conventional as well as tactical nuclear attacks—i.e., something like Massive Retaliation. Kahn's "Type III" deterrence (which he does not discuss in detail) appears to cover threats of tactical nuclear or conventional responses that would make any incursion "unprofitable"—i.e., everything else. Of course, all such typologies, including the one being employed here, are somewhat artificial.

and most theoretical questions. Doctrine was in hand to guide force posture planning and strategic declaratory policy, as well as war plans. By the early 1960s there was substantial consensus on the nature and requirements of strategic deterrence, and by the late 1960s on the desirability and feasibility of strategic sufficiency. Subsequently, most analytical attention from political scientists and international relations specialists has shifted elsewhere.[2]

United States strategic deterrence policy, like the theory, has remained relatively stable and unambiguous since the early 1960s. "Assured Destruction" was pronounced to be the core strategic deterrence policy in 1962 (to be supplemented for awhile, at least declaratively, with Damage Limiting and Flexible Response).[3] Successive presidents and secretaries of defense have repeated that Assured Destruction (or its logical equivalent, "sufficiency") is the *sine qua non* of American security. For the last decade the engineering and technical imple-

[2] Not only Raymond Aron has concluded that "since about 1963 . . . there is not really much more to be gained from the study of . . . the nuclear threat." Aron, "Evolution of Modern Strategic Thought," pp. 4–5.

Deterrence theory on the strategic level can be represented in mathematical terms. A representative example of this technical deterrence theory is Daniel Ellsberg's mathematical deterrence model; Ellsberg, "Crude Analysis of Strategic Choice." See also Hunter's expansion and analysis of Ellsberg's model, "Aspects of Mathematical Deterrence Theory." Rush has formalized this kind of deterrence theory in an inventory of propositions: "Deterrence of Unlimited War." Since about the mid-1960s strategic deterrence has been primarily a technical specialty for systems analysts and operations researchers associated with the services and the Office of the Secretary of Defense, and more recently with the National Security Council and the Arms Control and Disarmament Agency, and some of these organizations' contractors, rather than an active area of inquiry by political and other social scientists.

[3] "Damage Limiting" refers to measures, offensive or defensive, intended to reduce as far as possible the damage suffered in a strategic nuclear war. It played a relatively important role in U.S. strategic policy until the latter part of the 1960s, when the great growth in Soviet strategic capabilities suggested its increasing infeasibility. In the strategic context "Flexible Response" means the capability and doctrine for making highly controlled, limited, and selective strategic strikes; it is principally relevant for strategic war which grows out of a lesser conflict by escalation. A lucid representation of Flexible Response in the strategic context is given in Schelling, "The Strategy of Controlled Response."

mentation of this policy has altered rapidly to keep pace with technological developments, but (quite unlike the previous decade) official strategic policy and doctrine have remained relatively stable.

Deterrence of conventional *limited war* has received significantly less attention. Conceptually and analytically, the study of deterrence on this level has lagged. With few exceptions, mathematical methodologies like systems analysis are not useful in this area.[4] But by the mid-1960s a handful of ideas—largely drawn from the Korean experience—had won general acceptance. For instance, deterrence of limited attacks upon an area the U.S. wishes to protect has seemed to depend to an important degree on the quality of the U.S. commitment to defend the area; some means for lending credibility to, and signaling, such commitments have been discussed. Should deterrence fail, the avoidance of escalation in the resulting conflict has been recognized as depending in part upon respecting "firebreaks" and situational "saliencies," [5] as well as upon maintaining superior potential power at higher levels of violence—"escalation dominance"—to discourage the opponent from resorting to escalation.[6]

In the 1950s the U.S. seemed to be attempting to substitute the policy of Massive Retaliation for any deterrence policies aimed specifically at this level of threat. When in the early 1960s Flexible Response and "multiple options" were substituted for Massive Retaliation, the new policy reflected a sense that ideas and theory about the deterrence of limited war had somewhat progressed. (It also reflected the confidence of the Kennedy Administration that U.S. conventional forces had been

[4] War-gaming has been used in studying the possible development of major limited wars on the Central European front, as well as in limited applications elsewhere. But such war-gaming almost never aspires to the quantitative rigor, or reliability of results, of strategic war-gaming.

[5] See, for example, Schelling, *Strategy of Conflict*, chapter 3 in Appendix A, and the same author's *Arms and Influence*, chapter 4. Also Enthoven, "American Deterrent Policy."

[6] The term is Kahn's: *On Escalation*.

greatly improved over their 1950s levels.) Flexible Response, however, never represented a strategy in the same sense as deterrence by Assured Destruction. Assured Destruction was the policy product of a systematic theory of strategic deterrence in which decision-makers had high confidence, whereas Flexible Response was the policy product of a few ideas suggesting, with only moderate confidence, the usefulness of precise and careful application of limited force. More specifically, Assured Destruction and the underlying theory of strategic deterrence could offer relatively precise criteria for contingency planning of operations and for decisions on force structure and procurement.[7] They could also offer a relatively precise guide for proper declaratory policy concerning U.S. strategic forces. Flexible Response, however, offered a much less complete guide to policy. While it could recommend that a complete range of forces and types of forces be procured ("multiple options") and that intelligence, command/control, and operational doctrine be developed to employ them flexibly to meet limited attack, it could not make recommendations concerning the amount of any one kind of force to procure, what to declare publicly about the force, where the force should be deployed, or—most importantly—when, how, and under what circumstances it should be used. (These questions, it will be recognized, could be answered only with reference to the specifics of U.S. foreign policy, not by the Flexible Response strategy itself.) Exaggerating slightly for the sake of clarity, one might say that whereas Assured Destruction and its ancillary policies successfully *chose among* a range of possible decisions by specifying what to procure, where to deploy it, what to declare about it, and when and how to use it, Flexible Response *widened* the range of deci-

[7] These criteria are not, of course, exact in intelligence and technical terms in the way, for instance, the meaning of "invulnerable basing" is quite precise, given known Soviet missile accuracies. But they nevertheless greatly lessened the range of uncertainty. "An intolerable level of destruction to the enemy's society," for example, is a policy criterion which can never be precisely quantified; but a value can be assigned to it with much greater confidence than a value can be to one's estimate of the costs and risks that must be threatened to deter an attack on, say, Yugoslavia.

sions by recommending that some of *all* kinds of forces be procured and held in positions of highest flexibility, thereby deliberately maximizing the options available (and hence maximizing the number of deployment, operational, and action decisions that would have to be made later). It is not too much of an exaggeration to say that Flexible Response represented what could be termed a "second-order" policy to procure everything and be ready for anything. It was necessary precisely because theory was lacking which could guide specific choices.[8]

This limited scope and character of the Flexible Response policy is revealed by the ad hoc character of measures taken by the United States during the 1960s to enhance deterrence in areas where limited war threatened, and to reinforce deterrence on occasions, such as Berlin 1961, Cuba 1962, and Vietnam 1965, where it appeared to be failing or about to fail. Later we will examine in some detail various expedients tried by the United States in such situations. But generally it appears that throughout this period the United States characteristically discovered, when limited war threatened, that Flexible Response had secured many kinds of forces, and hence options, for enhancing deterrence, but neither it nor any other available doctrine could provide criteria for deciding whether, when, where, and how to employ or threaten to employ what forces, or to activate which options.

But if deterrence theories have been somewhat underdeveloped and deterrence policies somewhat ad hoc when applied

---

[8] An implication of this "second-order" character of the Flexible Response policy which is rarely if ever mentioned by its advocates is that by widening and complicating the range of options and the number and kinds of decisions required later, Flexible Response in effect demands *more* theory, not *less*. For multiplied options and multiplied kinds of options require a larger number of criteria to guide decision and hence richer and more powerful theory, both for understanding limited war in general and for diagnosing specific limited threats as they emerge. (In the last decade there has been some awareness of this need.) But lacking such theory, the U.S. to some extent acted in an intellectual vacuum during the 1960s, improvising, for instance, ad hoc measures to reinforce deterrence (discussed subsequently) and otherwise resorting to primitive and inadequate hypotheses. For a more detailed discussion of some of these hypotheses, see George, Hall, and Simons, *Limits of Coercive Diplomacy*.

to the problem of limited war, the situation is still less satisfactory on the third level—deterrence of threats of conflict below limited war on the spectrum of violence. Here lies a range of phenomena which comprise by far the largest volume of conflict-related events that U.S. foreign policy attempts to deal with. Violence is covert, low-level, or not yet visible; but conflict predominates in a wide variety of situations, including sublimited, counterinsurgency, and guerrilla warfare, espionage and "black" operations, "crisis diplomacy," and "crisis management." Operationally this range of problems represents all those activities which aim at preventing crises or halting them prior to outbreak of conventional limited war. (Usually these problems are perceived by American policy-makers as deriving from the activities of the United States' major opponents.) Let us term this the level of "crisis and crisis-preventive diplomacy."

On this level the deterrence of potential actions of likely opponents is nearly always a major, and often the predominating, United States objective. Yet both the theory and the practice of deterrence here are highly unsystematic and undeveloped. Deterrence on this level has lacked an accepted nomenclature, any kind of regular methodology for analysis, and apparently even a consensus on the intellectual definition of the problem. "Theory" has been largely limited to, again, an emphasis upon the signaling of diplomatic commitments and upon their credibility, on an analogy from the limited-war case. Reflecting the very undeveloped state of the theory, U.S. policy for the deterrence of threats on this level has had a highly ad hoc, opportunistic, and proximate character. If Flexible Response is a much less ambitious doctrine than its analogue, Assured Destruction, the analogous doctrine or announced policy principles for deterrence at the level of crisis and crisis-preventive diplomacy do not exist at all. (Indeed, even in declaratory policy, "deterrence" has been mentioned relatively infrequently in this context, though with respect to limited as well as strategic war "deterrence" has very often played a vital role in U.S. declaratory policy.) At this third level the United

States has had no deterrence doctrine—either for planning the acquisition of forces and other capabilities, for declaratory policy, or for diplomatic, military, or other action plans.

One important consequence of the lack of doctrine for this level has been an attempt to apply the forces and "options" procured under the doctrine of Flexible Response to this lower level of the threat spectrum as well. In practice, the "deterrence" of threats at this level has too often been interpreted as a matter of deploying *military* capabilities and implicitly or explicitly threatening their use to deal with a primarily *diplomatic* crisis or emergent crisis. This attempt to extend the applications of Flexible Response into the lower portion of the spectrum is exactly analogous to the earlier attempt to extend, through Massive Retaliation, the applications of strategic deterrent forces into the next lower portion of the spectrum, to try to deter limited war. Both have been tried for the same reason: a lack of adequate theory on the lower levels.

Characteristics of Deterrence Theory at the Three Levels

Some interesting general characteristics of overall deterrence theory in the current era emerge from a comparison of these three levels.

Quite clearly, the degree of theoretical development varies directly with the level of violence under consideration. The theory of strategic thermonuclear deterrence is highly refined, but the quality and quantity of theory fall off steadily as the degree of violence lessens, until for crisis-preventive diplomacy we have very little theory at all. This generalization holds true for all the significant aspects of theory—the precision of concepts, the formality and exactitude of their logical relationships, the degree to which the theory can be expressed in mathematical or quantitative terms, the degree of general consensus enjoyed by the major ideas and the relative comprehensiveness of these agreed-upon ideas, the stability of theory over time, and the level of confidence in the theory held generally and especially by policy-makers.

Largely because deterrence theory at the strategic level has been so much better developed in so many respects, there has been a marked tendency for theorists *to employ strategic deterrence as the paradigm case* for thinking about deterrence in general. Strategic deterrence theory has been highly visible, coherent, and logically crisp. By contrast, attempts to examine the workings of deterrence at the level of limited war and below have discovered deterrence to be less sharply visible and less easy to isolate in such contexts. Accordingly, a great many discussions of such cases, or of deterrence in general, have approached the subject from the "purer" strategic problem and employed it as the paradigm case of deterrence.[9] (This tendency will be discussed and criticized in more detail subsequently.)

At the same time, however, in the last ten years or so there has been a gradual shift of interest among analysts to the problems of deterrence at the lower end of the scale of violence. Recognition of the extremely underdeveloped state of deterrence theory for these levels and of consequent inadequacies in U.S. deterrence policies has stimulated increasing attention to this difficult area.

Historical and Intellectual Factors Shaping Deterrence Theory

It is important to understand why deterrence theory has developed as it has. The antecedents of the theory in the current era, both historical and intellectual, have been several.

[9] See, for example, Brodie's "The Anatomy of Deterrence" (chapter 8 of *Strategy in the Missile Age*); chapters 2 and 3 of Singer's *Deterrence, Arms Control, and Disarmament;* Kahn's *On Escalation;* chapter 14 of Aron's *Peace and War;* and Snyder's *Deterrence and Defense.*

Two major historical factors shaping the development of deterrence theory have been the *locus of the most salient threat* to the United States, and somewhat related, analysts' and policy-makers' *image of the relevant conflict.* Until relatively recently, by far the most salient threat has been the strategic. Indeed, the emergence during the 1950s of a Soviet strategic strike capability against the American homeland represented the first occasion in modern times that the United States itself became vulnerable to attack. The impact of this novel threat was greatly enhanced by the unprecedented level of damage a strategic nuclear strike could inflict upon U.S. civil society, and by the unprecedented speed with which an attack could be delivered. (Furthermore, the West expected Soviet strategic forces to grow even more rapidly in size and quality during the late 1950s than they actually did.) The novelty, great danger, potential speed of attack, and rapidity with which the strategic threat grew and altered in character all raised the problem of strategic deterrence to dramatic prominence.

The development of deterrence theory was also substantially influenced by the Cold War image held by analysts and policy-makers of a sharply bipolar political and diplomatic universe. Under these circumstances analysts tended to focus upon the aspects of deterrence (and other politico-military) theory that emphasized the logic of acute, highly polarized conflict. Thus the deterrence of strategic war, the ultimate in stark, bipolar conflict, received precedence over the problems of lower-level conflict, where "cooperation" with opponents in keeping conflict from escalating is a major dimension of the conflict, and where there are likely to be complex interactions among opponents, proxies, and allies which mitigate bipolarity.[10]

[10] Incidentally, it is worth noting that the "degree of polarity" of a conflict is an ambiguous term with several possible meanings, not all of which vary directly with "the level of threat to be deterred." "Degree of polarity" can mean the extent to which the universe of players is clustered into two opposing centers of decision and action. It can mean the level or worth of the stakes at issue in a conflict (and hence, presumably, the degree of motivation or commitment of players in the struggle). It can mean the degree to which (in the language of game theory) the game is one of pure conflict, or contains elements of coopera-

But contemporary deterrence theory has been shaped by intellectual as well as historical factors. We observed in the previous chapter that the idea of deterrence began to be discussed in the period between the world wars when the capacity to inflict pain (with bomber aircraft) was separated from the necessity first to defeat military forces. The emergence after World War II of a special class of weapons delivered by a special instrumentality (SAC) that was supremely capable of inflicting "unacceptable costs" raised the concept of deterrence to high visibility. It was therefore strategic deterrence in particular which was sharply distinguished from the entirely traditional and familiar form of "deterrence" represented by the power physically to halt opposing forces at the border, deny them territory, and/or degrade them. Strategic deterrence is almost solely "deterrence by punishment," whereas other cases include "deterrence by denial." We might say that strategic deterrence thus presented the deterrence concept in its purest form, and allowed it to be isolated, identified, and analyzed. Only after this isolation of "pure" deterrence have we been able to gradually reintegrate our new comprehension of deterrence with the complexities that arise when the same forces or actions both deter and serve other goals, including denial.

The strategic case was instrumental in isolating and identifying deterrence intellectually for another reason as well. In its simplest form, deterrence is merely a contingent threat: "If you do x I shall do y to you." If the opponent expects the costs of y to be greater than the benefits of x, he will refrain from doing y; he is deterred.[11] Rarely in the real world does deterrence actu-

---

tion as well. Frequently, all these variables correlate well, but they do not have to. The Cuban missile crisis, for example, was a largely (but not entirely) bipolar conflict over the deployment of the most powerful strategic weapons which saw virtually no violence actually used, and which featured great "cooperation" between the major parties. Deterrence theory, though, has been best developed for and best applied to those situations where bipolarity in *all* its senses is great, and has received but little analysis distinguishing its forms and roles in more complex situations where polarity is differentiated.

[11] Bruce Russett suggests a slightly more complex formulation in his articles on "Calculus of Deterrence" and "Pearl Harbor." He points out that a potential at-

ally work in this simple a way. But strategic deterrence can approach it. Assured Destruction is nearly this: if the Soviets launch an atomic attack upon the United States, the nuclear destruction of the Soviet Union will be assured.[12] Of course, technology provides a variety of ways to implement Assured Destruction, as well as giving the opponent options for strategic defense. But however great may be the technical and engineering problems of "operationalizing" this kind of deterrence in the fast-changing technological context of modern weapons, the logic of the threat is straightforward.[13] (This fact of straightforward logic also permitted the previously existing game theory to be applied to the deterrence problem. This intellectual antecedent of contemporary deterrence theory will be taken up in the next chapter.)

But deterrence at the level of limited war and below is usually much more complex and involves additional variables, many of them difficult to measure. The intellectual history of deterrence has thus consisted, naturally enough, of identifying and elucidating the logic of the simplest case first, and then extending the analysis to progressively more complex cases. Historically, the *complexity* of problems and the *measurability* of their variables have comprised another major determinant of the focus of analysts' attention. We mentioned in chapter 1 the special features of strategic deterrence which simplify its analysis; but it is worth examining in a little more detail the complexities imbedded in the other cases.

---

tacker will actually challenge deterrence only if the utility of doing so successfully, minus the utility of having to fight a war (each of which must be weighted by his subjective estimate of the probability of war), exceeds the utility of doing nothing. A similar formulation appears below at the outset of chapter 3.

[12] Not even Assured Destruction is quite this simple. Certain other events, such as a Soviet atomic attack on Western Europe, would also trigger the U.S. response, it has been declared. And of course, the Soviets must at all times be convinced that enough of the American strike forces would survive a Soviet first strike, and penetrate to their targets in the USSR, to accomplish the Assured Destruction.

[13] The various "hurdles" implicit in operationalizing strategic deterrence are lucidly discussed in Wohlstetter, "The Delicate Balance of Terror."

At the strategic level the *objectives* of both players are clear-cut and have remained constant for many years. A single objective—preventing a strategic strike by the other party—is of overriding importance. On the lower levels, however, the players usually have objectives of several kinds. In limited-war situations, each wishes to attain tactical objectives, keep conflict limited, and gain or keep various advantages with respect to alliances, proxies, and neutrals, as well as domestic opinion. Practical achievement of these objectives often proves difficult because usually some of the requirements conflict. Each side is therefore likely to be unsure of his motivation to achieve various objectives. For this reason, and because objectives and motivation both are variables, changing over time, each player will attempt to influence the incentives and utilities of the other.

All these observations apply as well to crisis and crisis-preventive situations, where subsidiary players are likely to play larger roles and thus multiply the complexities. Furthermore, since the situation is still emerging, it is highly indefinite and ambiguous. Accordingly, psychological and subjective considerations will make up a larger proportion of both one's image of one's own objectives and one's image of the opponent's; and ideological and "operational code" [14] variables may play a heavy role. In crisis-preventive diplomacy it may not be clear that a crisis is likely, or even that other players' objectives conflict seriously with one's own. The limits of the conflict, on the other hand, have not yet been defined; so the number of potentially relevant factors and the number of national interests that may be affected are still highly uncertain. Accordingly, it will be difficult to judge such questions as (1) how motivated one ought to be; (2) what aspects of the problem, if any, to bring before the highest-level decision-makers; (3) how to calculate the relationship of this problem to other national policies, interests, and problems; (4) approximately how other players will

[14] The "operational code" is a technique for analyzing the presuppositions, attitudes, and characteristic modes of behavior of an opponent. See Leites, *The Operational Code of the Politburo;* George, "The 'Operational Code.'"

calculate which of their interests are involved in what degree; and so forth. It may not appear that deterrence is a relevant policy at all; if opponents' objectives seem limited and/or the unfavorable consequences of conceding them appear containable and acceptable, a policy of conciliation may be more appropriate.

Somewhat similar observations apply when we turn from objectives to *means*. For strategic deterrence, both sides need consider only one kind of capability, strategic forces. To be sure, there are choices, such as the tradeoffs among offensive and defensive forces or the mix of bombers, ICBMs, and submarine-launched missiles. But there is little problem of selecting among incommensurable means: one does not have to debate whether to send a diplomatic brief, a bribe, or a battalion. The comparative simplicity of means calculations for deterrence on the strategic level is demonstrated precisely by the fact that they can be almost entirely mathematicized. But deterrence of lower-level conflict, unlike Assured Destruction, cannot be implemented by threatening a specific level of damage; and it does not involve a single kind of military power. Selection among kinds and quantities of military means in limited war, for example, is complicated not only by uncertainty about tactical requirements, but much more importantly, by the necessity to subordinate tactics to considerations of escalation control and to the political objectives of the conflict. Deterrence at levels below the strategic differs strikingly from the strategic case in that it is primarily a question of influencing the opponent's political calculus of the acceptable costs and risks of his potential initiative rather than simply threatening overwhelming military costs. The operational criteria for selection among means are dominated not by technical or tactical but by diplomatic and political factors.

In crisis and crisis-preventive diplomacy, such factors are numerous and highly complex. Besides the agonizing decision on whether to resort to any military means, there are choices available among a wide variety of diplomatic, political, economic, declaratory, covert, and other means—many of which are

A Checklist of Varying Characteristics of Deterrence

	Strategic Case	Limited-War Case	Crisis and Crisis-Preventive Diplomacy
Own objectives:			
Number	one	few	many
Are they in conflict with each other?	—	sometimes	usually
Are such conflicts serious and difficult to resolve?	—	sometimes	often
How motivated should one be?	totally	uncertain	very uncertain
Opponent's objectives:			
Number	one	few	many
Are they clear?	yes	often	rarely
Is it clear what their limits are?	yes	sometimes	rarely
Is it clear how motivated he is to attain them?	yes	rarely	hardly ever
Own means:			
Number of kinds appropriate	basically one	very few	many
Criteria for selection among	—	fairly clear	unclear
Criteria for selection of quantity	clear	fairly clear	unclear
Opponent's means:			
Number of kinds	basically one	very few	many
Difficulty in estimating which means or how much he will use	none	often some	usually considerable

mutually somewhat incommensurable. Means of different kinds may need to be combined: for example a military "show of force" may also be an important part of a diplomatic or declaratory strategy. In these situations, the requirements for implementing deterrence are much less a matter of acquiring, proving possession of, or using raw military capabilities than a matter of demonstrating concern, motivation, and commitment, and/or of

	Strategic Case	Limited-War Case	Crisis and Crisis-Preventive Diplomacy
Degree of polarization of actual or potential conflict	absolute	acute	variable and mixed
Difficulty in estimating whether deterrence is succeeding or not	none	not much	often consider-able
General ambiguity in the situation	very little	sometimes considerable	usually very great
Number of other national policies that intersect with the deterrence policy	very few	a number	many
Likelihood of conflicts among these policies that will be difficult to resolve	no	sometimes	usually
How many possible outcomes are there to the situation	very few	moderately few	a great many
Does a crisis in deter-rence last long enough to alter many of the above-listed variables and considerations?	no	yes	yes
Is the nature of "ratio-nality" in dealing with the crisis problem-atical?	no	slightly	considerably
Uncertainties	minimal	considerable	enormous

communicating intentions. It is not much of an exaggeration to say that in the strategic case the content and surety of the adversaries' (contingent) intentions are not in doubt, and attention focuses upon the adequacy of their capabilities, whereas in the other cases the availability on both sides of adequate raw capabilities is rarely in doubt, and attention focuses upon their intentions.

Other dimensions of deterrence besides the problem of objectives and the problem of means are also more complex at the lower levels of threat. Complications are introduced by the existence of other policies that intersect and overlap a nation's deterrence policies (often in a contradictory or at least ambiguous way) and by the fact that a very large number and variety of outcomes are possible, more than one of which may be acceptable to either or both sides. Crises and limited wars last long enough so that almost all the variables discussed here will change over time. In these situations it may also be difficult to assess whether deterrence policies are proving effective or not; other policies pursued at the same time may be the source of the emerging outcome, or it may result from fortuitous factors rather than from policy. Indeed, in crisis and crisis-preventive diplomacy especially, the number of possible outcomes and uncertainties may be so large, and the variables so intractable, that nearly all "calculations" seem of problematical usefulness, and doubt may begin to arise about the usefulness of "calculating" at all. Under these circumstances, the meaning of "rationality" itself may seem to become questionable, although the essential logic of deterrence rests upon the assumption that all players will be "rational" in assessing expected costs and benefits.[15]

The major differences among the strategic, limited war, and crisis and crisis-preventive diplomacy varieties of deterrence, as they emerge from the foregoing terse review, are summarized in the checklist on the preceding pages. But they can be compressed into the proposition that in the latter two cases deterrence is very largely a *context-dependent* problem. It is dependent not upon comparatively few technical variables, known with high confidence on both sides, but upon a multitude of variables, many of them partially "subjective," that fluctuate over time and are highly dependent upon the context of the situation. But this high degree of context-dependency and its implications for deterrence theory and deterrence policy have by no means been clearly recognized to date. The attention given

[15] See below, pp. 73–77, for additional remarks about rationality.

to the strategic case has left comparatively underestimated and unappreciated the much greater complexities of deterrence as applied to the cases of limited war and crisis and crisis-preventive diplomacy—and indeed has left largely unrecognized the limits of the applicability of "deterrence" to this realm at all.

The remainder of this study explores these ideas at length. We will consider the problem of strategic deterrence no further, but examine in detail deterrence at the lower levels. We hope to show, using case examples as well as analysis, why the application of deterrence here is a difficult and complex task, and how this task can be approached and understood.

Bibliography

Aron, Raymond. "The Evolution of Modern Strategic Thought," *Problems of Modern Strategy*. Adelphi Paper No. 54. London, International Institute for Strategic Studies, February 1969.

——. *Peace and war*. Garden City, N.Y., Doubleday, 1966.

Brodie, Bernard. *Strategy in the Missile Age*. Princeton, Princeton University Press, 1959.

Ellsberg, Daniel. "The Crude Analysis of Strategic Choice," *American Economic Review*, LI, No. 2 (May 1961), 472.

Enthoven, Alain C. "American Deterrent Policy," in *Problems of National Strategy*, ed. Henry A. Kissinger. New York, Praeger, 1965, p. 120.

George, Alexander. "The 'Operational Code': A Neglected Approach to the Study of Political Leaders and Decision-Making," *International Studies Quarterly*, 13, No. 2 (June 1969), p. 190.

——, David Hall, and William Simons. *The Limits of Coercive Diplomacy*. Boston, Little, Brown, 1971.

Halperin, Morton. *Limited War in the Nuclear Age*. New York, Wiley, 1962.

Hoffmann, Stanley. *The State of War*. New York, Praeger, 1965.

Hunter, Douglas E. "Aspects of Mathematical Deterrence Theory." Security Studies Project Document No. 19. Los Angeles, University of California at Los Angeles, n.d.

Kahn, Herman. *On Escalation: Metaphors and Scenarios*. New York, Praeger, 1965.

——. *On Thermonuclear War*. Princeton, Princeton University Press, 1961.

Leites, Nathan. *The Operational Code of the Politburo*. New York, McGraw-Hill, 1951.

Rush, Myron. "Deterrence of Unlimited War: A Propositional Outline." RAND P-1465. Santa Monica, Calif., The RAND Corporation, April 1960.

Russett, Bruce. "The Calculus of Deterrence," *Journal of Conflict Resolution*, 7, No. 2 (June 1963), 97.

——. "Pearl Harbor: Deterrence Theory and Decision Theory," *Journal of Peace Research*, No. 2 (1967).

Schelling, Thomas C. *Arms and Influence*. New Haven, Yale University Press, 1966.

——. *The Strategy of Conflict*. Cambridge, Harvard University Press, 1960.

——. "The Strategy of Controlled Response." Adelphi Paper No. 15. London, International Institute for Strategic Studies.

Singer, J. David. *Deterrence, Arms Control, and Disarmament.* Columbus, Ohio State University Press, 1962.
Snyder, Glenn. *Deterrence and Defense.* Princeton, Princeton University Press, 1961.
Waskow, Arthur. *The Limits of Defense.* Garden City, N.Y., Doubleday, 1962.
Wohlstetter, Albert. "The Delicate Balance of Terror." *Foreign Affairs*, 37, No. 2 (January 1958).

Two useful bibliographies to the literature on deterrence theory are:

Brody, Richard A. "Deterrence Strategies: an Annotated Bibliography," *Journal of Conflict Resolution*, 4, No. 4 (December 1960), 443.
Raser, John R. "Theories of Deterrence," *Peace Research Reviews*, 3, No. 1 (1969).

Chapter 3

The Normative Use of
the Abstract Deterrence Model

The Content of the Contemporary
Model of Deterrence

WE HAVE NOTED that the greatest development of deterrence theory has taken place in analyzing the strategic threat of all-out thermonuclear war, and that deterrence theory covering lesser threats has remained comparatively underdeveloped. And we have suggested a few reasons to account for this development. But much remains to be said about the nature and characteristics of such theory as exists regarding deterrence of threats less than the strategic.

The fact that the United States shares no borders with any hostile powers has introduced a certain kind of simplicity into American deterrence theory. Leaving aside a few bizarre exceptions, it is not possible for any opponent to make a comparatively limited attack on or threat to United States territory. The only plausible attacks upon the United States itself would be of the comparatively unlimited strategic kind. Thus for the United States the deterrence of *limited* probes, challenges, or attacks has been the same as the deterrence of challenges or threats to U.S. *interests* beyond her own territory. The problem for American foreign policy has been that of "projecting" deterrence beyond her own borders to cover other parts of the world, seeking to protect some third party—an ally, or a neutral we wish to safeguard. Accordingly, theory about the deterrence of limited threats to the U.S. has focused almost exclusively upon a "three-nation problem" involving an aggressor nation, the U.S., and some smaller nation which is the object of the aggressor's designs and which the U.S. seeks to protect. The goal of this theory has been to discover how the U.S. can successfully project its deterrent power to protect a third nation or group of nations.[1]

A relatively simple set of ideas about this problem has emerged [2] which without much oversimplification could be presented in the form of a simple model embracing the following propositions: [3]

(1) The principal communist powers perceive an interest in attacking or encroaching upon various nations or regions within which the U.S. has an interest in preserving self-determination.

[1] It is important to realize that this simple separation does not apply to the Soviet Union, Western Europe, or China. These powers do share borders with hostile nations. Therefore, each of them must consider the possibility of a probe, incursion, or attack upon the homeland which is nevertheless *not* a strategic strike. For these powers deterrence is thus somewhat more complicated intellectually. But for the U.S. the deterrence of limited attack is the same as what Glenn Snyder calls the problem of "secondary deterrence." Snyder, *Deterrence and Defense*, p. 17.

[2] A bibliography of the works we have taken to represent the principal statements of deterrence below the strategic level appears at the end of this chapter. While the propositions presented here are not taken from any one of these works explicitly, we believe they represent a fair and recognizable condensation of the contemporary wisdom. Where certain authors have clearly gone beyond this simple model in their theorization, appropriate indication will be made later. Writers who have criticized contemporary deterrence theory are mentioned in a separate listing at the close of this chapter.

[3] This simple model is drawn especially from Russett's "Pearl Harbor" study and from chapter 1 of Snyder's *Deterrence and Defense*. The model is worded from the viewpoint of the United States, since this is most theorists' perspective. By appropriate changes in the proper names it can, of course, be generalized to describe any deterrent situation.

(2) Such attacks can be deterred if these powers calculate that the expected costs and risks (negative utilities) of attacking outweigh the expected benefits (positive utilities):

$$C + R > B$$

(3) Such expectations will be held if these powers believe that the United States will defend the attacked nation. More precisely, the expectations will result if the estimated probability of U.S. defense, multiplied by the costs and risks that that defense would impose, exceeds the expected benefits that would result in the event of no U.S. defense: [4]

$$p(C + R) > (1 - p)(B)$$

(4) Generating this belief—or more exactly, raising this estimated probability—is therefore the object of U.S. deterrence policy.[5]

(5) The requirements for generating this belief are that the principal communist powers perceive a U.S. "signal" of intent to defend and find the signal "credible."

(6) The signal requires appropriate declaratory and action moves by the United States, communicating the intent.

(7) Credibility requires that the U.S. appear to become *committed* to carrying out its intention to defend the attacked nation.

Additional ideas have grown up concerning appropriate policy if deterrence failed and war ensued. Based largely on the Korean War experience, this "limited war theory" need not be discussed here.[6] The above list of propositions summarizes contemporary theory about how to make deterrence succeed.

[4] In his article on "Pearl Harbor," Bruce Russett suggests a similar formula for the deterrent relationship, and subsequently points out that the potential attacker also always possesses the option of striking directly at the defending great power rather than at the pawn. Most analysts have assumed this option to be an unlikely one in the thermonuclear era.

[5] The reader will recall that strategic deterrence of an all-out attack on the United States is now excluded from the discussion, and that "deterrence" refers to deterrence of threats below the strategic level.

[6] Limited war theory is discussed by Halperin in his *Limited War;* this work also possesses a valuable bibliography of literature on the topic to 1962.

Condensing contemporary deterrence theory into this propositional form highlights a very important feature of the theory which is frequently overlooked. The character of the theory is fundamentally *normative-prescriptive*, not *historical-explanatory*. This is not to say that deterrence theorists have necessarily always or even usually had in mind the direct transmittal to policy-makers of their conclusions. But it is to say that the logic of the theory is purposive in character: it presupposes that the United States has a deterrent purpose and it explicitly takes the accomplishment of this purpose as its subject matter. In principle, if not in all theorists' behavior, the maker of policy is the intended recipient of the conclusions of the theory. This character of the theory is clear not only from a propositional summary such as this one, but also from the most casual survey of the deterrence literature. Only very rarely does it contain retrospective explanation of past events, and the tiny number of such explanations which do exist have simply not been incorporated into the mainstream of deterrence theorizing.[7] Quite the contrary: the large deterrence literature has grown up with almost no systematic attention to historical cases of deterrence, to the explanation thereof, or to inductive theory-building therefrom. These time-consuming activities have been sidestepped, for reason of theorists' understandable sense of urgency during the Cold War era, so that theory could be created which, even if only in a general way, could offer norms and prescriptions serving the U.S. purpose.

Like other normative-prescriptive theories, deterrence theory has grown up structured fundamentally in the form of certain assumptions, a specified goal or purpose, and a set of means for accomplishing this purpose. Without criticizing any particular deterrence theorist, we find it intellectually productive to examine the elements of deterrence theory critically.[8]

[7] These few attempts will be discussed in the next chapter.

[8] In the analysis of contemporary deterrence theory that follows, we do not mean to suggest that we believe the theory is either more or less well developed in various directions than it actually is. Defining the range of "the" existing body of theory in a way that would be widely acceptable is difficult, be-

The principal assumptions of deterrence theory are given above in propositions 1 to 3. The first of these propositions constitutes an assumption about "the state of the world." There is, in fact, room for considerable debate about how many nations and regions have been actually threatened. A major power which takes on the role of protector of allies, as the United States has done, may frequently be deterring a threat which does not exist. It is very difficult to know, since the absence of attack could mean either that no attack was ever intended or that deterrence has succeeded. But the United States has tended to assume that at a minimum, those nations lying near the borders of the major communist powers are likely to be in danger.

The second and third propositions constitute assumptions about how the deterrence mechanism works. They represent propositions of "decision theory" and rest upon the premise of decision by calculation of utilities. We will return shortly to ex-

---

cause the perspectives of scholars, policy-analysts, and policy-makers differ greatly. We are aware, on the one hand, that from the viewpoint of the highly abstract theorist, deterrence "theory" can readily appear to consist of very little indeed. His concern is refining the right way to formulate a proposition, with learning what one can and cannot derive from a particular hypothesis, or perhaps with showing that the theoretical possibilities are more variegated than had previously been thought. From this viewpoint, there are hazards in criticizing, as we do here, the "theory" for what may more plausibly be seen as imperfections in its concrete interpretation or application in a specific policy context. On the other hand, from the viewpoint of the policy-analyst and others interested in the richly detailed playing out of deterrence logic in various real-world problems, the analysis presented here could seem rather abstract. His concern is with precisely that panoply of coloring details which, in a sense, we shall be criticising the "theory" for lacking; but he is fully aware of them and may, indeed, refer to many of them as "theory" since they are, after all, more abstract than what Khrushchev said about Berlin on June 4, 1961. We seek to steer a middle course between these viewpoints. We believe that the critical analysis which follows will be of relevance to almost any kind of theorist or analyst concerned with deterrence, although what specifically will be most relevant and the nature of the relevance will vary. And we believe our points about the general nature of deterrence theory, of the way people think about it, and of the way they use it, are valid without these points applying in toto to any particular theorist's or analyst's views about deterrence.

amine these somewhat complicated aspects of deterrence theory in detail.

In combination, the first three propositions, plus an apparently obvious value judgment, seem logically to yield the fourth proposition defining the object of action. In fact, though, the conclusion does not follow in an entirely unambiguous manner. *One* major object of U.S. deterrence policy, indeed, will be to suggest that the costs and risks of an opponent's initiative are too great. However, this is only a formula for frustrating the perceived aggressive intent. As many deterrence theorists have realized it needs to be supplemented with attempts to *reduce the motivation* underlying that intention, and/or to *provide alternative goals* that may be relatively satisfactory to the deterred power. These are also appropriate objects of U.S. policy and may be viewed as other kinds of "influence" complementing deterrence. Furthermore, the apparently obvious value judgment behind the fourth proposition—that in any case, the U.S. should hope to prevent a challenge to the status quo—may also be not quite self-evident, even in cases where a legitimate U.S. interest is likely to be damaged. For the opponent may be only temporarily deterred and may wait for or prepare more propitious circumstances; or if forestalled at one point, especially if no alternative paths are provided, the opponent may turn to other actions which could damage U.S. interests more. These lines of reasoning will be pursued at greater length in the last chapter of this book.

To date, the assumptions and goals of deterrence have received little critical attention of a systematic character. Only a few, comparatively formal treatments of deterrence have attended to these elements explicitly and analytically.[9] The assumptions and goals, rather, have often been taken for granted

---

[9] For example, the Snyder chapter, both Russett essays, and Milburn's essay on "What Constitutes Effective U.S. Deterrence?" See also Patchen, "Deterrence Theory in the Study of National Action," pp. 164–76; Singer, "Inter-Nation Influence: A Formal Model"; Baldwin, "Inter-Nation Influence Revisited," pp. 471–86, and "The Power of Positive Sanctions," pp. 19–38.

and explicit attention focused upon norms and prescriptions: the means of implementing deterrence—or as it is often put, the "requirements" of deterrence.

These requirements may be thought of as falling into three broad classes: (1) the full formulation of one's intent to protect a nation; (2) the acquisition and deployment of capacities to back up the intent; and (3) the communication of the intent to the potential "aggressor." Usually none of these is as simple or as easy as it might appear at first glance. The full formulation of a deterrent intent involves not only the decision to attempt deterrence in a given case, but also the perception and analysis of the threat (including both the opponent's motivation and his capabilities), the calculation of the U.S. national interest in the case, and the determination of what kinds of responses might be appropriate to the challenge and how "expensive" they should be allowed to become in terms of resources consumed or other opportunities foregone. The acquisition and deployment of capacities to back up a deterrent intent—the second requirement—may involve delicate judgments to balance the relative advantages and disadvantages of different and somewhat incommensurable options—political, diplomatic, economic, and in the end, military. The third step is then communicating in a credible way to the opponent the intention and capacity to carry the intention out.

Of these three classes of deterrence requirements, theorists have concentrated very largely upon the last. Deterrence theory to date has not explored in any depth the variety of problems imbedded in the first two issues. Instead, these matters have been taken to be either nonproblematical or outside the scope of deterrence theory, and analysts have gone on to focus upon the third problem of credibly communicating deterrent intentions. Thus the last three propositions on the list of seven above have received most of the attention. We have learned a good deal about the intricacies of "signaling" in an environment of competing messages and multiple audiences; [10] and a

---

[10] For instance, Jervis, *The Logic of Images.*

subtle intellectual analysis has been performed on the nature of "commitments" and the means by which a nation can commit itself credibly.[11] The dimension of signaling and commitment is the best-developed and most visible aspect of contemporary deterrence theory, and has dominated its literature in recent years.

But while these issues are important, concentration upon them to the partial neglect of the other requirements of deterrence, and the wider assumptions and objects of deterrence, has given the theory a somewhat narrow, mechanistic, and technical character. Deterrence theory to date has seemed to presume, de facto, that the scope, desirability, form, and appropriateness of a deterrent relationship among the U.S., a potential aggressor, and a third nation were either not problematical or not germane issues, and has passed on to the technician's questions—by what tactics does one become committed once the decision has been made to do so, and how then can the commitment be effectively signaled?

One reason why this aspect of deterrence has been emphasized is the experience of Korea. The conclusion was widely drawn that the communists felt free to attack because in previous official declarations the United States had seemed to exclude South Korea from the list of nations to whose defense it was committed. The lesson, reinforced by experiences in the years prior to the outbreak of World War II, seemed to be that for deterrence to succeed, the U.S. needed to signal to the opponent a credible commitment to the potentially threatened third nation.

A second reason is the peculiar location of the United States, mentioned above. Geographically isolated from the centers of threat, America's deterrence problem has been to project deterrence far beyond its own vicinity to protect third nations seemingly threatened by nearby potential aggressors. Geography not having made a connection between these third nations and the U.S. interests obvious, establishing and adver-

[11] Thomas Schelling in particular has offered penetrating insights on these points. See, e.g., chapter 2, "The Art of Commitment," in Schelling, *Arms and Influence.*

tising this connection has seemed to be the most salient problem in deterrence. Thus the U.S. deterrence problem has been generally defined as the question of how to bind threatened nations to the distant United States. Establishing and signaling commitments has seemed to be the answer most relevant to policy; so this aspect of deterrence has been best studied.[12]

The Abstract, Deductive Nature of the Theory

But there has been another important reason why the central propositions of deterrence theory have developed in the way just summarized: nearly all of them have been significantly influenced by the methodology with which deterrence has been approached to date.

The special strategic case—the deterrence of the outbreak of central thermonuclear war—has necessarily been studied by the use of formal, abstract models since, fortunately, we lack any concrete experience of the subject. But there is no shortage of historical experience of deterrence situations of the kind we are now focusing upon: the deterrence of limited war and crisis. The Cold War and post–Cold War periods have, regrettably, provided a plethora of cases where decision-makers felt it necessary to consider applying deterrence policies, often did so, and sometimes saw those policies fail in various ways. But despite the existence of this historical experience, deterrence theory nevertheless has been developed with very little refer-

[12] For this reason and for others already discussed, we think it is readily understandable why deterrence theory has the character it does. At the same time, we have felt free, in the discussion that follows and at other points in this book, to be unrestrained in including a considerable critical component in our assessment of it. Understanding and sympathizing with the motives and reasons that have yielded contemporary deterrence theory does not, we feel, relieve us of the responsibility for being searching in our evaluation and even for putting emphasis at various places in this work on its deficiencies, where doing so can help lead to correctives.

ence to empirical research! With a very small number of comparatively uninfluential exceptions to be discussed later, the theory has been developed *deductively*, not inductively. (In this we notice again the use of the strategic case as the paradigm—now in methodology as well as in substance.) What Thomas C. Schelling said of his own work applies readily to that of the overwhelming majority of deterrence theorists: "I have used some historical examples, but usually as illustration, not evidence." [13]

Contemporary deterrence theory has been developed substantially as a deductivist product of the field known as "decision theory." Analysts have begun by applying the premises and logic of decision theory to the problem of deterrence and constructed abstract models which have then been presented as embracing the essential analytical issues. Often this use of decision theory has been in words, without recourse to symbols and other formalities of theory. But some discussions of deterrence have explicitly labeled their analyses "decision theory" and have presented their conclusions in probabilistic form, in the manner of propositions 2 and 3 above.[14] Often, however, probability has been left aside and the analysis has been cast in the forms of that branch of decision theory called "game theory." And, unlike Schelling, theorists sometimes have neglected to emphasize that they are using an abstract-deductive method or to indicate what this may mean.

A typical game-theory presentation of a deterrence situation might be the one shown in the figure.[15] Let us suppose that

[13] Schelling, *Arms and Influence*, p. vii.

[14] For example, Russett's essay, "Pearl Harbor." In this paper Russett makes the same case as the one being developed here, that contemporary deterrence theory has been constructed principally on decision theory, and calls for analysts to push beyond this framework to develop a richer and more empirical theory of deterrence. The need for more empirical research on these matters has been emphasized also by McClelland, "The Reorientation of the Sociology of Conflict," and Sullivan, "International Bargaining Behavior."

[15] This example is a modified version of one employed by Snyder, *Deterrence or Defense*, pp. 17–19. Closely related is the illustrative problem discussed by Schelling on pp. 126–27 of *Strategy of Conflict*.

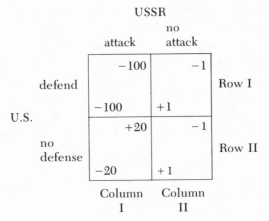

Game-Theory Example of a Deterrence Situation

the United States has given some indication that it will defend, say, Yugoslavia, from a Soviet attack, and the USSR is now deciding whether or not to make such an attack. Possible numerical "payoffs" are as shown: in the event of a Soviet attack and an American defense, both sides lose greatly (− 100); however, in the event the U.S. does not defend Yugoslavia in the actual attack, the Soviets make a moderate gain and the Americans suffer a moderate loss, in "credibility" and other diplomatic values (+ 20 and − 20, respectively). We may assume that the U.S. gains very slightly and the Soviets lose very slightly in the absence of a Soviet attack, since world opinion may believe that U.S. deterrence is successful (+ 1 and − 1, respectively).

From the game-theory standpoint, the most interesting aspect of this example is the fact that, by the nature of the case, the United States must decide whether to actually defend Yugoslavia only after an attack has begun. The "column" player chooses his move before the "row" player. Once "column" has chosen Column I ("attack"), it is in the interest of "row" to choose Row II ("no defense"), thereby losing only 20 rather than 100.

This way of conceptualizing the deterrence problem intrinsically highlights the dimensions of "commitment" and "signaling." For if row (the United States) does not find some way of committing himself to choose Row I ("defend") *under any circumstances* and signaling this commitment to column (the USSR), the latter will not find such a choice credible in the pinch. He will, quite reasonably, expect row, once actually confronted with an attack, to choose the path yielding the smallest losses. This is the essence of the "problem of deterrence" in its game-theory formulation.

Game theory has thus been useful in sharpening our understanding of certain important aspects of deterrence. But though they can be valuable, game and decision theory should constitute only one approach to the problems of deterrence. For game theory—a point not always clearly communicated by game theorists—is useful largely as a *methodology*. For the study of deterrence and of many other specific problems in the social sciences, game theory provides a structure for analysis rather than a set of theorems or conclusions. Thomas C. Schelling, perhaps the most creative of those who have applied game theory to deterrence and related problems, has suggested this:

> What may be of most interest to a social scientist is [the] rudiments, . . . [not] the subtle or elaborate analysis that has attracted the attention of mathematics. . . . The rudiments can help him to make his own theory, and make it in relation to the particular problems that interest him. One of the first things that strike a social scientist when he begins to experiment with illustrative matrices is how rich in variety the relationships can be. . . . For this reason, game theory is more than a "theory", more than a set of theorems and solutions; it is a framework for analysis. And for a social scientist the framework can be useful in the development of his own theory. Whether the theory that he builds with it is then called game theory, sociology, economics, conflict theory, strategy, or anything else, is a jurisdictional question of minor importance.[16]

Specialists in international conflict and others interested in applying game theory to the problems of deterrence may have been less than clear about game theory's status as a methodology rather than a substantive doctrine partly because the word

[16] Schelling, "What Is Game Theory?" pp. 219–20.

"theory," while meaningful to the mathematician, is something of a misnomer from the viewpoint of the social scientist:

> There is another problem of nomenclature: game theory already has the word "theory" in its name. We find it useful to draw distinctions between economics and economic theory, statistics and statistical theory, decisions and decision theory; but there is no accepted name for whatever the field is of which "game theory" refers to the theoretical frontier. Most game theory in fact has been substantially mathematical . . . [but] for the social scientist, what is rudimentary and conceptual about game theory will be, for a long time, the most valuable . . . as a framework . . . on which to build his own theory in his own field.[17]

That its value is very largely methodological is particularly true of so-called "mixed-motive" game theory, which is the branch of the theory which applies to situations involving the deterrence of threats below the strategic. Where the players have interests in common as well as in conflict there is, Schelling points out, no formal deductive solution: ". . . The principles relevant to successful play, the strategic principles, the propositions of a normative theory, cannot be derived by purely analytical means from a priori considerations." [18] Accordingly, Schelling suggested that:

> One [conclusion] is that the mathematical structure . . . should not be permitted to dominate the analysis. A second one, somewhat more general, is that there is a danger in too much abstractness. . . . A third conclusion . . . is that some *essential* part of the study of mixed-motive games is necessarily empirical.[19]

But for some ten years, Schelling's advice has not been followed in any careful or systematic way, at least so far as research in deterrence is concerned. The inductive approach, which might have extended and supplemented the insights of game theory by examining empirically how deterrence has actu-

---

[17] *Ibid.*, pp. 237–38.   [18] Schelling, *Strategy of Conflict*, p. 163.
[19] *Ibid.*, p. 162; emphasis in the original.

ally worked in various cases, has gone largely neglected.[20] As a result, deterrence theory has retained the abstract, deductive character of its original methodology.

This might have had no worrisome consequences had deterrence theory been offered merely for heuristic purposes or as a rudimentary explanatory theory. But it has been presented as a normative-prescriptive theory—as an actual guide for policy. *To employ an abstract, deductive theory in the normative-prescriptive mode is to run a significant intellectual—and potentially, a policy—risk.* There is a danger that the theory's norms and prescriptions will be limited in their scope, utility, or accuracy by the simplifications inherent in any small number of abstractions and in the deductivist methodology by which they are derived.

Simplifications of the Abstract Theory of Deterrence

Contemporary deterrence theory in fact *does* embody a number of significant simplifications, the number, full extent, and far-reaching consequences of which have not always been

---

[20] There has been a good deal of laboratory experimentation, in an effort to inject empirical content into game theory. But there has been little inductive analysis of historical deterrence situations. For a review of an analysis of experience with experimental games, see Rapoport, "Prospects for Experimental Games," printed in the *Journal of Conflict Resolution*. This journal is the principal forum for experimental game research of kinds interesting to specialists in political science and international affairs; it has published articles on the subject in nearly every issue since 1962. For a discussion of games that experiment with explicitly deterrent relationships, see Rapoport, "Games Which Simulate Deterrence and Disarmament."

Among those who have critically reviewed experimental evidence regarding the effects of threats on cooperative behavior are Nardin, "Communication and the Effects of Threats in Strategic Interaction"; Jervis, *Perception and International Relations;* and Milburn, "When Do Threats Provoke Violent Responses?"

thoroughly appreciated. These simplifications merit some attention.

1. *The Unitary Player*. A necessary assumption of decision and game theory is that each side is a *unitary* and *purposive* player. As applied to relations between nations, the method presumes that one may compress a nation into a single decision-maker: "the player" perceives a situation, consults "the" national interest and constructs "his" payoffs, and then selects the strategy that will maximize "his" utility. In fact, of course, this simplification does great violence to the reality—in many cases sufficient violence that a national decision will seem either incomprehensible or "irrational" if viewed through the spectacles of this model. Almost any interesting decision taken by a modern state is the product of tugs-of-war among institutions within its society or bureaucracy, and of the personal and self-interested maneuverings of many top decision-makers. All these players have their own interpretation of the "national interest" in a given situation and, of course, also have their own purposes, which are not necessarily the same as "the national" purpose. At one time, this was virtually a platitude of political science. However the rapid growth during the last twenty years of game-theory and other formal approaches to national strategy which presume the unitary decision-maker and encourage analyses employing this assumption has necessitated a reemphasis upon the realities. Graham Allison, in particular, has forcefully and lucidly stressed the role of organizational processes and bureaucratic politics in foreign policy decision-making.[21]

With respect specifically to deterrence theory, it is vital to keep constantly and clearly in mind the fact that one must deter not an opponent "nation" or "player" but rather at least a majority of the relevant individuals, groups, and/or institutions in decision-making circles within that nation. (We will have many occasions in the later case studies to note differing perceptions and strategies with regard to deterrence from different ele-

[21] Allison, *Essence of Decision*.

ments within the U.S. government. The same clearly applies to other states.)

2. *Rationality*. Somewhat related is the assumption of *rationality* in decision theory. As the theory has been adapted to the study of conflict, attention has been given to its apparent assumption of "perfect rationality" in decision-making. Theorists concerned with the basis of deterrence theory in decision theory have at times confused the "rationality" assumption. Again, most of the confusion has resulted from the attempt to employ or adapt the abstract theory of deterrence as a normative-prescriptive theory for action without clear recognition of the inherent limits of this practice.

Considered strictly as an abstract, formal theory, "rationality" in decision theory presents little difficulty and small grounds for criticism. On this level, the theory requires only that the decision-maker be able to make the mathematical calculations correctly on the basis of the matrix of payoffs. "It is assumed that all the elements of his value system are displayed—everything that matters to him is allowed for—in the ranking or valuation of cells in the matrix." [22] In effect, the payoffs display the choice as hypothetically it would appear to "the final" national decision-maker (e.g., the President) *after* the situation it describes has been perceived, interpreted, and weighed by the governmental machinery and possible outcomes have been weighed in terms of values, including the final decision-maker's own values. In short—and this can hardly be emphasized too strongly—the payoffs are *final subjective* estimates. On the basis of these estimates it is not hard to perform correctly the calculations needed to make a choice, and this is all that decision theory means by "rationality."

This is a useful simplification for purposes of formal deductive analysis. It would not be reasonable to expect abstract theory to do more, or to abandon "rationality" in this sense, which is a requisite for theory-building. The difficulties begin

[22] Schelling, "What Is Game Theory?" pp. 236 and 237.

to arise when attempts are made to apply directly or to adapt the abstract theory in the normative mode as a guide for policy. For in terms of the familiar three-step functional model of decision-making—"search," "evaluation," and "choice"—decision theory has focused exclusively upon the last.[23] There are at least four important considerations falling under the former two headings which the abstract theory compresses into the payoff numbers, but which the policy-maker must deal with explicitly.

First, there is a problem in *values*. Decision theory presumes within the concept of rationality that the actor's value hierarchy is itself internally consistent.[24] But in the real world of the policy-maker, it is notoriously difficult to construct an unambiguous and consistent ordering of values.

Second, there is a problem is assessing possible *outcomes*. Decision theory presumes that the cells define the outcomes and that the payoffs within each cell define the players' valuations of the outcomes. But the real policy-maker will often find it difficult to define the principal, possible outcomes of an actual situation. Thus even if he knows his values—his preferences among various hypothetical outcomes—he may have difficulty in estimating the various actual outcomes possible and in connecting these unambiguously to his values.

Third, there is a problem is assessing possible *courses of action*. In decision theory, "to describe an action as 'rational' is to say that it is consistent with the actor's values, whatever those may be." [25] But in the real world, moving from "values" to the assessment of actions is a process of two steps, both prob-

[23] Regarding game-theory models, Karl Deutsch points out in *The Nerves of Government* that "they gain their power by focussing attention on the 'payoff' situation, but must take the goals of all players as simple, and the inner structure of each player as given. Game models are hard to imagine visually, or as a flow of processes. They are likely, therefore, to supplement other models rather than to replace them . . ." (p. 72).

[24] This presumption, often stated explicitly in decision theory, is a necessity if the theorist holds that the player is in any sense making preferences among a set of possible outcomes. If he holds only that the player is selecting among numbers (payoffs) then these numbers must already reflect value judgments.

[25] Maxwell, "Rationality in Deterrence," p. 3.

lematical. One must decide how various predictable outcomes are to be related to values, as just mentioned. But one must also decide what actions on one's own part are likely to generate any particular outcome. Since it is often hard to predict how any outcome may be produced, selecting among possible courses of action is often difficult even if one knows what outcome one desires.

Fourth, there is a problem of *information* which affects all the foregoing considerations, as well as one's overall grasp of the nature of the situation or problem. In decision theory, both the cells themselves and the payoffs within the cells embrace the information defining the situation, and present either insufficient data for any decision at all (empty cells—a mathematically "degenerate case") or data adequate for a formally correct and rational decision. But the real world too often will provide the policy-maker with information insufficient for a high-confidence "definition of the situation" (yet sufficient to indicate that a problem exists and that action is required). The real decision-maker, therefore, may not have information suggesting the possibility or feasibility of an option he would like to select if he knew about it; information important to the previous considerations of assessing values, outcomes, and courses of action; or even information indicating that no action is required after all.

Finally, all the above considerations apply as well when one is trying to estimate the opponent's payoffs. In the real world the opponent does not provide one with a matrix, his own half filled in; yet critical choices depend upon one's reconstructing the opponent's probable subjective payoffs. In doing so, one must estimate what a fairly consistent value hierarchy for the opponent might be, how he may connect this to various perceived possible outcomes, what actions he can take and what actions he may decide can serve a given outcome, and the pattern and quantity of his information. In all these estimates, one's own information about the opponent is likely to be deficient.

The burden of the foregoing is that there are a number of

factors which abstract decision theory may properly treat as fixed assumptions, but which the real decision-maker must face up to as issues when trying to employ abstract deterrence theory in the normative-prescriptive mode. These issues will raise in his mind the question of what degree of confidence he should properly place in his calculations. In many real-world situations, the uncertainties are likely to appear numerous enough and complex enough to alter choices themselves, usually in the direction of greater caution. Or the uncertainties may be unrecognized or become affected by wishful thinking, thereby increasing the likelihood of serious miscalculations.

Rationality in decisions therefore will appear to the policy-maker more as a goal to be sought—under the severe "cognitive constraints" just mentioned—than a premise to be assumed. In attempting to cope with the limitations imposed by the just-named considerations, decision-makers employ a variety of devices to strive for rationality in the operational context. Not merely reforms in decision-making procedure but also, for instance, the use of relatively explicit models of the opponent's values and beliefs reflect these efforts to "operationalize" rationality.[26] And these efforts vary significantly among different nations and within the same nation in different times or circumstances.

[26] Strategies designed to assist decision-makers in coping with cognitive constraints on rationality are listed by Alexander George in "Adaptation to Stress in Political Decision-making," in *Coping and Adaptation*, ed. by G. V. Coelho, D. A. Hamburg, and J. Adams (New York, Basic Books, 1974). These coping strategies include: (1) "Satisficing" rather than an "optimizing"; (2) Tactics of "incrementalism"; (3) "Consensus politics"—deciding on the basis of what will command support rather than attempting to master the problem by analysis; (4) Using historical models and analogies to diagnose and prescribe for present situations; (5) Reliance upon ideology, general principles, or morality as a guide for action; (6) Beliefs about the nature of politics, society, and history, about correct strategy, and about one's "national purposes."

The latter three—as employed by others or oneself—may be usefully examined with the structure of "the operational code": Alexander George, "The 'Operational Code': A Neglected Approach to the Study of Political Leaders and Decision-making," *International Studies Quarterly*, XIII, No. 2 (June 1969).

For another approach to the problems of rationality and cognitive constraints in policy-making, see Steinbruner, *The Cybernetic Theory of Decisions*.

This opens the way for a significant line of research of the inductive variety. Abstract theory with its formal notion of rationality needs to be supplemented with empirical theory that can suggest how rationality has been approached and operationalized under different circumstances. Specifically with respect to deterrence, both the abstractness of the theory and its normative use to date have encouraged the notion that there is only one kind of rationality. Critics of the theory have challenged the relevance of any supposition of this "perfect" rationality while its defenders have emphasized its normative and intellectual value.[27] But both positions are somewhat tangential to the actual practice of deterrence in the contemporary period, where the quest for rationality has proceeded in different ways at different times, and by different nations. These multiple kinds of approaches to rationality need to be studied if we are to comprehend how deterrence policies are actually formulated and applied; and this is a task for empirical research.[28]

3. *Scope.* Abstract deterrence theory has been simplistic in that to date it has lacked the means of defining its own scope or relevance. We have already remarked that it needs to be supplemented with a broader theory concerning the reduction of

---

[27] In a widely quoted passage Thomas Schelling notes that he has employed the assumption of rationality and points out that "the premise of 'rational behavior' is a potent one for the production of theory. *Whether the resulting theory provides good or poor insight into actual behavior is . . . a matter for subsequent judgment*" *Strategy of Conflict*, p. 4; emphasis added. Schelling did not note, but it is equally true, that the same premise is a virtually mandatory one for a prescriptive or normative theory. We do not aim to deny the utility of Schelling's premise but hope to take up his hint that actual deterrence behavior may be somewhat different from prescriptive deterrence theory.

[28] There is another aspect of the problem of rationality in deterrence which is germane but somewhat tangential at this point. This is the strategy of "the rationality of irrationality."

In his essay, "Rationality in Deterrence," Stephen Maxwell subjects this strategy to a searching criticism. His theme is that contemporary deterrence theory has given too much emphasis to this strategy without specifying various reasons why it must remain a relatively uncertain one, or recognizing that policy-makers are usually sharply limited in the extent to which they can manipulate commitments, and hence become "irrationally" committed at will.

the threat against the nation we wish to protect, and/or the re-channeling of the threat into a more acceptable form. But even before such a theoretical development is attempted, we need criteria suggesting *when* a deterrence policy should be applied. Such criteria are not a part of today's abstract deterrence theory. This theory has been offered in contingent form: "if the U.S. seeks to apply deterrence, then such-and-such means should be employed." There has been little effort to determine when deterrence should be applied, to distinguish circumstances under which deterrence is likely to succeed or fail, or to differentiate among those threats that may be deterred with one kind of policy response, those threats that may require another kind, and those threats that are not likely to be successfully deterred at all.

Again, the identification of its scope must be an empirical element in deterrence theory, requiring analysis of the inductive variety and outside the reach of abstract theory. The complexities of the decision as to whether and how to attempt deterrence will be taken up in chapter 19.

4. *Emphasis on Military Threats.* Deterrence theory to date has focused largely on the threat of military attack. Other forms of threat to U.S. interests have not been carefully distinguished in theory from open attack, or their special features identified. Rather, there seems to have been an implicit, simplified assumption that whatever policies were potent enough to deter "the worst case"—military attack—would certainly be potent enough to deter lesser threats. This is a precise conceptual analogue of the argument used in the 1950s by advocates of deterring limited war by the threat of Massive Retaliation: "the dog we keep to lick the cat can lick the kittens." The analogue was applied to policy, too. As noted in the previous chapter, the U.S. has made efforts to extend downward the doctrine and forces of Flexible Response to deter threats lower on the scale of violence than limited war, rather than have to deal with the greater complexities of deterrence at that level.

But it is usually not true that policies designed to deter a limited military attack will automatically deter any less violent threat. Often, open attack will not be "the worst case," merely the most obvious and unambiguous one, and for that reason in many ways the easiest, not the hardest, to deal with.

In any event, military attack does not appear to be a plausible contingency in very many cases. The actual extensions of communist influence in the Cold War and post–Cold War world have derived either from nonmilitary expansionist diplomacy of a traditional form—e.g., the Soviet Union's diplomatic offensive in the Middle East in recent years—or from the rise toward power of internal communist elements where communism has come in the name of reform (e.g., China, Cuba) and/or nationalism (e.g., Vietnam). Yet as Kennan and many others have pointed out,[29] since the late 1940s the U.S. erroneously has tended to interpret "containment" primarily in terms of containing a *military* threat, and accordingly deterrence theory has focused largely upon deterring military attack.

In this respect the theory has also reflected concerns aroused by the traumatic experience of Korea, a striking instance when the threat did indeed come in the form of open military attack. A broader range of experience with other kinds of challenges has generally not been exploited in developing deterrence theory. Of course, the intellectual problems of deterring outright military attack, even at a low level, are simpler than those of deterring nonmilitary "offensives."

The various kinds of simplification in deterrence theory appear to be reflected in the United States' experience in Southeast Asia in the early to mid-1960s. In retrospect there seem to be good reasons for believing that the threat posed by Hanoi to South Vietnam, at least (and perhaps to Laos as well), was simply not deterrable by any deterrence policy the United States could have been willing to attempt. If at that time the U.S. had possessed a deterrence theory with a better-defined scope which was capable of differentiating deterrable from nondeterrable threats, the U.S. might not have made the deterrence com-

[29] Kennan, *Memoirs*, p. 365.

mitments it later felt it had to fulfill in order to maintain its general credibility. There is also reason to believe that the U.S. interpreted what was primarily a nonmilitary threat to South Vietnam as a military one, and activated Flexible Response and related options designed to deter such a threat.

5. *Tendency toward a Binary View of Commitments.* Despite the emphasis in deterrence theorizing to date upon the concept and role of commitments, this aspect of the theory is in fact significantly oversimplified. Almost all theoretical treatments of deterrence have presumed that a commitment by the United States to protect some smaller power is an "either-or" matter—either the U.S. is committed to protect the nation or it is not. But in fact, with the possible exception of the American commitment to NATO, no U.S. commitment is absolute. Rather, commitments explicitly or implicitly are given to protect a nation against some threats, under some circumstances, for some time. As Stephen Maxwell has noted, "The weakness of these [i.e., deterrence theory's] versions of commitment is that they reduce a complex political fact to a military or diplomatic process." [30] Commitments, in fact, are a complex political phenomenon; they are made for many purposes, and their significance in terms of American willingness to defend a smaller nation, if need be, can vary greatly depending upon a variety of factors. (This aspect of "commitments" will be analyzed in considerable detail in chapter 19.) The assumption, contrary to ample and readily available historical experience, that commitments are a simple either-or matter is a particularly striking instance of the willingness of deterrence theorists to be abstract and unempirical.

6. *Restriction to Negative Influence.* To date deterrence theory has focused too narrowly on the role of threat in influence among nations. Except occasionally, when theorists have pointed out the need to couple "promises" with "threats" to make the latter work, the emphasis has been almost exclusively upon the engineering of proper threats. We have already al-

[30] Maxwell, "Rationality in Deterrence," p. 18.

luded to the need for theory concerning the reduction and re-channeling of challenges to legitimate U.S. interests as well as their frustration. More generally, theory needs to give as much attention to the role of "inducement" or "promise" as to that of threat. For the manipulation of inducements to affect other states' behavior is likely to be at least as complex as the manipulation of threats. (Some of the same considerations will apply to the "signaling," "credibility," and "commitments" of promises or inducements as to these aspects of threats; but there are likely to be important differences as well.)

Deterrence theory has focused upon threats rather than promises for the understandable reason that the theorists were strongly influenced by the Cold War image of acute international conflict, enhanced by the rapid growth of the strategic strike potential of the Soviet Union. In the post–Cold War era of less acute conflict, it would be appropriate for the theory to be extended. The need for a wider theory, be it called "deterrence," or "influence theory" of which "deterrence" would be one portion, is taken up in more detail in the last chapter.

7. *Inattention to Deterrent Capabilities.* Deterrence theory has significantly simplified the requirements of implementation measures for deterrence. Attention has been diverted from the question of whether "back-up capacities" are available or applicable by the assumption that the military power of the United States should be ample to meet any contingency.[31] This assumption is not correct. In any given case, even if the formulation of one's intent to deter has turned out to be well calculated, appropriate, and adequate, one's capacity to back it up may not be. The enormous raw military power of the United States would seem her least doubtful set of capacities. But it is not America's general capacities that will help deter a specific threat but her capacity to deal with the particulars of that threat. The United States must possess practical, usable, and specific

[31] This remark applies to deterrence theory since the early 1960s. It was, of course, a major criticism of Massive Retaliation that it did not provide the requisite capacities for deterrence of nonstrategic threats. But it would appear that the great buildup in U.S. conventional capacities under the doctrine of Flexible Response led to the assumption that the "capacities" problem was solved.

military options, and applying these options must be politically feasible.[32]

In this respect, too, U.S. deterrence policy failed in Southeast Asia in the early and mid-1960s. Hanoi never doubted overall American military power, nor the intent of American decision-makers to protect South Vietnam and Laos. What Hanoi doubted—essentially rightly—was first, America's capacity to find specific military options that would be effective against guerrilla attack; and second, the domestic political feasibility for the U.S. of applying effective military options over an extended period of time.

The full adequacy of one's capacities is likely to seem even more problematical when one turns from military to the more complex nonmilitary capabilities needed to back up deterrence in many situations. In the political, economic, and diplomatic spheres there is the same requirement as in the military field for practical specific options, but these options may be even harder to find.

The Normative-Prescriptive Use of an Abstract-Deductive Model

The seven simplifications in contemporary deterrence theory (which could be broken down into a smaller or larger number) are a natural consequence of the essentially abstract, deductive approach that analysts have taken to deterrence. This should be clearly recognized. The unitary actor, rationality, and the other assumptions and simplifications we have discussed are necessary ones to make manageable the logical tracing out of abstract theory. So long as it is kept clearly in mind that deterrence theory *does* have an abstract-deductive character, they are harmless enough.

The hazard begins to enter in when this simplified model is

[32] A similar argument is made on pp. 7–11 and 224–25 of George, Hall, and Simon, *The Limits of Coercive Diplomacy.*

used in a normative-prescriptive mode. As a rudimentary explanatory theory, or as a heuristic tool in more empirical studies, the simplified model can be and is very valuable. But there has been a marked tendency to employ the abstract-deductive model as a source of norms and prescriptions for policy, while ignoring or greatly deemphasizing the methodological and substantive prerequisites of a good normative-prescriptive theory.

We discuss some of the wider aspects of general normative-prescriptive theorizing for public policy in the Appendix. Here we wish to emphasize the many respects in which current *deterrence* theory fails to satisfy the prerequisites of normative-prescriptive theory. Methodologically, deterrence theory simply has not been adequately tested against historical experience, as we have indicated in this chapter and will show at greater length subsequently. Substantively, deterrence theory is seriously incomplete, to say the least, for a normative-prescriptive application. Most or all of the seven simplifications just discussed vitiate the theory's genuine policy relevance. (Of these, the theory's inability to define its own scope and applicability may be the most serious of all.) Furthermore, as discussed earlier in this chapter, two necessary elements of a normative-prescriptive theory, its assumptions and its goal, have been largely passed by in the race to generate the third element, the norms and prescriptions (which, however, have focused to date, as noted earlier, only on one segment of the relevant spectrum).

Many specialists in international relations, of course, have been aware in a general way of most of these simplifications in the abstract theory of deterrence. But the simplifications seemingly have not been visible enough to inspire major, systematic efforts to supplement the abstract theory with inductive analysis.[33] However, there have been a very few attempts to test some of the propositions of deductivist deterrence theory against historical evidence. To these we now turn.

[33] Other students of the problem who have shown awareness of the deductive character of deterrence theory and the need to supplement it with inductive examinations include, besides Thomas Schelling, William W. Kaufmann in "The Requirements of Deterrence" and Bruce Russett in his later "Pearl Harbor" article.

Bibliography

We have taken the following to be the principal contributions to deterrence theory at the levels below strategic war. The nature of each author's conceptualization of deterrence at this level, the extent to which he chooses to embrace formal or even mathematical models of deterrence, and the degree to which he focuses on deterrence to the relative exclusion of potentially related topics, naturally differ considerably.

Aron, Raymond. *Peace and War*. Garden City, Doubleday, 1966; chapter 14.

Brodie, Bernard. *Strategy in the Missile Age*. Princeton, Princeton University Press, 1959; chapter 9.

Fink, Clinton. "More Calculations About Deterrence," *Journal of Conflict Resolution*, 9, No. 1 (March 1965), 54.

Halperin, Morton. *Limited War in the Nuclear Age*. New York, Wiley, 1963.

Hoffmann, Stanley. *The State of War*. New York, Praeger, 1965; see especially chapter 6, "Roulette in the Cellar" and chapter 8, "Terror in Theory and Practice."

Jervis, Robert. *The Logic of Images in International Relations*. Princeton, Princeton University Press, 1970.

Kahn, Herman. *On Thermonuclear War*. Princeton, Princeton University Press, 1961; see especially pp. 126, 138–44, and 282.

——. *On Escalation, Metaphors and Scenarios*. New York, Praeger, 1965; chapters 3, 4, and 5.

Kaufmann. William W. "Limited Warfare," in W. W. Kaufmann, *Military Policy and National Security*. Princeton, Princeton University Press, 1956.

——. "The Requirements of Deterrence," in Kaufmann, *Military Policy*.

Maxwell, Stephen. "Rationality in Deterrence." Adelphi Paper No. 50. London, Institute for Strategic Studies, August 1968.

Milburn, Thomas. "Design for the Study of Deterrent Processes." China Lake, Calif., U.S. Naval Ordnance Test Station, April 1964.

Raser, John R. "Deterrence Research: Past Progress and Future Needs," *Journal of Peace Research*, No. 4 (1966), p. 297.

Russett, Bruce. "The Calculus of Deterrence," *Journal of Conflict Resolution*, 3, No. 2 (March 1963) p. 97.

——. "Pearl Harbor: Deterrence Theory and Decision Theory," *Journal of Peace Research*, No. 2 (1967), p. 89.

Schelling, Thomas C. *Arms and Influence*. New Haven, Yale University Press, 1966; principally chapters 2 and 3.

——. *The Strategy of Conflict*. Cambridge, Harvard University Press, 1960; see especially chapters 2, 3, 5, and 8.

—— "What Is Game Theory?" in James Charlesworth, *Contemporary Political Analysis*. New York, Free Press of Glencoe, 1967.

Snyder, Glenn. *Deterrence and Defense*. Princeton, Princeton University Press, 1961; see especially chapter 1, part C, and chapters 3, 4 and 5.

We have taken the following to be the principal statements by the *critics* of deterrence theory, who severally have raised a number of the points made in this chapter:

Boulding, Kenneth E. "National Images and International Systems," *Journal of Conflict Resolution*, 3, No. 2 (June 1959), 120.

——. "Toward a Pure Theory of Threat Systems," *American Economic Review*, May 1963.

Deutsch, Karl W. *The Analysis of International Relations*. Englewood Cliffs, N.J., Prentice-Hall, 1968; see especially pp. 112–32.

——. *The Nerves of Government*. London: Free Press of Glencoe, 1963, pp. 51–72.

Etzioni, Amitai. *The Hard Way to Peace*. New York, Collier, 1962.

Green, Philip. *Deadly Logic*. New York, Schocken, 1968.

Holsti, Ole. *Crisis, Escalation, War*. Montreal, McGill–Queen's University Press, 1972.

Knight, Jonathan. "Risks of War and Deterrence Logic," *Canadian Journal of Political Science*, 6, No. 1 (March 1973), 22.

Maxwell, Stephen. "Rationality in Deterrence." Adelphi Paper No. 50. London, International Institute of Strategic Studies, August 1968.

Milburn, Thomas W. "The Concept of Deterrence: Some Logical and Psychological Considerations," *Journal of Social Issues*, 17, No. 3 (1961), 3.

Osgood, Charles. *An Alternative to War or Surrender*. Urbana, Ill., University of Illinois Press, 1962.

Payne, James L. *The American Threat*. Chicago, Markham, 1970.

Rapoport, Anatol. *The Big Two*. New York, Pegasus, 1971.

——. *Strategy and Conscience*. New York, Harper & Row, 1964.

Raser, John R. "Deterrence Research: Past Progress and Future Needs," *Journal of Peace Research*, No. 4 (1966).

——. "Theories of Deterrence," *Peace Research Reviews*, 3, No. 1 (1969).

Russett, Bruce M. "Pearl Harbor: Deterrence Theory and Decision Theory," *Journal of Peace Research*, No. 5 (1967).

Singer, J. David. *Deterrence, Arms Control and Disarmament*. Columbus, University of Ohio Press, 1962.

——. "Threat Perception and the Armament-Tension Dilemma," *Journal of Conflict Resolution*, 2, No. 1 (1958), 90.

Other sources drawn upon in this chapter include:

Baldwin, David A. "Inter-Nation Influence Revisited," *Journal of Conflict Resolution*, 15, No. 5 (December 1971), 471.

——. "The Power of Positive Sanctions," *World Politics*, 24, No. 1 (October 1971), 19.

Bloomfield, Lincoln P., and Amelia C. Leiss. *Controlling Small Wars*. New York, Knopf, 1970.

Fisher, Roger. *International Conflict for Beginners*. New York, Harper & Row, 1969.

——, ed. *International Conflict and Behavioral Science*. New York, Basic Books, 1964.

Jervis, Robert. *Perception and Mis-perception in International Politics*. Princeton, Princeton University Press, forthcoming.

Kissinger, Henry A. "Military Policy and Defense of the 'Gray Areas,' " *Foreign Affairs*, 33, No. 3 (April 1955), 416.

Luard, Evan. "Conciliation and Deterrence," *World Politics*, 19, No. 2 (January 1967), 167.

McClelland, Charles. "The Reorientation of the Sociology of Conflict," *Journal of Conflict Resolution*, 6, No. 1 (March 1962), 88.

Milburn, Thomas W. "What Constitutes Effective U.S. Deterrence?" in *International Stability*, ed. Dale J. Hekhuis, G. G. McClintock, and A. L. Burns. New York, Wiley, 1964.

——. "When Do Threats Provoke Violent Responses?" Paper presented before the International Studies Association annual meeting, March 1973.

Nardin, Terry. "Communication and the Effects of Threats in Strategic Interaction." Paper of the Peace Research Society International, Cambridge, Mass., November 1967.

Osgood, Robert E. *Limited War*. Chicago, University of Chicago Press, 1957.

Patchen, Martin. "Deterrence Theory in the Study of National Action: Problems And a Proposal," *Journal of Conflict Resolution*, 9, No. 2 (June 1965), 164.

Ponturo, John. "The Deterrence of Limited Aggression," *Orbis*, 6, No. 4 (Winter 1963), 593.

Pool, Ithiel de Sola. "Deterrence as an Influence Process." China Lake, Calif., U.S. Naval Ordnance Test Station, November 1965.

Rapoport, Anatol. *Fights, Games and Debates*. Ann Arbor, University of Michigan Press, 1960.

——. "Games Which Simulate Deterrence and Disarmament," *Peace Research Reviews*, 1, No. 4 (1967).

——. "Prospects for Experimental Games," *Journal of Conflict Resolution*, 12, No. 4 (December 1968), 461.

Shubik, Martin. "Some Reflections on the Design of Game Theoretic Models for the Study of Negotiation and Threats," *Journal of Conflict Resolution* 7, No. 1 (March 1963), 1.

Singer, J. David. "Inter-Nation Influence: A Formal Model," *American Political Science Review*, 57, No. 2 (June 1963), 420.

Steinbruner. *The Cybernetic Theory of Decisions: New Dimensions of Political Analysis*. Princeton, Princeton University Press, 1974.

Sullivan, Michael P. "International Bargaining Behavior," *International Studies Quarterly*, 15, No. 3 (September 1971), 359.

Waskow, Arthur. *The Limits of Defense*. Garden City, N.Y., Doubleday, 1962.

Weinstein, Franklin. "The Concept of a Commitment in International Relations," *Journal of Conflict Resolution*, 13, No. 1 (March 1969), 39.

Wolfers, Arnold. *Discord and Collaboration*. Baltimore, Johns Hopkins University Press, 1962.

Young, Oran. *The Politics of Force*. Princeton, Princeton University Press, 1969.

Chapter 4

The Empirical Study of Deterrence

Empirical Studies to Date: Statistical Attempts

ONLY A HANDFUL of attempts have been made to date to examine deterrence empirically. On the whole they tend to throw light upon some of the deficiencies just described in the deductivist theory of deterrence and to suggest some important lessons for the methodology of future research. These lessons will be discussed in this chapter, followed by a presentation of the somewhat novel methodology of the present study. A more detailed examination of methodological problems of research in this and similar areas appears in the Appendix.

The first significant effort to study deterrence empirically was Bruce Russett's 1963 article, "The Calculus of Deterrence." [1] Russett begins from the premise that the critical factor

---

[1] In addition to this piece, there are a handful of other empirical examinations of deterrence questions, some of which we will have occasion to refer to again later in this chapter: deLeon, MacQueen, and Rosecrance, *Situational Analysis;* Fink, "More Calculations about Deterrence"; Naroll, "Deterrence in History"; Naroll, Bullough, and Naroll, *Military Deterrence in History;* Russett, "Pearl Harbor." In addition, at the time of this writing empirical research related to deterrence is being conducted by Professor Raymond Tanter and his associates at the University of Michigan and Professor Gerald Shure and his associates at UCLA. Tanter and his associates are combining a case study approach to problems of deterrence with computer-based laboratory exercises. Their work em-

determining the success or failure of a particular deterrence policy is the credibility of the "defender's" commitment to the "pawn"—that is, the credibility of the explicit or implicit threat by a great power that it will come to the military assistance of a small nation which may be attacked by another power. He chose to examine the potential of nine postulated factors for enhancing this credibility. The chosen factors were objective and situational:

—the pawn/defender ratio in population;
—the pawn/defender ratio in GNP;
—the presence or absence of a prior formal commitment;
—strategic superiority by the defender;
—local superiority by the defender;
—defender's political system (dictatorship or democracy);
—the existence of formal military cooperation between
    defender and pawn;
—political interdependence between defender and pawn;
—economic interdependence between defender and pawn.

Employing an arithmetic correlation technique, Russett determined the presence or absence of each of these factors in seventeen recent historical cases where a major power apparently had attempted to deter attack on a pawn. Only one factor, economic interdependence (as measured by the percentage of the pawn's imports provided by the defender), demonstrated a high correlation with deterrence "success" ("success" being defined to include not only forestalling attack but also repulsing an attack without conflict between the attacking forces and regular combat units of the major-power defender).

That this research method provides only rather rudimentary

---

ploys both a nonstrategic model, which includes attention to bureaucratic politics and other constraints on rational behavior, and a strategic model.

At UCLA new methodological tools are being developed to aid in the design, analysis, and evaluation of complex crisis games. These range from multiteam on-line computer-administered simulations to paper-and-pencil scenarios that are structured to allow for systematic evaluation of large numbers of independent and dependent factors in specific crisis contexts. Two of these studies were reported in the abstracts for the Fourteenth Annual Convention of the International Studies Association, March 14–17, 1973, New York, New York.

information about deterrence was recognized by the same author in his 1967 essay, "Pearl Harbor: Deterrence Theory and
Decision Theory." Here Russett pointed out that his previous
attempt made

> two substantial inferential leaps. One is from the existence of . . .
> bonds between the defender and pawn to their perception by . . .
> the potential attacker, and the second is from their perception to
> their entry in a significant way into the calculations [of the potential
> attacker].[2]

There are, in short, a number of intervening variables between
the actions of the defender and the deterrence of the potential
attacker—variables of perception and assessment. While the selection of "hard," objective factors of the kind employed by
Russett in his earlier study may facilitate the study and scoring
of cases, it is these subjective factors imbedded in the minds
and calculations of the potential attacker's policy-makers—i.e.,
decision-making variables—that are of the essence in deterrence.

It is not impossible to consider such intervening variables
while retaining a statistical-correlative methodology. Peter
deLeon, James MacQueen, and Richard Rosecrance included
some in their study, "Situational Analysis in International Politics." [3] In this study, 49 cases from the period 1931–1965 were
selected where a "committor nation" (the term "aggressor" was
avoided) took "threatening action" with respect to some "con-
tested area" which a "responder nation" attempted to forestall.
"Threatening action" was interpreted to mean any overt move
to upset the status quo. The cases were grouped according to
various mathematical tests. Correlations were then performed
against 40 independent variables, including such decision-making variables as:

—the apparent objectives of the players;
—the players' estimated probabilities of success for their policies;

[2] Russett, "Pearl Harbor," p. 94.

[3] See also Rosecrance, "Categories, Concepts and Reasoning."

—the players' assessments of the importance of the issue;
—the players' respective "determination";
—the players' respective perceptions of the likelihood of major war arising from the threatening action;
—the state of morale in the player populations.

Certain variables (and certain groupings of the cases) enjoyed significant correlation with the "failure or success" of the threatening action.

But in general it appears that adequate attention cannot be given with the statistical-correlative methodology to the intervening, decision-making variables in deterrence, at least at the present time. One salient reason is that these intervening variables tend to alter from case to case in complex ways which cannot readily be compressed into a small number of predefined values for coding. In his second article Bruce Russett agrees:

> To go further we must move from the examination of many cases to the study in depth of one or more particular instances to discover whether these [objective] factors were really observed by the decision-makers and what importance they took on [in their calculations].[4]

He then proceeds with a fairly intensive case study of the Pearl Harbor attack. In this instance, he establishes, the Japanese decision-makers did indeed perceive tight bonds between defender (the U.S.) and pawns (U.S. allies in the Far East); and these perceptions entered in a significant way into their calculations. Thus in this instance the intervening variables were present, and one is justified in concluding that the Japanese decision-makers appropriately observed the American deterrence attempt. But of course, the correlation between "commitment" and "deterrence success" *fails* in this case! Deterrence failed *even though* the Japanese leaders (as Russett demonstrates) accepted the high credibility of the U.S. commitment.

What this result immediately suggests is that a researcher's assessment of the Japanese utility calculations must not only be more comprehensive than a mere correlation of objective, situa-

[4] Russett, "Pearl Harbor," p. 94.

tional factors with deterrence success/failure. It must also be more comprehensive than a simple scoring of the presence or absence of "perceptions" and "calculations" of these factors. The Pearl Harbor case, in fact, provides a particularly good demonstration of the need to develop deterrence theory to become richer and more differentiated. In this case another decision-making variable must be brought in: Japanese policymakers were strongly *motivated* to challenge the status quo even though they accepted that war was probable thereafter. This instance also shows that where the potential initiator is highly motivated, a deterrence policy may backfire, bringing attack upon the deterring power as well as upon the pawn.[5]

Empirical Studies to Date: Intensive Case Studies

One concludes, therefore, that the statistical-correlative approach to deterrence needs to be supplemented with relatively intense analyses of individual cases, embracing a variety of decision-making variables. Some attempts of this kind have been made. Most of the major crises of the Cold War era by now possess a literature of case studies, many of which at least take up issues of deterrence, and a few of which, like Glenn Paige's *The Korean Decision*, consider these issues in some detail. Roberta Wohlstetter's *Pearl Harbor: Warning and Decision* also shows how complex and fragile a deterrence policy can be.

[5] Furthermore, it is important to recognize that the United States was not merely trying to deter the Japanese government from further encroachments in the Far East; it was also trying to *coerce* the Japanese into undoing some of their earlier conquests. Coercion is much more difficult and risky than deterrence, and more likely to inspire an unpleasant response from the opponent. See George, Hall, and Simons, *The Limits of Coercive Diplomacy*. From the viewpoint of the Japanese Government, the United States had confronted it with a difficult choice between highly unpalatable alternatives. The option of attacking the United States in this situation was regarded as the lesser evil, compared to doing nothing or agreeing to abandon the expansionist policy on which Japan had embarked some years earlier.

But these intensive case studies, although they all employ decision-making approaches, generally are not strictly comparable. Hence their findings do not cumulate and prove little more than suggestive for theory-building. Not only do these studies vary widely in the degree and manner in which they examine deterrence questions; they also employ somewhat different decision-making models—and differing degrees of attention to any explicit model. With the passage of time and the accumulation of research experience, the early attractiveness and promise of "the" decision-making approach to the study of foreign policy has given way to a more sober realization of its intricacies and the variety of ways in which it can be conceptualized. We have not one but many decision-making approaches.[6]

A scrutiny of these individual case studies does suggest, however, the richness of the deterrence phenomenon. The most elementary and nonrigorous comparison of, say, the several Berlin crises, the Taiwan Strait crises, and the Cuban missile crisis serves to indicate deterrence's potential complexity. For instance, a brief perusal of just these cases will suggest to the analyst that deterrence "success" or "failure" is not a one-time event. Crisis policy-making within both the defending and the potentially initiating powers is a process composed of a series of interrelated decisions, each of which must therefore be seen as imbedded in a sequential as well as a "cross-sectional" policy context. Hence, deterrence is likely to succeed or fail through time and in stages. A glance at these cases also suggests that deterrence does not succeed or fail in just one way. Rather, there is likely to be more than one causal pattern by which the deterrence mechanism may work, or fail. And simple "success" or "failure" is frequently an inadequate typology for organizing the outcomes of deterrence attempts. (These analytical points will be taken up again in much greater detail in Part Three.)

Individual case studies, then, possess a set of virtues and deficiencies just contrary to those of statistical-correlative studies.

[6] For an incisive discussion of the failure of intensive case studies of foreign policy to cumulate scientifically, see Rosenau, "Moral Fervor, Systematic Analysis, and Scientific Consciousness in Foreign Policy Research."

They embrace deterrence's richness and diversity, but they fail to accumulate scientifically.

The Methodological Problem

What seems required, therefore, is a research methodology which is capable of differentiating and identifying the variations in a number of relevant decision-making variables from one set of deterrence circumstances to another and assessing their significance, while remaining "cumulable" across multiple cases.

As a matter of fact, scholars seem to be coming to a very similar conclusion in several fields within the social sciences where multiple case studies need to be examined from the viewpoint of a single research interest. For example, Sidney Verba has introduced the term "disciplined-configurative" to describe this kind of study in comparative politics ("macropolitics"). Such studies, he says, should examine "a large number of factors" across many cases, where "the uniqueness of the explanation for any particular case arises from the fact that the *combination* of relevant factors that accounts for a nation's pattern of politics will be different from the combination in other cases." [7] The factors themselves, however, remain the same; hence analyses are cumulable. (We consider Verba's views and others at greater length in the Appendix.)

In the field of foreign policy studies, what is essentially this method has also been independently discovered and applied by several analysts in recent years. In *The Politics of Force* Oran Young formulated a small number of specific hypotheses and discussed them in the context of a specific set of Cold War crises, attempting to account for variations in the outcomes. Lincoln Bloomfield and Amelia Leiss, in their *Controlling Small Wars*, examined fourteen post–World War II cases, employing

[7] Verba, "Some Dilemmas in Comparative Research."

13 general groups of factors that encourage the escalation or de-escalation of conflict and attempting to explain variations across cases in factors that might be relevant to conflict-control. Alexander George, David Hall, and William Simons, in *The Limits of Coercive Diplomacy*, examined three cases in depth, attempting to uncover variables explaining the failure of a particular foreign policy technique in one instance and different degrees of success in two others. Ole Holsti's *Crisis, Escalation and War* compared two cases in detail—the outbreak of World War I and the Cuban missile crisis—and several other cases in lesser degree, with respect to psychological and decision-making factors in escalation. Richard Smoke's *Controlling Escalation* examined five pre–World War II cases in depth, employing a standardized set of six questions in each, in an effort to elucidate escalation control measures.

As these examples suggest, there can be substantial variation in scholars' efforts to cope with the problems of combining "cumulability" and detailed differentiation of variables. But what these have in common is an effort to study multiple case studies employing the *same* variables, while accounting *explicitly* for the variation in these factors from case to case.

The Method of Focused Comparison

The method of "focused comparison," as we would like to call it, resembles the statistical-correlational approach discussed in the first section of this chapter insofar as it examines multiple cases and establishes its results, in the main, by making comparisons among them. Also like the statistical-correlational approach, it proceeds by asking a limited number of questions or testing a limited number of hypotheses, all of which are usually closely related to each other. (Our questions for this study will be discussed shortly.)

But the focused comparison method also resembles the intensive case study approach discussed in the second section of this chapter in that it examines each case in some depth; for all practical purposes, therefore, only a small number of cases can be studied. All cases are approached by asking identical questions. This standardized set of questions or hypotheses insures the comparability of results. (Additional questions, of course, may be asked of any given case if it seems desirable to bring out unique features it may possess, so that the method has some built-in flexibility.)

With this method the investigator is able, of course, to uncover similarities among cases that suggest possible generalizations; but he is also able to investigate the differences among cases in a systematic manner. Analysis of differences can be just as useful as analysis of similarities for the development of theory. By specifying the differing circumstances or causes that led to different results in the various cases, the investigator can illuminate in an explicit, orderly fashion the complexity of deterrence phenomena and the variation in outcomes. Comparison of cases can thus lead to what might be termed "contingent generalizations"—"if circumstances A then outcome O"— which can be an important part of theory and have important implications for practice.

The focused comparison method has, of course, its own limitations. Unlike the statistical-correlative approach to multiple cases, it does not and cannot determine the relative frequency with which any given conjunction of independent and dependent variables occurs, since it does not employ either a complete or a representative sample of cases.[8] And because the number of cases employed is small, findings will enjoy a lower degree of formal verification than do statistical generalizations grounded in quantitative analysis of a large number of cases.

But what the focused comparison method can offer in place of a high degree of formal verification may be something more

---

[8] Statistically based predictions of the probability of some event are therefore not possible, although a different kind of "prediction" can be made (see below). It should also be noted that there is no obstacle in principle to combining the method of focused comparison with a statistical-correlative approach to a larger set of cases, representative or complete.

valuable—potentially a significantly greater degree of relevance to real policy problems than is usually enjoyed by statistically validated generalizations (or, for that matter, the conclusions of a single case study). This greater relevance can exist for several reasons. The researcher does not select variables for their measurability. He does try to specify the circumstances under which his variables are likely to apply. Furthermore, the standardized set of questions can employ variables which policymakers themselves find useful and tend to employ in dealing with fresh problems. If carefully designed, the questions should then uncover results of potential policy relevance by focusing in detail on the more useful decision-making or utility-calculus considerations.

Finally and most importantly, the capacity of the focused comparison method to differentiate among cases offers a greater *diagnostic* potential than does the scoring of variables preselected for their measurability. Since variation among cases is addressed explicitly and analytically by the focused comparison method, conclusions can be drawn with this method that can assist directly in the diagnosis of a fresh case, historical or contemporary. For example, one can in principle use this method to arrive at the discovery of certain patterns of success and failure in deterrence, as will be discussed at greater length in Part Three below. Such patterns are of obvious diagnostic assistance to the policy-maker in coping with a current deterrence problem, and can offer him a kind of "contingent prediction" about the way his current situation would be likely to develop, given the presence or absence of various conditions or factors. (The importance of policy-relevant theory and the needs of policymakers are addressed in greater detail in the Appendix.)

Questions on Deterrence

The investigator who approaches the problem of deterrence with the focused comparison method discovers almost at the outset that neither the few statistical-correlative and intensive case studies in existence nor the deductive, normative-prescriptive theory he has inherited provide him with hypotheses or questions which are precise, operationally significant, and adequate. Rather, the thin body of existing empiricism, and the thicker but not very policy-relevant body of theory, provide at most a set of starting-points or "kernels" around which he can begin to crystalize his own questions. The result is that his research design becomes, at least informally and for practical purposes, an iterative one. Tentative questions and ideas are tried out against two or three case studies in a preliminary way, and are then refined and expanded upon on the basis of the tentative results. A new trial is made, and the process of question-asking and -answering iterates back and forth, until a satisfactorily full menu of hypotheses or questions can be arrived at for more formal application to all one's case study material.

In the case of deterrence, again, the questions which can be asked usefully of a complete set of cases must, at the present time, remain moderately (but only moderately) general ones. Such is the nature of the questions employed in this study. The requirement for fairly general questions about deterrence, it might be emphasized, does not flow from any limitation in the focused comparison method, which is quite capable of successfully utilizing quite specific and concrete hypotheses. Rather, it is the presently quite underdeveloped state of empirically based and policy-relevant deterrence theory (as discussed in chapters 2 and 3) that accounts for the moderate generality of the most useful questions at the present stage of research.

Implicit in these questions is, in effect, a preliminary image or model of the deterrent situation derived from the iterating process just mentioned. The simplicity and generality of this model does considerable violence to reality, of course; but since its purpose is simply to derive a set of questions to ask about the empirical material, it is only heuristic (in a very strict sense of that often misused term).

We begin, then, at the point where U.S. policy-makers are considering the relationship between the United States and the "third area," an area which may become threatened by an opponent. The relationship between the area and the U.S. is not necessarily either obvious, foreordained, or unlimited. Rather, U.S. policy-makers are likely to consider that the U.S. has various goals or objectives with respect to the third party which can be valued for differing reasons and to a greater or lesser degree. Hence, an interesting first question to ask concerning any case is:

QUESTION 1: What valuation of what objectives was made by U.S. decision-makers vis-à-vis the third area?

(The reader should remind himself that "U.S. decision-makers" are not usually a monolithic body. Rather, as pointed out in the previous chapter, there will usually be diverse interpretations of all the matters embraced by these questions, by differing institutions and individuals. The case studies to come will give considerable attention to this point, as appropriate.)

Ex hypothesi the potential opponent also has various goals with respect to the third party which can be valued for differing reasons and to a greater or lesser degree. Hence a second question, logically parallel to the first:

QUESTION 2: What valuation of what objectives was made by the opponent's decision-makers vis-à-vis the third area?

The same caveat regarding the multiplicity of organizational and bureaucratic players applies to the opponent as well, of course. While there are obvious limitations in the extent to which the researcher can determine the interests of various of the opponent's policy-makers, and indeed of the summation of interests that motivates the opponent's actual policy, nevertheless it frequently turns out that judgments of analytical significance can be made.[9]

Likewise *ex hypothesi*, United States policy-makers be-

[9] See, for instance, Graham Allison's effort to reconstruct the political processes of the Soviet Union in his *Essence of Decision*, chapters 4 and 6.

come aware of a potential threat or action inimical to U.S. interests (as they have been defined) in the third area:

> QUESTION 3: What was the perception of U.S. decisionmakers of the kind and magnitude of the opponent's explicit or implicit threat to the third area, and of the objectives this threat appeared to serve?

At this point U.S. policy-makers do not necessarily decide that a deterrence effort is called for. The potential threat may be assessed as an insignificant one or a bluff. Even if it is assessed as real and significant, the decision may be reached that the cost to the United States of the opponent's carrying out his threat is acceptable. In fact, there are a number of variables involved in the perceiving and interpreting the implications of the threat:

> QUESTION 4: How did U.S. decision-makers perceive and assess their policy problem and the major policy alternatives, including deterrence?

Related to this question will be policy-makers' perceptions of the deterrence option itself. As pointed out in the previous chapter, activating the deterrence option involves the full formulation of a deterrence strategy and analysis of the requirements of that strategy in the context at hand. Additionally, perceived constraints may limit one's ability to meet the full requirements of one's preferred option:

> QUESTION 5: How did U.S. decision-makers formulate the deterrent option(s) available to them, and how did they assess the requirements of these option(s)? What constraints on meeting the requirements were perceived?

Also closely related to these matters is the question of policymakers' views regarding events should the deterrence attempt fail. Would the United States then allow the opponent's challenge to the third area to stand, thus revealing the American deterrence effort as a bluff? (Was it meant as a bluff in the first place?) Or would some "action policy" then be adopted to protect perceived U.S. interests? Needless to say, what the United States actually does when deterrence has failed may be different, but policy-makers' *expectations* regarding this eventuality are part of the deterrence problem itself:

QUESTION 6: What expectations concerning action policy in the event deterrence failed were held by U.S. decision-makers?

For purposes of analysis we presume at this point that U.S. policy-makers do in fact select a deterrence strategy and begin to execute it. The opponent's perception of this attempt is critical:

QUESTION 7: What were the perceptions of the opponent's decision-makers of the nature and extent of the U.S. deterrent commitment, and of the kind and magnitude of the risks it posed to their projected initiative in the third area?

Finally, of course, the opponent may choose to continue, extend, or modify his challenge to the third area rather than withdrawing it, thereby manufacturing at least a partial failure for the U.S. deterrence attempt. His decision to go forward with an initiative will depend upon his policy-makers' concluding that their objectives, as they value them, outweigh the projected risks of challenging the U.S. deterrence commitment:

QUESTION 8: What new action by the opponent resulted from what reassessment of his objectives in the light of the perceived risks?

The reader will have noticed that this last question resembles and can be connected to question 2, and that if the opponent makes a new threat or takes a threatening action, the remainder of the questions can be asked again in the new situation. In other words, the sequence of questions can be—and in most real-world cases, must be—iterated. This reflects the fact, which we have mentioned before and will have occasion to stress again, that deterrence usually fails or succeeds over time and in stages. An initial deterrence commit-

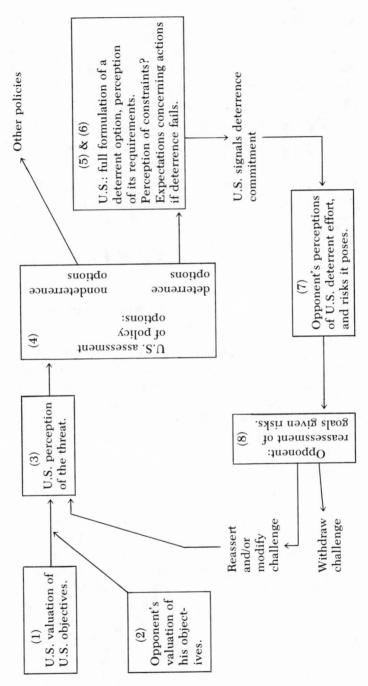

Flow Chart of Questions on Deterrence

Note: Numbers in parentheses refer to the list of questions.

ment may fail to prevent the opponent from making some sort of preliminary probe into the third area. With this new evidence, the U.S. may choose to issue a stronger commitment, to mobilize troops or otherwise "send a signal," and in other ways to strengthen the deterrence effort. The opponent may respond with a further and deeper probe, designed to ferret out the real lengths to which the U.S. will go without bringing down the full weight of a military response in a major crisis. And so forth. At each stage of the back-and-forth sequence of deterrence efforts and probes, the complete set of eight questions can be asked. This iterating process is illustrated by the figure, which lays out in "flow-chart" terms the sequence of events embraced by the eight questions.

Nearly all the eleven cases treated in Part Two of this study demonstrate this sequential, gradual failure of deterrence. In the interest of readability, we have not included the explicit lists of questions and answers, since in several cases the whole set of eight questions had to be asked several times over during the sequential, step-by-step unfolding of the deterrence problem. The reader will, however, be able to see for himself the implicit framework of questions and answers within the text of each case study.

We turn now to our eleven case studies. Some conclusion can and will be adduced *within* each study, simply on the basis of the intensive analysis of that individual case. Many more conclusions, of the focused comparison variety, will follow in Part Three.

Bibliography

Allison, Graham. *Essence of Decison*. Boston, Little, Brown, 1971.

Bloomfield, Lincoln P., and Amelia Leiss. *Controlling Small Wars*. New York, Knopf, 1970.

deLeon, Peter, James MacQueen, and Richard Rosecrance. *Situational Analysis in International Politics*. Unpublished manuscript, UCLA Political Science Department, 1967. A summary report under the same title appears in *Behavioral Science*, 14, No. 1 (January 1968), 51.

Fink, Clifton. "More Calculations about Deterrence," *Journal of Conflict Resolution*, 9, No. 1 (March 1965), 54.

George, Alexander, David Hall, and Williams Simons. *The Limits of Coercive Diplomacy*. Boston, Little, Brown, 1971.

Holsti, Ole. *Crisis, Escalation, and War*. Montreal, McGill–Queen's University Press, 1972.

Naroll, Raoul. "Deterrence in History," in *Theory and Research on the Causes of War*, ed. Dean G. Pruitt and Richard C. Snyder. Englewood Cliffs, N.J., Prentice-Hall, 1969.

——, Verne R. Bullough, and Frada Naroll. *Military Deterrence in History: A Pilot Cross-Historical Survey*. Albany, State University of New York Press, 1973.

Paige, Glenn. *The Korean Decision*. New York, Free Press of Glencoe, 1968.

Rosecrance, Richard N. "Categories, Concepts and Reasoning in the Study of International Relations," *Behavioral Science*, 6, No. 3 (July 1961), 223.

Rosenau, James M. "Moral Fervor, Systematic Analysis, and Scientific Consciousness in Foreign Policy Research," in *Political Science and Public Policy*, ed. Austin Ranney. Chicago, Markham, 1968.

Russett, Bruce M. "The Calculus of Deterrence," *Journal of Conflict Resolution* 7, No. 2 (June 1963), 97.

——. "Pearl Harbor: Deterrence Theory and Decision Theory," *Journal of Peace Research*, No. 2 (1967), p. 89.

Smoke, Richard. *Controlling Escalation*. Forthcoming.

Verba, Sidney. "Some Dilemmas in Comparative Research," *World Politics*, 20, No. 1 (October 1967), 114.

Wohlstetter, Roberta. *Pearl Harbor: Warning and Decision*. Stanford, Stanford University Press, 1962.

Young, Oran. *The Politics of Force*. Princeton, Princeton University Press, 1968.

Part Two
🏵
Case Studies

THIS PART OF THE BOOK presents eleven case studies of major United States deterrence efforts between 1948 and 1963. These case studies are of twofold value. First, they provide an empirical base for the theoretical analysis in Part Three. Anticipating this, some aspects of these cases are given special prominence in the chapters that follow, as preparation for that later analysis.

But second, the case studies are intended to stand in their own right as historical explanations of the outcomes of many of the major deterrence efforts of the Cold War period. They are "historical" in the sense that they are, of course, retrospective. However, they are also analytical in the sense that we employ a variety of tools and concepts in attempting to explain the *reasons* behind a particular outcome in terms of the inner logic of the deterrence process. They are therefore as much "political science" as they are "history," but since each is intended to stand by itself as a reasonably complete treatment of the issues it chooses to raise, somewhat more explanatory detail is provided than would be necessary for a narrow-gauged analysis of deterrence dynamics alone. We have not hesitated, in other words, to give attention to background, contextual, and idiosyncratic features of each particular case in order to construct a more adequate explanation of the events of that case itself.

Chapter 5

The Berlin Blockade, 1948

Résumé of the Crisis

THE STEADY deterioration of relations between the Western powers and the Soviet Union in the post–World War II period culminated on June 24, 1948 with the Soviet blockade of Allied ground access to West Berlin. The United States had made no special effort to deter the Soviets from making this move. Prior to the blockade, it is true, the Truman Administration had asserted a general policy of "containment" toward the Soviet Union. While containment implied the need for something like deterrence, as well as utilization of other means for reducing the vulnerability of noncommunist states to various forms of Soviet encroachment, American leaders were slow to see this implication. As discussed in chapter 1, the Truman Administration rarely thought of implementing containment with specific deterrence strategies. The major exception to this, of course, was the NATO treaty; but this came later, in 1949, and the blockade crisis contributed to bringing it about. Prior to the NATO treaty's effort to deter Soviet aggression against Western Europe, and for other parts of the world even after the formation of NATO, the Truman Administration was inclined to wait for a Soviet initiative or probe and then respond to it.

As we shall see, there was ample warning of a Soviet move against West Berlin prior to June 1948. But Truman took no specific measures to deter it. Confronted on June 24 with the dilemma of attempting to maintain the isolated Western position in West Berlin without risking war, President Truman rejected both advice to withdraw from West Berlin and advice to respond with military force. The Western Allies did not directly challenge the ground blockade; instead, they hastily organized an airlift of supplies to West Berlin. The airlift was not conceived initially as an instrument for thwarting the blockade, since its estimated maximum capability was expected to fall far short of the minimum needs of the West Berlin population and Allied forces in the city. It was resorted to rather as a means of buying some time for diplomatic discussions with the Soviet government. Initial negotiations, however, failed to resolve the dispute. The blockade continued and the crisis dragged on. The Soviets occasionally threatened but did not seriously attempt to interfere with Allied aircraft employing the established air corridors to fly supplies from Western Germany to West Berlin.

The Allies were reluctant to escalate their response or to engage in coercive threats in an effort to force Stalin to relax the blockade. They chose to work instead within the existing framework of limitations, or ground rules, that had evolved in the early days of the crisis. More and more resources were poured into the airlift and, developing great skill at improvisation, the Allies eventually transformed it into an effective weapon for breaking the blockade. With the addition of a selective and increasingly effective counterblockade of East Germany, the Allies succeeded in reversing the expected outcome of the Soviet blockade. The Soviet leaders now had to make the onerous decision as to whether to engage in a risky escalation or to accept the failure of their blockade to pressure the West into withdrawing from Berlin or making major diplomatic concessions on other European issues. The crisis was eventually resolved in 1949 through negotiations which left the Western position in Berlin substantially intact.

The General Structure of
the Deterrent Situation

The onset of the Berlin crisis of 1948 provides a rather sobering example of the difficulty of translating the concept of deterrence into a well-designed, well-implemented attempt to discourage efforts to change the status quo. Deterrence is easiest and clearest in uncomplicated situations where the line between "defender" and "initiator" is clearly drawn and where the "initiator" is clearly engaged in an effort at unjustified aggrandizement. A review of the complex origins of the Berlin crisis makes it clear that the Soviet blockade of West Berlin cannot be regarded as a simple effort at aggrandizement, or even as an act clearly or exclusively aimed at altering the territorial status quo in the Soviets' favor. The threat to West Berlin, rather, was embedded in a much broader set of issues and emerged as the culmination of a complex series of interactions between the two sides. A full understanding of the deterrent situation of 1948 requires some attention to these complexities. In recapitulating this background, we do not attempt to judge questions of responsibility in any moral sense. Rather, we seek to demonstrate how the deterrence problem of 1948 grew out of complex interactions that were not entirely planned by either side.

Following the end of World War II, hopes for continued postwar cooperation in Europe between the former allies were undermined gradually by increasing conflict and rivalry. In much of Europe the situation remained fluid and unstable, and the lines of acknowledged control and influence were not to be clearly and finally drawn for several years. In this dangerous situation, the policies and actions of both sides combined offensive and defensive components. The tendency of each side to perceive its own behavior as largely "defensive," and that of its opponent as mainly "offensive," encouraged mutual suspicion and accentuation of conflict.

In 1945 and early 1946 many officials in Washington were

still disposed to believe that, however disagreeably the Soviets were behaving in Eastern Europe, they were perhaps acting largely out of a "defensive" need to enhance the security of the Soviet Union by obtaining friendly regimes on its borders. This image of limited Soviet objectives changed, however, in 1946 with what was taken to be evidence of Soviet expansionist aims in Iran, Greece, and Turkey. The Soviets were now seen as attempting to extend control over areas that lay outside their security needs. Secretary of State Byrnes now stated: "I do not doubt that their ultimate goal is to dominate, in one way or another, all of Europe." The Truman Administration moved to mobilize resources to aid Greece and Turkey, which led to the statement of the Truman Doctrine and the formulation of the Marshall Plan.

In February of 1948 the Western world was shocked by the communist coup in Czechoslovakia which unseated the democratic government of Eduard Benes. This event evoked memories of the earlier fall of Czechoslovakia to Hitler in 1939 and hardened the Western image of Soviet leaders and their intentions. Shortly thereafter, relations between Stalin and Tito rapidly deteriorated, culminating in the expulsion of the Yugoslav government from the Cominform on June 28. This might well have provided considerable incentive for the Soviets to attempt to consolidate their interests in Eastern Europe, including the area of Berlin. The events in Yugoslavia and Czechoslovakia demonstrated to Allied leaders the Russians' concern for the solidarity of their position and their willingness to adopt extreme measures to protect it. The Soviet government was also encountering difficulties in Finland, where Finnish-Soviet military negotiations were bogged down and the elections of early July yielded another defeat for a European communist party.

Soviet aspirations were being fiercely challenged in Western Europe as well. Despite agitation sponsored by the local communist parties, France had finally, if reluctantly, aligned itself with Britain and the United States in Germany; and Italy had given the local communists a severe setback in the elections of April 1948. There were, in addition to these specific losses, two trends involving the influence of the United States in Europe which the Soviet Union must have been eager to stem. The first was the emergence of the European Recovery Program. This important economic commitment to Europe, formally signed on April 4, 1948, was especially distasteful to the Russians because of its inclusion of the Western zones of Germany. This must have appeared in Moscow to be yet another indication of the Allies' intentions to add a German state to the balance of power on the Western side of the scales. Obviously, this was perceived as a major threat to Soviet interests in Europe.

The second general trend was the rearmament of the United States and its increasing reinvolvement with Western Europe militarily. American domestic politics was punctuated throughout this period by discussion of rearmament, the draft, and the controversial universal military training proposal. Externally the United States, in conjunction with its European allies, was attempting to bolster the security arrangements of the North Atlantic region. One step in this process was taken in April when Great Britain, France, and the Benelux countries signed an agreement in Brussels pledging military cooperation among the five nations for a period of fifty years. In addition to this display of Pan-Europeanism, an event which received the full support of American leaders, the United States indicated its readiness to assume a role of active involvement in European affairs by its approval of the Vandenberg Resolution. Passed by the Senate on June 11, 1948, this statement prepared the ground for American participation in mutual security alliance systems. These two events clearly portended the formation of NATO within a year.

As for Germany, it had become evident by the fall of 1947 that plans for administering it through four-power cooperation had foundered on a fundamental disagreement as to the way in which that country should be treated. The Western Allies believed that at least West Germany should be allowed to become an economically viable member of a rebuilt, noncommunist Western Europe. The Soviet Union preferred to keep the Western zones of Germany, as well as its own Eastern zone, economically weak and dependent. Pursuing its policy for Europe, the United States, supported by England and to a lesser extent by France,[1] came to favor divided arrangements for administration of Germany. In sharp contrast, the Soviet Union wanted to maintain a centralized occupation mechanism, since this would enable it to maximize its influence over the Western zones of Germany. Frustration and stalemate for the evolving policy of the Western Allies was engendered by the fact that unanimity was required in the Allied Control Council, the highest-level quadripartite agency for Germany, and in the Berlin Kommandatura, the four-power agency for administering Berlin, which was also divided into four zones.

Disenchantment was a familiar feeling at higher levels of negotiation as well. On December 15, 1947, the Council of Foreign Ministers of the four powers adjourned after having failed to reach an agreement on the Austrian and German peace treaties. This had serious consequences for Germany, since that country was in great need of decisive action of both a political and an economic nature. Although certainly not in complete agreement on what was to be done, the Allies began to see the need for the development of interzonal German administrative agencies which could assume some of the load being carried by Allied military establishments. Additionally, December 1947 and January 1948 marked the nadir of the faltering German economy. Changes were clearly essential in both fields, and they did not appear likely to come within the four-power structure. With these considerations in mind, the three Western powers along with the Benelux countries convoked the London

[1] France, after being devastated in two world wars, was anxious to insure against the reemergence of a powerful German nation. French leaders, therefore, were deeply disturbed by the American insistence that the three Allied occupation zones in Germany be united. As the confrontation over Berlin developed, the French continually urged moderation in dealing with the Russians. This hesitancy continued well into the critical phase of the crisis. Britain, on the other hand, took a firm position early in the crisis. Some British officials even spoke publicly in favor of adopting a strong military response to the Soviet provocations. Windsor, *City on Leave*, p. 196; *New York Times*, April 2, 1948; p. 2.

Conference for the consideration of German affairs in February 1948. The six nations discussed the coordination of economic policies among the zones, the inclusion of West Germany in the European Recovery Program (the Marshall Plan), and the establishment of a German federal government. All these items were bitterly opposed by the Soviet Union. In anticipation of the Russian reaction, an interim communiqué, issued on March 6, stressed the urgency of developing an interzonal government but advised that "ultimate Four Power agreement is in no way precluded" by the discussions being held at the conference.[2] It was only a short time later that quadripartite negotiations on currency reforms, an essential requirement for the economic rejuvenation of Germany, ended, and forced independent Western planning in that area as well.[3]

The wording of the London announcement did not soothe the Soviets' sense of indignation. Even before the conference had begun, the Soviet government had expressed its feeling on being excluded from any discussion of issues related to Germany. They contended that the London meetings violated the Potsdam agreement, which called for four-power consideration of all German affairs and the joint administration of Germany as a unit rather than separate disjointed parts.[4] On March 20, 1948, Marshal Sokolovsky, the Russian military commander for Germany, demanded during an Allied Control Council meeting that he be informed of the proceedings of the London Conference. Upon Allied refusal, he read a prepared speech charging the Western powers with sabotaging four-power control and walked out of the meeting. This marked the last of the Council's sessions and the beginning of the accelerated phase of Soviet efforts to break down the control machinery and to isolate Berlin.

On March 31 the Soviets began interference with access of Allied military trains to West Berlin, which soon led to what in retrospect came to be called the "baby blockade." We shall

[2] Congress, Senate, *Documents on Germany*, p. 56.

[3] Mezerik, *Berlin and Germany*, p. 34.

[4] Gablentz, *Documents on the Status of Berlin*, p. 53.

discuss the significance of the baby blockade, which lasted ten days, later in this account. Soviet imposition of a full ground blockade at the end of June was triggered by the series of events set into motion by the Allied decision in the spring to introduce currency reform into West Germany. Not only was the German economy stagnating, but because of the effects of runaway inflation, a major effort was needed to establish a firm monetary basis for Germany's trade and industrial revival. Even the Soviets, despite their continuous interference, admitted the need for renovation of the monetary system; but unfortunately, this was the extent of East-West agreement. The Allies and the Russians were at loggerheads over the details of any attempt to implement currency reform. One of the most crucial differences separating the two sides on this problem concerned control of the rate and manner of issue. The Allies demanded a single printing plant under four-power authority, while the Russians were equally insistent upon securing separate plates for unsupervised use within their zone. The Western experts were not in the least willing to accede to this Soviet condition. They remembered too well the experiences of 1945 with the Allied Military Mark when the Soviets had flooded Germany with paper money, much of which eventually had to be redeemed by the United States.[5] As time passed, the situation became more and more pressing. Frustrated by continued Soviet refusal to cooperate in overhauling the German economy, the Western powers decided to introduce currency reform into their own zones of occupation. The announcement of this move on June 18 indicated that it would be implemented two days later. The Allied initiative specifically excluded all portions of the city of Berlin. Unmoved by this concession, the Soviets decided to introduce their own new currency into *all* Berlin, without Allied control, on June 23. The Western powers saw this Soviet move as a challenge to their rights in Berlin. To recognize the Soviet-supported currency throughout the city would not only generate practical problems of exchange but would be implicit

[5] Robert Spencer, "The Berlin Dilemma," in McInnis et al., *Shaping of Postwar Germany,* p. 118.

acceptance of the Soviet claim that there existed a special relationship between the Eastern zone and Berlin because of its
geographical location. As a result, on the next day the Western
powers reversed their position (the French going along reluctantly) and introduced a special currency of their own into West
Berlin to counter the Soviet initiative.

The process of move and countermove continued. The Soviets quickly responded on June 24 by closing the gate on all
modes of supply to West Berlin except air traffic. (The "baby
blockade" in April had been restricted to Allied military traffic.)
On the pretext of technical difficulties, the Helmstedt-Berlin
rail line, chief route for shipping food consignments, was included. This generated immediate concern among the Allied
administrators and the population of Berlin over the problem of
feeding the city. The East German news agency distributed an
article which contended that reserve food stores were nonexis-
tent in the French sector and none too large in the British and
American sections. "Great apprehension about the food supply
for the three western sectors of Berlin has arisen," the release
continued without undue exaggeration.[6] In an effort to calm the
German populace, Colonel Frank Howley, the American commandant of Berlin, announced that thirty-six days of food rations
had been stocked and would be distributed as they were
needed.[7] To prolong the period of grace before this reserve was
consumed, General Clay called General Curtis LeMay at the air
force headquarters in Weisbaden on June 25 and requested the
initiation once again of an airlift of supplies. Unlike the situation in early April when the Soviets had soon allowed ground
traffic to West Berlin to resume, this time they did not.

Accordingly, the Western Allies found themselves confronted
with a grave challenge not only to their position in Berlin but to
their entire policy for rebuilding a noncommunist Western
Europe. On the surface a legal dispute over rights of access to
West Berlin,[8] the crisis over the blockade was at bottom the

[6] Davison, *Berlin Blockade*, p. 99.   [7] Howley, *Berlin Command*, p. 201.

[8] We need not review here the preparations the four allies had made toward the
end of World War II for joint occupation and administration of Germany, and

consequence and symptom of the broader struggle over the future of Europe. As a result, Berlin, the scene of the first major confrontation between the East and the West, became the enduring symbol of the Cold War.

Our review of the general structure of the deterrence situation in 1948 has called attention to the complex interactions between the two sides that heightened each side's perception of the threat to its interests. Disagreement and conflict fed on themselves extending to a host of interrelated issues. Each side came to feel not merely that the stakes were high but that the issues in dispute were inextricably entangled. From the Soviet standpoint it became increasingly important to take some action—and the blockade of Berlin was chosen precisely for this reason—that would offer the hope of arresting and perhaps reversing the drift of events in the complex situation in Europe that was both thwarting Soviet aspirations and threatening what she saw as her security interests. As for the Allies, the value they placed on remaining in West Berlin was much strengthened by the diplomatic context in which the Soviet blockade was imposed and the perceived connection of the blockade with a larger set of issues. Noteworthy is the fact that a firm Allied commitment to remain in West Berlin and to defend it, if necessary, had *not* been formulated prior to the inception of the full ground blockade in late June. Such a commitment emerged, rather, as a result of the ensuing crisis. The contest over West Berlin was quickly perceived by Truman and some, though not all, of his advisers as an intrinsic part of the overall struggle for Europe. To allow the Western powers to be forced out of Berlin or to "buy off" the Soviet threat by major concessions with regard to West Germany and Western Europe would have given the Soviets major advantages in the continuing struggle over Europe; and so these options were rejected.

---

the circumstances that left the three Western occupying powers without formal Soviet recognition of their land access rights to West Berlin. Since land access was so tenuously established, it was fortunate for the Western allies that air access to West Berlin had been secured in the formal, written agreement of November 30, 1945. Davison, *Berlin Blockade*, pp. 33–37; see also Franklin, "Zonal Boundaries and Access to Berlin."

Truman's dilemma had novel aspects which were to become all too familiar in subsequent episodes of the Cold War. On this and other occasions American policy-makers had to decide whether it was better to "defend" a threatened outpost or a third country that was not in itself of vital importance to U.S. security or to attempt by other means to limit the political-diplomatic costs of losing it. Such a policy dilemma could arise in an acute form at the time of the Berlin blockade because American policy-makers had come to believe that the international system was an increasingly polarized, unstable one in which a setback in one locale could have profound destabilizing effects in other locales as well. The parts of the international system were seen as tightly "coupled," so that perturbations in one locale tended to cause strong repercussions in other areas that could throw the rest of the international system into great disequilibrium.[9]

The Initiator's Motives, Calculations, and Strategy

Our review of the events leading up to the Soviet imposition of the blockade makes amply clear that the Soviet move cannot be viewed as a simple effort by an aggressor to change the local territorial status quo. Let us try to characterize more adequately, therefore, the complex motives, calculations, and strategy that lay behind the choice of the blockade.

The Soviets' primary objective in imposing the blockade was to pressure the Western powers into giving up policies that were leading to the creation of a separate West Germany that would no longer be subject to Soviet control through the instrumentalities of four-power occupation. This was explicitly spelled out on July 3 by Marshall Sokolovsky, the Soviet military governor. According to General Clay, Sokolovsky said that

[9] For an incisive analysis of the impact of such beliefs about the international system on foreign policy, see Singer and Wildavsky, "A Third World Averaging Strategy."

the "technical difficulties" earlier alleged to have caused the closing of railways and highways from the Western zones of Germany to Berlin "would continue until the West abandoned plans for a West German government." [10]

In brief, the blockade was Moscow's way of saying to the West, you may set up a separate West German government or you may continue to exercise your powers in Berlin, but you cannot do both. To exercise sole power over West Berlin was a secondary objective of less value to the Soviets. Nonetheless, it would constitute a significant payoff in the event that the blockade did not succeed in persuading the Allies to modify their policies.

The Soviets hoped that the blockade would help to achieve their primary objective by shattering Western unity. The blockade provided almost perfect leverage for exerting political-diplomatic pressure. It squeezed the Western powers in a painful fashion without using Soviet military force. It placed the Western Allies in the invidious position of having to pay a heavy diplomatic price to get the blockade lifted; and it confronted them with the alternative of having to use force or to make aggressive moves to challenge the blockade that might result in bloodshed and war. Disagreements among the Allies in this situation would be natural.

At the same time, from the Soviet standpoint the blockade was a *controllable* and *reversible* gambit. Soviet leaders were not committed to persisting in the blockade; they could at any time find a solution to the "technical difficulties" and open up ground access to West Berlin. Nor need the Soviets persist in the blockade if the Western powers threatened to overreact to it in ways that raised the danger of war.

The blockade of West Berlin is, indeed, a classical example of a low-risk, potentially high-gain strategy. Of the various options available to the Soviet government for indicating its disapproval of Western policy toward Germany and for inducing changes in that policy, the blockade of West Berlin seemed to

[10] Clay, *Decision in Germany,* p. 367.

be almost perfect. It offered a low-cost opportunity to secure by political-diplomatic means an important objective of Soviet foreign policy. Failing that, or in addition to it, it offered the prospect of a variety of other useful payoffs. The blockade enabled the Soviet leaders to test the strength of the U.S. commitment not only to maintaining its position in West Berlin but to Germany as a whole. In 1948 it was by no means clear what value the United States and its Allies would place on the evolving policy of reconstituting Western Europe, or what costs and risks they were prepared to accept on its behalf. This policy was controversial within the United States, and important elements of opinion in England and France were by no means sympathetic with efforts to revive the German economy. Even if this policy ultimately was retained and pursued, the strain on the Allies' mutual relations could be severe.

Deterrence Fails in Stages: The Problem of the Defender's Response

We return now to the three-month period from the end of March, when the partial "baby blockade" was temporarily imposed, to the end of June, when a fuller blockade was imposed on all ground access to West Berlin, to remain in effect unti May 1949.

The events of this period exemplify one of the central themes of this study, namely, that deterrence often fails *in stages*. This is a phenomenon that deterrence theory, as presently constituted, does not clearly envisage.

Abstract deterrence theory tends to focus on hypothetical situations in which the initiator, if he challenges deterrence, decides to do so at a well-defined point in time and then implements his decision with a relatively simple and rapid sequence of events. This is indeed one way in which deterrence can fail. But the Berlin crisis of 1948 and other cases to be taken up later indicate that the initiator's decision to challenge the status quo may be made in stages and implemented in stages over a longer period of time. A rather complex set of preliminary, tentative actions may precede the final commitment to action that unmistakably challenges the defender. In this way, the initiator may rely on feedback either to perfect his utility calculations, to condition his opponent to the forthcoming challenge, or to gauge and control the risk of an overreaction to the challenge by the opponent. This period during which the initiator is preparing his action and feeling out the situation may be critical. For when deterrence fails in stages, the defender receives considerable "warning," and opportunities may arise for strengthening deterrence or making other responses.

This is not to imply that "warning" is always easy to recognize and to act upon. It is tempting to suggest that the defender should make use of the available warning, even if equivocal and ambiguous, to engage in an eleventh-hour, ad hoc strengthening of deterrence in various ways, signaling strong commitment and making threats designed to induce the initiator to pull back from his potential challenge, even at the last minute. It is certainly rational in principle for the defender to use available warning in this way. But in practice he may experience various constraints on his ability to do so.

Despite substantial warning, United States decision-makers were caught by surprise at the time of the blockade. That the Western outpost in Berlin was a likely magnet for Soviet pressure had been clearly recognized by only a few Western officials. From the vantage point of Berlin, General Lucius Clay and his political adviser, Robert Murphy, advised the National Security Council as early as October 1947 that the United States "must be prepared for Soviet action to force our withdrawal from Berlin." [11] Apparently, however, at this early date they did not think that a blockade was a likely form for such a Russian move. Major General Williams Hays, Clay's deputy commander, announced in January 1948 that he could not "see the Russians being so foolish as to deliberately and publicly starve

[11] *Ibid.*, p. 239.

the people of Berlin. . . . This is not the way to win friends and influence people. . . ." [12] On the other hand, the *New York Times* later the same week cautioned against this optimistic line of thinking by observing that given the strength of the Soviet position around Berlin a blockade would be fairly simple to implement.[13]

As this indicates, the problem of recognizing and interpreting warning was an inextricable part of the broader task of estimating Soviet intentions. That the Soviets were strongly motivated to oppose the evolving Western policy with respect to Germany was clear enough. What was not perceived and anticipated was that the Soviets would take the *tactical* initiative around Berlin in an effort to bolster their slipping *strategic* position in Europe. How far the Soviets would go in pursuit of their broader objectives in Germany and Europe was a subject of considerable disagreement among American policy-makers in the spring of 1948. American leaders may have assumed that Soviet leaders would recognize that a move against West Berlin constituted a *high*-risk strategy and, hence, would not be acceptable. If so, U.S. leaders displayed a tendency on this as on subsequent occasions to misinterpret what in fact were *low*-risk Soviet initiatives as implying a willingness to risk war.

The initial complacency of officials in Washington was violently shattered on March 5 by the receipt of the following message from General Clay:

> For many months, based on logical analysis, I have felt and held that war was unlikely for at least ten years. Within the last few weeks, I have felt a subtle change in Soviet attitude which I cannot define but which now gives me a feeling that it may come with dramatic suddenness. . . . I am unable to submit any official report in the absence of supporting data but my feeling is real. . . .[14]

Clay noted that intelligence reports did not support his opinion, but he felt Washington should be aware of his concern. This cable sent the various intelligence groups scurrying in an effort

[12] *New York Times*, January 13, 1948, p. 10.

[13] *Ibid.*, January 18, 1948, p. 10.   [14] Davison, *Berlin Blockade*, p. 73.

to assess the validity of Clay's impression. Many officials in Washington dismissed the report as unnecessarily alarming, and the CIA reported on March 16 that war was unlikely in the next sixty days.[15] Others were apparently convinced a threat did exist. But noticeably lacking in these efforts to assess Soviet intentions was the ability to differentiate the lesser and less risky options available to the Soviets for exerting effective pressure against West Berlin from military actions that might indeed trigger a war.

Clay wrote later that his cable of March 5 "led to a speed up in our preparations for defense." [16] But Clay does not indicate what those preparations were, and it is obvious that they did not suffice to deter the Soviets from shortly taking threatening moves in Berlin.

Within a few weeks of Clay's warning, indeed, the Soviet military governor in Berlin on March 31 announced that, after only twenty-four hours' notice, all baggage and passengers on military trains to Berlin would be checked by Russian personnel. This move was made necessary, according to the Soviets, by the increasing infiltration of "subversive and terrorist elements" into the Berlin area.[17]

It should be noted that the conditions which the Soviets placed on the movement of Allied military traffic did not in themselves constitute a blockade; nor can we be certain that at this time (as against late June, when the full blockade went into effect) the Soviets viewed their interference with Allied ground access to West Berlin as the precursor of a possible blockade. In a sense, it was the nature of the Allied response on this occasion that transformed the Soviet demand for checking baggage and passengers into a blockade. Allied authorities chose not to submit to the Soviet demand for inspecting military trains and, as we shall note, made an abortive effort to defy it.

British and American authorities deemed the Soviet de-

---

[15] *Ibid.* On April 2, the CIA extended indefinitely its prognosis that war would not occur.

[16] Clay, *Decision in Germany*, p. 354.   [17] Davison, *Berlin Blockade*, p. 64.

mand for inspection of their military trains as, in effect, a blockade, something grossly unacceptable and a violation of their rights of free access. Although this was not the first instance of Soviet interference with traffic to Berlin, it was the first which directly involved the Allied garrisons in the city.[18] General Clay decided in early April to test the Soviets' determination by sending a train with armed guards toward Berlin with orders not to submit to a search. The train was finally switched onto a siding, where it remained until it ignobly withdrew to the American zone. As Clay remarked, "It was clear that the Russians meant business." [19]

Clay now responded by ordering a small-scale airlift in order to supply members of the Berlin garrison. Within a few days a Russian fighter plane, attempting to buzz and harass a British transport plane over the Gatow airport in West Berlin, collided with it, resulting in the crash of both planes and loss of life. The British and American military governors promptly ordered fighter escorts henceforth for all unarmed planes engaged in the airlift, whereupon Marshall Sokolovsky issued an immediate apology and assured the Western commanders that no harassment in the air corridors had been intended.[20] Since only the rail shipments destined for consumption within the military outpost were affected, the airlift did not involve an operation of a very large scale. A capacity of 60 to 100 tons a day was quickly achieved; this proved sufficient until April 10, when the Soviets inexplicably allowed the rail service to resume.

[18] The Soviets had tightened their borders to unauthorized passage as early as the summer of 1947 and had restricted the movement of German household goods from Berlin to the West in December 1947. These are the first Soviet restrictions mentioned. Nettl, *The Eastern Zone and Soviet Policy in Germany*, p. 262; and Bennett, *Berlin Bastion*, p. 23.

[19] Clay, *Decision in Germany*, p. 359.

[20] Evidently in the period between the apology and its retraction, Moscow decided to use this accident in an attempt to gain some control of Allied traffic in the flight corridors. The Soviets even established their own investigating team which found the British pilot had been negligent and recommended that measures be taken "to establish order and to save Soviet fliers from further losses." *New York Times*, April 24, 1948, p. 1.

ASSESSING THE BABY BLOCKADE

The "baby blockade," as it came to be known, was over. We turn now to noting the limited impact it had in generating a response on the part of the United States to the possible need to reinforce or otherwise modify deterrence. The temporary blockade did indeed serve to reinforce Clay's earlier malaise over a possibly serious Soviet move against West Berlin. Washington was concerned enough at least to discuss several options open to it. In response to Clay's request for instructions on how to deal with the Soviet move, a number of suggestions were made to Truman by his advisers in Washington: (1) send a message to Stalin warning him of the provocative nature of the restrictions; (2) call congressional leaders for a conference; (3) instruct Clay to prevent Soviet soldiers from boarding U.S. trains,[21] with orders to shoot only in self-defense; and (4) contact the British to see what they intended to do. Truman did issue the instructions to Clay. However, he preferred not to put too much emphasis on the Soviet restrictions or to add to the impression of a dangerous crisis. Thus, he elected not to call a meeting of congressional leaders and, despite the ten-day period of obstruction of Allied access to West Berlin, Truman did not send a diplomatic protest to the Soviet government.

The baby blockade did not appreciably heighten Washington's concern about a future Soviet move against West Berlin. Nor was it perceived as part of a slowly developing case in which deterrence might fail in stages. The U.S. leaders seem to have given little attention to the possibility that the way in which they responded to this interference in Berlin in early April might give Soviet leaders useful information regarding the utility of exerting further pressure in an effort to deal with the complex German and Western European situation. Whether or not the Soviets intended their interference with Allied access as a dry run for a full blockade (and we have already suggested the possibility that they did not), it is certain that the Allied re-

[21] The Soviet military government had insisted on the need for close Soviet inspection of supply trains and trucks.

sponse to the small blockade in April did provide Soviet leaders with a useful opportunity to assess in advance the risks of the full blockade which they introduced in late June. The small airlift suggested that the United States was willing to accommodate as best it could, at least temporarily, to Soviet efforts to redefine Allied access to West Berlin. Even Clay's armed train in April, the solitary American attempt at anything resembling a coercive response to test Soviet resolution, indicated clearly the limitations the United States would set upon its actions. The air disaster at Gatow also served to define the "rules of the game" for the forthcoming blockade. The Western response to the event served to establish for the Russians how far they could safely go in their efforts to isolate the city. They recognized the possibility that serious interference with the air corridors might become a *casus belli*.[22]

The baby blockade also provided the Western powers with an opportunity to learn how to accommodate themselves to such a threat to West Berlin. Certainly the responses the Allies made to the baby blockade served to condition their response to the reimposition of the blockade in late June. The "baby airlift" of April became what organizational theorists call a "conspicuous" alternative,[23] a fact which increased the probability of its being resorted to again in June.

Since the events of April contributed to the gradual failure of deterrence in ways that Allied leaders might have but did not perceive at the time, it is tempting to employ hindsight to criticize Allied leaders for lack of clearer foresight at the time. Such

[22] The extreme caution the Soviets exercised in this respect during the full blockade is all the more striking because it deprived them of an important option. It has been estimated that the Soviets would have been able to sabotage the effectiveness of the airlift if they could have curtailed its performance by as little as 10 or 15 percent. Davison, *Berlin Blockade*, p. 198. That American decision-makers used Soviet interference with their air rights as a prime indicator of the likelihood of war was implied in Truman's memoirs. At a National Security Council meeting in July, Clay said he was convinced that the Soviets would "not attack our planes unless they had made the decision to go to war." Truman, *Years of Trial and Hope*, p. 125.

[23] Cyert and March, *Behavioral Theory of the Firm*, p. 46.

a judgment would oversimplify the task Allied leaders faced and constitute an overly facile interpretation of the lost opportunity to deter the Soviets from imposing the full blockade. We have to note that the temporary partial blockade of April could hardly be regarded by Allied leaders as a conclusive indication of Soviet intentions to impose a *prolonged and full* blockade later on. Besides, the Soviet authorities did lift their restrictions on ground access after ten days of interference. To be sure, there was no guarantee that interference with access would not be resumed at some point; but it is also noteworthy that Soviet leaders did not threaten or warn that a more severe, prolonged blockade would be imposed if the Western powers did not give them satisfaction on policy toward Germany.

The events of April, therefore, constituted only equivocal warning of what was to come in late June. In the weeks preceding the reimposition of the blockade, American officials in Berlin continued to warn Washington of the dangers latent in the situation, but it is not clear how precise and consistent these warnings were. One official who insists that the warning was both explicit and precise is Robert Murphy in his memoir, *Diplomat among Warriors.* Murphy reports that he and Clay repeatedly advised their superiors that land access to the city could be severed by the Soviets at any time. They also requested that Washington decide what would be done in such a case, but evidently they did not receive a satisfactory reply.[24] General Clay's own account of the crisis, published before Murphy's book, does not mention the numerous warnings referred to by Murphy. Clay's recollection of this period is also somewhat inconsistent with regard to his assessment of the likely Soviet tactics, which makes it difficult to establish whether or not he actually anticipated the blockade or to determine the specificity of the warning he forwarded to Washington.[25]

---

[24] Murphy, *Diplomat among Warriors,* pp. 311–12.

[25] Clay relates that during the miniature blockade in April when Army Secretary Royall asked for his interpretation of the situation he replied that he did not think a comprehensive blockade was likely. He reasoned, as General Hays had earlier, that the Russians would not be so foolish as to make a move which

It is possible, therefore, that Murphy was the only one who actually predicted a blockade and that Clay and Hays, though recognizing the possibility of such a maneuver, thought it unlikely that the Russians would adopt such a strategy. If this interpretation is correct, the fact that the two ranking American representatives in Berlin offered discrepant estimates of Soviet intentions could have contributed to the reluctance of officials in Washington to attach high probability to reimposition of a blockade. In addition, the impact on Washington planners of these diverging opinions might well have been exacerbated by the dual nature of the communication system between American headquarters in Berlin and Washington, which had Clay corresponding with the Department of the Army and Murphy with the State Department.

But the Soviets themselves certainly acted in ways which provided ominous clues as to their intentions. The Soviet authorities had tampered with various parts of the communication and transportation systems connecting Berlin and the Allied zones on and off since mid-1947. Even after the ten-day blockade of April, however, there does not seem to have been any high-level U.S. attempt to decide what would be done if the situation were repeated at full scale. There is no evidence available in public sources which would indicate that serious contingency planning for the eventuality of a blockade was conducted in Washington at this time.[26] It is incredible; but, at the peak of the decision-making structure, as John Foster Dulles said, "No one took this very seriously." [27] Successive issues of *The Economist* (June 26 and July 3) illustrate the comic tragedy that developed. The first article stated: "In particular it is to be hoped that General Clay's instructions are specific and firm. . . . If

---

would alienate the German people so thoroughly. From this it would seem likely that even if the possibility of a blockade had been mentioned in official reports, Clay's personal deprecation of that eventuality lessened the impact of the warning. Yet later in his narrative, General Clay asserts that he "had foreseen the Soviet action for some months." Clay, *Decision in Germany*, pp. 361, 365.

[26] Davison, *Berlin Blockade*, p. 75.   [27] Dulles, *War or Peace*, p. 55.

not, the situation might become perilous." [28] The second carried this shocked rejoinder: "What is alarming is to discover how little the Western Powers had apparently foreseen such a siege or prepared for it." [29] Only within the Berlin garrison itself had preparations been ongoing. There Colonel Howley had directed the development of "Operation Counterpunch." Assuming only that the Russians would try to split their sector from the rest of the city, it provided for a buildup of certain food reserves and outlined emergency administrative procedures. This immediate action plan for the city, of course, did not treat the deeper question of what the United States should do to maintain its position in the city.[30]

Two hypotheses may be advanced to help account for this astounding oversight on the part of Allied planners. First, Western leaders may have been lulled into complacency by certain Soviet tactics which, whether or not intended for the purpose, served to blunt their perception of the developing threat. In the period of almost a year during which the Russians had tampered with ground traffic to and from Berlin before imposing the full blockade the new regulations had rarely caused extreme inconvenience or directly involved Allied personnel. It is at least plausible that this interference was regarded as simple harassment of no real consequence and became more or less an accepted part of the Berlin environment. The absence of diplomatic protest over any of the restrictions until the final closure of the border adds some support to this hypothesis.

The second phenomenon which might explain the lack of Allied preparation is a form of wishful thinking that Erich Fromm has labeled "possibilistic thinking." This refers to the tendency to exaggerate the probability of a desired event which on the basis of an objective appraisal of the evidence should be seen as merely possible. American decision-makers seem to have convinced themselves that the Soviets would not take advantage of the vulnerable Allied position. A full blockade would

[28] *The Economist*, June 26, 1948, p. 1055.   [29] *Ibid.*, July 3, 1948, p. 1.
[30] Howley, *Berlin Command*, p. 201.

have confronted the Western powers with an extremely difficult situation for which they would have no ready answer. Rather than considering that the tough and determined opponent was capable of pursuing this invidious course of action, it was tempting to find reasons why he would not and to exaggerate the role these reasons would play in his calculations. Thus, U.S. policy-makers preferred to believe that the Soviets would realize that it was not in their overall interest to undertake such a despicable plan as a blockade of the entire population.[31]

The inability of U.S. leaders to face up to and plan for the worst contingency that awaited them may be contrasted with their handling of the currency problem. In this matter, the disadvantages faced by the Western powers were minor compared to those that faced them in maintaining ground access to Berlin. With less need to engage in wishful thinking, therefore, the Allies proceeded to develop thoughtful contingency plans to counter anticipated Soviet actions. As discussed earlier, the "B mark" was introduced by the Western nations hours after the Russian currency change. This eventuality had received careful attention.[32] Judging by their preparedness in this area, it seems that planners may have begun to see this as the probable form of any Russian move. It is possible that decision-makers ignored the warnings of a blockade because they had prepared for a different type of challenge, a currency reform, and did not wish to face the far more difficult problem of a blockade.

Both the Western decision-makers' tendency to be lulled into complacency by Soviet moves and their tendency toward possibilistic thinking became more pronounced in this case because to take the possibility of a full blockade seriously would have required administration officials to face up to extremely difficult and controversial policy questions they had not yet decided. We would suggest that not the least of the reasons why Washington could not respond to Murphy's and Clay's

[31] Windsor, *City on Leave*, p. 103. See also *New York Times*, January 13, 1948, Sect. 4, p. 7.

[32] Davison, *Berlin Blockade*, p. 78.

queries as to what to do if access to Berlin were cut off was that administration officials were in fact badly divided over the wisdom of trying to defend the Western position in Berlin, should that become necessary. Evidently, the familiar phenomenon of "bureaucratic politics" within the executive branch did affect decision-making on the Berlin problem to some extent; but limitations of data on this aspect of the crisis exclude informed speculation here of its role in American policy-making.

The latent division among policy-makers was to emerge visibly when the blockade was reimposed in June. Only the firm position Truman took at that time on remaining in Berlin kept the division among his advisers from having a greater impact on the Western response to the new crisis. In the weeks before the Soviets once again cut off ground access to the city, the disagreement on the feasibility and desirability of staying in Berlin had a more subtle effect on contingency planning: it tended to paralyze the ability of the administration to use the available warning of a possible blockade to reinforce deterrence by means of suitable signals to the Soviets.

It must be remembered that in 1948 there was as yet no formal, firm Western commitment to Berlin. The baby blockade would appear to have provided the Western powers with an excellent opportunity to resolve this ambiguity by strengthening and making more explicit their commitment.[33] But this "opportunity" is, in fact, more correctly described as a dilemma. Murphy, seconded to some extent by Clay (although, as noted, this is not entirely clear) was urging that a clear and firm position be asserted on Berlin lest Moscow be encouraged to act in ways that would raise the danger of war. Washington officials were less certain as to what behavior on the part of the United States would or would not add to the danger of a war they wanted desperately to avoid. Some officials argued that the United States should stay in Berlin at all costs, but confessed they did not

---

[33] We shall note later several crises in which the administration did in fact respond to equivocal warning that deterrence was failing by strengthening and making more explicit its commitment to defend certain territories or small allies.

know how it could be managed without war if the Soviets proved obstreperous. Others argued that West Berlin was indefensible, with a small number of Allied troops there surrounded by hundreds of thousands of Soviet troops, and that the United States should consider leaving Berlin before it was forced to do so. Still others said it was possible to work things out with the Soviets since Moscow, too, did not want a war. This debate was still in progress when the blockade was reimposed on June 24.[34]

One may wonder at the failure of American policy-makers in this case (as in some others to be noted) to seize upon available warning—however inadequate for estimating Soviet intentions with high confidence—at least to take some readily available measures for strengthening deterrence. Even equivocal or ambiguous warning that deterrence may be about to fail would seem on the surface to be sufficient reason for taking sensible measures to strengthen deterrence. But acting upon this principle sometimes involves difficulties that have not been anticipated by deterrence theorists.

In the present case, using equivocal warning to attempt to reinforce deterrence was certainly a possibility and, indeed, was recognized as such by some policy-makers. It is even possible, though by no means certain, that the Soviets might have been deterred from reimposing the blockade had the United States, following the baby blockade, formulated and conveyed to the Soviet leaders a strong commitment on behalf of West Berlin and coupled it with a credible threat to use force promptly if the blockade were reinstituted. But, as we have suggested, such a course of action required a significant change in U.S. policy, namely the formulation of a new commitment laden with possible costs and risks.

To "reinforce" deterrence in the spring of 1948, then, meant not the reaffirmation of an existing commitment and additional communications designed to enhance its credibility to the opponent. Rather, to reinforce deterrence in this case would

[34] Murphy, *Diplomat among Warriors*, pp. 312–13; Clay, *Decision in Germany*, p. 359; Davison, *Berlin Blockade*, p. 75.

require U.S. policy-makers to decide whether to make a new commitment and to accept significant costs and risks on its behalf. We belabor the point in order to emphasize that efforts to reinforce deterrence on the basis of warning are not always cost-free.

The Defender's Response: The Role of the Image of the Opponent

Another part of the explanation for the American "failure" in this case to evaluate correctly the available warning and to respond to it effectively concerns the role of the U.S. leaders' image of the opponent. It is by now a truism that specific intelligence available for estimating an opponent's intentions rarely speaks for itself. To interpret it correctly requires a theory or model of how this particular opponent perceives different kinds of situations and calculates the utility of different options available to him. A blanket assumption of a single kind of rationality will not do for this purpose. Rather, one must be able to understand the opponent's peculiar approach to rational calculation, which is a function of his idiosyncratic ideological values, his operational code belief system, the organizational and bureaucratic processes that affect his formation and implementation of policy, and also the possible role of personality variables. Together these constitute what may be called the "image of the opponent," or the opponent's "behavioral style."

The interpretation of available facts that bear on estimating the opponent's intentions and likely responses is often subtly influenced by one's underlying, often unspoken and untested, image of the opponent. An incorrect or defective model of his behavioral style can lead one to distort even reasonably good factual information as to what the opponent is up to.

We do not have enough data to reconstruct fully the image of the Soviet opponent that U.S. leaders held during this crisis. It is evident, however, that this image was not held in clear focus and that, moreover, top-level American policy-makers disagreed on it in important respects.

Despite an image of Soviet hostility and aggressiveness widely shared by U.S. policy-makers, most of them, as we have noted, failed to foresee the Soviet move against West Berlin. This event demonstrated to U.S. officials once again that their knowledge about Soviet leaders was somehow inadequate for anticipating the way in which the Soviets would calculate the utility of available policy options. The shock of the blockade could hardly have reinforced whatever confidence U.S. leaders might have had that they were operating with a correct image of the Soviet opponent. Some American leaders, as we noted, reacted to the unexpected Soviet move against West Berlin with the interpretation (incorrect in our view) that Soviet leaders had deliberately chosen a high-risk strategy. The implications of this interpretation of Soviet behavior for the U.S. response to the blockade were, of course, more ominous than the alternative that the Soviets were really engaged in a low-risk strategy and would refrain from accepting greater risks.

In assessing Soviet intentions U.S. officials were generally agreed that Moscow wanted to test the strength of U.S. determination to stay in Berlin. But they disagreed in their judgment as to how far the Soviets would go in pursuing this and other objectives. Some officials, such as General Clay and Ambassador Murphy, maintained that the Soviets were bluffing and would back down before a strong show of force. Noteworthy, however, is Truman's unwillingness to resort to either bluff or intimidation in dealing with the Soviet threat to West Berlin. We have already noted his reluctance to give Stalin a warning during the small blockade of early April for fear of provoking him. Later in this crisis, too, Truman rejected recommendations for action that might raise the risk of war.

Truman's caution stemmed in part from his image of the opponent. Unlike General Clay and some other officials, who tended to perceive the Soviet Union as something of a neighborhood bully, full of fight and tough talk until challenged, Truman and other advisers saw the USSR as a wily adversary—

deceitful to be sure, but also unstable and, worst of all, unpredictable! (Secretary of Defense Lovett remarked that the heads of Soviet leaders were "full of bubbles.") Contrary to the view of his hard-line advisers who believed that the Soviet Union would not run any risk of World War III until ready for it, Truman believed that the crisis indicated that Moscow was willing to "risk a military incident" to test U.S. "firmness and patience." In his view it was also possible that Soviet leaders might even be looking for a pretext to begin a war. The National Security Council, too, thought the Soviets were capable of provoking and engaging in war.

Thus the different images of the Soviet opponent within Truman's administration at this time produced different perceptions not only of Moscow's intentions and its willingness to accept high risks, but also of the utility and risks of different measures the West might undertake to maintain its position in Berlin. The fear of needlessly "provoking" the Soviets in some way was an important consideration in Truman's mind in this and other crises; it served as an important constraint on the means he would employ in protecting American interests in crisis situations.[35] Strange as it may seem from today's perspective on the Cold War, American leaders in 1948 were trying not to antagonize or provoke the Soviets in certain ways even while—one must add—antagonizing them in other ways.

Deterrence Success or Failure?

Some observers are disposed to regard the Berlin crisis of 1948–1949 as an example of successful deterrence by the Western powers, in that the Soviets confined themselves to the

---

[35] The President later said he had been worried that even if the blockade of Berlin was not a Soviet pretext for a European war, "a trigger-happy Russian pilot or hot-headed communist commander might create an incident that could ignite the powder keg." (Truman, *Years of Trial and Hope*, p. 124).

ground blockade and did not resort to stronger measures against the Western position in Berlin. It is true that stronger options were available to the Soviets for taking political control of West Berlin and/or evicting Allied occupation forces from the Western sectors of the city. It is difficult, however, to speak of the Soviets as being deterred, at least at the outset of the crisis, from the use of these stronger options. In the first place, as we have noted, Soviet objectives were evidently complex; they included the hope that pressure on Berlin might succeed in modifying emerging Allied policies in Western Europe and West Germany to which the Soviets objected. The option of pressure via a blockade of Berlin may have seemed to the Soviets not merely as less risky than seizure of the city but also as a more appropriate means of pursuing their broader objectives. In the second place, the argument that this case is to be regarded as an example of successful deterrence would seem to rest on the dubious assumption that the Soviets were obliged to settle for the blockade because they felt deterred from using stronger options against West Berlin. Far from being a second-best strategy, however, the blockade may have been viewed by Stalin as a *preferred* option for pursuing his complex objectives. At the outset the Soviets had every reason to believe that the blockade would be effective and lead to a successful outcome of the crisis.

A better case, of course, can be made for the thesis that the Western powers succeeded in deterring the Soviets from escalating the conflict later on when the airlift began to frustrate the impact of the blockade on West Berlin. So far as the initiation of the Soviet blockade itself is concerned, however, it seems quite reasonable to regard it as a *failure* of deterrence from the standpoint of the Western powers. Certainly the blockade confronted the Allies with a serious challenge to the status quo; and it provided the Soviets with seemingly effective leverage for obtaining important diplomatic concessions.

The Berlin crisis of 1948 was one of the first Cold War confrontations to demonstrate the limitations of deterrence as an instrument of American foreign policy. It would become increasingly evident in the following years that while overt warfare between the two nuclear powers might be deterred or otherwise avoided, lower-level confrontations stemming from the clash of interests would periodically occur.

Bibliography

While there are many accounts of the origins and development of the Berlin blockade, none have considered its implications for deterrence theory and practice. The memoirs of Truman, Clay, and Robert Murphy contain useful materials on American decision-making. The most useful analyses of the crisis are the books by Davison, Gottlieb, Windsor, and Young, all of which contain materials on Soviet as well as American policy-making. Useful interpretations of Soviet policy are also contained in Ulam, Kolko, LeFeber, and Shulman.

For earlier research on this case we are indebted to Jane Howland and John Oneal.

Bennett, Lowell. *Berlin Bastion.* Frankfurt, Fred Rudl, 1951.
Berlin: Crisis and Challenge. New York, German Information Center, n.d.
Berlin: The City That Would Not Die. Compiled by the editors of the *Army Times,* New York, Dodd, Mead, 1968.
Campbell, John C. *The United States in World Affairs, 1948-49.* New York, Harper & Bros., 1949.
Clay, Lucius D. *Decision in Germany.* Garden City, N.Y., Doubleday, 1950.
Cyert, Richard M., and James G. March. *A Behavioral Theory of the Firm.* Englewood Cliffs, N.J., Prentice-Hall, 1963.
Davis, Franklin M., Jr. *Come as a Conqueror.* New York, Macmillan, 1967.
Davison, W. Phillips. *The Berlin Blockade.* Princeton, Princeton University Press, 1958.
Dulles, John Foster. *War or Peace.* New York, Macmillan, 1950.
Economist, The. January–October, 1948.
Ferrell, Robert H. *George C. Marshall,* New York, Cooper Square Publishers, 1966.
Franklin, William M. "Zonal Boundaries and Access to Berlin," *World Politics,* XVI (October 1963), 1-31.
Gablentz, O. M. von der, ed. *Documents on the Status of Berlin.* Munich, R. Oldenbourg Verlag, 1959.

Gaddis, John Lewis. *The United States and the Origins of the Cold War, 1941–1947.* New York, Columbia University Press, 1972.

George, Alexander L. "The 'Operational Code': A Neglected Approach to the Study of Political Leaders and Decision-Making," *International Studies Quarterly,* XIII (June 1969), 190–222.

Gimbel, John. *The American Occupation of Germany.* Stanford, Stanford University Press, 1968.

Gottlieb, Manuel. *The German Peace Settlement and the Berlin Crisis.* New York, Paine-Whitman Publishers, 1960.

Great Britain. *Monthly Report of the Control Commission for Germany.* British Element. January–October 1948.

———. *Germany,* Number 2. Great Britain Foreign Office, October 11, 1948.

Halle, Louis J. *The Cold War as History.* London, Chatto and Windus, 1967.

Howley, Frank. *Berlin Command.* New York, Putnam's, 1950.

Iklé, Fred Charles. *How Nations Negotiate.* New York, Harper & Row, 1964.

Kennan, George F. "The Sources of Soviet Conduct," *Foreign Affairs,* XXV (July 1947), 566–82.

———. *Memoirs 1925–1950.* Boston, Little, Brown, 1967.

Kintner, William R. "The Strength of the West," in *Berlin and the Future of Eastern Europe,* ed. David S. Collier and Kurt Glaser. Chicago, Henry Regnery, 1963.

Kissinger, Henry A. *Nuclear Weapons and Foreign Policy.* New York, Harper & Bros., 1957.

Kolko, Joyce and Gabriel. *The Limits of Power.* New York, Harper & Row, 1972; pp. 488–98.

LaFeber, Walter. *America, Russia, and the Cold War, 1945–1966.* New York, Wiley, 1967.

Mander, John. *Berlin: Hostage for the West.* Baltimore, Penguin, 1962.

McClelland, Charles A. "Access to Berlin: The Quantity and Variety of Events, 1948–1963," in *Quantitative International Politics,* ed. J. David Singer. New York, Free Press, 1968.

McInnis, Edgar, et al., eds. *The Shaping of Postwar Germany.* New York, Praeger, 1960.

McLellan, David S. "Who Fathered Containment?" *International Studies Quarterly,* 17 (June 1973), 205–26.

Mezerik, A. G., ed. *Berlin and Germany.* New York, International Review Service, 1962.

Millis, Walter, ed. *The Forrestal Diaries.* New York, Viking, 1951.

———, with Harvey C. Mansfield and Harold Stein. *Arms and the State.* New York, The Twentieth Century Fund, 1958.

Murphy, Charles J. V. "Berlin Air Lift," *Fortune,* November 1948, pp. 89–93, 218–29.

Murphy, Robert. *Diplomat among Warriors.* New York, Doubleday, 1964.

Myers, Shirley. *Berlin: Free City in a Communist Country.* Johannesburg, South African Institute of International Affairs, 1966.

Neal, Fred, W. *War and Peace and Germany.* New York, Norton, 1962.

Nettl, J. P. *The Eastern Zone and Soviet Policy in Germany, 1945–50.* London, Oxford University Press, 1951.

New Times. Russian English-language journal published by Trud. January–October 1948.

New York Times. January–October 1948.

Possony, Stefan T. "Berlin: Focus on World Strategy," in *Berlin and the Future of Eastern Europe*, ed. David S. Collier and Kurt Glaser. Chicago, Henry Regnery, 1963.

Richardson, James L. *Germany and the Atlantic Alliance.* Cambridge, Harvard University Press, 1966.

Robson, Charles B., ed. *Berlin: Pivot of German Destiny.* Chapel Hill, University of North Carolina Press, 1960.

Rodrigo, Robert. *Berlin Airlift.* London, Cassell, 1960.

Sheinman, Lawrence, and David Wilkinson, eds. *International Law and Political Crisis.* Boston, Little, Brown, 1968.

Shulman, Marshall D. *Stalin's Foreign Policy Reappraised.* Cambridge, Harvard University Press, 1963.

Singer, Max, and Aaron Wildavsky, "A Third World Averaging Strategy," in *U.S. Foreign Policy: Perspectives and Proposals for the 1970's*, ed. Paul Seabury and Aaron Wildavsky. New York, McGraw-Hill, 1969; pp. 13–35.

Smith, Jean Edward. *The Defense of Berlin.* Baltimore, The Johns Hopkins Press, 1963.

Smith, Walter Bedell. *My Three Years in Moscow.* New York, Lippincott, 1950.

Truman, Harry S. *Memoirs.* Volume II, *Years of Trial and Hope, 1946–1952.* New York, Doubleday, 1956.

Ulam, Adam B. *Expansion and Coexistence: The History of Soviet Foreign Policy, 1917–67.* New York, Praeger, 1968.

U.S. Congress, Senate Committee on Foreign Relations. *Documents on Germany 1944–1959.* Washington, U.S. Government Printing Office, 1959.

U.S. Department of State. *The Berlin Crisis.* Washington, U.S. Government Printing Office, 1948.

Warburg, James P. *Germany: Key to Peace.* Cambridge, Harvard University Press, 1953.

Westerfield, H. Bradford. *The Instruments of America's Foreign Policy.* New York, Crowell, 1963.

Willis, F. Roy. *The French in Germany, 1945–49.* Stanford, Stanford University Press, 1962.

Windsor, Philip. *City on Leave.* New York, Praeger, 1963.

Young, Oran R. *The Politics of Force.* Princeton, Princeton University Press, 1968.

Chapter 6

The Outbreak of the Korean War

Introduction:
The Significance of the Case

AS ROBERT E. OSGOOD has noted, the Korean War is "one of the truly decisive events that shaped the pattern of war and politics in our era." [1] It profoundly influenced American postwar strategy, powerfully stimulated military expenditures, globalized the containment policy and severely exacerbated relations with Communist China.

As part of President Truman's quick move to assist South Korea, he ordered the U.S. Seventh Fleet to provide temporary protection to Formosa. Thus began the process of recommitment to Chiang Kai-shek, from whom the administration had painfully disengaged. Before the outbreak of the Korean War, the island of Formosa to which the defeated Chinese Nationalist forces had retreated was expected to fall to the Chinese Communists later in 1950. As a result of the Korean War, Formosa became the "bone in the throat" in Peking's relations with the United States, preventing any possibility of a détente for over two decades.

Given the fateful consequences of the Korean War, it is particularly important to examine its origins and outbreak closely

[1] Osgood, *Limited War*, p. 163.

from the standpoint of deterrence theory and practice. Was the Korean War, as some observers have held, "essentially accidental and avoidable?" [2] Or, as revisionist historians have suggested, was the war an event that occurred in large part because of American duplicity of one kind or another? Or did the shifting Cold War objectives and strategies of the two sides play an important role in setting them on a collision course in Korea that neither side foresaw and that could not easily have been prevented? The last interpretation is favored here and will be developed in detail in this chapter.

Deterrence Failure or Failure to Employ Deterrence?

The Korean War is often included among those wars that occurred as a result of miscalculation. Such tragic occurrences are often cited to emphasize the need for more effective use of deterrence strategy in foreign policy. If the "aggressor" had only known that the United States would eventually join in the struggle against him, John Foster Dulles used to emphasize, World Wars I and II might have been avoided. This "lesson of history," applied to the outbreak of the Korean War, argues not unreasonably that had the United States clearly committed itself to the defense of South Korea ahead of time, the all-out North Korean attack of June 1950 probably would not have occurred. The same point was made in anticipation of the event by Syngman Rhee, President of the Republic of (South) Korea. In May 1949, shortly before the remaining U.S. occupation forces were pulled out of South Korea, Rhee emphasized that deterrence required an unambiguous U.S. commitment:

> Whether the American soldiers go or stay does not matter very much. What is important is the policy of the United States towards the security of Korea. What I want is a statement by President Tru-

[2] Halle, *Cold War as History*, p. 204.

man that the United States would consider an attack against South Korea to be the same as an attack against itself.[3]

The Truman Administration was willing to give such an unequivocal guarantee to NATO but nothing like it was forthcoming on behalf of South Korea.

We agree that the Korean War is less a failure of attempted deterrence than it is a failure to employ deterrence more effectively. But it is all too easy to misuse the benefit of hindsight to say that American leaders should have foreseen that they would respond to a flagrant attack on South Korea and, hence, should have foreseen the desirability of making a firmer commitment to South Korea in the interest of deterrence.[4] To rely on hindsight to criticize the Truman Administration for failing to employ deterrence more effectively is to ignore the substantial difficulties the leaders of a country can experience in deciding when to use deterrence strategy as an instrument of foreign policy.

One of the limitations of deterrence theory noted in chapter 3, therefore, is particularly relevant to this case. Deterrence theory per se, we noted, does not define its own scope or its relevance as an instrument of foreign policy. That is, the general theory of deterrence does not contain very useful criteria for indicating when a state should attempt to apply deterrence strategy to protect a weaker country. The answer to this question can be determined *only by a country's foreign policy, not by deterrence theory*. While deterrence is sometimes a necessary or useful instrument of foreign policy, correct use of this strategy in foreign policy is by no means self-evident or easily determined in all circumstances.

[3] Oliver, *Syngman Rhee*, pp. 295–96; cited by Higgins, *Korea and the Fall of MacArthur*, pp. 9–10.

[4] Of course, even effective deterrence of an all-out attack against South Korea would not necessarily have extended to lesser forms of pressure, subversion, and guerrilla warfare. These the North Koreans had already tried, and they might have continued to do so if deterred from undertaking a stronger attack.

Résumé of the
Background of the Case

The "two Koreas" problem emerged as a result of ad hoc wartime arrangements with the Russians to divide responsibility for accepting the surrender of Japanese forces in Korea on either side of the 38th Parallel. By mid-1947 the rapid demobilization of U.S. armed forces required the Truman Administration to consider withdrawal of the 45,000 men then in South Korea. The administration hesitated, however, fearing that American withdrawal would quickly lead to North Korean Communist control of the whole Korean peninsula. To avoid such an outcome the United States helped organize South Korean military forces along the lines of a constabulary force and worked through the United Nations to achieve a simultaneous withdrawal of Soviet and American forces. U.S. troop withdrawals began in September 1948 but were delayed when guerrilla warfare threatened the stability of the new South Korean Republic. The withdrawal was completed in June 1949. The Soviet Union announced that the removal of its troops from North Korea had been completed in December 1948.

Before withdrawing their forces, the two powers had encouraged the establishment of local governments, both of which promptly claimed jurisdiction over the whole country. There were some important differences, however, in the way in which the two governments were established. In November 1947, the General Assembly of the United Nations had called for elections throughout Korea, under the observation of a U.N. commission, to choose a representative national assembly for the purpose of drafting a constitution and establishing a national government. The Soviet Union refused to permit U.N. supervision of elections in North Korea and, hence, the North Korean government was not recognized by the U.N. as the validly elected, lawful government of the area.

In the South, on the other hand, the Republic of Korea came into being through elections held under U.N. supervision. It had the advantage, therefore, of recognition by the U.N. and by many of its member states as the lawful government in the area south of the 38th Parallel. Thus not only the United States but the United Nations as well played a major role in the birth of the South Korean Republic. Thereby, the U.N. assumed a special responsibility for South Korea. This must be kept in mind if we are to understand the strong support the U.N. gave to the Republic of Korea when it was invaded by the North Korean army.

Despite opposition from North Korea in October 1949, the General Assembly decided to continue the U.N. commission in Korea and requested it to investigate any matter that might lead to military events in Korea. In March 1950 the Secretary-General assigned eight military observers to observe incidents along the 38th Parallel. And, in fact, the reports of these U.N. observers immediately after the outbreak of the war played an important role in obtaining U.N. support for South Korea.

During the previous year the United States had withdrawn its forces from Korea and thereafter seemed to lean more heavily on a U.N. role in South Korea. But as Leland Goodrich was to note some time after the Korean War, the U.N. obviously "did not have the means at its disposal to guarantee the security of the new Republic. This responsibility only the United States could discharge." [5] We are led to inquire, therefore, into the nature of the commitment that Washington retained on South Korea's behalf.

The Development of
the Defender's Commitment

In the early morning of June 25, 1950, the North Korean Democratic People's Army launched a massive offensive employing over 7 divisions and 150 tanks in an effort to take over

[5] Goodrich, *Korea*, p. 207.

South Korea. The North Korean attack not only surprised American leaders, it revealed their political and military unpreparedness to intervene. President Truman's decision to commit U.S. military forces to aid South Korea was entirely an ad hoc, improvised action. Such a course had not been envisaged by U.S. foreign policy and had not entered into American strategic and military planning. After the withdrawal of U.S. occupation forces from South Korea in 1949 only a small military advisory group of 500 officers and enlisted men had been left behind. South Korea had then become the "responsibility" of the State Department; only after Truman decided to employ American military forces to oppose the North Korean attack did South Korea come under the jurisdiction of General MacArthur's headquarters in Tokyo.

While at first glance it seems that American policy toward South Korea reversed itself after the North Korean attack, a more careful appraisal explains the unforeseen and improvised nature of the U.S. military intervention in terms of a major gap in American strategic and foreign policy planning in the years that preceded the outbreak of war.

The Truman Administration had long considered South Korea to be of minor strategic significance. Withdrawal of U.S. occupation forces from that country was determined not merely by pressures generated by the rapid demobilization of American forces following World War II. Military planners judged that there was no U.S. security requirement to maintain forces in South Korea. On several occasions the Joint Chiefs of Staff (JCS) and civilian policy-makers carefully considered American security interests and foreign policy in the Far East. The criterion employed in these assessments was the "strategic" importance of these areas and, on this basis, Korea was clearly not of importance to the security of the United States. In the autumn of 1947 the JCS stated its views as follows: "from the standpoint of military security, the United States has little interest in maintaining the present troops and bases in Korea." The JCS went on to note that "in the event of hostilities in the Far East, our present forces in Korea would be a military liability and could not be maintained there without substantial reinforcement prior to the initiation of hostilities. . . ." [6]

Noteworthy is the fact that on this and subsequent occasions the "strategic" significance of South Korea was assessed exclusively with reference to the contingency of another *general war*. Since the fate of Korea in a general war would be decided in other theaters of war, and since Soviet occupation of Korea would not constitute a major liability in a general war, Korea lacked strategic significance for the global pattern of American security. The concept of limited war was still a novel one and did not enter into the framework of American military-strategic planning. Similarly, the special calculus of Cold War considerations, which might have qualified the tendency to view Korea solely in "strategic" terms, was not yet fully developed in the calculations of American policy-makers and did not yet enter into their definition of the situation in Asia to the extent that it did for Europe.

The "gap" in politico-military planning sprang from the failure to envisage that considerations other than Korea's strategic importance in a general war might require a U.S. commitment to its defense. And yet it was precisely these other considerations which suddenly became paramount following the North Korean attempt to take over South Korea. It is not without significance that Truman's initial decision of June 26 (announced the following day) to use American air and naval forces to help the South Koreans was taken on the initiative of the State Department. As Secretary of Defense Louis Johnson later recalled, "The military neither recommended it nor opposed it," although they did emphasize the "difficulties and limitations" of such an action.[7]

It is true that United States policy had excluded South Korea from its own "defense perimeter" in the Far East (and, thereby, from the protection of a unilateral American guarantee). Nonetheless, it is equally true, as Acheson noted in his

[6] Truman, *Years of Trial and Hope*, p. 325.

[7] Congress, *MacArthur Hearings*, IV, 2581, 2584 f.

well-known address of January 12, 1950, that the United States was prepared, if an attack against South Korea occurred, to invoke "the commitments of the entire civilized world under the Charter of the United Nations, which so far has not proved a weak reed to lean on by any people who are determined to protect their independence against outside aggression." [8] Later, when criticized for having inadvertently encouraged the attack on South Korea by his public announcement that it lay outside the U.S. "defense perimeter," Acheson reminded his critics of the passage in this speech which referred to the important role of the United Nations. But a closer examination of the policy planning behind Acheson's reference to the role of the U.N. does not relieve the administration from the main burden of the criticism that its public statements weakened rather than strengthened deterrence of a North Korean attack. It was true, but only in a quite limited sense, that U.S. plans called for immediately taking the matter of an attack on South Korea to the United Nations. Indeed, outlines of a draft resolution had been drawn up against this contingency within the State Department.[9] But there is no indication that U.S. contingency planning envisaged going beyond this kind of politico-diplomatic response to providing a military defense of South Korea either under the aegis of the United Nations or through unilateral action. If Truman and Acheson believed that the United States had an "obligation" or "commitment" under the United Nations Charter to help defend South Korea, there is no indication that the military implications of such a commitment were taken into account in American national security policy and military planning.

The fact of the matter is that the administration was taken by surprise not merely by the timing of the North Korean attack

---

[8] Dean G. Acheson, "Crisis in Asia—An Examination of U.S. Policy," *Department of State Bulletin*, XXII, No. 556 (January 23, 1950), p. 116; quoted in Paige, *Korean Decision*, p. 67.

[9] Testimony of John D. Hickerson, Assistant Secretary of State for United Nations Affairs, June 5, 1951. Congress, *Senate, Hearings on . . . Appropriation for 1952*, p. 1086.

and to some extent also by the strength of the North Korean army; it suddenly became aware of the *political* as against the "strategic" importance of South Korea. Truman's decision to oppose the North Koreans was not motivated by a sudden discovery that the strategic importance of Korea to American military security was greater than had been calculated earlier. Rather, the administration now assessed the expected damage to U.S. interests from allowing the North Koreans to take over South Korea on the basis of a much broader and more complex calculus than the earlier strategic criterion. Once South Korea was attacked it was perceived by the administration, Truman and Acheson in particular, to have much greater Cold War significance than had been anticipated, a Cold War significance which overshadowed its quite limited strategic significance.

This lack of prescience *cannot* be explained in terms of the inadequate procedures for orderly policy-making that are familiar in other historical cases. The Truman Administration's decision to downgrade the importance of South Korea after World War II was eminently rational, given the set of premises and constraints that governed formulation of U.S. foreign policy at the time. It was also a well-considered decision, arrived at through careful and responsible procedures for considering U.S. interests and security requirements in Asia and the best allocation of available resources. Furthermore, the administration's position on South Korea was not unilaterally determined by one department in the executive branch or unduly influenced by parochial or narrow views of national interest. Rather, the administration's policy stance toward South Korea had been developed through full, unhurried discussions and ample coordination among the departments having responsibility for foreign policy and national security. What is more, U.S. policy toward South Korea was remarkably free of major controversy either within the executive branch, between the administration and Congress, or in the arena of alert public opinion. It should also be noted that the acute controversy over the Truman Administration's China policy in the late forties did not extend to its policy on South Korea. Thus, when Secretary of State Dean

Acheson, in his oft-cited speech of January 12, 1950, excluded South Korea from the U.S. "defense perimeter" in the Far East, hardly anyone in Congress or within the country took special note of it, whereas critics of the administration's China policy reacted sharply and predictably to Acheson's similar omission of Formosa from the defense perimeter.

We therefore cannot resort to institutional or bureaucratic "irrationalities" to explain U.S. policy for South Korea, even though that policy itself contributed to the North Korean and Soviet decision to move against South Korea. What this case highlights is the unusual difficulty foreign policy–makers can encounter in attempting to judge and foresee the "value" of a weaker country within the framework of the objectives and means of their overall foreign policy. Deterrence theory needs to cope with this better than it has. Judgments of this kind can be exceedingly difficult to make when, as in this case, the perceived "value" of a small country is determined not by a simple calculus—such as the strategic importance of that country to the stronger power's security—but by a more complex calculus governed by a variety of considerations which are not stable over time but, rather, are sensitive to changes in the historical situation as it unfolds. Judgments of the "value" of a small country and of the "expected utility" of a commitment to defend it, then, can be highly *context-dependent*, often in ways which policy-makers only dimly and perhaps inaccurately perceive. Indeed, if one agrees with the administration's decision to intervene in the Korean War, then one might plausibly argue that global and regional developments connected with the intensification of the Cold War were making the administration's policy of no military commitment to South Korea obsolete even before the war broke out, but *without* the administration's realizing it.

The context-dependency of deterrence commitments is an important theme in this book, as well as one of the most important analytical problems of this case. Let us look into it somewhat more deeply.

Four interrelated developments in the context of U.S. policy for Korea were under way in the period prior to June 24, 1950:

(1) the shift in U.S. grand strategy for Asia away from the post–World War II objective of a strong, united, democratic China toward greater reliance on a stable, viable, friendly Japan;

(2) the emerging U.S. view that some kind of containment of Communist China was necessary;

(3) the growth in Soviet military power and the changing U.S. view of Soviet strategic intentions;

(4) the gradual spread of the Cold War to Asia and the emerging U.S. view that the Cold War was global in nature.

We shall attempt to show that these developments were only beginning to make themselves felt in U.S. policy for Korea in the precrisis period—hence the administration's general unawareness of the political importance of the peninsula—but were thrown into bold relief, as by a sudden flaring light, by the North Korean attack—hence the administration's rapid decision to intervene.

The development of American policy toward China is an important part of the shifting context in which U.S. policy on South Korea was being formulated. With the failure in 1947 of General Marshall's efforts to obtain a negotiated settlement between the Nationalists and the communists, the administration was faced with the necessity of considering the extent to which it would become actively involved in the Chinese civil war. The fact that only limited American military forces were available and the fear of being drawn into an eventual full-scale military intervention helped to defeat proposals for improving the efficiency of the Nationalist armies by greater use of U.S. military advisers. It was believed that massive U.S. involvement would be necessary to insure Chiang's success. The price tag attached to achieving the traditional U.S. objective of a united, democratic China was so large that it encouraged policy-makers to undertake a fundamental reevaluation of the U.S. national interest in China. A policy review was conducted in 1947 by the State Department's Policy Planning Staff, headed by George

Kennan. It concluded, as he recalls in his *Memoirs*, that the loss of China to the communists would not constitute "any intolerable threat" to U.S. security, though it would "heighten greatly the importance of what might now happen in Japan. Japan, as we saw it, was more important than China as a potential factor in world-political developments. It was . . . the sole great potential military-industrial arsenal of the Far East. We Americans could feel fairly secure in the presence of a truly friendly Japan and a nominally hostile China. . . ." [10]

In readjusting U.S. policy to the expectation of defeat for the Chinese Nationalists, the administration altered its conception of American security requirements in Asia. Abandoning the elusive, frustrating, and costly objective of a united, democratic, and friendly China, American policy shifted emphasis to insuring that a stable and friendly Japan would emerge after the end of the U.S. military occupation.

The search for an agreed-upon policy regarding the nature and timing of a Japanese peace treaty, however, encountered many difficulties within the administration. The Joint Chiefs of Staff opposed early termination of the military occupation of Japan and, later, emphasized that security considerations required provision for continuing American military bases if a peace treaty were to be concluded. The complex international environment surrounding the issue of a Japanese peace treaty offered additional difficulties. It was clear to administration leaders that a comprehensive multilateral peace treaty would be virtually impossible to achieve, given the different interests of the many countries that had been involved in the war with Japan and their conflicting views regarding the desirability of a conciliatory or a punitive peace. During the winter of 1949–1950 the administration moved somewhat uncertainly toward the goal of achieving an early peace treaty that would take the form of a bilateral U.S.-Japanese agreement and insure in some way continuation of U.S. military bases in Japan.

We cannot confidently infer the impact of this development on Soviet perceptions of the changing situation in Asia, or the

[10] Kennan, *Memoirs*, pp. 373–75.

role this played in their policy toward Korea; but the increasing importance of Japan in American policy calculations must have been evident enough to Moscow. Similarly evident to Soviet leaders must have been the fact that the United States was searching for a means of consolidating Japan's position on the anticommunist side of the Cold War. As George Kennan has noted, and Dean Acheson has confirmed, few American policy-makers gave any thought to the effect their plans for a separate peace treaty with Japan might have on Soviet policy in the Far East.[11] That Soviet concern over developments in Japan may have played a role in the decision to move against South Korea was inferred by U.S. policy-makers only after the attack took place.

The administration's decision to disengage itself from Chiang Kai-shek left open, of course, the question of its future relationship with the Chinese Communists. Taking note of the important issues that complicated Soviet relations with the Chinese Communists, some U.S. officials had hoped at one time for an early development of "Titoism" among the Chinese Communists. But the task of withdrawing the United States from its limited involvement in the Chinese civil war proved difficult and laborious. Truman's decision to reverse the U.S. commitment to the Chinese Nationalists was extremely controversial at home and became enmeshed in acute partisan politics. As a result, the administration was not able to withdraw support from Chiang as promptly and completely as it thought desirable. The administration felt obliged to continue, reluctantly, limited economic and military aid to Chiang Kai-shek in order to prevent congressional opponents of its China policy from retaliating by voting against its European security program. This added, of course, to the already difficult task of nurturing an early rapprochement with the Chinese Communists. The administration's inability to make a clean break with the Chinese Nationalists led predictably to increased friction and hostility in its relations with the Chinese Communists.

[11] *Ibid.*, p. 395; Acheson, *Present at the Creation*, pp. 429–31.

In early July 1949 Mao issued a historic pronouncement on foreign policy. He declared that the emerging Chinese Communist state would have to ally itself with the Soviet Union and rejected as illusory the idea that China could follow a "third road" or "lean to the side of imperialism." [12] Shortly thereafter, Acheson turned to the difficult task of developing a containment policy for preventing the further spread of communism in Asia. In October Mao proclaimed the establishment of the People's Republic of China, and the issue of diplomatic recognition was posed. But even before this, the steady worsening of U.S.– Chinese Communist relations and the domestic political context in the United States impressed upon the State Department the impracticality and imprudence of any early effort to seek normal diplomatic relations with the new communist regime in China. As a matter of fact, for several months the State Department had been attempting to dissuade other noncommunist governments from any haste in moving toward recognition.

In December Mao journeyed to Moscow and engaged in prolonged and secret negotiations with Stalin culminating on February 14, 1950 in the signing of a defense treaty. This provided for mutual assistance against aggression by Japan or "any other state which should unite with Japan, directly or indirectly, in acts of aggression." [13] There was no reference to Korea and, after the outbreak of the Korean War, Western observers were left to speculate as to whether Stalin had discussed with Mao the possibility of a North Korean move against South Korea.

During this period the Truman Administration stubbornly maintained its policy of no commitment to the defense of Formosa, even while initiating a containment policy toward Communist China. During the winter of 1949–1950 and, indeed up until the North Korean attack in late June, Truman and Acheson vigorously warded off pressures from domestic critics of their China policy to give the Chinese Nationalists greater assistance

[12] Cited in Tsou, *America's Failure in China*, p. 505.

[13] Whiting, *China Crosses the Yalu*, p. 27.

and to use the U.S. Navy to protect Formosa from an invasion from the mainland.

In other ways as well, the administration's emerging policy of containing communism in Asia lacked the urgency and high level of priority displayed in its efforts to establish bulwarks against the Soviet Union in Europe. The intensification of the Cold War in Europe had not yet made itself fully felt in Asia. However, in one area, Indochina, a direct linkage was established between Europe and Asia even before the outbreak of the Korean War. The development can be only briefly mentioned here.

When late in 1949 the Chinese Communists suddenly emerged as the victor in the civil war, Washington's previous ambivalence toward assisting the French in Indochina changed. The objective of containment now increasingly dominated the administration's attitude toward the conflict in Indochina. At the end of 1949 Truman approved a National Security Council study on Asia (NSC 48/2) which stated that the United States should "be prepared to help within our means" to meet the threat of communist aggression "by providing political, economic and military assistance and advice where clearly needed to supplement the resistance of other governments. . . ." The NSC document concluded that "particular attention should be given to the problem of French Indochina.[14]

Following Peking's and Moscow's recognition of Ho Chi Minh in January 1950, Washington agreed to provide economic and military aid to the French in Indochina. It should be noted, at the same time, that Indochina was not included in the U.S. "defense perimeter" which Acheson disclosed in his January 12 speech. It was clear, therefore, that while the U.S. was now extending a commitment to the defense of Indochina it went no further than the commitment to South Korea. In both cases the commitment was limited to economic and military equipment, and deliberately excluded any military guarantee involving U.S. forces.

[14] *Pentagon Papers,* I, 39.

The world strategic context was shifting in other respects as well that would affect the response the United States would make to the North Korean attack. After some internal debate within the administration during 1947–1948 regarding the level of U.S. military forces needed to sustain the policy of containment, Truman had resolved the issue in favor of Secretary of State Marshall and those who believed that a major increase in forces-in-being was not necessary. Considerations of domestic economy strongly influenced Truman's decision to keep to a military ceiling of $15 billion annually.

The first Soviet A-bomb test in August 1949, coming several years earlier than had been expected by U.S. planners, led Truman in early 1950 to approve development of the H-bomb. The breaking of the American atomic monopoly at this time and other developments—the intensification of the Cold War in Europe and the communist victory on the mainland of China— combined to lead the administration in early 1950 to initiate a major review of American foreign and national security policy. The results of this appraisal, embodied in NSC-68, were submitted to President Truman in early April 1950, less than three months before the outbreak of the Korean War.

The principal conclusion of NSC-68 was that American military strength would have to be increased substantially over its then current level. It was anticipated that when the Soviet Union acquired an operational stockpile of atomic weapons in a matter of some four years, American strategic nuclear strength could no longer serve as a deterrent to Soviet employment of its superior conventional forces. A substantial strengthening of American conventional forces therefore would be necessary. While Truman neither approved nor disapproved of NSC-68, he did request a study of the costs of implementing the strategy it recommended. This study was under way when the Korean War broke out. In the meantime, beginning in February, Acheson embarked on a series of public addresses throughout the country in which he articulated the premises, conclusions, and implications of NSC-68. His purpose was to arouse public support for creating "situations of strength" in order to implement containment of the Soviet Union more effectively. This could be done only through military spending considerably in excess of the current annual ceiling of $15 billion. (Some estimates within the administration regarded an annual military budget of $50 billion as desirable and also feasible from the standpoint of the domestic economy.) However, given Truman's conservatism on fiscal matters and the difficulty of generating sufficient public and congressional support for higher military outlays, most observers agree that a substantial increase in the military budget would probably not have occurred were it not for the Korean War.

The U.S. view of Soviet strategic intentions was indeed changing. At the same time, however, a serious intensification of the Soviet threat was not expected for several years. The basic assumption of American policy was still that Soviet leaders were not immediately ready to risk a world war, and would not be at least until they had acquired an adequate operational A-bomb capability. In the meantime, the Soviets were expected to continue to press for their objectives indirectly, avoiding overt forms of aggression that might risk a general war. Modifying this view of Soviet intentions were mounting intelligence indications in the spring of 1950 that some kind of communist military action at one point or another was to be expected. While Korea was on the list of possible targets, it was thought unlikely that it would be singled out for Soviet probing. Action in other danger spots, such as Berlin, Turkey, Greece, Iran, Finland, Yugoslavia, Formosa, or Indochina, was deemed more likely.

We have reviewed the major historical changes that were providing a new context within which American leaders would reconsider the significance of South Korea when the North Korean attack occurred. We have also noted that American policy-makers were already in the process of assessing and adapting to these changes. A hardening of the U.S.–Communist Chinese relationship was already under way before the outbreak of the Korean War.

But it was by no means obvious or predetermined that the

administration's search for some kind of discriminating containment of Communist China would lead to a reversal of Washington's no-commitment policy toward the Chinese Nationalist
regime on Formosa and, for the first time, to active U.S. military
intervention in the Chinese civil war. This was a direct consequence of the North Korean attack.[15] Similarly, whereas the
conflict with the Soviet Union had hardened in Europe, intensification of the Cold War there had not made itself fully felt in
Asia. The outbreak of the Korean War quickly resulted in the
globalization of containment. It also seemed to confirm the fears
expressed in NSC-68 regarding Soviet strategic intentions, and
it served to catalyze and expedite acceptance of many of the
policy recommendations and implications of NSC-68.

The Initiator's Motivations and Calculations

Although the North Korean attack was widely interpreted
as proof of malignant Soviet intentions, there are in fact critical
questions regarding the motivations and calculations of the
leaders in the Kremlin. The North Koreans themselves were obviously strongly motivated to eliminate the anticommunist
regime in South Korea and to unify their country. Whether the
Soviets initiated or merely approved the North Korean attack, it
is no secret that they were instrumental in equipping and training the North Korean army and in retaining close involvement
through Soviet military advisers.

The possibility that the North Koreans may have invaded
the South without the knowledge or approval of the Soviets has
frequently been mentioned, but it has been supported thus far
only by fragmentary bits of circumstantial evidence that do not
lend sufficient overall plausibility to the thesis.[16] Most special-

---

[15] We disagree in this important respect with the revisionist interpretation advanced by Joyce and Gabriel Kolko; see p. 173 below.

[16] See, for example, Stone, *Hidden History of the Korean War*.

ists on Soviet foreign policy who have examined the available evidence remain unpersuaded. "That the North Koreans would have attacked on their own," Adam Ulam concludes, "is inconceivable." [17] It is less certain that the Chinese Communists were consulted in advance and approved the North Korean venture.[18] From this standpoint, as Herbert Dinerstein notes, the origins of the Korean War "are still clouded in obscurity, it being one of the pieces of dirty linen the Chinese and the Russians have not yet elected to wash in public." [19]

We need not dwell on the nature of the objectives that Soviet leaders may have sought to further. Whatever specific payoffs the Soviets envisaged, it is obvious they had much to gain from a quick seizure of the Korean peninsula. Soviet leaders looked at Asia with increasing interest in 1950. It is not necessary for our purposes to reconstruct in detail the perceptions and motives that led to a shift in communist pressure from Europe and the Mediterranean to Asia. "In retrospect," however, as Robert Osgood has noted,

> nothing seems more logical than the shift of the main thrust of Communist expansion from an area of relative Western strength, where expansion entailed large risks of total war, to an area of greater vulnerability and weakness, where the West had scarcely applied the strategy of containment, where the risks of total war were minimized, and where neither local resistance nor massive retaliation was an effective deterrent.[20]

Indeed, much of Asia was economically, politically, and militarily weak and appeared ripe for social change, as was evidenced by the unexpectedly easy and rapid victory of the Chinese Communists in 1949. The relatively mild reaction of

[17] Ulam, *Expansion and Coexistence*, p. 517

[18] Ulam (*Ibid.*, pp. 517–18) believes it possible that Peking was not consulted or fully informed in advance, and did not approve of the North Korean attack. Whiting, however, regards it highly unlikely that Stalin did not inform Mao of the forthcoming attack; *China Crosses the Yalu*, p. 45. In *Khrushchev Remembers* the Soviet premier states that Mao was consulted in advance and approved.

[19] Dinerstein, *Intervention against Communism*, p. 14.

[20] Osgood, *Limited War*, p. 163.

American leaders to this greatest shift of power since World War II may have surprised Soviet leaders; perhaps it also encouraged them to look more closely at other opportunities for reducing Western influence in key areas of Asia. Korea was indeed a prime candidate from this standpoint. The Soviet perimeter would be greatly strengthened by possession of the Korean peninsula. A Soviet-oriented regime in firm control of the entire Korean peninsula would further the Soviet quest for hegemony in Northeast Asia; it would counterbalance the growing significance of Communist China and provide leverage for greater influence over developments in Japan. Indeed, stirred by the possibility of a separate U.S.-Japanese peace treaty, Soviet leaders may have calculated that unification of Korea by communist forces might stimulate Japanese neutralism and arouse serious doubts about the wisdom of signing a treaty with the United States.

One can think of various reasons for the timing of the North Korean attack. As Marshall Shulman notes, the decision to use force was preceded by "a long and unsuccessful effort to undermine South Korea by means of Communist penetration units and by border harassments of increasing intensity." [21] North Korean and Soviet leaders might have continued to rely on subversion, but the South Korean elections of May 1950, while revealing discontent with Syngman Rhee's government, were generally interpreted as an endorsement of the democratic system. An early move against South Korea may have recommended itself not only from the expectation that, given time, the democratic regime in the South would further consolidate itself, but also by concern that American foreign policy might be moving toward a stronger containment policy in Asia which, in turn, might lead it to giving greater aid to South Korea. The North Korean move may have also been timed to disrupt the thrust of U.S. policy toward Japan before it succeeded in converting that country into a military ally.

In accounting for Moscow's calculations, however, the criti-

[21] Shulman, *Stalin's Foreign Policy Reappraised*, p. 144.

cal question is not what it hoped to gain but how it assessed the risks of a North Korean effort to overrun the South. We do not believe that Soviet motivation was so compelling as to lead it to accept a high-risk strategy. Rather, it seems much more likely that Soviet leaders sanctioned the North Korean attack as a low-risk venture. There was ample foundation for such a view. Acheson's oft-noted omission of South Korea from the American "defense perimeter" in Asia was but one of many indications that the United States was not deeply committed to its survival. The administration's low estimate of Korea's strategic importance was reflected in the words of other high military and political authorities as well, and also by the low priority assigned to economic and military aid to South Korea. Nor can the possibility be excluded that Soviet espionage also turned up evidence that the U.S. commitment to South Korea was limited.

The lack of any response by the administration to increasing indications that the build up of the North Korean army imperiled South Korea must have tended to confirm the Soviet view that the administration had written off South Korea. To reach this conclusion Soviet leaders did not have to rely on their ability to read U.S. intentions correctly. It was obvious that the severe shortage of American troops, combined with the clear priority the administration placed on strengthening Western Europe's defenses, made it highly unlikely that the U.S. would divert troops to the defense of South Korea. In any case, it would take at least a week to move elements of U.S. occupation forces from Japan to Korea; and even those troops were understaffed and inadequately trained for combat.

Well might Soviet leaders conclude that Washington had neither the intention nor the capability for opposing a strong North Korean attack. They were amply justified in believing that, at most, the American response to such an attack would be minimal and probably confined to the diplomatic level, whether through the United Nations or through bilateral channels. Soviet leaders no doubt took note of Acheson's disclosure in his defense perimeter speech that U.S. plans called for taking the matter of an attack on South Korea to the United Nations, but they were amply justified in regarding this as a *substitute* for

unilateral U.S. military intervention rather than, as it turned
out, a vehicle for it.

That the critical asymmetries imbedded in the situation
would exclude any "rational" American decision to intervene
militarily on South Korea's behalf was, after all, not merely the
judgment of Soviet leaders. Ample indications were available to
them that their conclusion was shared by all leading American
policy-makers. For example, when Senator Tom Connally,
chairman of the Senate Foreign Relations Committee, was
asked in an interview published only seven weeks before the
Korean War broke out, "Do you think the suggestion that we
abandon Korea is going to be seriously considered?" he replied:

> I'm afraid it's going to be seriously considered because I'm afraid
> it's going to happen, whether we want it to or not. I'm for Korea.
> We're trying to help her. But South Korea is but right across by this
> line [the 38th Parallel]—north of it are the Communists with access
> to the mainland—and Russia is over there on the mainland. So that
> whenever she takes a notion she can over-run Korea just like she
> will probably over-run Formosa when she gets ready to do it. I hope
> not, of course.[22]

Statements like this by congressmen on sensitive issues of
foreign policy often force administration officials to issue dis-
claimers in order to reduce damage to the conduct of foreign
relations. But in this case, evidently, no one in the administration found it possible or desirable to take issue with Senator
Connally's pessimistic and presumably well-informed prediction. The alert observer, whether in Washington, Seoul or Moscow, might well conclude that Connally was trying to prepare
public opinion for the loss of South Korea as well as Formosa.

We might finally consider why the communist leaders
chose to mount an all-out attack against South Korea rather than
employing force in more discretely controlled increments to
"test" the U.S. reaction before proceeding to complete the conquest of South Korea. Given their confident reading of the
asymmetries of the situation and of American policy toward
South Korea, Soviet leaders evidently found it entirely reason-

---

[22] *U.S. News and World Report*, XXVII, May 5, 1950, p. 40.

able to conclude that the best strategy for taking South Korea was an all-out attack aimed at achieving a quick fait accompli.[23] The North Korean army was equipped and trained to enable it to mount a decisive offensive against the constabulary-type defense forces of South Korea. A pounce-and-snatch strategy promised success with very low risk of U.S. military involvement. Use of satellite military forces—"war by proxy"—insured against the remote possibility that the United States would regard an attack against South Korea as a *casus belli* against the Soviet Union. Perhaps more importantly in Moscow's view, a quick, decisive use of force would give the political decision-making process in Washington—regarded, not without reason, as being generally sluggish—very little time to reconsider and possibly reverse its standing policy of no military commitment to defense of South Korea. An all-out attack would be perceived to be less risky in this respect than a military campaign that deliberately moved slowly and cautiously against South Korea in order to "test" the U.S. commitment. If Soviet leaders had been highly uncertain of the U.S. commitment, then a "limited probe" action against South Korea would have made sense. But since Moscow had ample reason to believe that Washington had written off Korea, a "limited probe" strategy would have had the severe disadvantage of giving U.S. leaders ample time to reconsider their no-commitment policy and to collect military forces for intervening on South Korea's behalf.

The Defender's Response to Warning

Thus far, we have treated the outbreak of the Korean War as a "failure to employ deterrence" rather than as a "failure of at-

[23] This interpretation is explicitly supported by Khrushchev's memoirs, although its full authenticity remains uncertain. Khrushchev recalls that the plan for an attack was initiated by Kim Il-sung, the North Korean Premier, and received Stalin's approval. Stalin "was worried that the Americans would jump in, but we were inclined to think that if the war were fought swiftly—and Kim Il-sung was sure it could be won swiftly—then intervention by the U.S.A. could be avoided." *Khrushchev Remembers*, p. 368.

tempted deterrence." This distinction is analytically useful but one must be careful not to apply it without qualification to complex historical cases that, like the present one, actually combine elements of both types of "failure."

During the spring of 1950, U.S. intelligence discovered that the Soviets were engaged in a substantial buildup of the offensive strength of the North Korean army. The question of the opponent's intentions now became particularly salient for American policy-makers. And, with it, one would have supposed, would arise the question of whether the U.S. policy of attempting to maintain the independence of South Korea through limited means—essentially, political and economic support—was likely to continue to be successful and, if not, what changes in that policy might be considered.

When it appears that the opponent may be getting ready to challenge or test the defender's limited commitment to a weak ally, the defender has a choice of several responses. He may increase his commitment to include the promise of direct military support to defend against an attack. He may maintain his limited commitment but increase the amount of indirect economic, military, and diplomatic support. He may decide to reduce even his limited commitment; or he may prepare in other ways to cushion the costs of the possible failure of his policy of maintaining the weak ally's independence.

Early in 1950 ample warning that the policy of limited commitment to South Korea might soon undergo a severe test was available to American policy-makers. What is curious is that they did not respond in *any* of these three ways. Indeed, very little use of the available warning was made. This was not a "rational" response to the changing situation. Warning provided an opportunity for careful reevaluation and reassessment of the current policy and the various premises on which it was based. It also provided an opportunity for rehearsal of how the administration might respond to the unpleasant contingency of a strong North Korean attack, even though such an attack might still be regarded as improbable.

The value which a more rational use of available warning might have had in this case cannot be easily dismissed. If one believes that Truman's military intervention on behalf of South Korea was a correct and necessary decision, then one must deplore the fact that the administration did not utilize available warning of the North Korean attack to strengthen its commitment to South Korea in the hope of deterring it. A costly and tragic war through miscalculation might then have been avoided. If, on the other hand, one believes that Truman's intervention was an unwise and unnecessary decision, and that he overreacted to the North Korean attack, then one must deplore the administration's failure to make better use of warning for different reasons. If Truman and his advisers had rehearsed the contingency of a North Korean attack, they might have minimized its shock effect on their calculations. They might also have decided against military intervention and taken steps to cushion the effects the attack would have on the general position of the U.S. around the world. Either way, the importance of the available warning demands a closer analysis of the administration's lack of receptivity and response to it.

In assessing receptivity to available warning it is useful to distinguish between strategic and tactical warning. The former term refers to long-range indications of the opponent's plans and preparations; the latter refers to indicators of an imminent attack. Warnings of both kinds are seldom conclusive. The indicators may be equivocal regarding whether the opponent will take some kind of action and/or ambiguous regarding the precise nature, timing, and location of the action. The warning indicators themselves may be quite good, but receptivity to them may be degraded by various factors.

In the Korean case U.S. officials were somewhat more receptive to strategic warning than to tactical warning of the North Korean attack. Indications of North Korean intentions prior to the attack were plentiful, but they were systematically downgraded and misinterpreted by U.S. officials. Thus, as Truman's memoirs acknowledge, there had been warnings for some time of a full-scale North Korean attack: "Throughout the spring the Central Intelligence reports said that the North Koreans might at any time decide to change from isolated raids to a full-scale attack. The North Koreans were capable of such an attack at any time. . . ." However, implicitly distinguishing between good strategic warning and equivocal, uncertain tactical warning, Truman adds that intelligence had not pinpointed "whether an attack was certain or when it was likely to come." [24] Secretary of State Acheson, too, recalled that intelligence appraisers had agreed that such an attack, while possible, was not imminent and that it was more probable that North Korea would continue its efforts to gain control over South Korea by lesser means.

What this indicates is that the entire burden of avoiding surprise had come to rest upon the receipt of good *tactical* warning of an imminent North Korean attack, without policy-makers being clearly aware of this. But there can never be assurance that unequivocal tactical warning will be available or that receptivity to it will remain unimpaired. To avoid surprise and to take advantage of available warning usually requires that policy-makers begin to consider what they will do on the basis of good strategic warning, or strategic warning coupled with equivocal tactical warning. It courts trouble to remain passive until and unless high-confidence tactical warning is available.

In the present case strategic warning might have been utilized by American officials in several ways: (1) To step up intelligence efforts designed to clarify the estimate of North Korean intentions and to improve arrangements for receipt and processing of indicators of tactical warning. (2) To initiate a study of the expected damage to general U.S. interests in the event of an all-out North Korea attack. This might have created awareness among policy-makers that South Korea was assuming a political and Cold War significance that outweighed the lack of "strategic" significance attributed to it years earlier when the basic decision was made to withold a full-fledged commitment of American military support in case of attack. (3) To anticipate some of the special psychological and political pressures and decisional dilemmas that might confront U.S. leaders in the

[24] Truman, *Years of Trial and Hope*, p. 331.

event of a North Korean attack. A rehearsal of this kind, as we have already noted, might have enabled the administration to make a calmer and more restrained response to the attack when it actually occurred.

Available information indicates that very little use was made of this warning. The burden placed on receipt of good tactical warning was clearly excessive and, in retrospect, unjustified. Since reasonably good strategic warning did not succeed in getting U.S. leaders to reopen the question of the adequacy of current policy toward the defense of South Korea, it is hard to see how tactical warning could have possibly triggered a quick policy reappraisal resulting in a heroic last-minute effort to strengthen deterrence of the North Korean attack.

As it was, tactical warning, predictably enough, was ambiguous. In the years preceding the attack there had been innumerable minor border violations, as well as two limited invasions of South Korea. These border violations had become so regular an occurrence that Secretary of Defense Louis Johnson referred to them as "Sunday morning excursions." [25] Their very frequency evidently conditioned U.S. intelligence estimators to be suspicious of a "cry-wolf" attitude and to downgrade new indicators of a large-scale North Korean attack. Nor was suspicion aroused by a sharp drop in the frequency of border incidents in the weeks before the attack; evidently no one thought this might signal the lull before the storm. South Korean leaders frequently expressed their concern about the danger of a strong North Korean attack, but even when reinforced by the American Ambassador's own warning, this did not suffice to perturb the dominant U.S. intelligence interpretation. After all, the South Korean leaders were making a case for obtaining heavier military equipment to counter North Korean acquisition of Soviet tanks; and the concern expressed by the U.S. Ambassador in Seoul could be discounted as a normal case of special pleading by a conscientious representative in the field.

Administration leaders confined themselves to taking note

[25] *MacArthur Hearings,* IV, 2584.

of the malaise that the shifting balance of military power between North and South Korea, which the United States was doing nothing to rectify, was creating among South Korean political leaders. The most noteworthy of efforts to calm the South Koreans' invasion jitters was John Foster Dulles' address to the South Korean National Assembly on June 17, a week before the attack occurred. Dulles assured his audience that the American people remained "faithful to the cause of human freedom and loyal to those everywhere who honorably support it." He concluded: "You are not alone; you will never be alone, as long as you continue to play worthily your part in the great design of human freedom." [26]

Some writers have drawn attention to Dulles' statement as indicating that the United States was committed after all to the defense of South Korea.[27] But such an interpretation obscures the significant difference between a policy of full-fledged commitment to military support and the actual U.S. policy of limiting its commitment to provision of economic aid, military equipment, and diplomatic support. Dulles' statement was consistent with the latter policy. His speech had been cleared by Assistant Secretary of State Dean Rusk and the last paragraph, from which we have quoted, had in fact been drafted by Rusk and the director of the State Department's Policy Planning staff, Paul Nitze. Both of them evidently agreed with Dulles' suggestion that something should be said during the course of his visit to South Korea to "firm up" the public American policy position on South Korea.[28]

[26] Cited by Paige, *Korean Decision,* p. 74.

[27] Some writers (e.g., I. F. Stone) have even questioned whether Dulles was conniving in some way to strengthen the U.S. commitment or, even, to bring about a war. The more careful analysis by Joyce and Gabriel Kolko of Dulles' trip and of his speech would appear to reject all these interpretations. "Too much," they say, "has been read into these words." The Kolkos' own analysis is largely consistent with that offered here of the purpose and limited significance of Dulles' speech; though they also call attention to the view he expressed earlier regarding the need for a strong U.S. response in the event of a crisis in the Far East. (*Limits of Power,* pp. 576–77, 562.)

[28] Paige, *Korean Decision* pp. 65, 74.

There is little reason to believe that the statement in question by Dulles was intended to convey a strengthening of the U.S. commitment toward an assurance of American military intervention, if needed, to contain a powerful North Korean attack. It is always possible that Dulles himself and other members of the administration believed that the U.S. commitment should be strengthened, but there is no evidence to support this and no indication of a policy debate within the administration on the matter. Acheson recalls that the thought of visiting Korea during the course of his visit to Japan had been Dulles' own idea, and he does not recall having seen the speech Dulles gave to the South Korean National Assembly.[29]

Furthermore, the primary audience for Dulles' statement was the South Koreans, whom he wanted to reassure. While the possibility cannot be entirely excluded that the statement was also intended to impress North Korean and Soviet leaders as well, it would constitute a rather meager way of reinforcing deterrence; and, most likely, this was not its purpose. Certainly we have no evidence of any other efforts to reinforce deterrence. In fact, the administration appears to have felt no particular need to do so. Most policy-makers seem to have found one reason or another for downgrading the significance of the available warning indicators of a North Korean attack. Three are especially worth noting.

First, the North Korean communists were seen as being under the direct control of the Soviet Union. Hence, so the logic of interpretation proceeded, an all-out North Korean move was unlikely, since it would create the risk of a general war for which the Soviets were not yet prepared. No one seemed to question the premise, imbedded in this interpretation, that the Soviets would regard an attack by their proxy as a high-risk strategy. And no one seemed to consider that the absence of a U.S. commitment to defend South Korea might encourage Soviet leaders to reduce their estimate of the risks of an attack.

Second, underestimation of the strength of the Soviet-

[29] *Ibid.*, p. 74.

equipped and -trained North Korean army further encouraged the view that the North Koreans would not attack. Coupled, as this was, with overestimation of the South Korean army's defensive capability, U.S. officials persuaded themselves that the communist leaders, too, would not rate a major North Korean attack as an attractive or viable option, and would prefer to rely on the somewhat greater potential of subversion and other indirect strategies for undermining the South.[30]

Third, U.S. officials may have underestimated the desire of the Soviet Union to strive for hegemony in Northeast Asia and failed to grasp the role Soviet leaders would assign to a North Korean attack as furthering this objective. Soviet experts in the government were unable to perceive clearly enough the way in which the Soviets were viewing developments in Asia and in the Cold War more generally. We have already commented on the possibility that the move against South Korea may have appealed to Soviet leaders as a way of countering emerging U.S. plans for a separate peace treaty with Japan, and on the fact that American officials were not sensitive to this possibility.

George Kennan has frequently drawn attention to and deplored the chronic tendency during these years for U.S. planners, particularly military planners, "to view Soviet intentions as something existing quite independently of our own behavior. It was difficult to persuade these men that what people in Moscow decided to do might be a reaction to things we had done."[31] But even Kennan and other Soviet experts had difficulty in ferreting out Moscow's intentions in the spring of 1950. "Why had it [the attack on South Korea] been authorized by Moscow? True, we had not foreseen it. But once it had happened, it stood as a clue to what had been transpiring in recent weeks and months in the thinking of the Kremlin leaders; and

---

[30] In his *Memoirs* (p. 485), Kennan recalls that the effort of Soviet experts in State Department to interpret indications of a possible attack in Korea went awry because they accepted erroneous military intelligence estimates that credited the South Korean army with such great defensive capability as to render a North Korean attack unrealistic.

[31] *Ibid.*, p. 497.

much that was previously unintelligible then fell into place." [32]

Some revisionist historians and radical critics of American foreign policy have suggested that important U.S. officials were not really surprised by the North Korean attack. They point to the fact that ample warning was available and, glossing over the problem of receptivity to warning, infer from the lack of response to it a conspiracy or secret decision to allow the North Korean attack to take place rather than to deter it. These officials, it is further alleged, wanted to use the forthcoming North Korean attack to further their desire to mount a much stronger Cold War policy.[33]

A different interpretation can be placed, however, on the lack of a fuller response to available warning. (This phenomenon, incidentally, is not unique to the Korean War; witness, for example, the problem of interpreting warning indicators of the Japanese attack on Pearl Harbor or, to take a quite different case, Stalin's lack of receptivity to the indications that Hitler was going to attack the Soviet Union.) We described earlier the policy background and the shift in the historical context in some detail because we believe these factors to be an important part of the explanation not merely for Truman's unexpected military intervention in the Korean War, but also for the administration's curious passivity and lack of receptivity in the face of available warning of a possible North Korean attack. Let us recall briefly some of the relevant components of the policy background.

In excluding South Korea from the American defense perimeter in the Far East on the ground that it was not of strategic importance in a general war, U.S. planners did not foresee or gauge properly the broader political and Cold War considerations that would suddenly enhance the importance of South Korea once it was attacked. Defense planning for Asia had been geared to the contingency of a general war in which, clearly, it

---

[32] *Ibid.*

[33] See, for example, Stone, *Hidden History of the Korean War*, pp. 27, 39–40. Most of these extreme revisionist theses were quietly rejected in the detailed work of two other revisionist writers, Joyce and Gabriel Kolko. A discussion of their own interpretation of the origins of the Korean War is presented below.

made no sense to attempt a direct defense of South Korea. No
military plans or preparations were made for lesser contingencies which might involve South Korea. Both military and political planners operated at this time without a clearly defined
image of the threat of limited war and of strategies for dealing
with such threats.

In this policy context, the possibility of "receiving" and
utilizing available warning to reinforce deterrence was particularly difficult to realize because it required a reversal of the U.S.
policy of no military commitment to South Korea. Psychologically as well as politically, it was difficult for the Truman Administration to be receptive to indications that the North
Koreans might attempt to overrun South Korea. We must recall
that the administration's decisions in 1947–1949 to withdraw
American forces from South Korea and to limit its commitment
to economic aid, military equipment, and diplomatic support
were part of a larger Asian policy, painfully arrived at following
the disillusionment with the Chinese Nationists, for reducing
and redefining U.S. commitments in the Far East. Not only
South Korea but, more importantly, Formosa, to which Chiang's
remaining Nationalist forces had retreated, were also denied
any direct U.S. military support or guarantee. Furthermore, in
the chorus of criticism of Truman and Acheson over the
disengagement from Chiang, few voices were raised on behalf
of South Korea.

When warning indications multiplied concerning a possible
attack on South Korea, therefore, it was easier to dismiss them
than to take them seriously. For to take them seriously would
carry the penalty of deciding what to do about it. It would have
been extremely difficult for Truman and Acheson to respond to
warning of a North Korean attack by improvising an effort to
deter it. This would have required that they be willing to reconsider their earlier decision on where to draw the line in the Far
East. To act upon warning with a belated effort to deter North
Korea would have required the administration to tell the American public that it had suddenly decided to make a new commitment on behalf of the defense of South Korea. Such a reversal of

U.S. policy on behalf of South Korea was politically inconceivable unless it extended also to the defense of Formosa. The close linkage of the two was demonstrated after the North Korean attack when the administration immediately deployed the Seventh Fleet to "neutralize" Formosa, to protect it from Chinese Communist attack, and to disarm the voluble and powerful critics of its China policy before they could attack the administration for coming to the assistance of South Korea while continuing to leave Formosa to its fate. (A Chinese Communist attack on Formosa was expected to take place later in the year.)

This is not to say that Truman and Acheson rejected or downgraded available warning after *consciously* considering the implications of accepting it. The problem of receptivity to warning is more subtle than this. The failure to perceive warning in this case is a prime example of the subtle influence the dominant policy background itself can have in reducing receptivity to available warning. (We shall see its influence in other cases as well.) Acceptance of available warning of an attack on South Korea would have forced the administration to reopen policy matters on which decisions had been reached earlier only with great difficulty. It was easier to hope and believe that this would not be necessary or could somehow be avoided. Wishful thinking also played a role in downgrading the likelihood of a large-scale North Korean attack, as against the further efforts at subversion of South Korea which U.S. leaders expected. A large-scale attack was clearly something U.S. policymakers hoped and expected would not occur and which they were not prepared to deal with until it happened.

This was then no simple intelligence failure: fundamental considerations of U.S. policy, strategy, and domestic politics abetted the failure to recognize, accept, and act upon warning. It is difficult to envisage how these subtle but potent factors could have been neutralized to the point where U.S. leaders could have accepted warning of the forthcoming North Korean attack as requiring them to recalculate policy toward South Korea.

Epilogue: Origins of the Korean War— Some Competing Views

We have attempted to reconstruct Soviet perceptions and calculations in a way that is consistent with available historical facts and with the logic of the situation at the time. But the origins of the Korean War, as we have tried to suggest, are quite complex. Many of the essential historical facts are not yet available and, indeed, may never be known. More material (but by no means the full historical record) is available on American perceptions, calculations, and actions than on North Korean and Soviet policy-making. Scholars who bring different general theories and frameworks to bear on the question are likely to reconstruct the origins of the war in somewhat different ways. Before concluding this case study we shall consider an account of the origins of the Korean War published recently be the historians Joyce and Gabriel Kolko that promises to become an authoritative revisionist interpretation for some years to come.

It is noteworthy that their detailed examination of the large number of American sources that have become available in recent years leads the Kolkos to put aside two of the more bizarre of the earlier revisionist hypotheses: namely, that the South Koreans attacked first and thereby deliberately or inadvertently provoked the North Korean attack; and that important U.S. officials knew the North Koreans were planning to attack but did nothing to deter it because they wanted to use the attack to intervene, and to launch a stronger Cold War policy more generally.

Instead, the Kolkos develop an alternative interpretation that is closer in important respects to the orthodox view of the origins of the Korean War. The revisionist context of their thesis is complex and cannot be easily summarized, but the essentials of their view are these: (1) the attack on South Korea was exclusively the North Koreans' own idea; the Soviets were not behind it and were surprised by the North Korean move; (2)

the North Korean attack was deliberately made to appear more powerful and more successful than it was by Syngman Rhee, the President of South Korea, in order to bring about U.S. military intervention; General MacArthur cooperated with Rhee in this respect; (3) Truman and Acheson deliberately overreacted to the North Korean attack because it provided them with a "useful crisis," i.e., an unexpected but welcome opportunity to break the logjam that was hampering fuller and more effective pursuit of their Cold War objectives and politics.

Detailed evaluation of all aspects of the Kolkos' interpretation of the origins of the Korean War is not possible here. Important elements of their argument are necessarily based on conjecture (which they acknowledge) and on selective interpretations (which they are less aware of, or less willing to acknowledge) of available facts and evidence that permit of alternative interpretations which, if correct, do not support their overall thesis.

These weaknesses are particularly evident in their interpretation of North Korean motives for launching the attack and their view of Soviet noninvolvement. It is indeed useful to have, finally, a carefully reasoned version of the long-standing hypothesis that the North Koreans acted on their own. But, if the Kolkos' detailed exposition of this hypothesis now permits one to see better the elements of plausibility that can be attached to it, their elaboration of the thesis also serves to expose more specifically than heretofore the important weaknesses imbedded in it.

The Kolkos raise more questions than they answer when they argue that the Soviet military buildup of the North Korean army (which included approximately 150 tanks and other heavy equipment the South Koreans lacked) was designed merely to give it a defensive capability in order to stabilize the situation and assure peace in the region; that the Soviets did not intend to provide the North Koreans with an offensive capability against South Korea.[34]

[34] Kolko and Kolko, *Limits of Power*, p. 585. The Kolkos generally minimize the military superiority of the North Korean army over the South Korean forces.

The Kolkos' thesis that the Soviets were not aware of the North Korean plan to attack South Korea strains plausibility, especially since they make no effort to explain how this alleged effort at deception of the Soviets by the North Koreans could have succeeded in evading the scrutiny of Soviet military advisors in the North Korean army.[35] Central to the Kolkos' thesis regarding Soviet noninvolvement in the North Korean attack is a rejection of the orthodox interpretation that Soviet leaders approved the attack on the mistaken premise that the United States had written off South Korea and would not intervene militarily against a determined North Korean attack. The Kolkos do not take direct issue with this interpretation of the role that Soviet miscalculation (and, indeed, North Korean miscalculation as well) played in the outbreak of the war. Instead, they confidently assert that the Soviets could not have miscalculated. Rather, Soviet leaders "must have realized" and foreseen that a war in Korea would trigger U.S. military intervention and a strong Cold War response that would be contrary to Soviet interests; hence, the logic of the Kolkos' interpretation proceeds, the Soviets certainly could not have approved or even known about the forthcoming North Korean attack.[36]

In addition to crediting the Soviet leaders with an unusual capacity to foresee and calculate correctly their foreign policy interests in the rather complex situation at the time, the Kolkos also argue, again against the orthodox interpretation, that Soviet foreign policy lacked any motivation to extend its control over the entire Korean Peninsula. By crediting the Soviet Union with strictly defensive, status quo objectives in Northeast Asia,

---

A fuller statement of the important elements of qualitative superiority over the South Korean army is noted in the official U.S. Army history by Appleman in *South to the Naktong, North to the Yalu*, pp. 17–18.

[35] The official U.S. Army history of the Korean War cites intelligence reports as indicating that about 3,000 Russians were active in the North Korean army program before June 1950. "In some instances as many as fifteen Soviet officers served as advisers on an N.K. infantry division." Appleman, *South to the Naktong, North to the Yalu*, p. 7.

[36] Kolko and Kolko, *Limits of Power*, p. 585.

the Kolkos are able to set aside (without discussion) the possibility that Soviet leaders attached value to acquiring control over the entire Korean Peninsula and, besides, had ample reason to assume that the United States had written off South Korea and would not give it military assistance. For the orthodox interpretation of Soviet complicity in the North Korean attack (based on the calculation that this was an attractive high-gain, low-risk strategy for advancing Soviet interests), the Kolkos substitute the interpretation that Soviet foreign policy attached "low priority" to Korea and that Moscow would have prevented the North Koreans from attacking had it known what they were up to, since such an attack conflicted with the global political strategy that the Soviet Union was then pursuing.[37]

The Kolkos attempt to buttress this thesis in various ways. For example, they point to indications of aloofness and reticence in Soviet behavior after the North Korean attack took place.[38] They ignore, however, the at least equally plausible interpretation that Soviet leaders simulated aloofness to facilitate international acceptance of the North Korean action and then, taken by surprise by U.S. military intervention on South Korea's part, continued to remain aloof and reticent because they were now all the more motivated to avoid direct responsibility for the North Korean attack so as to reduce and control the risks of American overreaction. The Kolkos' evidence and reasoning are thus insufficient to require abandonment of the orthodox thesis of Soviet involvement in the North Korean attack.

Moreover, it is noteworthy that they acknowledge that the North Korean attack was no ordinary border incursion but was designed to capture Seoul and topple the Rhee government.[39] For some curious reason—perhaps because they believe that the North Koreans did not initially employ all their forces—the Kolkos feel that for the North Koreans the attack must be regarded as a "limited campaign" and refer to it as a "limited war."[40] This confuses the issue, since the *objective* of the North Korean attack was, as acknowledged by the Kolkos, certainly anything but limited. If successful in achieving its objec-

---

[37] *Ibid.*, pp. 585–86.   [38] *Ibid.*, p. 586.   [39] *Ibid.*, p. 574.   [40] *Ibid.*, p. 578.

tive, the North Korean attack would have set the stage for unifying Korea along political lines much more to their liking.

Given the North Koreans' objective, it could hardly come as a surprise to them that Rhee would try to save his government, even if it meant not taking an all-out military stand to save his capital. However, the fact that Rhee chose to evacuate the government to the South—thus frustrating the objective of the North Korean attack—becomes the basis for another strand in the Kolkos' overall interpretation. Ignoring the fact that the South Korean army's retreat (by no means entirely voluntary or carried out in good order) was a rational defensive strategy, the Kolkos hold that Syngman Rhee's "premature" abandonment of Seoul, together with the fact that the South Korean army did not attempt a firm, decisive stand, constitutes circumstantial evidence that Rhee deliberately pretended to be losing in order to make sure that American ground forces as well as air and naval power would be employed on his behalf. In this, they say, MacArthur cooperated—but whether in coordination with Rhee or not "is a matter of conjecture," [41] and "whether consciously or not" is uncertain [42]—by deliberately exaggerating the pessimistic reports he sent to Washington in order to insure U.S. intervention and to obtain larger forces for a counteroffensive—and, indeed, a larger war.

That the South Koreans might reasonably have lacked confidence in their ability to stop rapidly the tank-supported North Korean advance, the Kolkos ignore. Instead, the Kolkos are quite confident that the South Koreans had the capability to make a successful defense against the "limited" North Korean attack, that they knew they could, and that they chose not to do so.[43] The Kolkos argue, further, that U.S. military intervention

[41] *Ibid.*, p. 582.   [42] *Ibid.*, p. 592.

[43] Compare this with the official U.S. Army historian's analysis of the failure of the South Korean army's counterattack, designed to relieve pressure on Seoul, and his account of the premature blowing up of the Han River bridges which resulted in a "military catastrophe" for the South Korean forces. "The main part of the [South Korean] army, still north of the river, lost nearly all its transport, most of its supplies, and many of its heavy weapons. . . . The disintegration of the ROK Army now set in with alarming speed." Appleman, *South to the Naktong, North to the Yalu*, pp. 34, 28–29.

need not have gone beyond provision of air and naval support. In this event, they believe that the North Korean objective would have been foiled and the Korean War would have been only a "mild crisis," an "episode . . . essentially like many earlier ones" in Korea.[44]

Not merely did Rhee and MacArthur wish to turn it into a more severe crisis but, according to the Kolkos, from the outset Acheson and Truman "appreciated the value of a moderate crisis in getting numerous global projects and appropriations out of an indifferent and hostile Congress."[45] They were peculiarly receptive and insufficiently critical, therefore, of the pessimistic reports from Korea.[46]

It is probably true that the "Cold War significance" of South Korea for the Truman Administration included the perception that the North Korean attack made it much easier to put into effect stronger defense measures, which were then under consideration, as necessary to implement more effectively the containment of the Soviet Union. The element of truth in this perceptive observation, however, is distorted by making this motive the exclusive or primary one for U.S. military intervention in South Korea. Thus, the revisionist thesis would have it, the administration intervened solely out of a cynical calculation that the North Korean attack gave it a badly needed opportunity, a "useful crisis," to effect heavier military expenditures and to whip up support for stronger Cold War policies. This ignores and downgrades the ample evidence of far more complex motives and calculations on the part of leading administration officials. There is little need to attribute cynicism to Truman and Acheson when idealism legitimized and supported hardboiled judgments regarding the Soviet-communist threat. One can disagree with the administration's response to the North Korean attack without insisting that Truman and Acheson perceived it and reacted to it merely as a "useful opportunity." The evidence cannot be dismissed that they actually perceived considerable damage to American foreign policy interests as likely if they did not come to South Korea's assistance.

[44] *Ibid.*, p. 582.   [45] *Ibid.*, p. 580.   [46] *Ibid.*, p. 583.

To emphasize that fear of the Cold War consequences played a critical role in shaping the administration's response to the North Korean attack is not necessarily to agree with its assessment of them. Under the shock of the unexpected North Korean attack and the need for rapid decision-making if a seizure of South Korea were to be prevented, Washington had to assess the Cold War significance of these events all too hurriedly. Had there been an opportunity either before or after the North Korean attack for more leisurely and careful analysis of what was at stake from the standpoint of vital U.S. interests, and for consideration of alternative ways of limiting the expected Cold War damage from the loss of South Korea, Truman and Acheson might have been more restrained in their response.[47] As it was, however, the North Korean attack not only seemed to confirm their worst fears about Soviet intentions but, in fact, added substantially to them.

Prior to the Korean attack, as Seyom Brown has noted,[48] the administration's containment policy had not yet been "globalized." To be sure, certain developments in this direction were already under way in U.S. policy in Asia prior to the Korean War, as we shall note later. But Truman and Acheson recognized that the situation in Asia differed in important respects from that in Europe and had ruled out the possibility of a Pacific pact similar to NATO.[49] While interested in finding a viable version of containment in Asia, the administration was feeling its way cautiously and with considerable restraint. Severely complicating the emergence of a stronger and more comprehensive containment policy in Asia was the administration's decision to disengage from the Chinese Nationalists and to accept the Chinese Communists as victors in the civil war. At the time

[47] One of the authors raised a number of questions of this kind in an earlier analysis and critical evaluation of the U.S. decision to intervene; see George, "American Policy-Making and the North Korean Aggression." A more comprehensive critique of malfunctions in the policy-making process on this and other occasions is presented in the same author's recent study, "The Case for Multiple Advocacy in Making Foreign Policy."

[48] Brown, *Faces of Power*, p. 59.

[49] Tsou, *America's Failure in China*, p. 506.

of the North Korean attack, the administration was still waging a reasonably successful struggle to ward off the pressure of Republican critics of its China policy to recommit itself to the defense of Formosa. The bold North Korean attempt to take over South Korea had the effect of pulling the rug out from under the administration in its struggle with domestic critics of its China policy; it served as a catalyst that globalized containment overnight.

We may note, finally, that even if one accepts (as we do not) the Kolkos' thesis that the North Koreans acted alone, the problem remains of explaining the North Korean failure to anticipate American military intervention and, similarly, the failure of U.S. leaders to make a stronger commitment to South Korea in order to deter a possible North Korean attack. In other words, the outbreak of the Korean War would still invite attention from the standpoint of deterrence theory and practice, though in that event the explanations and lessons drawn would differ in some important respects from those presented in our treatment of the case.

Bibliography

The most detailed account of the American response to the North Korean attack is Paige's study, based on interviews with most of the leading American policy-makers and other sources. On this aspect of the case see also Truman, *MacArthur Hearings*, Smith, Warner, Higgins, Mills, Spanier, Hoyt, and the two articles by George. With the exception of Khrushchev's memoirs (the full authenticity of which is in doubt), information on Soviet and North Korean policy-making is lacking; interpretations of available clues are provided by Shulman, Ulam, LaFeber, Kolko, and Stone.

For earlier research on this case we are indebted to Jane Howland.

Acheson, Dean. *Present at the Creation.* New York, Norton, 1969.

Appleman, Roy E. *South to the Naktong, North to the Yalu.* Washington, D.C., U.S. Government Printing Office, 1961.

Bell, Coral. *Negotiation from Strength.* New York, Knopf, 1963.

Brown, Seyom. *The Faces of Power.* New York, Columbia University Press, 1968.

Bundy, McGeorge, ed. *The Pattern of Responsibility.* Boston, Houghton Mifflin, 1952.

Collins, J. Lawton. *War in Peacetime: The History and Lessons of Korea.* Boston, Houghton Mifflin, 1969.

Cottrell, Alvin and James E. Dougherty, "The Lessons of Korea," *Orbis*, Spring 1958, pp. 39–65.

De Weerd, H. A., "Strategic Surprise in the Korean War," *Orbis*, Fall 1962.

Dinerstein, Herbert D. *Intervention against Communism.* Baltimore, Johns Hopkins Press, 1967.

Finletter, Thomas K. *Power and Policy.* New York, Harcourt, Brace, 1954.

Futrell, Robert Frank, Lawson S. Moseley, and Albert F. Simpson. *The United States Air Force in Korea 1950–1953.* New York, Sloan and Pearce, 1961.

Garthoff, Raymond. "War and Peace in Soviet Policy," *Russian Review*, April 1966, pp. 121–33.

George, Alexander L. "American Policy-making and the North Korean Aggression," *World Politics*, VII, No. 2 (January 1955), 209–32.

——. "The Case for Multiple Advocacy in Making Foreign Policy," *American Political Science Review*, LXVI, No. 3 (September 1972), 751–85.

Goodrich, Leland M. *Korea: A Study of U.S. Policy in the United Nations.* New York, Council on Foreign Relations, 1956.

Hall, David K. "Operationalizing the American National Interest in Post-War China," unpublished MS, Stanford University, August 1969.

Halle, Louis J. *The Cold War as History.* New York, Harper & Row, 1967.

Halperin, Morton H., *Limited War in the Nuclear Age.* New York, Wiley, 1963.

Hammond, Paul Y. "NSC-68: Prologue to Rearmament," in Warner R. Schilling, Paul Y. Hammond, and Glenn H. Snyder, *Strategy, Politics and Defense Budgets.* New York, Columbia University Press, 1962.

Higgins, Trumbull. *Korea and the Fall of MacArthur: A Precis in Limited War.* New York, Oxford University Press, 1960.

Hoyt, Edwin C. "The U.S. Reaction to the Korean Attack: A Study of the U.N. Charter As A Factor in American Policy Making," *American Journal of International Law*, LV (January 1961), 45–76.

Kennan, George F. *Memoirs 1925–1950.* Boston, Little, Brown, 1967.

Kolko, Joyce and Gabriel. *The Limits of Power*, New York, Harper & Row, 1972.

Khrushchev Remembers, with an introduction by Edward Crankshaw. Boston, Little, Brown, 1970.

Lekie, Robert. *Conflict: The History of the Korean War.* New York, Putnam's, 1962.

LaFeber, Walter. *America, Russia, and the Cold War, 1945–1966*, New York, Wiley, 1967.

May, Ernest R. "The Nature of Foreign Policy: The Calculated versus the Axiomatic," *Daedalus*, Fall 1962, pp. 653–67.

——. *"Lessons" of the Past: The Use and Misuse of History in American Foreign Policy.* New York, Oxford University Press, 1973.

Millis, Walter, Harvey C. Mansfield, and Harold Stein. *Arms and the State: Civil Military Elements in National Policy.* New York, The Twentieth Century Fund, 1958.

Mosely, Philip E. *The Kremlin and World Politics: Studies in Soviet Policy and Action.* New York, Vintage, 1960.

Murphy, Robert. *Diplomat among Warriors.* New York, Doubleday, 1964.

Oliver, Robert T. *Why War Came to Korea.* New York, Fordham University Press, 1950.

——. *Syngman Rhee: The Man Behind the Myth.* New York, Dodd, Mead, 1954.

Osgood, Robert Endicott, *Limited War: The Challenge to American Strategy.* Chicago, The University of Chicago Press, 1957.

Paige, Glenn D. *The Korean Decision.* New York, Free Press, 1968.

Pentagon Papers, The. Senator Gravel edition, Vol. I. Boston, Beacon Press, n.d.

Poats, Rutherford. *Decision in Korea.* New York, McBride, 1954.

Rees, David. *Korea: The Limited War.* New York, St. Martin's Press, 1964.

Rovere, Richard H. "Letter from Washington," *New Yorker*, July 8, 1950.

Royal Institute of International Affairs, *Survey of International Affairs, 1949–1950.* London, Oxford University Press, 1953.

Sallager, Frederick M., and Jean M. Scott. "Background for American Policy toward Korea." Unpublished MS, 1955.

Shulman, Marshall D. *Stalin's Foreign Policy Reappraised.* Cambridge, Harvard University Press, 1963.

Simmons, Robert R. "The Korean War: Containment on Trial." Paper presented at the annual meeting of the American Political Science Association, September 1972.

Smith, Beverly. "The White House Story: Why We Went to War in Korea," *Saturday Evening Post,* November 10, 1951, p. 22 ff.

Snyder, Richard C., H. W. Bruck, and Burton Sapin, eds. *Foreign Policy Decision Making: An Approach to the Study of International Politics.* New York, Free Press of Glencoe, 1962.

——, and Glenn D. Paige. "The United States Decision to Resist Aggression in Korea: The Application of an Analytical Scheme," *Administrative Science Quarterly,* III (1958), 342–78.

Spanier, John W. *The Truman-MacArthur Controversy and the Korean War.* Cambridge, Harvard University Press, 1959.

Stone, I. F. *The Hidden History of the Korean War.* New York, Monthly Review Press, 1952.

Taft, Robert A. *A Foreign Policy for Americans.* Garden City, N.Y., Doubleday, 1952.

Tsou, Tang. *America's Failure in China.* Chicago, University of Chicago Press, 1963.

Truman, Harry S., *Memoirs.* Volume II, *Years of Trial and Hope, 1946–1952.* Garden City, N.Y., Doubleday, 1956.

Ulam, Adam B. *Expansion and Coexistence,* New York, Praeger, 1968.

U.S. Congress. *Congressional Record,* Vol. 96, Part 7 (June 28, 1950), pp. 9319–27.

U.S. Congress, Senate Appropriations Committee, *Hearings on State, Justice, Commerce and the Judiciary Appropriation for 1952.* Washington, U.S. Government Printing Office, 1951.

U.S. Congress, Senate Committee on Armed Services and Committee on Foreign Relations. *Military Situation in the Far East (MacArthur Hearings).* 5 vols. Washington, D.C., U.S. Government Printing Office, 1951.

U.S. News and World Report, XXVII, May 5, 1950. Interview with Senator Tom Connally.

Warner, Albert L. "How the Korea Decision was Made," *Harper's,* June 1951, pp. 99–106.

Willoughby, Charles, and John Chamberlain. *MacArthur 1941–1951.* New York, McGraw-Hill, 1945.

Whitney, Courtney. *MacArthur: His Rendezvous with History.* New York, Knopf, 1956.

Whiting, Allen S. *China Crosses the Yalu.* New York, Macmillan, 1960.

Chapter 7

Chinese Communist Intervention in Korea

The Background of the Problem

THE DAMAGING EFFECTS of the North Korean invasion of South Korea on the subsequent course of international affairs might have been substantially limited and circumscribed had it not led within five months to a new war with intervening Chinese Communist forces. Historical perspective serves only to deepen the tragic feeling held by many at the time that this "new war" with China was unnecessary and avoidable. The conflict of interests imbedded in the historical situation was genuine enough; but, once again, it led to war only because of misperceptions, miscalculations, and inept actions. It is sobering to reflect that the Chinese-American military confrontation in Korea was one which neither side wanted and both tried to avoid.

The events which led to the new war in Korea are familiar enough and need to be recapitulated only briefly. Following the North Korean invasion of the South on June 25, 1950, the United States intervened with U.N. support. Seoul, the capital of South Korea, was lost on the third day. Thereafter, for a period of many weeks the U.N. forces fought a rearguard action, attempting to slow the North Korean advance and to gain time for the deployment of U.S. forces from Japan and the United

States. The North Korean forces pushed steadily southward in a desperate effort to drive out the U.N. troops before they could secure a toehold around the southern port city of Pusan from which to build up forces for a counteroffensive. By mid-August, however, it became evident that the North Korean forces were unlikely to succeed. It was at this point that Peking began to express open concern at the course of events and indicated its active interest in how the war would be settled and, in particular, in the fate of the North Korean regime. At about this time, too, it was clear that Soviet efforts to arrange a favorable negotiated settlement had failed, and prominent U.S. spokesmen were talking of unifying Korea by force.

Peking believed that the United States and the United Nations might later cross into North Korea with the idea of liquidating the communist regime and unifying the country. She therefore put into effect several means of deterrence: an initial deployment of 60,000 forces into Manchuria, to bring the total there to 180,000 by mid-July; a massive domestic propaganda campaign to prepare the Chinese for possible intervention in Korea; official warnings and statements that Peking would intervene if U.S. troops crossed into North Korea; an additional deployment of forces into Manchuria beginning in mid-September that brought the total there by mid-October to approximately 320,000.

Peking's anxiety and its effort to make its deterrence effort credible both mounted after MacArthur launched his counteroffensive at Inchon. Within a week or ten days it was clear that the North Korean army had been badly defeated and that only remnants would succeed in getting back across the 38th Parallel. Thereafter, events moved quickly. In late September and early October Peking's warnings of potential intervention became more explicit and more urgent. But South Korean troops crossed into North Korea on October 1, to be followed by U.S. troops on October 7, the same day that the U.N. General Assembly passed a resolution that endorsed the new war objectives of occupying North Korea and unifying it with the South. Peking's deterrence effort had failed to achieve sufficient credibility or

potency to persuade Washington and its U.N. supporters to hold
back from invading North Korea.

Accordingly, on October 17 Chinese "volunteers" in large
numbers began to cross the Yalu River into North Korea, in
secrecy and without detection. On October 26 and November 2
they engaged in sharp tactical combat with South Korean and
U.S. units that were approaching the Yalu. On November 5
General MacArthur reported to the U.N. the presence of Chinese Communist forces in Korea and stated that the U.N. forces
under his command now faced a new war. On November 17
the Chinese Foreign Ministry acknowledged the presence of its
"volunteers" in Korea. But on November 8 the Chinese forces
had disengaged from further contact on the battlefield; and as
the days passed, optimism revived in MacArthur's headquarters
and in Washington.

The continued crossing of Chinese forces into North Korea
remained undetected, and their numbers were grossly underestimated by MacArthur's intelligence network. Its estimate of
only 60,000 Chinese troops in North Korea was less than one-
fourth of the actual number.

On November 24 MacArthur announced his "end-the-war"
offensive and sent his forces to the Yalu. Two days later the
Chinese launched a full-scale offensive that took MacArthur's
forces by surprise and sent them reeling backward into the
longest retreat in U.S. military history. After great military difficulties and the loss of Seoul for the second time in the war, a
stable defensive line was finally established. A long, costly, and
painful war of attrition developed that was to last until the summer of 1953, when a cease-fire was finally arranged.

Overview of the Case: A Double Failure of Deterrence

As this account recalls for us, the confrontation occurred
because the United States, with the backing of the United Na-

tions General Assembly, decided not merely to pursue the defeated North Korean army across the 38th Parallel but also to adopt a new war aim of unifying Korea through force of arms. The Chinese clearly attempted to deter the United States and the United Nations from taking these steps. The United States, for its part, attempted to dissuade China from carrying out its threat to send military forces into North Korea.

We can speak, therefore, of a double failure of deterrence. Each side attempted and failed, in turn, to deter the other from moving into North Korea. Each side employed various means of signaling its intentions and influencing the opponent's calculations so as to persuade it at first to stay out of North Korea and, when that failed, to limit its actions and objectives. The Chinese deterrence effort began in mid-August. Peking's concern and the urgency and level of explicitness of its deterrence threats increased as diplomatic efforts to bring the war to a halt failed and, particularly after the North Korean army was virtually destroyed by General MacArthur's bold Inchon landing in mid-September.

As Chinese concern and Chinese threats mounted, the United States responded with increasing assurances that its actions did not and would not threaten Chinese interests. Over a period of several months official administration statements repeatedly emphasized the limits on U.S. goals in Korea and the peaceful intentions of the United States toward China. Some observers have suggested that the American policy for persuading the Chinese to stay out of North Korea can hardly be called deterrence, since it relied so heavily on reassurances and made very little use of threats. However, the reassurances were backed by the threat implicit in the presence of American military forces, particularly air power, in Korea.

The dual failure of deterrence cannot be accounted for on the ground that this was an intense, short crisis which did not provide an opportunity for more thoughtful design and implementation of deterrence strategy. Ample time was available and was used by both sides—whether with the highest proficiency is another matter—to pursue their deterrence efforts. As a result, the case provides scholars interested in deterrence theory with ample historical materials for a critical assessment of why deterrence failed. It has also tempted them to direct the search for an explanation of the deterrence failure to possible flaws in the way in which each side attempted to signal its intentions and to achieve credibility for its communication of threat or reassurance.

FLAWS IN SIGNALING

Indeed, important flaws in signaling on both sides can be easily identified, and they have been discussed at some length by numerous scholars.[1] The chief flaw of this kind on the American side, it might be fairly said, was the fact that the credibility of Truman's and Acheson's official reassurances of their limited goals in North Korea and their peaceful intentions was called into question for Chinese Communist leaders by a continuing stream of hostile, aggressive statements from other members of the administration and from influential Americans in Congress and elsewhere outside the government. Truman disavowed such statements and took severe disciplinary action against several members of his administration (dismissing Secretary of the Navy Francis P. Matthews, and Commandant of the Air War College General Orvil A. Anderson). But, as specialists on Communist China have emphasized, these statements undoubtedly reinforced Peking's worst suspicions as regards American duplicity and hostility. Thus, Truman's efforts to signal credible reassurances of his intentions were placed in jeopardy by what specialists in communications theory refer to as the problem of "noise," i.e., conflicting background events that hamper receptivity to and/or correct interpretation of the intended message.

In contrast, unusual consistency and lack of "noise" characterized Peking's efforts to signal its intentions. There were, however, other flaws in its signaling which scholars have cited as possibly important contributing causes for Peking's failure to

[1] See in particular Zelman, "Chinese Intervention."

make its threats credible to Truman and Acheson. First, lack of diplomatic contacts and more direct channels of communication undoubtedly complicated and possibly hurt Peking's deterrence effort. Peking transmitted some of its most critical, weighty statements through Indian diplomatic channels which, however, the United States regarded as unreliable. (This applied particularly to K. M. Pannikar, Indian Ambassador to Peking, who was regarded by American officials as procommunist and gullible.) Second, the effectiveness of Peking's signals was hurt by the secrecy and caution with which the Chinese moved across the Yalu in mid-October, evidently to safeguard the security of their forces against American air power and to test the American response. Thereby, American intelligence was led to grossly underestimate the number of Chinese involved; and this, in turn, reduced the full impact the Chinese move into North Korea might have had on U.S. perceptions of the seriousness of Peking's intentions.

Useful lessons for deterrence theory and practice can indeed be extracted by a detailed examination of these and other flaws in signaling and by noting the factors that constrained more effective signaling in the present case. It would be a serious error, however, to fasten upon these flaws in signaling as decisive or critical factors for explaining either or both deterrence failures in this case.

BROADER LESSONS:
THE LIMITED UTILITY OF DETERRENCE

We call attention elsewhere in this study (especially in chapters 3 and 16) to the tendency of deterrence theory to oversimplify matters by focusing too narrowly on technical aspects of the problem of signaling as being somehow critical for achieving the much-sought-for credibility of commitment and of communication of one's intentions. The lessons for theory and practice imbedded in the dual failure of deterrence in this case go far beyond the signaling problems encountered by the two sides. More fundamental factors were at work; indeed, scholars who have discussed these flaws in signaling have generally avoided or have explicitly warned against regarding them as the primary factors in the breakdown of deterrence efforts.[2]

We choose in this account to emphasize the broader lessons the present case illustrates with regard to the limitations of deterrence and the risks of overreliance upon it. One writer has concluded that "it seems quite likely that the Chinese involvement in Korea was mainly the result of confusion and not of considered policy on either side." [3] We can agree with this conclusion, but it is imperative at the same time to discourage optimistic expectations that deterrence theory can be perfected so as to avoid similar "confusion" on future occasions.

What the Chinese Communist intervention in the Korean War demonstrates above all else is the fact that *deterrence cannot be an effective substitute for a sensible foreign policy or be utilized to cover up gross foreign policy errors.* Deterrence cannot be used, as in this case by Truman and Acheson, to avoid the consequences of a "provocative" and dangerous foreign policy. The fact that the administration did not intend or desire to provoke Chinese intervention by its move to unify Korea by force did not make deterrence a more justifiable or viable strategy for trying to avoid the consequences of a fateful policy error. Neither did the fact of United Nations legitimization and support for the administration's foreign policy error make deterrence any more suitable or feasible a method of dealing with the dangerous confrontation with China that ensued. Finally, the fact that Washington had inadvertently alarmed and provoked Peking by its *actions* did not provide rational grounds for the administration's hope that mere *verbal reassurances* of its nonhostility and limited aims should suffice to calm down Peking and persuade it that intervention in Korea was unnecessary.

Only a timely and credible abandonment of the policy of unifying Korea by force of arms could have reliably reduced the

[2] *Ibid.*, pp. 15, 17, 29, 31, 33; De Weerd, "Strategic Surprise," pp. 446, 451; Rees, *Korea*, p. 113.

[3] Lindsay, *China and the Cold War*, p. 37.

danger of war with China by removing or substantially diminishing its motivation to intervene. But a reversal of policy was so unpalatable to the administration that it was unwilling to face up to the necessity for modifying its war objective before it was too late. A policy reversal would have meant admitting that it had gravely erred in embracing the objective of Korean unification and accepting the severe political costs, domestic and international, of backtracking from this policy commitment.

We emphasize this aspect of the administration's policy perspective because we believe that it reduced U.S. receptivity to indicators of the growing threat of Chinese intervention. For scholars to attribute the failure of Chinese warnings to achieve credibility to Peking's lack of skill in signaling is superficial and misleading. The administration's rigid adherence to its new war objective of Korean unification made extremely difficult Peking's task of signaling credible warnings to deter the United States. The administration preferred to believe that a painful reversal of its war policy might not be necessary. It found reasons to believe that the Chinese threat of intervention was either a bluff or something which could be counterdeterred. When deterrence of Chinese intervention failed and Chinese forces crossed into North Korea and demonstrated their willingness to fight, the administration was shaken and momentarily considered modifying its war objective and military strategy. But once again it succumbed to wishful thinking and grasped at the possibility that Chinese intervention might have very limited objectives, or that MacArthur might succeed after all in employing his understanding of "oriental psychology" to intimidate the Chinese into pulling out.

Our analysis will emphasize that *both* failures of deterrence had a common root cause in the administration's rigid persistence in its policy error of attempting to unify Korea by force. Washington's reluctance to accept information that challenged the premises and wisdom of its policy strongly encouraged its tendencies to misread the frame of reference with which Peking perceived events in Korea, to misinterpret available intelligence, and to underestimate Peking's motivation and willingness to take risks.[4]

It is also true that the risks and damage stemming from the administration's fundamental error in foreign policy were compounded and severely exacerbated by General MacArthur's effort to push the U.S. onto an even riskier path and, if necessary, into a larger war with China. We shall note, however, that Washington's problem of controlling the headstrong General was partly of its own making, and that reluctance to reverse its policy of unifying Korea contributed importantly in November to its fateful decision, after the Chinese had intervened, to allow the General to implement his risky plan for sending his army to the Yalu.

The Double Deterrence Problem is Set Up: The Decision to Unify Korea

On October 7, 1950 the General Assembly of the United Nations passed a resolution which, "recalling that the essential objective was the establishment of a unified independent and democratic Korea," recommended that "all appropriate steps be taken to assure stability" throughout North as well as South Korea. Thereby the General Assembly did not merely sanction the movement of forces under MacArthur's command across the 38th Parallel into North Korea but also endorsed a new and more ambitious U.S. war aim of securing a unified, noncommunist Korea. While the administration did not formally sponsor the resolution, it had sought it and helped to draft it. The intention to pursue unification of Korea by force of arms was clear, even though euphemistic and ambiguous language was employed in the General Assembly's resolution.

[4] As these remarks imply, cognitive dissonance theory is quite relevant to the working of the psychological processes. For applications of cognitive dissonance theory to analysis of foreign policy–making see, for example, Holsti, *Crisis, Escalation, War;* and De Rivera, *Psychological Dimension of Foreign Policy.*

This was no modest extension of the objective for which the war was being fought. In effect, Washington had made a truly historic. decision to go beyond containment of communism to seek for the first time the elimination of a communist regime. True, the decision was not part of a general change in American grand strategy from containment to liberation; rather, it took place under exceptional circumstances in which the United States had received widespread support for resisting "aggression" by the communist government in one half of a divided country against the anticommunist government in the other half. It is also true that the decision to occupy North Korea and unify the country emerged quite slowly, following the refusal of its government to honor the United Nations request that it pull its forces back into North Korea and the failure of various diplomatic efforts during the summer of 1950 to work out some mutually acceptable way of terminating the war.

Notwithstanding these extraordinary circumstances that help to explain the escalation of the war objective, the fact remains that the policy decision to eliminate the communist regime in North Korea and to replace it with an anticommunist regime on the borders of both the Soviet Union and China could not but activate the strongest motivation in both Moscow and Peking to find a way of preventing so distasteful and dangerous an outcome to the Korean War.

Leading officials in the Truman Administration were by no means unaware of the risks of this policy decision, though they misjudged them. At the outset of the Korean War, in coming to South Korea's assistance, Truman and Acheson had defined the objective of their action as limited quite strictly to pushing the North Koreans back behind the 38th Parallel.[5] For various reasons, however, a return to the status quo ante proved to be difficult. North Koreans did not voluntarily pull back their forces; and while they continued their advance, the Soviet Union maneuvered at the United Nations and through other diplomatic channels during the summer in an attempt to impose conditions

[5] Truman, *Years of Trial and Hope*, p. 341; Acheson, *Present at the Creation*, p. 450.

for a cease-fire and return to the 38th Parallel. They also wished to tie termination of the war to the issue of seating Communist China in the United Nations, over which the Soviet representative had walked out of the Security Council five months before the onset of the Korean War.

As for Washington, not only did it reject the idea that the communists should be allowed any gains from the North Korean "aggression," it was also reluctant to envisage a termination of the fighting that left open the possibility that the North Koreans would be free to resume hostilities at some later date. The Truman Administration further complicated the diplomatic search for a way of terminating the war by refusing to agree to the status quo ante insofar as Formosa was concerned. Having announced at the outset of the war that the Seventh Fleet would be used to "neutralize" Formosa temporarily while U.S. forces were engaged in the defense of South Korea, the Truman Administration thereafter refused to return to its pre–Korean War policy of tacitly allowing Formosa to fall to the Chinese Communists. On January 5, 1950, it may be recalled, Truman had unequivocally declared that the U.S. government regarded Formosa as Chinese territory and would not use its armed forces to assist in Formosa's defense or pursue a course of action that would lead to involvement in the Chinese civil war. After the Korean War broke out, even though Truman and Acheson resisted pressures for allying the United States with the Chinese Nationalists, they did alter their policy on Formosa. The administration now took the position that the future status of Formosa would have to await international action and welcomed United Nations consideration of the problem. But the clear implication was that, in the meantime, "neutralization" of Formosa by the Seventh Fleet would continue.[6]

Even while MacArthur's forces were falling back and retreating into the Pusan perimeter, and particularly after the General unveiled plans for a daring landing at Inchon to trap the North Korean forces, some officials in the administration were giving

[6] Truman, *Years of Trial and Hope*, pp. 349–58; Acheson, *Present at the Creation*, p. 418.

serious attention to the longer-range problem of what to do after the invasion was repelled. In mid-July Truman decided that nothing should be said on the subject until the course of the fighting was clearer. At the same time he asked the National Security Council to prepare recommendations on the subject. A sharp difference of opinion developed within the State Department which, as Acheson admits,[7] "inhibited clear-cut thinking and led to a wait-and-see attitude." Acheson recalls that Paul Nitze's Policy Planning Staff, influenced by George Kennan's views, argued that under no circumstances should MacArthur's forces cross the 38th Parallel. On the other side of the issue, Dean Rusk and John Allison in the Far Eastern Division argued that a crossing of the parallel to destroy the invader's forces and to restore security in the area should not be precluded.[8]

As for Acheson himself, it is evident that he did not grasp the importance of resolving this policy dispute among his closest advisers in a fashion that would enable the State Department to exercise a controlling influence over the administration's evolving policy. Within two weeks, at the end of July, he was suddenly confronted by a detailed proposal from the Pentagon which recommended that MacArthur be permitted to cross the 38th Parallel, defeat the North Korean forces, and occupy the country, provided that the President, Congress, and the United Nations adopt the war aim of a united, free, and independent Korea.[9]

In his memoirs, Acheson derides the ambitious Pentagon plan and the assumptions on which it was based. He also claims that he succeeded in substantially modifying the Pentagon proposal before it emerged as an NSC paper on September 1. According to Acheson's recollection, the NSC paper dealt solely with military operations in implementation of the original, more restrictive objective which the U.N. had approved on June 27; that is, it was *not* intended to endorse the expanded war aim the Pentagon planners had recommended.[10]

Truman's more detailed account of the NSC paper of Sep-

[7] *Ibid.*, p. 451.   [8] *Ibid.*, pp. 445, 451.   [9] *Ibid.*, p. 451.   [10] *Ibid.*, p. 454.

tember 1, however, does not fully support Acheson's interpretation of it. According to Truman the NSC paper authorized MacArthur not only to conduct military operations beyond the 38th Parallel to destroy the North Korean forces but also "to make plans for the occupation of North Korea." [11] While this language stopped short of indicating a new war aim of unifying Korea, it certainly opened the door in that direction.

It should be noted that in allowing MacArthur to proceed beyond the 38th Parallel Acheson and Truman were attempting to make a distinction between flexibility in military tactics needed to defeat the North Korean forces decisively, which they approved, and the question of adopting a new war aim, which they set aside for the time being. It is apparent that the NSC decision reflected Acheson's belief that the issue on which his advisers in the Department had disagreed so sharply could be straddled for the time being, and that the risks of allowing MacArthur's forces to go into North Korea could be controlled. "Until the actual military situation developed further, no one could say where the necessity for flexibility in tactics ended and embarkation upon a new strategic purpose began." [12]

The decision to unify Korea had not yet been made, to be sure, but the important first step toward making it *in stages* had been taken. In retrospect, the NSC recommendation of September 1 appears much more significant in this respect than it did at the time. The distinction between tactical flexibility and adoption of a new strategic purpose was quickly eroded and lost as Truman responded to a series of fast-moving events. There is little evidence in the record that adopting the new war aim ever became a rational, deliberate choice after the NSC discussions that preceded the recommendations of September 1. Instead, it would appear that the administration thereafter slid into the new war aim without ever making an explicit, well-formulated decision to do so.

It may be recalled that the U.S. Ambassador to the U.N.,

[11] Truman, *Years of Trial and Hope*, p. 359.

[12] Acheson, *Present at the Creation*, p. 445.

Warren Austin, had already put up a trial balloon on behalf of the idea in an August 17 speech in the Security Council; and the possibility had also been discussed with India's Sir Benegal Rau.[13]

President Truman had inched forward toward the new war aim in a broadcast to the nation on September 1, when he stated, "We believe that Koreans have a right to be free, independent, and united," and went on to issue an implicit threat against Chinese intervention.[14]

As Acheson implies in his memoirs, he did not realize that the ambiguous NSC statement was to be the first step on a slippery slope. In retrospect, Acheson also admits that the U.N. resolution of October 7 was "not thought through and it masked in ambivalent language the difficulties and dangers [of] which Kennan had warned. . . ." [15]

Acheson refers to a memorandum he had received from Kennan in late August which emphasized, as Acheson recalls, that "it was not essential to us or within our capabilities to establish an anti-Soviet regime in all of Korea." [16] While Acheson obscures the full measure of his misjudgment of this fundamental point by flailing MacArthur in his account, he tacitly admits having succumbed to the tempting opportunity which MacArthur's success at Inchon appeared to create for unifying Korea.[17]

As Richard Neustadt has argued so persuasively, Truman and Acheson allowed the favorable turn of military events and their desire for U.N. approval of tactical military operations in North Korea to lead them to commit the United States and the United Nations to a new war aim. "In practice Truman's chief advisers, and the President himself, seem to have taken as a matter of course the need for something more . . . once it had

[13] *Ibid.*, p. 454.

[14] Truman, *Years of Trial and Hope*, pp. 358–59; see also Neustadt, *Presidential Power*, pp. 211–12n19.

[15] Acheson, *Present at the Creation*, p. 454.   [16] *Ibid.*, p. 446.

[17] *Ibid.*, p. 454.

been decided that MacArthur should go north. . . . 'That is a matter for the U.N. to decide,' said Truman on September 21, when queried at press conference about crossing the parallel; thereafter, U.N. action was not only logical, it had to happen." [18]

Truman and Acheson did not regard it as a vital or even very important objective of U.S. foreign policy that Korea be unified. They drifted into the new war aim because they did not see offhand another way of terminating the war satisfactorily and because unification of Korea seemed to them (and it must be said to many others as well) an extremely attractive, low-risk bonus for defeating the North Korean aggression. The satisfaction gained from having worked through the U.N. to defeat aggression was heady wine. It aroused unrealistic fantasies of taking giant steps toward establishing a system of collective security that might henceforth buttress Free World interests. It also encouraged a dangerously foolish attempt to make the U.N. General Assembly serve as an international sovereign agent that could impose its will on the Soviet Union and China in matters that strongly engaged their interests. Instead of facing up to the need, however difficult and unpleasant, for recognizing the interest of the Soviet Union and Communist China in the fate of North Korea and for drawing them into meaningful diplomatic conversations to find a settlement that would be minimally acceptable to them, Acheson was willing to gamble on his ability to calculate and control the risks of an aggressive strategy. He did not foresee that his ability to control the international risks of attempting to unify Korea would be jeopardized by his imperfect control in the days ahead over the President, General MacArthur, and other officials in the administration whose words and actions hardened the American commitment to the new war objective and robbed it of its initially tentative character.

The NSC paper of September 1, which Truman approved on September 11, left many of the critical decisions regarding

[18] Neustadt, *Presidential Power*, p. 132; also pp. 123–37.

adoption of a new war aim and military strategy to be decided later on the basis of subsequent developments, fuller information bearing on Chinese and Soviet intentions, and further consideration of the usefulness of pressing into North Korea. But the surprising momentum of MacArthur's Inchon offensive pressured Washington into making these critical decisions more rapidly than had been expected. The Inchon landing took place on September 15, and before the end of the month the North Korean forces had been badly defeated, with important remnants, however, fleeing back into North Korea. MacArthur's forces, gathering on the 38th Parallel urgently required a new directive. At the time this directive was being drafted, around September 24 or 25, the danger of Chinese and Soviet intervention did not seem to be great, though Chinese concern over events in Korea actually had been steadily mounting since mid-August.

It must be noted that the reluctance with which the Chinese moved toward intervention [19] and the unexpectedly rapid demise of the North Koreans on the battlefield created an unusual situation far from favorable to the Chinese effort to deter the U.S. move. As it turned out, the more serious Chinese deterrence statements either coincided with or followed the decisions being made in Washington to authorize the pursuit of the North Koreans across the 38th Parallel and to seek U.N. approval of a new war aim.

Neither Washington nor Peking desired a confrontation with the other. But both sides' tasks—Washington's effort to assess Peking's attitude before embarking on the move into North Korea, and Peking's effort to deter the move—were made more difficult by the unexpectedly swift momentum of military events in the last two weeks of September. The decision processes and the actions of the two sides at this critical juncture were somewhat out of phase with each other.

[19] Whiting, *China Crosses the Yalu*, pp. 88, 108.

The First Deterrence Attempt:
The Chinese Try to Deter the U.S.

In late August, following the failure of Soviet diplomatic efforts to promote a negotiated settlement in Korea, Peking had
attempted to persuade the West that a negotiated settlement
was preferable to pursuing victory over North Korea. Thus on
August 20 Chou En-lai addressed a cable to the U.N., his first in
more than six weeks, focusing this time on Korea rather than, as
before, on Taiwan. Demanding Chinese representation at the
U.N. Security Council when the Korean question was to be discussed, he stated: "Korea is China's neighbor. The Chinese
people cannot but be concerned about the solution of the
Korean question. . . . It must and can be settled peacefully."

On September 6, 11, and 19 various resolutions offered in
the United Nations requesting North Korean and/or Chinese
participation in U.N. discussions of the war were defeated.
Beginning immediately after the Inchon landing, it will be recalled, the buildup of Chinese forces in Manchuria increased
until by mid-October it had reached an estimated level of
320,000 troops. Beginning on September 22 Chinese deterrence
statements became more explicit and more urgent. However,
the out-of-phase character of the interaction between the two
sides, to which we have referred, hampered the efficacy of
these statements.

Chou En-lai's first public warning in a speech on September
30 [20] came *after* Washington's directive to MacArthur on the
27th authorizing him to proceed beyond the 38th Parallel.
Moreover, preparations for the U.N. resolution that would ap-

[20] It was preceded on September 22 with a Peking foreign ministry statement
acknowledging MacArthur's charge of having transferred troops of Korean eth-
nic origin to North Korea prior to the outset of the Korean War and affirming
that Peking would "always stand on the side of the Korean people." On September 25 the acting chief of staff of the Chinese Communist army issued an indirect warning through Indian Ambassador Pannikar, that China would not "sit
back with folded hands and let the Americans come up to the [Sino-Korean]
border." Cited in *Ibid.*, pp. 105, 107.

prove that action and endorse the new war aim were already well under way in Washington and, in fact, the resolution was formally presented to the General Assembly on September 30. On the same day Chou En-lai issued another warning that focused more directly upon the crossing of the 38th Parallel as a possible *casus belli*. There was hardly time for his warning to sink in. On the next day, October 1, Republic of Korea troops crossed into North Korea and MacArthur broadcast his first ultimatum ordering Pyongyang, the North Korean capital, to surrender. On October 2 Chou En-lai summoned Indian Ambassador Pannikar to a dramatic midnight meeting and, dismissing the move of South Korean forces across the 38th Parallel as inconsequential, declared that should U.S. troops invade North Korea, China would enter the war.

Peking had now finally defined an explicit *casus belli*, but caught in the momentum of their own policy development American officials and U.N. representatives found it easy to dismiss Chou's warning as a maneuver designed to influence the forthcoming vote on the U.N. resolution. On October 7 the U.N. resolution was passed and the U.S. First Cavalry Division crossed into North Korea, followed immediately by the rest of the Eighth Army. On October 8 General MacArthur addressed a second surrender ultimatum to Pyongyang. Within a week Chinese Communist troops crossed the Yalu River into North Korea, unannounced and undetected. Peking had failed to deter the United States from going into North Korea either by large-scale military deployments or by verbal warnings.

We have indicated that Peking's initial effort to deter the United States failed in part for reasons of timing, and U.S. suspicion of the Indian "channel" for the signals. But there were deeper reasons as well, reasons which went to the heart of the American decision-making process.

The U.S. Accepts the Risk
of Chinese Intervention

We have noted that the decision to pursue the defeated North Korean forces across the 38th Parallel, and to occupy the country as a prelude to its unification with South Korea, was made in stages over a period of several weeks. Washington did indeed consider the possibility that its actions and plans might trigger Soviet or Chinese military intervention. It is important to recall that Truman's awareness of these risks led him initially to give only *provisional* approval to the movement of Mac-Arthur's ground forces across the 38th Parallel. Thus, the basic NSC planning document of September 1 carefully linked its recommendation that MacArthur be allowed to extend his operations into North Korea to the prior condition that there be "no indication or threat of entry of Soviet or Chinese Communist elements in force." [21] A JCS directive, based on this NSC recommendation, was sent to MacArthur on September 15, the same day the Inchon offensive began. Even this initial directive, it may be noted, envisaged the possibility that events might lead to an occupation of North Korea. Thus the directive instructed MacArthur "to make plans for the occupation of North Korea." [22]

In response to the northward movement of the combat zone, the administration soon began to harden its initially provisional authorization of military operations beyond the 38th Parallel. The success of the Inchon offensive required a new directive to MacArthur; and this need, in turn, extracted new decisions from Washington regarding the extent to which it was prepared to risk Chinese or Soviet intervention. It is not too much to suggest, as some scholars have,[23] that tactical military requirements and the search for a military strategy to guide operations

---

[21] Truman, *Years of Trial and Hope*, p. 359.   [22] *Ibid.*

[23] Spanier, *Truman-MacArthur Controversy*, p. 89; Millis, Mansfield, and Stein, *Arms and the State*, pp. 272–75.

in North Korea intruded into and decisively shaped the more slowly developing war objectives and grand strategy in Washington. Instead of a well-defined, carefully considered overall policy determining the answers to questions of military strategy and tactics, grand strategy itself was being shaped by incremental decisions geared to the evolving military situation.

Thus on September 27 the JCS transmitted, with Truman's approval, a new directive to MacArthur that went significantly beyond the earlier directive of September 15 in accepting the risk of Russian or Chinese intervention. MacArthur was now, in effect, authorized to resist Chinese forces that entered North Korea covertly, so long as their intervention was unannounced and did not comprise "major" forces. At the same time, however, the directive still reflected the thought that the administration would be reluctant to proceed with operations in North Korea in the face of an announced Soviet or Chinese threat to intervene. Thus, the directive stipulated that authorization of MacArthur's operations in North Korea applied only so long as there was "no announcement of an intended entry, and no threat by Russian or Chinese Communists to counter our operations militarily in North Korea." [24] Taken at face value, this would seem to imply that the administration was ready to be deterred by a credible threat of Soviet or Chinese intervention. But, in fact, these provisos in the directive of September 27 were soon to fall by the wayside when, within a few days, Peking indeed began to issue sharp warnings that it would intervene if U.S. forces moved into North Korea.

For the time being, however, the September 27 directive indicated that any commitment Washington had to occupying North Korea was still very much a provisional one, and that the administration was not ready to accept the risk of a clash with "major" Chinese or Soviet forces. Nonetheless, qualified though it may still have been, the possibility of occupying North Korea as a prelude to unifying the country that had entered into the first directive to MacArthur on September 15 was

[24] Truman, *Years of Trial and Hope*, p. 360.

now even more explicitly referred to. As quoted by MacArthur
(but missing from Truman's and Acheson's accounts of the JCS
directive of September 27), MacArthur's instructions included
the following passage:

> When organized armed resistance by the North Korean Forces has
> been brought substantially to an end, you should direct the R.O.K.
> forces to take the lead in disarming remaining North Korean units
> and enforcing the terms of surrender. Circumstances obtaining at the
> time will determine the character of occupation of North Korea. Your
> plans for such an occupation will be forwarded for approval to the
> Joint Chiefs of Staff.[25]

It should not have come as a surprise to Washington, therefore, when on October 1 MacArthur broadcast an ultimatum to
the commander-in-chief of the North Korean forces calling upon
him "forthwith to lay down your arms and cease hostilities
under such military supervision as I may direct." This was
clearly a demand for unconditional surrender and MacArthur
justified it in terms of the need to carry out "the decisions of the
United Nations . . . without further loss of life and destruction
of property." [26]

Before moving ahead with our account of the gradual erosion of the cautious position taken in the September 1 NSC
paper, we should note that the JCS directive of September 27
did, however, also reflect Washington's reluctance to permit
MacArthur to use his forces in ways that might provoke intervention. He was instructed that, "as a matter of policy, no non-
Korean ground forces were to be used in the northeast provinces bordering on the Soviet Union or in the area along the
Manchurian border." And, "under no circumstances" was Mac-
Arthur to cross these borders with air, ground, or naval forces.

The first of these two constraints on MacArthur's use of his
forces was eroded within a few days. MacArthur quickly com-
plied with the request to submit a plan of operations to Washington that would indicate how he meant to implement the JCS

[25] MacArthur, *Reminiscences*, p. 358.

[26] *New York Times*, October 1, 1950, p. 5.

directive of September 27. Mindful of the injunction therein, MacArthur proposed to use only South Korean troops north of the Chungjo-Yongwon-Hungnam line. Acheson recalls that he and Secretary of Defense George Marshall approved of the plan because it "seemed excellently contrived to create a strong military position from which to exploit the possibilities of the North Korean defeat—either to insure the South by a strong defensive line against a renewal of the attack or, *if the South Koreans were strong enough and the Chinese did not intervene,* to move toward the U.N. goal of a united, free, and independent Korea." [27]

Thus, if Acheson's memory is correct, his account clearly implies that at this time, September 29, he and presumably Truman and Marshall had moved toward a partial and qualified acceptance of the new war aim of unifying Korea. The conditions they attached to it, however, were both significant: (1) only South Korean troops to be used in the northern reaches of North Korea bordering China and the Soviet Union, and (2) no Chinese intervention.

The first condition was immediately placed in jeopardy on September 29 by Marshall's private telegram to MacArthur, commenting sympathetically on the constraints placed on his operations by the directive of September 27: "We want you to feel unhampered tactically and strategically to proceed north of the 38th parallel." To this MacArthur replied, "Unless and until the enemy capitulates, I regard all Korea as open for our military operations." [28] MacArthur was later to cite this exchange of telegrams with Marshall as releasing him from the prohibition against using other than South Korean troops in the northern border regions. Whatever Marshall's intentions were at the time—a question that does not appear to have been adequately clarified—the exchange of telegrams obviously contributed to Washington's difficulties in imposing tactical constraints on Mac-

[27] Acheson, *Present at the Creation*, p. 453; emphasis added.
[28] Cagle and Manson, *Sea War in Korea*, p. 116; Acheson, *Present at the Creation*, p. 463; Truman, *Years of Trial and Hope*, p. 372.

Arthur's military operations to control the risks of Chinese intervention. (In his offensive of mid-October, MacArthur ordered the drive to the Yalu to be spearheaded by American troops, with South Koreans to take their places after the border was reached where this was feasible. When questioned on this by the JCS, MacArthur cited the message from Marshall.)

South Korean forces crossed the 38th Parallel on October 1, with American forces following on October 7. In between, as noted earlier, Chou En-lai issued his strongest warnings of Chinese intervention. With Chinese intervention now explicitly threatened, the administration proceeded to *harden* its policy commitment to unifying Korea rather than, as earlier directives to MacArthur had suggested it might, becoming more reluctant to push ahead into North Korea. On October 9 the U.N. resolution was passed, endorsing the new war aim of unification. Reflecting these developments and taking into account the possibility of Chinese intervention, Truman now instructed the JCS to issue MacArthur a new directive which for the first time unequivocally authorized him to resist any Chinese troops that entered Korea. The relevant portion of the new October 9 directive read as follows:

> Hereafter in the event of the open or covert employment anywhere in Korea of major Chinese Communist units, without prior announcement, you should continue the action as long as, in your judgment, action by forces now under your control offers a reasonable chance of success. . . .[29]

The weeks that followed the initially cautious authorization of military operations north of the 38th Parallel saw a curious and increasingly bizarre drama enacted. Even while indications of Chinese Communist threats, warnings, and preparations for intervention multiplied, Truman hardened his provisional commitment to the new war aim. Logically, the mounting indica-

---

[29] *Ibid.*, p. 362. There is no indication in Truman's account that Acheson participated or concurred in this new directive to MacArthur. Truman merely states that, in response to his request, the JCS "submitted their recommendation to me through the Secretary of Defense . . . and I approved. . . ." Acheson's own memoir makes no reference to the directive of October 9.

tions of probable Chinese intervention should have reinforced the administration's initial caution and confirmed the wisdom of having given only provisional authorization of the move into North Korea. But precisely when there was increasing reason for Truman to keep policy flexible, he consistently acted in ways that made it more rigid. As Richard Neustadt wonders, having incurred the risk of authorizing MacArthur's move into North Korea before Chou En-lai's warnings came, why did Truman make it worse thereafter? "The question arises," Neustadt continues,

> because Truman spent October adding to his power risk with every choice he made. The new war aim had been announced by the U.N. in cautious words; Truman promptly and repeatedly restated it himself without equivocation. MacArthur's northward march had been approved with qualifications; Truman promptly waived the major qualification. . . .[30]

The Chinese deterrence effort of late summer and early fall of 1950, therefore, failed for reasons which it would hardly have been easy for Peking to predict. Despite Chou's signals, Washington chose simply to accept the risk of Chinese intervention, and to proceed with the policy of unifying Korea by force. Implicitly, Washington considered the risk it was accepting to be low—a central miscalculation which demands our attention.

The U.S. Miscalculation of Chinese Intentions

Throughout the three-month period ending with the all-out Chinese attack in late November, U.S. leaders consistently failed to discern the way in which Peking was perceiving the developing Korean situation, weighing what was at stake, and calculating the utilities and risks of its alternative courses of action. This was *not* an intelligence failure in the narrow sense of

[30] Neustadt, *Presidential Power*, p. 137.

the word. The available intelligence on the deployment of Chinese forces and other indicators of Peking's intentions was good enough to require American leaders at an early stage to take the threat of Chinese intervention more seriously than they did. Later, after the Chinese move into North Korea, intelligence was good enough, if not to avert the military surprise of the Chinese offensive, at least to correct the maldeployment of MacArthur's forces that made them peculiarly vulnerable to the Chinese attack.

Scholars who have examined this case agree that the explanation of the American miscalculation of Peking's intentions is complex and many-faceted. The momentum of events following MacArthur's landing at Ichon, the intoxication of success, domestic political considerations, and wishful thinking no doubt abetted the miscalculation. We have already suggested that behind the administration's wishful thinking lay its reluctance to accept and weigh properly information that challenged the premises and wisdom of its goal of occuping North Korea as a prelude to unification of the country.

But the miscalculation of Peking's intentions was by no means confined to top-level policy-makers. It also characterized the most careful and responsible estimates of professional intelligence specialists.

U.S. INTELLIGENCE ESTIMATES

A review of available accounts of these intelligence appraisals indicates that they did not challenge sharply or early enough the widespread euphoria and optimism within the administration. Rather, intelligence estimates appear to have consistently minimized in the process of interpretation the numerous indications that the Chinese threat of intervening was a serious one. The intelligence appraisers were evidently subject to some of the same psychological influences and misperceptions that distorted the views of top-level leaders.[31]

[31] It should be noted that at this time MacArthur's headquarters was solely responsible for intelligence acquisition in and around Korea. His daily in-

Only belatedly, and more in response to events as they unfolded than in anticipation of them, did U.S. intelligence estimates gradually move toward a more correct view of the opponent's intentions. This conclusion emerges from an examination of the partial information presently available on four estimates of Chinese intentions formulated by the CIA in the critical six-week period before the Chinese launched their major offensive on November 25. It will be noted that the most sober and valid CIA estimate came too late to goad top-level decision-makers into correcting policy errors already made.

On October 12, well after Peking had defined the *casus belli* in a futile deterrence effort and was concentrating large forces in Manchuria, the CIA gave a generally reassuring estimate of Chinese intentions. It granted that the Chinese had the capability for effective intervention but held that such intervention would not necessarily be decisive. Furthermore, the CIA estimate saw no convincing indication at that time that the Chinese intended to resort to a full-scale entry into the war. The estimate concluded that Peking feared the consequences of war with the United States and that its intervention was thus "not probable in 1950." [32] Three days later Chinese Communist forces began to cross the Yalu into North Korea.

Washington's estimate of Peking's objective and intentions was revised upwards several times in October and November in response to events, but the correction was always minimal and inadequate. Thus when the earlier thesis that the Chinese threat of intervention was a bluff had to be abandoned, U.S. intelligence appraisers then favored the hypothesis that the Chi-

---

telligence reports to G-2, Department of the Army, in Washington constituted the main sources of information on Chinese forces in regard to Korea. In addition, CIA combined reports from its own sources, chiefly the Chinese Nationalist government on Formosa and others operating out of Hong Kong, with reports from MacArthur's headquarters in attempting to discern Communist Chinese intentions. Collins, *War in Peacetime*, pp. 173–75, 198–99, 213; *MacArthur Hearings*, II, 1234; De Weerd, "Strategic Surprise," p. 445; Appleman, *South to the Naktong, North to the Yalu*, p. 757.

[32] Collins, *War in Peacetime*, p. 175; Higgins, *Korea and the Fall of MacArthur*, p. 59.

nese were interested in no more than setting up a small "buffer area" near the Yalu to protect their interest in the hydroelectric dams in that area. This hypothesis was advanced by the CIA in a memorandum to the President on October 20, evidently without knowledge of the fact that five days earlier Chinese forces had begun their covert deployment into North Korea.[33]

The estimate of Chinese objectives was nudged upward once more in early November, again in response to sobering developments in the field. In late October and early November Chinese forces had clashed sharply with U.N. forces and temporarily checked their advance northward toward the Yalu. Reflecting these developments, the CIA estimate of November 6 took on a more sober tone. Noting that as many as 200,000 Chinese Communist forces were concentrated in Manchuria, the CIA warned that their entry might stop the United Nations advance and force a withdrawal to defensive positions further south. The CIA estimate concluded ominously but rather vaguely that, with their entry into Korea, the Chinese Communists had staked not only some of their forces but also their prestige in Asia. It had to be taken into account, the CIA held, that the Chinese knew what risks they were taking; in other words, that they were ready for general war.[34] A similar note of increased sobriety and concern was suddenly conveyed in MacArthur's communications of November 6 and 7 to Washington, again as a result of the check his forces were receiving from Chinese troops.

Administration leaders were now by no means certain that Peking's objective was limited to creating a buffer area along the Yalu. An NSC meeting of November 9 considered the possibility that Peking was pursuing more ambitious objectives.[35] If so, it seemed definitely more likely to U.S. leaders that the Chinese intention was to impose a war of attrition on the U.S. forces in North Korea than that Peking would opt for a more ambitious and riskier attempt to drive U.N. forces completely out

[33] Truman, *Years of Trial and Hope*, p. 372.   [34] *Ibid.*, pp. 376–77.
[35] *Ibid.*, pp. 378–80; McLellan, "Dean Acheson and the Korean War," pp. 27–29.

of the peninsula. There was another possible aim which, unfortunately, U.S. leaders did not recognize at this stage—namely, Peking's desire to maintain the existence of a communist state in North Korea.[36] Recognition that Peking was pursuing this objective was to come later; but this would have been the opportune moment to consider whether the Chinese would settle for it. For in early November the administration was suddenly struck with the realization that negotiations with the Chinese would probably be necessary to salvage the aim of unifying Korea to whatever extent was possible. As it turned out, Washington had only a short while to find out what the Chinese would settle for and then possibly to modify its own objectives. But just at this time, the impetus for a reassessment of overall policy in the war again declined appreciably.

Around November 9 the Chinese Communist forces disengaged from contact with U.S. and U.N. forces along the entire battlefront. This disengagement was to continue until the Chinese struck in full force on November 25. As the days passed without combat, the acute anxiety as to Chinese intentions that Washington had felt in early November gradually declined.

On November 24, on the eve of the all-out Chinese offensive, the CIA produced its most disquieting estimate.[37] It stated that the Chinese "at a minimum" would increase their operations in Korea—a significant prediction in view of the fact that the Chinese had disengaged their forces from combat on the battlefield since November 9. The CIA estimate added that the Chinese would seek to immobilize U.N. forces, subject them to attrition, and maintain the semblance of a North Korean state. It also stated that the Chinese possessed sufficient strength to

---

[36] Contradicting this is testimony by Acheson at the congressional hearings on MacArthur's dismissal in which he stated that "the general view in Wasington" as of November 9 was that the Chinese objective "was to halt the advance of the UN forces in Korea and to keep a Communist regime in being on Korean soil." *MacArthur Hearings*, Part 3, p. 1834. This is not consistent with other accounts and, as Lichterman suggests, it is possible that Acheson's memory was in error in assigning this view of the Chinese objective to U.S. estimates in early November. Lichterman, "To the Yalu and Back," p. 614.

[37] Truman, *Years of Trial and Hope*, p. 381.

force U.N. forces to withdraw to defensive positions.[38] The CIA estimate stopped short of attributing to the Chinese the intention of trying to drive U.N. forces out of Korea; but it was indeed sober enough and laden with important implications for policy. It came, however, too late.

FAILURE TO UNDERSTAND PEKING'S FRAME OF REFERENCE

During October and November Washington moved belatedly toward a more correct view of Peking's objectives and, closely related to this, its military intentions. Part of the explanation for earlier miscalculations—but only part of it—lies in the fact that Washington underestimated Chinese Communist military capabilities. And perhaps even more importantly, it overlooked the possibility that Peking might rate its own capabilities much more highly than did Washington. The remainder of the explanation concerns *the strength of Peking's motivation,* which U.S. leaders consistently and seriously underestimated. The erroneous estimates of Peking's capabilities and motivations were mutually reinforcing. Together they buttressed the view that the

---

[38] Given the disappearance of Chinese forces from the battlefield since November 9, the basis for this sober CIA estimate is not clear. Perhaps CIA estimators in Washington were influenced by a telecon report from General MacArthur's G-2 on November 17. Far from lending credence to optimistic interpretations that were being attached to the quiescence of the Chinese Communist forces, MacArthur's G-2 reported a buildup of approximately four Chinese divisions in the Changin Reservoir area and called attention to the vulnerability of the west flank of MacArthur's X Corps. Presumably this information was also passed on to MacArthur and to X Corps by G-2. Perhaps it was taken more seriously by the CIA in Washington than by MacArthur. Collins, *War in Peacetime,* p. 213.

In his testimony, Acheson went further than the account of the CIA estimate presented here. He stated that on November 24 "we concluded here in Washington that the Chinese objective was to obtain United Nations withdrawal [from North Korea] by intimidation and diplomatic means, but in case of failure of these means there would be increasing intervention, and it was said that there was not available evidence sufficient for a conclusion as to whether the Chinese Communists were committed to a full-scale offensive." *MacArthur Hearings,* III, 1834.

Chinese would pursue only limited objectives and would surely want to avoid a major war with the United States.

Of these two factors, we wish to stress the role played by the strong Chinese motivation, and the critical impact of underestimating it on U.S. policy. Let us examine these elements more closely.

Available intelligence indicators of Chinese intentions were systematically misinterpreted and minimized by American decision-makers for reasons that are as simple as they are fundamental. U.S. leaders miscalculated because they failed to understand *the frame of reference from which the Chinese Communist leaders assessed the significance of what the United States was doing in Korea.* In Peking's eyes, U.S. policy in Asia had begun to harden and to assume an increasingly threatening posture with the outbreak of the Korean War. Chinese Communist leaders saw in Truman's "neutralization" of Formosa during the first few days of the Korean War an ominous "reversal" in U.S. policy toward China. This was by no means a totally irrational suspicion on Peking's part. Had not the United States in 1949 finally acquiesced in the Chinese Communist victory over Chiang's Nationalist forces? And had not Washington in early 1950 publicly written off Formosa as well as South Korea in defining its defense perimeter in the Far East? Now in June 1950 not only did the United States suddenly intervene militarily in the Korean "civil war," it also immediately reversed its policy of tacitly allowing Nationalist-held Formosa to fall to the Chinese Communists. And during the summer, as we have already noted, the administration gave unmistakeable indications of moving toward a new position calling for an "international" solution to the problem of Formosa before the Seventh Fleet was removed.

Peking felt threatened also by the success of MacArthur's military operations against North Korean forces in the summer. It may have seen in U.S. actions in Korea the beginning of a repetition of the course of aggression pursued earlier by Japan. Not only historical precedent but ideological perspectives as well colored Peking's view of U.S. strategic intentions as American forces moved across the 38th Parallel in pursuit of the remnants of the North Korean forces. If the United States remained unopposed, Peking felt, it would soon pose a direct threat to Chinese Communist territory and exacerbate internal instability. In announcing its intention to occupy and unify Korea, was not the United States for the first time using force to eliminate a communist regime? Was it not for the first time going beyond containment to "roll back" communism? Could Peking expect that the United States would be content to stop with the conquest of North Korea? Were there not already strong and important voices, like MacArthur's, being raised on behalf of a more aggressive U.S. policy in Asia? Much indeed seemed at stake not only for Peking but for the communist world as a whole. Indications of Peking's perception of the threat and its calculus were available to U.S. policymakers, but they were discounted, so that U.S. leaders grossly underestimated the strength of Peking's motivation to intervene.

Some specialists on Chinese Communist foreign policy have speculated that Peking's total motivation combined "offensive" with "defensive" motives. They suggested that the hardening of Washington's policy on Korea and Formosa not only increased Peking's doubts as to the reliability to American declarations; it may have strengthened Peking's disposition to push its broader objectives in Asia. If an opportunity arose to inflict a humiliating defeat on U.S. forces and to evict them from Korea, Peking would be prepared to accept the risks, since such a success would greatly enhance its broader objectives.[39]

With the benefit of hindsight, to be sure, this is the picture of Peking's perceptions and strong motivation that has emerged as the accurate one. It contrasts sharply with the way in which U.S. leaders at the time perceived their opponent. In the U.S. view, the perspective of the new Chinese regime was more "nationalist" than "communist" in orientation. Peking was seen as calculating its policy toward Korean developments conservatively from the standpoint of its true "national interests." Wash-

[39] Whiting, *China Crosses the Yalu*, pp. 6–8, 159; Tsou, *America's Failure in China*, pp. 576–80.

ington leaders were confident that Peking would regard its interest in Korea as quite limited.[40]

Estimates of Chinese intentions, then, were based on a faulty premise—namely, the belief that the Chinese leaders were calculating their interests in much the same way as we did. Since Truman and Acheson had evidently convinced themselves that legitimate Chinese national interests were not importantly threatened or affected by the U.S. occupation of North Korea or by plans for unifying it with South Korea, they believed that Chinese leaders also saw it in this way or could be persuaded to do so.

In sum, therefore, the miscalculation in this case developed as follows: operating with an incorrect image of the opponent and of his frame of reference, U.S. intelligence analysts and top-level leaders failed to grasp Peking's perception of the threat. As a result, Washington misread Peking's perception of the magnitude of what was at stake. Underestimation of Peking's motivation and of Peking's estimate of its military capabilities, in turn, distorted the U.S. estimate of the way in which Chinese leaders were calculating the risks and deciding what level of risks to accept.

There is no indication in the voluminous materials on this case that U.S. intelligence appraisers employed anything like the method of "analytical predictions" in assessing Chinese intentions. From late August to late November, U.S. intelligence analysts assessed and reassessed the relative probability of the courses of action open to Peking and attempted to provide a responsible judgment of what it seemed most likely the opponent would do. We have already noted the pronounced and consistent tendency in these estimates to regard Peking as acting conservatively. This view of the opponent was never challenged or tested by examining the assumptions on which it rested. Thus, there is no indication that U.S. intelligence officials attempted to construct a working hypothesis that made

[40] Whiting, *China Crosses the Yalu*, pp. 169–70; Spanier, *Truman-MacArthur Controversy*, pp. 96–100; McLellan, "Dean Acheson and the Korean War," pp. 17–21; Rees, *Korea*, pp. 113–14.

the strongest possible case for the seemingly implausible view
that Peking might choose or feel itself obliged to pursue a more
ambitious policy in the conflict. The rationale on Peking's part
for such a course of action was evidently never adequately explored by U.S. estimators; or, if so, it was not brought effectively to the attention of top-level decision-makers.

Similarly, we find no indication in the available record that
any individual or group in the administration was asked to or
allowed to play a vigorous "devil's advocate" role in order to
test the assumptions and expectations on which official policy
was based. Several members of the administration were indeed
dubious, if not seriously concerned, over the decision to occupy
North Korea. This included, as we have seen, not only George
Kennan, who had recently left his position as director of the
Policy Planning Staff in the State Department, but also Thomas
Finletter, Secretary of the Air Force, and Admiral Sherman,
Chief of Naval Operations. Kennan is reported as having repeatedly warned the administration of the risks of a Chinese reaction to the crossing of the 38th Parallel. The concerns felt and in
part expressed by these individuals, however, were not converted into a systematic challenge of the dominant view within
the adminstration.[41]

The Second Deterrence Attempt: The U.S. Tries to Deter China by Reassurances

In considering Washington's response to the available
warning of a possible Chinese intervention it is useful to distinguish the initial phase of Chinese threats and preparations for
intervention, which lasted for about two months, from subsequent phases in which warning became clearer. In the first
phase, U.S. leaders regarded Chinese threats and preparations

[41] Kennan, *Memoirs,* pp. 488–49; Higgins, *Korea and the Fall of MacArthur,* pp.
78–9; Lee and Henschel, *Douglas MacArthur,* p. 204; James Reston in the *New
York Times,* November 16, 1950.

to intervene as a bluff intended for purposes of diplomatic pressure. At the same time, Washington recognized to a degree that Peking may have been genuinely concerned over the threat advancing U.N. forces posed to its interest in the hydroelectric power dams in North Korea and, more generally, over the possibility that the United States might entertain more far-reaching hostile designs against the Chinese mainland.

During this initial phase, U.S. leaders regarded Chinese intervention as unlikely but a possibility that could not be altogether ignored. Even before the Chinese deterrence effort was in full swing, U.S. leaders relied upon *reassurances* to Peking and not threats as the means of reducing the likelihood of Chinese intervention in Korea. Repeatedly during the three months preceding the all-out Chinese offensive of November 25, Truman and Acheson attempted to reassure Peking that the United States had no military or political designs on the Chinese mainland. Despite increasingly belligerent Chinese statements, mounting Chinese military preparations for intervention and, finally, the deployment of Chinese forces across the Yalu, the administration continued to believe that the Chinese could be influenced by expressions of the "traditional friendship" of the United States and its peaceful intentions.

The administration's decision to rely on reassurances and largely to forego threats as a means of preventing Chinese intervention is incomprehensible unless we keep in mind Washington's fundamental misjudgment, to which we have already referred, of Peking's frame of reference and its calculus.

The administration was extremely resourceful in thinking of all the many reasons why Peking should not want to intervene, but singularly lacking in the imagination and empathy that might have uncovered the even stronger reasons the Chinese leaders had for intervening. It is not altogether surprising, therefore, that Washington should have felt that reassurances of our peaceful intentions would suffice. This belief was supported, no doubt, by the fact that Truman and Acheson did not regard themselves as entertaining hostile designs against the Chinese Communist regime. Evidently they did not realize that whatever the value of their own assurances of friendship and peaceful intentions, Peking may have been equally if not more impressed with the contradictory "noise" of statements hostile to Communist China and the Soviet Union emanating from other high-level American officials, such as MacArthur, Secretary of the Navy Matthews, Major General Orvil Anderson, and echoed by others within the country. Such statements were much more consistent with Peking's view of American imperialism and with the harder line U.S. policy had taken in Asia since the onset of the Korean War; no doubt they reinforced Chinese Communist fears that U.S. policy would become even more hostile if not checked in Korea.

It is possible that Truman and Acheson avoided making deterrent threats for other reasons besides the fact that they thought it unnecessary to do so. Explicit threats to bomb the Chinese mainland might have reinforced the already strong voice and influence of those within the country who wanted a harder policy toward Communist China and the Soviet Union and, hence, might have made it more difficult to keep the war limited. Moreover, a policy of threatening the Chinese—particularly when it seemed unnecessary—might have had an adverse effect on the administration's ability to keep alive the longer-range goal it had adopted in 1949 of seeking an eventual *modus vivendi* with the Chinese Communist regime and of attempting to woo it away from the Soviet Union.

If at first Chinese threats and preparations to intervene could be dismissed as bluff, there came a point when the available warning had to be regarded as at least equivocal. With the knowledge that substantial Chinese forces were entering or already had entered North Korea, and with the sharp tactical engagements of late October and early November, the hypothetical threat of Chinese intervention became a bitter reality for U.S. leaders. The question was no longer whether the Chinese would intervene but what they were after, how far they would go, and what they would settle for.

Washington had a month to address itself to these questions and to attempt to influence Chinese intentions and behavior before the Eighth Army was struck by the unexpected Chinese offensive of November 25. How did Truman and Acheson utilize this opportunity? We have already noted that in the policy reassessment of November 9 the NSC appeared ready to accept the fact that negotiations would be necessary to deal with Peking's intervention. On this occasion, no serious consideration was given to the possibility of coercing Peking into withdrawing its forces. The President was firmly opposed to any actions or statements that might risk a widening of the war. There is no indication that he considered threatening Peking with an extension of the war to its own territory in order to induce greater prudence in its behavior. MacArthur was instructed to take every precaution not to violate Manchurian territory "because it is vital in the national interests of the United States to localize the fighting in Korea." Truman considered it urgent to refocus attention and resources to shoring up Western Europe; he was deeply concerned over the possibility (supported by CIA estimates) that the Soviet Union wanted to embroil the United States in Asia so as to have a free hand in Europe.[42] Given this judgment of priorities, the administration decided in early November that an attempt should be made to come as close as possible to realizing its objective of unifying Korea, but within the confines of presently authorized military operations and possibly with the help of negotiations through the United Nations, to which representatives of China and North Korea were now invited.

In the new situation created by entrance of Chinese forces into North Korea, therefore, Truman and Acheson remained reluctant to threaten actions against the Chinese mainland because, at bottom, they were not really prepared to carry them out. Interestingly, General MacArthur apart, there was no substantial disagreement in this respect between the civilian heads of government and their top-level military advisers. Thus, for example, the JCS recommended to the President that "every effort should be expended as a matter of urgency to settle the

[42] Truman, *Years of Trial and Hope,* p. 378.

problem of the Chinese Communist intervention in Korea by political means. . . ." [43]

Whether threats to extend the war to the Chinese mainland would have been credible and potent enough to deter the Chinese from intervening, or at least to persuade them to limit the aims and scope of their intervention, is another matter. This question is both hypothetical and complex. To a considerable extent the answer hinges on the view one takes of the risk calculations that accompanied Peking's decisions on the objectives and scope of its intervention. It has been plausibly argued that Chinese leaders were so strongly motivated to intervene that they were willing to accept the risk and also the *likelihood* of a strong U.S. military response, even one including the use of atomic weapons against the mainland. [44] In considering Peking's risk calculations, we must keep in mind that the Chinese had several intervention options, graduated according to the scope of the objectives they wished to pursue. They ended (but did not necessarily begin) by opting, with their offensive of November 25, for the objective of inflicting a major defeat upon the U.N. forces and possibly evicting them from Korea. The Chinese might also have considered and settled for a lesser objective: if not a "buffer zone" of some kind along the Yalu, then a viable communist regime in North Korea. It is possible that Chinese leaders might have limited the scope and objective of their intervention if this had been thought necessary for limiting the risks of an American military overreaction.

This leaves open, of course, the question of whether Washington would have been able or willing to generate threats of retribution sufficiently strong and sufficiently credible to influence Chinese leaders to opt for the lesser and safer intervention option. Since U.S. leaders did not grasp the need for a strong deterrence effort, either to prevent Chinese intervention or, later, to discourage an all-out offensive, they did not take up the

[43] *Ibid.*

[44] See, for example, Whiting, *China Crosses the Yalu*, pp. 134–39, 160–62; and Zelman, "Chinese Intervention," pp. 26–28.

difficult question of whether and how to employ threats to play upon Peking's calculations.

But even had a stronger deterrence effort been made, it is questionable that it would have led the Chinese to forego intervention altogether. We need to consider in this connection a fundamental underlying factor that greatly reduced Peking's vulnerability to stronger efforts the United States might have made to deter it from intervening. What U.S. leaders apparently did not grasp was the fact that beneath this slowly developing crisis there was an *asymmetry of motivation* in Peking's favor. The Chinese Communist leaders were the more highly motivated to prevent American troops from occupying North Korea than U.S. leaders were (or could be) to carry out the occupation against Chinese military opposition. The United States was indeed much stronger militarily than Communist China. But the Chinese placed a higher value on denying us North Korea than we placed on occupying it and unifying it with South Korea.

When objectives conflict sharply, the efforts the parties to the dispute will make in pursuit of their respective aims are by no means a simple function of their relative strengths, nor is the outcome of the conflict. The weaker side, if it has more at stake, may overcome its reluctance to pit its strength against a stronger opponent. In such a case the weaker side may be willing to accept greater costs and risks than its opponent, whose lesser motivation makes him reluctant to employ fully his superior resources. This intangible but fundamental factor of motivation made it inherently less likely that U.S. leaders would be able to generate credible threats of strong magnitude and that Peking could be sufficiently intimidated thereby into staying out of Korea altogether.[45]

In fact, given the magnitude of Peking's concern over what it perceived to be at stake, probably only a substantial reduction of the U.S. objective and a curtailment of its military effort to occupy North Korea would have sufficed to prevent Chinese intervention. Peking's motivation was probably too strong to be

[45] The importance of relative motivation is considered in more detail in George, Hall, and Simons, *Limits of Coercive Diplomacy*, pp. 215–20.

influenced solely by threats, let alone the general reassurances that were actually offered. Its incentive to intervene could probably be modified only by a reversal of some of the U.S. policies and actions that were motivating Peking to intervene. There are limits to what deterrence can be expected to accomplish. It required no remarkable historical memory to recall that deterrence had failed in December 1941 to prevent the Japanese from moving further into Southeast Asia. In fact, the very credibility of the American deterrence effort on that occasion had contributed to the desperate Japanese decision to strike at Pearl Harbor as well as attacking Southeast Asia. As Walter Zelman has concluded in his analysis of the implications of the Chinese intervention for deterrence theory: "The lesson here may be that if one party wishes to deter another, it should not let the penalties of non-action (being deterred) appear as great as the potential risk of action.[46]

The Last Chance

In some foreign policy crises there is little time or opportunity to correct an initial miscalculation of the opponent's intentions. When the situation requires the decision-maker to act quickly, he cannot afford to spend time making efforts to obtain better intelligence appraisals before he acts. This axiom does not apply, however, to the present case, since the threat of Chinese intervention developed slowly and was implemented in stages. In principle, therefore, there was plenty of time and ample opportunity for reassessing Chinese intentions.

It is not often that history is generous enough to provide policy-makers with several opportunities to correct initial mistakes in perception and judgment that would lead, if unchecked, to catastrophe. But in this case it was. Even as late as the second or third week in November, Washington had the op-

[46] Zelman, "Chinese Intervention," pp. 28, 32.

portunity to take steps to reduce Peking's incentive to engage in
a major war by modifying the U.S. war objective and restricting
military operations. The final "point of no return" for U.S. policy was not passed until shortly before the Chinese launched
their all-out offensive on November 25. Until then, at the very
least Washington could have avoided the worst damage of the
Chinese attack by calling off MacArthur's offensive to the Yalu
and pulling his forces back to a better defensive position at the
narrow neck of the peninsula. This last opportunity lay entirely
in Washington's hands; it required no new signals to persuade
Chinese leaders of anything, nor negotiations, nor indeed any
form of tacit cooperation on Peking's part.

It is agonizing to see how close policy-makers in Washington came to seizing their last chance to avoid the catastrophe
that followed. By early November, as we noted earlier, the hard
fact that the Chinese had not only intervened in substantial
numbers but were obviously willing to fight finally sobered
American political and military leaders. In late October and
early November, Chinese units had engaged in sharp tactical
engagements with South Korean and U.S. forces. On November
6 MacArthur reported to the United Nations that his forces were
facing "a new and fresh army" with adequate reserves and supplies. On the next day his headquarters warned that "if the
Chinese build-up continued, further advances might be prevented, and a 'retrograde movement' forced upon the United Nations Command." On November 8 top-level political and military leaders in the administration (excluding Truman, who
could not attend) gathered in a special meeting of the National
Security Council in order to review Chinese intentions. They
recognized that the war objective of unifying Korea probably
could not be realized any longer through military means alone.
Furthermore, they accepted the fact that negotiation with the
Chinese would probably be necessary to salvage the objective as much as possible. It was at this meeting that Acheson
suggested that a "buffer area" be established in Northeast
Korea under a U.N. commission. It was agreed that the State
Department would try to find out whether negotiations with the

Chinese Communists were possible. The door was now open at last to a reassessment of U.S. war policy.

The President's top military and political advisers recognized the risk which the Chinese posed to MacArthur's maldeployed forces. Although keenly disturbed, they failed to summon the necessary will to take the problem to the President for a top-level decision to halt MacArthur's advance to the Yalu and to order him to pull back his forces to less vulnerable positions. The fact that all the President's top advisers could agree on the need for new instructions to MacArthur and yet found narrow bureaucratic and political reasons for not informing the President of this constitutes a breakdown of the first magnitude in the advisory process.[47]

We have noted that the JCS as well as Truman's top political advisers recognized that negotiations would now be necessary to terminate the war and that it would be necessary to settle for something less than full unification. Logically this implied that military force by itself could not be relied upon to achieve a favorable outcome. Rather, military strategy and tactics would now have to be adapted to serve a new political and diplomatic approach to the conflict. But a clear and consistent concept regarding the reorientation of military strategy to this end never emerged. Within a few weeks the administration allowed a headstrong, self-confident MacArthur to implement his own military strategy of marching to the Yalu.

How can we account for the administration's failure to implement its recognition that reliance would now have to be placed on diplomacy rather than military action? Why did it waver and allow MacArthur to pursue military victory? The answer to this puzzle has been partially obscured for many years. The catastrophe which followed the successful Chinese offen-

---

[47] These facts were noted initially by Lichterman (*To the Yalu and Back*, p. 602) and, especially, by Neustadt, *Presidential Power*, pp. 144–46. Their interpretation was largely confirmed by Acheson in the course of his denial of one factual component of their account; see *Present at the Creation*, p. 468. In this he was supported by Collins, *War in Peacetime*, p. 202. A detailed review of the case as an example of malfunctions in the policy-making process is presented by George, "The Case for Multiple Advocacy," pp. 751–85.

sive and Truman's eventual relief of MacArthur from his command inevitably led to bitter recriminations and efforts to manipulate blame. MacArthur and his followers charged that by
imposing constraints on the conduct of the war the administration had encouraged the Chinese to believe that they could attack his forces without fear of retaliation. The administration
charged that MacArthur had brought about the defeat of his
army by plunging ahead recklessly to the Yalu against repeated
advice from Washington that he pursue a more cautious pattern
of operations. As a result, a confusing picture emerged of the
General as having been both overconstrained and undercon-
strained by Washington.

In time more dispassionate analyses of the available record
were to indicate that, while the administration had indeed *advised* caution in early November, it had not changed Mac-
Arthur's directives or imposed a more cautious strategy on
him when he rejected its advice. It also emerged that whereas
MacArthur had interpreted his military directives broadly, he
had rarely violated them and that, certainly, his bold attempt in
mid-November to end the war by going to the Yalu—a "recon-
naissance-in-force," he was to call it after it had boomeranged—
did not violate any directives.

To understand the problem Washington faced in attempting
to persuade and control MacArthur's operations in these critical
weeks of November, we must recall that before the Chinese
actually intervened, Truman had delegated to the General a
large measure of discretion over military strategy and tactics in
Korea. In the event of covert or overt intervention of "major"
Chinese forces, the October 9 directive to MacArthur had
stated, "you should continue the action as long as, *in your judgment*, action by your forces now under your control offers a reasonable chance of success." [48] As Neustadt points out, the
definition of a "reasonable chance of success" was delegated to
MacArthur's judgment: "In the weeks to come he would
misjudge with tragic consequences, but it cannot be charged

[48] Truman, *Years of Trial and Hope*, p. 362; emphasis added.

that he exceeded his instructions. . . . The discretion given to
MacArthur in October contributed directly to disaster in November." [49]

By not taking back the discretionary authority granted Mac-
Arthur, Truman in effect allowed the General to determine for
Washington the level of costs and risks that was acceptable in
pursuing the war objective in the dangerous situation that developed in November. Truman's passivity in this respect is all
the more remarkable in that it was amply clear to everyone in
Washington that MacArthur attached more importance to
achieving the full objective of unifying Korea, even in the face
of Chinese intervention, than Washington did. Accordingly, it
was logical for MacArthur to be willing to accept greater risks
than Washington would in an effort to intimidate the Chinese
into withdrawing from northern Korea and, thence, to proceed
with the unification of North and South Korea. But it was both
illogical and irresponsible for Washington, which did not think
the war objective was worth great risks, to allow MacArthur to
determine the level of risks that were to be accepted.[50]

The question remains, however, why top-level officials in
Washington, alarmed as they were in early November over the
Chinese intervention and disposed as they were at that time to
modify their war objective, did not *impose* greater caution on
MacArthur's proposed operations while they explored the possibility of a negotiated settlement. This modification of war aims
and military strategy would have been difficult for Washington
under the best of circumstances. Time would have been needed
to change course through a series of incremental steps to condition opinion and prepare the ground for a new policy. But to
gain the necessary time, the tempo of military operations would
have had to be slowed down. This might have been possible
had MacArthur cooperated. But, since he was not disposed to

[49] Neustadt, *Presidential Power*, p. 138; Lichterman, "To the Yalu and Back,"
pp. 594, 611.

[50] The implications of this error for the subsequent theory and practice of presidential control of force are discussed in George, Hall, and Simon, *Limits of Coercive Diplomacy*, pp. 1–5.

do so, the administration was required to exert itself to the utmost to curb MacArthur's desire to push quickly to the Yalu. This it did only half-heartedly and ineffectually. Truman was indeed reluctant, as some scholars have noted, to depart from the traditional American practice in wartime of giving military commanders considerable freedom to decide how best to employ their forces in order to achieve the mission assigned. Truman and his advisers also held back from imposing a more cautious strategy on MacArthur because they were aware of the political outcry that would have surely followed from the General and others to the effect that Washington was depriving him of an opportunity to achieve the victory he thought lay within his grasp. Finally, Washington had no inkling that the number of Chinese troops already in Korea was over four times the 60,000 to 70,000 that was estimated by MacArthur's headquarters. From the very beginning, military intelligence had consistently underestimated the number of Chinese involved in the intervention.[51]

There is another important element in the explanation which was obscured for many years, possibly because administration officials were reluctant in the aftermath of mutual recriminations and blame-shifting to present opponents with ammunition that could have been used to force them to share greater responsibility with MacArthur for his reckless mid-November drive to the Yalu. The facts now available show that Washington's anxiety over the Chinese intervention in early November declined appreciably in the next few weeks and, with it, Washington's motivation to impose greater caution on MacArthur gave way to a willingness to let him proceed with his bold plan. It was not simply a question of resolving their doubts in favor of the General's plan because, with the memory that he had been proven right in insisting on the Inchon landing against everyone else's judgment, Washington felt obliged to accord special weight to his view. Rather, the facts of Chinese military intervention also appeared to be changing.

[51] Appleman, *South to the Naktong, North to the Yalu*, pp. 769–70.

On November 8, when anxiety over the Chinese intervention was at a peak, the Chinese forces disengaged from any contact with U.N. forces on the battlefield. Their whereabouts became increasingly a mystery in the following twenty days. It is
possible that the Chinese disengagement was purely tactical, in
accord with Mao's guerrilla warfare doctrine of pulling back to
recuperate or to prepare a trap for advancing enemy forces.
However, this does not exclude the possibility that the
disengagement had another purpose as well. Peking may have
disengaged its forces also in order to assess the risks of increasing its intervention and to observe, before doing so, whether
the willingness it had already demonstrated to engage U.N.
forces in combat would suffice to lead the United States to modify its policy and its plans for occupying North Korea.
Curiously, it apparently did not occur to U.S. leaders that the
Chinese disengagement might be either a tactical stratagem or a
military pause deliberately designed for political purposes, to
give Washington an opportunity to clarify and possibly reconsider its basic policies. If the latter was the reason for the
disengagement of Chinese forces, however, it had the opposite
effect! The disengagement inadvertently signaled the wrong
message to U.S. leaders.

The Chinese disengagement evidently nourished Mac-
Arthur's illusions and encouraged him to gamble; for did not the
disengagement signify that Peking was having second thoughts
and might be persuaded to back down altogether by a bold effort on his part to exploit "oriental psychology"?[52] As for the

[52] MacArthur's calculations and rationale for resuming his march to the Yalu in
mid-November may never be fully clarified. Evidently, it was a risk that he
calculated and thought to be acceptable under the circumstances as he perceived and evaluated them. Quite possibly, MacArthur was even willing to accept appreciable risks in the matter, though he obviously did not foresee their
full magnitude because he grossly underestimated the capability of the Chinese
forces and the damage they could inflict on his forces. The war aim of unifying
Korea obviously appealed to MacArthur, as it did to others. He placed a higher
value on achieving this objective than did the more cautious administration
leaders. Hence, he was personally prepared, and thought the country should be,
to accept the risks and possible costs of his march to the Yalu. In other words, as
the Kolkos emphasize, MacArthur was by no means averse to a war with China,

administration leaders, they were puzzled and wary at first over the Chinese disengagement. But the fact that days passed without any further sign of the Chinese forces strengthened in their minds the sanguine possibility to which they had subscribed earlier, namely, that the Chinese had decided after all to restrict their intervention to minor activity.

Although a number of earlier writers had already called attention to the possible effect of the Chinese disengagement on MacArthur and Washington,[53] concrete evidence that it eroded Washington's disposition to control MacArthur's operations did not emerge until 1968.[54] As a result, it is now clear that the acute concern that all Truman's top advisers had felt during the first week of November over the riskiness of MacArthur's military strategy had largely evaporated by November 21. Having examined the minutes of two meetings Acheson had on that day, first with his staff and then with Marshall, Bradley, and other officials, David McLellan finds that "Far from revealing great anxiety or trepidation about MacArthur's advance to the Yalu, Acheson seems to have shared the prevailing confidence that MacArthur could accomplish his mission and that Chinese intervention, if it did occur, could be contained within a buffer zone along the Yalu." McLellan continues, "It would be a mis-

though it would appear that he thought that his strategy would succeed in coercing them to withdraw. Kolko and Kolko, *Limits of Power*, pp. 596–97, 600–602. As viewed by MacArthur, the alternatives to resuming the march to the Yalu in mid-November—namely, standing still or retreating to the narrow waist of North Korea—probably appeared more distasteful than accepting the risk of a strategy which, while admittedly somewhat bold, offered the possibility of a major gain.

[53] For example, Lichterman, "To the Yalu and Back," p. 607; Neustadt, *Presidential Power*, p. 143; Appleman, *South to the Naktong, North to the Yalu*, p. 754; Zelman, "Chinese Intervention," pp. 12–13; Fehrenbach, *This Kind of War*, p. 297.

[54] An article published in 1968 by David S. McLellan, based on original research on materials made available to him by Dean Acheson, adds substantially to our knowledge of developments in top-level policy calculations in Washington during the middle of November 1950. The account presented here relies heavily on McLellan's disclosure of the minutes of two meetings in which Acheson participated on November 21. McLellan, "Dean Acheson and the Korean War," pp. 16–39.

take to believe that Acheson was a convinced opponent of Mac-Arthur's campaign, constrained to silence by virtue of his civilian role or by political expediency." [55]

Continued Chinese quiescence on the battlefield evidently had strengthened the possibility in Acheson's mind, as no doubt in the minds of other administration leaders, that MacArthur might succeed after all in forestalling or repelling the Chinese intervention. At the meeting with his staff on November 21 Acheson expressed the belief that the directive to MacArthur should not be changed until the General had had a chance to probe the situation and push forward his planned offensive.[56]

Thus, if the Chinese had disengaged in early November in order to allow time for a change in U.S. policy, they received an unmistakable answer when MacArthur was allowed to resume his march to the Yalu. Under the circumstances, Peking could hardly be expected to credit earlier indications that Washington was interested in working out a compromise settlement. Whether or not Washington realized it, it had behaved in such a way as to confirm the most extreme form of the Chinese Communist image of American insincerity and duplicity. The Chinese then launched their major offensive of November 25, beginning a long and bitter war. Whatever opportunity had existed earlier in November for avoiding this was now irretriev-

[55] *Ibid.*, pp. 32–33. McLellan is hard put to explain the relative optimism displayed at the November 21 meetings, which he finds "strangely unreal" when compared with the "dread of Chinese involvement" under which these same policy-makers had been laboring earlier in November. The explanation for their change of mood, which McLellan overlooks, can undoubtedly be traced to the Chinese disengagement on the battlefield, which he fails to mention.

[56] McLellan, "Dean Acheson and the Korean War," p. 30. In his memoirs Acheson offers a quite different account of the meeting with Marshall and the Chiefs of Staff on November 21 than do the minutes of the meeting available to McLellan. Acheson states that he expressed his concern over MacArthur's dispositions and was reluctantly persuaded not to oppose MacArthur's "probe," since the General claimed that he could not otherwise determine the degree of Chinese intervention. Acheson also states that Marshall and Bradley felt they could not presume to direct the theater commander's dispositions from a distance of 7,000 miles. It is clear from Acheson's account that he regards Marshall and Bradley, and not himself, responsible for failing to restrain MacArthur; *Present at the Creation*, p. 467.

ably lost because of Washington's indecisiveness, its wavering and inconsistent attitude toward the possible military and diplomatic strategies before it, and its gross ineptness at what has come to be called "crisis management." Instead of creating the time needed for developing its new diplomatic strategy by halting the momentum of action on the battlefield or, at least, insuring that military actions would be consistent with and supportive of its new diplomatic approach, the administration wavered in its adherence to the evolving diplomatic strategy and allowed MacArthur to revert to the earlier strategy for unifying Korea by force.[57]

The "textbook" requirements of deterrence, while they are relatively simple to conceptualize in general terms, are nonetheless often tragically difficult to apply effectively in real-life situations of some complexity. The environment, beliefs, expectations, and policies of the decision-maker invariably include a variety of constraints that may hamper his ability to send—or to receive—clear and effective signals of the kind needed to prevent deterrence from failing. The events of the autumn of 1950 are, above all, a tragic illustration of the inapplicability of deterrence strategy when used by the United States on behalf of a provocative and mistaken foreign policy.

[57] For a fuller discussion of this case, specifically from the standpoint of crisis management, see George, Hall, Simons, *Limits of Coercive Diplomacy*, pp. 11–15.

Bibliography

There are many good studies of the Chinese intervention into the Korean War. For analysis of American policy-making we have drawn on the memoirs of Truman, Acheson, MacArthur, and Collins; the *MacArthur Hearings;* and, among secondary accounts, particularly those by Lichterman, Neustadt, Spanier, De Weerd, Millis *et al.*, Higgins, Goodrich, Westerfield, Osgood and McLellan. The best analysis of the development of Chinese policy is still that by Whiting, with Tang Tsou providing a less detailed but useful account. Soviet policy is covered by Ulam, Shulman. Zelman provides an excellent analysis of the case from the standpoint of deterrence theory and practice; useful theoretical frameworks for the same purpose are presented by Jervis and by Holsti. Detailed revisionist interpretations are contained in the books by Stone and the Kolkos. We are indebted to earlier research on this case by Jane Howland.

Acheson, Dean. *Present at the Creation*. New York, Norton, 1969.

Appleman, Ray E. *South to the Naktong, North to the Yalu*. Washington, D.C., U.S. Government Printing Office, 1961.

Barnett, A. Doak. *Communist China and Asia*. New York, Harper & Bros., 1960.

Cagle, Malcolm W., and Frank A. Manson, *The Sea War in Korea*. Annapolis, U.S. Naval Institute, 1957.

Collins, J. Lawton. *War in Peacetime: The History and Lessons of Korea*. Boston, Houghton Mifflin, 1969.

De Rivera, Joseph. *The Psychological Dimension of Foreign Policy*. Columbus, Ohio, Merrill, 1968.

De Weerd, Harvey A. "Strategic Surprise in the Korean War." *Orbis*, Fall 1962.

Fehrenbach, T. R. *This Kind of War*. New York, Macmillan, 1963.

George, A. L. "The Case for Multiple Advocacy in Making Foreign Policy," *American Political Science Review*, LXVI, No. 3 (September 1972), 751–85.

George, A. L., D. K. Hall, and W. E. Simons. *The Limits of Coercive Diplomacy*. Boston, Little, Brown, 1971.

Goodrich, Leland M. *Korea: A Study of U.S. Policy in the United Nations.* New York, Council on Foreign Relations, 1956.

Halperin, Morton H. *Limited War in the Nuclear Age.* New York, Wiley, 1963.

Higgins, Trumbull. *Korea and the Fall of MacArthur.* New York, Oxford University Press, 1960.

Holsti, Ole R. *Crisis, Escalation and War.* Montreal, McGill–Queen's University Press, 1972.

Jervis, Robert. *The Logic of Images in International Relations.* Princeton, Princeton University Press, 1970.

Kennan, George F. *Memoirs 1925–1950.* Boston, Little, Brown, 1967.

Kolko, Joyce and Gabriel. *The Limits of Power.* New York, Harper & Row, 1972.

Lee, Clark, and Richard Henschel. *Douglas MacArthur.* New York, Holt, 1952.

Levi, Werner. *Modern China's Foreign Policy.* Minneapolis, University of Minnesota Press, 1953.

Lichterman, Martin. "Korea: Problems in Limited War," in *National Security in the Nuclear Age,* ed. Gordon B. Turner and Richard D. Challener. New York, Praeger, 1960.

——. "To the Yalu and Back," in *American Civil-Military Decisions; A Book of Case Studies,* ed. Harold Stein. University, University of Alabama Press, 1963.

Lindsay, Michael. *China and the Cold War.* Melbourne, Melbourne University Press, 1955.

MacArthur, Douglas. *Reminiscences.* New York, McGraw-Hill, 1964.

McLellan, David S. "Dean Acheson and the Korean War," *Political Science Quarterly,* March 1968.

Marshall, S. L. A. *River and the Gauntlet.* New York, Morrow, 1953.

Millis, Walter, with Harvey C. Mansfield and Harold Stein. *Arms and the State: Civil Military Elements in National Policy.* New York, The Twentieth Century Fund, 1958.

Neustadt, Richard E. *Presidential Power: The Politics of Leadership.* New York, Wiley, 1960.

Newsweek, all issues from July 3, 1950 to December 25, 1950.

Osgood, Robert E. *Limited War: The Challenge to American Strategy.* Chicago, University of Chicago Press, 1957.

Panikkar, Kavalam Machava. *In Two Chinas: Memoirs of a Diplomat.* London, Allen & Unwin, 1955.

Reston, James. *New York Times,* November 16, 1950.

Rees, David. *Korea: The Limited War.* London, Macmillan, 1964.

Rovere, Richard H., and Arthur Schlesinger, Jr. *The MacArthur Controversy and American Foreign Policy.* New York, Farrar, Straus and Giroux, 1965.

Shulman, Marshall. *Stalin's Foreign Policy Reappraised.* Cambridge, Harvard University Press, 1963.

Spanier, John W. *The Truman-MacArthur Controversy and the Korean War.* Cambridge, Harvard University Press, Belknap Press, 1959.

Stebbins, Richard C. *The United States in World Affairs 1950,* New York, Harper & Bros., 1951.

Stone, I. F. *The Hidden History of the Korean War.* New York, Monthly Review Press, 1952.

Sulzberger, C. L. "Foreign Affairs: Charting the China Storm," *New York Times,* March 8, 1967.

Truman, Harry S. *Memoirs.* Volume II, *Years of Trial and Hope, 1946–1952.* New York, Doubleday, 1956.

Tsou, Tang. *America's Failure in China, 1941–1950.* Chicago, University of Chicago Press, 1963.

——, and Morton H. Halperin, "Mao Tse-tung's Revolutionary Strategy and Peking's International Behavior." *The American Political Science Review,* March 1965.

Ulam, Adam B. *Expansion & Coexistence.* New York, Praeger, 1968.

United Nations Official Records, Fifth Session, First Committee, 346–53 meetings, September 30 to October 4, 1950.

U.S. Congress, Senate Committee on Armed Services and Committee on Foreign Relations. *Military Situation in the Far East (MacArthur Hearings).* 5 vols. Washington, D.C., U.S. Government Printing Office, 1951.

U.S. Department of State, *Department of State Bulletin.* Vol. 23, Nos. 576–97 (July 17 to December 11, 1950).

Westerfield, H. Bradford. *The Instruments of American Foreign Policy.* New York, Crowell, 1963.

Whiting, Allen S. *China Crosses the Yalu: The Decision to Enter the Korean War.* New York, Macmillan, 1960.

Willoughby, Charles, and John Chamberlain. *MacArthur 1941–1951.* New York, McGraw-Hill, 1954.

Zelman, Walter. "Chinese Intervention in the Korean War: A Bilateral Failure of Deterrence." Security Studies Paper No. 11, UCLA, 1967.

Chapter 8

Deterrence through "Massive Retaliation" Threats: Korea and Indochina, 1953–1954

Résumé

DWIGHT D. EISENHOWER and his Secretary of State, John Foster Dulles, entered office in January 1953 committed to bringing the war in Korea to an end and to drawing a tighter containment line around Communist China. The new administration identified itself more closely with the Chinese Nationalist regime on Taiwan, and it increased the flow of economic and military aid to Indochina to assist the French in turning back the Vietminh threat.

Eisenhower also introduced important changes in the articulation and employment of deterrence strategy on behalf of containment objectives. This was evident particularly in the administration's policies in Asia, where it employed threats of the kind that came to be associated with the term "Massive Retaliation" on behalf of its most pressing objectives in Korea and Indochina. First, in order to bring about an armistice, in Korea the administration threatened to widen the war through use of nuclear weapons on the Chinese mainland. Then, once the armistice was achieved the administration, backed by its allies,

STEPHEN J. GENCO is coauthor of this chapter.

made a similar threat to deter any resumption of the war by the communist side later on. Finally, the administration attempted to employ its deterrence power in order to assist the French in Indochina by warning Peking against intervening militarily on behalf of the Vietminh.

The structure of the situation was, of course, rather different in these three cases. The threat to expand the Korean War was, strictly speaking, an instance of "compellance" or coercive diplomacy rather than deterrence, since it was intended to get the other side to stop the fighting and to sign an armistice.[1] Deterrence, on the other hand, attempts to persuade an opponent not to do something he has not yet done. This became the situation once the armistice had been signed. The problem now, as perceived by the administration, was to provide sanctions to "enforce" the armistice. The threat to expand the fighting beyond the borders of Korea if the other side broke the armistice and resumed the war, therefore, was clearly an example of deterrence rather than compellance.

Similarly, the U.S. threatened to strike at targets in China if Peking sent its forces into Indochina, and this was also an example of deterrence strategy. In other important respects, however, the structure of the situation in Indochina differed greatly from the circumstances of the Korean War. The United States was not directly engaged in the Indochina War, as it was in Korea. While the United States and some of its allies agreed upon the necessity of preventing a communist takeover by force in South Korea, it was much more difficult to apply the containment objective effectively to Indochina, because there it became inextricably connected with the French effort to maintain its colonial position.

The major threat to the French position in Indochina was the internal one posed by the Vietminh. The United States could assist the French by providing economic and military aid; but to deter the Vietminh from pursuing their efforts in the in-

[1] On the distinction between "compellance" and "deterrence" see Schelling, *Arms and Influence*, pp. 69–78. The concept of compellance is analyzed further in George, Hall, and Simon, *Limits of Coercive Diplomacy*, pp. 21–32.

ternal struggle was another matter. For various reasons, the United States could not intervene with its own forces to prevent a Vietminh success over the French and, indeed, did not threaten to do so until late in the day. What the administration did do was to direct its deterrence efforts toward the less likely contingency of a major Chinese military intervention into Indochina. The Massive Retaliation threat Dulles posed for the purpose, however, left an important gap in deterrence. What remained undeterred was continued indirect Chinese military assistance to the Vietminh, which played an important role in their eventual success.

Achieving a Korean Armistice

By the summer of 1951 the Korean War had reached the stage where both sides were ready for truce discussions. But the wrangling over the terms of the settlement was bitter and prolonged. Meanwhile, fighting continued at a high level throughout the remainder of the Truman Presidency.

The new administration came into office in January 1953 with a pledge to end the costly and frustrating war of attrition. Eisenhower notes in his memoirs that "several possible lines of action" were under consideration.[2] A continuation of the situation then present was viewed as "intolerable." An attack on the North to gain an all-out military victory by conventional means was, for a variety of reasons, seen as "the least attractive of all plans." An atomic attack on either North Korea or mainland China was viewed as feasible but would most likely lead to "other problems, not the least of which would be the possibility of the Soviet Union entering the war." Thus it seemed that escalation of the war would generate more difficulties than it would solve. The only choice perceived to be open, therefore, was to attempt to reach a favorable agreement through the framework

[2] Eisenhower, *White House Years*, pp. 178–81.

that had been developed during the Truman Administration—the stalled armistice talks. To get the talks moving again, Eisenhower employed a type of strategy that would later become known as a Massive Retaliation threat:

> The lack of progress in the long-stalemated talks . . . and the nearly stalemated war both demanded, in my opinion, definite measures on our part to put an end to these intolerable conditions. One possibility was to let the Communist authorities understand that, *in the absence of satisfactory progress, we intended to move decisively without inhibition in our use of weapons, and would no longer be responsible for confining hostilities to the Korean Peninsula.* . . . *In* India and in the Formosa Straits area, and at the truce negotiations at Panmunjom, we dropped the word, discreetly, of our intention. We felt quite sure it would reach Soviet and Chinese Communist ears.[3]

Eisenhower had apparently decided at least six weeks before he was sworn in as President that he would use the threat of nuclear escalation to stimulate the talks and thereby bring the war to a close. Following a visit to Korea from December 2 to 5, 1952, the President-elect met with his future Secretary of State aboard the cruiser *Helena*. According to an account given by Presidential Assistant Robert Donovan, "he and Dulles had determined to make it clear to the Communists that to delay the truce indefinitely would be to invite the United States to enlarge the war and to strike at China not only in Korea but on two or three other fronts of its own choosing." [4] Upon his return to New York, Eisenhower made some oblique references to the new strategy but refrained from revealing it *in toto*.

According to Eisenhower's memoirs, the administration first "dropped the word" some time during February 1953. Eisenhower believed that this hint was largely responsible for the first breakthrough in negotiations on February 22, which resulted in the exchange of seriously sick and wounded prisoners.[5] After this encouraging turn, however, the talks once again bogged down over the issue of the exchange of the rest of the prisoners of war. In the meantime Joseph Stalin died in

[3] *Ibid.*, p. 181; emphasis added.   [4] Donovan, *Eisenhower*, p. 115.

[5] Eisenhower, *White House Years*, p. 181.

March, a development that probably led to a major reconsideration of policy on the Korean War by his successors in Moscow.

Seeing that its initial Massive Retaliation threat had failed to bring about the desired outcome, the administration decided to put together a more credible display of its intentions by employing several channels of communication simultaneously. General Mark Clark, the chief U.N. negotiator at Panmunjom, was instructed to present to the communists the "final" allied proposals concerning the prisoner of war question. Clark states further: "If . . . the Communists rejected this final offer and made no constructive proposals of their own, I was authorized to *break off* the truce talks rather than to recess them, and to carry on the war in new ways never yet tried in Korea." [6] These proposals were tabled when the delegation met in executive session on May 25. Concurrently, on May 22, Secretary Dulles arrived in India for three days of talks with Prime Minister Nehru. According to his own account,[7] Dulles had confidence in Nehru's "ability to communicate speedily with Peking" and informed him that "if the war continued, the U.S. would lift the self-imposed restrictions on its actions to hold back no effort or weapon to win." [8] Although, as Rees points out,[9] Nehru reportedly denied any personal knowledge of the atomic threat, other Indian officials that Dulles met could have easily passed the message on to Peking. As an additional warning to the Chinese that the U.S. intended to carry out its threat if necessary, missiles with atomic warheads were transferred to Okinawa in the early spring.[10]

While the effect of this series of coordinated moves on the other side cannot be determined conclusively, it is certainly possible that they contributed to breaking the logjam. At the

---

[6] Clark, *From the Danube to the Yalu*, p. 252.

[7] Shepley, "How Dulles Averted War." Shepley's article was based on Dulles' personal recollections.

[8] *Ibid.*, p. 71.   [9] Rees, *Korea*, p. 417.

[10] Donovan, *Eisenhower*, p. 116; Adams, *Firsthand Report*, p. 48.

next plenary session of the armistice talks on June 4, the communists accepted, with minor changes, the final allied proposal on prisoners.[11] With this issue now finally removed, negotiations moved quickly and compromise settlements were worked out on one after another of the remaining points of contention. As a result, the Korean armistice was finally signed on July 27, 1953. The military truce was to be followed within three months by a peace conference to deal with the larger political questions of a divided Korea.

Enforcing the Armistice Through Deterrence

As the armistice went into effect, the United States was faced with what appeared to be another serious problem: how to insure that the communists would not break off the cease-fire and resume their offensive. Eisenhower certainly had no desire to continue stationing a large contingent of U.S. and U.N. troops along the armistice line in order to deter the resumption of hostilities by the other side. Therefore, some other type of deterrent was seen to be necessary. Eisenhower's solution was to extend the applicability of his Massive Retaliation threat to this new situation.

On August 7, 1953, General Clark announced in a report to the U.N. Security Council that the sixteen U.N. members who had contributed armed forces to the Korean conflict had signed a statement in Washington on July 27, the day of the armistice. In addition to declaring that the allies fully intended to uphold the terms of the agreement, this "Declaration of Sixteen" also contained a careful description of the probable consequences of a resumption of the fighting by the communists:

> We affirm, in the interests of world peace, that if there is a renewal of the armed attack, challenging again the principles of the United Nations, we should again be united and prompt to resist. The consequences of such a breach of the armistice would be so grave that, in

[11] Rees, *Korea*, p. 417.

all probability, it would not be possible to confine hostilities within the frontiers of Korea.[12]

This declaration was followed shortly on August 8 with the announcement of a U.S.–South Korean mutual defense treaty. No further serious fighting occurred along the armistice border and the United States was able to withdraw 6 of its 8 divisions stationed in Korea by mid-1955. Brushing aside other considerations and developments, such as Stalin's death, which may have contributed to the communist side's decision to conclude the armistice, both Eisenhower and Dulles credited the atomic threat as having been primarily responsible for ending the war.[13] Encouraged thereby, the administration was led to apply its new deterrence strategy to other situations where the Chinese Communists seemed to be threatening Western interests.

Deterring Chinese Communist Intervention in Indochina

EXTENSION OF CONTAINMENT TO SOUTHEAST ASIA

We noted in chapter 7 that the communist takeover of the Chinese mainland in 1949 had prompted the United States to take a

---

[12] Text in Department of State, *American Foreign Policy 1950–1955: Basic Documents*, p. 2662.

[13] Speaking to the Geneva Conference in April 1954, Dulles stated that the truce had come "only after the Communists realized that, unless there was quick armistice, the battle area would be enlarged so as to endanger the sources of aggression in Manchuria. Then and only then did the Communist rulers judge that it would be expedient to sign the Armistice." Quoted in Rees, *Korea*, p. 418.

Sherman Adams reports on Eisenhower's confirmation of the importance of the threats: "talking one day with Eisenhower about the events that led up finally to the truce in Korea, I asked him what it was that brought the Communists into line. 'Danger of an atomic war,' he said without hesitation. 'We told them we could not hold it to a limited war any longer if the Communists welched on a treaty of truce. They didn't want a full-scale war or an atomic attack. That kept them under some control.'" Adams, *Firsthand Report*, pp. 48–49.

greater interest in extending the policy of containment from Europe to Asia. Both the Truman and, later, the Eisenhower Administration believed that the process of devolution from colonial empires to independent states could create "power vacuums" and conditions of instability which would make large parts of Asia susceptible to the type of communist strategy that had resulted in the overthrow of the Nationalist government in China. The North Korean attack on South Korea and the concurrent attempt by Ho Chi Minh's regime to oust the French from Indochina were seen as Asian manifestation of a worldwide communist aggressive intent. The ability of South Korea to resist the North, and the ability of France together with the Associated States it sponsored in Laos, Cambodia, and Vietnam to resist Ho, were seen as crucial to the West's attempt at erecting a line of containment against the expansion of communism.

Before the outbreak of the Korean War, the Truman Administration's perception of the communist threat in Asia focused primarily on the Soviet Union itself; the newly emerging Chinese Communist regime was seen as becoming a serious threat only in the more distant future. However, Peking's unexpected intervention in the Korean War substantially increased Washington's fear of communist expansion throughout Asia, and the Chinese Communists now replaced the Soviet Union as the major and direct source of the danger of further communist expansion in Asia. What is more, as a result of the Chinese military intervention in Korea and the heavy fighting that followed, the acute Cold War beliefs that characterized the dominant American view of the conflict with the Soviet Union were now extended to Communist China as well.

As a result of these developments, American leaders attached steadily greater importance to preventing a "communist takeover" in Indochina. From an early stage, the attitudes of American leaders toward Ho Chi Minh and his aspirations for an independent Indochina had been distorted by their perception of "monolithic communism." The tendency to inflate the value of Indochina to the Free World by viewing a possible French defeat there in terms of its "row-of-dominoes" consequences had been evident already in Washington during the Truman Administration. This distortion increased as China began to give Ho Chi Minh assistance.

Chinese Communist military aid to the Vietminh had begun shortly after Peking extended recognition to Ho Chi Minh's Democratic Republic of Vietnam (DRV) in January 1950. The Chinese sent small arms and military technicians, improved communications between China and northern Vietnam, and trained Vietnamese military and civilian personnel on Chinese soil. During the Korean War, Chinese military aid to the Vietminh remained at a relatively low level, with Peking content to supply enough aid to enable the Vietminh to maintain themselves against the French.

Peking's intervention in Korea in late November of 1950 immediately raised the possibility of a large-scale Chinese military "intrusion" into Indochina as well. Indeed, in December a national intelligence estimate regarded Chinese intervention in Indochina as "impending." [14] As time passed, however, and as the Vietminh demonstrated an ability to do well enough on their own, Washington's fear that the Chinese would move into Indochina was replaced by concern over the deterioration of the French position. Thereafter, American policy-makers continued to note the possibility that the Chinese might intervene in either one of two circumstances: as a response to the success it was hoped and believed the French would eventually enjoy against the Vietminh; or as a reaction to possible American intervention on behalf of the French and the Associated States. But the chief threat to Indochina perceived by American policy-makers over the next few years was not the possibility of external aggression by the Chinese but rather the inability of the French to deal with the internal threat of the Vietminh. That the Chinese would continue to supply the Vietminh was taken for granted and accepted as something which could not really be prevented. Besides, Washington did not believe that Chinese military aid to the Vietminh could in itself be decisive;

[14] *Pentagon Papers*, I, 84.

despite Washington's persistent criticism of the French performance in Indochina, it continued to believe that the French had the *capability* for controlling and eventually removing the internal threat, so long as Chinese forces did not intervene on a large scale, as in Korea.

In any case, Washington gave little or no thought to the possibility of deterring the Chinese from continuing and increasing indirect military aid to the Vietminh. The government steadily increased the amount of American aid to the French and emphasized the importance of Indochina, but it did not employ the threat of American military intervention in any form as a means of discouraging the Chinese from supplying the Vietminh. Deterrent threats for this purpose were not made, it must be surmised, because Washington did not regard them as having any credibility. So far as Indochina was concerned, Washington had the capability and resolution for a deterrent threat of the Massive Retaliation type but for little else. The Korean War was a heavy drain on available American military forces. Moreover, Washington had to give clear priority to the defense of Western Europe over Indochina in considering the allocation of programmed increases in force levels.

But even had there been a surplus of U.S. ground and other forces available for commitment to Indochina, such forces could not have been the basis for deterrence threats because the French were firmly and clearly opposed to any form of direct American military participation in their conflict with the Vietminh. Indeed, the French even resisted more active participation by U.S. personnel in the training of indigenous forces. Finally, as already suggested, Washington in any case did not regard Chinese military aid to the Vietminh as the critical factor on which the outcome of the war depended. Rather, throughout the period up to and including the Dienbienphu crisis in the spring of 1954, Washington felt that the performance of the French in dealing with the internal threat in Indochina was severely hampered by various factors of their own making, which were derived largely from the colonialist objectives they were pursuing.

APPROACHES TO THE USE OF DETERRENCE:
ACHESON AND DULLES

While direct Chinese military intervention was regarded as unlikely, both the Truman and Eisenhower administrations were
obliged to consider what the American response to this event
would be and, in addition, what might be done to deter such a
move by Peking. Truman and his advisors decided not to issue
explicit deterrence warnings to the Chinese against intervention in Indochina, whereas Eisenhower and Dulles decided to
do so.

Acheson felt that the United States "would have to do
something" if the Chinese entered Indochina. Furthermore, he
felt that a warning to deter them from doing so was "highly
desirable." Nonetheless, he decided against giving such a warning. In his mind deterrence warnings should not be issued until
and unless the government made a policy decision that it would
definitely act if the contingency in question arose or, if it were a
question of joint action with allies, as in this case, until a political agreement with them had been reached regarding the action
that might be taken if the warning went unheeded. To issue deterrence warnings in the absence of such intra- or intergovern-
mental policy decisions, Acheson felt, was risky and should be
avoided. It is clear that he feared being caught bluffing.[15]

But the Eisenhower Administration entered office determined to develop a new defense policy that would place greater
reliance on U.S. strategic power and on air and naval forces, and
would make greater and more explicit use of threats of employ-

[15] On June 26, 1952, in a memorandum of conversations on the subject of Indochina with British Foreign Secretary Anthony Eden, Acheson summarized
what he had said on the matter of a warning to the Chinese as follows: "He
[Acheson] felt it would be desirable to issue a warning statement of some sort,
whether public, private, detailed and specific, or otherwise, but it would be essential to have a general understanding as to the action we might take if the
warning were to go unheeded. To issue a warning and take no effective action
would be calamitous." Acheson had expressed similar views earlier to Sir
Oliver Franks in Washington. To be caught bluffing, Acheson felt, "would make
us look very silly and would weaken the effect of any other warning." *Pentagon
Papers*, I, 391, 381; see also Acheson, *Present at the Creation*, p. 676.

ing these forces to deter encroachments on the boundaries of containment. We have seen examples of this in the efforts of the new administration first to bring about the Korean armistice and then to provide sanctions to enforce the armistice by means of an explicit deterrence warning that if the communist side resumed the war the allied response would not be confined to Korea. Before the summer was over, less than nine months after Eisenhower entered office, the threat of Massive Retaliation (as it was soon to be called) was extended to Indochina, ostensibly to deter a large-scale Chinese military intervention.

This is not to say that Eisenhower and Dulles thought that such a Chinese move had now become likely or was becoming more likely. Rather, the major reasons for issuing the deterrence warning were evidently three: first, to avoid any possible Chinese miscalculation; second, to emphasize the American commitment to prevent a communist takeover in Indochina; and, third, to provide the French with psychological assurance that they could proceed with a new and more costly plan for bringing the Vietminh threat under control. It is also possible—but here lack of firm information forces us into more speculative analysis— that Dulles and other American officials believed that the threat of Massive Retaliation might succeed in intimidating Chinese Communist leaders not merely from engaging in open military intervention but also from granting the increased indirect military aid that the Vietminh would need in order to cope with the enhanced French effort called for in the new plan.

Generally speaking, Dulles placed greater hope in intimidating opponents than Acheson had and was less inhibited in trying to do so. Dulles was not as concerned as Acheson had been with the need to avoid making threats that one was not prepared to carry out. Moreover, in Dulles' theory of deterrence it was not necessary that declaratory policy on behalf of deterrence should hue closely to the specific actions the government intended to take should deterrence fail. He believed that it was generally sufficient for deterrence purposes to make a credible threat that the United States would respond in *some* way to aggression; it was not necessary to indicate more specifically how it would respond. Particularly in the defense of "gray areas," such as Indochina, Dulles employed threats in order to get as much deterrence mileage as possible from uncertainty connected with possible use of American military power.[16]

CONSTRAINTS ON THE USE OF
DETERRENCE STRATEGY ON BEHALF OF THE FRENCH

Given Dulles' views on these matters and his open espousal of deterrence policy on behalf of Indochina well before he be-

[16] As a sympathetic biographer concludes, Dulles' policy of deterrence "contained degrees of uncertainty and ambiguity and a tendency to view overstatement as a better bargain than understatement, which may well have included a degree of bluff in some cases." Guhin, *John Foster Dulles*, p. 235.

In some respects Dulles exceeded even Eisenhower in the reliance he placed upon the possible utility of deterrence strategy and threats to defend weaker allies. When Dulles visited General Eisenhower, then commander of NATO forces in Paris, in May 1952, he presented him with a memorandum containing his thoughts on the role of deterrence in American foreign policy which foreshadowed very closely the Massive Retaliation statements he was to make later as Secretary of State. Shortly thereafter, the memorandum was published in *Life* Magazine. The article, entitled "A Policy of Boldness," declared that in dealing with communist expansionism, *"There is one solution and only one: that is for the free world to develop the will and organize the means to retaliate instantly against open aggression by Red armies, so that, if it occurred anywhere, we could and would strike back where it hurts, by means of our choosing." Life,* May 19, 1952, p. 151; italics in original.

While in substantial agreement, Eisenhower felt that Dulles oversimplified matters and, specifically, called his attention to the inability of threats of all-out attack to deter local minor aggressions and internal subversion. Later that year, when Dulles was helping to draft the Republican platform on which Eisenhower would run, the General "once more reminded Dulles that reliance on retaliation was not a sufficient and workable deterrent to 'broad' Soviet threats." Gerson, *John Foster Dulles*, pp. 74–75, 84; Guhin, *John Foster Dulles*, p. 227. (Eisenhower's civilian chief of staff, Sherman Adams, records that the President took exception later to Dulles' efforts in 1956 to extol the administration's willingness to go to the "brink." Adams, *Firsthand Report*, pp. 117–20.

During the same visit to Paris, Dulles gave an address to a French audience in which he applied his ideas of deterrence strategy directly to Indochina. The threat of American air and naval bombardment of the Chinese mainland, he suggested, could keep Peking from intervening directly in Indochina. Interestingly, Dulles also expressed the view that the general doctrine of deterrence that he was espousing would not only neutralize the external threat of communist aggression to which Asian allies were vulnerable but also assist them in coping with the threat of internal subversion. Gerson, pp. 76–78; Guhin, pp. 226. As we shall see in chapter 11, Dulles expressed similar ideas in 1957 when explaining the rationale for the Eisenhower Doctrine in the Middle East.

came Eisenhower's Secretary of State, what is surprising is not
that the new administration should employ the threat of Massive Retaliation against China in order to defend Indochina but
that such a declaration was withheld until Dulles' speech of
September 2, 1953 to the American Legion. In fact, the new administration was finding that it was not easy to develop a viable
policy for assisting the French to cope with the Vietminh. The
rhetorical commitment to Indochina was one thing; operationalizing the commitment in terms of a viable plan to deal effectively with the various threats to Indochina was quite another matter.

Responsibility for the defense of Indochina quite clearly
had to remain with the French, first because the French government was adamantly opposed to any direct or indirect military
involvement by the United States or other allies that might undermine its war objectives and its control of political and military strategy. Then in addition, the Eisenhower Administration
was severely constrained by its own emerging defense policies
from designing plans for the defense of Indochina in the event
of a French collapse or withdrawal. Whatever the meaning of
the "New Look" (the term Eisenhower's defense specialists
gave to the new military posture the administration was designing), it did *not* mean the employment of American ground
forces in another war on the Asian mainland. The Eisenhower
Administration was committed not only to ending the Korean
War but to avoiding another one of this kind in the future. It
was virtually unthinkable that, once an armistice was obtained
in Korea, American military forces should then be redeployed
in Indochina. Not only considerations of domestic politics but
Eisenhower's own defense strategy prohibited the employment
of large U.S. ground forces in local wars of this kind. However
the employment of U.S. air and naval forces was not similarly
constrained, and it was on this (but only this) basis that the
Eisenhower Administration undertook the deterrence of a major
Chinese Communist intervention in Indochina.

Therefore, no American troops would supplement the
ground forces that the French supplied themselves and attempted to raise from the local populations. Washington was

perforce limited to encouraging the French to continue their effort in Indochina by paying for an increasingly larger proportion of the total war costs,[17] and by providing military aid and advice on how to improve the motivation and capability of the indigenous forces the French had raised. In addition, the Eisenhower Administration attempted to exhort the French by declarations regarding the importance of Indochina to the containment of communism.

Even before the Korean Armistice was finally signed in July, the administration had been concerned that the Chinese Communists might be tempted to take advantage of the end of the fighting in Korea to shift their attention and resources to the war in Indochina. Washington's apprehension, however, did not go so far as to lead it to attach any considerable likelihood to such a Chinese move. The national intelligence estimate of June 4, 1953 (NIE-91) continued to regard Chinese intervention as unlikely "whether or not" an armistice was reached in Korea. (The NIE took a pessimistic view of the steadily deteriorating internal situation in Indochina and the inability of the French to cope with it, politically or militarily.) [18]

Apprehension regarding possible Chinese intervention was understandably greater among the French, who were having sufficient difficulty with the Vietminh without having to contemplate the prospect of increased Chinese activity on its behalf. As early as March, Washington felt it desirable to reassure Paris that it viewed the Indochinese and Korean conflicts as parts of the same pattern of aggression, and that, should Peking take advantage of an armistice in Korea to pursue aggressive war elsewhere in the Far East, such action would have the most severe consequences.[19] For the time being, however, the ad-

[17] American assistance to the French effort in Indochina, which had begun modestly with $10 million in early 1950 before the outbreak of the Korean War, increased steadily thereafter until it reached over a billion dollars in fiscal year 1954, which consistuted 78 percent of the total cost of the French war burden. Gurtov, *First Vietnam Crisis*, pp. 24–25; *Pentagon Papers*, I, 77.

[18] *Ibid.*, 391–404.

[19] The linkage between the two theaters had been suggested in earlier statements by administration leaders and was now emphasized in the weeks and months that followed in public statements by Eisenhower and Dulles; in a joint

ministration would not go so far as to threaten massive retaliation to deter Chinese military intervention. The impetus to do
so came with the emergence in mid-1953 of a military plan
devised by a new French commander in Indochina, General
Navarre, for bringing the Vietminh threat under firm control.
The Navarre Plan called for a substantial increase in indigenous
forces and deployment of additional French forces. It also
required the United States to provide an additional $400 mil-
lion in aid to France for fiscal year 1954. Armed with the Laniel
government's assurance that it would grant genuine independence to the Associated States in Indochina, the State Department strongly urged that the Navarre plan be given the backing
it needed from the United States.[20] Other administration officials were noticeably less confident that the Navarre Plan
would be implemented effectively but agreed that the United
States government should support it.[21]

There was apprehension both in Paris and in Washington
that the Chinese might increase their own role before the Navarre Plan, which would require a year or so in preparation,
could make itself felt on the battlefield. It appeared useful to
Washington, therefore, to issue an explicit Massive Retaliation
threat against the possibility of Chinese military intervention.
On September 2 Dulles delivered the administration's most
forceful warning to date. Noting that Communist China was
"training, equipping and supplying the Communist forces in
Indo-China," Dulles noted that there was a risk that, "as in

---

statement on July 4 by the foreign ministers of the United States, Great Britain,
and France; and also in the sixteen-nation declaration that accompanied the announcement of the Korean armistice on July 27.

[20] "The present French government is the first in seven years," the State Department observed, "which seems prepared to do what needs to be done to
wind up the war in Indochina." Warning that "The Laniel government is almost
certainly the *last* French government which would undertake to continue the
war in Indo-China," the State Department added that the sentiment for a negotiated settlement of the Indochina conflict was growing steadily. *Pentagon Papers*, I, 405, 407. This appraisal of the Laniel Government is reflected also in
Eisenhower's *White House Years*, p. 343.

[21] *Ibid.*, pp. 410–11.

Korea, Red China might send its own army into Indo-China."
He then warned that "The Communist Chinese regime should
realize that such a second aggression could not occur without
grave consequences which might not be confined to Indo-
China." [22]

THE GAP IN DETERRENCE AND
IN POLICY PLANNING

Thus, the Massive Retaliation policy of deterrence was finally
applied to Indochina some seven months after the Eisenhower
Administration entered office. Whether Dulles' declaration was
relevant and responsive to the immediate and overriding problem in Indochina was, as Gurtov notes,[23] another matter. An important gap in deterrence remained. Whether or not Dulles actually believed that the threat to retaliate against a major
intervention by the Chinese would also prevent them from continuing and increasing their indirect military assistance to the
Vietminh, such hopes were not justified. Peking continued to
supply and assist the Vietminh, who were now moving ahead
with their own plans for a showdown in Indochina before the
results of the Navarre Plan could make themselves felt. Whatever Washington's original hopes for its deterrence strategy, it
tacitly accepted Peking's role as supplier to the Vietminh.

It was obvious, therefore, that an important gap in deterrence policy remained open. Hence the question became
whether the Navarre plan could so revitalize the effort against
the Vietminh as to counterbalance continued Chinese assistance. During the winter of 1953–1954 it became increasingly
clear in Washington that French implementation of their plan
was proceeding sluggishly and ineffectively.[24] In January 1954

[22] The warning was given, it may be noted, despite the fact that a low probability was attached to the possibility of such a Chinese intervention. Gurtov, *First
Vietnam Crisis*, pp. 175–76 n47.

[23] *Ibid.*, p. 33.

[24] This was accompanied by considerable criticism of the French on the part of
American military officers connected with the U.S. military advisory program in
Indochina. See, for example, *Pentagon Papers*, I, 90, 93, 410–11.

a National Security Council paper (NSC 5405) emphasized once
again that

> by far the most urgent threat to Southeast Asia arises from the strong
> possibility that even without overt Chinese Communist intervention
> the situation in Indochina may deteriorate as a result of the weaken-
> ing of the resolve of France and the Associated States of Indochina
> to continue to oppose the Viet Minh rebellion, the military strength
> of which is increased by virtue of aid furnished by the Chinese
> Communist and Soviet regimes.[25]

There was ample warning, therefore, that current and projected French and American efforts to deal with the deteriorating situation in Indochina were not likely to succeed. But
U.S. policy-making circles did not respond to this warning in a
timely fashion. Although the gap in the deterrence protection
was recognized clearly enough, policy-makers did not go on to
analyze the contingency that the attack on the Western position
might in fact flow through this gap. In short, the gap in the deterrence screen was soon being accompanied by a gap in American policy planning.

To be sure, during the winter, the contingency plans for
dealing with an overt Chinese military attack were again studied.[26] But as is so often the case, it was easier to analyze this
clear-cut contingency than the more ambiguous and intractable
but more likely possibility of a Vietminh success achieved without Chinese intervention. The circumstances in which this latter development might occur were, of course, nebulous and difficult to anticipate. Yet from an early stage, American planners
had recognized and even emphasized the important role politi-

---

[25] *Pentagon Papers*, I, 436.

[26] NSC-5404, January 16, 1954 (*Pentagon Papers*, I, 422–23) called for a series of
actions, including use of U.S. air and naval forces to interdict Chinese Communist communication lines, and possibly for a naval blockade of China and for
bombing of military targets in China that contributed directly to the war in Indochina. But any military response by U.S. forces to Chinese intervention, it
was clearly stipulated, should not be on a unilateral basis but under U.N. auspices or as part of a joint effort with France, the United Kingdom, and any other
friendly governments. Noticeably lacking, futhermore, was any statement that
U.S. ground forces would be employed in Indochina.

cal and psychological factors would play in any eventual French defeat in Indochina. Thus for instance NSC-5405, while otherwise pessimistic over the deterioration of French resolve, also emphasized that "with continued U.S. economic and material assistance, the Franco-Vietnamese forces are not in danger of being militarily defeated by the Viet Minh unless there is large-scale Chinese Communist intervention." [27] More difficult to envision or to predict was the effect of lesser military Vietminh successes over a period of time or of a dramatic but localized military success such as Dienbienphu on the political resolution of the French government.

It was only during the winter of 1953–1954 that American policy planners began to give serious study to the question of how to respond should the French appear ready to abandon the struggle, or should they unexpectedly reverse their standing opposition to U.S. involvement and interference in their conduct of the war and demand that American forces be brought in. A substantial interagency debate over U.S. military intervention took place within the administration during the entire winter.[28] Important disagreements emerged quite early among and within the Defense and State Departments and the CIA; and the debate evidently clarified many questions connected with different forms of American military intervention.[29] Despite a strong consensus that Indochina was important to American and Free World security interests, the dilemmas and constraints affecting direct U.S. military intervention were recognized and given substantial weight. What emerged during the interagency debate was a strong and persistent questioning of both the feasibility and the expected effectiveness of available military options. The role army leaders played in the interagency debate was of particular importance: they aggressively challenged the prevalent assumption that U.S. air and naval forces might sal-

[27] *Pentagon Papers*, I, 437.

[28] Important new details of this interagency debate are documented and usefully analyzed in the *Pentagon Papers;* see I, 88–95, 429–54.

[29] The value of multiple advocacy in policy-making is well demonstrated in this case. See George, "The Case for Multiple Advocacy," pp. 751–85.

vage the situation in Indochina without need for substantial U.S. ground forces. In this respect, it may be noted, Army Chief of Staff General Matthew Ridgway was also implicitly challenging a fundamental premise of Eisenhower's New Look defense posture, namely, the hope that the United States could deal with local conflicts in the future by relying on air and naval power to supplement the ground forces of the local defender and, hence, avoid "another Korea."

Since most officials taking part in the interagency debate did not really favor commitment of U.S. ground forces, the question of military intervention hinged on these competing estimates regarding the expected effectiveness of air and naval power (and, of course, the complex and frustrating issues connected with improving the performance and morale of the French). Army spokesmen and the studies they provided reinforced doubts felt within the other services and civilian officials regarding the expected effectiveness of air and naval power; they also warned that initial use of air and naval forces would commit the United States openly to a losing cause and thereby create pressure for commitment of large ground forces. Proponents of U.S. air and naval intervention were sobered by the specter of another Korea; and Eisenhower and his leading defense advisors had to consider whether, notwithstanding the importance they assigned to Indochina, they would scuttle the New Look defense policy even before it had been fully implemented.[30]

Washington's Response to the Dienbienphu Crisis

The battle for Dienbienphu, which had started in January, suddenly reached the stage of crisis in late March and a

---

[30] As Randle notes, the New Look simply did not allow for a major unilateral American commitment of combat ground forces in an area such as Indochina. "Such a commitment would require a major revision of the New Look military strategy as well as a revision of the budget on which that strategy was based." Randle, *Geneva 1954*, p. 49.

fresh and urgent appraisal of the question became necessary. By this time, the administration had already rehearsed the problem of whether and how the United States should intervene militarily. Admittedly, the interagency debate had not settled the issues and was, in fact, still in progress when the Dienbienphu crisis came to a head. The crisis gave fresh momentum to the arguments and pressure for intervention and the administration came very close to intervening; but, the arguments and internal pressures against this course of action that had developed within the administration during the interagency debate, now fortified by congressional opinion, prevailed.

On March 19, 1954, having struggled since January to overcome the critical interpretations placed both at home and abroad on the unfortunate way he had described the administration's reliance on deterrence power,[31] Dulles categorically declared that the policy of Massive Retaliation had "no application" to events within Indochina per se but only to the possibility of Chinese intervention. He acknowledged that there were no suitable targets for nuclear weapons in Indochina and that the war there was "a complicated military-political struggle in which strategic air power was almost totally irrelevant." [32]

Dulles now hurriedly and belatedly moved to strengthen deterrence of the real threat in Indochina, the Vietminh, by attempting to find some other basis for intimidating the Chinese

---

[31] In his January 12, 1953 address to the Council on Foreign Relations Dulles had used the term "massive retaliatory power" in emphasizing that the United States would rely on "a great capacity to retaliate instantly, by means and at places of our choosing." This and other aspects of his speech aroused concern that the administration planned to respond instantly and automatically to any communist aggression with a large strategic nuclear strike. Admiral Radford, Chairman of the Joint Chiefs of Staff, recalls that he was "somewhat appalled" when he read Dulles' speech and later told the Secretary of State that the words he had employed were not descriptive of the administration's new military program: "It was massive deterrent power rather than massive retaliatory power" that the New Look defense program had in mind. Dulles has used "an unfortunate phrase." Quoted in Gerson, *John Foster Dulles*, p. 338; for a detailed account of Dulles' "Massive Retaliation Speech," see also Guhin, *John Foster Dulles*, pp. 221–39.

[32] Quoted in Randle, *Geneva 1954*, p. 71.

and thus preventing the kind of limited, indirect assistance that was providing the Vietminh with the critical margin of superiority they needed and were now utilizing so effectively at Dienbienphu.[33] In a major speech on March 29, Dulles recognized that Peking had "avoided the direct use of their own Red armies in open aggression against Indochina," but he went on to emphasize that U.S. policy was opposed to imposition of communist rule on Southeast Asia "by whatever means." The implication Dulles wished to convey was that the United States might intervene after all, even if there were no major Chinese intervention. In other words, Dulles was deliberately redefining and extending the *casus belli* for American participation to cover contingencies other than Chinese military intervention. At the same time, however, he avoided committing the United States to intervene to avoid a French defeat by employing ambiguous language.[34]

As the Dienbienphu crisis moved toward a possibly catastrophic climax, it revealed the seriousness of the gap in deterrence and in U.S. planning that had been left open since Dulles' September 2 speech. The administration had committed itself only to responding to a major, overt Chinese intervention, thus leaving it to the French to cope with the impact of the in-

---

[33] On Chinese military assistance to the Vietminh, see Chen, *Vietnam and China*, pp. 260–78; Zasloff, *Role of the Sanctuary;* Fall, *Hell in a Very Small Place*, pp. 294, 298; and Gurtov, *First Vietnam Crisis*, pp. 74, 76, 81, 93, 98–99.

On April 15, 1954, Dulles gave a detailed account of the importance of Chinese aid in his testimony before the House Committee on Foreign Affairs; reprinted in *Department of State Bulletin*, XXX, No. 773 (April 19, 1954), pp. 579–83.

[34] Thus, Dulles stated that the possibility of a communist takeover in Indochina "should not be passively accepted, but should be met by *united action . . .*" (emphasis added). Randle, *Geneva 1954*, p. 59 ff. emphasizes that Dulles' threat of "united action" was intended for deterrence purposes and did not signify a decision to intervene should it become necessary. The *Pentagon Papers*, I, 93, support this interpretation in part by revealing that the administration had by no means reached a decision to intervene at this time. Rather, Eisenhower, still opposed to unilateral U.S. intervention, had evidently encouraged and authorized Dulles to explore the possibility of some form of collective action. Thus, besides its intended deterrence value, Dulles' call for "united action" was the beginning of a more intensive effort in the next few weeks to come to an agreement with France and the U.K. for some kind of joint action.

creasing Chinese military aid and supplies. During the autumn and winter the United States had tardily and slowly begun to study what it might do if the Vietminh appeared to be winning even without overt Chinese intervention. Dulles finally moved to fill the gap in the deterrence effort in his "United Action" speech of March 29 and in subsequent statements.

Whether a similar declaration substantially earlier would have deterred or reduced Chinese aid is, of course, an open question. Also open is the question of whether such a declaration would have softened the psychological blow to Paris of the fall of Dienbienphu.

We believe it is more likely, however, that much earlier systematic attention in United States policy-making circles to the gap in U.S. deterrence and to the probability that the opponent would utilize it might well have led to consideration of possible fall-back positions. In actuality, the calculated ambiguity of Dulles' "United Action" speech and subsequent, similar, statements failed to deter the Chinese and Vietminh, while nevertheless succeeding in extending the American commitment and announced interest in Indochina. This policy therefore set the stage for the the later proposals within the administration to intervene in Indochina with air and naval strikes, and even with nuclear weapons. It is at least possible, on the other hand, that an earlier effort to fill the gap in planning and analysis would have uncovered some of the difficulties inherent in this kind of "calculated ambiguity." If so, policy-makers could then have begun analyzing the possibility of retrenching the containment line. Whether the United States could have avoided its later agony in Vietnam by writing off the Associated States and drawing its containment line at, say, Thailand, can naturally never be known.

Conclusions

We have examined three situations in which the Eisenhower Administration, in its first year in office, employed

threats of Massive Retaliation to advance important policy objectives in Korea and Indochina. There were, as noted at the
outset of this chapter, important differences in the structure of
these three situations from the standpoint of the applicability of
deterrence strategy. Whatever might be said about the necessity
and effectiveness of such threats for bringing about the Korean
armistice and for deterring resumption of the war, we note that
the threats were at least suited to the character and relative simplicity of these two situations. Threats to expand the war
beyond the geographical limits of Korea were clearly relevant to
the problem of exerting leverage in the armistice negotiations
and to the additional problem of "enforcing" the armistice
thereafter.

The same cannot be said for the third situation we have examined. Deterrence strategy employing Massive Retaliation
was at best of peripheral relevance for the complex structure of
the situation in Indochina.

We shall focus our conclusions on Indochina, since it illustrates clearly some of the special difficulties Washington encountered in trying to transfer the policy of containment from
Europe to Asia. (We shall see other evidences of this in chapter
9 when we discuss the Taiwan Strait crisis of 1954–1955.) In
Western Europe, the inhabitants had sufficient will to defend
themselves against insurrection and subversion; as a result, the
Soviet Union could expand only by direct military action.
Whether or not Moscow entertained such intentions of doing so,
apprehension that it might had an unsettling effect in Western
Europe, which could be alleviated by the formation of NATO
and the American commitment. In Asia, on the other hand,
powerful anticolonialist and nationalist strivings created internal turmoil and instability in which, as in Indochina, the issue
of communism assumed only peripheral importance. The magnitude and the nature of the resulting internal instability made
it difficult to apply containment. As Robert Osgood notes,

> The significant feature of the Communist advance in Indochina was
> that the Chinese did not need to resort to direct intervention in order
> to attain their objective. Their capacity to support a successful insur-

rection indicates the crucial difference between the problem of containment in Asia and in Europe.[35]

The structure of the conflict in Indochina and its root causes were such as to make it *a nondeterrable phenomenon*. The fact that a nationalist revolt for independence from French colonialism was underway could not be erased by focusing, as American policy-makers did, on the threat of communist expansion implicit in the circumstance of native communist leadership of the struggle. Ho Chi Minh was indeed a communist, but his allegiance was to Vietnam, not to Peking or Moscow. While some American policy-makers toyed with the idea that Ho might prove to be another Tito, this possibility was never explored or encouraged. Instead, from an early stage Acheson decided to regard him as a communist whose aspirations could be viewed only as a threat.[36] French support was needed for containing the Soviet Union in Europe, and, under the circumstances, Acheson was hardly motivated to take a more friendly view of Ho's aspirations at the risk of alienating the French. Added to this, the ideological blinders with which American policy-makers viewed the situation distorted perceptions from an early stage during Truman's Administration. Washington's view of a monolithic worldwide communist threat led by Moscow limited the ability of American leaders to differentiate among different communist opponents and their different motives and goals. Thus, Ho Chi Minh's effort to oust the French from Indochina came to be regarded as part of an Asian manifestation of a worldwide aggressive communist strategy.

At the same time, Washington was well aware of France's colonialist objectives and disapproved of them. This created a genuine dilemma for U.S. policy, but it was one that was eventually resolved in a quixotic attempt to use the French colonialist struggle to further the American policy of containment. Such an attempt was unrealistic as well as unjustified. Not only did the United States seriously damage its liberal international image by giving only lip service to the anticolonialist and na-

[35] Osgood, *Limited War*, p. 223.   [36] *Pentagon Papers*, I, 50–52.

tionalist aspirations in Indochina; its effort to compensate for this by attempting to use the French colonial war for purposes of containment was never more than a poor gamble. For Washington's containment objective became inextricably connected with the French effort to maintain a colonial position in Indochina. The unreality of Washington's policy consisted in its inability or refusal to see that French colonialist objectives would frustrate and defeat its desire to make Indochina into a bastion of containment against Communist China.

Imbedded in the structure of the situation in Indochina was the stubborn and fundamental fact that France and the United States were pursuing different and conflicting objectives. Unlike Truman and Eisenhower, the French were not interested in erecting a containment barrier against Communist China in Southeast Asia; rather, they hoped to salvage as much of their colonial position as possible. Conflicting American and French objectives in Indochina created, in turn, fundamental disagreements over the means to be employed. In Washington's view the French should grant genuine independence to the Indochinese states in order to rouse the population's motivation to participate more effectively in military and administrative efforts to prevent a Vietminh success. Washington hoped that viable, noncommunist states and armies might be established that would permit eventual French military disengagement without risk of a communist takeover. But the French government was unwilling to adopt such political measures to enhance its war effort because, quite simply, full independence for the Associated States of Indochina was not compatible with its war objectives or its conception of the national interests engaged in the conflict in Indochina.

The Pentagon Papers are replete with indications that U.S. military and civilian officials alike were well aware that France's colonialist objectives and policies in Indochina were severely hampering efforts to bring in the local inhabitants on the French side of the struggle against the Vietminh. Apart from advising that this situation be changed, the U.S. could do little. Washington lacked leverage to impose on Paris policy recommendations that were anathema to the French; and recognizing this, U.S. policy-makers gradually placed greater emphasis and hopes on the military side of the struggle.

Given this structure of the situation, the outcome of the colonialist war in Indochina was not likely to be dependent upon or very sensitive to the application of deterrence strategy against Communist China by the United States. The more important threat was the internal one, and French policy itself did much to exacerbate it. What is more, the French were not as strongly motivated to remain in Indochina as Washington wished them to be. Ironically, Washington placed greater value on *its* objective of containment in Indochina than the French did on *their* objective of maintaining a colonialist position. Apart from paying an increasingly large proportion of the costs of the war to the French, thereby doubtless prolonging the conflict in Indochina, there was little the United States could do to enable the French to deal with the Vietminh. Not only was Washington reluctant to send its own forces, particularly ground forces, into Indochina, but in any case French policy consistently and firmly excluded any direct U.S. military participation, until the catastrophe at Dienbienphu became imminent. Even then, the French government wanted only limited American air support. The French opposed any kind of internationalization of their war or military coalition—at first because they did not want to jeopardize achievement of their colonialist objective by sharing control of the war with allies; and later, at the time of the Dienbienphu crisis, because they did not want to jeopardize their effort to negotiate their way out of the war by allowing the Geneva conference to become enmeshed in the Cold War policies and calculations of the Eisenhower Administration.

From the standpoint of deterrence theory, therefore, the Indochina case indicates once again that deterrence strategy cannot be expected to make up for or rescue a poorly conceived or unrealistic foreign policy. This case also exemplifies a theme discussed in chapter 2 regarding the frustrations and dangers of attempts to employ strategic and limited-war concepts of deterrence to the complex crisis-preventative type of situation. Deterrence strategy is not easily applied, we have seen, to dissuading a major power (Communist China in this case) from giving military and economic assistance to one side in a colonial or civil war. The threat of Massive Retaliation to deter a major Chinese military intervention did not affect Peking's important role as a supplier of the Vietminh. If anything, it offered Peking indirect assurance that it was safe to do so. For by specifying that the threat of retaliation applied to Chinese military intervention Dulles thereby defined the *casus belli* or threshold for an American response in such a way as to suggest that the Chinese could safely supply the Vietminh without triggering a U.S. military response.

There was, therefore, an important gap in U.S. deterrence policy which, as we noted, reflected another gap in policy planning. The administration simply had not decided what it would do if it appeared the French were about to be defeated by the Vietminh without a Chinese military intervention. Washington's ability to design a more comprehensive deterrence policy, covering all threats and contingencies, was severely constrained by political and military considerations. Unfortunately for Washington's effort to promote containment in Indochina, the gaps in its deterrence effort and in its policy plans included precisely the most serious threats and the most likely contingencies. For, despite all its posturing about the critical importance of Indochina, the fact was that Washington had not really made a commitment to prevent a Vietminh success under any and all circumstances. The administration was constrained from doing so by its unwillingness to intervene unilaterally, without some form of joint action with Britain and France; by its justified reluctance to put American military power at the disposal of French colonialist objectives; and by its determination in any case to avoid committing large ground forces. Eisenhower reflected the dilemmas and constraints that lay at the root of the administration's ambivalence and apparent indecisiveness about intervention when he explained to reporters at the end of April that the administration had been "trying to steer a course between the unobtainable and the unacceptable in Indochina."

Bibliography

The major sources on the strategy employed by the Eisenhower Administration to bring the Korean armistice negotiations to a close are Eisenhower, Adams, and Donovan. Rees provides a good summary and interpretation. For the Indochina account we have relied on the detailed analyses of Gurtov, Randle, and the *Pentagon Papers* (Senator Gravel edition, Vol. I); the last source includes documentation of important details in U.S. policy planning. Useful accounts of the development of Dulles' deterrence theory and his use of Massive Retaliation type threats are provided by Gerson (pp. 68–80, 144–51, 156–57) and by Guhin (pp. 221–39).

For earlier research on some aspects of the Indochina case we are indebted to Jane Howland.

Acheson, Dean. *Present at the Creation.* New York, Norton, 1969; chapter 70.

Adams, Sherman. *Firsthand Report: The Story of the Eisenhower Administration.* New York, Harper & Bros., 1961.

Baldwin, Hanson. "Lessons of Dienbienphu: Too Little and Too Late," *New York Times,* May 16, 1954, sect. 4, p. 5.

Bator, Victor. *Vietnam—A Diplomatic Tragedy: The Origins of the United States Involvement.* New York, Oceana, 1965.

Beal, John Robinson. *John Foster Dulles: 1888–1959.* New York, Harper & Bros., 1959.

Chen, King C. *Vietnam and China, 1938–1954.* Princeton, Princeton University Press, 1969.

Clark, General Mark. *From the Danube to the Yalu.* New York, Harper & Bros., 1954.

Donovan, Robert J. *Eisenhower: The Inside Story.* New York, Harper & Bros., 1956.

Dulles, John Foster. "A Policy of Boldness," *Life,* May 19, 1952, pp. 146–60.

Eden, Anthony. *The Memoirs of Anthony Eden: Full Circle.* Boston, Houghton Mifflin, 1960.

Eisenhower, Dwight D., *The White House Years: Mandate for Change: 1953–1956.* Garden City, N.Y., Doubleday, 1963.

Fall, Bernard B. *Hell in a Very Small Place: The Seige of Dienbienphu.* New York, Lippincott, 1967.

——. *The Two Viet-Nams: A Political and Military Analysis.* New York, Praeger, 1963.

George, Alexander L., David K. Hall, and William E. Simons. *The Limits of Coercive Diplomacy.* Boston, Little, Brown, 1971.

Gerson, Louis L. *John Foster Dulles.* New York, Cooper Square Publishers, 1967.

Guhin, Michael A. *John Foster Dulles: A Statesman and His Times.* New York, Columbia University Press, 1972.

Gurtov, Melvin. *The First Vietnam Crisis: Chinese Communist Strategy and United States Involvement, 1953–1954.* New York, Columbia University Press, 1967.

Hinton, Harold C. *Communist China in World Politics.* Boston, Houghton Mifflin, 1966.

Kahin, G. M., and J. W. Lewis. *The United States in Vietnam.* New York, Dial, 1967.

Lacouture, Jean, and Philippe Devillers. *La Fin d'une guerre: Indochine 1954.* Paris, Editions du Seuil, 1960.

Lancaster, Donald. *The Emancipation of French Indochina.* London, Oxford University Press, under the auspices of the Royal Institute of International Affairs, 1961.

Morgenthau, Hans J. "John Foster Dulles," in *An Uncertain Tradition: American Secretaries of State in Twentieth Century* ed. Norman A. Graebner. New York, McGraw-Hill, 1961.

Osgood, Robert Endicott. *Limited War: The Challenge to American Strategy.* Chicago, University of Chicago Press, 1957.

Pentagon Papers, The. Senator Gravel Edition. 4 vols. Boston, Beacon Press, n.d.

Randle, Robert F. *Geneva 1954.* Princeton, Princeton University Press, 1969.

Rees, David. *Korea: The Limited War.* New York, St. Martin's Press, 1964.

Ridgway, Matthew B., as told to Harold H. Martin. *Soldier: The Memoirs of Matthew B. Ridgway.* New York, Harper & Bros., 1956.

Roberts, Chalmers H. "The Day We Didn't Go to War," *The Reporter,* XI (September 14, 1954), 31–35.

Salisbury, Harrison E. "Image and Reality in Indochina," *Foreign Affairs,* 49, No. 3 (April 1971), 381–94.

Schelling, Thomas C. *Arms and Influence.* New Haven, Yale University Press, 1966.

Shepley, James. "How Dulles Averted War," *Life,* January 16, 1956, pp. 70–80.

Snyder, Glenn. "The 'New Look' of 1953" in Warner R. Schilling, Paul Y. Hammond, and Glenn H. Snyder, *Strategy, Politics, and Defense Budgets.* New York, Columbia University Press, 1962.

U.S. Department of State. *American Foreign Policy 1950–1955: Basic Documents.* 2 vols. Washington, D.C., Department of State Publication No. 6446, 1957.

"What Ridgway Told Ike—War in Indo-China Would be Tougher than Korea," *U.S. News & World Report,* June 25, 1954, pp. 30–33.

Zasloff, J. J. *The Role of the Sanctuary in Insurgency: Communist China's Support to the Vietminh 1946–1954.* RAND RM-4618-PR. Santa Monica, The RAND Corporation, May 1967; pp. 54–67.

Chapter 9

The Taiwan Strait Crisis, 1954–1955

The Significance of the Crisis

THE INDOCHINA CRISIS was hardly over when another major confrontation developed between the United States and Communist China, this time in the Taiwan Strait. In Eisenhower's words, the Strait crisis which began in September 1954 and dragged on for nine months was to "threaten a split between the United States and nearly all its allies, and seemingly carry the country to the edge of war, thus constituting one of the most serious problems of the first eighteen months of my administration." [1]

If, as seems likely, Peking did intend to wrest Quemoy and Matsu, the most important of the offshore islands in the Taiwan Strait, from the Nationalists, then one can regard American actions during the crisis as achieving a partial deterrence success. The Chinese Communists did not launch an all-out attack, and the islands remained in Nationalist hands. But the success was achieved at considerable cost, as Eisenhower's reflection suggests. Despite the obvious difficulties of attempting to protect an isolated outpost, so vividly demonstrated by the Berlin blockade of 1948, the administration proceeded to enter into a commitment to islands that lay only a few miles from the Chinese mainland and within range of direct artillery fire from Chi-

[1] Eisenhower, *Mandate for Change*, p. 459.

nese Communist batteries. Moreover, if the American commitment deterred an all-out Chinese Communist attack on Quemoy and Matsu, it did not deter Peking from employing lesser options at its disposal to create controlled pressures with which to test and, if possible, to erode the U.S. commitment. This case, therefore, must be regarded as an example of a partial failure of deterrence, as well as a partial success.

The crisis did much to erode confidence in the judgment and good sense of the administration at home and abroad. It aroused keen anxiety regarding the administration's apparent willingness to risk war to help the Nationalists retain control of Quemoy, "the Staten Island of Communist China," as it was called by critics of the administration's policy.

If deterrence was successful in the end, it must also be said that deterrence strategy had been stretched to the limit in this crisis. Had the time bought by this success been used to persuade Chiang Kai-shek to evacuate the offshore islands, so that the basis for a similar crisis in the future would be removed, one might be able to find some justification for the administration's stubborn unwillingness to allow the Chinese Communists to acquire territory through military action or pressure. But after the crisis ended, the administration made only half-hearted, ineffectual efforts to persuade Chiang to downgrade the political and psychological significance of Quemoy and Matsu to the Nationalist cause. The Chinese Communists were free, therefore, to apply controlled pressure against these islands again whenever they thought it useful to do so. It came as no surprise when a similar crisis over Quemoy erupted in the summer of 1958.

The Development of the Deterrence Commitment

Prior to the Korean War, President Truman had held firmly to his controversial policy of avoiding American military involvement on the Nationalist side in the Chinese civil war. Truman had been prepared to accept the fall of Taiwan, to which Chiang Kai-shek's forces had retreated from the mainland in 1949. This development was expected, in fact, before the end of 1950, and it would have signified for all practical purposes the end of the Chinese civil war. However, shocked into action by the North Korean attack on South Korea, Truman at once reversed his policy on Taiwan. At the same time that he ordered American military force to be used to assist the South Koreans, he found it expedient to use the Seventh Fleet to "neutralize" Taiwan and the nearby Pescadores. At first this appeared to be a temporary move that would be undone once peace was restored in Korea. During the weeks that followed the decision, however, it became increasingly evident that Truman would find it difficult to reverse policy once again, and that he did not contemplate withdrawing protection from Taiwan in the event that a return to the status quo ante could be arranged in Korea. During the summer the administration began to suggest that the future status of Taiwan should be determined by "international action," perhaps through the United Nations.

The intervention of the Chinese Communists in the Korean War further strengthened ties between the United States and Nationalist China. In a bilateral Mutual Defense Assistance Agreement in February 1951 the United States undertook to provide military assistance to Taiwan. At the same time, however, Truman sought to limit the scope and objectives of this assistance by stipulating that the Nationalist government confine the use of American military aid to maintaining "internal security" and "legitimate self-defense." Support for Nationalist operations against the mainland was thereby excluded. In addition, the training and equipment furnished Nationalist forces on Taiwan were tied to the understanding that they would not be sent to the offshore islands, which were still held by Nationalist forces.

The offshore islands include several groups of small islands, numbering altogether about thirty, that are close to the mainland in the Taiwan Strait. The Quemoys, comprising 60 square miles altogether, block the port of Amoy, only two miles away on the Chinese mainland. Further north in the Strait are the 19 Matsu islands, covering 12 miles altogether, but placed only 10 miles away from the port of Foochow on the mainland. The Quemoy and Matsu islands, it should be noted, had always been under the control of the government on the mainland. Unlike Taiwan and the Pescadores, they had not been held by Japan after the Sino-Japanese war of 1894–1895. The Tachen Islands, lying about 200 miles north of Taiwan, were much less significant to the Nationalists than were Quemoy and Matsu, and were also more difficult for the Nationalists to defend. The Nanchi (Nanki) Islands, lying to the south of the Tachens, were some 75 miles closer to Taiwan and hence somewhat easier to defend.[2]

Earlier, when Truman ordered the Seventh Fleet to patrol the Taiwan Strait to prevent Communist Chinese attacks on Taiwan, he had excluded the offshore islands from his protective "neutralization" order. However, although not prepared to defend these islands, the administration was also unwilling to provoke the strong supporters of the Nationalists within Congress and in the country by making a clear statement to this effect.

Despite Truman's effort to limit the American commitment strictly to the defense of Taiwan and the Pescadores, it had become evident well before Eisenhower came into office in January 1953 that the Nationalist regime was going to play a role in the gradually evolving policy of containment of Communist China. Two developments, the prolongation of the Korean War and the election of Eisenhower, gave new impetus to containment, and, in fact, pushed U.S. policy toward Communist China *beyond* containment. In order to put pressure on the communist side to negotiate an armistice in Korea, Eisenhower announced shortly after coming into office that the Seventh Fleet would no longer prevent Chinese Nationalist forces from

[2] When the artillery shelling of Quemoy began on September 3, Nationalist forces numbered approximately 9,000 on the Matsus and 15,000 on Quemoy. Eisenhower, *Mandate for Change*, pp. 461–62.

mounting operations against the mainland from Taiwan. During the presidential election, Republican campaign oratory had emphasized that the United States should move beyond the containment of communism to the goal of "liberation" of the communist satellites. Eisenhower's "unleashing" of Chiang Kai-shek created the impression that his administration was prepared to use more vigorous methods to "roll back" communism.

Although Eisenhower's "unleashing" order was designed largely for purposes of psychological warfare and was accompanied in private by U.S. constraints in Chiang's freedom of action, it encouraged important elements of his administration and, of course, the Nationalist government as well, to press for a more "positive" policy of support for Taiwan. While a detailed, authoritative account of these developments is not yet available, the memoirs of the U.S. Ambassador to Taiwan, Karl Rankin, provide glimpses of complicated maneuvers and bargaining between American and Nationalist officials which deepened and extended the U.S. commitment. It is clear that in mid-1953 American military and diplomatic officials in Taiwan pressed a reluctant Chiang Kai-shek to increase and strengthen his forces on the offshore islands.[3]

Behind this advice to Chiang lay a rigid conception of containment that sought to exclude loss of any territory, even islands a few miles from the mainland that were admittedly not necessary for the defense of Taiwan and not easily defensible against a determined Chinese Communist attack. George Kennan was later to deplore the "militarization" of containment that was brought about by the Korean War. One example of it was American pressure on Chiang in 1953 to build up his forces on the offshore islands in order to deny the Chinese Communists an easy conquest of them. This was a short-sighted and costly extension of containment. Chiang was gratuitously provided with bargaining leverage to press for increased U.S. sup-

[3] Rankin, *China Assignment*, pp. 167–69; Alsop, "The Story Behind Quemoy," pp. 86–87; Alsop, "Quemoy: We Asked For It," p. 18; Tsou, *The Embroilment over Quemoy*, pp. 6–7; Halperin and Tsou, "United States Policy Toward the Offshore Islands," pp. 122–23.

port and, after committing larger forces and his prestige to the defense of the offshore islands, he would then be in a position to convert Chinese Communist action against these islands into a vehicle for trying to entice the United States into a larger war with Communist China.

In other ways as well, the requirements of containment as interpreted by Dulles drew the United States closer to Chiang Kai-shek and gave the Generalissimo leverage with which to nourish hopes of U.S. assistance in regaining the mainland. The collapse of the French in Indochina in 1954 led Dulles to organize the Southeast Asia Treaty Organization (SEATO) which, because of the coolness of some of the member states to Chiang Kai-shek, omitted Nationalist China from membership. Earlier, the United States had concluded a separate peace treaty with Japan and signed a mutual defense treaty with South Korea. These events led the Nationalist government to press the United States for a similar treaty. The commitment which Truman had made to defend Taiwan and which Eisenhower had continued was simply a unilateral assertion of U.S. policy and, as such, did not constitute as firm or as stable a commitment from the Nationalist standpoint as would a mutual defense treaty. Dulles, in fact, needed little persuasion from Chiang to move in this direction, since a treaty with the Nationalist government coincided with his own desire to establish a ring of military alliances around Communist China.

Negotiations between the two governments regarding the defense treaty were well under way when on September 3 the Chinese Communist shore batteries began a heavy artillery shelling of Quemoy Island. Thereafter, Chiang Kai-shek sought to have the offshore islands included within the scope of the defense guarantee. Further, he tried to obtain a wording of the treaty that would imply not merely U.S. support for Nationalist claims to the mainland but also a tacit willingness to assist in defending any former territory that the Nationalist government might regain in the future! [4] The dominant opinion in Washing-

[4] Rankin, *China Assignment*, pp. 195–6.

ton was opposed to these requests, and the administration would commit itself in the treaty to defend only Taiwan and the Pescadores. The offshore islands were not mentioned in the treaty, which was finally concluded in December 1954, and it was understood that they lay outside the defense commitment.

Indeed, as a *quid pro quo* for granting Chiang the defense treaty, the administration received assurances that the Nationalists would not undertake offensive action against the mainland without prior American approval. At the same time, however, the administration passed up the opportunity afforded by Chiang Kai-shek's desire for a defense treaty to insist that the Nationalists withdraw from the offshore islands. Moreover, the treaty included a minimal concession to the desire of the Nationalist government and its American supporters that some allusion, at least, be made to Chiang's aspirations for returning to the mainland. Thus, the treaty contained a stipulation that its provisions would "be applicable to such other territories as may be determined by mutual agreement." This did not commit the United States in any way to extend the defense commitment; but it could be regarded as leaving the door open to possible reconsideration of the matter in the future. This loophole served to nourish the hopes of those who wanted stronger U.S. assistance to the Chinese Nationalist cause.

Assumptions behind the Development of the Deterrence Commitment

In the light of later history this drift toward a stronger commitment to the Nationalist Chinese may seem difficult to understand. But it was consistent with assumptions which were widely accepted at the time. Many officials in Eisenhower's administration operated with what might be called a "devil image" of the Chinese Communists. For them Peking was the "lawless aggressor" of the Korean War who had defied the United Nations and succeeded in fighting the United States to a standstill. There was little appreciation of the true reasons for the Chinese intervention in the Korean War, analyzed earlier (see chapter 7). The fact that Peking had felt obliged to respond to the provocative American policy of attempting to unify Korea through force of arms was ignored and, instead, American policy-makers overgeneralized from the fact of Chinese military intervention to conclude that Peking relied on military force as the chief instrument of its foreign policy. Dulles and other leading administration officials perceived the Chinese Communists as having aggressive designs throughout Asia, but particularly Southeast Asia, which they would carry forward if not resolutely opposed and deterred by the threat of U.S. military power.

Of particular significance for this case study is the additional fact that many officials in the Eisenhower Administration did not regard the Chinese Communist victory over the Nationalists as the final outcome of the Chinese civil war. The Chinese Communist leaders' hold over the Chinese people was regarded as tenuous, and their ability to develop and maintain a viable, stable central government was questioned. To the premise that the communist regime on the mainland might well be a transitory phenomenon was added a desire to find ways of encouraging its demise. While Eisenhower was sympathetic with these views and ready to pursue the goal of containing and eroding, if possible, the Chinese Communist regime, he was unwilling to do so by means that risked another war. In this he differed from some of the hawks in his own administration.

The application of deterrence strategy to contain Communist China during these years was much more problematical and risky than it was against the Soviet Union in Europe, since the structure of the situation in Asia differed in important respects from the European one. Applying containment and deterrence against the Soviet Union was made easier by the fact that the Soviets were, in a sense, willing to be contained. They had no unsatisfied irredentist claims; moreover, they had enhanced their security by acquiring control of countries on their border in Eastern Europe. In contrast, the Communist Chinese were by no means a satisfied power. They had yet to liquidate their rival in the civil war and to recover Taiwan. The threat which the Nationalist regime posed to Peking's security interests was much magnified by the fact that the United States was drawing closer to Chiang and giving him increasing support.

In Asia, therefore, the United States was attempting to apply containment to a dangerously fluid situation in which fundamental issues of sovereignty and boundaries were not yet settled. The rhetoric of "liberation" and the means, however limited, thus far employed on its behalf by the United States were highly threatening to the Chinese Communists. And this was all the more true since, in contrast to the Soviet Union, the Chinese Communist government was not recognized diplomatically by the strongest and most hostile of its opponents. Not only did the United States withhold diplomatic recognition and effectively oppose Peking's admission to the United Nations; it also allied itself with the Chinese Nationalists, thus intervening in the Chinese civil war.

Moreover, there was as yet little articulate sentiment within the Eisenhower Administration for a "two Chinas" solution to the conflict between the communists and the Nationalists. Instead, important members of the administration favored a policy of improving the offensive as well as the defensive capability of the Nationalist forces in order to pose a threat to the mainland and to keep open the possibility, should favorable circumstances develop, of permitting and assisting the Nationalists to return to the mainland. Thus, for example, in a congressional hearing in 1954, Congressman Coudert asked the Assistant Secretary of State for the Far East, Walter Robertson, the following question: "Did I correctly understand you to say that the heart of the present policy toward China and Taiwan is that there is to be kept alive a constant threat of military action vis-à-vis Red China in the hope that at some point there will be an internal breakdown?" Robertson replied: "Yes, sir, that is my conception." [5]

Peking, then, was amply justified in regarding the United

[5] Quoted by Sigal, "The 'Rational Policy' Model and the Formosa Straits Crisis," p. 126.

States as fundamentally hostile and unwilling to accept the continued existence of the communist regime.[6] At the same time, it is probably true that Peking perceived American intentions as being more dangerous than they actually were. Whereas in the Korean War Truman and Acheson had acted more provocatively than they knew, even while offering Peking assurances that their intentions were not hostile, the Eisenhower Administration, on the other hand, spoke more threateningly than it acted. In part, this was because of Dulles' penchant for a strong declaratory policy—for example, Massive Retaliation—in the interest of deterrence. But not all the harsh and threatening statements by hawks in Eisenhower's administration reflected administration policy. Like Truman earlier, Eisenhower, too, had a problem with hawks in his administration who expressed their sentiments too openly.

The situation in Asia, we are emphasizing, was not neatly structured for a classical *defensive* application of deterrence strategy. The containment lines were not as clearly or as firmly drawn in Asia as in Europe. The U.S. assertion of deterrence in order to defend the Chinese Nationalists on Taiwan was in fact a provocative, offensive encroachment from the standpoint of Peking. This was a situation in which who was defending what against whom was perceived quite differently by the two sides, a fact which, of course, lay at the root of the special risks attending the effort to use deterrence to implement containment.

Unlike the Russians in Europe, as we have suggested, the Chinese Communists could not cooperate by accepting containment for several reasons. Not only would accepting containment require Peking to sacrifice some of its vital interests, it would also commit Peking to sitting passively while Chiang and the United States decided how far to go in assisting the hoped-for collapse of the Chinese Communist regime on the mainland. In other words, given the peculiar and fluid structure of the sit-

[6] Peking's view of U.S. intentions in this regard was shaped both by the various public indications of the Eisenhower Administration's increased support for the Nationalist regime and by its awareness of CIA activities launched against the mainland from the various offshore islands.

uation at this time in Asia, "containment" and "liberation"
overlapped and could not be easily distinguished as separate
policies by either Peking or Washington. In this dangerous situation it would have been surprising if crises had not developed
that threatened to plunge the United States and Communist
China into a new war.

The Initiator's Motivation and Calculations

From this review of the assumptions of American policy in
the Far East, it is clear that Peking was fully justified in perceiving acute dangers to its security. Furthermore, Peking had to
anticipate that at any time a combination of pressure from Taiwan and from hawks in Washington might succeed in pushing
American policy on a truly aggressive path, aimed at undoing
the outcome of the civil war on the mainland. Nor were Peking's fears eased by the rapid growth during the period of
1952–1955 of American nuclear capabilities, both strategic and
tactical.

The fundamental policy question for Peking, therefore, was
whether or not to wait passively and act nonprovocatively in the
hope that the dangers latent in this situation would not materialize. The alternative would be to take initiatives from time to
time in carefully controlled probes, generating political, military, and diplomatic pressures that might resolve the ambiguities of the situation in a more favorable manner or, at least,
weaken the ability of the Nationalists and hawks to conspire effectively against Communist China's interests.

On several occasions Peking chose to take the initiative in the
Taiwan Strait rather than accepting the risks of passivity. The
result on one occasion was the crisis of 1954–1955, which we
are considering in the present chapter. Several years later, another "initiative" or "response" by Peking to actual, imagined,
or expected maneuvers by its opponent was to result in the
Quemoy crisis of 1958, which we shall discuss in chapter 12.

Still another crisis, though of lesser proportions, erupted in the Taiwan Strait in 1962.

Given lack of access to the policy calculations of Chinese Communist leaders, it is difficult to infer reliably the *detailed* perceptions they had of the opportunities and threats, or the *precise* definition of the situation which led Peking to initiate controlled pressures in 1954–1955, 1958, and 1962. But for our purposes it is not necessary to strive for a fine-tuned image of these variables. The essentials of the deterrence situation can be derived from an outline (in which we can have considerable confidence) of the logic of Peking's position.

The Chinese Communist regime was sustaining, actually and potentially, many kinds of damage and risk from the Nationalist control of the offshore islands. From these vantage points the Nationalists launched guerrilla, intelligence, and propaganda activities against the mainland and denied Peking control and free use of its own harbors, coastline, and coastal waters. Nationalist occupation and military use of these islands also had great political and symbolic significance for both sides. It was an affront to Peking and a reminder of the military weakness and vulnerability that contributed in some measure to its domestic instability. For the Nationalists, as Peking was only too well aware, their military occupation of islands just a few miles from the mainland served to keep alive their hope of an eventual return to the mainland. Peking's controlled pressures on these islands were its way of deterring and eroding these Nationalist aspirations. Whether or not Peking was really bent on wresting control of these islands at this time, its willingness to use military force against them and to generate a controlled confrontation with U.S. military power in the straits signified and reemphasized its continuing commitment to "liberate" Taiwan eventually and to complete its defeat of the Nationalists, which U.S. intervention had prevented.

Seen in this light, the risks of passivity on Peking's part become clearer. The Chinese Communists did not have the military capabilities for defying the U.S. commitment to Taiwan and saw no reason to engage in a heroic but highly risky direct military challenge. On the other hand, lesser military options were available to Peking for protecting and advancing its interests through a strategy of controlled pressures that entailed limited risk of provoking an overreaction from the U.S. military forces. By exercising low-level military actions, such as artillery shelling of Quemoy, Peking could call attention to the danger of another major war inherent in American support for the Nationalist regime. It could hope that antiwar sentiment within the United States and elsewhere might exert effective pressure to limit and erode the American commitment to Chiang. A controlled but tense crisis in the Taiwan Strait might also strengthen the influence on American policy of those members of the Eisenhower Administration and Congress who either were only lukewarm supporters of the Chinese Nationalists or who were unwilling to accept risks of another major war as the price of supporting Chiang's aspirations. A controlled crisis might also appear attractive to Peking as a means of introducing more sobriety into Washington's calculations and motivating it to impose greater constraints on the deployment and on the activities of Nationalist forces in order to prevent Chiang from dragging the United States into another war with Communist China, this time on his behalf. Thereby, too, Peking could hope to exacerbate latent tensions in U.S.-Nationalist relations and put itself in a position to widen any fissures that developed.

Inducing more sobriety in Taipei and Washington may have seemed particularly necessary to Peking as 1954 progressed. In his New Year's message that year, Chiang Kai-shek had pledged an attack on the mainland "in the not too distant future." Later, in an Easter message, Chiang called for a "holy war" against the communists, and during the month of May air and naval clashes occurred between the two sides in the Formosa Straits. In July Syngman Rhee, President of the South Korean Republic, gave a speech before a joint session of the U.S. Congress in which he called for American air and naval support for a combined Nationalist and South Korean invasion of the Chinese mainland.

On August 11 Chou En-lai, Premier of the People's Republic of China, denounced American support for the Nationalist regime and called for the "liberation" of Taiwan. Eisenhower concedes that Chou's speech came "as if in reply" to the earlier statements of Chiang and Rhee. Indeed, between the lines of his carefully phrased account Eisenhower tacitly recognizes that Chou was responding to the provocative threats which Chiang and Rhee, and their American supporters, were direct-ing toward Peking.

At the same time, however, it is unlikely that Eisenhower appreciated the full impact such statements and promotional ac-tivities had upon Peking's perception of the threat. Eisenhower himself had no intention of encouraging or supporting an in-vasion of the mainland. He had defined his famous order "un-leashing" the Nationalists to exclude such adventures. But Pe-king was forced to formulate its view of American intentions without benefit of firm indications of the constraints which Ei-senhower imposed on support of Nationalist aspirations. Thus, for example, Chinese Communist leaders probably were not aware that at the time of the "unleashing" statement Ambas-sador Rankin had privately indicated to Chiang Kai-shek that this constituted no change in the American policy of nonsupport for an invasion of the mainland, and that the United States ex-pected to be consulted by the Nationalists before any decision of this kind was made.[7] From Peking's standpoint, rather, there was sufficient indication that U.S. policy-makers had not drawn a firm line on how far to go in supporting Chiang. Hence a pol-icy of vigorously asserting Communist China's claim to Taiwan and demonstrating its resolution by artillery shelling of Que-moy may have recommended itself to Peking as the best way of influencing the fluid situation.[8]

[7] Rankin, *China Assignment*, p. 155.

[8] It is also possible, as Alice Hsieh suggests, that Peking may have hoped that its controlled probe in the strait would feel out Soviet deterrent capabilities and Moscow's willingness to bring them into play on behalf of Chinese Communist objectives vis-à-vis Taiwan. Hsieh, *Communist China's Strategy* pp. 17–19. But if so, it soon became evident that the Soviet Union was reluctant to back Pe-king's moves. Khrushchev arrived in Peking in late September after the artillery shelling of Quemoy had commenced. He contented himself, however, with very cautious, noncommital expressions of sympathy with Peking's desire to "lib-erate" Taiwan.

The Defender's Response to Warning

In his memoirs Eisenhower acknowledges that the heavy Chinese Communist artillery shelling of Quemoy which began on September 3 "did not come as a complete surprise." [9] There is no indication that the administration took Chou's statement of August 11 as a warning of serious Chinese Communist military action against Taiwan in the near future. Nevertheless, when coupled with reports of a buildup of Chinese Communist strength on the mainland opposite Taiwan, Chou's statement constituted warning, however equivocal, of some kind of new action by the Chinese Communists in the Taiwan Strait. And perhaps Eisenhower was additionally moved to reinforce deterrence by Chou's explicit warning against American interference with Peking's efforts to "liberate" Taiwan. And so, when Eisenhower was asked in a press conference on August 17 "what would happen . . . if the Communists did attack Taiwan in force," he felt obliged, or took the opportunity, to remind Peking that the Seventh Fleet's orders to protect Taiwan were still in force. "Therefore," he added in response to the question, "I would assume what would happen is this: any invasion of Taiwan would have to run over the Seventh Fleet."

What was to be called into question, however, was not the U.S. commitment to Taiwan and the Pescadores but rather whether it extended also to the offshore islands. Peking continued to call for the "liberation" of Taiwan, communist troops assembled at bases opposite the offshore islands, and military activity increased in the Taiwan Strait. Then on August 26 forty Chinese Communist raiders struck on Quemoy Island, killing ten Nationalists. Heavy artillery bombardment of Quemoy began on the morning of September 3 and continued sporadically thereafter.

Peking had initiated a limited probe. How far it would go was not clear; perhaps this would depend on how Washington

[9] Eisenhower, *Mandate for Change*, p. 462.

clarified and signaled its policy with regard to Quemoy and the other offshore islands. From Peking's standpoint the response Eisenhower had made to its initiative thus far was incomplete. Not only did additional questions connected with U.S. support for Chiang Kai-shek remain to be clarified; in addition, there was the important question of how the United States would cope with the difficult task of "operationalizing" its commitment to the Nationalists when it was subjected to carefully controlled pressures.

The clarification of U.S. support for Chiang came in stages. The preexisting U.S. commitment to defend Taiwan and the Pescadores was emphatically reiterated by Eisenhower in the August press conference, and imbedded in the mutual defense treaty of a few months later. As the crisis deepened, a new commitment was made, extending U.S. protection—albeit with some ambiguity—to the Quemoys and Matsus lying just a few miles off the Chinese mainland. But at the same time, Washington also made it clear that no American help would be given to the defense of the Tachens and Nanchis, other offshore islands which were also occupied by Nationalist forces for awhile. The problems of how these differentiated commitments were generated, and how the U.S. would try to operationalize them demand some further attention.

The Problem of the Defender's Response: the Struggle to Define American Policy

The Chinese Communist shelling of Quemoy in September initiated a major policy debate among Eisenhower's principal advisers that extended far beyond the immediate question of what response to make to the threat to Quemoy. Indeed, this question could not be separated from the larger one of defining more clearly the nature of American commitment to the Nationalist regime on Formosa. At this time, the administration had under active consideration Chiang Kai-shek's request for a formal defense treaty. Important questions concerning the extent to which Washington would wish to go in encouraging and assisting Chiang to return to the mainland were brought to the surface by the need for a careful consideration of the provisions and language to be incorporated into the treaty and by Chiang's other requests.

Eisenhower quickly found himself at the center of a major disagreement within his circle of advisers.[10] He was also subjected to extreme pressures for and against a strong stand from domestic opinion and from abroad. Eisenhower's problem over the next six months, working under these severe pressures, would be to define and apply the U.S. commitment without being drawn into the Chinese civil war in such a way as to risk a general war with Communist China.

As we shall see, Eisenhower was finally led to extend the U.S. commitment to Quemoy and Matsu, despite his considerable reluctance to do so. While the materials for a detailed historical analysis of policy-making are not available, enough is known to make certain general observations with confidence. Faced with extreme pressures both for and against support of the Nationalists, Eisenhower attempted to find a middle ground that would represent the least departure from current U.S. policies toward the Chinese problem.

Illustrated here, therefore, is one of the major limitations of traditional deterrence theory that were noted in chapter 3. Deterrence theory, we may recall, has been based on an oversimplified assumption drawn from decision and game theory that the government of each side in the conflict situation is a *unitary* actor. That is, deterrence theory views each government as if it were a single decision-maker who perceives the situation as an individual would, constructs his payoffs and selects a strategy that is expected to be of maximum utility to him. In fact, however, the decisions taken by a government are often

[10] Opposition within the administration to stronger support for the Nationalist government is described in some detail in Alsop, "The Story behind Quemoy." Army Chief of Staff General Matthew Ridgway's opposition is noted by Eisenhower, in *Mandate for Change*, p. 463.

the result of a many-sided tug-of-war among various agencies and advisers who participate in the policy-forming process inside and outside the executive branch. Decisions which define commitments and structure deterrence policy are often made in the same way that other policy matters are settled. Far from being the unalloyed, pure judgment of a single rational actor, i.e., the chief executive, such decisions may be the "negotiated" outcome of a complex process of resolving, reconciling, and compromising sharp disagreements over policy among various interested parties.

In this case, there were several policy-making arenas where decisions had to be made regarding various aspects of the American commitment. Besides the vigorous controversy over some of these questions within his own administration, Eisenhower had to contend with (1) strong and conflicting pressures from Congress; (2) concerned and divided public opinion within the country as a whole; (3) persistent pressures and maneuvers from the Nationalist government, which saw in the evolving crisis opportunities for advancing its cause as well as dangers to its interests; (4) antiwar and anti-Nationalist pressures from U.S. allies, in particular Great Britain. Drawn into these many overlapping arenas of policy debate, Eisenhower was influenced to some extent by discussion, persuasion, negotiation, and tacit bargaining with the various partisan advocates which the crisis had aroused. This is not to say that analysis of the issues played an insignificant role in resolving the policy dilemmas confronting Eisenhower; but many fundamental questions connected with the U.S. national interest that were imbedded in efforts at cost-benefit evaluation of alternative courses of action could not be rigorously or conclusively analyzed.

In order to command the desired minimal degree of consensus for the decisions he would make, Eisenhower was inclined to make only marginal changes in existing American policies toward the two Chinas. He was driven by the conflicting pressures on him to seek a middle ground that wholly satisfied few of the principal actors or constituencies who participated in the policy debate. In the end, Eisenhower and Dulles attempted to provide a cohesive rationale for the set of decisions that clarified the U.S. commitment and applied deterrence to some of the offshore islands. But it is clear that these decisions were influenced by political considerations and were responsive to some extent to the pressures mentioned above.

Within the circle of Eisenhower's closest advisers, for example, there were vocal and persistent advocates of more "positive" measures on behalf of the Nationalists. When the artillery shelling of Quemoy began in September, the Joint Chiefs of Staff quickly agreed that the offshore islands were not militarily essential to the ability of the United States to defend Taiwan. On strictly military grounds, therefore, there was no need for U.S. intervention to prevent the loss of these islands. However, three of the four members of the JCS felt that the loss of the offshore islands, inevitable without American assistance, would have serious political and psychological effects on the Nationalists' morale. Therefore, they favored extending the U.S. commitment to include the defense of some of them. These three JCS members also recommended that the United States help the Nationalist air force undertake preemptive strikes against communist staging areas on the mainland.

Eisenhower rejected this recommendation on the ground that to bomb the mainland would risk a major war. He also turned down the recommendation that the United States help defend Quemoy, preferring Dulles' suggestion that the matter be taken to the United Nations Security Council in an effort to obtain a cease-fire in the Taiwan Strait. However, as Eisenhower notes, "To this plan Chiang Kai-shek objected; going to the Security Council, he contended, was the first step toward letting it decide who owned Taiwan and which China had a right to United Nations representation." [11]

In December Eisenhower refused once again to extend the U.S. commitment to any of the offshore islands. The defense treaty with Nationalist China had only recently been signed

[11] *Ibid.*, p. 465.

when the Nationalist Ambassador brought Eisenhower a suggestion from Chiang Kai-shek that it would be good psychological warfare for the United States to go beyond the provisions of the treaty and assure at least logistic support for the defense of the offshore islands. Eisenhower turned down this request.[12]

It should be noted that while the United States had been deliberating its response to the artillery shelling of Quemoy and completing arrangements for the defense treaty with Taiwan, the Chinese Communists had been careful not to step up action against Quemoy. Instead they shifted the focal point of their probe to the Tachen Islands, some 200 miles north of the Taiwan Strait. On November 1 Chinese Communist planes bombed these islands. The buildup of forces on the mainland and the construction of jet airfields opposite Taiwan continued. Then on January 10 a hundred communist planes raided the Tachens. A week later, on January 18, an amphibious invasion employing almost 4,000 Chinese Communist troops, supported by heavy air bombardment, overwhelmed the 1,000 Nationalist irregulars on the island of Ichiang, which lay about 7 miles north of the Tachens. On the next day 200 communist planes—the largest air strike thus far—hammered the Tachen Islands.

In public statements both Eisenhower and Dulles downgraded the importance of the Tachens to the defense of Taiwan. At the same time, as Eisenhower put it at a policy meeting on January 19, he and his advisers felt that "the time had come to draw the line." [13]

At this point Eisenhower was more amenable to the recommendation he had rejected in September, that the United States commit itself to defending some of the offshore islands. He also accepted Dulles' proposal that Chiang be persuaded to evacuate the Tachens with the assistance of American forces. This was approved by Eisenhower over the opposition of most of the members of the JCS, who felt it to be both unwise and difficult to evacuate the Tachens. The *quid pro quo* which Chiang received for evacuating the Tachens was a private assurance that

[12] *Ibid.*, p. 466.   [13] *Ibid.*

the U.S. would fight if necessary to help defend the Quemoy and Matsu islands.[14] Nationalist evacuation of the Nanchi Islands followed when the administration informed Chiang that it would not assist in their defense.[15]

Eisenhower's memoirs are silent on the matter of a private assurance to Chiang but indicate no disagreement on his part when at the high-level policy meeting on January 19 Dulles stated, "we should assist in the evacuation of the Tachens, but as we do so we should declare that we will assist in holding Quemoy and possibly the Matsus, *as long as the Chinese Communists profess their intention to attack Taiwan.*" [16]

Dulles' private language on this occasion regarding the American commitment to defend Quemoy and Matsu was unequivocal; and it is noteworthy that his proposal was linked to Peking's declaratory policy rather than to its preparations for an attack on Formosa. In public, however, the administration deemed it politically expedient to profess that its commitment to these two small island groups off the mainland was tied very closely to whether an attack on them was part of, or a clear preliminary to, an attack on Taiwan.[17] Partly this may have been intended to allow the administration to give slightly different in-

[14] Rankin, *China Assignment,* p. 221; Beal, *John Foster Dulles,* p. 221; Halperin and Tsou, "United States Policy toward the Offshore Islands," pp. 125–26; Sigal, "The 'Rational Policy' Model and the Taiwan Straits Crisis," p. 131.

[15] Rankin, *China Assignment,* p. 223.

[16] Quoted by Eisenhower, *Mandate for Change,* p. 467 (emphasis added).

[17] The Formosa Resolution was passed by the House of Representatives on January 25 by a vote of 410 to 3. It encountered considerable more questioning in the Senate before approval on January 28 by a vote of 83 to 3. The resolution authorized the President "to employ the armed forces of the United States as he deems necessary for the specific purpose of securing and protecting Taiwan and the Pescadores against armed attack, *this authority to include the securing and protecting of such related positions and territories of that area now in friendly hands and the taking of such other measures as he judges to be required or expedient in assuring the defense of Taiwan and the Pescadores.*" (quoted in *Ibid.* pp. 469, 608; emphasis added). In the message to Congress requesting passage of the resolution Eisenhower had indicated he would use the authority only "in situations which are recognizable as parts of, or definite preliminaries to, an attack" against Taiwan and the Pescadores.

terpretations of its commitment to different audiences and in different circumstances. But some accounts of the crisis have it that Dulles' recommendation for a more sweeping pledge to defend the two offshore islands was softened in the language of the draft resolution which Eisenhower requested Congress to approve, because the President and some of his advisers feared that a request for an unconditional commitment would encounter severe congressional and public opposition.[18]

Such an interpretation is not merely plausible but compelling. It is difficult to account otherwise for the deliberate introduction of equivocal language into a declaratory policy that was supposed to reinforce deterrence. Eisenhower and Dulles both believed that ambiguity in declaratory policy was not in accord with the dictates of sound deterrence strategy. This in itself constitutes strong indirect evidence that, as Harding argues,[19] rhetorical obfuscation in declaratory policy was forced upon them by the expectation otherwise of strong domestic and international opposition to an appearance of further embroilment with the Nationalists that might lead to a major war with Communist China.

The question remains whether the deliberate ambiguity of the Formosa Resolution reflected a similar, only conditional, commitment in the administration's classified *action* policy and war plans. This we do not know for certain. It was characteristic of Eisenhower to rebel at efforts to get him to decide in advance just how he would respond to hypothetical crisis situations in the future. In this instance he retained for himself the actual decision and, of course, its timing in the event that the Chinese Communists should launch an all-out attack against Quemoy. But by endorsing an extension of the U.S. commitment, even in the conditional terms of the Formosa Resolution, he had substantially narrowed if not virtually lost his freedom of action to withhold use of American forces to prevent the loss of Quemoy, should it become necessary to do so. If such a contingency had

[18] S. Alsop, "The Story behind Quemoy," pp. 26–27, 86–88.
[19] Harding, "The Domestic Sources of Foreign Policy: The Quemoy Crises."

arisen it seems inconceivable that Eisenhower would not have invoked the Formosa Resolution. For, as Eisenhower himself practically admitted on various occasions, it was difficult to imagine a full-scale Communist Chinese attack on Quemoy which was not part of a campaign against Taiwan as well.[20]

Indirect evidence that the administration was, for all practical purposes, committed to defend Quemoy can be seen also in the decision Eisenhower now made to give logistical assistance to Nationalist forces attempting to defend the offshore areas from the beginning of an attack, without waiting to see whether the Chinese Communist action was part of a campaign against Taiwan.[21] In addition, in a show of force, three aircraft carriers were dispatched from Manila to the Formosa Straits and a wing of F-86 Sabrejets was flown to Taiwan from Okinawa.[22]

The Problem of the Defender's Response: Operationalizing the Commitment

Eisenhower had wanted a resolution on Taiwan from Congress, of course, in order to strengthen the deterrent impact of his policy on the Chinese Communists. It was Eisenhower's practice to seek consultation and support from Congress before commiting the United States or initiating military intervention in third-area conflicts. In April 1954 he had sought and failed to obtain advance congressional support when an air strike was being considered to assist the beleaguered French forces at

[20] Eisenhower, *Mandate for Change,* pp. 468, 471, 480.

[21] In December, we noted earlier, Eisenhower had rejected Chiang's suggestion, relayed by the Nationalist Ambassador in Washington, that it would be a good idea from the standpoint of psychological warfare to give the Nationalists an assurance of logistic support for the defense of these offshore islands. After the critical decisions of January 19, however, Eisenhower reversed himself, as the account in his memoirs of his cable to Dulles indicates. Eisenhower, *Ibid.,* p. 474.

[22] *New York Times,* January 22 and 27, 1955.

Dienbienphu. In addition to the Formosa Resolution of 1955, Eisenhower was to obtain another congressional resolution in 1957 with regard to the Middle East. (And in August 1965 President Johnson was to follow the precedent set by Eisenhower in obtaining the Tonkin Bay Resolution from Congress.)

In Eisenhower's practice of seeking congressional endorsements in advance of his intended commitments and actions there was, of course, an element of shrewd manipulation of the norms of crisis bipartisanship as well as respect for the necessary role of Congress in foreign policy.[23] However, if Eisenhower expected Congress' approval of the Formosa Resolution to constitute a blank check for his subsequent handling of the crisis in the Formosa Straits, events were to prove that this was not the case.

The administration had been remarkably successful, it is true, in isolating and neutralizing both the extreme left and extreme right critics of its China policy during the debate preceding the adoption of the resolution. But no sooner was the resolution approved than congressional demands for its clarification and restriction emerged. These demands were triggered by Nationalist claims that the United States had promised to defend Quemoy and Matsu and that these offshore islands were essential to the defense of Taiwan and the Pescadores. The claims were rebutted gently by the State Department, which emphasized the conditional nature of the commitment to the offshore islands.

Never one to settle for half a loaf, Chiang Kai-shek further aggravated the anxiety of congressmen and others who feared that the administration would become embroiled in a war over the offshore islands by renewing his exhortations to "counterattack the Communists and recover the mainland" and by asserting that he expected Washington's "moral support, sympathy, material and logistical support" but not "ground forces." [24] Ei-

[23] Harding, "The Domestic Sources of Foreign Policy: The Quemoy Crises."

[24] *New York Times*, February 8 and March 2, 1955; quoted by Sigal, "The 'Rational Policy' Model and the Formosa Straits Crisis," p. 131.

senhower was immediately faced with demands in Congress that he dissociate American policy from these Nationalist claims and demands. On March 2 the President strongly rejected Chiang's request for U.S. aid in the attack against the mainland which Chiang claimed to be readying: "I thought that this whole thing had been discussed so thoroughly, there could be no question of America's attitude in this matter. The U.S. is not going to be a party to aggressive war; that is the best answer I can make." [25]

The administration's efforts to assure the dove critics of its policy predictably aroused the suspicion and displeasure of the hawks, who now feared that the commitment to the offshore islands was not as reliable as they had believed earlier. It was clear that the continuation of the crisis was eroding the administration's earlier success in neutralizing extreme critics on both the right and the left. Eisenhower was also unsuccessful, as his memoirs indicate, in holding the support of his British ally, despite the fact that he had a Conservative government under his old friend and comrade, Winston Churchill, to deal with.[26]

During March the administration's anxiety about the situation in the Taiwan Strait deepened. The Chinese Communists gave no indication that their determination to pursue their action was lessening, and they continued to build up forces across from Quemoy and Matsu. It was feared that an attack might come in mid-March before the Nationalists could complete defensive preparations on the islands.[27]

It was painfully evident to the administration that its new commitment to the offshore islands was not deterring Peking's continued use of low-level options against Quemoy; and worse, that it might not discourage the Chinese Communists from escalating their probe into a stronger attack. Paradoxically, therefore, the danger of being drawn into a war with Communist China increased *after* the U.S. commitment had been ex-

[25] *New York Times*, March 2, 1955, quoted in *Ibid.*, p. 131.

[26] Eisenhower, *Mandate for Change*, pp. 470–76.   [27] *Ibid.*, pp. 476–77.

tended to deter an attack against Quemoy and Matsu. For now, having committed itself to help defend Quemoy, the administration was obliged to decide just how to operationalize its commitment, should the Chinese Communists step up their action and threaten to overrun the island. Caught in this situation, Eisenhower felt obliged to issue new deterrent threats. On March 16 he stated in a press conference that the United States would use tactical atomic weapons in a war with Communist China, hoping, as he later explained in his memoirs, that this "would have some effect in persuading the Chinese Communists of the strength of our determination." [28]

With the mention of nuclear weapons the crisis entered a new phase of heightened public consciousness. A full-blown war scare emerged on March 26 when the press leaked an off-the-record statement by Admiral Carney, the Chief of Naval Operations, predicting a Chinese Communist attack on the offshore islands in April and indicating that the JCS advocated an all-out attack on China in response. This created an immediate groundswell of criticism of the administration's policy, which Eisenhower attempted to allay. Support for his commitment to the offshore islands was now so tenuous that he felt obliged to send two members of his administration to Taipei in an effort to persuade Chiang Kai-shek to thin out his forces on Quemoy and Matsu in order to reduce their political and psychological importance. The instructions given to Admiral Radford, Chairman of the Joint Chiefs of Staff, and to Assistant Secretary of State Robertson before they left for Taiwan clearly implied an interest on Eisenhower's part in finding a way out of the commitment to defend Quemoy and Matsu.[29] But whether this mission was in full earnest or by way of alleviating congressional criticism, the choice of two men strongly committed to support of the Nationalist cause was hardly likely to provide the degree of pressure needed to get Chiang Kai-shek to agree to a downgrad-

[28] *Ibid.*, pp. 477–78.

[29] *Ibid.*, p. 481; S. Alsop, "Story behind Quemoy," p. 88.

ing of the offshore islands and a lessening of the new U.S. commitment to them that he had gained, after much effort, only four months earlier.

At about this time, Peking evidently decided to turn off its bombardment of Quemoy and to seek a relaxation of tensions in the Taiwan Strait.[30] In a speech to the Bandung Conference on April 20, Chou En-lai stated that Peking had no desire to go to war with the United States and indicated his willingness to negotiate. The crisis was now over, and talks between Chinese and American ambassadors began in Geneva several months later.

The U.S. commitment to the offshore islands survived the crisis. The Radford-Robertson mission to Taiwan failed to persuade Chiang to downgrade Quemoy and Matsu. The U.S. commitment, however, remained of limited value from the standpoint of deterrence. As the crisis of 1954–1955 had shown, Peking did not have to engage in an all-out attack against Quemoy and Matsu in order to test and, if possible, erode the U.S. commitment. Lesser military options, such as sustained or periodic artillery fire, and threats of an invasion were available for this purpose.

Despite the obvious difficulties of attempting to protect an isolated outpost and of deterring low-level controlled pressures against it, so vividly experienced in the Berlin blockade of 1948, the United States had permitted itself (with much less reason) to enter into a similar commitment to islands that lay only a few miles from the Chinese mainland within easy interdiction range of artillery as well as air attack. Deterrence had been pushed to its limits in the 1954–1955 crisis in the Taiwan Strait. Peking retained the possibility of taking the initiative in the future to create another controlled crisis in the Taiwan Strait. It would do so again in 1958, once more stretching deterrence to the limit and taking the United States to the brink of war.

[30] Tsou, *Embroilment over Quemoy*, p. 8.

Bibliography

Detailed scholarly studies of the Taiwan Strait crisis are still to appear. This crisis has generally been treated briefly by most scholars as a precursor of the Quemoy crisis of 1958, to which they have given more detailed attention. And yet the Taiwan Strait crisis of 1954–1955 is an important one from the standpoint of the effort to use deterrence strategy as an instrument of foreign policy. The early studies which Tang Tsou published in 1959 remain of considerable value. The development of American policy on the offshore islands is traced by Halperin and Tsou in their 1966 article, which also contains perceptive observations on the constraints of bureaucratic politics on Eisenhower's decision-making. The multiple political pressures on the administration's handling of the crisis are discussed in Harry Harding's unpublished 1970 study. Leon Sigal's revisionist interpretation (1970) contains useful insights and raises important questions. The most important and revealing of the memoir sources on American policy-making are the books by Dwight D. Eisenhower and Karl Lott Rankin. Important details, however, are available only in journalistic accounts which are useful though at times of uncertain factual reliability.

For earlier research on this crisis we are indebted to Harry Harding.

Adams, Sherman. *Firsthand Report: The Story of the Eisenhower Administration.* New York, Harper & Row, 1961.

Alsop, Joseph. "Quemoy: We Asked for It," *New York Herald Tribune,* September 3, 1958.

Alsop, Stewart. "The Story behind Quemoy: How We Drifted Close to War," *Saturday Evening Post,* December 13, 1958, pp. 26–27, 86–88.

Beal, John Robinson. *John Foster Dulles, 1888–1959*. New York, Harper & Bros. 1959.

Brown, Seyom. *The Faces of Power*. New York, Columbia University Press, 1968.

Clubb, O. Edmund. "Formosa and the Offshore Islands in American Foreign Policy, 1950–1955," *Political Science Quarterly*, LXXIV, No. 4 (December 1959), 517–31.

Donovan, Robert J. *Eisenhower: The Inside Story*. New York, Harper & Bros. 1956.

Eisenhower, Dwight D. *The White House Years: Mandate for Change, 1953–1956*. Garden City, N.Y., Doubleday, 1963.

Gerson, Louis L. *John Foster Dulles: A Statesman and His Times*. New York, Cooper Square Publishers, 1967.

Halperin, Morton H., and Tang Tsou. "United States Policy toward the Offshore Islands," *Public Policy*, XV (1966), 119–38.

Harding, Harry. "The Domestic Sources of Foreign Policy: The Quemoy Crises of 1954–55 and 1958." Unpublished paper, Stanford University, 1970.

Hinton, Harold C. *Communist China in World Politics*. New York, Houghton Mifflin, 1966.

——. "Sino-Soviet Relations in a U.S.-China Crisis: The Chinese Attitude," in *Sino-Soviet Relations and Arms Control*, ed. Morton Halperin. Cambridge, MIT Press, 1967.

Holsti, Ole. "The 'Operational Code' Approach to the Study of Political Leaders: John Foster Dulles' Philosophical and Instrumental Beliefs," *Canadian Journal of Political Science*, III, No. 1 (March 1970), 123–57.

Hsieh, Alice L. *Communist China's Strategy in the Nuclear Era*. Englewood Cliffs, N.J., Prentice-Hall, 1962.

Hughes, Emmet John. *The Ordeal of Power*. New York, Dell, 1964.

Morgenthau, Hans J. "John Foster Dulles, 1953–1959," in *An Uncertain Tradition: American Secretaries of State in the Twentieth Century*, ed. Norman A. Graebner. New York, McGraw-Hill, 1961.

Mozingo, David. "Containment in Asia Reconsidered," *World Politics*, XIX, No. 3 (April 1967), 361–77.

Rankin, Karl Lott. *China Assignment*. Seattle, University of Washington Press, 1964.

Rovere, Richard H. *Affairs of State: The Eisenhower Years*, New York, Farrar, Straus, 1956.

Shepley, James. "How Dulles Averted War," *Life*, January 16, 1956, pp. 70–80.

Sigal, Leon V. "The 'Rational Policy' Model and the Formosa Straits Crisis," *International Studies Quarterly*, 14, No. 2 (June 1970), 121–56.

Tsou, Tang. *The Embroilment over Quemoy*. International Study Paper No. 2. Institute of International Studies, University of Utah, 1959.

——. "Mao's Limited War in the Taiwan Strait," *Orbis*, III, No. 3 (Fall 1959), 332–50.

Chapter 10

The Hungarian Revolution, 1956

Résumé of the Crisis

THE TWENTIETH CONGRESS of the Communist Party of the Soviet Union convened in February 1956 and, as one aspect of "de-Stalinization," adopted liberalized economic and social policies for the Eastern European satellites. These policies had the unanticipated effect of encouraging demands for even greater reforms, especially in Poland and Hungary. During the summer of 1956 Erno Gero, First Secretary of the Hungarian Communist Party, attempted to deal with these pressures by a combination of repression and appeasement. The situation did not improve during the summer and fall, however, and on October 4 Gero readmitted to the Party Imre Nagy, a former premier who had been expelled by Gero's predecessor a year before. Nagy was recognized as a symbol of liberalization and reform policies, and Gero hoped his vindication would neutralize the mounting criticism in the country. But instead, the gesture inspired the popular forces to even greater militance.

On the night of October 23, fighting and rioting broke out in Budapest, and police opened fire on crowds of demonstrators. Some time during the night Soviet troops were requested to enter the city and restore order.

STEPHEN J. GENCO is the author of this chapter.

The next day it was announced that Imre Nagy had been reinstated as Premier. Apparently Gero hoped to use Nagy's popularity to disarm the resistance and counteract the effect of the Soviet intervention, which was now in full force. Gero and Nagy urged a halt to the violence and even offered surrender deadlines with full amnesty, but the fighting continued. Two members of the Soviet Presidium, Anastas Mikoyan and Mikhail Suslov, arrived in Budapest to observe the crisis.

On the 25th, Mikoyan and Suslov decided that Gero was no longer capable of alleviating the situation, and he was replaced by Janos Kadar, a party official who was considered to have less of a Stalinist stigma than Gero. Kadar and Nagy made renewed but unsuccessful efforts to stop the fighting. Mikoyan and Suslov returned to Moscow.

Nagy reorganized the government on October 27. He formed a "popular front" cabinet which included two noncommunists. The new government, designed as a compromise to the dissidents' demands, evoked little enthusiasm among the revolutionaries, who had by now taken over exclusive control of the provinces. On the 28th, negotiations were taking place between the government and the Soviet troop commanders for withdrawal from Budapest, and a cease-fire was announced. Some troops began to leave, and order was gradually restored. By the 29th, all Soviet troops had withdrawn from Budapest and had been replaced by Hungarian army units.

Nagy's new government took office on October 30. Its first act was to announce that the one-party system had been abolished and that negotiations were to begin for the immediate withdrawal of Soviet forces from all of Hungary, not just from Budapest. Also on October 30, a major policy statement was released by Moscow concerning Soviet relations with the satellite countries. The statement took a conciliatory position with respect to the Hungarian situation and affirmed that the Soviet Union and the satellites could "build their mutual relations only on the principles of complete equality . . . and of non-interference in one another's internal affairs." It admitted to previous mistakes in mutual relations and stated the general principle that troops should be stationed in other countries only with the consent of the host state. With specific reference to the course of events in Hungary, the announcement promised that the Soviet government would completely withdraw its troops as soon as the Hungarian government considered withdrawal necessary. The declaration also warned, however, that "to guard the Socialist achievement of people's democratic Hungary is the chief and sacred duty of the workers, peasants, intelligensia, of all the Hungarian working people at the present moment." In light of this warning, it announced that Moscow "expresses confidence that the peoples of the Socialist countries will not permit foreign and domestic reactionary forces to shake the foundations of the people's democratic system." [1] In other words, the Soviets would not allow Hungary or any other of their Eastern European satellites to abandon the system of Communist Party rule or the hegemony of the Soviet Union over that area.

In spite of the statement's explicit promise to withdraw Soviet troops from Hungary, however, by November 1 no move had been made to do so. Nagy became convinced that the Soviets had no intention of following through on their declaration. As a result, he ignored the clear warning contained in the declaration and announced Hungary's withdrawal from the Warsaw Pact, proclaimed Hungarian neutrality, and asked the United Nations to consider means of aiding the Hungarians in their struggle. With this move, Nagy overstepped what had been set as the permissible limits of behavior for a socialist country. He had reintroduced the multiparty system, and had thereby divested the Communist Party of its monopoly of power and, consequently, had denied the Soviet Union its supremacy over Hungary. Surprisingly, however, the Soviets appeared to be monitoring the situation and still seemed to be attempting to reach a negotiated settlement, even after these announcements.

On November 3, Nagy pushed his reforms even further and again reorganized the government, this time formally including several independent parties. Soviet forces were still present in growing numbers throughout the country, and nego-

[1] Quoted in Vali, *Rift and Revolt*, p. 346.

tiations for their withdrawal were continuing. It was beginning to appear, at least to the Nagy government, that perhaps an agreement could be reached. On the morning of November 4, however, these hopes were shattered as Soviet troops again invaded Budapest in full force. Nagy appealed for Western aid to protect Hungary's neutrality. The Soviet forces soon overran the city and, although bitter fighting continued for several days, Nagy's government toppled and a new regime headed by Janos Kadar took over.

During the most critical period of the Hungarian revolution—the seven days directly preceding the massive second Soviet intervention on November 4—events in Hungary were forced to share world attention with another crisis that unexpectedly broke out in the Middle East on October 29, when Israeli military forces attacked Egyptian installations on the Sinai Peninsula. When Britain and France joined in the attack on October 31 by bombing military targets in Egypt, in preparation for landing their own armed forces in the Suez Canal area, the situation became an international crisis of major proportions. The United States did not support the French and British actions and, as a result, was forced to admit that a serious rift existed between the policies of the U.S. and those of its two major Western allies. Of course, this turn of events could not have come at a worse time for Imre Nagy and his new provisional government, or at a better time for the leaders of the Soviet Union. The Suez crisis acted to divert the attention of both the United States and the United Nations away from the question of Hungary and consequently decreased the chances of Western action being taken in support of the Nagy government.

The U.S. Response:
Clarification of U.S. Noncommitment

The news of an outbreak of a full-scale revolution in Hungary on October 23, 1956, must have been received by the

United States government with mixed feelings of encouragement and concern. It may have felt encouraged because the uprising seemed to substantiate John Foster Dulles' prediction that "the Communist structure is over-extended, over-riding, and ill-founded. It could be shaken if the difficulties that were latent were activated." [2] But concern also was evident in a remark of President Eisenhower: "with the deterioration of the Soviet Union's hold over its satellites might not the Soviet Union be tempted to resort to extreme measures, even to start a world war?" [3] The fear of this second possibility proved to be the more important influence on the United States' response to the crisis.

For our purposes, that response may be summed up as the clarification for the Soviets that the United States did *not* have a commitment to Hungary and was not attempting to deter them from reasserting their hegemonic position in Hungary. While the Eisenhower Administration would, of course, have been very pleased if the Hungarians had somehow managed to achieve freedom on their own, it was anxious to communicate to the Soviets that the U.S. would not employ nor even threaten to use force in Hungary.

The fact that the Soviets delayed their intervention in force until November 4 may have been due in part to a desire fully and clearly to obtain this reassurance (although it was certainly also due in part to purely bilateral Soviet-Hungarian factors and to delays in the internal Soviet policy debate). Certainly the Soviets would reasonably have wished for American reassurance, since previously there had been an appearance of a partial, ambiguous commitment to U.S. intervention in such situations. The 1952 Republican Party platform, on which President Eisenhower had been elected, had specifically promised a policy of "liberation" of the "captive nations" of Eastern Europe as an alternative to the Truman policy of mere "containment" of any

[2] Press conference, June 30, 1953. Text in U.S. Department of State, *American Foreign Policy 1950–1955*, II, 1744–45.

[3] Eisenhower, *White House Years*, p. 67.

further Soviet aggression. A policy of "rolling back" communism, as it came to be known, had been repeated by Dulles in
his first address as Secretary of State: "To all those suffering
under Communist slavery . . . let us say: you can count on
us." [4] The USSR therefore had good reason to believe that "roll-
back" was now part of U.S. foreign policy, and that there was a
reasonable probability that the U.S. might actually act to implement this strategy in certain contingencies. If so, the Hungarian
situation in the autumn of 1956 would certainly seem to be almost as favorable a contingency as the U.S. could hope to find.

It is true that in its first opportunity to operationalize its
roll-back policy, the workers' uprisings in East Germany in
June 1953, the Eisenhower Administration had done nothing
more in response than make protests and send foodstuffs. But at
that point the administration had barely taken office. Moreover,
that opportunity was not nearly as favorable to a roll-back policy
as the Hungarian one, where the established government was
potentially pro-Western and might at any time make a formal
appeal, legitimate under international law, for American assistance. Furthermore, Soviet intelligence was doubtless aware in
the fall of 1956 that many Hungarian revolutionaries themselves
believed—largely on the basis of continuous encouragements
over the previous years from the Voice of America and Radio
Free Europe—that the United States had committed itself to aid
an anti-Soviet Hungarian revolution. Announcement of this belief by the Nagy Government, which by no means could be
ruled out, might serve to *activate* such a commitment by the
U.S., even if previously it had not really existed. (A somewhat
similar course of events, after all, had taken place in Korea in
1950, and at that time America had possessed a less belligerent
government.) Finally, and perhaps most importantly, in 1956
the United States possessed massive strategic nuclear superiority over the Soviet Union, and the Soviet leaders knew this. [5]

[4] Quoted in Brown, *Faces of Power*, p. 110.

[5] It appears that in reality the "roll-back" or "liberation" policy was originally
intended as a true action policy by Eisenhower and Dulles but was reduced to
purely rhetorical significance under the "New Look" defense policy that was

In light of all these factors, the Kremlin might well have looked anxiously in the waning days of October for signs that the U.S. would not actually intervene in Hungary. Such signs were not long in forthcoming. As early as October 25, President Eisenhower released a statement merely deploring the (first) Soviet military intervention. The *New York Times* article accompanying it reported that "there was no indication from White House personnel . . . that the President intended to do more than speak out sharply." [6]

The National Security Council met on the 26th and concluded that the Soviet position in Europe was seriously threatened, and that nothing should be done that might provoke the USSR into an irrational overreaction. (It was at this meeting that Eisenhower expressed anxiety that the Soviets might start a world war rather than see their East European hegemony unravel.) The next day Secretary Dulles delivered a speech in Dallas stating that the "U.S. has no ulterior purpose in desiring the independence of the satellite countries" and offering *economic* aid to any of them attempting to free itself from exclusive dependence upon the Soviet Union, without posing a rejection of communism as a condition.[7] (It should be noted that this

later adopted. "Liberation" was one of three grand strategies, along with Massive Retaliation and Truman-style "containment," that were studied by the administration's task forces on defense policy during 1953. The resulting document, NSC-162, recommended a mixture of Massive Retaliation and containment and did not even mention "liberation." It cannot be assumed, however, that by 1956 Soviet intelligence had been able to report confidently the conclusion of NSC-162, which was, of course, a highly classified document. And even if it had, there remained the serious problem that Hungarian events might activate a commitment previously only rhetorical and latent.

[6] *New York Times*, October 26, 1956, p. 14. There may have been some uncertainty about the precise meaning of the President's statement. Robert Murphy, for instance, remarks in his memoirs that he interpreted the statement as implying that Washington sought to sponsor the Hungarian revolt; Murphy, *Diplomat among Warriors*, p. 429. If Moscow also found the statement ambiguous, this may have been a motive, though probably a minor one, for the Soviet withdrawal from Budapest that occurred on October 28 and 29.

[7] This paragraph of Dulles' speech was seen as important enough, in President Eisenhower's view, to convey directly to the Soviet leadership. It read: "The U.S. has no ulterior purpose in desiring the independence of the satellite coun-

NSC meeting and the Secretary's speech occurred days before
the Suez crisis broke out, indicating that that crisis was not a
factor in the administration's original decision to avoid overt
U.S. involvement in Hungary.)

On October 31—two days after Soviet troops left Budapest
and five days before they returned—the President made his policy even more explicit. In a televised address Eisenhower repeated the U.S. offer of economic assistance without "any particular form of society as a condition." He said that U.S. policy
supported East European nations' quest for true sovereignty,
but that the United States "could not, of course, carry out this
policy by resort to force." [8]

No further major statements were made by administration
leaders, who by this time were becoming more and more caught
up in the mushrooming Suez crisis. On November 2 in his only
material response to the crisis, Eisenhower did authorize $20
million in food and other relief for the Hungarian people. But
the "no commitment" signal had already been clearly communicated. After the massive second Soviet intervention, the
President merely sent a note of protest to Premier Bulganin,
containing no explicit or implicit threats of U.S. counteraction.[9]

The United States did sponsor a resolution in the United
Nations on November 5. There had been previous efforts, en-
joying tacit U.S. approval, to bring the Hungarian question to
the attention of the U.N., but both the Security Council and the
General Assembly had been preoccupied with the Suez affair.
The U.S.-sponsored resolution did not pass until after the Nagy
Government had been crushed by the massive and very rapid

---

tries. Our unadulterated wish is that these people, from whom so much of our
own national life derives, should have sovereignty restored to them, and that
they should have governments of their own choosing. We do not look upon
these nations as potential military allies. We see them as friends and as part of a
new and friendly and no longer divided Europe. We are confident that their independence, if properly accorded, will contribute immensely to stabilize peace
throughout all of Europe, West and East." Quoted in Eisenhower, *White House
Years*, p. 71.

[8] *New York Times*, November 2, 1956, p. 14.

[9] The text of the note is given in *Documents on International Affairs*, p. 491.

Soviet intervention.[10] In retrospect it seems likely that the USSR deliberately accepted the fairly high ruble costs of such a large-scale and speedy Hungarian operation in order to stabilize that situation as quickly as possible. This action gave the United Nations little opportunity for more than a condemnatory, but purely verbal, resolution; it also reduced to a minimum any residual anxieties the Soviets may have had regarding a possible reversal of the reassuring United States policy.

Sources of the United States Policy

When President Eisenhower and other U.S. officials later explained why the United States did not intervene in the Hungarian crisis, they emphasized the limited U.S. capabilities for doing so. The U.S. failure to use deterrence seems to have been highly dependent on the belief that there was no credible foundation for a deterrence effort, given the difficulties and risks of implementing any kind of effective action. Eisenhower pointed this out at length in his memoirs:

> The launching of the Soviet offensive against Hungary almost automatically had posed to us the question of employing force to oppose this barbaric invasion.
> . . . I still wonder what would have been my recommendation to the Congress and the American people had Hungary been accessible by sea or through the territory of allies who might have agreed to react positively to the tragic fate of the Hungarian people. As it was, however, Britain and France could not possibly have moved with us into Hungary. An expedition combining West German or Italian forces with our own, and moving across neutral Austria, Titoist Yugoslavia, or Communist Czechoslovakia, was out of the question. The fact was that Hungary could not be reached by any United Nations or United States units without traversing such territory. Unless the major nations of Europe would ally themselves spontaneously with us (an unimaginable prospect), we could do nothing.[11]

[10] A good chronological account of U.N. actions during the Hungarian Revolution is given in Gordon Gaskill, "Time-table of a Failure," in Kovacs, *Facts about Hungary*, pp. 129–54.

[11] Eisenhower, *White House Years*, pp. 88–89.

It also seems that flying in supplies to the Hungarians was not possible either, since the only air space potentially available was over Austria, which had "declared in no uncertain terms that it would resist any form of overflights." [12] This declaration was, of course, in line with the provisions of the 1955 Austrian Peace Treaty, which guaranteed absolute Austrian neutrality in international affairs. This landmark treaty was certainly not one which the U.S. wished to violate, either on the ground or in the air. Thus, the U.S. was faced with a situation in which a threat to take substantive action appeared to be simply impossible to carry out.

Britain and France, of course, could not move with the United States because a large proportion of their readily available forces was committed to the Suez operation, which the United States strongly opposed. The Suez crisis deeply divided the principal Western Allies at just the time when the greatest unity would have been needed to deter a Soviet intervention in Hungary; and that crisis also diverted the attention of Washington, London, and Paris from events in Eastern Europe much more than it diverted Moscow's attention. It is doubtful, however, that the West could have found usable conventional options to back up a deterrence effort, even in the absence of the Suez crisis, because of the isolated geographical position of Hungary, surrounded by communist nations and neutral Austria.

Nuclear options remained, however, made credible by the doctrine of Massive Retaliation and the known fact of great U.S. strategic superiority over the Soviet Union. Janos Radvanyi, a former Hungarian diplomat who had been assigned to Moscow, reports that Khrushchev took these possibilities seriously: "In the course of private conversations at which I was present, the Soviet premier always felt it necessary to explain that the Soviet leadership had to take into account the possible effect on Soviet actions of the U.S. nuclear striking capability." [13] Khrushchev,

[12] Murphy, *Diplomat among Warriors*, p. 430.

[13] Radvanyi, *Hungary and the Superpowers*, p. 11.

no doubt, was further concerned because President Eisenhower had proved at the end of the Korean War that he was capable of using nuclear threats to achieve politico-military ends (see chapter 8).

Why, then, did Washington not employ its doctrine of Massive Retaliation in the Hungarian situation? One reason may be that U.S. decision-makers, perhaps because of insufficient intelligence information, had underestimated the actual effect that their rhetoric and their superior striking power had had on the Soviet leadership. Second, as we have already seen, Eisenhower definitely believed that the Soviets were highly motivated to defend their hegemonic position in Hungary—even to the point of nuclear war. Although it appears certain that the Soviet leadership made no explicit, overt attempts to deter the U.S. at the time, Eisenhower obviously placed much emphasis on their frequent statements of "firm interest" in preserving the socialist states, interpreting these statements as implying at least an indirect deterrence commitment. Implicitly, Eisenhower may have recognized that the situation generated a tremendous asymmetry of motivation, favoring the Soviets. Third, and most basically, the American leaders simply did not consider the fate of Hungary to be worth an atomic war. As John Foster Dulles reportedly said at a private meeting, intervention "would risk a nuclear war with the Russians, and the American government was not prepared to take this risk on the Hungarian issue." [14] Given this assessment of the risk, a threat of Massive Retaliation also had to be avoided; otherwise the U.S. leaders might very well have found themselves either accused of bluffing or forced to back up their words with actual employment of nuclear weapons.

We can conclude, then, that the United States—probably quite properly—*deterred itself* from taking or threatening action in the Hungarian case, partly by accepting as its relevant image of the opponent an image of Soviet leaders irrevocably committed to maintaining their Hungarian position, and partly by rec-

[14] Drummond and Coblenz, *Duel at the Brink*, pp. 180–81.

ognizing its own lack of capability and motivation to influence the situation effectively. Although Eisenhower's and others' view of the proximity of World War III if the U.S. had intervened in Hungary may have been somewhat alarmist, the basic perception of the Soviet commitment, capabilities, and motivation seems to have been essentially correct. Unless the American people were prepared to run a significant risk of nuclear war for the sake of Hungary—and they probably were not—the administration's decision not to attempt deterrence of the Soviet intervention there appears to have been well taken.

Bibliography

The Hungarian Revolution is fairly well documented with several good sources. Perhaps the best is the book by Vali, which covers the 1949–1961 period with thorough documentation and contains an excellent bibliography. The United Nations report provides a valuable account of the revolution. Important documents are included in the Zinner and Lasky books.

Memoirs dealing with American decision-making in this case are provided by Eisenhower, Murphy, and Adams. In addition, Dulles' role and policy views are covered in Gerson, Beal, and Drummond and Coblenz. Useful secondary analyses and interpretations are presented in the books by Kovrig, Brown, and Radvanyi.

Adams, Sherman. *Firsthand Report: The Story of the Eisenhower Administration.* New York, Harper & Row, 1961.

Beal, John R. *John Foster Dulles, 1888–1959.* New York, Harper & Bros., 1959.

Brown, Seyom. *The Faces of Power.* New York, Columbia University Press, 1968.

Documents on International Affairs, 1956. London, Oxford University Press, 1959.

Drummond, Roscoe, and Gaston Coblenz. *Duel at the Brink.* New York, Doubleday, 1960.

Eisenhower, Dwight D. *The White House Years: Waging Peace, 1956–1961.* Garden City, N.Y., Doubleday, 1965.

Gerson, Louis L. *John Foster Dulles: A Statesman and His Times.* New York, Cooper Square Publishers, 1967.

Halasz de Beky, I. L. *A Bibliography of the Hungarian Revolution.* Toronto, University of Toronto Press, 1963.

Kovacs, Imre, ed. *Facts About Hungary: The Fight for Freedom.* New York, Walton Press, 1966.

Kovrig, Bennett. *The Myth of Liberation.* Baltimore, Johns Hopkins Press, 1973.

Meray, Tibor. *Thirteen Days That Shook the Kremlin.* New York, Praeger, 1959.

Murphy, Robert. *Diplomat among Warriors.* New York, Doubleday, 1964.

Lasky, Melvin J., ed. *The Hungarian Revolution: A White Book.* New York, Praeger, 1957.

New York Times, October 26, November 2 and 5, 1956.

Radvanyi, Janos. *Hungary and the Superpowers.* Stanford, California, Hoover Institution Press, 1972.

U.N. General Assembly. *Report of the Special Committee on the Problem of Hungary.* Eleventh Session, Suppl. 18 (A/3592), 1957.

U.S. Department of State. *American Foreign Policy 1950–1955: Basic Documents.* Washington, Government Printing Office. Vol. II.

Vali, Ferenc A. *Rift and Revolt in Hungary.* Cambridge, Mass., Harvard University Press, 1961.

Zinner, Paul E., ed. *National Communism and Popular Revolt in Eastern Europe.* New York, Columbia University Press, 1956.

Chapter 11

The Eisenhower Doctrine:
Deterrence in the Middle East, 1957–1958

Résumé

ON JANUARY 1, 1957, President Eisenhower and Secretary of State Dulles met with a bipartisan group of congressmen to ask their support for a new declaration of American policy in the Middle East. This was necessary, Eisenhower believed, because the withdrawal of the French and British following the Suez crisis of November had greatly increased the danger of communist encroachments throughout the Middle East. He requested that a joint resolution be passed by Congress declaring the new policy, allocating funds for the economic assistance of Middle Eastern nations, and authorizing the President to use force in the area in the event of communist aggression if he should consider it necessary. Thus, the baton of Western influence in the Middle East was passed from Britain and France to the United States.

The congressional resolution, which soon came to be known as the Eisenhower Doctrine, extended the policy of containment to the region directly below the "northern tier" states

STEPHEN J. GENCO is the author of this chapter.

flanking the Soviet Union's southern border. Eisenhower and Dulles were aware that their policy did not come to grips with regional factors, which were primarily responsible for the general instability of the area—factors such as the Arab-Israeli dispute, the issues of Arab nationalism, neutralism, and anticolonialism, the drive for modernization, and the rivalry between Egypt and Iraq for leadership in the Arab world. However, they believed that Middle Eastern instabilities per se threatened U.S. and Western interests only insofar as they were exacerbated by the Soviets. They hoped that regional problems could eventually be worked out through the United Nations, on terms favorable to the West, once the danger of communist takeover had been deterred by the U.S.[1]

The assumption of the preeminence of the communist threat, however, was to prove questionable later when it was tested in the four major crises that rocked the Middle East in 1957 and 1958. Only in the Syrian crisis of August and September 1957 was there a potentially serious possibility of communist takeover; and the Eisenhower Administration discovered, much to its chagrin, that such an outcome would be essentially nondeterrable, since the Syrian government was pursuing closer ties with the Soviets through its own volition. In the other three crises—Jordan in April 1957, Lebanon in May 1958, and Iraq and Lebanon in July 1958—American interests were put in what was perceived to be severe jeopardy by conflicts whose origins were to be found in regional instabilities which U.S. policy had previously considered to be of secondary importance. Communist involvement was only minimal in these three cases. When American troops landed in Lebanon the day after the Iraqi coup of July 15, 1958, President Eisenhower justified the intervention as necessary to "stop the trend toward chaos"; [2] he made no mention of communist "aggression" in either country.

[1] See the discussion of this issue in President Eisenhower's January 5, 1957 speech in *Current Documents*, p. 789, and in Secretary Dulles' statement made before the Senate Foreign Relations and Armed Services Committees, *Ibid.*, pp. 799–800.

[2] Eisenhower, *White House Years*, p. 270.

The use of deterrence policy in this case may have been somewhat useful for discouraging the Soviets from pursuing their ambitions in the Middle East too directly.[3] At the same time, however, the Eisenhower Doctrine was clearly insufficient for dealing with the overall problems of instability and social unrest which faced most of the nations in the area. The root causes of the region's instabilities were essentially nondeterrable phenomena incapable of being altered by a policy such as the Eisenhower Doctrine. The administration lacked appropriate policies for adapting to regional forces in ways that would minimize damage to U.S. and Western interests in the Middle East.

Formulation of the Deterrence Commitment

THE CONGRESSIONAL RESOLUTION

Eisenhower formally requested the joint congressional resolution concerning the Middle East in a special message to Congress on January 5, 1957. In this address, he conveyed a fairly explicit, though somewhat simplistic, perception of both the communist threat in the region and the American actions that would be necessary to respond to that threat. Soviet motives and goals were drawn in broad and somewhat vague historical terms:

> Russia's rulers have long sought to dominate the Middle East. This was true of the Czars and it is true of the Bolsheviks. . . .
> The reason for Russia's interest in the Middle East is solely that of power politics. Considering her announced purpose of Communizing the world, it is easy to understand her hope of dominating the Middle East.[4]

---

[3] It would be premature to conclude that the U.S. achieved a "deterrence success" in the Middle East vis-à-vis the Soviet Union as a result of its formulation of the Eisenhower Doctrine. The Soviets may have had no intention of taking aggressive action in the area, even if the doctrine had not been declared (see also chapter 16, pp. 516–17).

[4] *Current Documents*, p. 784.

Given the fact that the Soviets had not yet acted aggressively to achieve this goal, the administration's perception of the threat was evidently connected with an assumption that the presence of Western power had so far thwarted Soviet desires to take over the region. Thus, as Eisenhower saw it, a renewal of that presence was necessary to maintain the deterrence effect.[5] The weakening of Anglo-French influence in the Middle East, the President contended, made it imperative for the United States to announce an unequivocal commitment to the area. He proposed a resolution with three primary features:

> It would, first of all, authorize the United States to cooperate with and assist any nation or group of nations in the general area of the Middle East in the development of economic strength dedicated to the maintenance of national independence.
>
> It would, in the second place, authorize the Executive to undertake in the same region programs of military assistance and cooperation with any nation or group of nations which desires such aid.
>
> It would, in the third place, authorize such assistance and cooperation to include the employment of the Armed Forces of the United States to secure and protect the territorial integrity and political independence of such nations, requesting such aid, against overt armed aggression from any nation controlled by International Communism.[6]

Eisenhower emphasized that the need for an American commitment was urgent. Accordingly, Congress quickly began to evaluate his proposals through hearings before the House Committee on Foreign Affairs and the Senate Committees on Foreign Relations and Armed Services. After two months of extensive testimony at both hearings,[7] the *Joint Resolution to Pro-*

---

[5] The reader might note that this perception is essentially self-confirming. The possibility that the Soviets had not wanted to attack was evidently dismissed as incompatible with the image held by U.S. leaders of Soviet motives and goals. We will discuss this "image of the opponent" in more detail further on.

[6] *Ibid.*, p. 788.

[7] Hearing testimony can be found in Congress, House, *Economic and Military Cooperation* and Senate, *President's Proposal*. Given the nearly identical testimony made at the two hearings, we will cite only the Senate hearings in this study.

mote Peace and Stability in the Middle East was passed by both Houses of Congress. It contained all the essential points requested by the President and was signed into law on March 9, 1957.[8]

AMERICAN ECONOMIC AND STRATEGIC INTERESTS IN THE MIDDLE EAST

The interests which the Eisenhower Doctrine was designed to protect encompassed not only those of the United States, but those of the whole Western alliance as well. They were of two interrelated types—economic and strategic. Western economic interests centered around the vast oil reserves located in the Middle East. Containing in 1957 nearly 70 percent of the world's known oil deposits, the Middle East was supplying 20 percent of the oil used by the Free World and a formidable 75 percent of the oil used by Western Europe. The State Department estimated that "the Middle East can be expected to supply a constantly increasing proportion of the oil supplies of

[8] The Resolution stated in part: "*Resolved by the Senate and the House of Representatives of the United States of America in Congress assembled,* that the President be and hereby is authorized to cooperate with and assist any nation or group of nations in the general area of the Middle East desiring such assistance in the development of economic strength dedicated to the maintenance of national independence.

"Sec. 2. The President is authorized to undertake, in the general area of the Middle East, military assistance programs with any nation or group of nations of that area desiring such assistance. Furthermore, the United States regards as vital to the national interest and world peace the preservation of the independence and integrity of the nations of the Middle East. To this end, if the President determines the necessity thereof, the United States is prepared to use armed forces to assist any nation or group of such nations requesting assistance against armed aggression from any country controlled by international communism. . . ." Text in Dept. of State, *Policy in the Middle East,* pp. 44–47.

The statement in the doctrine that held the independence and integrity of these nations to be vital to the U.S. national interest, it should be noted, was not contained in the draft proposal that the administration presented to Congress. The statement was added at the suggestion of Senator Mike Mansfield. Later, Mansfield denied that he had intended any broad interpretation of his amendment to justify military intervention. *New York Times,* May 22, 1958; p. 1. See the discussion on pp. 321–23.

most areas, particularly the United States, Western Europe, Asia, and the Far East." American oil companies were heavily involved in Middle Eastern oil producing operations. A 1956 study estimated that U.S. companies had invested $1,290 million in fixed assets in the Middle East as of December 31, 1955. This constituted 47 percent of the total international investment in Middle Eastern oil.[9]

The Eisenhower Administration considered the economic interests of Western Europe to be directly related to those of the United States. Thus, when it accepted the dominant Western role in the Middle East, it did so with the knowledge that one major purpose of the U.S. presence would be to protect the economic interests of Western Europe.[10] The most important of these interests, of course, was Middle Eastern oil.[11] In addition, however, Western Europe had other substantial economic interests in the area. It supplied about 58 percent of the total Middle Eastern imports and purchased about 57 percent of their total exports.[12] The Suez Canal was a vital transportation link for Western Europe, particularly for France and Britain, who together accounted for nearly half the ships going through the canal each year.[13] Some interests, such as banking and investment advantages, were less tangible but of equal if not greater importance.[14]

[9] *Current Documents*, p. 820; *President's Proposal*, pp. 34–35. In a country-by-country breakdown, the five major U.S. oil companies (Standard Oil of New Jersey, Standard Oil California, Texas Oil, Socony Mobil, and Gulf Oil) together controlled 100 percent of the oil production in Saudi Arabia, 100 percent in Bahrein, 50 percent in Kuwait, 35 percent in Iran, 24 percent in Iraq, and 24 percent in Qatar. *President's Proposal*, p. 35.

[10] This point was made repeatedly by U.S. officials. See, for example, Eisenhower's comments in his January 5 speech in *Current Documents*, p. 785; Dulles' statement before the House Foreign Affairs Committee in *Policy in the Middle East*, p. 26; and Robert Murphy's address at Georgetown University, *Ibid.*, p. 52.

[11] *President's Proposal*, p. 351.   [12] *Ibid.*, p. 38.

[13] Thomas, *Suez Affair*, p. 66.

[14] A State Department analysis reported that: "Western Europe . . . derives sizeable benefits (which cannot be quantitatively estimated) from such services

The economic interests of the United States and the Western alliance were viewed as interlocking with the strategic importance of the area. Should the Middle East, and consequently these Western interests, fall under the control of the Soviet Union, then, U.S. leaders believed, a massive communist victory in Western Europe would surely follow.[15]

Beyond these potential effects in Europe, the Eisenhower Administration envisioned worldwide repercussions from a communist takeover of the Middle East. Soviet power would be extended to the Indian subcontinent and to Africa. Thus, the Soviets would outflank India on the one hand and Europe on the other. They would gain control of ports on the Mediterranean, the Persian Gulf, and the Arabian Sea. The U.S. would lose its air bases in Saudi Arabia, Libya, and possibly even in Morocco. As a result, according to the Senate committees' report on the proposed resolution, "all of Africa would be seriously endangered, and Western Europe itself would be in grave peril, as would south and southeast Asia. Such an event, in short, would have extremely adverse consequences upon the security and economy of the United States." [16]

Thus, strategically as well as economically, the Eisenhower Administration perceived that the loss of the Middle East to

---

as maritime and air transport, construction contracts, and profits of trading firms established by their nationals in the Middle East, several concessionary companies, insurance, and especially banking.

"Many of the Western European banks have a key position in the financial and commercial life of Middle Eastern countries." *President's Proposal*, p. 38.

[15] In testimony before the Senate committees, Dulles remarked that the Soviets were "very eager to get control of Western Europe. The vast manpower, industry, raw materials, that exist there would, if it fell under their control, decisively alter to their advantage and our disadvantage the balance of power in the world.

"Now there are two ways of their getting that control. One is by fighting to get it. The other is to get control of its economy so that it cannot exist except on Soviet Communist terms.

"And if international communism gets control of the Middle East, they will be in precisely that position. . . . And I would not expect under those conditions it would be feasible for Europe to stay independent of Soviet Communist control." *President's Proposal*, p. 66.

[16] *Current Documents*, p. 821.

"international communism" would constitute a severe, and possibly fatal, blow to American national interests. It should be emphasized that it was primarily these interests, and only secondarily the well-being of the nations of the Middle East, that the U.S. was attempting to promote with the Eisenhower Doctrine. As is evident from a close reading of the doctrine itself, socioeconomic progress per se was only encouraged as it related to "U.S. vital interests" and "the maintenance of national independence" (which basically meant that a nation should stay independent of communist influence). The administration saw no urgent need to promote modernization, democratic institutions, or the raising of standards of living if they did not directly benefit the American position vis-à-vis the Soviet Union.[17]

THE DEFENDER'S PERCEPTION OF THE THREAT

Three questions concerning the U.S. perception of the threat in this case are important to this study. One has already been examined: what were the interests that U.S. decision-makers felt were being threatened in the Middle East? The second and third question will be considered here: why did U.S. officials perceive the Soviet Union to be the primary source of the threat to Western interests? And how was the Soviet Union perceived to be threatening these interests?

The question of why the U.S. focused its policy in the Middle East on deterring the Soviet Union instead of dealing more directly with the numerous other destabilizing factors at work in the region is central to understanding the eventual failure of the policy. At first glance, the policy seems to have been simply a result of U.S. ignorance of the realities of Middle Eastern politics. But statements made by policy-makers throughout 1955 and 1956 show that ignorance was not the issue; the U.S. was well aware of Arab nationalism, the Iraqi-Egyptian split, etc. The real reasons underlying the American policy were much more complex. Although the Soviet Union was perceived as the

[17] See the exchanges concerning this distinction between Secretary Dulles and Senators Morse and Wiley, *President's Proposal*, pp. 260–63, 454–55.

primary threat to Western interests in the region, it apparently was not perceived as the only threat. As we shall see, U.S. leaders felt that a broad "umbrella" effect could be achieved by the proclamation of their deterrence commitment vis-à-vis the Soviet Union, so that these other threats would also be effectively deterred. But for now, let us examine this Soviet threat more closely.

As early as September 1955, Secretary Dulles had felt a deep concern over the possibility of Soviet entrenchment in the Arab world. The arms-for-cotton deal that Moscow made with Nasser at this time, with Czechoslovakia as an intermediary, was in his opinion "the most serious development since Korea, if not since World War II." [18] In the period between this sale and the Suez crisis of November 1956, U.S. policy-makers found what they considered to be substantial evidence of a vigorous economic, if not military, offensive being waged in the area.[19] Available data showed that whereas the Soviet Union had negotiated only 20 trade and payment agreements with Middle Eastern countries by the end of 1953, the number had arisen to 60 by August 1956. Soviet bloc economic and technical assistance programs had by that date been extended to Egypt, the Sudan, Syria, Turkey, and Yemen and had been offered to Iran, Israel, Lebanon, Libya, Pakistan, and Saudi Arabia. In addition to Egypt, Soviet bloc arms had been shipped to Syria and Yemen and had been offered to Saudi Arabia and Sudan.[20]

The administration viewed this aid as a blatant attempt by the Soviets to use economic and military assistance in an effort to create pro-Soviet "client" states—Egypt and Syria were often considered to be already in this category—who would then be encouraged to undermine more conservative pro-Western regimes in other Arab countries. When the Suez crisis broke out, bringing an end to British influence in the area, the potential threat posed by these "client" states appeared to have been

[18] Finer, *Dulles over Suez*, p. 28.

[19] Soviet activities in the Middle East from mid-1955 to the end of 1956 are discussed in Laqueur, *Soviet Union and the Middle East*, pp. 211–46.

[20] *Current Documents*, p. 822.

greatly increased. In fact, it could be said that the Suez debacle was the critical turning point of the Cold War rivalry in the Middle East in the 1950s.

From the American perspective the effect of Suez was disastrous. Not only had it shaken the foundations of Western supremacy and severely strained Western ability to uphold a favorable status quo in a region vital to U.S. and European security; it had also provided an excellent opportunity for the Soviet Union, at minimum cost and risk, to appear as a firm supporter of Arab nationalism and an active ally against Anglo-French-Israeli aggression. The Soviets did not let the opportunity go by. During the fighting they gained the respect of many Arab leaders by adopting a militant, provocative stand against the West. In the course of the fighting they threatened to send "volunteers" to aid Egypt in its battle, and at the same time sent messages to the French and British governments obliquely threatening them with missile attacks on their homelands if they did not withdraw their troops.[21] Not incidentally, this behavior also confirmed the fears of many U.S. leaders that the Soviets were indeed the primary threat to Western interests in the area. By the end of 1956, then, it seemed clear to the Eisenhower Administration that the USSR was well on its way to becoming a full-fledged Middle Eastern power.

Despite this evidence of growing Soviet interest and activity in the Middle East, however, the administration was unable to support its assessment of the grave threat to the Middle East by pointing to actual communist political (as opposed to psychological and economic) victories in the area. During the Senate hearings, Dulles was forced to admit that: (1) there was no

[21] The threats to send "volunteers" were made on November 6 and 10. See Congress, Senate, *Events in the Middle East*, p. 21. The U.S. reacted quite strongly to these threats, possibly because of their similarity to the Chinese Communists' threat, eventually carried out, to send "volunteers" to Korea in 1950. Texts of the letters from Khrushchev to Britain and France (and also the U.S. and Israel) can be found in *Documents on International Affairs*, pp. 288–93. A good discussion of the Soviets' use of nuclear threats to gain policy ends during the Suez crisis and in other cases can be found in Speier, "Soviet Atomic Blackmail," pp. 301–28.

evidence of Soviet "volunteers" present in any Middle Eastern country, (2) no country in the Middle East appeared to be under communist domination, (3) no country in the Middle East appeared to be in imminent danger of subversion by communist coup, and (4) no country in the Middle East appeared to be going communist by choice.[22] Furthermore, the suppression of local communists by all Arab regimes at the time, with the exception of Syria, was common knowledge. However, Dulles contended, now that the Western deterrent in the region had been eliminated, these conditions could be expected to change unless the United States took precautionary measures.

A critical gap between action and response becomes apparent in the structure of U.S. policy at this point. We have seen that although the Soviet Union was quite active in Middle Eastern affairs throughout 1955 and 1956, the activity was manifested in terms of propaganda and economic aid, not in terms of military preparations or undertakings. Yet, the Eisenhower Doctrine, which was apparently designed as a response to these nonmilitary Soviet activities, addressed itself exclusively to the question of military attack and/or takeover. We can identify two important elements that help explain this gap. The first is the dominant image of the Soviet Union held by U.S. leaders at the time. This image, encompassing both implicit and explicit assumptions about Soviet motives, goals, and capabilities, was revealed quite clearly in innumerable administration statements.

Basically, the Eisenhower Administration viewed the Soviet Union with the utmost distrust and was firmly convinced of the treachery, ruthlessness, and lack of moral scruples of the Soviet regime.[23] A corollary to this image was the premise that the Soviets would take advantage of any global situations where Western powers had faltered or shown weakness. In such a situation,

[22] *President's Proposal*, pp. 40–41.

[23] Dulles: "No one can reliably predict whether, and if so, when, there would be Communist armed aggression, but three things are known: (1) the Communist capability, (2) the temptation, (3) the lack of any moral restraints." *President's Proposal*, p. 5.

it was believed, the Soviets would attempt to achieve the greatest and quickest advance of their interests through the most expedient means they could employ.[24] In light of this image, we
can even go so far as to say that if the Soviet activities noted
above had *not* occurred, U.S. officials would still have been extremely fearful of a communist move into the Middle East because of the putative "vacuum" created by the withdrawal of
France and Britain. This leads us to the conclusion that the administration's fear of an imminent Soviet attempt to take over
the Middle East was at least as much a function of the U.S.
leaders' image of the Soviets' motives and capabilities as it was
based on a considered evaluation of the record of Soviet activities, accomplishments, and problems in the region.

In order to identify the second element that contributed to
the action-response gap inherent in the Eisenhower Doctrine,
we must turn to the question of how the Soviet Union was perceived to be threatening Western interests in the Middle East.
An examination of public speeches and of testimony given at
the Senate hearings on the proposed resolution reveals that U.S.
leaders saw a dual threat emanating from the Soviet Union.
The first aspect of the threat was the possibility of overt
armed attack, direct aggression, and the second was the possibility of subversion, indirect aggression.[25] Direct aggression, as we
have seen, was considered a serious threat *not* because it appeared to be likely, but simply because the Soviets were capable of carrying it out. However, subversion, either by the Soviet
Union or by its client states, was viewed as the primary threat to
U.S. interests. Dulles made the distinction quite clear before
the Senate committees when he stated, "I would say I think
that subversion is the greatest immediate danger in the area, although the military danger is not to be ignored, because there

[24] For example, when Dulles discussed the possibility of a Soviet attack on
Turkey and Iran, he stated that although it would be highly unlikely, "It must
always be accepted as a possibility when there exists the power and the capacity to use it suddenly." *President's Proposal*, p. 335.

[25] *President's Proposal*, pp. 48–49, 157, 288–89, 328, 339, 350, 373.

exists ample military power. . . ." [26] Because the doctrine specifically mentioned only armed aggression and said nothing at all about subversion, it is clear that U.S. leaders envisioned a relationship between the two that would allow the U.S. implicitly to bridge the gap between them and deter the latter by explicitly deterring the former.

PREMISES UNDERLYING
THE AMERICAN DETERRENCE EFFORT

The relative simplicity of the wording of the Eisenhower Doctrine belies the complex effect it was intended to have in the Middle East. The doctrine was meant to deter the dual communist threat, first by putting the Soviet Union "on notice" that the U.S. considered the Middle East to be vital to American national interests and second by bolstering the confidence of pro-Western governments in the area. The first goal was to be achieved by declaring a credible commitment that would effectively deter the Soviets from initiating any aggressive actions. The second goal was to be achieved by eliminating pro-Western governments' fear of overt attack by international communism and by offering economic assistance that would allow them to build up their internal security forces and to improve their economic conditions.[27]

Although the administration considered the danger of subversion to be the most important threat to Western interests, it felt constrained from attempting to deter it by direct means because of at least two important and related factors. First, there was the risk of overstepping United Nations provisions concerning collective self-defense. The U.N. Charter recognized "the inherent right of . . . collective self-defense" [28] only in cases of

[26] *Ibid.*, p. 328.

[27] *Current Documents*, p. 806; *President's Proposal*, pp. 289, 339.

[28] This phrase is found in Article 51 of the Charter. See *Yearbook*, pp. 831–50. We will come across it again later in this study when discussing the U.S. reaction to the Lebanese civil war. The whole article is quoted below, footnote 63.

armed attack and not in cases of subversion.[29] Eisenhower realized that an open breach of this provision by the U.S. would
generate considerable criticism from both the Soviet bloc and
the Third World nations and would thus seriously endanger the
hoped-for acceptance of the doctrine. Second, a U.S. declaration
of an intention to respond with military intervention to an internal change of government which it considered to be the result
of a subversive takeover would be strenuously rejected by
every Middle Eastern nation. Officials in the U.S. were quite
conscious of the imperialist aura surrounding the Western presence in the Middle East, and were anxious not to give the area's
leaders an opportunity to transfer their fear and distrust of the
European powers to the United States. Accordingly, the administration placed its emphasis on more covert means of deterring internal communist subversion.

As for the explicit U.S. declaration opposing overt aggression, there were apparently no factors like the two discussed
above which might have acted to constrain this aspect of the administration's policy. Indeed, American officials were quite
confident that their commitment to respond with troops to a
request for assistance from any Middle Eastern country threatened by "armed aggression from any country controlled by international communism" would be regarded as credible by the
Soviets. Given the administration's assumption that a Soviet
military attack on the Middle East would be an extremely unlikely event almost certainly leading to all-out nuclear war, U.S.
leaders felt that their deterrence strategy in this respect was
quite secure. By the same token, however, it was practically
meaningless. This aspect of the doctrine was designed to deter
an action that would probably not take place in any event because it was deterred by other, more global and more direct
means. In fact, the doctrine's only claim to credibility in this
sense was in relation to aggression not by Soviet-bloc countries,
but by regimes "controlled by international communism" within
the Middle East area. When and how a government could be

[29] *President's Proposal*, p. 48.

branded as being under international communist control (as well as what constituted "subversion") were left unspecified by the doctrine and presumably subject to determination on a case-by-case basis, as the need arose. To the anti-Western regimes in the area who were establishing close ties with Moscow, however, the Eisenhower Doctrine could be interpreted as a clear warning.

The Soviet Union and its client states were not the only audience the U.S. hoped to reach with its declaration against armed aggression. The commitment was also meant to increase the confidence of certain pro-Western governments in the area. During the Senate hearings, Secretary Dulles stated that one of the main reasons the U.S. had decided to create the Eisenhower Doctrine was because several of those countries had pleaded for a stronger American commitment in the Middle East. Under examination, Dulles revealed that Turkey, Iran, Iraq, and Pakistan were "the ones that I can mention." [30] These four nations, along with Britain, were the members of the Baghdad Pact, the only Western alliance existing in the region at the time.[31] Apparently, they considered a Soviet attack to be a more plausible possibility than did the U.S. In any case, they were eager to embrace an American initiative that would bring not only a better assurance of U.S. support for their regimes, but also a windfall in terms of economic aid and military equipment (just as two years earlier, and for similar reasons, they had been as

[30] *Ibid.*, p. 341. Dulles stated: "One of the factors which led us to made this recommendation, the President to make his address, was the very urgent, almost desperate, plea which we received from a number of countries in the area that, unless we were prepared to do something like this, they saw no hope of staving off a rather early collapse and takeover by international communism . . ."; *President's Proposal*, p. 338; see also pp. 73, 351, 373.

[31] The Baghdad Pact began as a mutual defense treaty between Turkey and Iraq signed in February 1955. Soon after, it became a part of the Western defense system when Britain, Iran, and Pakistan joined. The U.S., although instrumental in creating and supporting the pact, decided not to join because it was not viewed as a "unifying force" among the Arab nations. *President's Proposal*, pp. 50, 334. How it divided the area will be briefly examined further on. For a brief discussion of the Baghdad Pact, see Campbell, *Defense of the Middle East*, pp. 49–62.

eager to take up Dulles' northern-tier concept and build on it the Baghdad Pact alliance, with an alacrity that took Dulles himself by surprise).

Economic and military assistance were the two principal means by which the doctrine was expected to aid in counteracting the problem of internal subversion.[32] This money would be added to the extensive aid program that the United States already had under way in the area, started under Point Four of the 1947 Truman Doctrine. The approximately $200 million per year now requested by the Eisenhower Administration was primarily designed to finance the strengthening of "loyal security forces" in Middle Eastern countries subscribing to the doctrine, and was clearly meant to provide the material inducement necessary to secure local adherence to the new policy.[33] Military aid agreements with Saudi Arabia, Iraq, Greece, and Jordan were signed following congressional passage of the doctrine, and $174 million in aid was distributed in the first four months of its existence.[34]

It was this aspect of the program, however, that contained the premises which would eventually cause the U.S. to attempt to employ the doctrine in situations involving *non*communist threats to American interests and thereby plunge itself into the

[32] Dulles outlined these three conditions for deterring subversion during the Senate hearings: "Experience in history, I think, demonstrates that there is no internal subversion or, if it should occur, that it cannot last, except under three conditions: "One is that there is an element of danger and possibility of the use of overt military power.

"Second is that the country is not able to maintain an adequate loyal security force of its own.

"And the third is that economic conditions be such that the people in desperation will turn to communism.

"Now, if you can stop those three conditions, you have done, I think, everything that is possible, and I think everything that needs to be done, to stop subversion." *President's Proposal*, p. 157; see also pp. 48–50, 288–89.

[33] The bolstering of internal security forces was the only use for U.S. economic assistance offered under the doctrine that Secretary Dulles mentioned during the Senate hearings as definitely projected by the administration. Nonmilitary aid, such as budgetary assistance, help for refugees, and development assistance he said "may prove desirable." *Current Documents*, p. 812.

[34] Royal Institute, *Survey*, p. 170n.

regional disputes it had originally hoped to avoid. Even though Dulles denied it vehemently, the goal of strengthening internal government security forces to counter communist opposition would also strengthen the government's position against legitimate noncommunist opposition within a country. Given the authoritarian nature of nearly every government in the Middle East, this type of American aid would unavoidably help to perpetuate the internal status quo in the pro-Western countries of the area.[35]

Whether Dulles actually believed that security forces would be used only against communists or whether he expected those forces to be used against any opposition is a question that cannot be resolved conclusively. In any case, the result—even if not the intention or the expectation—was that the United States, while ostensibly attempting to extend its global deterrence strategy vis-à-vis the Soviet Union to the Middle East, was also tampering with the internal and regional politics of the area. This led directly to U.S. involvement in the four crises we will examine further on, and eventually to the ultimate failure and abandonment of the Eisenhower Doctrine following American intervention in Lebanon in July 1958.

THE EISENHOWER DOCTRINE VS. ARAB NATIONALISM: THE REACTION OF THE ARAB STATES

One ingredient which the administration perceived to be necessary to insure the success of its deterrence strategy for the Middle East was the support and cooperation of the nations of the region which the Eisenhower Doctrine was meant to defend.

[35] In response to pointed questioning from Senator Ervin, Dulles stated: "I think to maintain security forces, to maintain law and order in [a Middle Eastern] country, is something which is entirely appropriate for us to assist in. We are doing that all around the world. . . .

"I do not believe that the kind of internal security forces we are trying to build up here would be used against the general will of the people unless it is stirred up and organized by international communism. That is the great danger, and if that is the purpose of it, then we want to have forces to resist them." *President's Proposal*, pp. 344–45.

On January 7, 1957, two days after stating the new policy, President Eisenhower announced that he would send Ambassador James P. Richards to the Middle East to confer with as many countries as were interested in the provisions of the new doctrine in order to "explain the purposes of the resolution . . . and to report to me on the most effective ways of carrying out those purposes." [36]

Long before the Richards mission arrived in the Middle East, however, it became fairly clear that the Eisenhower Doctrine was going to generate far more opposition among the Arab states than the administration had anticipated. It was understood in Washington that the doctrine would be opposed by those governments who enjoyed good relations with Moscow and against whom the American policy was, in a very real sense, primarily directed.[37] What U.S. policy-makers misinterpreted was the general mood prevailing in the region in the aftermath of the nationalization of the Suez Canal and the tripartite invasion of Egypt. They counted on rallying the support of the pro-Western governments to the new doctrine; this would provide a working basis for the doctrine, and, just as importantly, would constitute a clear test for distinguishing between the true friends and the enemies of the Free World in the Middle East. With the enemies thus conspicuously marked, they could be easily isolated, their forces weakened, and their influence curtailed. But the originators of the doctrine had not reckoned with the immense surge of nationalist feeling and of popular support for the Nasser regime that had swept across the Arab world precisely because of Nasser's successful challenge of Western "imperialist" tutelage, first in concluding the 1955 arms deal

[36] Quoted in *State Department Bulletin*, 36 (January 21, 1957), 86–87.

[37] Thus, it was not surprising that although Richards toured no less than 15 Middle Eastern capitals in March and April 1957, he declined to visit Egypt, Syria, and Jordan (a strongly pro-Egyptian nationalist government had been formed in Amman the previous October under Premier Suleiman al-Nabulsi) despite the expressed willingness of these countries to receive him. The countries Richards did visit were Afghanistan, Ethiopa, Greece, Iraq, Israel, Lebanon, Libya, Morocco, Pakistan, Iran, Saudi Arabia, the Sudan, Tunisia, Turkey, and Yemen.

and then at Suez. Nor, apparently, had they reckoned with the atmosphere of intense suspicion—if not outright hatred—of the West, combined with gratitude and admiration for the Soviet opposition to the Anglo-French attack on Egypt in collusion with Israel only a few months earlier.

These feelings were only magnifications of traditional Arab attitudes. The Eisenhower Doctrine did not adequately cope with the fact that the traditional enemy of the Arabs was Western imperialism, not communism. Only slowly and painfully had the Middle Eastern nations, one by one, extricated themselves from French and British control after World War II. They could easily interpret the doctrine as proclaiming that the United States was now prepared to take over the "burden" of Western domination. Eisenhower's reference to a "power vacuum" in the Middle East reinforced this interpretation of American objectives, and although U.S. officials later disclaimed the validity of this formulation, Arab Nationalist leaders were not inclined to believe that it had been merely a rhetorical slip. The Arab states—unlike Greece, Turkey, and Iran—had never experienced Tsarist or Soviet imperialism, and did not seek to be aligned along Cold War boundaries. The Egyptians and the Syrians in particular saw themselves as genuinely attempting to pursue a policy of "positive neutralism" in the spirit of the 1955 Bandung Conference.[38]

Under these circumstances, governments having close and friendly ties with the West could embrace the Eisenhower Doc-

---

[38] In 1955, 29 nations of Asia and Africa, led by Prime Minister Nehru of India, met at Bandung, Indonesia to evolve a new policy for the Third World vis-à-vis the Soviet Union and the West. The policy of "positive neutralism" was developed. It rejected alignment with either side in the Cold War, recommended offering trade to any nation on a mutually acceptable basis, and sought to create an international environment where small, nonaligned countries could be relatively free of the pressures of big-power politics. Nasser attended the conference, was extremely impressed by the new policy, and attempted to implement it in Egypt as soon as he returned. By opening relations with the Soviets, he was able to force his way out of dependence on the West and to begin to pursue his neutralist policies. The United States, still unable to accept neutralism as a viable alternative to Cold War alignments, interpreted his actions as almost tantamount to joining the communists and began to treat Egypt accordingly.

trine only at the risk of further exacerbating already tense relations with other Arab regimes, stirring up internal opposition, and laying themselves open to charges of collusion with Western imperialism and betrayal of pan-Arab aspirations. President Chamoun of Lebanon and Prime Minister Nuri Es-Said of Iraq, the two Arab leaders who associated themselves most closely with the doctrine, came to grief barely fourteen months later, partly because of their unequivocal espousal of pro-Western policies, of which the Eisenhower Doctrine was the most explicit symbol.

Moreover, the doctrine offered protection against communist aggression, a threat most Arabs did not recognize, but ignored the threat of expanding Zionism, which they felt was of paramount importance. The United States was intimately associated with the problem of Israel and was seen by the Arabs as largely responsible for its existence. Thus it is not surprising that Arab nationalists saw the doctrine as an attempt by the U.S. to divert their attention from the real enemy. To make matters even worse, the Richards mission visited Israel and the Israelis came out in full support of the American initiative. They "eagerly welcomed any indication of further United States involvement in the area, and regarded the more general references to the Middle East as an advance on the previous United States statement in support of the Baghdad pact, at which time the State Department had categorically refused to make a similar statement about threats against the security and integrity of Israel." [39]

This short exposition of the Arab reaction to the Eisenhower Doctrine highlights the important fact that, by ignoring crucial regional considerations and designing its Middle East policy as merely one aspect of its global Cold War strategy, the United States seriously damaged its ability to deal creatively with the problems facing the Middle East. As a result, U.S. policy proceeded to exacerbate the tensions that were at the heart of Middle Eastern instabilities and which were the primary causes of the four crises to be examined next in this account.

[39] Royal Institute, *Survey,* p. 166.

Implementation of the Deterrence Attempt

JORDAN—APRIL 1957

In 1957 Jordan was among the least stable of all the Arab states. Traditionally, the Hashemite monarchy had depended upon British subsidies and British influence to insure the stability of its rule. After Britain's general exit from the area, which in Jordan's case began with King Hussein's dismissal in March 1956 of the British commander of Jordan's military forces, General Sir John B. Glubb, this stabilizing force was no longer available. Bowing to strong domestic pressures emanating from sectors both of the public and of the officer corps, Jordan was forced to move closer to Egypt and Syria who, along with Saudi Arabia, offered in January 1957 to share in replacing the annual British budgetary subsidy to the Hashemites, hoping thereby to destroy the remnants of Whitehall influence in Amman. In return Hussein had to accept a joint military command with Syrian and Saudi Arabian troops stationed in Jordan.[40] Parliamentary elections held in October 1956 had paved the way for this switch in Jordan's orientation by returning a majority for the nationalist, anti-Western parties, including the National Socialists, who advocated Jordanian union with Egypt and Syria. A new government was formed under the premiership of pro-Egyptian Suleiman al-Nabulsi.

Although King Hussein was personally sympathetic to Western interests in the Middle East and was uncomfortable with Nasser's attempts to unite the Arab countries into a neutralist bloc under Egyptian leadership, he realized the precariousness of his pro-Western position and temporized, sanctioning several of Nasser's views. One result of this realignment was that Jordan initially condemned the Eisenhower Doctrine with the same vehemence as did Egypt and Syria. However, this apparent solidarity began to crumble almost as quickly as it had appeared. Of the three countries that had offered to take

[40] *Current Documents*, pp. 1015–17.

over Britain's subsidy, only Saudi Arabia paid its share. Hussein concluded that either Egypt and Syria were too poor to pay or they were intending to use their aid as a means of political domination. He was further alarmed by the increasingly radical policies of the al-Nabulsi Cabinet, which included recognition of the Soviet Union, diplomatic relations with Moscow, and willingness to accept Soviet military and other aid.

Becoming increasingly concerned over the fate of his regime and encouraged by the prospects of U.S. assistance opened up by the Eisenhower Doctrine, Hussein decided to try to halt the pro-Nasser trend in Jordan, which was being led by his Prime Minister. Hussein dismissed Nabulsi on April 15, 1957 and precipitated a civil struggle. The King was supported only by his Bedouin troops and a few veteran politicians and was challenged by several powerful political leaders and by some of the highest-ranking officers in the army.[41] The leaders of Syria and Egypt were apparently highly sympathetic to the cause of the King's opposition, but the extent of their active participation in the struggle was never clearly established. Neither Egypt nor the Soviet Union had openly committed itself to the overthrow of Hussein.

As the crisis became more acute, however, King Hussein began to claim that the independence and integrity of Jordan were threatened by "international communism"—a charge obviously meant for American ears—and the Eisenhower Administration did not fail to respond to the call. Later, Hussein's claims would prove extremely difficult to substantiate; but at the time Washington did not subject them to a thorough scrutiny because of its desire to safeguard Hussein's regime and the apparent urgency of the situation. Besides, regardless of whether a communist threat did in fact exist, salvaging the monarchy had become an end in itself, since it was perceived by the Eisenhower Administration as a crucial test of the credibility of the new approach and of the U.S. commitments embodied therein. On April 24 Eisenhower's press secretary, James

[41] Campbell, *Defense of the Middle East,* p. 128.

Hagerty, told a press conference that he had been authorized to say that both the President and the Secretary of State regarded the independence and integrity of Jordan as vital. A State Department spokesman interpreted Hagerty's statement as "a reminder to the world by the President that a finding has been made in the Joint Resolution of the Congress on the Middle East that the preservation of the independence and integrity of the nations of the Middle East were vital to the national interest of the United States and to world peace." This reminder was appropriate because of the threat to the independence and integrity of Jordan by international communism as King Hussein himself stated.[42]

Thus the first step was taken toward interpreting the Eisenhower Doctrine more broadly as a mandate to intervene in any situation that, in the President's opinion, threatened the independence and integrity of any nation in the area.[43]

Accordingly, on April 26, the Sixth Fleet was ordered into the eastern Mediterranean as a display of U.S. support for King Hussein. Soon after, on April 29, $10 million in emergency aid was granted to Jordan. Luckily, Egypt and Syria failed to intervene in the struggle on the side of the antiroyalists, and the Soviet Union chose to limit its role in the crisis to issuing denunciations of the American actions. Israel also decided not to become involved. As a result, the conflict remained primarily domestic; and King Hussein was able to suppress the pro-Nasser faction, reconstitute a more loyal government, and establish firmer control over the army.

The effect that invoking the Eisenhower Doctrine had on the outcome of the crisis is debatable. Most observers have concluded that Hussein's success was primarily based on his own courage and good luck. He also received much needed help and encouragement from King Saud, who placed the Saudi Arabian troops stationed in Jordan under Hussein's direct command, and from the Iraqi monarchy, which concentrated its troops

---

[42] *State Department Bulletin*, 36 (May 13, 1957), 768.

[43] Lafeber, *America, Russia and the Cold War*, p. 198.

along the Jordanian border and promised to move into the country if Syrian troops should attempt to enter the conflict.

In Washington, however, the rapid settling of the incident was seen as a direct result of bringing King Hussein under the protection of the Eisenhower Doctrine. It was viewed as a setback for both Nasser and the Soviet Union and as a diplomatic success for the United States which confirmed the utility of the Eisenhower Doctrine. The administration failed to consider, however, that the successful intervention on Hussein's behalf also entailed important costs, and that it did not remove the fundamental instabilities in Jordan and in the region. The United States had now assumed a commitment to Hussein and enmeshed itself in what was basically an inter-Arab struggle. Its use of the Sixth Fleet raised cries against "gunboat diplomacy" and, as John C. Campbell notes, placed the United States in the eyes of many Arabs in a position "hardly distinguishable from that which the British had just been forced to relinquish." [44]

SYRIA—AUGUST AND SEPTEMBER 1957

As the crisis in Jordan began to cool down, administration officials were almost immediately forced to focus their attention on an increasingly disturbing situation in Syria. The Syrian regime had been developing a closer relationship with the Soviet Union throughout the spring and summer of 1957. It may be noted that whatever its value for discouraging Soviet military ventures in the Middle East, the Eisenhower Doctrine had not succeeded in deterring the Soviets from giving traditional forms of economic and military assistance to Middle Eastern regimes. In August the Syrian Defense Minister visited Moscow and arranged large-scale Soviet credits for expanded trade and for Syria's development program. The Soviets then announced that they were sending the Syrian army heavy shipments of military supplies, some of which had already arrived in Syria. Soon thereafter, on August 13, the Syrians announced that they had uncovered a U.S.-sponsored plot to overthrow the government

[44] Campbell, *Defense of the Middle East,* pp. 130–31.

of Shukri al-Quwatli, and they expelled three American embassy officials in Damascus for alleged subversive activities. A few days later, the Syrian army's Chief of Staff, considered by the U.S. to be a moderate, resigned. He was replaced by General Afif al-Bizri, known for his anti-Western views and suspected of being a communist.[45]

As Eisenhower recalls, "The entire action was shrouded in mystery but the suspicion was strong that the Communists had taken hold of the government." [46] The administration was now apparently faced with a clear test of its premise that the United States had a vital interest in preventing the establishment of a communist state or Soviet satellite in the Middle East. In this case, the perceived communist threat was far more real than in Jordan, and again a U.S. response of some sort was viewed as vital if the administration was to avoid eroding the credibility of its commitments in the Middle East.

The nations surrounding Syria were also reportedly "deeply concerned" over the new activities going on within that country. Turkey, in particular, now saw itself potentially surrounded by Soviet power and feared for its southern port of Iskenderun, which it had retaken from Syria in 1939. Iraq, Lebanon, and Jordan, already unstable enough without a Soviet outpost on their border, feared increased infiltration and subversion emanating from a communist Syria. Saudi Arabia saw its hopes of increased Arab unity severely threatened; and Israel viewed its very existence as being placed in serious jeopardy.

Before any response to the situation could be formulated, the Eisenhower Administration needed to answer one crucial question: was the Syrian regime turning into a communist satellite, or was it merely expressing a radical form of Arab nationalism? As Eisenhower saw it: "If the government comprised only radical Arab nationalists and pro-Nasserites, that was one thing; if they were to go completely Communist, that would call for action." [47] However, the administration experienced considerable difficulty in deciding what response to make. Even though

[45] *Ibid.*, p. 131.   [46] Eisenhower, *White House Years*, p. 196.
[47] *Ibid.*, 197.

the threat of a communist takeover was perceived as being high, it appeared at first that the Eisenhower Doctrine could not be employed as a legal justification for intervening in Syria. As the doctrine itself clearly stated, it could only be invoked at the request of the government of a Middle Eastern nation which feared an attack by "international communism." Obviously such a request would not be forthcoming from the existing Syrian government. Thus the United States was left to find some other base for whatever leverage it would attempt to exert on the Syrian situation.

In order to gain more information about what was happening in Syria, the President sent Deputy Undersecretary of State Loy Henderson to the Middle East to confer with the leaders of Lebanon, Jordan, Turkey, and Iraq. Syria itself was pointedly left off his itinerary. After Henderson returned to Washington, Secretary Dulles issued a press release on September 7 describing the official U.S. view of the situation in Syria. It stated in part:

> He [Henderson] reported that he had found in the Near East deep concern at the apparently growing Soviet Communist domination of Syria and the large build-up there of Soviet bloc arms, a build-up which could not be justified by any purely defensive needs. . . .
>
> The President affirmed his intention to carry out the national policy, expressed in the congressional Middle East resolution which had been adopted, and exercise as needed the authority thereby conferred on the President. In this connection, the President authorized the accelerated delivery to the countries of the area of economic and other defensive items which have been programmed for their use.
>
> The President expressed the hope that the international Communists would not push Syria into any acts of aggression against her neighbors and that the people of Syria would act to allay the anxiety caused by recent events.[48]

The Administration stopped short of invoking the Eisenhower Doctrine, but it also appeared to define the situation as one in which the doctrine could be applied if Syria attempted to engage in provocative acts against its neighbors.

[48] Text in *State Department Bulletin*, 37 (September 23, 1957), 487.

As a demonstration of the availability of U.S. military power and also as a means of exerting pressure on Syrian internal political developments, the Sixth Fleet was again ordered into the eastern Mediterranean, and some American aircraft were redeployed from Western Europe to the U.S. base at Adana, Turkey. The Strategic Air Command was put on alert, and U.S. arms began flowing into the countries surrounding Syria.

Through these statements and acts, described by Eisenhower as "preliminary," the United States was coming close to committing itself to the overthrow of the Syrian government. The Eisenhower Doctrine was again being employed in an attempt to influence an internal situation. The Syrians certainly must have felt that the United States was poised to strike at the slightest provocation. Sensing imminent danger, they were careful not to engage in any actions which might have justified an American intervention. The regime repeatedly proclaimed itself to be Arab nationalist, not communist. Washington, although still extremely suspicious, became somewhat less apprehensive, as did the Arab states surrounding Syria. In fact, Lebanon and Jordan, although always willing to accept additional arms shipments from the United States, began to speak reassuringly of the priority they gave to the concept of solidarity among the Arab states, and made it clear that they wanted no conflict which would benefit the common enemy, Israel. At an Arab summit meeting in Damascus, the Prime Minister of Iraq spoke of a "complete understanding" between his country and Syria. Even King Saud, the Arab leader with whom the administration had the closest association, claimed to see no clear threat to any other Arab nation from Syria, and pledged to aid Syria in the event that *it* became a target of aggression.[49]

The reaction of the pro-Western Arab states came as a surprise to the Eisenhower Administration, which was not looking at the situation in the same way as the Arabs were. The administration was responding to its own Cold War premises which, as we have mentioned, were insensitive to the realities

[49] Campbell, *Defense of the Middle East*, p. 133; Brown, *Faces of Power*, p. 132.

of Arab nationalism. However, noting that the Arabs now saw Syria as an ally and not an enemy, the administration began to back away from its previous position. In a press conference on September 10, Secretary Dulles stated that action under the Eisenhower Doctrine now seemed unlikely in Syria, and he felt that the situation would work itself out peacefully. "There has been as yet no determination that Syria is dominated by international communism within the meaning of the Middle East resolution," he explained.

Dulles' press conference was noteworthy in that he laid down for the first time the explicit requirements which would have to be met before the intervention clause of the doctrine could be implemented. He was also quick to add that he did not feel these requirements had been met in the Syrian situation:

> There have to be three findings before there is direct armed intervention by the United States. There has to be a finding by the President that one of the countries was dominated by international communism; secondly, there has to be an act of aggression by that country; third, there has to be a request by the country attacked for that aid. . . . And I might say at the present time I don't think it likely that those three things will occur. . . .[50]

As the crisis was subsiding, the Soviets made a quick attempt to derive political advantage from the situation. Claiming that the United States, along with Turkey and Israel, was planning a major military attack on Syria, the Soviets announced that they "could not remain passive" and, in an obvious reference to Turkey, stated that "if the rifles fire, the rockets will start firing." The Soviet delegate to the U.N. demanded that the General Assembly discuss the "intolerably dangerous" situation and affirmed the Soviet Union's willingness "to take part with its forces in suppressing aggression and punishing the violators of peace." [51] Dulles attempted to rebut the Soviet charges and also felt obliged to counter the rhetorical Soviet threat of inter-

[50] *State Department Bulletin*, 37 (September 30, 1957), 527, 532.

[51] Campbell, *Defense of the Middle East*, pp. 133–34.

vention with a rhetorical deterrent threat of his own. ("Certainly, if there is an attack on Turkey by the Soviet Union, it would not mean a purely defensive operation by the United States, with the Soviet Union a privileged sanctuary from which to attack Turkey.") [52] Dulles' retort notwithstanding, the Soviets had succeeded, as in the Suez crisis, in presenting themselves as the Arabs' benefactors and supporters against the imperialist designs of the Americans, while at the same time expending very little energy and incurring very little risk.

The Syrian crisis demonstrated the difficulty Eisenhower's evolving Middle East policy was encountering in attempting to combine deterrence of possible Soviet "aggression" in the Middle East with protection of Western interests that were affected by domestic and regional instabilities having little or only an indirect relationship to the threat of "international communism." More than the earlier Jordan affair, the Syrian crisis revealed that Arab nationalism and neutralism placed important constraints on the behavior of even those pro-Western Arab governments that benefited from certain aspects of Washington's new Middle East policy.

It was now amply clear that the Eisenhower Doctrine, already proven powerless to deter the Soviet Union from giving either military or economic assistance to Middle East governments, was also incapable of supplying inducements with which to dissuade Egypt and Syria from seeking a closer relationship with the Soviet Union. And whatever the nature of the clandestine American effort to influence internal Syrian politics (the scanty evidence available suggests it was substantial) [53] it failed to generate a serious threat to the government of Shukri al-Quwatli. While American pressure may have induced greater caution in his government, there was no practical way in which the United States could have halted the Syrian government's movement toward the Soviet Union without incurring risks and costs much higher than it was willing to accept.

[52] *Current Documents*, p. 1047.   [53] Seale, *Struggle for Syria*, pp. 293–94.

LEBANON—THE FIRST PHASE,
MAY–JULY 1958

The eventual outcome of the Syrian crisis was not the communist takeover which the Eisenhower Administration had so greatly feared. Instead, the United States was surprised to learn in January 1958 that Syria and Egypt were planning to merge their two countries into one nation—the United Arab Republic (UAR). This development was still viewed with suspicion by U.S. leaders, however, because they perceived it as yet another communist-inspired move in the Middle East. At first, as Eisenhower recalls, "it was unclear whether this union was prompted by Communist influence or whether the Communists were merely going along with Nasser's ambition eventually to unify the Arab world." [54]

Paradoxically, however, it appears that the Syrian move toward Egypt was prompted not by the communists at all, but rather by Syrian army officers who feared that the communists were becoming too powerful a political force within Syria. Along with several politicians who were also growing suspicious of the communists, they hoped that the formation of the UAR would stabilize the fluid internal situation. The gambit was apparently successful. As one of his terms for accepting a merger, Nasser remained as President of the new republic. He immediately abolished all political parties, including the communists, in Syria. The result was a quick reversal of the influence which the Syrian communists had acquired. The Soviet Union, having lost the chance to increase its influence in Syria beyond that which it enjoyed in Egypt, chose to make the best of the situation and recognized the new republic on the day it officially came into being. For its part, however, the Eisenhower Administration was still perceiving the world as a bipolar system where any country's dealings with the Soviets were taken as evidence of potential for a communist takeover in that country.

[54] Eisenhower, *White House Years*, p. 262.

Another perceived blow to Western interests in the Middle East occurred in March 1958. Nasser and other leaders of the UAR began a violent press and radio campaign against King Saud, who was apparently involved in "intrigues" aimed against the new republic. These attacks came at a time when Saud's domestic policies were being subjected to severe criticism within his own country. The combination of the internal difficulties and the attacks by the UAR precipitated a crisis which resulted in Saud's turning over control of foreign, internal, and financial affairs to his brother, Prince Faisal, who was generally—and mistakenly—viewed in Washington as pro-Nasserite. Eisenhower described King Saud in his memoirs as "the man we had hoped might eventually rival Nasser as an Arab leader." The president was clearly concerned by Saud's fall from power. He stated reluctantly that, "as a potential bulwark against Communist expansion efforts in the Middle East, King Saud's usefulness was temporarily, at least, at an end." [55]

These and other developments since the Suez fiasco reinforced the feeling in Washington that the Western position in the Middle East was rapidly deteriorating and becoming more precarious. Therefore, when an internal conflict in Lebanon erupted into civil war in May 1958, U.S. leaders viewed it not as an isolated incident, but instead as another in a long line of threats to American and Western interests in the Middle East. The magnitude of the threat perceived by the administration in this case was no doubt greatly affected by this sense of a chain of events which seemed to be inexorably leading to the elimination of United States influence in the area. Thus, Washington felt itself under pressure to take more drastic action in Lebanon than it would otherwise have contemplated in order to reaffirm its interests throughout the Middle East. The eventual intervention in Lebanon on July 15, 1958, can be explained partially as a last resort by which U.S. leaders hoped to reverse, or at least arrest, this anti-Western trend. Indeed, throughout the Lebanon crisis, the administration showed far less flexibility and a much

[55] *Ibid.*, pp. 263–64.

quicker tendency to declare that some action would *have* to be taken than in either the Jordanian or Syrian crises we have already examined.

The crisis in Lebanon resulted from a complex web of causes, some internal, some regional, and some international. Fundamentally, all these causes emanated from the social cleavages which split Lebanese society into several conflicting groups. The most important cleavage was the religious one between Muslims and Christians. On nearly all important matters of controversy in Lebanon, the population tended to split into these two rival factions. Four basic sources of the civil war which broke out in May 1958 can be identified: (1) The feeling of the Muslim segment of the population that the government of Camille Chamoun was discriminating against them socially, politically, and economically; (2) the belief held by a large sector of the population that Chamoun's administration was basically corrupt; (3) the widespread feeling that the result of the 1957 elections, which filled the Cabinet and the Chamber of Deputies with Chamoun's supporters, was achieved through fraudulent means; and (4) the attempt by Chamoun to succeed himself as President in contravention to the Lebanese constitution.

The last two issues alienated a substantial number of Christians from the government, and were probably the ones most responsible for the eventual outbreak of violence in the country. Exacerbating them, however, were disagreements over regional and international issues. On the regional level, the Lebanese population found itself divided over the government's poor relations with Egypt and Syria, the issue of Arab nationalism under the leadership of Egypt, and the polarization of the Arab world into two hostile camps led by Egypt and Iraq. At this level, the country was split into two groups constituting the government and its supporters, including most of the Christian half of the country, on the one hand, and the Muslim half of the population as well as many disaffected political leaders on the other. The latter group was sympathetic with (Muslim) Nasser's brand of Arab nationalism and neutralism, whereas the government was seen as being aligned with Iraq against Egypt, opposed to the nationalist movement, and heavily reliant on the

(Christian) West for political and economic support. Viewed from this standpoint, of course, the Eisenhower Doctrine and Chamoun's adherence to it could only increase the internal cleavages in Lebanon.

The Lebanese government had given enthusiastic support to the doctrine and the principles upon which it was based. Chamoun and his strongly anti-Egyptian, influential Foreign Minister, Charles Malik, had seen in it what they thought was a timely instrument with which to counterbalance the gravitation of the Muslim half of the country toward Nasserist Pan-Arabism. On March 16, 1957, only seven days after the Eisenhower Doctrine became law, Lebanon and the United States issued a joint communiqué announcing that the two countries were in full agreement on the efficacy of the new resolution. This announcement was hailed in Washington as a vindication of the American policy. The effect in Lebanon, however, was quite different. By accepting the doctrine, the government was in effect openly entering the Cold War conflict on the side of the West. Second, it was obviously backing the United States against Egypt and Syria. Both these moves were viewed by the great majority of Muslim Lebanese and some Christian leaders as being in direct violation of the traditional policy established by the National Covenant of 1943, which demanded Lebanese neutrality in foreign affairs and Lebanese support of Arab states against foreign states.

The consequences of Chamoun's acceptance of the Eisenhower Doctrine were twofold. First, it added more fuel to the already bitter factionalism dividing the country. Second, it convinced the governments of Egypt and Syria that Lebanon was now fully in the enemy camp and was therefore a serious threat to their own security. As a result, they began to work actively for the removal or overthrow of the Chamoun regime. To this end, Lebanon became the target of an intense and sustained attack by the Egyptian and Syrian radio and press. This was complemented by attacks from the Soviet Union and from communist parties in the Middle East. These attacks, in turn, heightened the level of conflict within Lebanon even more.

All these factors—internal, regional, and international—fed

upon each other and formed a vicious spiral of antagonism that finally exploded into civil war on May 8, 1958, when a newspaper publisher and severe critic of the Chamoun regime was assassinated by unknown gunmen. As the fighting in and around Beirut became more intense, reports began to appear that Syrian infiltrators were entering Lebanon and aiding the rebel cause with men and matériel. Syrian and Egyptian radio broadcasts stepped up their attacks on Chamoun and urged that he be immediately overthrown.

The revolt might have been brought under control quickly had not the Lebanese army refused to take sides in the struggle. The commander-in-chief, General Fuad Chehab, did not come to the support of the government because he feared a split between the two religious factions in the army. Chehab realized that his army was a reflection of Lebanese society and felt that any attempt to put down the revolt would result in the army's dissolution into Christian and Muslim armed cliques.

As for Washington's view of the situation at this time, Eisenhower reports that "Behind everything was our deep-seated conviction that the Communists were principally responsible for the trouble, and that President Chamoun was motivated only by a strong feeling of patriotism." [56] In response to a request from Chamoun on May 13 inquiring what U.S. action would be taken if the Lebanese government were to request military assistance, Eisenhower replied that the United States would respond favorably to a request for assistance, but only under certain conditions. They were:

> First, we would not send United States troops to Lebanon for the purpose of achieving an additional term for the President. Second, the request should have the concurrence of some other Arab nation. Third, the mission of United States troops in Lebanon would be twofold: protection of the life and property of Americans, and assistance to the legal Lebanese government.[57]

In addition to reassuring Chamoun that the U.S. was behind him to this extent, Eisenhower ordered "preliminary actions"

[56] *Ibid.*, p. 266.   [57] *Ibid.*, p. 267.

paralleling the earlier U.S. moves during the Jordanian and Syrian crises. The Sixth Fleet was once again ordered into the eastern Mediterranean and the number of available Marines in the area was increased. The U.S. sent tear gas and small arms ammunition to the Lebanese government. On May 17, the State Department announced that the U.S. was considering whether to send American troops.[58]

Thus, the Eisenhower Administration went through the familiar motions of attempting to reinforce its deterrent role in the Middle East. Once again, a primarily internal conflict was being approached as if it were a case of communist encroachment. Once again, American policies were partially responsible for the crisis. And once again, the U.S. saw no way to deal with the problem except through military action.

Up to this point, however, the administration had not made its customary threat to invoke the Eisenhower Doctrine. This one missing item of its repertoire was added by Secretary Dulles during his press conference on May 20. By this time, despite Eisenhower's fears quoted above, the doctrine's declaration against "armed agression from any country controlled by international communism" had fallen into virtual disuse as the criterion of the doctrine's applicability. The administration had already seen the difficulties involved in attempting to prove such an allegation in the complex crises which it had previously faced in the Middle East. Now Dulles fell back on another phrase in the doctrine as the main justification for action. In response to a press conference question regarding its applicability to the situation in Lebanon, the Secretary of State replied:

> . . . the Eisenhower doctrine . . . contains several provisions. It is not just one thing. . . .
>
> Now we do not consider under the present state of affairs that there is likely to be an attack, an armed attack, from a country which we would consider under the control of international communism. That doesn't mean, however, that there is nothing that can be done. There is the provision of the Middle East resolution which says that the independence of these countries is vital to peace and the na-

[58] Qubain, *Crisis in Lebanon*, p. 113.

tional interest of the United States. That is certainly a mandate to do something if we think that our peace and vital interests are endangered from any quarter.[59]

The implicit aspects of the doctrine—its availability for use against indirect aggression and subversion from either communist or noncommunist sources ("any quarter")—were now in the forefront. Previously, in the Jordanian and Syrian crises, the "independence and integrity" phrase of the resolution had been mentioned as applicable to each situation. However, in both those cases, the administration's claim that communist maneuverings were involved was used as the primary justification for threatening to introduce American military power into the conflict. Now, the relative importance of the two clauses had been reversed. After May 20, the administration refrained from any public statements claiming that a communist threat was an important element in the Lebanese crisis. Apparently, some time between Eisenhower's response to Lebanon on May 13 and Dulles' statement on May 20, the administration had concluded that there was no adequate basis for branding the crisis as communist-inspired.

Following its decision of May 13 to assist Chamoun's government, the administration began conferring with Britain regarding the possibility of employing military intervention to stabilize the situation in the Middle East. Both powers feared that if Chamoun were toppled, the pro-Western regimes in Jordan and Iraq would suffer a similar fate. On May 22, American and English military personnel met on the island of Cyprus to develop a plan for combined intervention in Lebanon and Jordan.[60] The plan was meant to be activated only if the Syrian army, which at the time was located between Damascus and the Israeli border only a few hours from Beirut, should openly attempt to attack the government's forces in Lebanon.

While these actions were taking place, Lebanon was preparing to present its case before the United Nations Security

[59] *State Department Bulletin,* 38 (June 9, 1958), p. 945. See also footnote 6.

[60] *New York Times,* May 20, 1958, p. 10.

Council, charging Syria with supplying men and arms to the antigovernment forces in Lebanon. On June 6, Lebanese Foreign Minister Charles Malik brought before the council evidence to prove his charge of "massive, illegal, and unprovoked intervention in the affairs of Lebanon by the United Arab Republic." [61] In the ensuing debate, the United States and Britain backed Malik's claims, while the Societ Union joined the UAR in rejecting the charges. The outcome of the discussion was a decision on June 10 to send a United Nations observation group to Lebanon to get a first-hand report. The first members of the team arrived in the area two days later.

Eisenhower admitted in his memoirs that "the failure of President Nasser to object to a United Nations observation team in Lebanon was puzzling." [62] The puzzle was somewhat cleared up, however, when the observation group's first report minimized the outside support for the rebellion and stated that the vast majority of those fighting were undoubtedly Lebanese. United Nations Secretary-General Dag Hammarskjöld visited Lebanon on June 18 and also concluded that Syrian infiltration was not so heavy as President Chamoun had claimed. This turn of events left the United States discouraged and a bit embarrassed. Officials in Washington tended to feel that the observation group was too small to be able to effectively monitor the whole Syrian-Lebanese border, and American intelligence services contradicted the group's conclusions about Syrian infiltration, claiming that such infiltration was actually on the increase. However, the U.S. did not want to openly attack the U.N. efforts for fear of appearing to undermine the international organization's ability to handle the situation.

Time wore on, and the situation remained fairly stable. By early July, the administration was confident that the Lebanon crisis, like those before it, would pass with a minimum of damage to U.S. interests. President Chamoun had made several important concessions to the rebels. He agreed not to run for re-

[61] Agwani, *Lebanese Crisis*, p. 124.
[62] Eisenhower, *White House Years*, p. 268.

election and announced that he would cooperate in finding a candidate acceptable to both Christians and Arab nationalists. It appeared there would be no need for Western intervention.

The administration was still not completely satisfied that the United Nations would be able to handle the situation effectively, however. If the U.N. effort should prove unsuccessful, due to some unanticipated turn of events, the U.S. was still prepared to move unilaterally, if necessary, to protect Chamoun's government. A new justification for such an action was introduced by Secretary Dulles at a press conference on July 1. In an attempt to show that a much wider foundation existed for U.S. action than merely that which was expressed in the Eisenhower Doctrine, Dulles now announced that, should U.N. efforts to stabilize the situation fail, the U.S. could act under Article 51 of the United Nations Charter.[63] He emphasized however, that he hoped the problem could be solved by the U.N. and that American action would only come as a last resort.[64]

Thus, the Eisenhower Doctrine slipped even further into the background. Now even the "independence and integrity" clause was of secondary importance. The original purpose of the doctrine—to defend the nations of the Middle East from armed attack, ostensibly from international communism—was now to be carried out under another instrument of policy implementation, namely Article 51 of the U.N. Charter. The doctrine itself, if not the precepts it was based upon, was being mentioned less and less as a basis of American policy.

---

[63] Article 51: "Nothing in the present Charter shall impair the inherent right of individual or collective self-defense if an armed attack occurs against a Member of the United Nations, until the Security Council has taken the measures necessary to maintain international peace and security. Measures taken by members in the exercise of this right of self-defense shall be immediately reported to the Security Council and shall not in any way affect the authority and responsibility of the Security Council under the present Charter to take at any time such action as it deems necessary in order to maintain or restore international peace and security." *Yearbook*, pp. 831–50.

[64] *State Department Bulletin*, 39 (July 21, 1958), 105.

LEBANON—THE SECOND PHASE, JULY–OCTOBER, 1958

On July 14, 1958 Iraqi General Abdul Karim Qassim and his army entered Baghdad, the capital of Iraq, captured the radio station and the bridges, and then took over the King's palace. The Iraqi premier, Nuri Es-Said, and the royal family were assassinated. With unexpected suddenness the "unanticipated turn of events" referred to by Secretary Dulles on July 1 had occurred. The Iraqi coup came as a complete surprise to U.S. intelligence, leaving President Eisenhower particularly shocked. Iraq had been, as he recalled in his memoirs, "the country we were counting on as a bulwark of stability and progress in the region." [65] If such a surprising turn of events could occur in what had been regarded as the most stable and reliable of pro-Western Arab states, then, Eisenhower rightly wondered, how could the United States have any confidence at all in its ability to assess developments in the rest of the Middle East? The administration now feared the worst:

. . . *This somber turn of events could, without vigorous response on our part, result in a complete elimination of Western influence in the Middle East.* Overnight our objective changed from quieting a troubled situation to facing up to a crisis of formidable proportions.[66]

Indeed, the collapse of the Iraqi monarchy meant that the regime which had been the keystone and founding member of the Baghdad Pact, and which had also been the principal opposition within the Arab world to Nasser's drive for hegemony—and supposedly to communism as well—had been violently swept away overnight. Now in its place stood a completely new, untried revolutionary government. No one in Washington or in any other Western capital knew how to assess the political complexion of Qassim's new government or to predict how it would

---

[65] Eisenhower, *White House Years*, p. 269.

[66] *Ibid.*, p. 269 (emphasis added).

conduct itself vis-à-vis its Arab neighbors, Israel, or the Western nations involved in the Middle East. As a result, the whole of Western policy in the region was thrown into confusion.

The Eisenhower Administration, however, was quick to come to one conclusion: that the Iraqi coup would have a profound effect on the ongoing crisis in Lebanon. The balance in that country which was now being worked out between the Chamoun government and the opposition forces would probably, as a result of the coup, be altered in favor of the rebels. Certainly their morale would be boosted by the news of the overthrow of the Western-oriented monarchy. In addition, Chamoun's forces would suffer political and financial losses due to the sudden elimination of assistance they had been receiving from the previous Iraqi regime. Thus, in terms of its effect on the relative strength of the opposing factions in Lebanon, the Iraqi coup altered the situation substantially.

An even more important result of the coup, however, was its psychological effect on both President Chamoun and the Eisenhower Administration. Chamoun had previously tried to request U.S. intervention on several occasions between May and the outbreak of the coup in July, but had been dissuaded each time by the U.S. Ambassador. He had also managed to obtain authority from his Cabinet to request intervention without prior consultation if he deemed it necessary. Following the coup, his desperation reached new heights. Early on the morning of July 14, Chamoun separately called into his office the French, British, and American ambassadors. He told each of them that unless a Western intervention was forthcoming within the next forty-eight hours, "he would be a dead man, and Lebanon would become an Egyptian satellite." [67]

Upon receiving news of the Iraqi coup, Secretary Dulles reportedly advised the President that "the risks of not taking action were greater than those of doing so." [68] He also counseled Eisenhower that if the new Iraqi regime turned out to be com-

[67] Qubain, *Crisis in Lebanon*, p. 115.

[68] Drummond and Colbenz, *Duel at the Brink*, p. 193.

munist controlled, it would mean that the Soviet Union had "leap-frogged the northern tier," thus dealing a devastating blow to the Western position in the Middle East. If, on the other hand, the coup had been prompted by Egypt, that would mean that Nasser had now managed totally to surround Lebanon, Jordan, and Israel—the last Western-oriented countries in the region.[69] Further, Eisenhower was informed that there was very reliable evidence that a similar coup d'état had been scheduled against King Hussein for July 17.[70] Thus the situation seemed to portend not just one but several possible outcomes which were viewed as being capable of irreversibly damaging U.S. and Western interests in the area. This gloomy state of affairs left Eisenhower with the feeling that the United States would not be able to recover from this new situation as easily as it had from the other crises it had faced in the area during the previous year, and that the U.S. would therefore in all likelihood be forced to employ military intervention in a final attempt to stabilize the deteriorating situation. Accordingly, he described in his memoirs the sense of inevitability with which he entered the NSC meeting called to consider Chamoun's request:

> . . . Because of my long study of the problem, this was one meeting in which my mind was practically made up regarding the general line of action we should take, even before we met. The time was rapidly approaching, I believed, when we had to move into the Middle East, and specifically, into Lebanon, to stop the trend toward chaos.[71]

At the same NSC meeting Secretary of State Dulles called attention to some of the risks of an American intervention. He

[69] Beal, *John Foster Dulles*, p. 332. In his memoirs, on the other hand, Eisenhower recalls that although CIA Director Allen Dulles reported that the coup was executed by pro-Nasser elements in the Iraqi army and the new government included many pro-Nasser people, he had no evidence as yet that Nasser himself was behind the coup. Dulles made no mention of any evidence that might point to the coup being the work of "international Communist aggression." Eisenhower, *White House Years*, p. 270.

[70] McClintock, "The American Landing in Lebanon," p. 69.

[71] Eisenhower, *White House Years*, p. 270.

believed that the Soviets would make threatening gestures toward Turkey and Iran but that they would probably not act
because they feared a general war with the U.S. The oil pipe-
lines across Syria would most likely be cut, and U.S. access to
the Suez Canal might be impeded or denied. The British would
have to move into Kuwait to protect their oil interests, and the
U.S. would have to substantially increase strength at Dhahran
Air Force Base in Saudi Arabia. Finally, "If the United States
went into Lebanon we could expect a very bad reaction from
most Arab countries." [72] It is clear, therefore, that the administration was not entertaining hopes of achieving a very low-cost
intervention in Lebanon. Even so, however, Eisenhower was
still convinced that "The time had come to act." [73] The consequences of not acting were seen as involving nothing less than
"a complete elimination of Western influence in the Middle
East"; and the NSC quickly approved the intervention plan.

On the afternoon of July 14, Eisenhower, Allen Dulles, and
John Foster Dulles met with a bipartisan group of congressmen.
Some of them were skeptical about the operation. Senator William Fulbright voiced his doubt that the crisis was actually communist-inspired. House Speaker Sam Rayburn was fearful that
the U.S. might be getting into something that was strictly a civil
war. Eisenhower challenged Rayburn's view, which was based
primarily on the U.N. observation group's reports. The President pointed out that the U.N. group's reports only covered the
limited time when the group was at its stations, and mentioned
that "some of our own observers definitely doubted the compe-
tence of the team." [74] No specific refutation was made of Senator Fulbright's observation, however, which actually seemed
quite reasonable, since the administration had been unable as
yet to pinpoint any evidence of serious communist involvement
either in Lebanon or in Iraq. Although admitting that the congressmen were not completely satisfied with his explanations,
the President stated that "authority for such an operation lay so

[72] *Ibid.*, p. 271.   [73] *Ibid.*, p. 270.   [74] *Ibid.*, p. 272.

clearly within the responsibility of the Executive that no direct objection was voiced. In any event, the issue was clear to me—we had to go in." [75] Eisenhower did not feel that a renewed expression of congressional approval was necessary for him to take action, and he fully intended to employ the authority which he had received fifteen months before with the passage of the Eisenhower Doctrine. Directly after the congressional meeting, Eisenhower ordered the Sixth Fleet to land U.S. Marines in Lebanon on the following afternoon, July 15.

The administration's decision to send troops into Lebanon was announced in three separate statements issued on July 15. Following a White House press release which was issued in the morning, the President spoke before a joint meeting of Congress in the afternoon and then delivered a nationwide address over radio and television in the evening. In each of these statements, Eisenhower pointed out both the objectives and justifications of the intervention.

In terms of objectives, the President was quite specific but, as we shall see, refrained from publicly mentioning some considerations which probably weighed heavily in his decision. As it was, he professed in his congressional speech two objectives of the intervention by declaring that U.S. troops were sent to Lebanon "to protect American lives and by their presence to assist the Government of Lebanon in the preservation of Lebanon's territorial integrity and independence, which have been deemed vital to United States interests and world peace." [76]

The justifications for the intervention were less specifically spelled out. It appears this resulted from the administration's reluctance to abandon the Eisenhower Doctrine in the midst of a serious crisis, even though the doctrine seemed as inapplicable to this case as it had been to the previous three. Thus in his radio and television address, Eisenhower did not hesitate to

[75] *Ibid.* See also Adams, *Firsthand Report*, p. 291.

[76] *State Department Bulletin*, 39 (August 4, 1958), p. 182.

declare the importance of the doctrine's role in the American response.[77] He did not, however, go so far as to say that the intervention had been an example of the doctrine in action. The failure to uncover any significant communist involvement in the crisis precluded such a formulation. Indeed, now that Secretary Dulles had publicly enunciated the three necessary requirements for invocation of the doctrine, the administration could not very well attempt to use it as primary justification for its actions when two of those requirements had definitely not been fulfilled.

Therefore, the legal justification for the intervention was allowed to rest on Article 51 of the U.N. Charter. As Eisenhower told Congress, "the United States will be acting pursuant to what the United Nations Charter recognizes as an inherent right—the right of all nations to work together and to seek help when necessary to preserve their independence." [78] The only prerequisite for action under Article 51 was that the U.S. receive a request to intervene from the legal Lebanese government. Chamoun supplied that request in an action which was clearly within his constitutional rights as President of Lebanon.

Let us return to the objectives of the intervention. So far we have mentioned only the two official reasons for the action: (1) to protect American lives and property, and (2) to preserve "Lebanon's territorial integrity and independence." But we need not search far in order to discover other objectives. In the thirty pages of his memoirs devoted to the landing in Lebanon, President Eisenhower was particularly elusive as to why he felt

[77] In that speech Eisenhower stated:

"Last year the Congress of the United States joined with the President to declare that 'the United States regards as vital to the national interest and world peace the preservation of the independence and integrity of the nations of the Middle East.'

"I believe that the presence of United States forces now being sent to Lebanon will have a stabilizing effect which will preserve the independence and integrity of Lebanon." *State Department Bulletin*, 39 (August 4, 1958), p. 185.

[78] *Ibid.*, pp. 182–83.

there was no choice of means other than intervention to bring the situation under control. He states: "In Lebanon the question was whether it would be better to incur the deep resentment of nearly all the Arab world (and some of the rest of the Free World) and in doing so to risk general war with the Soviet Union or to do something worse—which was to do nothing." [79]

Other U.S officials who were involved in the decision have shed additional light on the reasons behind it. After he ordered the troops into Lebanon, the President asked Robert Murphy, who was then Deputy Undersecretary of State, to go to Beirut as a personal emissary and to explain to the Lebanese the purposes of the intervention. Murphy states that in a discussion with Eisenhower before his departure "the President elaborated a little on his purpose in ordering U.S. Marines to land in Lebanon."

> He said that the sentiment had developed in the Middle East, especially in Egypt, that Americans were capable only of words, that we were afraid of Soviet reaction if we attempted military action. Eisenhower believed that if the United States did nothing now, there would be heavy and irreparable losses in Lebanon and in the area generally. He wanted to demonstrate in a timely and practical way that the United States was capable of supporting its friends.[80]

This explanation of the purpose of the intervention is quite consistent with Eisenhower's Cold War policy as a whole. The administration intervened in Lebanon not merely to improve the situation there but primarily for the purpose of influencing Soviet and Egyptian images of the United States and enhancing the credibility of American commitments around the world.

Presidential Assistant Sherman Adams was candid about what the U.S. accomplished and what it did not accomplish through the intervention:

> Dulles said that he and Eisenhower were under no illusions that they had solved any problems in sending the Marines to Lebanon; they were using military force only to prevent the dangerous situa-

[79] Eisenhower, *White House Years*, p. 274.

[80] Murphy, *Diplomat among Warriors*, p. 398.

tion in the Middle East from getting any worse, and to reassure many small nations that they could call on us in time of crisis. There can be no question that they achieved that purpose.[81]

Although Eisenhower admitted suffering many "anxious hours" as he waited to see what the repercussions of the intervention would be, we find that after July 15 the conflict began to work itself out very quickly. As events developed, it appeared that the U.S. intervention and the coordinated British intervention to help King Hussein in Jordan, which finally took place on July 17, would incur less costs and risks than Dulles had predicted at the July 14 meeting. The United States gave no indication of any intent to intervene in Iraq. The Soviets refrained from any particularly provocative reactions to the Lebanese landings or the British move into Jordan, and contented themselves with labeling the interventions as "aggression" and began a vigorous diplomatic campaign for a summit conference to settle the conflict and to limit the flow of weapons into the Middle East. Eisenhower rejected these proposals, arguing that the matter should be dealt with through the United Nations Security Council. Nasser, not particularly enthusiastic over the possibility of a Soviet intervention coming on the heels of the Western incursion, apparently assured the Soviets that there would be no need for them to take military action unless the Western powers invaded Iraq or the UAR.[82] He then proceeded to keep his assistance to the Lebanese rebels at a minimum and began to use his influence to help in achieving a political compromise inside Lebanon.

In Lebanon the internal conflict reached a somewhat unexpected solution. Finding that Chamoun's regime could not be

---

[81] Adams, *Firsthand Report*, p. 293. Adams also claims that the Soviet government "was astonished and taken aback by our display of strength and determination at Lebanon. There was a change in the tone of Khrushchev's letters to the President in subsequent months, a more conciliatory note and a stronger inclination to negotiate rather than to threaten." *Ibid.*, p. 293. For a brief analysis of Khrushchev's reponse to the Lebanon crisis and its impact on the Sino-Soviet dispute, see Zagoria, *Sino-Soviet Conflict*, pp. 195–99, 350.

[82] Brown, *Faces of Power*, p. 137.

saved, Robert Murphy, to the chagrin of most pro-Western Lebanese who had welcomed the U.S. landings, proceeded to negotiate with the rebels and convinced them that the United States would be willing to support a compromise candidate for President. In a special election on July 31, the Lebanese Parliament overwhelmingly elected General Chehab, who had emerged as a presidential candidate acceptable to both camps even before the U.S. intervention, and the fighting quickly died down. On August 21, the U.N. General Assembly passed a resolution sponsored by the Arab states which pledged noninterference among the Arab countries in each other's affairs and paved the way for withdrawal of American forces from Lebanon and British forces from Jordan within a few months.

Thus, although the American intervention had been intended to bolster the pro-Western Chamoun government, it served to insure a measure of success for the coalition of forces opposing him on various grounds. Moreover, the new Lebanese government under President Chehab rejected his predecessor's adherence to the Eisenhower Doctrine and Lebanon rejoined the ranks of other neutralist regimes in the region, leaving King Hussein of Jordan as the only dependably pro-Western leader in the Middle East. Having exacerbated more problems than it had solved, the Eisenhower Doctrine was now quietly put aside.

Conclusions

This brief history of the Eisenhower Doctrine provides striking examples of several of the simplifications and limitations of deterrence theory discussed in chapter 3. It illustrates once again the fact, emphasized throughout this study, that deterrence strategy cannot be expected to support, make up for, or rescue a poorly conceived and misdirected foreign policy. In its practical aspects if not in its rhetoric, U.S. policy in the Middle East during 1957–1958 was profoundly insensitive to forces

such as nationalism, anticolonialism, and desire for modernization which were root causes of major tensions in the area. For
the most part American policy increased regional instabilities
rather than harnessing the underlying forces in a constructive
manner.

Important roots of the administration's failure in the Middle
East are to be found in its premises regarding the nature of the
Cold War and its implications for American foreign policy. The
fact that it viewed the world as a tight bipolar system in which
"third areas" such as the Middle East were battlegrounds for
great-power struggles contributed to the United States' insensi-
tivity and blundering in this region during 1957 and 1958. The
Eisenhower Doctrine, we have seen, was a direct reflection of
this worldview. Added to it was the dubious assumption that
the United States could control events in the Middle East
which might prove detrimental to Western interests by somehow reducing the Soviet Union's intrusion into the area. If
indeed the Soviet Union had been tempted to engage in direct
military adventures in the Middle East, then use of deterrence
policy in some more appropriate form by the administration
may have been necessary and useful. But the Eisenhower Doctrine, essentially a military threat, did not and could not succeed
in deterring the Soviet Union from providing arms or economic
aid to Middle Eastern regimes. Nor did the administration find
means of dissuading Egypt and Syria from seeking such assistance or from adopting a pro-Soviet and anti-Western stance. In
fact, by allowing the doctrine to be construed, both by its
friends and by its opponents in the Middle East, as aimed at
Nasserist Pan-Arabism as much as at the spread of communism,
the United States practically pushed the nationalists into closer
cooperation with the Soviets. "This alliance between nationalists and Communists was cemented by the western failure
clearly to distinguish between them." [83] While an attitude of
better understanding of Arab nationalism and a more conciliatory approach toward Egypt and Syria would not have resulted

[83] Seale, *Struggle for Syria*, p. 287.

in the elimination of Soviet influence from the Middle East, they would have enabled Washington to counteract Moscow's actions more effectively, to play a more constructive role in the area, and to better safeguard legitimate Western interests in the Arab world.

This case also illustrates the dangers, noted in chapter 2, of attempting to employ "strategic" and "limited war" concepts of deterrence in the far more complex "crisis-preventive" type of situation. The Eisenhower Adminstration did not clearly differentiate between these three levels of conflict, and it attempted to employ deterrence strategy in a mechanical and clumsy way to deal with all three types of contingencies. The assumption behind the Eisenhower Doctrine that a deterrence commitment against the danger of external attack by the Soviet Union or "international communism" would also strengthen Arab states against internal communist subversion proved to be ineffectual and largely irrelevant for maintaining stable pro-Western governments. The causes of internal instability were manifold, and, in fact, they were probably aggravated insofar as American policies that attempted to strengthen Arab governments internally against communist subversion posed a threat also to legitimate noncommunist opposition within those governments. To many Arab nationalists, the United States was guilty not only of trying to extend the Cold War into the Middle East but also of using the exaggerated danger of communism as a pretext for intervention to protect Western economic and other interests in the area.

Finally, the Eisenhower Doctrine case contributes to a major thesis of this study, namely that deterrence theory cannot successfully define the boundaries of its own use as an instrument of foreign policy. When to use deterrence is a decision which must be based on premises existing outside the scope of conventional deterrence theory. As developed to date the theory offers no criteria for distinguishing between deterrable and nondeterrable situations. The root causes of Middle East instabilities were essentially nondeterrable phenomena. The Eisenhower Administration either did not see this limitation or did not give it sufficient weight. Despite the administration's avowal of the need for a "multifaceted" approach to the problems of the Middle East, it stressed military policy over economic measures. It acted during 1957 and 1958 as if it believed that almost any situation which appeared to affect American interests adversely could be deterred if the proper type of credible commitment were made. This belief led U.S. leaders to attempt to employ the Eisenhower Doctrine as a deterrent to actions it had not originally been designed to deter, hoping that it would somehow succeed in precisely those respects in which U.S. foreign policy in the region itself had failed. Deterrence strategy thus usurped the policy which it was supposed to help support, and thereby became the main instrument of American influence in the Middle East.

The ultimate result of this attempt to substitute deterrence strategy for a coherent foreign policy was a considerable loss of United States influence and prestige in the region. It is not surprising that following the Lebanon intervention no more was heard of the Eisenhower Doctrine. Instead, the remaining years of the administration were marked by a search for a more flexible and differentiated policy in which economic assistance was assigned a larger role, and in which efforts were made to establish better relations with Nasser.

Bibliography

Any analysis of the formulation of the Eisenhower Doctrine and the Middle Eastern crises of 1957–1958 inevitably suffers from the lack of detailed scholarly sources. Since no careful evaluation of the doctrine's formulation has as yet been made (due in part, no doubt, to the paucity of official information available concerning the actual decision-making process) we have found it necessary to attempt to discover how and why the doctrine was meant to work by examining the Senate and House hearings and the public statements made by Eisenhower and Dulles during the January–March 1957 period. This method has its merits but cannot be expected to yield "conclusive" results. Thus, our conclusions can only be tentative. Many of the more important public documents are found in several of the collections listed below.

Interpretations of the doctrine's role in the Middle East vary extensively both in quality of scholarship and in the conclusions reached. Eisenhower's memoirs offer some insights but have little to say about the objectives of either the doctrine itself or the Lebanese intervention. Murphy and Adams also contain some interesting information. The other memoirs and biographies deal mainly in hazy generalities. Copeland offers some intriguing "inside" views.

Barnet offers an excellent analysis of the idea of "American responsibility" (which seems to underlie U.S. perceptions in this case), in addition to a capable short discussion of the case itself. Brown also contributes valuable insights. O'Bannon's thesis pulls together many sources and reaches some interesting conclusions. Safran offers the best analysis of the strategic implications of the Middle East for U.S. policy. Binder, Halpern, and Lafeber deal more peripherally with the issues with which we have been concerned, but are good summaries.

Information on Soviet decision-making concerning the Middle East is expectedly sparse. Laqueur's is the best study, but only covers the period up to the Syrian crisis. Ulam and Speier are slightly less useful.

The studies that deal with Middle Eastern politics are much more valuable in explaining the complexities of the various crises and the relative inadequacy of U.S. policy-makers' appreciation of them. Seale is excellent at unraveling the complexities of the inter-Arab political scene in the period 1945–1958. Meo, Campbell, and Qubain are also good, the last two being well documented. Kerr's concise but incisive account of the Lebanese crisis includes a good analysis of the U.S. performance and its motives.

The effect of the Suez crisis on U.S. perceptions is discussed in Thomas, Love, and Speier.

We would like to thank John C. Campbell, Louis Gerson, and Malcom Kerr for reading and commenting on an earlier version of this chapter, and Fuad Jabber for incorporating their suggestions and his own into a later version.

Documents

Documents on International Affairs, 1956. London; Oxford University Press, 1959.

United Nations. *Yearbook of the United Nations, 1946–1947.* Lake Success, New York, 1950.

U.S. Congress, House Committee on Foreign Affairs. *Economic and Military Cooperation with Nations in the General Area of the Middle East, Hearings on H. J. Res. 117.* 85th Cong., 1st sess., January 7–22, 1957.

U.S. Congress, Senate Committee on Foreign Relations. *Events in the Middle East: A Select Chronology 1946–1957.* 85th Cong., 1st sess., January 11, 1957.

———. *United States Foreign Policy, Middle East: Staff Study.* 86th Cong., 2d sess., January 9, 1960.

——— and Committee on Armed Services. *The President's Proposal on the Middle East, Hearings on S. J. Res. 19 and H. J. Res. 117.* 85th Cong., 1st sess., January 14–February 4, 1957.

U. S. Department of State. *American Foreign Policy: Current Documents, 1957.* Publication No. 7101, General Foreign Policy Series 117. Washington, Government Printing Office, 1960.

——. *State Department Bulletin*, Vols. 35–39 (July 1956–December 1958).

——. *United States Policy in the Middle East September 1956–June 1957.* Publication No. 6505, Near and Middle East Series 6505. Washington, U.S. Government Printing Office, 1960.

United States Decision-making Memoirs and Biographies

Adams, Sherman. *Firsthand Report: The Story of the Eisenhower Administration.* New York, Harper & Bros., 1961.

Beal, John R. *John Foster Dulles: 1888–1959.* New York, Harper & Bros., 1959.

Drummond, Roscoe, and Gaston Coblenz. *Duel at the Brink.* Garden City, N.Y., Doubleday, 1960.

Eisenhower, Dwight D. *The White House Years: Waging Peace, 1956–1961.* Garden City, N.Y., Doubleday, 1965.

Hughes, John Emmet. *The Ordeal of Power: A Political Memoir of the Eisenhower Years.* New York, Atheneum, 1963.

McClintock, Robert. "The American Landing in Lebanon," *United States Naval Institute Proceedings*, 88, No. 10 (October 1962).

Murphy, Robert. *Diplomat among Warriors.* Garden City, N.Y., Doubleday, 1964.

Analyses

Barnet, Richard J. *Intervention and Revolution.* New York, World, 1968.

Binder, Leonard. "The Middle East as a Subordinate International System," in Hancock and Rustow, *American Foreign Policy in International Perspective.* Englewood Cliffs, N.J., Prentice-Hall, 1971.

Brown, Seyom. *The Faces of Power.* New York, Columbia University Press, 1968.

Campbell, John C., *Defense of the Middle East, Problems of American Policy.* Rev. ed. New York, Harper & Bros., 1960.

Copeland, Miles. *The Game of Nations.* New York, Simon and Schuster, 1969.

Finer, Herman. *Dulles over Suez.* Chicago, Quadrangle, 1964.

Halpern, Manfred. *The Politics of Social Change in the Middle East and North Africa.* Princeton, Princeton University Press, 1963.

Lafeber, Walter. *America, Russia and the Cold War, 1945–1966.* New York, Wiley, 1967.

O'Bannon, George W. *The Lebanon Crisis of 1958, A Case Study of United States Foreign Policy in the Middle East.* Unpublished masters thesis, Stanford University, 1965.

Polk, William R. *The United States and The Arab World.* Rev. ed. Cambridge, Harvard University Press, 1969.

Safran, Nadav. *From War to War: The Arab-Israeli Confrontation, 1948–1967.* New York, Pegasus, 1969.

Thomas, Hugh. *The Suez Affair.* Harmondsworth, England, Penguin Books Ltd., 1970.

Soviet Decision-Making

Laqueur, Walter. *The Soviet Union and the Middle East.* New York, Praeger, 1959.

Speier, Hans. "Soviet Atomic Blackmail and the North Atlantic Alliance," *World Politics*, IX, No. 3 (April 1957).

Ulam, Adam. *Expansion and Coexistence*. New York, Praeger, 1968.

Zagoria, Donald S., *The Sino-Soviet Conflict, 1956–1961*. Princeton, Princeton University Press, 1962.

Middle Eastern Politics

Agwani, M. S., ed. *The Lebanese Crisis, 1958*. New York, Asia Publishing House, 1965.

Binder, Leonard, ed. *Politics in Lebanon*. New York, Wiley, 1965.

Kerr, Malcolm, "The Lebanese Civil War," in *The International Regulation of Civil Wars*, ed. Evan Luard. London, Thames & Hudson, 1972.

Love, Kenneth. *Suez, the Twice-Fought War*. New York, McGraw-Hill, 1969.

Meo, Leila, M. T. *Lebanon, Improbable Nation, A Study in Political Development*. Bloomington, Ind., Indiana University Press, 1965.

Qubain, Fahim I. *Crisis in Lebanon*. Washington, The Middle East Institute, 1961.

Rondot, Pierre. *The Changing Patterns of the Middle East, 1919–1958*. London, Chatto & Windus, 1961.

Royal Institute of International Affairs. *Survey of International Affairs, 1956–1958*, ed. Geoffrey Barraclough. London, Oxford University Press, 1962.

Seale, Patrick. *The Struggle for Syria*. London, Oxford University Press, 1965.

Chapter 12

The Quemoy Crisis, 1958

Résumé of the Crisis

ON AUGUST 23, 1958, Chinese Communist shore batteries began a heavy bombardment of the Quemoy and Matsu island groups, which developed over the next days and weeks into an effort to blockade by artillery fire the resupply of the islands. Peking had chosen to take advantage once again of the vulnerability of this Nationalist Chinese outpost, in order to initiate controlled pressure on behalf of its objectives in the residual civil war.

The artillery barrage was extremely heavy and effective. It is estimated that 50,000 shells fell on the islands on August 23, and the bombardment continued unabated until September 4. Together with the operations of Chinese Communist patrol torpedo (PT) boats in the nearby waters, it succeeded in preventing the Nationalists from resupplying Quemoy until September 7, when the U.S. Navy began to escort Nationalist convoys to the island.

At first Washington was disposed to regard the artillery shelling as having only political-diplomatic objectives. An invasion of Quemoy was not regarded as a serious possibility, and the idea that Peking may have been attempting to impose an effective artillery blockade that would bring Quemoy to its knees was slow to emerge. It was only after a high-level Chinese

Communist army spokesman on August 29 called upon the Nationalist commander on Quemoy to surrender that Washington took account of the possibility that a blockade was under way. By September 2 an official spokesman for the administration was finally ready to admit that the blockade was seriously interfering with supplies to Quemoy.

Between September 2 and 4 the administration reassessed the situation and formulated a detailed policy position in the form of a classified memorandum which Eisenhower reproduces in his memoirs. The basic conclusion of the paper was that the United States could not allow Quemoy to be lost by either invasion or blockade. The value of Quemoy was rationalized in a detailed "row-of-dominoes" assessment of the far-reaching adverse consequences of its loss. The paper foresaw the necessity for prompt U.S. military intervention in the event of an *all-out* communist invasion. Conventional weapons might suffice to defeat an invasion if they were used promptly; otherwise, nuclear weapons might be necessary. As for the possibility of a Chinese Communist effort to blockade Quemoy, the policy memorandum was notably silent on what the administration would do if it failed in its efforts to assist the Nationalists in keeping Quemoy supplied. This, indeed, was the point of vulnerability in the American defense commitment, for in this contingency Washington would be forced either to escalate itself, or to try somehow to negotiate its way out of the crisis.

The decisions taken by Eisenhower after consultations with Dulles and others were announced on September 4 from Newport, Rhode Island, where he was vacationing. Eisenhower stopped short of invoking the Formosa Resolution in the formal statement he issued, though he did emphasize that "the securing and protecting of Quemoy and Matsu have increasingly become related to the defense of Taiwan." Dulles took a harder line in a news conference "backgrounder" on the Eisenhower statement; the Secretary of State strongly implied that the United States would intervene if Quemoy were invaded, and that such an intervention might involve the use of nuclear weapons. Dulles also indicated that the United States Navy would escort Nationalist convoys up to the three-mile limit and that U.S. pilots had been given orders permitting "hot pursuit" of Chinese Communist planes operating over the Taiwan Strait. Once again, noticeably, he was silent on what the United States would do if the blockade could not be broken by these means. It was evident that such a development would place the administration in a most serious and unpleasant dilemma.

The Eisenhower and Dulles statements made it clear to Peking that any hopes it may have had that the U.S. was no longer committed to Quemoy were ill-founded. Thereupon the crisis entered a second phase in which Peking attempted to control the risk of any American overreaction. On September 6, Chou En-lai took up Dulles' suggestion that ambassadorial talks be resumed and offered, in effect, to settle the Sino-American dispute in the Taiwan area through peaceful negotiations.

Chou's statement, however, did not necessarily mean that Peking sought a quick end to the crisis. And indeed, the Communist Chinese perceived potential payoffs which might still be won, while at the same time the risks of serious escalation were carefully controlled. Accordingly, the artillery shelling and related activities directed toward the blockade of Quemoy continued. In Peking's view there was no need as yet to call off the blockade just because the United States had declared its intention to prevent Quemoy's loss. If Peking had ever contemplated an invasion of the island, the strong deterrent statements by Eisenhower and Dulles on September 4 made this option much too risky. But it was quite a different question whether and how the United States would be able to deal with the artillery blockade. Peking's planners had initiated the blockade on the well-conceived premise that the United States might not be able to break it without using air power to attack the shore batteries and other targets on the mainland. The premise still appeared a plausible one.

Peking had also assumed that Washington would be most reluctant to extend the war to the mainland out of concern for the strong opposition such a move would generate at home and abroad, and also for fear that air attacks against the mainland might lead to a major war. To activate and/or reinforce these inhibitions, Peking and Moscow neatly orchestrated their efforts at crisis management. On September 7, in a well-timed move, Khrushchev sent a letter to Eisenhower in which he warned: "An attack on the Chinese People's Republic is an attack on the Soviet Union." This deterrent statement was obviously intended to discourage Washington from dealing with the blockade by means of air attacks against mainland targets. Khrushchev restated and clarified his position in a second letter to Eisenhower on September 19 and in a Tass statement on October 5.[1]

Of course, there was no way of being quite certain that the United States would not eventually undertake air operations against the mainland. But it was clear to Peking and doubtless Moscow that for the time being Washington was keeping its response at a low level, hoping to assist the Chinese Nationalists to develop an effective capability for resupply of Quemoy. Accordingly, in this second phase of the crisis, Peking could afford to wait and see whether the Nationalists, with limited American help, would be able to break the blockade. If they failed to do so, then the United States, it could be hoped, might back away from the risks associated with escalating its response.

At first, U.S. planners were by no means optimistic that limited U.S. assistance to the Nationalist navy would suffice to

---

[1] In his last statement Khrushchev made it clear that his defensive commitment to Communist China was limited to the case of an American attack against the Chinese mainland. He did not specify at any time during the crisis what would constitute an "attack" on China and what kind of Soviet response it would trigger. However, in the October 5 statement he did exclude any military support for Peking's effort to liberate Taiwan by making it clear that the Soviet Union would not intervene in the "civil war."

The Soviet role in the 1958 crisis has become the subject of some disagreement among specialists on Sino-Soviet relations. The interpretation that Khrushchev gave less support than Peking wished has been argued by Hsieh, Zagoria, and Thomas, among others. A "revisionist" thesis that Peking did not expect more from the Soviet Union has been advanced by Halperin and Tsou. The differences in these interpretations are not central for our purposes here; a clearer differentiation of the various issues involved in Sino-Soviet cooperation during the crisis may well enable future scholars to narrow considerably the differences between the two interpretations.

break the blockade. After a disappointing week or ten days, however, U.S. technology and skill at improvisation began to make themselves felt in improved convoy and offloading procedures. By September 21 it was clear that the blockade had been broken. Washington would now be spared the difficult decision of whether or not to escalate military operations against the mainland in order to prevent the gradual strangulation of Quemoy. Instead, the onerous burden of deciding whether to accept the existing situation or to escalate was passed back to Chinese Communists. Peking's decision was to accept the fact that the blockade had proven unsuccessful, and to settle for whatever gains it might still extract from the situation by diplomatic and propaganda means while finding a face-saving way of terminating the crisis. (Ambassadorial talks began in Warsaw on September 15 but successive meetings produced no agreement and, in fact, contributed little to the termination of the crisis.)

On October 6 Peking announced a one-week cease-fire, provided the U.S. Navy cease escorting Nationalist convoys to Quemoy. In this and other ways Peking attempted to exacerbate disagreements and suspicions between the United States and the Nationalists. The U.S. accepted the temporary cease-fire and the crisis gradually subsided. But once again, as in 1954–1955, the sources of the conflict remained unresolved. Peking's way of terminating the crisis was, as Oran Young notes, "a tactical move rather than a strategic defeat. . . . The CPR retained the option to reactivate the confrontation over the offshore islands at any time of its own choosing." [2]

The General Background of the Deterrent Situation

The earlier crisis of 1954–1955 in the Taiwan Strait offered, as we have suggested, some compelling lessons for American

[2] O. Young, *Politics of Force*, pp. 292–93.

policy which, however, were not taken to heart. This new crisis was in many respects a depressing replay of the earlier one and suggests some similar basic lessons.

It had been demonstrated in 1954–1955 that, while the U.S. might be able to deter an all-out attack on the offshore islands, it could not easily deter Peking from using lesser options and threats against these isolated outposts. Peking had it within its power to exploit the vulnerability of the islands which lay only a few miles from the mainland to create another acute but controlled crisis in the future. It should have required no great perspicacity on the part of American policy-makers to realize that the partial success of their deterrence stragegy in the 1954–1955 crisis had not resolved any of the sources of the conflict, but had merely gained time to develop a sounder policy. It had to be expected that Peking would remain highly motivated to find another occasion and a more favorable opportunity to pursue its vital national interests in the Taiwan Strait.

Another lesson the earlier crisis should have held for Washington stemmed from the unnerving experience of having found that its commitment to the offshore islands had threatened to deprive it of the minimum domestic and international support needed to weather the crisis. Indeed, as the war scare in March 1955 had demonstrated, the more imminent the need for U.S. military intervention on behalf of the defense of these offshore islands, the greater was the political pressure on the administration not to intervene. So much so that, as we noted earlier, Eisenhower had been forced by congressional pressure in March and April of the 1955 crisis hurriedly to seek a way out of his commitment to defend Quemoy and Matsu by sending high-level emissaries to persuade Chiang Kai-shek to downgrade their importance.

It was amply clear, therefore, that in supporting Chiang's determination to hold these islands, the administration had been pursuing a policy that strained its political resources almost to the breaking point. The events of January–April of 1955 had offered a sober lesson in the dependence of deterrence strategy on political support. It is one thing to muster enough political support to make a commitment and to direct deterrent statements against an opponent, as Eisenhower did in obtaining congressional backing for his Formosa Resolution in January 1955 (and, to take another instance, Lyndon B. Johnson was to do in obtaining congressional support for the Tonkin Bay Resolution in August 1965). It is quite a different matter to retain that political support when the opponent begins to challenge deterrence, and public awareness of the risk of war becomes more immediate, as was demonstrated by the effect of the war scare in March 1955 (to say nothing of the Vietnam case).

The prolonged crisis of 1954–1955 finally subsided, and ample time was then available to the administration for reappraising and modifying the decision taken in January 1955 to extend its commitment to Quemoy and Matsu. However, Radford and Robertson, the emissaries to Chiang, failed to persuade the Nationalist leader to downgrade the islands' importance. The Eisenhower Administration failed either to exert additional pressure on its ally or to withdraw its commitment from the offshore islands, so that there was no guarantee that the U.S. would not be dragged into another crisis and perhaps war over Quemoy.

Chiang Kai-shek, in the meanwhile, was proceeding to do everything he could to insure that the United States would have even less freedom of action in a future crisis in the strait. Between 1954 and 1958 the Generalissimo increased his forces on the offshore islands from 30,000 to 100,000. It is commonly believed that his purpose in doing so was to make it more difficult for Eisenhower not to invoke the Formosa Resolution in a future crisis. With one-third of the Nationalist army now on the offshore islands, a successful attack on them would indeed endanger Chiang's ability to defend Taiwan with his remaining forces. Moreover, the loss or forced withdrawal under communist pressure of 100,000 Nationalist troops on the offshore islands could well have profound psychological effects in Taiwan that might lead to a political collapse of the Nationalist regime. Not only did the Eisenhower Administration fail to insist that Chiang decrease the symbolic and morale value of the offshore islands, it also passively accepted the Generalissimo's shrewd maneuver to link the defense of these islands more tightly with the defense of Taiwan itself. That Chiang should have acted to bind his strong but somewhat reluctant ally more firmly to his interests and aspirations is perfectly understandable. That the United States should have allowed him thus to manipulate and control its policies is all but incomprehensible. We find in this case an illustration of one of the major risks and limitations of deterrence policies: namely, the opportunities it may give a weak ally to manipulate the nature of the commitment made to it.

Like the 1954–1955 case, the crisis of 1958 can be regarded as both a partial success and a partial failure of deterrence. American deterrence strategy failed in that it did not dissuade the Chinese Communists from initiating the heavy artillery shelling. But American deterrence strategy may possibly have gained a partial success, as well, in that the precrisis deterrence commitment by the United States may have at least dissuaded Peking from choosing the option of an all-out attack against Quemoy, in a sense, forcing it to settle for the less risky option of an artillery blockade.

Noteworthy about the Quemoy crisis of 1958 is that, in contrast to some other cases considered in this study, the deterrence failure was *not* because of a fundamental miscalculation by either side. The conventional wisdom that "war is the result of miscalculation" is not supported by this case, nor indeed by some other cases. In initiating their potent but limited probe via an artillery blockade, the Chinese Communists correctly perceived both the ambiguity of the U.S. commitment to Quemoy that had been written into the Formosa Resolution and the high probability that Washington would observe important limits on its military response if it decided to react to a low-level threat to Quemoy. Peking chose an appropriately cautious military option for testing and clarifying the U.S. commitment, and for exerting pressure to erode the administration's willingness to accept risks in order to help defend Quemoy.

Nor, for its part, did Washington miscalculate. It quickly

perceived the essentially cautious strategy Peking was undertaking and the limits which the Chinese Communist leaders wished to impose on the confrontation. The absence of important miscalculation on either side helps to account for the fact that the crisis could be contained at a low level of military confrontation and managed by both sides without erupting into large-scale warfare.[3]

The Initiator's Motivation and Calculations

Peking's precise motivations and calculations in the 1958 crisis, as in others we have discussed, cannot be known precisely at this time. But here as in other cases it is not difficult to trace the major outlines of the initiator's decision calculus, and to suggest interpretations of his motivation which are not merely plausible in retrospect, but could and should have been plausible to United States decision-makers at the time.

In our account of the Taiwan Strait crisis of 1954–1955 we presented an analysis of the basic strategic dilemma created for Peking by the U.S. intervention in the Chinese civil war through its backing of the Nationalist regime on Formosa. Private diplomatic conversations with the United States in Geneva since the autumn of 1955 had not loosened the American commitment to Chiang Kai-shek, or even indicated that it might be

[3] The interpretation advanced here seems at first glance to contradict Oran Young's thesis (*Ibid.*, pp. 129, 188–89) that there was an element of miscalculation in Peking's decision to initiate the crisis. However, it is clear that Young arrives at his conclusion because he focuses on Peking's unfulfilled hope of securing more important payoffs rather than, as we do, on Peking's shrewd calculation and control of the risks of its initiative. We agree that Peking did not achieve all the objectives it probably assigned to its initiative. However, Peking judged correctly that it was initiating a *controlled, low-risk* action of potentially high rewards. From Peking's standpoint it was worth engaging in such an initiative even though the probability of a large payoff was uncertain. It would be somewhat misleading and beside the point, therefore, to emphasize that Peking "miscalculated" because it did not obtain all or many of the results it may have been hoping for.

loosened in the future.[4] Accordingly, the basic structure of Peking's strategic problem had not changed by 1958, nor had the need of the Chinese Communist regime to forego passivity in favor of carefully controlled initiatives from time to time (as discussed on pp. 276–79 above).

Moreover, there had been fresh indications of the hostility of American intentions since 1955. Increased military and economic assistance from the United States had enabled the Nationalist regime to maintain 600,000 men in its armed forces, "proportionally more men under arms than any other country".[5] Nationalist activities harassing the mainland and coastal waters, and threats of wider attacks, continued unabated. In May of 1957 the United States announced that Matador tactical missiles, capable of firing nuclear warheads, would be installed on Taiwan, ostensibly as a response to Chinese threats to use force in the Formosa Strait area and the improvement of the Chinese Communist military posture on the mainland opposite Taiwan.

The situation in the Taiwan Strait, therefore, was not merely remaining highly unsatisfactory from Peking's point of view but was actually deteriorating. The moderate foreign policy line which Communist China had adopted with the Bandung Conference of the spring of 1955 had by mid-1958 netted all the gains it was likely to, without having generated any improvement in the Formosa Strait. By this time, it was evidently becoming clear to Peking that it could not protect its interests in the strait indefinitely, nor realize its aspirations vis-à-vis Taiwan, without resuming pressure against the U.S.-Nationalist alliance. As a number of China specialists have noted, Mao's thoughts turned to the possibility that the communist bloc might now pursue a policy of "brinkmanship" of its own in selected areas. In this he was encouraged by the enormous increase that had occurred since 1954 in the strategic nuclear striking power of the USSR.[6]

[4] K. T. Young, *Negotiating with the Chinese Communists*, pp. 12–13.

[5] Kallgren, "Nationalist China's Armed Forces," p. 35; also, Sigal, " 'Rational Policy' Model," p. 134. "Proportional," that is, to population.

[6] See, for example, Zagoria, *Sino-Soviet Conflict*, pp. 167–68; Hsieh, *Communist China's Strategy*, pp. 109–19.

In his policy review of February 1958, Chou En-lai referred to Peking's determination to liberate Taiwan and omitted to add the qualifier, "peacefully," that had been normal since 1955.[7] The decision to initiate another controlled probe in the strait may have been discussed at a meeting of the Military Committee of the CCP that occurred between May 27 and July 22, and may have been discussed with Khrushchev when he visited Peking between July 31 and August 3. It is uncertain how much encouragement Khrushchev gave Mao. Several options were available to the People's Republic of China and were presumably considered: an all-out invasion of a major offshore island, such as Quemoy; a determined artillery blockade of Quemoy designed to force an evacuation; or artillery shelling of Quemoy coupled with an invasion of one of the smaller islands held by the Nationalists (as Peking had done in the 1954–1955 crisis).

It is unlikely that Peking found an all-out invasion of a major island, such as Quemoy, an attractive initial move, or seriously considered undertaking it before U.S. intentions were clarified. The quick, decisive seizure of territory was a risky option in view of the possible existence of a U.S. commitment to defend Quemoy, the equivocal language of the Formosa Resolution notwithstanding. It had to be accepted, furthermore, that Washington possessed ample forces in the area to make an unacceptably violent response to any invasion attempt, if necessary very rapidly. There is every reason to doubt that Peking was prepared to accept a high-risk strategy, such as an all-out invasion of Quemoy, in the face of America's capacity to destroy the invasion force and perhaps to escalate the conflict to the mainland in reply.

Rather, Peking selected a low-risk strategy, as it had in 1954–1955, and for the same reasons. The option Peking activated possessed several very attractive features. It was a "reversible" probe; the artillery shelling could easily be stopped, resumed, and stopped again as necessary in order to monitor and control the risks. The limited and controlled nature of the probe was signaled to Washington by excluding confusing or

[7] Hsieh, *Communist China's Strategy*, p. 93; Zagoria, *Sino-Soviet Conflict*, p. 175.

alarming background "noise," and no troops were mobilized or landing craft prepared. The risks involved were further reduced by obtaining from the Soviet Union appropriate deterrence statements to dissuade Washington from escalating against the mainland.

One might wonder why Peking initiated essentially the same option in 1958 that it had tried and found wanting in 1954–1955. But in the interim, the situation had changed to Peking's favor, militarily and—it may well have seemed in the Forbidden City—politically. Militarily, the Chinese Communists had gained from the increase in Soviet strategic power. While the United States retained overall strategic superiority, Eisenhower nonetheless felt himself obliged to recognize that "any large-scale conflict stimulated here was now less likely [than in the 1954–1955 crisis] to remain limited to a conventional use of power." The local balance of military power had also shifted so as to be more favorable to Peking. The Chinese Communists had built a complex of military airfields in the Fukien area opposite Taiwan "that would enable them to launch air attacks not only against the tiny offshore islands but against the main Chinese Nationalist base on Taiwan as well." Moreover, the Chinese Communists had greatly improved their artillery emplacements, which "now almost ringed Quemoy." As Eisenhower put it in comparing the two crises over the offshore islands: "This new challenge resembled the earlier one of 1955. But the current situation included new dangers that seemed to make our position more difficult." [8]

Furthermore, the Chinese decision-makers could readily believe that the United States would not prove motivated to defend Quemoy in the test. They knew that it had been with misgivings that the United States had moved the defense line westwards to the offshore islands during the earlier crisis. They knew that in the meantime Washington had made some efforts to persuade Chiang to pull back.

But the most compelling reason why the policy-makers in

[8] Eisenhower, *White House Years*, p. 293.

Peking believed that the situation of 1958 differed from the earlier one to their advantage, was they believed that now they could blockade Quemoy with artillery fire alone. The great strengthening of their ability to bombard the islands, which had moved forward steadily in the intervening three and a half years, led them to think that the islands could be cut off from resupply by shellfire alone and, if the local Nationalist commander refused to surrender, pounded and starved into submission. On this assumption, it would be difficult for the United States to operationalize a commitment to defend Quemoy, even if it made one, without escalating fairly drastically to attacks upon the mainland. Such a move would be very strongly opposed by American public opinion, and was additionally deterred by the Soviet statements. Thus Peking expected that its greatly enhanced artillery capabilities had much sharpened the latent geographical, military, and by implication political asymmetries inherent in the situation. Unlike the 1954–1955 case, the burden of escalating to rescue a fast-deteriorating military position would be shifted to the United States.[9] In all probability, decision-makers in Peking expected that their Washington counterparts would realize this when they observed the devastating artillery barrage of the last days of August, and would therefore avoid making any clear commitment to Quemoy in the first place.

The maximum payoff available with this strategy would be the capture of the offshore islands with the destruction of one-third of the Nationalist army; this would gravely weaken the Formosa regime and perhaps limit U.S. intervention in Chinese affairs. But if for any reason this maximum payoff were not obtained, the situation would still offer lesser but very attractive potential payoffs. Washington might pressure Chiang into withdrawing his forces and surrendering the islands. Or, if the United States offered to negotiate its way out of the crisis, Com-

---

[9] The reader will observe the similarity in the logic of this situation to that of various Berlin crises, where the Soviet Union also attempted to extract gains from sharpening favorable latent asymmetries, while thrusting onto the West the burden of escalating to reverse the deterioration in its position.

munist China could expect to make important diplomatic gains, such as recognition, admission to the United Nations, agreements by the U.S. to limit future support to the Nationalists, or perhaps a neutralization of the offshore islands at Chiang's expense.[10] Peking's initiative was thus a well-calculated one, offering opportunities for a variety of gains at low and controllable risks. It was not unrealistic of Peking to assign some respectable probability of success to even the most ambitious of the objectives it decided to pursue through its strategy of controlled pressure.

The Defender's Response to Warning

Although the policy-makers of the United States government had failed to penetrate in advance the probable motivations, perceptions, and calculations of their opponents across the Strait of Formosa, they were receptive to various warning signals that a new challenge might be mounted to their deterrent position. The difficulties they met with in trying to respond to this warning, however, are of analytical and theoretical as well as historical interest.

Tension in the Taiwan Strait area began to rise in the period following the landing of American troops in Lebanon on July 15, 1958. The Chinese launched a strong anti-American propaganda campaign, which included calls for the liberation of Taiwan. They stationed combat aircraft for the first time on the airfields constructed on the Fukien Coast in the preceding years, and stepped up military activity on land and in the air over the strait. In early August Khrushchev and Mao met for several days in Peking. At first Chinese intentions were not clear, but Eisenhower writes in his memoirs that on August 6 he had "definite word" through intelligence sources that the Chinese Communists might be contemplating a new attack on

[10] Tsou, "Mao's Limited War," pp. 332–50; Harry Harding, "Quemoy Crisis," p. 17.

the offshore islands. On the same day, Chiang Kai-shek declared a state of emergency and ordered increased defensive measures.

Washington's response to the warning indicators was more sluggish and cautious than one might expect, since the warning was being taken seriously. This can be partly explained by the fact that it was not absolutely certain that the Chinese Communists would resort to major force against the offshore islands. There had been threats and sporadic exchanges of violence between the mainland and Taiwan since the end of the 1954–1955 crisis. But a more important component of the explanation lies in the fact that the warning of a possible attack immediately revived the question of how Eisenhower should resolve the ambiguity in the declaratory policy put forward in the Formosa Resolution of January 15, 1955. The commitment to assist in the defense of Quemoy and Matsu, we may recall, had been couched in conditional terms: the President would have to determine whether an attack on the offshore islands was part of, or preliminary to, an attack on Formosa and the Pescadores.

If there had been some question as to the importance of the offshore islands in 1954–1955, there was none now. However reluctantly, the administration felt it now had no choice but to help defend Quemoy and Matsu, since Chiang had by this time placed about a third of his army on these islands. It is not clear just when in August the administration came to this policy conclusion; it is quite possible that it decided to defend the offshore islands, if necessary, *before* the artillery barrage began and *before* the exact nature of Peking's threat was known.[11]

Whenever the administration decided to defend Quemoy, it undoubtedly moved slowly and with difficulty in finding a way to signal its commitment in order to reinforce deterrence and try to forestall a direct challenge. We must therefore distinguish between the impact which the clearly perceived warning had on Eisenhower's *action* policy and its impact on his *declaratory and signaling* policy. It was easier for the administration to

[11] Harding, "Quemoy Crisis," p. 25.

decide privately in mid-August that it would prevent the fall of Quemoy than it was to announce its intention to do so publicly in order to persuade Peking to hold back. That a gap of this kind between action policy and declaratory policy can develop and persist during the critical early phase of a crisis points to a distressing and dangerous limitation that may be encountered in deterrence strategy. We need to inquire further, therefore, into the reasons why the administration's declaratory policy in August did not reflect more fully the firm policy of action to defend Quemoy that it had formulated.

After receiving the "definite" warning of August 6, it was obvious to administration officials that the danger of war lay in the possibility that the Chinese Communists would attempt to overrun the offshore islands on the mistaken assumption that the United States would choose not to become militarily involved. To avoid this possibility, moreover, administration officials realized that they should act promptly to remove any possible ambiguity in the minds of policy-makers in Peking as to whether there was an American commitment to the offshore islands.[12] Yet the administration did not carry out this intention until much later, which was too late. Why?

There is no single explanation for this contradiction. The administration's ability to issue an appropriate signal to the Chinese Communists was impaired by several constraints. In the first place, Eisenhower explains in his memoirs that he regarded the joint congressional resolution of 1955 on Formosa as requiring him "not to make absolute advance commitments, covering every contingency, but to use my judgment according to the circumstances of the time." Eisenhower chose to place a conservative interpretation on the discretionary power conferred on him by the resolution. He was sensitive to the possibility that to give an unequivocal public commitment to defend

---

[12] According to Eisenhower (*White House Years*, p. 295), the idea of issuing a strong statement to deter the Chinese Communists won heavy support from Dulles and others in the administration; but the President elected to follow the advice of the JCS, who felt it would be better to say little in order "to keep the Communists guessing."

Quemoy in advance of an attack would be construed by domestic and international critics as constituting a premature invocation of the presidential judgment required under the resolution in order to employ U.S. forces for this purpose. Thus, when questioned about U.S. policy on Quemoy at his press conference of August 21—two days before the artillery shelling of Quemoy began—Eisenhower replied: "You simply cannot make military decisions until the event reaches you." [13] Even after the artillery shelling had been under way for two weeks, Eisenhower was to authorize a circumspect statement indicating that he had not yet made a finding under the resolution that the employment of the armed forces of the United States was required or appropriate in insuring the defence of Formosa.

A second constraint on giving Peking an explicit warning was the belief that to do so would complicate U.S. relations with Chiang Kai-shek. As Eisenhower explained in his memoirs, "the effect on Chiang Kai-shek of a definitive statement might be undesirable. . . ." He adds: "to restrain him from his cherished ambition of aggressive action against the mainland was not always easy. One way of inducing some caution on his part was to keep some doubt in his mind as to the conditions under which the United States would support him." [14] Accordingly, another reason for diluting deterrence statements toward Communist China was the desire to discourage Chiang from attempting to maneuver the United States into a war with mainland China. Furthermore, U.S. leaders were reluctant to embrace a strong, unequivocal deterrence posture toward the offshore islands because it would encourage the Chinese Nationalist government to shift responsibility onto American forces for dealing with Chinese Communist actions in the Taiwan Strait. Wishing to avoid or minimize direct American military involvement if possible, Washington wanted the Chinese Nationalists to make a maximum effort of their own to resupply their Quemoy garrison rather than leaning on a U.S. guarantee.

A third constraint on giving Peking an explicit warning lay

[13] *New York Times*, August 22, 1958.   [14] *Ibid.*

in the fact that to do so would have exacerbated domestic and allied public opinion, which was strongly opposed to risking war over the offshore islands.

A fourth constraint grew out of the fact that the administration wished to defend only the largest of the Quemoy and Matsu islands. It made no sense to defend the smaller ones in each of these two island chains. Yet the administration was reluctant to specify in advance exactly which of the offshore islands it would defend. To do so, Eisenhower states in his memoirs, would have simply invited the Chinese Communists to occupy all the others. Accordingly, Washington favored an ambiguous declaratory policy which had the advantage of keeping the opponent guessing. This was the rationale behind the JSC's advice to Eisenhower to say little.[15]

All these constraints inhibited the administration's response to the warning it had received. By the time they had all been considered and a signal devised that reflected them all, its contents were much diluted—and too late. What finally emerged was a pallid, veiled warning to Peking which Dulles decided to incorporate in a letter to Representative Thomas Morgan on August 24. "It would be hazardous," Dulles observed somewhat circumspectly in deference to the constraints of the Formosa Resolution, "for anyone to assume that if the Chinese Communists were to attempt . . . to attack and seek to conquer these islands, that [it] could be a limited operation." [16] Whatever deterrence impact the Dulles letter might have had on Peking's decision to initiate its artillery blockade of Quemoy, the fact is that it was issued the day after the artillery shelling had begun. It seems unlikely that such a cautiously

[15] Eisenhower, *White House Years*, p. 295. Some JCS planners believed that the Chinese Communists might initially invade one or two of the smaller, less important offshore islands, which the United States should not and was not prepared to defend. Later, it was reported (J. Alsop, "War for the Islands?" p. 10) that American policy-makers had drawn a secret "must-defend" line around the two largest islands of the Quemoy group and the five largest of the Matsu group.

[16] *Department of State Bulletin*, 39 (September 8, 1958), 379.

worded declaration would have influenced Peking even if it had arrived in time.[17]

There is no indication in the available record that the administration gave thought to the possibility of using private diplomatic channels to transmit a much stiffer and more timely statement to Peking. Private channels would not have been subject to the political constraints, noted above, that affected what the administration felt it could say publicly. But the diplomatic channel that would have most recommended itself for this purpose was no longer open. The Sino-American ambassadorial talks that had been going on in Geneva since the end of the 1954–1955 crisis had been broken off by the United States in late 1957.[18] During the present crisis, therefore, as in the critical period preceding the Chinese intervention in the Korean War, Peking and Washington lacked a dependable channel of direct communication.[19]

There is no indication that the Eisenhower Administration considered using third parties, as Chou En-lai had done in the autumn of 1950, to communicate the American commitment to the offshore islands in the period *before* the communist bombardment began. Given the administration's realization of the value of removing any ambiguity on this point in Peking's calculations, this failure remains inexplicable. In the event, Washington responded *after* the bombardment began, by strengthening its military capabilities in the Formosa Strait. On August 26 the Seventh Fleet was placed on alert, and was soon reinforced by two aircraft carriers, one heavy cruiser, and four destroyers.

[17] Dulles' letter was followed a few days later by a statement from Eisenhower in a press conference which intimated but stopped well short of actually stating that he would be obliged to invoke the Formosa Resolution in view of the greater importance the offshore islands had assumed since 1955 in the defense system of Taiwan.

[18] K. T. Young, *Negotiating with the Chinese Communists*, pp. 132–34.

[19] When another crisis erupted in the Taiwan Strait in 1962, the ambassadorial talks, which had been resumed at the end of the 1958 crisis, proved useful to President Kennedy for clarifying U.S. policy and defusing the tension; *Ibid.*, pp. 250–51.

An additional squadron of U.S. Air Force jet fighters was also deployed to the theater.

The Defender's Response to the Partial Breakdown of Deterrence

After it became clear to Washington that its effort to signal a commitment to Quemoy was too late, and that deterrence had partially broken down, it was recognized that some sort of action policy would be required. The United States' response to the breakdown of deterrence can be divided chronologically into two phases.

The first phase proceeded during early and mid-September, during which period it seemed that the Chinese Communists might very well succeed in blockading the offshore islands by their artillery fire. United States decision-makers were therefore pressed by just the dilemma that their counterparts in Peking had anticipated—whether to escalate the conflict or in some fashion to try to evade the full implications of the commitment. During this phase Secretary Dulles chose to throw out important hints that a more flexible American position might be possible. In public statements and in the negotiations convened in Warsaw, Dulles sought to create a conciliatory image of his position. In part, this was an attempt to meet the strong domestic and international criticism to which American policy was being subjected. But in part, the conciliatory image was one aspect of a genuine effort to defuse the most dangerous aspects of the crisis.

To resolve the dilemma of choosing between escalation and evasion of the commitment, Dulles took the position that a dependable cease-fire in the Taiwan Strait must precede any substantive negotiation on the disposition of the offshore islands. From Peking's viewpoint, of course, this position represented less a genuinely conciliatory one than one designed to undercut the situational asymmetries which were Peking's principal advantage. Despite the conciliatory image and various vague hints of the possibility of "important changes" in the American position, there was no indication that the Eisenhower Administration intended to weaken its commitment to Taiwan itself. Yet if the negotiations were confined to the offshore islands alone, it was unclear why the United States should negotiate away its commitment *after* Peking agreed to the cease-fire. So it is not surprising that the Chinese Communists reacted very negatively to Dulles's "conciliatory" policy. Presumably they expected that a continuation of the artillery blockade would force a more genuinely conciliatory view in Washington.[20]

But Peking was cheated from the realization of its hopes by the unexpected skill of the Americans in designing a technical solution "around" the blockade. Just as had happened with the Berlin blockade of 1948–1949, the Americans surprised even themselves with their ability to improvise a technological answer—in this case principally new convoying and off-loading procedures for the supply ships—which neutralized the blockading power's situational advantage. By September 21 it was clear to Washington that the islands could be resupplied indefinitely, and hence that the blockade had been broken.

A second phase opened therefore in the United States' response to the deterrence breakdown. As it became clear to Dulles that the military pressure was off, and also that his "conciliatory" image had not seduced Peking into any negotiations from which some advantage could be extracted, he reverted to a harder position. On October 14, the day after Peking had declared an extension in the de facto cease-fire it had instituted, Dulles backed off from his conciliatory stand. Explicitly recognizing and deploring Peking's unwillingness to make a deal confined to the offshore islands, Dulles stated that under these

[20] It may be true, as Kenneth Young asserts, that Dulles was not contemplating an eventual "two Chinas" solution to the still unresolved civil war. Yet in his quite sympathetic and at times parochial account of Dulles' diplomacy, Young admits that "Washington's position at Warsaw may have seemed to advocate the concept of 'Two Chinas' to Peking leaders, and thus may have contributed to Peking's abrupt shying away from the course of the discussion at Warsaw." *Negotiating with the Chinese Communists*, p. 193.

circumstances he was no longer planning to exert pressure on the Nationalists to reduce their garrisons on the islands (as he previously had intimated he would do).

Of greatest analytical interest is the way in which Dulles then seemed to put out of his mind the need to bring about changes in the underlying situation that had generated the crisis he had managed to weather. (He behaved in this way on other occasions as well, for instance after the 1954–1955 crisis.) In other words, Dulles apparently was willing to introduce flexibility into the American position in some respects in order to survive a difficult crisis, but he was unwilling or uninterested in displaying the same flexibility afterward to avoid a new crisis. Dulles may have been a clever tactician in using diplomacy to support deterrence strategy when the latter seemed inadequate by itself to deal with a crisis. However, he lacked the wisdom of classical statesmanship in supplementing deterrence with conciliation and flexibility in order to reduce a situation's conflict potential before it erupted into dangerous crises.

In other respects as well, the Eisenhower Administration's practice of stretching deterrence strategy to the limit in order to achieve at least partial deterrence success incurred hidden costs that corroded sound statesmanship. In the 1958 crisis, as in others, Dulles and Eisenhower succumbed to the temptation of drawing upon the awesome military force available to them to generate threats with which to support a questionable application of deterrence strategy. The use of national power to enforce deterrence to protect marginal outposts invariably requires policy-makers to engage in rhetorical inflation of the values of the outpost in question. The costs of rhetorical inflation are not trivial, especially when policy-makers resort to it repeatedly to justify to themselves and to others their acceptance of the risk of war to uphold a questionable commitment which, they believe, circumstances have forced upon them. The more questionable the commitment and the more reluctant they are initially to enter into it and to uphold it, the more likely it is that policy-makers will end up believing the rhetorical arguments they employ to justify it. It is too psychologically uncomfortable, as well as politically risky, for policy-makers to persist very long in propagandistic bombast on important matters of this kind which they do not themselves believe.

Thus, to rationalize their commitment to the offshore islands during the early stages of the present crisis, top-level administration officials subscribed in all solemnity to an astonishing version of the "row-of-dominoes" assessment of the national interest. In the *classified* statement of policy which Eisenhower and Dulles formulated on September 4 and published later in Eisenhower's memoirs, the defense of the offshore islands was regarded as necessary because their loss would "probably" threaten not merely Nationalist control of Taiwan but also the American position in Japan, Korea, the Philippines, Thailand, and Vietnam; and would "probably" push neutralist Indonesia, Malaya, Cambodia, Laos, and Burma under communist influence! [21] As Morton Halperin and Tang Tsou note in their incisive analysis of the role of bureaucratic communications in policy-making, "ritualistic language comes to be believed by those writing and reading the policy proposals." [22] It is hard to account otherwise for the fact that in the September 4 statement of the administration's policy, Eisenhower and Dulles subscribed to a row-of-dominoes analysis which explicitly argued that the consequences of a loss of the offshore islands "would be even more far-reaching and catastrophic than those which followed when the United States allowed the Chinese mainland to be taken over by the Chinese Communists" in 1949! [23]

As in the latter stages of the 1954–1955 crisis in the Taiwan Strait, Eisenhower again felt obliged at the end of the 1958 crisis to send a high-level emissary to Taiwan to try to persuade Chiang Kai-shek to reduce somewhat his forces on the offshore islands and, in addition, to agree to renounce the use of force to regain control of the mainland. This time Dulles was the emissary and, as had Radford and Robertson in 1955, he met with

[21] Eisenhower, *White House Years*, pp. 691–93.

[22] Halperin and Tsou, "*U.S. Policy toward the Offshore Islands,*" p. 132.

[23] Eisenhower, *White House Years*, p. 692.

only limited success. Chiang agreed to a slight cutback of forces on the islands, but no sooner had he issued a joint statement with Dulles implying a renunciation of force to regain the mainland than high Nationalist officials denied that the Republic of China had thereby abdicated its right to invade the mainland.[24]

Certainly the agreement which Dulles obtained from the Generalissimo on this occasion did not prevent the latter in June 1962 from threatening harassment or invasion of the mainland. In reaction, Peking undertook military preparations and deployments near the offshore islands. Tension mounted once again, but the third Taiwan Strait crisis was quickly brought under control when President Kennedy used direct private diplomatic channels at Warsaw as well as public channels to assure Peking that the United States would not support any Nationalist attempt to assault the mainland. At the same time, however, it may be noted that Kennedy felt obliged to reiterate his predecessor's commitment to the offshore islands.[25]

And there the matter of the U.S. commitment to the offshore islands has stood. There was no direct reference to Quemoy and Matsu in the joint communiqué issued by President Nixon and Premier Chou En-lai following the former's visit to China in 1972.

[24] Hinton, *Communist China in World Politics*, pp. 269–70; O. Young, *Politics of Force*, p. 78.

[25] K. T. Young., *Negotiating with the Chinese Communists* pp. 250–51; Hinton, *Communist China in World Politics*, pp. 271–72; Halperin and Tsou, "U.S. Policy toward the Offshore Islands," p. 128; Sigal, " 'Rational Policy' Model," pp. 144–49; Hilsman, *To Move a Nation*, pp. 310–19; Sorensen, *Kennedy*, pp. 661–62.

Bibliography

Detailed scholarly studies are available on the Quemoy crisis of 1958. The early studies by Tang Tsou (1959) are still useful, and they have been extended in important directions in more recent collaborative articles with Morton Halperin. Harry Harding and Kenneth T. Young examine the development of the crisis in considerable detail. Oran Young's account is the most analytically oriented of the available studies; he singles out for separate discussion some twelve or thirteen questions having to do with the crisis behavior of the two sides. Young's treatment of the crisis from the standpoint of deterrence theory, however, is brief. Sino-Soviet relations, an important component of the crisis, have been the subject of somewhat competing interpretations by Hsieh, Zagoria, Thomas, Solomon, and Halperin and Tsou ("The 1958 Quemoy Crisis"). The Chinese Communist approach to the use of force as an instrument of policy is dealt with by Whiting and by Greene.

Much on American policy-making during the crisis remains to be clarified when additional documentary sources become available. However, the structure and development of U.S. policy emerges with reasonable clarity by synthesizing, as a number of scholars have done, contemporary official statements, journalistic reportage, and disclosures in memoirs, of which Eisenhower's is thus far the most important.

Critical reflections on the Eisenhower Administration's handling of the crisis are offered by most scholars, in particular Tsou, Halperin, Barnett, Harding, O. Young, and Sigal.

For earlier research on this case we are indebted to Harry Harding and Jane Howland.

Alsop, Joseph. "War for the Islands?" *New York Herald Tribune*, September 5, 1958.

Barnett, Robert W. "Quemoy: The Use and Consequence of Nuclear Deterrence." Cambridge, Harvard University Center for International Affairs, March 1960 (mimeographed).

Clubb, Edmund O. "Sino-American Relations and the Future of Formosa," *Political Science Quarterly*, LXXX, No. 1 (March 1965), 1–21.

Eisenhower, Dwight D. *The White House Years: Waging Peace, 1956–1961*. New York, Doubleday, 1965.

Greene, Fred. *U.S. Policy and the Security of Asia*. New York, McGraw-Hill, 1968.

Halperin, M. H., and Tang Tsou. "The 1958 Quemoy Crisis," in *Sino-Soviet Relations and Arms Control*, ed. M. H. Halperin. Cambridge, MIT Press, 1967; pp. 265–303.

——. "United States Policy toward the Offshore Islands," in *Public Policy*, ed. John D. Montgomery and Arthur Smithies. Cambridge, Harvard University Press, 1966; Vol. XV, pp. 119–38.

Harding, Harry. "The Domestic Sources of Foreign Policy: The Quemoy Crisis of 1954–55 and 1958." Unpublished study, Stanford University, 1970.

——. "The Quemoy Crisis of 1958." Unpublished study, Stanford University, 1968.

Hilsman, Roger. *To Move a Nation*. New York, Doubleday, 1967.

Hinton, Harold C. *Communist China in World Politics*. Boston, Houghton Mifflin, 1966; chapter 10, "Taiwan and the Offshore Islands."

Howe, Jonathan T. *Multicrises: Sea Power and Global Politics in the Missile Age*, Cambridge, MIT Press, 1971; pp. 161–282.

Hsieh, Alice Langley. "The Sino-Soviet Nuclear Dialogue: 1963," *Journal of Conflict Resolution*, June 1964.

——. *Communist China's Strategy in the Nuclear Era*. Englewood Cliffs, N.J., Prentice-Hall, 1962.

Irish, Marian D. "Public Opinion and American Foreign Policy: The Quemoy Crisis of 1958," *Political Quarterly*, 31, No. 2 (April–June 1960), 151–62.

Kallgren, Joyce. "Nationalist China's Armed Forces," *The China Quarterly*, 15 (July–September, 1963).

McClelland, Charles A. "Decisional Opportunity and Political Controversy: the Quemoy Case," *Journal of Conflict Resolution*, VI, No. 3 (September 1962).

——, Daniel Harrison, Wayne Martin, Warren Phillips, and Robert Young. "The Communist Chinese Performance in Crisis and Non-Crisis: Quantitative Studies of the Taiwan Strait Confrontation, 1950–1964." Report to the Naval Ordnance Test Station, China Lake, Calif., December 14, 1965.

Nitze, Paul. "Brinkmanship and the Averting of War," in *Military Policy Papers*. The Washington Center of Foreign Policy Research, December 1958.

Rovere, Richard. "Letter from Washington," *New Yorker*, September 20, 1958, pp. 91 ff.

Schelling, Thomas C. *Arms and Influence*. New Haven, Yale University Press, 1966.

Schlesinger, Arthur. *A Thousand Days*. Boston; Houghton Mifflin, 1965.

Sigal, Leon V. "The 'Rational Policy' Model and the Formosa Straits Crisis," *International Studies Quarterly*, 14, No. 2 (June 1970), 121–56.

Snow, Edgar. *The Other Side of the River: Red China Today*. New York, Random House, 1962.

Solomon, Richard H. *Mao's Revolution and the Chinese Political Culture*. Berkeley and Los Angeles, University of California Press, 1971.

Sorensen, Theodore. *Kennedy*. New York, Harper & Row, 1965.

Tsou, Tang. *The Embroilment over Quemoy: Mao, Chiang, and Dulles*. International Study Paper No. 2. Institute of International Studies, University of Utah, 1959.

——. "Mao's Limited War in the Taiwan Strait," *Orbis*, III, No. 3 (Fall 1959), 332–50.

——. "The Quemoy Imbroglio: Chiang Kai-shek and the United States," *Western Political Quarterly*, XII, No. 4 (December 1959), 1075–91.

Thomas, J. R. "Soviet Behavior in the Quemoy Crisis of 1958," *Orbis*, VI, No. 1 (Spring 1962), 38–64.

U.S. Department of State. *Department of State Bulletin*, 39 (September 8, 1958), 379. Dulles's letter to Representative Thomas Morgan, August 23, 1958.

Whiting, Allen S. "The Use of Force in Foreign Policy by the People's Republic of China," *The Annals*, 402 (July 1972), 55–66.

Young, Kenneth T. *Negotiating with the Chinese Communists*. New York, McGraw-Hill, 1968; pp. 137–98.

Young, Oran. *The Politics of Force*. Princeton, Princeton University Press, 1968.

Zagoria, Donald S. *The Sino-Soviet Conflict*. Princeton, Princeton University Press, 1962.

Chapter 13

The Berlin Deadline Crisis, 1958-1959

Résumé of the Crisis

FOR ALMOST TEN YEARS following the lifting of the Berlin blockade in the spring of 1949 there was no major Berlin crisis. But the city remained the symbol of, and a main crucible for, the ongoing Cold War: a topic of frequent abortive negotiations with the Soviets, the scene of recurrent Soviet harassment of Western access rights, and the starting point of all the most plausible scenarios of how a major war could begin.

In the summer and fall of 1957, the USSR demonstrated new missile and rocket capabilities, one reply to which was a NATO plan, adopted in December 1957, for stationing intermediate range strategic missiles in Europe, with nuclear warheads under American control. The Middle Eastern and Quemoy crises postponed an effective Soviet response, but in the autumn of 1958 the Kremlin's attention returned to its western front, where nuclear-armed missiles were soon to be installed on German territory for the first time.

On November 10, Khrushchev made a speech in Moscow denouncing the "remilitarization" of West Germany. Possibly on the spur of the moment but more probably by plan, he added that "the time had obviously arrived" for East Germany to take over control of access to Berlin. An apparently clear implication was the threat of a new blockade.

Neither the United States nor the other NATO powers took any public notice of this initiative for two weeks, and on November 27 the USSR sent identical notes to the three Western occupying powers of Berlin and to Bonn proposing "negotiations" to convert West Berlin into a "free city" under terms that would put it substantially under East German control. If "half a year" passed without reaching "an adequate agreement," then the Soviet Union would turn over to East Germany control of access to the city. The note thus contained all three elements of the classical ultimatum: a demand upon the recipient powers, a time limit for the fulfillment of the demand, and a threat of sanctions in the event of nonfulfillment.

However the note was also somewhat ambiguous, seeming to imply at another point that the six-month deadline might refer to the *start* of negotiations; and the same interpretation was given privately by Khrushchev two days later and publicly by Deputy Premier Mikoyan in January. Subsequently, the Soviets backed further and further away from any attempt to execute an ultimatum.

Despite the receipt of considerable warning, the United States took no steps prior to receiving the deadline note to reinforce its deterrent posture in Berlin. Secretary of State Dulles chose to react flexibly and in a somewhat conciliatory manner both to the warning and to the note itself. Later, the Soviet challenge became diluted in a maze of diplomatic messages, public declarations, and private discussions throughout the winter and spring; and, ultimately, the Kremlin agreed to postpone discussing the central Berlin issues until a Summit Conference scheduled for 1960. When this conference collapsed, however, the Soviets made it clear that they awaited only the election of a new American president before reopening the crisis.

The General Structure
of the Deterrent Situation

The Berlin blockade of 1948–1949 had served to create a firm U.S. commitment to the security of West Berlin, which commitment the intervening ten years, with their occasional Soviet probes, had only strengthened. In this period NATO was created and formidable forces gathered under an American general; NATO, too, had a commitment to West Berlin.[1] Within the city itself, French, British, and American garrisons not only remained but were if anything somewhat stronger than before.

From a strictly military viewpoint, of course, West Berlin represented a liability rather than an asset, and presented no advantages for the defense of the NATO powers. But from a wider diplomatic and political viewpoint, the defense of Berlin was perceived in Washington and in other NATO capitals as critical to the alliance and to the general position of the West. With the successful Berlin blockade, the city had become the symbol of the Cold War, and its citizens the symbol of the determination of the Western democracies to resist and contain encroachments by the Soviet Union and by communism generally. It was assumed in Washington and other Western capitals that to withdraw, particularly under Soviet pressure, would have an enormously demoralizing effect upon NATO and upon the West as a whole, would suggest the prospect of further withdrawals, and might positively encourage Soviet aggression. It would also have generated a major political crisis within West Germany. Accordingly, the United States and its NATO allies were highly motivated to defend their position and rights in Berlin and to deter any Soviet assault upon them.

In placing such a high valuation upon this object of policy, the decision-makers of the United States, in particular, perceived somewhat fewer constraints on the exercise of deterrence than had pertained elsewhere. Domestic opinion firmly

---

[1] Stanley, *NATO in Transition,* p. 301.

supported a defense of West Berlin, and on this issue the United States' Atlantic allies could be counted upon. While there were some differences in viewpoint among various members of NATO, it was clear that in this case their interests were strongly engaged (unlike some Far Eastern cases) and were fundamentally in parallel (unlike some Middle Eastern cases). Aside from manageable "alliance politics" constraints, therefore, the principal limits to U.S. policy for Berlin seemed to be those arising from its awkward geography and the ambiguity of the Western position in World War II documents.

A policy seemed required because U.S. decision-makers perceived a real and potentially serious threat to the Western position. For it was clear from their past behavior there, from their declaratory policies, and from their foreign policy in general that the Soviets were highly motivated to gain complete control of Berlin. (Therefore, the general deterrent situation surrounding Berlin, at least in the period of 1958–1962, was the by no means common one of a highly motivated defending power attempting a deterrence policy vis-à-vis a highly motivated initiating power.) A variety of options seemed available to the Soviets, ranging from small "salami" tactics to a large-scale military *coup de main*. Geography gave the Soviets a number of situational advantages, and they maintained quite overwhelming forces in the vicinity of the city.

The perception in Washington of the specific policy problem, therefore, was that deterrence would be difficult but not impossible. Certainly it would be impossible to defend West Berlin using purely local, conventional forces, and hence pointless to rest any deterrence attempt on the threat to do so. (The West Berlin garrisons were intended to be just large enough to force the Soviets to resort to large-scale military action, and hence a completely unambiguous action, to take over the city quickly. Later this would be termed the "trip-wire" or "plate glass" function of the garrisons.) Washington policy-makers instead relied for deterrence on a very strong declaratory policy that consistently emphasized the unwavering U.S. commitment to West Berlin, backed in a general way by the power of NATO and the U.S. strategic arsenal. Under its general doctrine of Massive Retaliation, the United States systematically threatened to launch strategic warfare if the USSR aggressed against the containment line, which most definitely ran through West Berlin. Whether or not this was fully credible, the Soviet Union at least had to consider the probability of a major NATO ground thrust to Berlin from West Germany in the event the city was seized. Such action would lead either to an ignominious Soviet backdown or to a major European conflict, one that could not reliably be prevented from escalating to attacks upon the USSR itself.

The consequences of a clear and distinct violation of the manifest deterrence commitment were sufficiently obvious and sufficiently grave that U.S. decision-makers felt reasonably confident that the Soviets would not make such a major miscalculation. What concerned them more were the possible, less clear violations: lower-level Soviet options, exploiting by a new blockade or other coercive action the asymmetries inherent in the geographical situation to block or seriously impair Western access rights to Berlin. Throughout the 1950s there were "innumerable meetings" in Washington, often attended by the President, where decision-makers "examined against the possibility of future emergency, methods of support" for the city.[2]

Western policy-makers were proven correct in their estimate that the Soviets might be highly motivated to find a challenge to the West in Berlin. In 1948–1949 the USSR had been prevented by the United States' quite unexpected airlift capabilities from forcing the West to choose between remaining in Berlin and going ahead with plans for the creation of an independent West Germany. The intervening years had seen not only the consolidation of the Federal Republic but also its rearmament and its inclusion in NATO. Simultaneously, West Berlin itself was increasingly a "bone in the throat," as Khrushchev termed it. The city was a haven, and as it prospered more than East Berlin, a magnet, for East Germans fleeing to the West. By the fall of

---

[2] Eisenhower, *The White House Years*, p. 336.

1958 some ten thousand arrived in West Berlin every month. In the Soviet view the city was a center for Western espionage and "subversive activities." The maintenance of Western troops— and institutions and media—over a hundred miles within Warsaw Pact borders was a continuing obstacle to the consolidation of Soviet control over Eastern Europe.

Accordingly, throughout this period Soviet foreign policy held as a maximum objective the detachment of West Germany from the Western camp—a novel version of this was proposed again later in the "deadline crisis"—and as a minimal, highly valued objective the removal of the West from all Berlin. But a policy reaching toward these objectives was stymied for some eight years by the firm American commitment to its position in Berlin, backed by clear U.S. strategic superiority.

During 1957, however, there was a development in the overall strategic balance which both gave the USSR an opportunity to activate its Berlin policy and heightened its motivation to do so. The Soviet demonstration of long-range missile and space-satellite capabilities during the latter half of that year gave Khrushchev the opportunity for publicly claiming, as he was to do consistently for the next four years, that the balance in strategic weapons had shifted sharply, even decisively, toward the Soviet Union. In Soviet declaratory policy—and also in Soviet strategic doctrine—such a shift logically implied and required a shift in the general politico-diplomatic balance of power, and the place where the Soviet Union proposed to collect its due was Berlin.

This Soviet declaratory position (and to some degree genuine belief) was to be the vehicle for a determined Soviet diplomatic offensive against West Berlin, which waxed and waned but did not stop for over four years. Indeed the deadline crisis of 1958–1959 and the crisis of 1961 can usefully be seen as all a single tapestry, a long duel over Berlin which did not fade away until, during the Cuban missile crisis in 1962, the United States again asserted its superiority in strategic weapons.

Khrushchev declared throughout this period that the alleged shift toward the USSR of the strategic armaments balance meant that the ultimate American sanction behind its deterrence policy in Berlin, the threat of a strategic strike, was effectively voided. If he could convince Washington and/or its allies that the Massive Retaliation threat was no longer credible, they should then conclude that nothing prevented the Soviets from employing their overwhelming superiority in local conventional forces in any Berlin crisis. In effect the Premier presented the West with this as the scenario of any clash around Berlin: the USSR could allow East Germany to close the access routes to the city at any time. If it did so, the Western powers would then have to choose between accepting this loss and initiating violence in an attempt to reopen the routes with conventional forces. Such forces, however, could be defeated by the superior local Soviet conventional forces. With such a defeat imminent, the West would again have to choose between accepting a loss and escalating to the use of nuclear weapons. The latter option would soon spiral into a general nuclear war, which the West could not win since it no longer—Khrushchev claimed—possessed strategic superiority. In this scenario, it was clearly pointless for the NATO allies to employ force, and hence not credible for them to threaten to do so. Accordingly, Khrushchev concluded, the Western strategic position in Berlin had become untenable, and the "free city" plan the Soviets offered late in 1958 provided the Allies a face-saving means of withdrawing.

The Kremlin's motivation to push this line was heightened, if any heightening was necessary, by a decision at the December 1957 NATO Foreign Ministers Conference to station intermediate range ballistic missiles (IRBMs), armed with nuclear warheads under American control, in Europe, including the Federal Republic. While the decision was not implemented for a considerable period, this response to Soviet strategic advances (and to Soviet missile-rattling during the Suez Crisis of the fall of 1956) meant that for the first time West Germany would have within its grasp, if not under its direct control, nuclear weapons with sufficient range to reach the USSR itself. In proportions that may never be known, this genuinely added to the Soviets' perceived security problem and provided a convenient symbol for the Soviets' well-advertised alarm over "revanchist German militarism." [3]

The immediate Soviet reaction to the NATO decision was intense, including a call for a new Summit Conference. The Western reply was negative; counterproposals and alternatives generated a diplomatic exchange lasting through the spring of 1958. Crises in the Near East and in the Taiwan Strait then diverted attention elsewhere, but thereafter Khrushchev returned promptly to the Berlin question with his November 10 speech.

The Initiator's Motivation and Calculations

There is some evidence to suggest that Khrushchev had not intended to include the statement that it was time for the West to leave Berlin in his address of November 10 but was carried away by his own emotional diatribe against "German militarism." [4] However, the Kremlin was clearly in process of launching a Berlin campaign, some opening guns of which (as will be discussed later) had already been fired in September and October; it seems more likely, therefore, that Khrushchev's passion was planned, as it was on other occasions. However this may be, there was no significant Western response, and the Soviet deadline note arrived seventeen days later with its threat to turn over control of the Berlin access routes to East Germany in six months.

The challenge evidently was a carefully selected one. In

---

[3] Schick, *The Berlin Crisis*, pp. 7–10. Adam Ulam asserts that "To us now it is clear that the main Soviet objective was to secure an agreement that would make it impossible for West Germany to obtain nuclear weapons. . . . One suspects that for the moment they would have settled for a firm pledge that West Germany would be barred from being a nuclear force." *Expansion and Coexistence*, p. 620.

[4] Barker, "The Berlin Crisis," pp. 60–61; E. L. Dulles, "Berlin—Barometer of Tension."

resuming pressure on West Berlin in 1958, Soviet leaders were even more cautious than they had been in 1948. There was no actual blockade this time, only the *threat* (and a somewhat ambiguous one) of a probable blockade at some point in the future. In a real sense, therefore, U.S. deterrence was successful, and remained so until the crisis temporarily subsided. Options at Khrushchev's disposal for challenging deterrence in ways that would have created an acute crisis were threatened but never actually carried out. Whatever the Kremlin's real beliefs may have been about the strategic balance and the credibility of the American nuclear arsenal, throughout it carefully avoided any serious risk of a military conflagration around Berlin.

While successful in this sense, United States deterrence policy proved unable to forestall a Berlin crisis which seriously challenged her and her allies' unity and determination, and which at one point saw the West offering the Soviets a significant package of concessions in Berlin. In this sense, U.S. deterrence was incomplete. It succeeded in preventing the *actuality* of a physical, coercive Soviet move in Berlin but failed to prevent the *threat* thereof. And the threat itself represented a politico-diplomatic actuality, one which nearly gained the Soviets a significant payoff, and which might have gained them a very much greater one had the West been less unified and less skillful in the management of the crisis after deterrence failed.

Indeed, it is not easy to imagine, even with benefit of long hindsight, how U.S. deterrence might have been modified to forestall *both* the military actuality and the politico-diplomatic threat. The deadline crisis case thus illustrates some of the built-in limitations of deterrence as a policy, even in the service of the basic objective of containment (quite apart from its limitations in the service of wider foreign policy objectives). Khrushchev was able to calculate only too shrewdly that however firm and consistent the American deterrence commitment might be in principle, it would prove difficult for the U.S. to fully implement the commitment in practice, within the particular circumstances of Berlin.

In effect, the Kremlin by launching the deadline crisis was

attempting to heighten and to capitalize upon the important latent asymmetries of that situation which had not yet fully come into play—military, diplomatic, and psychological advantages to the Soviets related to Berlin's peculiar geography and history and by 1958 quite imbedded in the structure of the situation. Employing these advantages they were able to "design around" the U.S. deterrence posture, to make gains along a front which that posture did not, and could not easily, face.

Many of the Kremlin's other options were risky ones. Another blockade might accomplish no more than the first (and no less: the unifying and galvanizing of the West). A military seizure, either straightforward or disguised as a political coup against the West Berlin city government, was another option that must have appeared highly risky. Options of these kinds and variations upon them were what U.S. deterrence policy had been designed to forestall. The Kremlin clearly perceived and respected U.S. deterrence, and despite its rhetoric evidently found that deterrence credible—or at least credible enough vis-à-vis the more overt options. Furthermore, the danger of an irrational American overreaction to any overt move was one which the Soviet leaders could not have dismissed, and this worked to strengthen deterrence (as it usually does). But the Kremlin was able to find another option which promised a reasonably high probability of eventually achieving the objective of removing the West from Berlin, at reasonably low risk, and in particular at very low risk of any irrational Western overreaction. Let us glance in slightly greater detail at these two major aspects of the option the Soviets discovered for designing around U.S. deterrence.

The "deadline note" option offered a reasonable probability of eventually achieving a Western withdrawal, principally through the effects it could be expected to have on Western determination and unity. (In the same manner it offered some probability of setting into motion developments that might result in at least a partial detachment of West Germany from the Western camp.) The somewhat ambiguous threat seemed to imply a potential new blockade, with the possibility of armed

clashes between Western and East German troops and the
dangers of escalation which that possibility suggested. Through
Soviet declaratory policy accompanying and following the note,
and in various other ways, Kremlin leaders sought to make this
threat and its risks as alarming and vivid as possible (which attempt may have been assisted by its calculated ambiguity). On
the basis of past experience, they had reason to hope that vicari-
ous experiencing of a really intense military crisis in Central
Europe would have a splintering effect upon the Western position. Important segments of the public would become alarmed
at the risk of a major war and would appeal to their governments to avoid it by meeting the Soviet demand, which, after
all, was only to "negotiate." The several NATO governments
would each have their own perception of the nature of the crisis
and the proper policy with which to meet it. The diversity of
positions would shatter allied unity and sap the allies' determination. Through the mechanism of "alliance politics," the
policy that was the lowest common denominator would emerge,
in this instance probably the least resolute one.

Thus the Soviets could hope that an ambiguous *threat* of
a new blockade (or worse) would have just the opposite effect
of the *actuality* of one: it would tend to divide the Western allies in internecine bickering, whereas an immediate and real
military crisis would unite them. While the specific pattern of
events that would gradually emerge could not be predicted exactly in advance, the Kremlin could believe that as an essentially monolithic entity facing a plurality of divided opponents,
it could cause its own will to gradually prevail in a complex and
shifting situation. The Western position would gradually erode,
and in time little of it would be left.

By presenting the West with a challenge containing aspects both of clarity—in the vividness of possible dangerous
outcomes—and of ambiguity—in the circumstances under
which these outcomes might be triggered—the Soviet Union
challenged deterrence in a complex and sophisticated way.
The publicly available evidence suggests that the U.S. and its
allies were not adequately prepared for this kind of challenge.
As remarked earlier, contingency planning for Berlin crises ap-

parently presumed that the USSR would not miscalculate the deterrent situation so badly as to launch a full-scale military attack on the city, and therefore concentrated on less violent coercive options, such as a new blockade. But there is little evidence of contingency planning for still lower-level Soviet options like the *threat* of East German control of access. Indeed, there are good administrative reasons why such planning in advance of the contingency would seem unproductive and even counterproductive. All the problems of alliance politics that the Soviets expected to arise after November 27 would have arisen in advance. The United States' allies would quite reasonably have resisted attempts to define alliance policy in advance on purely hypothetical (and complex) contingencies, and any U.S. attempt to bring pressure to bear to do so might have made agreement even more difficult. (Precisely these problems were encountered in 1961, when the U.S. did seek interallied contingency planning.) [5] The Soviet challenge to U.S. deterrence thus struck it on a flank where it both was not and could not be adequately prepared.

This sophisticated Soviet option, however, had its own uncertainties. The promise of a reasonable probability of a significant payoff rested upon the Kremlin's convincing the Western powers, or many of them, of two things: first, that they had lost strategic superiority, and hence that any escalation to violence around Berlin would follow essentially the scenario sketched above, by which the West could only lose; and second, that the Kremlin, by virtue of its newly acquired strength, as well as for other reasons, was more highly motivated to bring about its desired changes in Berlin than the West was, or ought to be, to resist them. Thus in a deterrence situation characterized, as noted earlier, by high motivation on the part of both initiator and defender, the Soviets needed to convince the West that there was an *imbalance of motivation* in their own favor.[6] In ac-

---

[5] Schick, *Berlin Crisis*, pp. 157–58.

[6] Khrushchev was adopting a variant of the strategy elsewhere termed "coercive diplomacy". For such a strategy to succeed, an ingredient that is usually indispensable is a demonstrable asymmetry of motivation in favor of the coercing power. George, Hall, and Simons, *Limits of Coercive Diplomacy*, chap. 5.

tuality, the NATO allies partially (but only partially) accepted the notion that their opponent had achieved at least strategic parity; but they largely rejected the Soviet scenario of what an armed clash around Berlin would have to be like. However, in the end the Soviets failed to make any major gains from the deadline crisis principally because they failed to establish among critical Western decision-makers the belief that the Kremlin was more highly motivated than the West was.[7] (They failed also because the West remained more confident in its strategic power than the Kremlin had intended, and because the NATO Allies displayed unexpectedly great skill in achieving the necessary degree of unity within the alliance.)

We remarked that the other important aspect of the option of "designing around" U.S. deterrence the Soviets implemented in the "deadline note" was its promise of relatively low risk. Clearly no very violent response would come because of the note itself, and the deadline was sufficiently distant for many indications to appear of likely Western responses to a positive Soviet action before any action needed to be taken. The more violent of Khrushchev's threats and scenarios were remote in time; his immediate action was altogether nonviolent.

In addition, the Soviets structured this crisis, like other ones, so as to maintain *control over* their own risks. (In Soviet doctrine, risks are acceptable not necessarily when they are low, but when they are controllable—i.e., when they can be unilaterally reduced at any time they may seem to grow too large.) What precisely would happen at the end of six months if the

---

[7] Implicitly, the Soviets were attempting to convince the West of a particular doctrine of escalation—that one's acceptance of risk should be proportional to one's expectation of a favorable outcome. That is, one might run comparatively high risks if one confidently expected a highly favorable outcome, lower risks if one was uncertain or expected a rough stalemate, and still lower risks (or in principle, none) for an expected loss.

This theory was implicitly rejected in the Berlin deadline case, but it was only afterward that an explicit countertheory was developed, especially by Thomas Schelling in the early 1960s. Schelling demonstrated with force and lucidity that "risk-acceptance" is a manipulable factor of many attributes, including one's ability to construct a set of opponent's objectives and expectations and one's effort to change or reinforce a prevailing bargaining system.

West did not cooperate was left sufficiently unclear in the deadline note as to be open to any interpretation. In other respects, too, the note of November 27, evidently carefully drafted, contained calculated ambiguities. The suggestion that after six months negotiations need only to have *begun* gave the Kremlin a built-in device for terminating the crisis (if this seemed prudent) in almost any eventuality, since any plausible Western responses over six months could be called "negotiations." Finally, Khrushchev's private remark two days later, and subsequent private and public communications from Soviet leaders, reinforced this "escape clause."

These calculated ambiguities had a double payoff, in controlling the USSR's risks and also in tending to confuse the West as to the hardness of the Soviet position, reducing the influence of those who wanted to react firmly to the Soviet challenge and encouraging those who thought the Soviets were or might become "reasonable" and that a compromise should be sought. By diluting its ultimatum, however, Moscow also lowered the pressure. As the months passed it became increasingly clear that the Soviets were attaching less and less significance to their own deadline, until in the end May 27 passed with hardly a ripple.

The Defender's Response to Warning

Both strategic and tactical warning were available to U.S. decision-makers prior to the onset of the deadline crisis, apparently with only marginal benefit for U.S. and Western responses. Strategic warning came from the intense Soviet reaction to the NATO plan of stationing long-range nuclear weapons on German soil, which response included an insistent call for a new Summit Conference, a step-up in Soviet harassment of West Berlin in January 1958, and in February the Rapacki Plan for a "neutralized zone" in Central Europe. The diplomatic exchanges over these developments provided clear indications that the Soviets considered technological developments to be shifting the balance of power in their favor, and that they might be considering a major new initiative on Berlin.[8] The interruption of events generated by the Near East and Taiwan Strait crises presumably could and should have been interpreted as representing only a postponement, not a cancellation, of a European crisis.

In addition to this strategic warning, tactical warning was provided by what one analyst has termed "a diplomatic fusilade" in the immediately preceding period.[9] In September 1958 the Soviets announced that they had received an urgent message from the East German regime requesting four-power negotiations to prepare a draft peace treaty for the two German states, and a commission composed of representatives of Bonn and Pankow to discuss reunification. The Soviets endorsed this proposal and called upon the Western powers to correct the "abnormal situation" existing in Germany in the absence of a peace treaty. Bonn, supported by Washington, responded with a counterproposal for a four-power commission to reunite Germany. Rebuffed by this, East German Premier Ulbricht escalated by publicly laying claim to West Berlin on October 27 and implying that his regime would exercise sovereignty over the access routes. While he had made similar remarks on previous occasions (including at the Party Congress in July), this time he also referred to West Berlin as having originally been "part of the Soviet zone of occupation," an assertion similar to that which the Soviet military governor had made prior to the Berlin blockade in 1948.[10] Also during the autumn, the Soviet Ambassador to Bonn had remarked that the USSR hoped to have the Berlin "problem" solved by Christmas.[11]

---

[8] Smith, *Defense of Berlin*, pp. 15–19; Richardson, *Germany and the Atlantic Alliance*, p. 264; Ulam, *Expansion and Coexistence*, pp. 619–28; Schick, *Berlin Crisis*, pp. 6–10.

[9] Smith, *Defense of Berlin*, pp. 157–62.

[10] Schick, *Berlin Crisis*, p. 5; Windsor, *City on Leave*, p. 199.

[11] Schick, *Berlin Crisis*, p. 12n.

These and other lesser warnings of the shape of things to come did not go completely unnoticed in the West. The U.S. National Security Council held a meeting devoted to Berlin policy in the fall; and more significantly, a special four-power working group, composed of representatives from the U.S., the Federal Republic, France, and Britain, was established in September to give "constant attention" to Berlin. As noted, however, the available evidence suggests that these responses to available warning consisted of another reanalysis and rehearsal of plans in the event of another blockade or more violent contingency. There is no indication that they included an examination of the kind of strictly politico-diplomatic initiative the Soviets put forth in November. Indeed, not only the form of the Soviet move but also its *timing* apparently came somewhat as a surprise. No nonroutine declarations of policy regarding Berlin were being delivered by Western leaders in this period. What impact a vigorous declaratory reaction to available warning might have had on Soviet action can only be speculated about.

If the Soviet deadline note of November 27 is regarded as the beginning of the crisis (as it usually is), then Khrushchev's speech of November 10 is the clearest tactical warning of all, though warning "of what" exactly remained unclear. Nonetheless, the demand to leave Berlin had come from the highest policy-making level of the Soviet Union, and a period of over two weeks followed during which the West had an opportunity to respond. If Khrushchev had indeed been carried away by emotion in that speech and had interjected an unintended demand, the importance of a prompt Western response would have been even greater, since presumably an appropriate one could have forestalled the formalization of the demand in a Soviet diplomatic note. The same is true if the November 10 speech was an experiment by the Soviet leadership to test the Western response.

If United States policy-makers at all recognized Khrushchev's statement as a possible warning, however ambiguous, that American deterrence policy in Berlin might be about to fail, it is difficult to understand why they did not make an immediate effort to reinforce deterrence. A vigorous declaratory reaffirmation of the very serious American commitment to the city, and of the U.S. leaders' *present* determination to maintain that commitment, would have had a positive impact (to an admittedly unknowable degree) at virtually no cost whatsoever.

But in fact Washington elected to maintain official silence for nearly two weeks. Eisenhower writes in his memoirs that he "at once recognized the dangerous potential" of Khrushchev's statement. He chose not to respond because it might suggest that American leaders were "edgy"—an impression he apparently felt would damage the image he wanted to maintain with the Kremlin.[12] Apparently no leading administration official recognized that it might be important for Moscow to know that the United States *was* "edgy" about Berlin, and that at the minimum, private channels might be utilized to express Washington's concern over Khrushchev's threat and intention to maintain its commitment fully. Of course, there can be no assurance that such a step would have altered the development of the crisis, but its potential payoff surely outweighed any plausible costs. The administration apparently did not recognize that the *absence* of an American reaction to the November 10 speech was more likely to have a negative effect on the Kremlin's image of the U.S. than the presence of an appropriate and expectable reaction.

Meanwhile the warnings did not cease. On November 14, four days after the verbal threat, Soviet personnel held three U.S. Army trucks for eight and a half hours on the Autobahn just outside of Berlin. With hindsight it is difficult to avoid the conclusion that Soviet leaders, possibly surprised at the lack of an initial Western reaction, were dipping a second toe in the water. At the time General Norstad, the Supreme Allied Commander in Europe, was evidently of the opinion that the Russians were indeed probing to test Allied reactions. He told Washington that in the absence of other instructions he would dispatch a test convoy to Berlin. If the Soviets detained it and if a protest did not extricate it within a few hours, he would res-

[12] Eisenhower, *White House Years*, pp. 330, 331.

cue it "by minimum force necessary." The Joint Chiefs of Staff wanted to put Norstad's plan into effect at once, but the President, despite his "sympathetic" view of the plan, believed that the Allies should be consulted first. To give time for consultation he suspended all convoys to Berlin. Eisenhower gives no indication whether he or his advisers were concerned lest the suspension of convoys encourage the Soviets to conclude that efforts to intimidate would meet with success. (The ban on convoys was later lifted by the President before November 27, and they passed without incident.)

After mid-month and the convoy incident, U.S. policy-makers took warning seriously, expecting an important Soviet move and a new Berlin crisis. On November 19 the *New York Times* reported that the Secretary of State considered it a "foregone conclusion" that the Soviets would accept the risks entailed in transferring the access control rights to East Germany. On the 20th the National Security Council met to discuss Berlin, and Dulles told the President that Khrushchev would "probably move soon to carry out his threat" to make this transfer, which would "create the most complicated situation in Berlin since . . . the 1949 blockade." [13] Nonetheless, the administration evidently still did not communicate to the Kremlin, publicly or privately, its concern over any threat to its rights or its determination to maintain its Berlin commitment. The next day, November 21, the White House Press Secretary replied in the most general way to questions on Berlin. British Prime Minister MacMillan, however, did send a message to Khrushchev reaffirming the British commitment to Berlin. One can only speculate on what conclusions the Kremlin may have drawn from the fact that the British, but not the American, leader should react to the threat with a reaffirmation of his rights and commitment.[14]

U.S. decision-makers decided to respond to the (now clear) warning with another strategy, which in fact would have been consistent with a reaffirmation of the commitment but which

[13] *Ibid.*, p. 331.   [14] *Ibid.*, pp. 331–32.

was apparently seen as competing with, and preferable to, any public or private declaratory effort to reinforce deterrence. Secretary Dulles held an image of the opponent different from that held by some other high-level U.S. governmental figures. He believed that on matters touching Berlin and Germany, the USSR was acting defensively, out of concern for its own security. Accordingly, he believed that the most appropriate American response to Khrushchev's November 10 speech was a signal of willingness to negotiate. A danger of war would arise, he felt, only if the U.S. failed to indicate this and instead reinforced its military forces in Germany—precisely the opposite estimate from that of the JCS and other officials.[15]

Evidently winning the internal policy debate, Secretary Dulles launched his policy of flexibility on some aspects of the Berlin question at a press conference on November 26, at which time he startled some listeners by indicating that he was "not surprised" at Khrushchev's threat, and that he could accept East German officials at the traffic control points as "agents" of the Soviet Union. This could be done, he added, without relieving the Soviets of their responsibility to insure unimpeded Western access. He asserted that nothing to date had indicated any Soviet intention to deny access. Rather, he suggested, the Soviet purpose was "to try to compel an increased recognition and the according of increased stature" to East Germany.[16] Clearly he was signaling to Moscow his sensitivity to and willingness to accommodate to legitimate Russian security needs, which he considered included a valid concern for East German security. Since he apparently expected the Soviets actually to turn over the access control to the East Germans, virtually at any moment, he may also have been attempting to forestall any drastic crisis by indicating that this could be acceptable if done in a certain way. (Whether similar signals had previously been sent Moscow via private channels is not known. There would have been precedent in the reassurances the U.S. privately sent the USSR during the Hungarian Revolution the previous year.)

[15] Schick, *Berlin Crisis*, pp. 29–35. This disagreement within the administration foreshadowed the sharper one of 1961. See below, pp. 433–37.

[16] *Ibid.*, pp. 30–34.

We see, therefore, that Dulles' response to warning that deterrence might be about to fail was not an attempt to reinforce deterrence by threats or military deployments or alerts, but rather an indication of limited, defined flexibility on the matter at issue. Dulles evidently had concluded that in any case the United States could not prevent the Soviets from transferring traffic management to the East Germans, and hence a signal of flexibility on this issue would, if this were all the Soviets intended, forestall any crisis, and if it were not, at least clarify and emphasize the essential issue in the Western viewpoint, namely, the rights of access to Berlin. He perceived that many possible techniques for reinforcing deterrence on receipt of warning would be at best irrelevant to a low-level politico-diplomatic challenge, and at worst provocative to the opponent, possibly obliging him to take similar measures and thus escalating the crisis. Dulles should therefore be credited with a real sophistication in grasping the limits of deterrence policies and looking for alternatives to threats in trying to ward off a crisis. He also avoided the ever-present temptation to signal one's commitment to oppose *any* change in the status quo; and he substituted instead a differentiated analysis of the national interest, distinguishing which interests could not be compromised in any way and which could be accommodated to the opponent's objectives when his motivation was high, in the interests of peace. Dulles apparently did not, however, recognize that fully consistent with this, and an important supplement to it, could be signals reaffirming one's full commitment to the protection of those interests which *were* deemed vital, thus nonprovocatively but credibly reinforcing deterrence.

The Crisis Trails Off

Dulles' public signals could hardly have reached the Kremlin in time to affect the "deadline note" sent on November 27. The text of the note effectively ruled out the Secretary's "agent theory" by insisting on more than "a shift of responsibility and authority" from Soviet to East German police. (The fact that this was done carefully strongly suggests that the Soviets may indeed have received messages from Dulles privately before his public statement.) Nevertheless, on receiving the note the State Department was relieved, both because the Kremlin had sent a piece of paper rather than taking physical action and because the initial interpretation placed on the "six months" clause was that it represented the postponement of all action for that time. A similar construction was deduced in the British Foreign Ministry and elsewhere.[17] The West thus found itself in the somewhat unusual position of feeling relief at the receipt of an ultimatum.

In the months that followed, Dulles and other U.S. leaders concentrated on two objectives: assuring the Soviet Union of a general American readiness to negotiate, although certain rights would not be given up; and attaining unity within the Western camp. In pursuit of the former, lengthy informal discussions, as well as more formal messages, were exchanged with the Soviets, in the course of which Dulles put together a package of minor concessions. (The Kremlin, however, declined this package, apparently in the expectation of being able to do better later.) In pursuit of allied unity, lengthy and complex negotiations were held among the principal Western powers, arriving first at an agreed position and later at agreed modifications to it for bargaining with the Soviets.

Neither of these somewhat winding trails is relevant to the present analysis of deterrence. Eventually the Soviets agreed to a foreign ministers' meeting in May in return for U.S. agreement to a new Summit Conference the following year. The six-month deadline was allowed to pass uncelebrated, and the Kremlin allowed the Berlin question to simmer pending the Summit.

Through the winter and spring of 1959 it became increasingly clear that, while anxious to be rid of the Western presence in Berlin and eager to badger the West into a greater recogni-

17 *Ibid.*, pp. 12 and 34.

tion of the East German regime, Moscow was not willing to risk a major confrontation. And the plan of signing a separate peace treaty and turning over control of access to Berlin to East Germany was not executed because in the last analysis it remained more useful to Moscow as a threat than as an actuality. The Soviet deadline note thus failed to achieve the goals for which it was intended. Yet it was not without payoffs for the Kremlin. It succeeded in its tactical objective of pressuring the reluctant Western powers into negotiations over Berlin; it obtained an invitation to the United States for Khrushchev; and it secured Eisenhower's agreement to another Summit meeting, which the President had consistently opposed since the Soviets first called for it in 1957.

Moreover, when the Paris Summit of 1960 collapsed, Khrushchev made it clear that he would reopen the Berlin question as soon as the new American president was elected. The Berlin crisis had not been terminated, only suspended.

Bibliography

There has not yet been written a comprehensive analysis of the Berlin deadline crisis of 1958–1959 (or the renewed crisis of 1961) which brings to bear the full reach of contemporary politico-military theory. The nearest approximation is Jack M. Schick's recent work, which covers the 1958–1962 period in rich and valuable detail, and which contains useful analysis as well. Other particularly valuable sources are the books of Jean Smith, James Richardson, Hans Speier, and Philip Windsor. Eisenhower's memoirs, the several pieces on Dulles, and Schick give important information about American decision-making in the crisis. Besides Schick, we have relied mainly on Horelick and Rush for the sources of Soviet behavior.

We are indebted to Jane Howland for earlier research on this crisis.

Alsop, Joseph. "Method in Khrushchev's Madness," *Washington Post*, July 20, 1959.
Barker, Elizabeth. "The Berlin Crisis 1959–1962," *International Affairs*, January 1963.
Bell, Coral. *Negotiation from Strength: A Study on the Politics of Power.* New York, Knopf, 1963.
Drummond, Roscoe, and Gaston Coblentz. *Duel at the Brink: John Foster Dulles' Command of American Power.* New York, Doubleday, 1960.
Dulles, Eleanor Lansing. *John Foster Dulles: The Last Year.* New York, Harcourt, Brace and World, 1963.
——. "Berlin—Barometer of Tension," in *Détente: Cold War Strategy in Transition.* New York, Praeger, 1965.
Eisenhower, Dwight D. *The White House Years: Waging Peace, 1956–1961.* New York, Doubleday, 1965.
——. "K Staged a Retreat on Berlin," *Washington Post*, September 26, 1965.
George, Alexander L., David K. Hall, and William E. Simons. *The Limits of Coercive Diplomacy.* Boston, Little, Brown, 1971.

Goold-Adams, Richard. *The Time of Power: A Reappraisal of John Foster Dulles*. London, Weidenfeld and Nicolson, 1962.

Halle, Louis. *The Cold War as History*. New York, Harper & Row, 1967.

Harriman, Averell. "My Alarming Interview with Khrushchev," *Life*, July 8, 1959.

Horelick, Arnold L., and Myron Rush. *Strategic Power and Soviet Foreign Policy*. Chicago, University of Chicago Press, 1965.

Mander, John. *Berlin: Hostage for the West*. Baltimore, Penguin, 1962.

Mezerik, A. G. *Berlin and Germany*. New York, International Review Service, 1962.

Mosely, Philip E. "Soviet Myths and Realities," *Foreign Affairs*, April 1961.

Richardson, James L. *Germany and the Atlantic Alliance: The Interaction of Strategy and Politics*. Cambridge, Harvard University Press, 1966.

Schick, Jack M. *The Berlin Crisis, 1958–1962*. Philadelphia, University of Pennsylvania Press, 1971.

Smith, Jean Edward. *The Defense of Berlin*. Baltimore, Johns Hopkins Press, 1963.

Speier, Hans. *Divided Berlin: The Anatomy of Soviet Political Blackmail*. New York, Praeger, 1961.

Stanley, Timothy W. *NATO in Transition: The Future of the Atlantic Alliance*. New York, Praeger, 1965.

Stebbins, Richard P. *The United States in World Affairs*. New York, Harper & Bros., 1959.

Ulam, Adam. *Expansion and Coexistence*. New York, Praeger, 1968.

Windsor, Philip. *City on Leave: A History of Berlin 1945–1962*. New York, Praeger, 1963.

Chapter 14

🏵

The Berlin *Aide-Memoire*
Crisis, 1961

Résumé of the Crisis

WHEN THE NEW AMERICAN PRESIDENT, John F. Kennedy, was elected, and even before he was inaugurated, the Soviets indicated that they would again address themselves to the "abnormal situation" in Berlin. On taking office, therefore, the new administration fully expected a new round, and probably a new crisis, over Berlin, and indeed sent a message to the Kremlin requesting time to prepare its position. In his initial survey, the President was alarmed to discover the few and very transient options available to him in any military showdown in Berlin before he would be faced with the necessity of using nuclear weapons to avert defeat. Accordingly, during the spring he initiated programs designed to increase his conventional capabilities in Europe, as well as his strategic capabilities.

Meanwhile, he sought ways of conveying to the Soviets that he would be no less resolute than his predecessor in protecting basic Western rights in Berlin, while at the same time seeking a *modus vivendi* with them there in the longer run. In February Kennedy suggested in a letter to Khrushchev that the two meet personally. The Soviet leader accepted in May, after the President had suffered a major diplomatic reverse (with no offsetting gain) at the Bay of Pigs. The two conferred in Vienna on June 3 and 4.

Kennedy, expecting no outbreak in Berlin until later in the year, tried to convey both his resolution and his eagerness to avoid a confrontation there. But the Premier surprised him by seizing the occasion to launch his new Berlin crisis. First he verbally renewed the threat to sign a peace treaty with East Germany unilaterally unless the West agreed to negotiate a "normalization" of the Berlin situation. Then he presented the United States with an *aide-mémoire* similar but not identical in content to the deadline note of November 1958. According to the *aide-mémoire,* the two Germanies themselves should negotiate a means of reunification; again the Soviet government considered that "six months" should be sufficient for this. If they were unable to reach agreement in this time, then each should sign a separate peace treaty with the four World War II victors. As in the previous note, West Berlin would become a "free city" on terms placing it substantially under East German control. Rights of access would have to be renegotiated with the Ulbricht government. The *aide-mémoire,* unlike the deadline note, did *not* indicate a date by which East and West Germany should have started or completed their "six-month" effort to negotiate reunification. But in subsequent speeches eleven and seventeen days later, Khrushchev stated that the USSR would sign a separate treaty with East Germany by the end of the year.

Kennedy's response came with a formal reply on July 17 and a television address to the American people on July 25. The position he established combined an expressed general willingness to negotiate with a strong reassertion of the Western rights in West Berlin, which he held to be in their essence non-negotiable. The President had received a commissioned report from Dean Acheson which had detailed steps the U.S. should take to bolster its deterrence posture in Berlin (as well as outlined contingency plans for any new blockade). To back up his strong declaratory position, Kennedy now asked and subsequently received from Congress yet additional monies to finance a further buildup in conventional forces in Europe and at home, authority to call up reserves or increase draft calls, authority to implement economic sanctions against the Warsaw Pact nations, and a tax increase to pay for these measures. He rejected, however, Acheson's advice to declare a national emergency.

Meanwhile, the Soviet Union had responded in kind to Kennedy's earlier decisions to refurbish American military power. Planned reductions in Red Army troop levels were rescinded, and supplementary funds were given the military equal to about one-fourth the regular annual announced defense budget. Khrushchev declared that Kennedy's response to his *aide-mémoire* had been belligerent, and tensions rose.

Early in August Khrushchev apparently decided finally to grant a request which Ulbricht had been pressing for some time, namely, to halt the ever-increasing flow of refugees fleeing East Germany through Berlin, a flow that was draining the state of some of its most productive citizens. On August 13, East Germans were forbidden to travel to West Berlin and barbed-wire barriers were erected on East Berlin territory to enforce the ban. When the following days saw no vigorous Western reaction, the barriers were solidified into a wall and extended around the whole of West Berlin. The U.S. reaction, besides a protest, was to send a detachment of troops down the Autobahn to exercise the access rights. There were also visits by Vice-President Johnson and later General Clay to raise the Berliners' morale. In the absence of any greater Western reaction, the Soviets pressed further to see what other gains might be made; they adopted a program of menacing gestures, including harassment of the air corridors and, at home, a resumption of nuclear testing in the atmosphere. Minor probes around Berlin were fielded by General Clay; the most spectacular of these was a tank confrontation at Checkpoint Charlie in October.

At the same time the Soviets and the Americans began conversations, formally through meetings between Rusk and Gromyko in New York in September, and less formally but more productively through the initiation of a private correspondence between Kennedy and Khrushchev soon afterward. Shortly thereafter the Premier announced to a Communist Party Congress that, since the West was negotiating, the *aide-mémoire* had been a success; and he lifted the "end of the year" deadline on results. Negotiations proceeded, as they had in 1959 and 1960 following the "deadline crisis," but as in May 1959 the intense period of the crisis was over.

The General Structure
of the Deterrent Situation

The *aide-mémoire* crisis of 1961 in certain respects closely resembles the deadline crisis of 1957–1958, of which it was essentially a resumption, but in other significant respects differs from it. An important resemblance to the deadline crisis is the Soviet success in "designing around" the U.S. and Western deterrent posture to generate a crisis promising politico-diplomatic gains for themselves. In this respect the deterrent situation in the *aide-mémoire* crisis moves within the same general structure as its predecessor, and much of the analysis presented in chapter 13 therefore applies in a general way to the *aide-mémoire* crisis as well. Recapitulating the relevant portion summarily: the Western deterrent posture was incomplete, due both to the intrinsic limitations of a deterrence strategy in a situation like that of Berlin and, to a lesser degree, to the failure of the Western powers to *attempt* to deter Soviet coercive options less overt than those of direct physical action. Exploiting the latent asymmetries inherent in Berlin's peculiar geographical and historical position, the Soviets exercised an option to threaten a coercive move rather than actually making it. In the circumstances reigning, the threat to turn over control of the access routes to the East Germans was at least as advantageous to the Soviet objectives, and probably much more so, than the actuality would have been. Avoiding the unifying and galvanizing effect which an overt military crisis would have had on the Western alliance, the threat, on the contrary, tended to splinter the alliance, and thereby offered the Soviets a reasonable probability of making significant politico-diplomatic gains. At the same time, this option offered them low and quite controllable risks, since the activating portion of the threat, the deadline, was somewhat ambiguous and could be modified, reinterpreted, or withdrawn at any time. All these propositions apply to the general structure of the deterrent situation in the *aide-mémoire* crisis.

In this chapter, therefore, we will not rehearse again these propositions as generalizations, but rather concentrate on ways in which their forms or mechanisms varied from those of the earlier crisis, and on ways in which the later crisis embodied new elements entirely. For the 1961 crisis was not simply a repetition in slightly differing detail of a Soviet game of diplomatic blackmail—making a verbal threat and then securing real concessions in return for a verbal withdrawal. Unlike its predecessor, this crisis included both actual (though limited) physical moves against the Western position in Berlin by the USSR (the Wall, the harassment of aircraft in the corridors) and physical responses by the West (the dispatch of troops down the Autobahn, the tank confrontation, and a number of very overt military preparations).

THE MOTIVATION OF THE ADVERSARIES

The *aide-mémoire* crisis reached the level of overt military moves in substantial part because by 1961 *both* adversaries were even more highly motivated than they had been in 1958–1959. In its response to the deadline crisis, the West had committed itself even more thoroughly to its position in Berlin than it had done before. And the mere existence of this crisis had once again, as in 1948, raised West Berlin and the Western position there to extreme visibility and saliency. Even more strongly than at the outbreak of the earlier deadline crisis, U.S. and Allied decision-makers believed that to retreat in Berlin might well unravel the whole Western defense structure; indeed, the mere fact of the earlier crisis, together with the commitments by which it had been weathered, reinforced this belief later. In a sense, the West had reaffirmed a self-fulfilling posture: making a stand in Berlin and asserting it to be the linchpin of the alliance in 1958 invested an even greater value in doing so again in 1961.

Whether the Soviets accurately perceived this seems somewhat dubious, given their statements and behavior in 1961. Rather, they may have had a variety of reasons for feeling that the Western position in Berlin had eroded or ought to have eroded. In the deadline crisis the West had offered significant concessions, and its negotiating position in the following eighteen months was not without similar concessions. The passing of John Foster Dulles, the apparent weakening of Chancellor Adenauer's political position in West Germany, political strains within NATO, the U-2 incident, the election of a new administration in America both inexperienced and untied to past dogmas—these and perhaps other events may have suggested to the Kremlin that the Western motivation to hold fast in Berlin or its capacity to do so, or both had declined in the period since the deadline crisis.

If so, then the general deterrent situation of 1961 embodied an asymmetry, for the West at this time *did* quite correctly perceive that the USSR was even more strongly motivated than before to achieve at least some alteration in the status of Berlin. Khrushchev's failure in the first round had been a conspicuous one. He had relaxed his six-month deadline and entered into negotiations which became ever more prolonged and during which the Allies unexpectedly managed to achieve sufficient unity to maintain their basic position. If, as some observers have speculated, the poor prospect of getting a favorable settlement on Berlin at the planned Summit meeting of May 1960 influenced Khrushchev's angry handling of the U-2 affair, the net outcome was nonetheless a further postponement of a Berlin solution, despite the Premier's oft-repeated claim that the situation was urgent. All this lent great plausibility to his words when in January 1961 he told U. S. Ambassador Llewellyn Thompson that his prestige was engaged in Berlin and he had waited long enough to make his move.[1]

[1] Schlesinger, *A Thousand Days*, p. 347.

Khrushchev's motivation was being further heightened by the increasing severity of East Germany's escapee problem. In 1960 the East German government had resumed agricultural collectivization and other measures to restructure society along more communist lines. The rate at which refugees escaped to the West via West Berlin thereafter increased steadily, and was stimulated further by the fear that escape to the West would soon become impossible. Despite severe police measures aimed at controlling the flow of East Germans to East Berlin, as well as traffic across Berlin, the escapee rate continued to rise throughout 1960 and into 1961. By early 1961 over a thousand East Germans a day arrived in West Berlin seeking refuge. A high percentage of these refugees were young people or individuals possessing important skills. The economy and society could not sustain such losses for very long. And Moscow could not tolerate the collapse of one of its satellites, both because of the ideological threat this would pose and because it would threaten to seriously erode the whole East European glacis which Moscow considered a vital security interest.

Finally, Soviet motivation to gain its Berlin objectives was also made more urgent by the Kremlin's knowledge that the claim to strategic superiority over the United States (upon which, as noted previously, the entire effort rested) was in fact doubtful at best, and could not be sustained much longer even as a bluff in the face of the ongoing American buildup in strategic weapons.

Thus, unlike the case in 1958–1959, this time the Soviets had at least two compelling and urgent reasons for challenging the West in Berlin beyond their more general fears of West German rearmament. (The latter, indeed, may have been somewhat weakened as the motor of policy in the intervening period as it became clear that Bonn was not going to obtain nuclear weapons through NATO.) By early 1961 both the deterring power and the power intending to challenge deterrence found themselves even more highly motivated in these policies than they had been in 1958, the potential challenging power perhaps especially so. It seems likely, however, that Khrushchev underestimated Kennedy's motivation to hold firm in West Berlin, and hence underestimated the resistance he would encounter or the risks he would run. The Bay of Pigs affair may have encouraged Khrushchev in his view of Kennedy as immature and lacking in judgment and nerve.

The Defender's Response to Warning

In 1961 the West enjoyed somewhat less tactical but at least as good strategic warning of the outbreak of a new Berlin crisis as it had in 1958. And as previously, the Western response to this warning was quite inadequate to forestall at least a partial failure of its deterrence policy—for rather more complex reasons than had pertained in 1958 (reasons to be analyzed in the two following sections).

Tactical warning in 1961 was insufficient to indicate when, or in what form, the new Soviet move against Berlin would come. Upon his inaugural Kennedy had asked Dean Acheson to lead a task force in studying the Berlin situation. His interim report, read by the President in April, warned that the new crisis was probable within that calendar year. Acheson drew upon American intelligence in making this prediction, for the intelligence community had already noted and reported the ample available strategic warning that a new Berlin crisis was approaching.

However, from Kennedy's surprise at Vienna when Khrushchev sprang his new Berlin initiative, it seems reasonable to infer that U.S. intelligence had not warned the President that the crisis was truly imminent, but had allowed him to believe that it might come later in the year.[2] If so, this was a true error. Walter Lippmann had had an interview with Khrushchev on April 10, and had come away from it with the impression that

[2] On Kennedy's surprise and dismay when Khrushchev told him that a treaty turning over Berlin to East Germany must be signed by December, see especially Schlesinger, *A Thousand Days,* pp. 372–75.

the Chairman felt real urgency about Berlin. A Soviet message to Bonn in February had warned, even more clearly, that the "abnormal situation" in Berlin could not wait for the next elections in the Federal Republic, which were scheduled for September. We must conclude, therefore, that clear and unequivocal tactical warning was lacking in 1961, but also that the Western decision-making apparatus misjudged available indications that the Soviet move on Berlin would come earlier rather than later. Perhaps the firm request Washington had made to Moscow after Kennedy's inaugural for time in which to prepare the American position had encouraged decision-makers to interpret the warning signs as implying that this time would be granted, rather than as implying that the granted time would be short.

When the crisis broke in June, the absence of clear, unequivocal warning of it suggested—perhaps intentionally—stronger and more urgent Soviet motivation to achieve its goals than had existed in 1958, when tactical warning was available. Prior to the deadline crisis, Khrushchev's speech and the later halting of trucks on the Autobahn had apparently represented a "testing strategy" by the Soviets, exploring Western reaction. Such a strategy was eschewed in 1961. The *aide-mémoire* was presented to the West simultaneously with Khrushchev's verbal message to Kennedy, and obviously both had been prepared in advance. Perhaps after the deadline crisis and two years of bargaining, in 1961 the Soviets had sufficiently high confidence in their expectation that the West would not drastically overreact to feel that further probing was unnecessary. Springing the *aide-mémoire* without preparatory moves may have offered predictable advantages of shock effect and, hopefully, of preventing the formation of a new Western "working group" to develop an alliance-wide position. The fact that the Soviets did not publish the *aide-mémoire* until five days after giving it to Kennedy may have represented a residual, low-cost hedge against an instantaneous drastic overreaction by the young new President.

Strategic warning was amply available prior to the crisis. In a public speech on January 6, Khrushchev had reasserted his intention to sign a separate peace treaty with East Germany. The following month the Kremlin sent an *aide-mémoire* to the West German government threatening a separate treaty with the Pankow regime and foreshadowing in other ways as well the contents of the communication Kennedy was to be handed a few months later. This note was widely publicized by Moscow on March 3. Later in January Khrushchev told Ambassador Thompson that his prestige was engaged in Berlin and he had waited long enough to make his move. In April he coupled similar intimations to Walter Lippmann with professed fears that Bonn was about to obtain nuclear weapons.[3]

Even without such specific warnings, it was widely understood in the West that the Soviets were only awaiting a good opportunity to reopen the Berlin crisis, and, indeed, that the Berlin crisis had never really ended after the withdrawal of the immediate deadline threat in 1959, but was merely proceeding for a period in low key. And Khrushchev had already made it clear that he would not wait longer than the installation of the new American President. Strategic warning, therefore, could hardly have been more ample and unequivocal.

The same cannot be said of the Western response to this warning. In the first place, the Eisenhower Administration in its closing year and a half apparently did not try to find a positive new policy for Berlin. After the major Soviet initiative of 1958–1959 had been dealt with, U.S. decision-makers continued to act defensively, fending off continuing low-level Soviet diplomatic probes. No major Western counterinitiative emerged implementing or even designing a strategy to shift the Berlin problem away from the context of Western deterrence and to give the city a more stable status that would still be consonant with Western interests. The difficulties involved in such an effort admittedly would have been formidable, including not only the inherent conflict of interest with the Soviets but also problems of alliance politics, as well as the more diffuse problems of fashioning any creative departure toward the close of a lengthy period in office. That such an effort was apparently not even

[3] *Ibid.*, pp. 353–56; *New York Times*, March 18, 1961; Lippmann, *Coming Tests with Russia*, p. 23; Speier, *Divided Berlin*, p. 130.

being studied, however, was precisely the criticism put forward by Senator Kennedy, among others, in this period.[4]

A consequence was that the new administration entered office to find little in the way of a planning base for any new policies on Berlin. This, in turn, was evidently the root of the administration's message to the Soviets that time would be needed to study Berlin, of President Kennedy's request to Acheson for a new analysis, and in part, of the initiative for the Vienna meeting. The accounts of that conference suggest that the President hoped to persuade Khrushchev that other means besides dangerously stark challenges to deterrence could be and should be sought to deal with conflicting East-West interests. Kennedy apparently was prepared to be flexible in this spirit in Berlin, and elsewhere, if the Soviets would grant the appropriate time for negotiating and would otherwise cooperate.[5] The Premier's refusal to understand this approach and his sharply renewed challenge to U.S. deterrence in Berlin may have been influenced (besides by his other reasons for urgency) by the fact that in the previous five months the new administration had essentially repeated its predecessor's declaratory policy on Berlin, having failed to inherit any planning base on which to do otherwise.

But the Kennedy Administration's response to strategic warning in Berlin was not limited to a search for new analyses and pleas for time to do it in. It also adopted a major action policy.

The Defender's Response: The Problem of Self-Image

Almost immediately upon entering office the new administration moved to enhance significantly the U.S. ability to back

[4] Schick, *Berlin Crisis*, pp. 141–45.

[5] Schlesinger, *A Thousand Days*, pp. 358–74; Sorensen, *Kennedy*, pp. 543–50.

up its deterrence policies with military force, at both the strategic and the conventional level. President Kennedy himself subscribed to the critique of Eisenhower's doctrine of Massive Retaliation, and staffed his defense agencies with appointees many of whom had played central roles in the development of that critique. The new administration came to power convinced that the threat to escalate rapidly to strategic warfare was not as credible as its predecessor had claimed, and, indeed, that the U.S. strategic arsenal would have to be improved quickly if it was even to be adequate to deter the Soviet counterpart forces.

With respect to the strategic forces themselves, Kennedy had campaigned on fears of a "missile gap," a sincere anxiety at the time, although new intelligence emerging later in 1961 dispelled fears of a developing Soviet strategic superiority. During his first six months or so in office, however, Kennedy partially believed the Soviet claim, trumpeted now for some three years, that the United States was the strategically inferior power, at least in offensive missile capabilities. To remedy this perceived weakness the President accelerated the Polaris and Minuteman missile programs, securing supplementary funds from Congress to do so.

The self-image of the United States held by key policymakers was disturbing in another way too. In Central Europe (and elsewhere as well) the U.S. seemed unacceptably inferior in conventional military power. The new President was alarmed to discover how few options he had (and how little time could be used up by exercising them) in any armed conflict in Germany before he would either have to accept defeat or initiate the use of nuclear weapons. While it was clear that in the immediate future NATO could not hope to match the Warsaw Pact man for man along the Central European front, the gross disparity in forces then pertaining struck Kennedy as both unnecessary and dangerous. He therefore sought ways to "lengthen the fuse on the bomb" represented by Berlin by adding effective conventional options to increase the number of steps of escalation he could take (and hence the amount of time available to both sides for sober thought) before having to make the fateful decision to resort to atomic weapons. In his spring messages to Congress seeking supplementary defense funds, he also requested and received monies to increase U.S. conventional capabilities both at home and in Europe; and he implemented this policy promptly.

Kennedy's response to his expectation of a challenge to deterrence was thus sharply different from Eisenhower's. The preceding President had sought to avoid giving any possible impression of being "edgy" about the credibility of U.S. deterrence in Berlin and had quite consciously vetoed the suggestions of some advisers to reinforce U.S. conventional capabilities in Europe out of his desire to avoid "provocative" acts. Eisenhower accepted with greater equanimity than his successor the West's gross inferiority in conventional military power in Central Europe. He did not intend to resort to nuclear weapons instantaneously in the event of a military clash around Berlin, but he was content to imply that he would do so fairly quickly, and otherwise to base his deterrence policy for Berlin on U.S. strategic power generally. He evidently felt that his deterrence policy was strengthened rather than weakened by reliance on the threat of reasonably rapid (which is not to say immediate or automatic) escalation to general strategic war.

Kennedy's view differed in at least three major respects. First, he feared a major Soviet miscalculation concerning the Western position in Berlin, as will be discussed in detail later. Second, he had little confidence that any European conflict, once nuclear weapons were introduced, could be halted short of a catastrophic world war. He therefore was anxious to lengthen the time span between the onset of military action and resort to atomic weapons.[6] In this he employed a more pessimistic assumption than did Eisenhower in estimating the Kremlin's will-

[6] There is some reason to believe that President Kennedy may have been more pessimistic than his predecessor regarding the amount of time that would be available after nuclear weapons were introduced "tactically" before all-out strategic exchanges began. That is, Eisenhower may have believed in a "longer and slower" escalation sequence following the first use of atomic weapons tactically than did Kennedy. Such, at least, was implicit in the Eisenhower Administration's doctrine of "Graduated Deterrence," which Kennedy did not fully accept.

ingness to bear risks. The new President considered it plausible that the Soviets might be so motivated to attain their Berlin objectives that they might accept the fairly high risks inherent in an overtly military move. If this was a plausible scenario, then he wanted means of dealing with it that would not trigger a general nuclear war.

Third, Kennedy was much less confident than Eisenhower of the general capabilities of U.S. strategic forces, given the strategic balance as he perceived it in 1961. Therefore he was logically compelled to doubt the credibility in a Berlin crisis of any threat, explicit or implicit, to use these forces. If this threat was to be inefficacious, another would have to be found. By threatening, rather, to use conventional forces on a large scale and for a significant time before resorting to atomic weapons, Kennedy felt he put forward a more credible sanction for his deterrence efforts. He did not expect to "win" a conventional European war against considerably superior Soviet conventional forces, but he expected his reinforcements on the Western front to "hold" the Soviets for a period. And once NATO was involved in a multidivision battle, *then* a threat to resort to nuclear weapons would be more believable. The Soviets would realize this, as they would also realize that Kennedy would indeed employ large conventional forces in a clash.

In this, again, Kennedy employed a more pessimistic assumption than had Eisenhower. It will be recalled that Kennedy's scepticism about the efficacy of the U.S. strategic threat was precisely what Khrushchev had attempted to persuade the West into in the 1958–1959 crisis, when he claimed that the threat to resort to nuclear weapons in an escalating Berlin crisis was no longer credible to him. This claim had not persuaded Eisenhower, but it did make a strong impression on the American critics of Massive Retaliation; indeed, Khrushchev's assertions were taken as evidence that their critique was justified. In effect, Kennedy went far toward buying Khrushchev's argument. Or at a minimum, he accepted at least partially the analysis suggesting American strategic inferiority and, hence, lessened credibility for deterrence; he noted that the Soviet leaders were putting forward this analysis; and he assumed that like himself they believed it (when in fact they knew the U.S. was not strategically inferior).

In sum, Kennedy, unlike Eisenhower, responded to strategic warning that deterrence might be challenged in the European theater by taking steps soon after entering office to *reinforce* deterrence, both with vigorous reaffirmations of the American commitment to Berlin and, even more importantly, with concrete measures to improve American conventional capabilities in that theater (as well as strategic capabilities in later years). This policy was consistent with Acheson's recommendations, and Kennedy also accepted Acheson's concepts as to how to break a new blockade with conventional forces as a basis for drafting new contingency plans to update those of 1958.

As a further technique for reinforcing deterrence, supplementary to the buildup in conventional forces and the vigorous declaratory effort, the new administration also responded to strategic warning in Berlin by disavowing the previous, somewhat conciliatory negotiating position of the Eisenhower Administration. After the crisis broke in June, the President further reinforced deterrence by deciding in July to seek authority to call up reserves or more draftees, to further increase U.S. conventional capabilities generally, and to send some new forces to Europe. This action was intended by the President not only to raise the probability of successfully dealing with any overt Soviet move but also to increase the chances that, as in 1958, the Kremlin would content itself with words and not resort to deeds.

It is difficult to imagine what more the incoming administration could have done in 1961 to reinforce deterrence on the receipt of strategic warning. Yet deterrence failed partially nonetheless—first as the Soviets designed around the deterrence policy to activate a low-level, politico-diplomatic option, as in 1958, and then later as they made actual coercive moves in Berlin. This case illustrates the great difficulty which the deterring power may encounter, even if highly motivated and possessed of major capabilities, in trying to maintain a deterrence policy against an opponent who is even more highly motivated and who possesses situational advantages that can be exploited at least partially to turn the flank of the deterrence effort. That the best efforts of the Kennedy Administration to respond vigorously to warning were unable to forestall a significant, although not complete, failure of deterrence in Berlin suggests something of the intrinsic limitations of deterrence as an element in foreign policy.

Furthermore, these efforts to reinforce deterrence were not without some inherent ambiguities and imponderables (as attempts to reinforce a failing deterrence policy often are). It is entirely possible that the Kremlin perceived Kennedy's buildup of American conventional power as at least partially an admission of weakness, as well as an attempt to regain strength. The American President, after all, was essentially endorsing Premier Khrushchev's position that U.S. strategic power was now inadequate to sanction the Berlin deterrence policy. Soviet policymakers may have decided to make their move in Berlin while the President still held this opinion and before his measures to bolster U.S. conventional forces could be effectively implemented. They would also want to move before U.S. strategic forces could be significantly improved. Kennedy's efforts to reinforce deterrence may therefore have been counterproductive, actually weakening it in the Soviet perception. Yet the President also had good reasons for not adopting a policy of reasserting Massive Retailiation. In the end, there was no way he could tell at the time, nor can we even now, which line of action would suggest weakness and which strength in Soviet eyes.

Kennedy's efforts to reinforce deterrence were imponderable then, and are now, in another respect as well. The Kremlin responded to his congressional messages requesting more defense funds in March and May (but not to his conventional buildup of July) with their own measures to enhance their military power. The President himself was later to speculate that these efforts to reinforce deterrence may have been counterproductive; that instead of acting as restraints, they may have forced the Soviets into hardening their own position.[7] This

[7] Schlesinger, *A Thousand Days*, pp. 347–48.

speculation is plausible if one takes the view that the Soviets had certain minimum objectives in Berlin for which they were willing to pay a very high price, plus additional objectives there on which they were prepared to be flexible if the West proved flexible. It will be recalled that Secretary Dulles had held this view at the beginning of the deadline crisis, when he opposed a policy of responding to warning by reinforcing deterrence. If this was the case in the spring of 1961, the image of intransigence and rearmament which Kennedy projected may have lowered the Kremlin's motivation to be flexible regarding its "additional" objectives. But there was no very clear evidence at that time that this *was* the pattern of Soviet objectives. And it is noteworthy that the President indulged in this speculation only later in the year after the actual limits of the most vital Soviet objectives in Berlin had emerged, and after new intelligence had revealed the comparative weakness of the actual Soviet strategic forces. The previous spring, when the full extent of Soviet ambitions in Germany was unclear and when the USSR appeared to possess strategic parity or perhaps even superiority, Kennedy's speculation would have seemed less plausible.

There are often several reasons for adopting measures to strengthen one's position, of which "reinforcing deterrence" is only one. (This was the case with Kennedy's measures, which were sought for other reasons besides a desire to improve U.S. forces in Central Europe.) In this way the calculus of one's deterrence policy becomes complicated; one may even decide to make an effort to reinforce deterrence because this is congruent with other policy objectives, where otherwise one might decide against such an effort. And often so little is known about the opponent's objectives that it is impossible to tell whether an intransigent reinforcement of deterrence will succeed in preventing him from mounting a challenge at all or merely reduce his incentive to be flexible about his nonessential objectives. Indeed, it was just this sort of question that comprised the most difficult aspect, which we have not yet addressed, of the problem of how to respond to strategic warning in 1961.

The Defender's Response:
The Problem of the Image of the Opponent

President Kennedy's efforts to reinforce deterrence were influenced by a different perception of his opponent from the one Eisenhower had had, for he came to office with a greater apprehension over the danger of a Soviet miscalculation concerning the Western position in Berlin. He had hopes of establishing a *modus vivendi* in Berlin involving internationalization of the access routes, but he was aware that the Kremlin had already turned down this notion when it was advanced by the Eisenhower Administration, presumably because the Soviets were not yet convinced that the West would not eventually accept some variant of their "free city" proposal. Kennedy recognized that achieving a *modus vivendi* therefore depended upon persuading a reluctant Kremlin that the U.S. would accept high risks to maintain its basic position in Berlin. It was precisely on this point that he feared the Soviets might miscalculate. He tended to believe that Khrushchev was indeed prepared to implement his threat to turn over control of the Western access routes to East Germany; and he tended to reject the conclusion others drew from the deadline crisis of 1958–1959 that Khrushchev had been engaging in a shrewd bluff, and would not accept the risks of war latent in carrying out his threat. More than Eisenhower and Dulles, Kennedy believed that the Kremlin was prepared, if necessary, to take *high* risks on behalf of its minimum objectives in Berlin (whatever these were), and that the Kremlin was basing its policies on the erroneous expectation that when and if the contingent threat to block access to Berlin was implemented, Washington would back away from the risk of a major war. The new President evidently did not, at least in the period prior to October 1961, subscribe to the alternative interpretation, which in essence had been Dulles' throughout most of the earlier crisis, that Khrushchev was pursuing a contolled, low-risk strategy in which the contingent threat of, in effect, another blockade was

solely a diplomatic lever to wrest major concessions through negotiation. Both the new administration and the old saw Khrushchev as strongly motivated to secure a change in Berlin; but
the old had been less apprehensive than the new as to the level
of risk he would be willing to accept, and less fearful that he
would miscalculate by underestimating Washington's resolution
in the event of a blockade. Kennedy seems to have believed
that his own resolution would not be as easily perceived by the
Soviet leader as Eisenhower had expected his to be; and expecting in addition that Khrushchev would pursue a high-risk
policy, if necessary, the President was deeply concerned about
the danger of war over Berlin from a Soviet miscalculation.

Thus the new President evidently decided that his first task
in approaching the Soviets must be to convince them that his
resolution equalled Eisenhower's. After the Bay of Pigs fiasco
this must have seemed particularly important. Kennedy therefore projected a hard-line declaratory policy during the spring
and he disavowed the flexible features in the Eisenhower
negotiating position. (This also accounts for the vigorous, almost
militant, language of his July 25 address to the nation, when following receipt of the *aide-mémoire* it seemed even more necessary to drive home his resolution to the Kremlin.)

Prior to the June outbreak of the crisis, Kennedy seems to
have had in mind a two-stage strategy for Berlin. The first stage
was to convince Khrushchev that he would not back away from
defending the basic Western interests in Berlin, even at the risk
of war. To succeed in this would remove or greatly lessen the
preoccupying danger of Soviet miscalculation. This seems to
have been one of the major motivations for the February 22
note to Moscow proposing the face-to-face meeting, and it was
the point the President began at once to make to Khrushchev
when the conversation turned to Berlin in Vienna.[8] Once this
message was clearly understood in the Kremlin, Kennedy apparently planned, he could move on to the second stage,
namely, to begin to explore possible bases for a *modus vivendi.*

[8] *Ibid.,* p. 371.

These intentions were wrecked, of course, when the Chairman
brought forth his new Berlin crisis in Vienna before Kennedy
could make his signal of resolution register.

Dean Acheson's final report, received by the President
three weeks later, accentuated a division of opinion on the appropriate image of the Soviet opponent within a Washington
policy-making community that was already debating the best
response to the *aide-mémoire*. In his report Acheson took the
position that the USSR was seizing upon Berlin as a pretext,
hoping to force a major defeat for U.S. foreign policy and a
grave weakening, if not dissolution, of the NATO alliance, accompanied perhaps by neutralist tendencies in West Germany.
Arguing that the West had already conceded everything that
could be conceded in Berlin, and hence that there was nothing
left to negotiate, the report urged a variety of mobilizations of
conventional military power, close consultation with the allies,
especially Germany, and the declaration of a national
emergency. Also included were contingency plans for a
sequence of military operations, culminating in a two-division
push down the Autobahn, if access to West Berlin were
blocked.

Acheson's conclusions typified the view of the "hard line"
school, which also included Vice-President Johnson, Paul Nitze
(Chairman of the State Department policy planning staff), General Maxwell Taylor, the JCS and many Pentagon civilians, and
the German desk in the State Department. It also closely ap-
proximated the position of Adenauer's Germany and De
Gaulle's France. The essence of the hard-line position was that
the Soviet Union was engaged in an *offensive* operation in Berlin posing serious dangers to the West, which could be contained only with a vigorous defense and deterrence effort. To
offer negotiations or an image of flexibility, it was argued,
would encourage the Soviets to press for the greatest possible
realization of their objectives, which, since the West would
have to stand and fight at some not-very-distant point, would
raise the danger of a major war. An unmistakable commitment
to hold fast in Berlin, backed by credible military capabilities,

on the other hand, would deter the Soviets from pressing their demands or executing their threats, and hence minimize the chances of war.

Opposed to this was a "soft line" school of thought, represented by Ambassadors Harriman and Thompson, Bohlen and other political appointees in the State Department, Adlai Stevenson, staffers Rostow, Sorensen, and Schlesinger in the White House, and Senators Fulbright and Mansfield, among others. (The positions taken by Secretaries Rusk and McNamara seem to have varied at different times during the crisis but tended in general toward this view also.) It represented the views of Macmillan's Britain as well. The essence of the "soft line" position was that the Soviet Union was engaged in an essentially *defensive* operation in Berlin, aimed at consolidating its system of East European satellites by ridding itself of the "escape hatch" which was draining East Germany and acting as a source of Western propaganda. This school accepted Acheson's statement of the three critical Western interests in Berlin—free access, the right to maintain troops, and the continued economic and political viability of West Berlin under democratic institutions—and also accepted the need for some buildup, preferably quiet, in Western conventional forces. But it urged active negotiations without delay as well, both for their own sake as an alternative to confrontation, and as a means of communicating to the Soviets that the West would attempt to be responsive in reducing the irritation value of West Berlin to the Soviets, consonant with protecting its basic rights. Only by opening negotiations promptly could we convince the Soviets that their legitimate, minimum security interests would be respected, thereby minimizing the risk of war. Intransigence, however, could generate war by leading the Soviets to make desperate moves.

This disagreement over Soviet intentions in Berlin reflected a more fundamental difference between the hard-line and soft-line schools in their more basic image of the Soviet opponent. The former held that, while the Kremlin may have softened its tactics and stretched out its schedule, it essentially retained the same basic Cold War objectives as ever—by gradual steps to extend its own and constrict America's influence until at some future date the whole of the West was in a subordinate status to itself. But the soft-line school represented those whose image of the USSR was in process of change from what it had been ten or even five years earlier. To this school it appeared that the expansionist dynamic of Soviet foreign policy, if indeed it had ever been as virulent as had been feared in the West, was becoming more moderate, and that the Kremlin was now acting and would continue to act increasingly out of "nationalist" and "defensive" motives—a trend which should be and could be encouraged by flexibility on the part of the West. From this more general difference over the "correct" image of the Soviet opponent came the two schools of thought on the best way to orient American and Western foreign policy in Berlin and in other specific problem areas of the same period.

In this respect the Berlin *aide-mémoire* case provides an excellent example of a general proposition relating to the implementation and applicability of deterrence policies. The immediately available indicators of the existence and form of a potential challenge to deterrence frequently do *not* provide much guidance concerning the opponent's intentions or objectives in the potential crisis. Rather one's estimates of these things will be based heavily upon one's more general and lasting image of the opponent and of his underlying foreign policies. The image one holds of the opponent's probable goals and behavior in a specific crisis therefore are part of one's *own* ideological view or belief system.[9]

President Kennedy attempted to mediate the debate between his two schools of advisers, apparently with some awareness that they were not as completely opposed as they might seem. Khrushchev might well be employing once again the classic Bolshevik strategy of pursuing multiple, but graduated objectives. Certain "defensive" objectives clearly were highly valued by the Soviets (for example, cutting off the flow of refugees to the West), while other objectives which were progres-

[9] This theme is discussed at greater length in chapter 20 below.

sively more ambitious and "offensive" evidently received a
more measured valuation and could sustain only more limited
risk-taking (for example, changing the status of West Berlin to
an extent and by means that would force the recognition of East
Germany and weaken NATO). Still other, even more ambitious
objectives (such as detaching West Germany from NATO de
jure, or at least de facto) would doubtless be realized with great
pleasure in the Kremlin, but were evidently valued too little to
sustain any significant acceptance of risk by the Soviets.

In his policy decisions the President tended to accept most
of the positive recommendations of both schools and to reject
most of their negative ones. He accepted the bulk of Acheson's
recommendations for contingency planning and for force augmentation, while rejecting the suggestion that no flexibility be
shown. He also accepted the recommendation of the soft school
that negotiations be attempted with the Soviets on a basis of
sensitivity to their security needs in East Europe, while rejecting this school's suggestion that military preparations be deemphasized.

An important decision consistent with the soft approach
that Kennedy apparently made toward the end of July was to ex-
empt "free access between East and West Berlin" from the list
of Western interests which he would consider vital. Acheson
and his school considered this point highly important because it
was guaranteed by the Potsdam Protocols which, it was argued,
had to be defended consistently and in toto—and also precisely
because a continuing drain on the communist empire was held
to be desirable by this school. But the President had to weigh
these considerations against the evidence that stopping this
hemorrhage was Khrushchev's most urgent and vital objective.
Apparently Kennedy decided that the Western interest in free
transit across Berlin could be sacrificed in the hope of terminating or lessening the crisis through appeasement—in its original
and honorable sense of allowing one's opponent his minimum
and absolutely necessary goals to save the peace. In any case,
the administration made no effort to contradict or object to a
public speech by Senator Fulbright on July 30 indicating that

for Pankow to close the Berlin border to its citizens would be an obvious and acceptable move (and even expressing surprise that it had not done so already). In an interview on August 10 the President made no reference to free movement in Berlin as a Western desideratum; nor did he mention Fulbright's statement. Furthermore, there is a possibility that the NATO foreign ministers in their conference on August 7 and 8 may have secretly decided that a closing of the border between East and West Berlin would not represent a *casus foederis*.[10]

With benefit of hindsight it is difficult to avoid the conclusion that the Fulbright address—delivered by a man intimate with the administration but in no way a responsible member of it—was a conscious signal to the Soviets suggesting that they relieve their most urgent distress in this manner.[11] Of course, no such thing has ever been acknowledged, for obvious reasons. And it is possible that the apparent tacit sanction of Fulbright's speech was merely an oversight on the part of the administration, although in light of the intense planning and analytical effort then under way throughout the government, this is unlikely. In any event, the Senator did not have long to wait to see his suggestion put into action.

Deterrence Fails a Little More

By the early spring of 1961 the outflow of refugees from East Germany was averaging over 1,000 a day. In a secret session of the Warsaw Pact Conference on March 28 and 29, Ulbricht demanded that he be allowed to close the border between East and West Berlin. But the other East European countries opposed such a move on grounds both of embarrassment and of the risk of a violent Western response; and the

[10] Schlesinger, *A Thousand Days*, p. 394; Richardson, *Germany and the Atlantic Alliance*, p. 284.

[11] President Kennedy remarked to an aide early in August that Khrushchev would have to halt the refugee flow. Schlesinger, *A Thousand Days*, p. 394.

USSR stated that it would be necessary first to determine how Kennedy's Berlin policies might differ from Eisenhower's. (Ulbricht's goal, however, remained unchanged, and during the summer he apparently leaked rumors of an imminent border closing to stimulate the refugee flow and thus obtain an unarguable case for proceeding to do so.) [12] The June *aide-mémoire* thus appears as an attempt to accomplish Ulbricht's basic purpose as part of a wider alteration in the German status quo that would further Soviet foreign policy objectives as well.

On August 4 and 5 the Warsaw Pact powers held another conference in Moscow at which the East German plan to close the border was approved and details worked out. [13] Whether on account of Fulbright's speech and the lack of contradiction by the American administration, or on account of the rapidly rising flow of refugees, or simply as the next step in the Soviet program of pressure on the West, Ulbricht received permission to take a step in clear violation of the Four-Power status of all Berlin and of the Potsdam Protocols—with Soviet military backing, naturally. The barriers between East and West Berlin began to go up at midnight on August 12/13.

Western reaction was slow. In West Berlin the Western commanding officers were taken completely by surprise and asked their capitals for instructions. Intelligence agencies in Washington were taken equally by surprise. The "ambassadors' group" on Berlin that had been formed in July convened, and together with the administration considered possible responses. It was not until four days later that a public protest was made by the Western allies, and Kennedy dispatched 1,500 troops down the *Autobahn* to West Berlin to confirm that access rights were unabridged. (The evidently genuine surprise of the Western governments suggests that this particular *way* of taking Senator Fulbright's suggestion was unanticipated, and/or that this signal—if it was that—was a very closely kept secret of the highest levels of the American government.)

[12] *Der Spiegel*, August 15, 1966, p. 27. The reliability of this account may be open to question.

[13] *Ibid.*, pp. 29–30.

Moscow and Pankow had evidently expected a sharper and more rapid Western reaction. The numerous armed forces guarding the workmen were not issued ammunition (although ammunition was available nearby), and the barriers first erected were flimsy, easily removable affairs of barbed wire, with some eighty-eight points left open for traffic.[14] Only when no physical reaction came were the temporary barriers replaced, in the following days and weeks, with a permanent wall, and the number of open points reduced to eight under tight East German control.

The erection of the Wall is another example of how deterrence may be designed around by a highly motivated power possessing important situational advantages. Unlike the case represented by the crisis as a whole, this was *not* an instance where no deterrence had been attempted. On the contrary, the right of free access from one part of Berlin to another was part of the Potsdam Protocols, one of the critical documents upon which the Western legal position in Berlin rested. But Pankow and Moscow were able to take advantage of the fact that their Wall, however aggressive it may have been in a moral sense against their own populations, was a "defensive" move in tactical and strategic terms. Erected on the territory of East Berlin, it placed upon the West the burden of making the first act of violence. For the West Berlin forces to have knocked it down would merely have invited its reerection further back. Clearly, the Western garrisons could not be making constant forays ever deeper into East Berlin, surrounded as they were by almost ludicrously overwhelming Soviet forces.

In erecting the Wall the Soviets played out in microcosm many of the advantages they possessed in somewhat more ambiguous ways in the Berlin situation as a whole. The location of Berlin over a hundred miles within communist territory placed squarely in Moscow's lap all the advantages provided by the distinction between *force* and *violence:* with the exception of any air action in the corridors, Moscow needed only to close off Berlin forcibly, then passively wait for the West to resort to vio-

[14] Windsor, *City on Leave,* p. 240; McDermott, *Berlin,* p. 30.

lence to reopen them. In the fifteen-year protracted conflict over Berlin, the West thus constantly had had to wrestle with the fact that, while strategically, legally, and morally it was the defensive power there, tactically it had to be the offensive one. Indeed, from the long view the most striking aspect of the Western deterrence effort in Berlin in this period may be how well it succeeded, not how often it nearly failed, given these underlying situational asymmetries. The same asymmetries were present and even more clear-cut in the case of the East Berlin Wall, and while violence as a Western response may not have been utterly infeasible, it clearly posed enormous risks for improbable gains. Considering that they could hope Khrushchev's incentive to take any further steps would now be reduced, it is not surprising that Western policy-makers decided to take no military action.

Kennedy found, however, that he had initially underestimated the need for major reactions, even nonmilitary ones. The anxiety in West Berlin became and remained so acute that he was obliged to send to the city first Vice-President Johnson and later General Clay, hero of the 1948–1949 airlift, as his "personal representative," with considerable authority to take necessary actions on the spot. In the succeeding months, indeed, Clay caused a number of very sharp Western reactions to local incidents, including the probably unnecessary confrontation of Soviet and American tanks at Checkpoint Charlie in October. While at times irritating his allies and even his sponsor in the White House, in hindsight Clay's vigor appears to have been useful in providing a local reinforcement of deterrence at a time when the Soviets were probably disposed to push for further gains.

For their success in erecting the Wall, together with the weakness of the Western reaction, clearly encouraged the Kremlin to immediately adopt a forward posture. Ten days after the first erection of the barriers, the USSR delivered a new note to the U.S. threatening Allied air rights in the corridors between Berlin and West Germany. This drew a sharp response from Washington, yet the Soviets adopted a policy of harassment.

East German and Soviet forces repeatedly "buzzed" Western aircraft in the corridors, and from the ground trained blinding searchlights on the pilot's compartment of incoming planes. (The Allies considered responding by using only military transport aircraft, and even with adding fighter escorts—a move which Britain rejected as too militant.)

Additionally, on August 30 the USSR resumed atmospheric testing of nuclear weapons (in direct violation of Khrushchev's pledge to Kennedy in Vienna not to be the first to do so); the testing program soon included the 50-megaton explosion which, having no possible military purpose, was taken in the West to be a "terror weapon"; a 100-megaton blast was later threatened. At the same time, Soviet naval maneuvers at sea included test nuclear detonations.

Evidently, the Kremlin was pleased—and perhaps even slightly surprised—at the lack of any overt Western reaction to the erection of the Wall. In such situations, Bolshevik doctrine calls for the application of additional pressure to extract maximum gains, and this policy the Soviets followed. Additionally, the Soviet decision-makers may have concluded that an earlier expectation of Western weakness in Germany had been proven correct, that Kennedy's implicit confession of strategic weakness was still salient (the testing program would underline *this*), and/or even that Kennedy, at the Wall as well as at the Bay of Pigs, was incapable of making a firm decision in a crisis.

Fortunately, however, the Soviets contented themselves with melodramatic but low-risk military activities, combined with declaratory demands that the West open negotiations on the basis of the *aide-mémoire.* They may have avoided going further because the Wall removed their most urgent and vital concern, and because they expected additional gains to be more likely to come from negotiations than from new coercive actions "in theater." It is possible that another influence toward restraint was their discovery through their intelligence network that the West (or at least Washington) now knew the Soviet claim of strategic superiority to be hollow. It was apparently in August and September that American intelligence uncovered

the fact that the USSR had deployed only a handful of ICBMs.[15]
Indeed, the new Soviet atmospheric testing program may have
been intended partly to compensate for this Western discovery.

The Crisis Trails Off Again

In his July 25 address, President Kennedy had sought to
strike a balance between military preparations for a confrontation in Berlin and the offer of negotiations to head off a confrontation. But the erection of the Wall, the Western attempts thereafter to shore up the morale of the West Berliners, and the
Soviet program of militant gestures had upset this balance, and
once again interfered with Kennedy's intended timetable for
first demonstrating resolution, then talking. (The difficulty—
much greater than in 1958–1959—of achieving agreement on a
negotiating position among the Western Allies had also delayed
Kennedy's graduation into the "talk" phase.) [16] By the end of
August Kennedy evidently believed that his resolution had
been demonstrated and that, with no developments in the Berlin air corridors requiring immediate action, it might be an opportune time for opening conversations with the Russians.

Apparently, Khrushchev had arrived at the same conclusion. Under cover of his atmospheric blasts, he sent a private
message to Kennedy via C. L. Sulzberger of the *New York
Times* suggesting communication between them outside normal
channels. To make sure the message got through, shortly thereafter he had a couple of Soviet diplomats visit Pierre Salinger,
the President's press secretary, with the same communication.
Kennedy and Khrushchev began to correspond secretly. While
no indication of the content of this correspondence has
emerged, knowledgable sources indicate that it was instrumen-

[15] Horelick and Rush, *Strategic Power*, pp. 35–36, 83–84, 125.

[16] For an account of this aspect of the crisis consult Schick, *Berlin Crisis*, pp.
154–58.

tal in cooling off the crisis.[17] Khrushchev evidently indicated his willingness to help the President find a Berlin solution that would not damage U.S. prestige. And it is possible that Kennedy offered Khrushchev concessions, perhaps concerning the use of West Berlin as a center of political and psychological warfare against the Eastern bloc, which led to Khrushchev's October decision to defuse the crisis.

Within more regular channels, Secretary Rusk and Foreign Minister Gromyko held meetings in New York in late September in connection with the opening of the new session of the U.N. General Assembly. Shortly thereafter the Minister talked with Kennedy.

The initiation of conversations on Berlin was apparently a factor in Khrushchev's decision to withdraw the deadline of "negotiations reaching an agreement this year," a decision he announced on October 17 at the first meeting of the Twenty-Second Party Congress. In his statement to the Congress, Khrushchev implied that the Wall and other politico-military moves around Berlin, together with his demands at Vienna and in the *aide-mémoire*, had paid off. The Rusk-Gromyko conversations indicated that the West was ready to negotiate seriously. Accordingly, the deadline was unnecessary and a hindrance, and should be lifted.[18] While neither Rusk nor Kennedy had said anything to indicate that the Soviet negotiating program as presented in the *aide-mémoire* represented an acceptable starting point, the Premier nonetheless may have concluded that he was more likely to get further negotiating without a deadline ten weeks away than with it. And to have come up to the end of the year with no additional substantive agreement might have placed him in an embarrassing position. (This was likely enough, and indeed did occur. The next major negotiations were between Ambassador Thompson and Gromyko in Moscow early in 1962.)

---

[17] Sorensen, *Kennedy*, pp. 599–600; Salinger, *With Kennedy*, p. 255; Sulzberger, "Foreign Affairs."

[18] Schick, *Berlin Crisis*, pp. 184–86.

But it seems likely that there were two additional major factors in Khrushchev's decision to lift the *aide-mémoire* deadline. First, his most important objectives may have been achieved, and the risks of continuing the crisis may have seemed too large to be worth running for only secondary objectives. With the erection of the Wall the Chairman had solved the most important and most urgent problem he had faced in Berlin—the escaping refugees—and had solved it in a way that could be perceived as a major politico-diplomatic victory over the West. (At the same time, Soviet fears about West German nuclear armament, which had been perhaps the major motivating factor in 1958, had been greatly reduced in the following three years, thereby lowering the Kremlin's motivation to press for wider German, as well as Berlin, gains.)

Second, by October the Kremlin could be sure that the West now was aware that the Soviet claim to strategic superiority was and had been a bluff. (The Soviet attempt to make political gains by means of strategic deception is discussed in more detail in the following chapter.) With this awareness the Western powers would now again have much greater confidence in their capacity to deter any major Soviet move against Berlin; and the mere existence of this confidence (whether actually justified or not) would make any such move highly dangerous and even continued probing somewhat risky. Khrushchev thus was obliged to withdraw his challenge to deterrence in Berlin until once more he could come up with a way of neutralizing or seeming to neutralize superior U.S. strategic power. His last and most dramatic attempt to do so came almost exactly one year later.

Bibliography

As with the Berlin deadline crisis, there is no completely adequate analysis of the *aide-mémoire* crisis yet in existence. However, Jack Schick's *The Berlin Crisis, 1958–1962* gives a wealth of information, combined with useful analytical insight. Also useful on the later crisis are Jean Smith, James Richardson, and Philip Windsor. American decision-making, with particular emphasis on the decisions of the President, is unusually well covered in the accounts of Sorensen and Schlesinger. As in the earlier crisis, Horelick and Rush are important supplements to Schick's portrayal of Soviet behavior. A detailed interpretation of Soviet policy-making is provided by Slusser.

For earlier research on this crisis we are indebted to Jane Howland, Raymond Morrow, Pamela Ellis, and Frederik Wiant.

Alsop, J. "Most Important Decision in U.S. History and How the President is Facing It," *Saturday Review,* August 5, 1961.

Ascoli, M. "The Wall," *The Reporter,* September 14, 1961.

Bailey, George. "The Gentle Erosion of Berlin," *The Reporter,* April 26, 1962.

Der Spiegel, August 15, 1966 ("Konjew Liess Augmarschieren") and August 29, 1966.

Dulles, Eleanor Lansing. "Berlin—Barometer of Tension," in *Detente: Cold War Strategy in Transition.* New York, Praeger, 1965.

"Excerpts from Kennedy's News Conference, Berlin, June 28, 1961," *Department of State Bulletin,* July 17, 1961.

Galante, Pierre, and Jack Miller. *The Berlin Wall.* London, Arthur Barker, 1965.

Halle, Louis. *The Cold War as History.* New York, Harper & Row, 1967.

Horelick, Arnold L., and Myron Rush. *Strategic Power and Soviet Foreign Policy.* Chicago, University of Chicago Press, 1965.

Lippmann, Walter. *The Coming Tests with Russia.* Boston, Little, Brown, 1961.

McDermott, Geoffrey. *Berlin: Success of a Mission?* New York, Harper & Row, 1963.

Mezerik, A. G. *Berlin and Germany.* New York, International Review Service, 1962.

Morrow, Raymond. "The Berlin Crisis of 1961 as a Failure of Deterrence." Unpublished seminar paper, Stanford University, December 1967.
Pachter, Henry. "JFK as an Equestrian Statue: On Myth and Mythmakers," *Salmagundi*, Spring 1966.
"Real Reason Why the Berlin Wall was Built" (W. Ulbricht interview), *U.S. News and World Report*, January 15, 1962.
Rees, David. *The Age of Containment: The Cold War 1945–1965*. New York, Macmillan, 1967.
Richardson, James L. *Germany and the Atlantic Alliance: The Interaction of Strategy and Politics*. Cambridge, Harvard University Press, 1966.
Salinger, Pierre. *With Kennedy*. New York, Avon, 1966.
Schick, Jack M. "The Berlin Crisis of 1961 and U.S. Military Strategy," *Orbis*, Winter 1965.
——. *The Berlin Crisis 1958–1962*, Philadelphia, University of Pennsylvania Press, 1971.
——. "American Diplomacy and the Berlin Negotiations," *Western Political Quarterly*, December 1965.
Schlesinger, Arthur, A. *A Thousand Days: John Kennedy in the White House*. Boston, Houghton Mifflin, 1965.
Slusser, Robert M. *The Berlin Crisis of 1961*. Baltimore, Johns Hopkins Press, 1973.
Smith, Jean Edward. "Berlin: The Erosion of a Principle," *The Reporter*, November 21, 1963.
——. *The Defense of Berlin*. Baltimore, Johns Hopkins Press, 1963.
Sorensen, Theodore C. *Kennedy*. New York, Harper & Row, 1965.
Speier, Hans. *Divided Berlin: The Anatomy of Soviet Political Blackmail*. New York, Praeger, 1961.
Stebbins, Richard P. *United States in World Affairs*. New York, Harper & Row, 1967.
Sulzberger, C. L. "Foreign Affairs, The Two K's and Germany," *New York Times*, November 6, 1966.
Tanter, Raymond. "International System and Foreign Policy Approaches: Implications for Conflict Modelling and Management," *World Politics*, 24 (Spring 1972), 7–39.
Trevor-Roper, H. R. "Berlin: The Large and Basic Issue," *The New York Times Magazine*, February 25, 1962.
Windsor, Philip. *City on Leave: A History of Berlin 1945–1962*. New York, Praeger, 1963.

Chapter 15

The Cuban Missile Crisis, 1962

The Sources of the Crisis:
the Cold War Use of Strategic Power

THE SOVIET ATTEMPT to deploy some 42 medium- and some 24 to 32 intermediate-range ballistic missiles secretly in Cuba during the late summer and early fall of 1962 triggered the most dangerous crisis of the Cold War. Never before or since have the Soviet Union and the United States been so close to a shooting war, one that could easily have escalated into a thermonuclear exchange. Unforeseen and unwanted by either side, the tense confrontation was resolved through careful crisis management by both Washington and Moscow and by a hastily arranged *quid pro quo* in which Khrushchev agreed to remove his missiles from Cuba in return for a pledge by Kennedy not to invade Cuba in the future.

The Soviet deployment of missiles into Cuba represented a major failure of United States deterrence policy, albeit one of an unconventional variety. The Soviet action was not one of the classical military actions that deterrence strategy is normally designed to discourage. Nor, despite its clandestine character, was the missile deployment intended to set the stage for a Soviet resort to military force. While the Soviets certainly wished to achieve surprise with their deployment, it was not part of a plan for a surprise attack upon the United States or any of its allies. Rather, the deployment was the grandest—and, as it turned out, the last—in a series of increasingly ambitious efforts the two superpowers had been making to exploit their strategic armories for politico-diplomatic purposes. President Kennedy's decision to demand the removal of the missiles, even at a significant risk of major war, was motivated not by fear that the Soviets would make some direct military use of them, but by his expectation that the Kremlin would transmute the improved strategic posture that Cuban-based missiles would give them into a variety of important Cold War gains.

Before examining the Cuban missile crisis itself, therefore, we should look with a little care into its roots in the Cold War. Until the latter part of the 1950s, the traditional pattern of U.S. Cold War policy had been to invoke America's strategic superiority over the Soviet Union not only to deter the Soviets from initiating general or limited war but also to impose constraints on their pursuit of foreign policy goals which the United States regarded as threatening or illegitimately expansionist. The doctrine of Massive Retaliation, of course, represented the apotheosis of this effort. It does not require much imagination to understand the frustration that Kremlin leaders must have felt at this strategy, and their eagerness to neutralize it and even, if possible, to turn it against its makers. As their own capabilities grew, the Soviet captains proved apt pupils of the American lesson on translating strategic power into a foreign policy tool. Even before the Soviets put Sputnik into orbit in the autumn of 1957, they had begun to employ strategic threats (as in the Suez crisis) for politico-diplomatic purposes. However, the shorter-range Soviet missiles, targeted on Western Europe, did not permit credible threats of this kind against the United States itself. So long as this situation obtained, the credibility of the American threat to retaliate directly against the Soviet Union protected weaker allies who were themselves at a disadvantage vis-à-vis Soviet military power.

This situation changed abruptly and in a most spectacular fashion when the Soviets demonstrated a technological breakthrough of far-reaching implications by successfully testing an intercontinental ballistic missile (ICBM) in late August 1957. The message that the United States was no longer invulnerable, and more, was in danger of being surpassed in military technology was driven home and absorbed deeply into the national consciousness when six weeks later the Soviets orbited the first earth satellite. The psychological impact on the United States was far greater than it had been when the Soviets had tested their first A-bomb and, later, demonstrated a capability for developing an H-bomb. The fact that Sputnik orbited directly and repeatedly over the United States did much to symbolize the nation's vulnerability to the Soviet ICBM. Public alarm mounted when in November Sputnik II demonstrated that Soviet missiles could put a very large payload into space and when, in due course, U.S. intelligence estimated that the Soviet ICBM production capability might be much larger than had been expected.

American uncertainty and anxiety regarding the development of Soviet strategic capabilities provided Khrushchev with a tempting opportunity to neutralize the Cold War advantages the United States had been realizing from its strategic superiority. He proceeded to use the ICBM threat to invigorate his own foreign policy. Increasingly, Khrushchev played upon American and Western fears that the Soviets were creating a "missile gap" in their favor. From 1957 to 1962 the Soviet government engaged in a deliberate, systematic, and sustained campaign of deception. It issued grossly exaggerated claims regarding the production and deployment of ICBMs and highly inflated statements of the strength and numbers of the Soviet ICBM force vis-à-vis that of the United States. After Khrushchev initiated the Berlin "deadline crisis" in late 1958 (chapter 13, *infra*), the effort to deceive the West with regard to Soviet ICBM capabilities became more contrived and systematic. Until the Cuban missile crisis, it occupied a central place in Soviet policy.[1]

While Moscow made a pretense of employing strategic threats for deterrence purposes in several diplomatic crises

[1] Horelick and Rush, *Strategic Power*, pp. 117–19.

(Syria, 1957; Iraq, 1958; Quemoy, 1958; Cuba, 1961) and for "compellant" (coercive) purposes in other cases (Suez, 1956; American U-2 flights over Russia, 1960), the most serious use it made of strategic threats in this period was in support of Soviet Cold War diplomacy in the Berlin crisis of 1958–1959, which resumed again in 1961. As Horelick and Rush observe,[2] the Soviet Union did not attempt to secure changes in the status quo of Berlin directly, by the use of strategic threats. Rather, strategic threats were employed (1) to increase the effect of the nonstrategic instruments of pressure that the Soviet Union brought to bear, and (2) to limit the West's freedom of action in opposing them.

Khrushchev attempted to use his strategic claims to erode the Western will to resist his demands and to deter undesirable responses the United States and its Western allies might make to the diplomatic pressure he brought to bear. As it turned out, however, he overestimated the West's willingness to make the concessions he demanded. He failed to undermine sufficiently Washington's confidence in its deterrence posture, although he came closer to doing so against Kennedy in the earlier phase of the 1961 crisis than against Eisenhower in the 1958–1959 crisis over Berlin. But it was President Kennedy who thoroughly discredited Khrushchev's strategic claims in September and October of 1961 by disclosing new intelligence that conclusively laid to rest the "missile gap" fear.

Indeed, the attempted use of strategic power for Cold War purposes during these years was interacting with the arms race in ways that were imperfectly understood by the leaders on both sides. Khrushchev did not in fact engage in a race with the United States to deploy ICBMs, but he spoke as if he were catching up to and surpassing the United States in strategic power. In addition to hoping that his strategic deception would facilitate his Cold War diplomacy, Khrushchev may have acted as he did between 1957 and 1962, to convince hard-liners in the Soviet Union that Moscow could realize the diplomatic fruits of

[2] *Ibid.*, pp. 11–13.

strategic power without having to make the expensive outlays needed to acquire it. Or perhaps Khrushchev was also buying time, trying to conceal from the United States that Moscow had decided not to deploy large numbers of inferior first-generation ICBMs while it proceeded to develop more sophisticated missiles for deployment later on.

But whatever the explanation for Khrushchev's behavior, his bombastic strategic claims created the illusion that the Soviet Union was engaged in a serious and successful strategic arms race with the United States. This could only stimulate American anxieties and increase the pressure for greater arms expenditures. The full impact was felt not in the defense policies of President Eisenhower, although he did reluctantly expedite certain programs as a hedge against a major missile gap in the future, but rather on the attitudes and defense policies of the Kennedy Administration when it came into office in January 1961. The intelligence capabilities available to Eisenhower were sufficient to give him confidence that the Soviet ICBM force remained quite small in numbers, Khrushchev's rhetorical exaggerations notwithstanding. Eisenhower saw the "missile gap" as arising, if at all, in the future and not reaching a peak until 1963, at which time the solid-fueled Polaris and Minuteman missiles were due to become operational in large numbers. Having in the meantime decided to forego any large U.S. deployment of the relatively unsatisfactory liquid-propellant, first-generation missiles, Eisenhower refused to be panicked into acquiring a substantially larger number of these inferior ICBMs by the threat of a missile gap. Such a gap could emerge, according to Eisenhower's intelligence specialists, only if the Soviets decided to procure and deploy large numbers of their own liquid-fueled, first-generation missiles. Eisenhower was willing to accept a missile gap if the Soviets moved in this direction, believing that a missile gap—if not too pronounced—would *not* be the equivalent of a "deterrence gap." In other words, Eisenhower counted on the overall level of strategic force available to the United States, including its large strategic bomber force, to maintain an adequate deterrent capability during the period in which the Soviets might possess a larger number of operational ICBMs than the United States.

However, Eisenhower did not succeed very well in allaying the growing concern of his defense critics that a dangerous "missile gap" was in fact emerging. Their long-standing dissatisfaction with his reliance on Massive Retaliation was compounded by a gnawing feeling that the conservative economic philosophy of his administration, manifested in a stubborn reluctance to increase the defense budget, was driving it into an attitude of complacency and myopia with regard to the growing Soviet strategic threat. These defense critics feared that the Soviets might well acquire enough ICBMs for a successful disarming attack on SAC bases.[3] In other words, they believed that the missile gap might indeed result in a "deterrence gap." They also feared that, in any case, the Soviets might succeed in making major Cold War gains from their growing superiority in missiles.

Intelligence on the actual Soviet missile force was, of course, a critical factor in this controversy over the adequacy of the current and projected U.S. strategic posture. Considerable confusion was created by the way in which U.S. intelligence chose to estimate the future as against the current number of Soviet ICBMs. For several years, U.S. intelligence attempted to deal with this question on the basis of Soviet production capabilities, rather than Soviet intentions. The U.S. estimate thus referred to the maximum number of ICBMs the Soviet Union could have, year by year, in the near future if it produced them at full capacity. This was, in other words, a "worst case" analysis that compared the maximum number of ICBMs the Soviets were *capable* of producing with the number of ICBMs the United States *intended* to produce within a given time period. Such a comparison was justified, of course, on the ground that there was no way of reading Soviet intentions and that the

[3] According to some calculations, as few as 175 Soviet ICBMs could take out all the vulnerable strategic air bases in the United States while Soviet MRBMs from Russia eliminated the overseas SAC bases. Quester, *Nuclear Diplomacy*, p. 151.

United States had to take into account the maximum possible future threat.[4]

In January 1960 Eisenhower's Secretary of Defense, Thomas Gates, introduced a new method of estimating the future Soviet ICBM force in terms of what it was expected the Soviets *would* choose to build and deploy. The new focus on Soviet intentions rather than on production capability considerably reduced the expected missile gap, but it also led, predictably, to a new criticism: that the administration was gambling with U.S. security by attempting to read the Soviet mind rather than basing U.S. requirements on Soviet capabilities. The administration was accused of doctoring the basis for its estimate of future Soviet ICBMs for domestic political purposes.

Controversy and confusion over the missile gap and the related question of the administration's own ICBM plans was compounded by secrecy. Unknown to most critics of Eisenhower's relatively sanguine attitude was a special intelligence source for his estimates of the Soviet missile force. The fact that the United States had been conducting U-2 photographic reconnaissance flights over the Soviet Union since 1956 was a well-kept secret until May 1960, when Khrushchev disclosed that the Soviets had finally succeeded in shooting down one of these planes and capturing its pilot, Francis Gary Powers. General knowledge from this time on that Eisenhower's intelligence estimates had been drawing upon the results of the U-2 flights did not, however, alleviate concern over the possible emergence of a missile gap in the near future. There were several reasons for this. First, of course, there was the fact that U-2 intelligence showing a limited Soviet ICBM deployment thus far did not exclude large-scale production and deployment in the future. Moreover, while acknowledging that U-2 flights had been taking place, the administration withheld specific information

---

[4] In January 1959 Secretary of Defense Neil McElroy provided a reduced estimate of Soviet production capabilities in an off-the-record statement. But even this suggested that if the Soviet Union worked at maximum capacity, it could have three times as many ICBMs by 1962 as the United States. Others estimated that the disparity would be even greater.

regarding the extent to which U-2 flights had covered the Soviet Union and the thoroughness of the information gained by this and other intelligence methods. Even within the administration itself, as repeated leaks indicated, the experts apparently disagreed in their interpretations of the available data, some of them—most notably the air force specialists—taking a less sanguine view than Eisenhower of the growing Soviet strategic threat. It was not immediately apparent to what extent the more pessimistic, alarmist estimates of Soviet capabilities within the administration were based on a legitimate interpretation of the uncertain evidence, and to what extent they went beyond this for parochial reasons, in order to develop a stronger case for expansion of American forces. Nor was the malaise of the outside critics relieved by one or two instances in which administration officials appeared to be manipulating the estimate of Soviet capabilities in order to counter public fears of a missile gap; and, indeed, went so far as to push the view that the adequacy of the American deterrent could not be judged mainly on the basis of the relative number of ICBMs possessed by the two sides. However accurate the administration's U-2–based estimates may have been, in any case Eisenhower called off further flights of this kind after Powers' U-2 was shot down in May 1960. Whether or not this cessation would create a serious gap in U.S. intelligence coverage of the Soviet missile force (the Eisenhower Administration was reluctant to clarify this question by revealing its plans for the use of intelligence-gathering satellites) it *would* serve to keep alive, if not indeed augment, anxiety over the possibility of a sudden missile gap in the near future, should the Soviet Union embark on a crash ICBM program.

Certainly this fear was nourished by Khrushchev's dramatic and chilling boasts regarding the rapid and substantial growth of the Soviet missile force, as well as his continuing efforts to make politico-diplomatic use of these threats. Later, it was to come as a distinct surprise to many of those most concerned about the missile gap that so large an element of deception entered into Khrushchev's boasts about Soviet intercontinental missiles. The fact of the matter was that the Soviet Union was deploying very few ICBMs and would not deploy many for a number of years.[5]

We have examined the history of the missile gap problem in some detail because it set the stage for the new strategic policies of President Kennedy—which, in turn, generated much of the pressure on Khrushchev to deploy strategic missiles in Cuba. Kennedy came into the Presidency genuinely convinced that Eisenhower had allowed grave deficiencies to develop in the U.S. military posture and determined to do something about it. During his campaign, Kennedy had taken the danger of the "missile gap" quite seriously and had promised increased expenditures on strategic and other forces. Sorensen reports that the U-2 evidence was not made available to Kennedy during the presidential campaign in the classified briefings he was given by the Eisenhower Administration.[6] However, the intelligence estimates handed over to the new administration, indicated that fear of a missile gap had been highly exaggerated, though some uncertainty existed for the future. The first SAMOS reconnaissance satellite was launched in January 1961, and it would be a while before the uncertainty affecting intelligence on the growth of the Soviet ICBM force, arising from the cancellation of U-2 flights, would be clarified by this new means of gathering intelligence.

Kennedy decided to proceed with plans for a substantial augmentation of American strategic forces. The Polaris program

[5] Sorensen suggests that the first Soviet ICBM had apparently been "too costly, too cumbersome and too vulnerable a weapon for mass production and deployment." The Soviet government then settled for deployment of a very few of these missiles "while pushing ahead on the deployment of medium-range missiles aimed at Europe and the development of a better ICBM." Sorensen, *Kennedy*, pp. 611–12. Hilsman indicates that American intelligence came to the conclusion that the giant rocket of 800,000 lbs. thrust which the Soviets developed initially (as compared to the 350,000 lbs. thrust of the American Atlas missile) proved "too bulky to serve as a practical weapon. A newer, smaller, more streamlined missile had to be designed instead, and the Soviet ICBM program must have been set back many months." Hilsman, *To Move a Nation*, p. 162.

[6] Sorensen, *Kennedy*, p. 612.

was accelerated by nine or ten months, ten additional Polaris submarines were added to the programmed force, the production capacity for Minuteman missiles was doubled, and the alert posture of the B-52 force improved. Kennedy undertook these measures to strengthen his strategic forces, not merely to redeem campaign promises, and not to cover embarrassment at learning that the missile gap about which he and his supporters had expressed alarm did not really exist. He still faced genuine and major uncertainties regarding Soviet development of strategic forces.[7] Kennedy also knew he would soon have to face another crisis over Berlin. Besides, he had four and possibly eight years in office to look forward to. It required no special imagination or paranoid anxiety to envisage how difficult it would be to cope with Khrushchev's already vigorous foreign policy as the Soviet Union acquired even more extensive strategic capabilities in the near future. Having seen how boldly Khrushchev utilized the limited strategic forces then available to him, Kennedy might well feel it to be prudent to push ahead with measures to retain a decisive margin of strategic superiority, in order to cope better with Khrushchev's Cold War tactics in the future. While Kennedy entered office hoping to bring about a modification of the Cold War during his presidency, he thought that a stronger and more flexible American military posture would be required at least until the Soviets gave up their claims on West Berlin and moderated the offensive thrust of their foreign policy.

Later in 1961, Khrushchev continued pressure on West Berlin even after erecting the Wall to seal off the flow of refugees from East Berlin. At this point Kennedy apparently decided to disclose the new intelligence at his disposal—evidently derived from the SAMOS program—to bring the weight of the actual,

---

[7] Hilsman states that "when the Kennedy Administration took office, the evidence on the Soviet missile deployment was still inconclusive. . . . even as late as June 1961 the evidence was contradictory and the intelligence community continued to be divided. . . . It was not until the summer and fall of 1961 that the Americans discovered the true situation—and decided to tell the Soviets that they knew." *To Move A Nation*, p. 163.

considerable American strategic superiority to bear in order to defuse the Berlin crisis. Kennedy had long been concerned that Khrushchev would miscalculate over Berlin; he authorized the disclosure of the new intelligence estimate, despite some misgivings, because he feared that otherwise Khrushchev might push the crisis dangerously close to war.[8] At first, leaks to the press in September indicated that the new U.S. intelligence estimates now credited the Soviet Union with but a fraction of the operational ICBMs that it had been expected to have by mid-1961. Then in October, Deputy Defense Secretary Roswell Gilpatric issued an authoritative and confident appraisal of the strategic balance. He unequivocally asserted that the U.S. had a wide and growing margin of strategic superiority over the Soviet Union. Gilpatric's speech and subsequent statements by other high officials reflected a top-level decision by Kennedy to correct the erroneous impression of a missile gap and, thereby, to deprive the Soviets of any further politico-diplomatic leverage derived from their exaggerated claims.

Confronted by this high-level American deflation of its strategic deception, the Soviet Union responded promptly with angry accusations; but most revealingly, it avoided contradicting the substance of Gilpatric's assessment of the strategic situation. In the months that followed, the Soviets modified their earlier claims of superiority, employing rhetorical devices which tacitly acknowledged the correctness of the new American appraisal.[9]

With his strategic deception of the last four years now unmasked, Khrushchev was left in a difficult position. He had no choice but to abandon the vigorous thrust of his foreign policy until he developed a real strategic capability. The costs of failure in strategic deception were not confined to frustration over the Berlin situation and the larger set of European security issues in which it was imbedded. There is reason to believe

[8] *Ibid.*, p. 163.

[9] Horelick and Rush, *Strategic Power*, pp. 83–102. See also Kahan and Long, "The Cuban Missile Crisis," pp. 565–66.

that Khrushchev's strategic claims had misled his Chinese Communist allies regarding Soviet power and encouraged them to press Moscow for new commitments to Peking's foreign policy goals which Soviet leaders were reluctant to assume. In addition to contributing indirectly to Sino-Soviet discord, Khrushchev's strategic deception had stimulated pressure for increased arms in the United States. As a result, the strategic situation facing the Soviet Union was now considerably worse than it would have been otherwise, and it was likely to remain so for some years unless a way could be found to achieve a rapid augmentation of the Soviet strategic capability.

In sum, events had come full circle since the mid-1950s, when Massive Retaliation had been in bloom. Once again, the Kremlin leaders were confronted by an opponent across the ocean who possessed strategic superiority, who knew it, and who was prepared to employ it (although no longer under the same name) for invidious politico-military ends—bolstering the deterrence of highly desired Soviet initiatives. (Indeed the situation was gloomier and more dangerous in 1962 than it had been seven years earlier, for now the Soviet leaders were confronted with a rising threat on their southeastern border.) Unless a way could be found—and quickly—to neutralize the growing American strategic superiority, the future would probably hold few successes for Soviet policy against the imperialists, which would also exacerbate problems with the Chinese.

In this way the ground was prepared for Khrushchev's 1962 gamble. The missile deployment in Cuba was the most dramatic strategic move in the competition, which both superpowers pursued, to extract maximum politico-diplomatic mileage from expensive and otherwise unusable thermonuclear weapons systems. More broadly, the Cuban missile crisis exemplified the ill-understood and "hidden," but increasing, risks of this competition. The gravest threat of thermonuclear war the world has thus far experienced resulted from the increasingly heavy reliance both sides were putting on their deterrent postures and forces in order to achieve too broad a range of foreign policy objectives. Fortunately the crisis itself made these risks visible and led the superpowers to pull back from this kind of competition. The Soviet leaders accepted the fact that they would have to neutralize the U.S. strategic position the hard way by shifting resources from other desired objectives to build up their advanced strategic forces. As this policy came to fruition in the late 1960s, the United States, for its part, accepted a position of parity or "sufficiency" in thermonuclear forces. Thus, the stage was set for SALT and related efforts to bring the arms race under control. Both superpowers, frightened by the Cuban missile crisis and distracted by the demands of an increasingly multipolar international system, tacitly agreed to stop trying to translate their strategic deterrent forces into politico-diplomatic advantage, at least vis-à-vis each other.

The Initiator's Motivation and Calculus

With this background in hand on the sources of the crisis, we may turn now to the deterrence dynamics of the crisis itself, beginning with a closer analysis of the motivations and calculations of the initiating power than we have made so far.

We may safely surmise that, having seen their campaign of strategic deception come to a bad end, Khrushchev and his closest supporters within the Soviet leadership group were under considerable psychological and political pressure to recoup the situation as quickly as possible. Knowledge that the real missile gap favored the United States rather than the Soviet Union restored Western self-confidence and altered the world political climate. By the end of 1961, it was evident that Soviet foreign policy had lost its forward momentum and was encountering disappointments on many fronts. And, as Horelick and Rush observe, "The Chinese Communist attack on Khrushchev centered precisely on the unfavorable trend in the cold war, which the Chinese attributed to Khrushchev's faulty and erratic leadership." [10]

[10] Horelick and Rush, *Strategic Power*, p. 139.

It is not known definitely how the idea of deploying strategic missiles in Cuba originated, whether with Castro or with the Russians themselves. (After the end of the crisis Castro issued contradictory accounts on this question.) [11] In any case, once the possibility of deploying some of their older, more plentiful medium and intermediate range missiles in Cuba was suggested, it must have recommended itself to Soviet leaders, as Hilsman notes, as "at least a temporary and expedient solution to their several problems. . . . It would give them a cheap and immediate substitute for the newer, more expensive ICBM's and let them stretch out the ICBM program to ease pressure on resources." [12]

No one can be certain as to exactly what specific and general benefits the Soviet leaders hoped to derive directly and indirectly from a successful deployment of their missiles in Cuba. One specialist on the USSR, Adam Ulam, suggests that a whole host of benefits may have been expected by Khrushchev and that, indeed, the missile deployment was the linchpin of an ambitious grand strategy which he concocted to deal with his major global and domestic problems.[13] Other writers attribute somewhat less ambitious goals to Khrushchev's missile gambit, though agreeing that the Soviet government was pursuing multiple Cold War benefits and not merely deterrence of an American invasion of Cuba. Hilsman reports that one group of Sovietologists in the State Department concluded that the decision to move missiles into Cuba was best viewed as "a generalized, strategic response to a whole set of problems, military, economic, and political" facing Soviet leaders in 1962. "A general improvement in the Soviet military position would affect the entire political context, strengthening their hand for dealing with the whole range of problems facing them. . . ." [14] Graham Allison's study raises useful cautions against the tendency of

---

[11] *Ibid.,* 134–36. In *Khrushchev Remembers* (p. 493) the former Soviet premier states that the Cuban missile deployment was his own idea.

[12] Hilsman, *To Move a Nation,* p. 164.

[13] Ulam, *Expansion and Coexistence,* pp. 668–69.

[14] Hilsman, *To Move a Nation,* pp. 161, 164.

these analysts to deduce Soviet objectives from American perceptions of what Americans in the Kremlin might see as benefits; at the same time, however, he too believes that a variety of goals motivated the Soviet deployment.[15]

In any case, whatever the full scope of Soviet objectives, the Soviet decision to proceed with deployment of strategic missiles was evidently made during the spring or early summer of 1962. It was part of a general Soviet arms buildup in Cuba that followed an easing of tensions in Soviet-Cuban relations. The first Soviet arms shipments began to arrive in late July and were cloaked in secrecy. No public announcement of the Soviet agreement to supply arms was made until Che Guevara's visit to Moscow of late August resulted in a joint communiqué on September 2. This communiqué stated that the Soviet Union had agreed to help Cuba meet threats from "aggressive quarters" by delivering "armaments and sending technical specialists for training Cuban servicemen." [16]

In retrospect it seems clear, however, that this communiqué was part of the Kremlin's tapestry of deception blanketing its true activities and motives in Cuba. The 42 MRBMs and 24 to 32 IRBMs being sent then to the island increased by half again the total destructive power which the Soviets could inflict upon the United States. Only a fraction of the "lower 48" states were out of range of the IRBMs, the number of which might, of course, have been increased later had Washington tolerated their presence. For these and other reasons we find it difficult to avoid the conclusion of Horelick and Rush that the Kremlin

---

[15] Allison prefers the explanation that various elements of the Soviet leadership group agreed upon the missile deployment for different reasons. This accords with a familiar observation about policy-making in complex organizations, namely, that various members often agree on a policy means without sharing the same notion of policy ends. But Allison applies this hypothesis to Soviet policy-making somewhat too rigidly, rejecting altogether the notion of "grand global planning" behind the Soviet decision to deploy the missiles. He slips into a false antithesis in assuming that overall planning is necessarily inconsistent with "a process in which a number of different individuals' quite distinct perceptions of separable problems snowballed into a single solution." Allison, *Essence of Decision*, p. 237.

[16] Pachter, *Collision Course*, p. 175.

was making "a bold effort to alter the unfavorable strategic environment in which the USSR found itself in 1962 as the result of the United States intercontinental buildup and the collapse of the 'missile gap' myth." [17] Although the missile deployment,

[17] Horelick and Rush, *Strategic Power*, p. 127. The thesis that the Soviet missile deployment was intended solely or primarily to deter a U.S. attack on Cuba, as claimed by Moscow, is examined and rebutted by Horelick, "The Cuban Missile Crisis"; Horelick and Rush, *Strategic Power*, pp. 127–36; Hilsman, *To Move a Nation*, pp. 161–65 and 201–202; and Ulam, *Expansion and Coexistence*, pp. 668–77.

Secret deployment of nuclear missiles, especially the IRBMs, to Cuba would have been an extremely unconventional way of providing deterrence protection to Castro, to say the least. Other options would have been much less risky. Moscow might have made vigorous deterrent statements, delivered a formal treaty guarantee, provided substantial military aid to strengthen Castro's own conventional forces, or deployed Soviet combat forces to Cuba to play a "plate glass" role like U.S. forces in Berlin. Moscow could have threatened to retaliate elsewhere, e.g. Berlin, should the U.S. attack Cuba, or brought Cuba into the Warsaw Pact.

Instead, Moscow took the unprecedented step of deploying major strategic weapons systems—never placed on the territory of its East European satellites despite the huge Soviet ground forces there—outside its formal alliance system. Moreover, unlike the United States, which had openly carried out the deployment of strategic missiles in allied territory, the Soviets moved secretly, under cover of high-level, systematic deception. At first, Moscow left dark the question whether Moscow or Havana would have operational control over these missiles. Finally, the presence of IRBMs as well as MRBMs in the deployed forces makes it extremely improbable that Moscow's motive was simply the protection of Castro. The MRBMs—cheaper, more mobile, and easier to handle— would have been ample to deter an attack on Cuba, as they could reach many American cities in the South. The IRBMs, however, extended the Soviet "reach" to most of the United States—useful for the general purposes of the Soviet Union but redundant so far as protecting Castro was concerned.

Allison is the sole major interpreter of the crisis who challenges this thesis; see *Essence of Decision*, pp. 113, 247. Allison's alternative explanation, that the IRBMs may have been included in the deployment as a result of the play of the routines or organizational goals of institutions within the Soviet government, has a serious weakness: it requires us to believe that the top-level Soviet leaders were either unaware of or indifferent to the implications of having suborganizations take the risk-enhancing step of adding IRBMs to the force.

In his reminiscences, the full authenticity of which remains uncertain, Khrushchev claimed the primary reason for putting missiles into Cuba was to deter a U.S. attack. However, the former Soviet Premier went on to say "In addition to protecting Cuba, our missiles would have equalized what the West likes to call 'the balance of power'." *Khrushchev Remembers*, pp. 493–94.

in the quantity existing when it was discovered, did not shift the military strategic balance in favor of the Soviet Union, it began to approach equalizing that balance. It would have placed Khrushchev once more in a position to make use of strategic threats in support of a broad range of foreign policy goals, this time with even greater credibility than when he attempted to exploit American uncertainty over Soviet ICBMs. As President Kennedy said later, the danger of the missile deployment lay not in the immediate military threat of the Cuban-based missiles; rather, as he put it, the missile deployment "would have politically changed the balance of power. It would have appeared to, and appearances contribute to reality." [18]

Clearly, an objective of this magnitude would have been sufficient motivation for the Soviets to accept moderate risks in its pursuit. There are good reasons for believing, however, that the Kremlin assessed its risks in this venture as reasonable and controllable ones. In the first place, the built-in capability of the MRBMs, especially, for very rapid deployment probably encouraged the Soviet leaders to think that these missiles could be made operational in Cuba before they were discovered by the Americans. Moreover, Moscow is presumed to have known that U.S. intelligence was not aware of this rapid-deployment feature of the MRBMs, and therefore to have hoped for a successful surprise deployment. (It is certainly true that U.S. intelligence had underestimated the rapid-deployment capability of the Soviet MRBM.) Once a few MRBMs were operational in Cuba, of course, they would serve to deter U.S. attacks while additional missiles, including the IRBMs, were being readied. Soviet leaders therefore had reasonable grounds for thinking they might achieve a fait accompli which, by its very nature, would be difficult for the United States to undo.

It is true, of course, that early in September President Kennedy committed himself to opposing any deployment of offensive missiles in Cuba. The Soviet deployment decision, however, was apparently made prior to the President's statement.

[18] Interview with President Kennedy, *Washington Post*, December 18, 1962.

While Kennedy's declaration might have had an effect had it come while the deployment was still being debated in the Kremlin, it was evidently inadequate to reverse the policy once it had been launched. Soviet leaders evidently thought that whatever the statements from Washington, once the missiles were deployed it would be difficult for the Americans to find practical options for securing their removal.

Furthermore, the Soviet leaders probably expected that the American political system would respond sluggishly to discovery of the missiles, and that the Kennedy Administration would be incapable of formulating a decisive course of action in the face of Soviet threats and political pressures. Such an expectation was certainly reasonable, and it would further encourage the Soviet belief that the critical MRBM portion of the missile deployment might be completed even if discovered by the United States in process. The elaborate cloak of deception the Soviets threw over the entire operation—consistently maintained up to and including direct falsehoods from the Soviet Ambassador to the President—was designed, of course, not only to delay the date of discovery of the missiles but also to delay a coherent American response thereafter. Indeed, if Kennedy's warning was meant to imply that he would take action to remove missiles in Cuba *immediately* upon discovering them, events justified the Soviets' scepticism.[19]

In calculating the risks of deploying the missiles, therefore, the Soviet leaders believed, first, that there was an excellent chance of a fait accompli; and second, that if by chance they were discovered in the process, that the initial U.S. response would probably be a hesitant one, and would amost certainly be diplomatic and political rather than military in character. The graver risk—to the Kremlin an unacceptable one—of a major

[19] Thus, there are indications that the Pentagon had prepared contingency plans for an invasion or air strike in the event offensive missiles were discovered; but when that event transpired these contingency plans were set aside. For, as Paul Nitze recalled, at that point top U.S. policy-makers "agreed that the U.S. must move with deliberation, not merely proceed with existing contingency plans." Abel, *The Missile Crisis*, p. 21.

shooting war with the United States would develop, if at all, only at a later point in the crisis, after intervening events had transpired which the Kremlin could probably manipulate to control its overall risks. Once again, therefore, we see the Soviet decision-makers willing to accept high risks in the later stages of a possible crisis scenario, *so long as* the initial risks were assessed as low, and the potentially dangerous later stages were sufficiently removed in time and by intervening events to allow crisis-control measures to be taken. As Roger Hilsman puts it,

> This is not to say that the Soviets thought the Cuba venture was without risk. But it does indicate that they thought of it as an easily manageable risk. As it turned out, the risk was manageable; the error was thinking that it would be easy.[20]

The error came partly from the Soviets' underestimation of the President. It is often remarked that Khrushchev viewed Kennedy as weak, inexperienced, and irresolute—a judgment seemingly derived from, or fortified by, the President's comparative youth, his handling of the Bay of Pigs fiasco, and his performance in Vienna in June 1961. Nearly everyone who has examined the Cuban missile crisis agrees that the Soviets were operating on an incorrect image of their opponent and were genuinely surprised when Kennedy reacted as firmly as he did. Clearly, this misestimate of their opponent could only strengthen their belief that the missile deployment would not entail excessive risk.[21]

[20] Hilsman, *To Move a Nation*, p. 182. In all probability, the Kremlin estimated that the very worst outcome it could plausibly conceive would be a U.S. air strike on the missile sites while still under construction. The *loss* to the USSR in this contingency would be serious, but the *risk* of uncontrollable escalation spiralling out of this event would be low, due to Cuba's isolated location, far from any other communist territory or interest. Note, furthermore, that events justified the Soviet estimate that this was an *improbable* U.S. action even if the missiles were discovered prematurely.

[21] It is interesting that Kennedy was aware of the Soviets' misperception of him and anxious to correct it (Schlesinger, *A Thousand Days*, p. 319). When he learned that Khrushchev had been secretly putting missiles into Cuba while systematically deceiving him with false assurances, he realized that Khrushchev

Further, their misperception of the President must have
been reinforced by an apparently erroneous interpretation of
his responses to the warnings he was beginning to receive by
September 1962.

The Defender's Response to Warning: The Policy Response

In late August and September of 1962 President Kennedy
obtained what might be considered strategic warning that the
steadily increasing Soviet military assistance to Cuba might develop along more ambitious, more dangerous lines. A U-2 flight
over Cuba on August 29 obtained photographic verification of
earlier indications that the Russians were bringing in surface-to-
air missiles (SAMs) of the kind that had shot down the U-2
plane piloted by Gary Powers. Although most members of the
administration thought it quite unlikely that the Soviets would
go so far as to introduce strategic missiles into Cuba or attempt
to convert it into a Soviet military base, they recognized that either eventuality would pose a grave challenge to American interests. A more immediate and urgent consideration in the administration's thinking at this time, however, was the fact that
mounting Soviet military assistance to Castro was seriously increasing political challenges within the United States. Criticism
of the administration mounted, as did pressure for a stronger
policy vis-à-vis Cuba. The Republicans announced that Cuba
would be the dominant issue in the November congressional
elections; Senators Kenneth Keating and Barry Goldwater—the

---

had made a dangerous miscalculation and that the only way to get the missiles
out of Cuba without war or major appeasement was to impress Khrushchev, as
never before, with his determination. The blockade option appealed to Kennedy because it offered him a badly needed opportunity to correct Khrushchev's misjudgment by means short of more dangerous, irreversible military actions such as the air strike option. The blockade, therefore, served a tactical
objective that was essentially psychological.

latter a possible presidential contender in 1964—were hitting especially forcefully.

Under these circumstances, the Kennedy Administration felt obliged to mobilize itself to reassure the voters that the danger was being exaggerated, that the government knew exactly what was and was not going on in Cuba, and that more aggressive measures would not be justified. In strong statements on September 4, and again on September 13, Kennedy declared that there was no Soviet buildup of offensive weapons on the island, and that should there be in the future, "the gravest issues would arise." Teeth were added to this statement by a presidential request to Congress on September 7 for standby authority to call up 150,000 reserves.

Kennedy's statements were issued more out of a desire to calm the American public than to warn the leaders of the Soviet Union.[22] What gave them a certain ambiguity for deterrence dynamics was that this was known in the Kremlin. It seems likely that the Soviet leaders heavily discounted the President's declarations, perhaps virtually to the point of ignoring them, precisely because they were so obviously motivated by internal political needs.

If it is true that Khrushchev and his comrades discounted Kennedy's warnings because they were "only political," this perception involved a dual error in their understanding of the American political system. In the first place, the President had not only pledged himself to act if missiles were introduced, but had consistently deemphasized this danger as unreal. Once the missiles were discovered, therefore, he would have a stronger, not a weaker, motivation to do something about them than he would if he had not made or accepted this issue as a "political"

[22] These statements were regarded within the administration as a rather inexpensive form of insurance that should eliminate any possible Soviet miscalculation, although it was assumed that any Soviet offensive activity in Cuba was extremely unlikely. Roger Hilsman, a member of the administration at the time, explicitly asserts that Kennedy's public statements were primarily motivated by his desire to deal with his domestic critics. Hilsman, *To Move a Nation*, pp. 196–97.

one. As one writer puts it, when the missiles were indeed discovered in October, "the United States might not be in mortal danger but the Administration most certainly was." [23]

In fact, President Kennedy's motivation in issuing the statements was complex and multidimensional, and it is this second aspect especially that one doubts was fully comprehended in the Kremlin. The Cuban missile crisis when it sprang forth engaged both the personal and political prestige of the President and the interests and national prestige of the United States. Some of Kennedy's critics have fastened on the President's personal and political motives and, deploring them, have argued that American interests were not sufficiently at stake to justify Kennedy's taking the United States and the world to the brink of thermonuclear war. We believe this interpretation exaggerates the role of Kennedy's personal and narrow political motivation at the expense of what he felt was at stake in terms of broader national interests. Certainly both aspects of his motivation were important, and it is impossible to separate the two. Whether we like it or not, a leader's sense of his personal and political stakes usually enters in some way into his judgment of his country's interests. Moreover, there is often some basis in fact to encourage a leader's tendency to identify his personal stakes in an issue with those of party and country. We must remember that nations are not disembodied entities; on many important matters, they deal with each other only through the actions, mentalities, and emotions of the persons who lead them. Moreover, domestic politics can seldom be neatly separated from the conduct of foreign policy. The leaders of each nation must take this into account when they deal with each other.[24]

This was particularly true in the Cuban missile crisis. In fact, it is only a slight exaggeration to say that Khrushchev could hardly have thought of a better way to insure that all aspects of

[23] *Ibid.*, pp. 196–98.

[24] Allison stresses these themes, and provides a persuasive account of the complexity and inseparability of the stakes from Kennedy's standpoint. *Essence of Division*, pp. 193–95.

Kennedy's motivation would be strongly aroused and so fused together as to become virtually inseparable. In the situation that Khrushchev had created, however hard the President might have tried, he could not have found a way to accept damage to his personal political stakes without also accepting damage to major U.S. interests.

The fact that the secret Soviet deployment of missiles would inflict personal and political humiliation on the President could not have escaped Khrushchev's attention when he *planned* the operation as well as while he was carrying it out. Of the several aspects of his bold gambit that show poor judgment on his part, his willingness to inflict such humiliation upon Kennedy is certainly among the most irresponsible.

This said, it also cannot be denied that the President's strong efforts early in September to reinforce the previously quite generalized deterrence of any offensive use of Cuba were quite inadequate for the purpose they were actually required to serve. Unknown to Kennedy, the deployment of offensive missiles had not merely been decided upon but was well along in implementation. The first missiles were already leaving their Soviet ports when Kennedy made his first statement.[25] At this late stage, it would have been very difficult for Khrushchev to reverse himself, even in the absence of complicating factors. The deployment operation was a complex one and had acquired its own momentum.

And there were complicating factors. If the available indications are correct that Khrushchev's original decision had en-

---

[25] It is true, as Allison observes (*Ibid.*, pp. 232–34), that before Soviet missiles actually reached Cuba on September 8, top-level officials (Sorensen and Robert Kennedy) did have an opportunity to indicate the administration's attitude in private conversations with Soviet Ambassador Dobrynin. Also, of course, the President's September 4 statement had been issued and, the previous day, his request for authority to call up reserves sent to Congress. The second, stronger, presidential statement followed before the deployment actually began on Cuban soil between September 15 and 20. But the purpose of Dobrynin's conversations apparently was merely to add to the deception in which the USSR was engaging. On both occasions Dobrynin, on instruction from Khrushchev, gave explicit assurance that no ground-to-ground missiles or other major offensive weapons were being brought into Cuba.

countered some opposition within the Soviet government,[26] then it would have been all the more difficult for Khrushchev to pull back now. To do so would have required him to tacitly concede the correctness of arguments others had made that a missile deployment would be too risky. It would also lay him open to charges from other Soviet leaders that he had retreated prematurely and perhaps unnecessarily, thereby depriving the Soviet Union of a chance for a major success. While classical Bolshevik doctrine enjoins good Bolsheviks to retreat when faced with danger, in practice this injunction has necessarily been incorporated into the Soviet approach to risk-acceptance already described, which appears to lie at the root of the Soviet government's unwillingness to call off its missile deployment on the basis of the two warnings Kennedy issued in early September.

Kennedy attempted to reinforce deterrence in Cuba without having before him a reasoned analysis, or working hypothesis, as to how the Soviet leaders might conceivably have persuaded themselves that the deployment of missiles was a calculable, controllable risk. Nor was it generally appreciated at this time in American decision-making circles that the Kremlin might find very significant risks calculable and controllable so long as they were expected to arise later rather than earlier in a crisis. The fact that the Kennedy Administration thought a Cuban missile deployment would be a high-risk, unacceptable option for the Soviets did not necessarily mean that the Soviets thought so.

The available record does not suggest that any attempt was made by the administration to construct a hypothetical Soviet risk calculus, however implausible initially, by which a Cuban deployment might seem reasonable given the *Soviet* attitude on high-but-deferred risks. Indeed, when the administration decided to draw the line on what it would tolerate in Cuba, there is no indication that either the President or his advisers thought

---

[26] Allison's discussion (*Essence of Decision*, pp. 112–13; 133–34; 234) of possible internal opposition to Khrushchev's decision draws upon Kolkowicz, "Conflicts in Soviet Party-Military Relations" and Michael Tatu, *Power in the Kremlin*.

the task sufficiently difficult, complicated, or interesting to warrant making any special effort to obtain the knowledge and judgment of American Sovietologists. Rather, the available record suggests that the task of designing means for reinforcing the deterrence of any dangerous Soviet moves in Cuba was handled through routine procedures.[27] At a minimum, it seems very safe to say that far less was done to assure high-quality policy planning to prevent deterrence from failing than was done to attempt to rescue the situation *after* it had failed. The fact that this is, in a sense, eminently understandable should not be allowed to obscure the point that prevention of deterrence failure is in actuality at least as important as coping with deterrence failure.

The American government's failure to reinforce deterrence adequately in September 1962 is the more striking because a properly designed effort might well have succeeded. What is known of Soviet behavior strongly suggests that Khrushchev's earlier calculations leading to the deployment would have included some kind of recognition of the possibility that it might have to be called off before it was completed—and even might well have included true contingency plans for such an event. Furthermore, the very existence of elements with the Soviet hierarchy who were skeptical of the value of the plan, or thought it too risky, might, depending upon their location in the communications flow, have meant great receptivity in the Kremlin to a properly designed deterrent signal.[28]

[27] Little information is available on this aspect of policy formation. Schlesinger reports that on September 4 "The Secretary of State brought over a draft of the warning. The President showed it to the Attorney General [Robert Kennedy], who recommended stiffening it with an explicit statement that we would not tolerate the import of offensive weapons." *A Thousand Days*, p. 798. Sorensen reports merely that a series of meetings were held at the White House preceding the President's decision to repeat his warning on September 13. *Kennedy*, p. 671.

[28] A public statement suggesting a rapid U.S. *military* response to any Cuban missile deployment might or might not have been difficult for the Kennedy Administration to make. But it is difficult to see why the administration could not have communicated privately to the Kremlin that—*because* of the heavy pressure from the Republicans and other "hawk" elements—the U.S. government

In the event, of course, the administration's actual efforts to reinforce deterrence had no effect, except possibly to accelerate the already rapid schedule for bringing the MRBMs to operational status. We have already suggested two reasons for this: the Soviets' scepticism about Kennedy's character and personal strength and their tendency to discount his public warnings as politically motivated. It seems likely that as September faded into October a third reason joined in reassuring the Kremlin. The continuing public statements out of Washington that nothing untoward was occurring in Cuba may have nourished Soviet hopes that their deployment would actually go undiscovered until the MRBMs were ready. Or, as time continued to pass and Soviet leaders assumed that Kennedy must have at least formed some suspicions and anxieties as to what they were doing, they may have thought that the President did not wish to make a public issue of it until after the 1962 elections.[29]

The Defender's Response to Warning: The Intelligence Response

Clearly, the Soviet gamble depended heavily for its success upon the United States' remaining blind to the fact that its deterrence policy for Cuba was being challenged until the missiles were operational and could exercise their own counterdeterrence—or at least until they were close enough to being operational so that they could be made fully ready while Washington was trying to fashion its response. The Cuban mis-

---

would be obliged to react immediately and decisively to such a contingency. This rather cheap signal would have played to the true vulnerability in the Soviet risk calculus—the fear that risks might be immediate and not remote after all.

[29] Hilsman offers the interpretation that Gromyko might well have concluded from Kennedy's failure to raise the issue of the missile deployment explicitly in their meeting on October 18 that the President did not intend to do anything really drastic, at least until after the elections; and so the Russian leaders were lulled into a false sense of security. *To Move A Nation*, p. 199; also pp. 166–67.

sile crisis is therefore quite distinctive in that the challenge to deterrence took the form of a force deployment rather than a military attack or other directly offensive action. This distinctive feature of the crisis put a premium on the defending power's intelligence apparatus—which, however, was called upon for once to discover merely the opponent's capabilities and not his intentions.

Those who have examined the question generally agree that the discovery of the Soviet missiles and the way in which this was accomplished must be considered a distinct success for U.S. intelligence. At the same time, they maintain that U.S. intelligence could and should have become suspicious of Soviet activities sooner than it did. The discovery of the missiles on October 14 came none too soon. The initial batch of MRBMs was nearing readiness; had these missiles become operational before or very shortly after they were discovered, President Kennedy would have been faced with just the difficult problem the Soviets were hoping to impose on him. In this crisis the *timing* of the intelligence discovery of the opponent's challenge to deterrence played a pivotal role, so that it is worth examining in some detail the roots of what must be classified as a near-failure of American intelligence. We have identified five factors that, when woven together and interacting, came fairly close to generating a U.S. intelligence and foreign policy failure of the first magnitude.

THE SPECIAL ROLE OF
THE U-2 AIRCRAFT

Both before the missiles were discovered and afterwards, critics of the administration's response to the Soviet military buildup in Cuba dwelt on the failure of U.S. intelligence appraisers to pay more heed to refugee and agent reports—one in particular had called attention to a truck convoy in Cuba that included exceptionally long trailers. In doing so, however, the critics failed to take into account the special role of U-2 overflights of Cuba in the administration's overall intelligence effort. As published accounts make clear, if and when reports from agents and refugees raised bothersome questions about activity in Cuba, intelligence officials then established a requirement for U-2 photographic coverage of the areas in which suspicious activity had been reported. Understandably, the fact that U-2 pictures were capable of providing relatively firm evidence on many possible military activities in Cuba made intelligence appraisers less dependent upon agents' and refugees' reports, and less inclined to rely upon them for conclusions regarding Soviet activities and intentions.

There are, of course, some risks in becoming overly dependent upon a single, generally superior source of intelligence information. An interesting and important aspect of this case concerns the fact that some of the latent risks of relying so heavily upon U-2 flights did materialize and led to a near-failure of intelligence. This part of the story was obscured in early disclosures and in testimony before congressional committees that held hearings in 1963 on various aspects of the missile crisis. In several early efforts to explain the sluggishness with which intelligence appraisers responded to available clues of the missile deployment, the peculiar role which overreliance on the U-2 had played was not recognized or given proper weight.[30]

But how could so excellent an intelligence source have been misused or have led the intelligence effort astray? The answer to this question lies in the impact which the faulty U.S. assessment of Soviet strategic intentions had on the U-2 effort. Until late August, two U-2 flights routinely covered Cuba each month.[31] If the weather permitted, each flight covered the whole island in a single trip. Following the discovery of the first SAM installations by the U-2 flight of August 29, the sched-

[30] Even before the crisis ended, suspicion had arisen that the U-2 flights over Cuba had not been scheduled in an optimal manner. See the bibliography to this chapter for a detailed discussion of the "photography gap" and its treatment in various sources.

[31] The following paragraphs draw primarily upon the accounts by Elie Abel and Roger Hilsman.

ule of overflights was stepped up. Between August 29 and October 7, six U-2 flights took place (September 5, 17, 26, and 29 and October 5 and 7) without discovering anything beyond SAM sites, MIG fighter planes on various Cuban airfields, and Komar torpedo boats armed with short-range rockets. But the disturbing fact is that all these flights except the one on September 5 *limited their photographic sweeps to that portion of Cuba lying east of Havana.* In the meantime, the medium-range missiles were being emplaced in *western* Cuba. They were to be discovered there by the U-2 flight of October 14.

The question arises, then, why U-2s did not overfly western Cuba during this critical period of well over a month. The answer lies in the fact that a high-level policy decision was taken on September 10 to alter the flight pattern of the U-2s in order to minimize the risk that one of these planes might be shot down over Cuba.[32] On the preceding day (September 9) a U-2 belonging to the Chinese Nationalists had been destroyed in the air over the Chinese mainland. Mindful of the U-2 incident of 1960, high-level officials in the administration feared that an incident of this kind in the tense Cuban situation might raise a political storm in the U.N. and throughout the world that might deny the United States further use of the U-2s over Cuba. Accordingly, they preferred to impose constraints on the flight paths taken by the U-2s rather than accept the risk that such flights might be cancelled altogether.

Ironically, the new policy of caution with regard to U-2 flights applied particularly to overflights of western Cuba. It was there that the Soviet deployment of SAMs had proceeded

---

[32] This decision resulted from a meeting on that day in McGeorge Bundy's office of the Committee on Overhead Reconnaissance (COMOR). Secretary of State Rusk, a member of the committee, is reported to have taken the lead in recommending that the usual flight patterns be modified to minimize the risk of a shoot-down. Instead of covering the whole island in a single flight, the alternative plan was adopted of scheduling shorter, more frequent flights that "dipped into" Cuban air space, and also a larger number of "peripheral" flights that would peer into Cuba from beyond the three-mile limit. Abel, *Missile Crisis*, p. 14; Hilsman, *To Move a Nation*, pp. 174, 190.

with "astonishing speed" and, hence, where the danger of a U-2 being shot down was the greatest.[33]

But it was also there that the need for U-2 photographic coverage was the greatest. The "astonishing speed" of the SAM deployment, after all, signaled that something needed to be heavily protected. There is even some reason to believe that U.S. intelligence officials considered the San Cristobal–Guanajay area of western Cuba to be the logical place for offensive missiles, if the Soviets had decided to deploy them.[34] But evidently, their disbelief that the Soviets would do so was strong enough to resolve the issue in favor of exercising greater caution with U-2 flights, so as not to risk a major incident.

There is, incidentally, no indication of any disagreement among the top officials who made the decision to curtail U-2 flight coverage of Cuba. Evidently they readily agreed that the proper course should be one of caution. It should be noted, however, that CIA Director John McCone, who had earlier advanced the thesis that SAMs were being deployed to cover and protect introduction of strategic missiles, was on a prolonged vacation outside the country when the decision was made. It is possible that McCone did not learn of the decision of September 10 until he returned in early October.[35]

---

[33] Abel (*Missile Crisis*, p. 14), more clearly than Hilsman, makes the point that the SAM deployment was known to have taken place with great speed, particularly west of Havana, and he implies that this dictated particular caution in authorizing overflights of western Cuba.

[34] Hilsman (*To Move a Nation*, pp. 175–76) refers to a CIA intelligence appraisal which held that the SAM deployment was "the most advanced" in the San Cristobal and Guanajay areas. He adds that in a special intelligence meeting of October 4 to discuss the resumption of U-2 overflights of western Cuba, "No mention was made . . . of the possibility of missiles in the area, but it was perfectly obvious that if missiles had been deployed in Cuba they would have to be in this region." *Ibid.*

[35] Abel's account implies that McCone did not: "McCone returned from his wedding trip to discover that western Cuba had not been overflown for a month. He promptly suggested, at a special conference on October 4, that the whole island be photographed at once with special attention to its western end." Abel, *Missile Crisis*, p. 15. It should be noted, however, that in other matters McCone was kept informed of developments in Washington during his absence.

If the caution displayed by high-level officials in curtailing the U-2 flights seemed reasonable at the time, nonetheless the incident strongly emphasizes the critical role played by the *belief* that the Soviets would not deploy offensive missiles. Given this belief, it seemed clearly justified to responsible top-level officials of the government to accept a partial degradation of the primary intelligence capability available to the United States for discovering and verifying Soviet intentions. It is also reasonable to conclude, as Hilsman does, that "there might have been a greater sense of urgency [to continue full coverage of Cuba by U-2s] if the overall judgment had been that the Soviets probably would put missiles into Cuba rather than that they probably would not." [36]

THE MISCALCULATION OF
SOVIET INTENTIONS

This leads us to search for the more fundamental factors and assumptions that lay at the root of the Kennedy Administration's belief that the Soviets would not go so far as to deploy offensive missiles. To this end, we shall now attempt to dissect the "anatomy of miscalculation" on the American side, and to show that it grew out of an inability to envisage how the Soviet leaders were calculating the risks of a missile deployment.

In late August, photographic intelligence had established that surface-to-air antiaircraft missiles were being installed in Cuba. This had reinforced speculation and rumors that the Soviet arms buildup might proceed along dangerous lines, that the Russians might be converting Cuba into a Soviet base, and that they might be tempted to install longer-range missiles in Cuba.

---

[36] Hilsman, *To Move a Nation*, p. 190. After a detailed assessment of the unfolding intelligence picture Hilsman concludes that had U-2s been used fully, "The soonest that the construction could have been recognized as missile sites was probably some time after September 15. . . ." Similarly, Sorensen reports the view of intelligence specialists that the missiles might have been discovered three weeks earlier than they were had photo-reconnaissance flights been made over western Cuba in late September, Sorensen, *Kennedy*, p. 675.

It was in this context that the United States Intelligence Board met on September 19 to consider the question of Soviet intentions in the light of the evidence available on the continuing arms shipments to Cuba. The board considered and approved a national intelligence estimate (NIE) on this subject. As reported by Elie Abel and Roger Hilsman, this NIE concluded, in effect, that the Soviets would not undertake a deployment of offensive missiles into Cuba.[37] An examination of available accounts of this NIE enables us to infer that the error in this intelligence appraisal rested not in underestimation of Soviet motivation but rather in an inability to understand how Soviet leaders would assess the risks of a missile deployment.

The NIE recognized that the Soviets might be tempted to put missiles into Cuba for several reasons: in Elie Abel's account, "chiefly for the psychological effect of such a move throughout Latin America" and because "Khrushchev might wish in this way to strengthen his position in preparation for some new move against Berlin." [38] Hilsman's account of the NIE mentions neither of these two considerations but adds another: "The estimate hedged, however, by noting that medium or intermediate range missiles in Cuba would significantly increase the Soviet capacity to strike at America's heartland and go far toward altering the strategic balance of power between East and West. It therefore urged the intelligence community to maintain a continuous alert." [39]

It is evident, therefore, that U.S. analysts did indeed foresee at least some of the substantial advantages that might tempt Soviet leaders to undertake the missile deployment. Where they erred was in assuming that the Soviet leaders would regard a missile deployment as a high-risk strategy, whereas with the benefit of hindsight it appears that the Soviets perceived it as a

---

[37] The two accounts coincide in their description of the conclusion the NIE came to and the general reasoning on which it was based; there is, however, some difference (though not necessarily contradiction) between them as regards the particulars of the NIE's reasoning. See Abel, *Missile Crisis*, p. 12, and Hilsman, *To Move a Nation*, p. 172.

[38] Abel, *The Missile Crisis*, p. 23.   [39] Hilsman, *To Move a Nation*, p. 172.

low-risk option. The U.S. estimators erred particularly in failing to envisage—by failing to ask?—how the Soviets might satisfy themselves that the missile deployment was a *calculable and controllable risk.*

Thus, the NIE of September 19 reasoned that the Soviets would decide against a missile deployment because they "realized the Americans would be likely to discover the missiles and would probably react strongly—that, in other words, the likelihood of exposure was high and the probable consequences bad." [40] (This was the critical point of error in the judgment of Soviet intentions; we shall return to it shortly.) The NIE's judgment that Soviet leaders would forego the temptation of a missile deployment was buttressed by additional considerations. In Hilsman's words,

> when it came to nuclear matters . . . the Soviets were cautious. Never, for example, had they positioned strategic nuclear weapons outside the Soviet Union—even in Eastern Europe, where they would have been less provocative and much easier to defend than they would be in Cuba. Both air and sea communications between Cuba and the Soviet Union were long, hazardous, and peculiarly vulnerable to American interdiction. Castro was a self-elected member of the bloc—which runs counter to Soviet conceptions of themselves and their world—and the regime and Castro himself were unstable, hardly to be trusted either as the recipients of really dangerous weapons or as the hosts for weapons that remained under Soviet control. [41]

On the face of it, the weight of these considerations seemed compelling to U.S. intelligence estimators; it drove them to conclude that Khrushchev would not deploy offensive missiles into Cuba. This was, clearly, the single best guess as to Soviet intentions, particularly in the absence of concrete intelligence, like the U-2 might furnish, to the contrary. And, as Elie Abel and Roger Hilsman indicate, few if any specialists on Soviet behavior inside or outside the government were disposed to regard it as plausible that the Soviets would take the action they did.

[40] *Ibid.* Hilsman's account is consonant with Elie Abel's in this respect.
[41] *Ibid.*

Hindsight in this case supports the familiar caveat that in matters of this kind it is never sufficient to define the task of estimating intentions in terms of a "single-best guess." This particular danger is widely recognized by analysts and is usually avoided by them. Alternative hypotheses as to the opponent's intentions are usually considered, and an effort is made to assign relative probabilities to them. The source of the error—in this case and elsewhere—was, rather, more subtle and more dangerous. It consists of the tendency to judge the relative probabilities of the alternatives prematurely, before all hypotheses, *including the seemingly unlikely ones,* have been subjected to the detailed analysis required to convert them into "conditional predictions."

In estimating an opponent's intentions, to avoid surprise one must ask whether there could possibly be something present in the situation at hand that might lead the opponent to act contrary to the way one regards as probable. The need for such an inquiry would be obvious enough even if it had not been demonstrated repeatedly in past cases of miscalculation that resulted in surprise. The real question, therefore, is how best to make this inquiry. The "conditional prediction" method attempts to construct a line of reasoning, however implausible initially, by which the opponent might find a seemingly undesirable option attractive and reasonable. By actually synthesizing a hypothetical set of circumstances under which the opponent might select the apparently implausible option, an analyst may suddenly discover that the opponent's "preconditions" for activating that option are closer to being realized in the situation at hand than he had thought.

If the method of conditional predictions had been employed in the Cuban case, some U.S. analysts would have been charged with formulating a detailed working hypothesis regarding Soviet risk calculations according to which the missile deployment *would* emerge as a feasible option in Soviet eyes. There is, however, no indication that anyone did present a reasoned, systematic case for the proposition that Soviet leaders might judge a missile deployment to be a calculable, controllable risk worth accepting in return for the great advantages it promised to bestow. We shall return to this aspect of the U.S. estimate when we consider the role of CIA Director John Mc-Cone, who attempted to play the devil's advocate.[42]

We have already noted the major assumptions which led the Soviet leadership to regard the missile venture as an initiative bearing acceptable risks: the plausible hope that the MRBM rapid-deployment capability would permit a fait accompli; the expectation that Kennedy's declarations regarding offensive weapons in Cuba were politically motivated and would not be seriously executed once the weapons were in place; the expectation that the cumbersome American political machinery would react sluggishly to any premature discovery of the missiles, and that Kennedy personally would be incapable of a firm and prompt response; and so on. None of these Soviet assumptions seem to have been considered in the U.S. assessment of the Kremlin's plausible options. Thus, we may say that Washington miscalculated by failing to consider how Moscow might miscalculate the risks of a missile deployment to conclude that they were acceptable. If this interpretation is correct, it strengthens the generalization that wars and dangerous crises often grow out of interacting miscalculations on both sides.

THE IMPORTANCE OF
THE POLICY BACKGROUND

Still to be considered is the question whether, as in the Korean War case, the dominant U.S. foreign policy attitude prevalent at that time exercised a subtle, yet perhaps potent influence in reducing the receptivity of U.S. policy-makers and intelligence analysts to the available warning of the opponent's intentions. Two distinctly different interpretations of the impact of the dominant policy attitude have been offered that are on the face of it sharply contradictory. On the one hand, Roberta Wohlstetter suggests that there was a distinct lack of receptivity to early

---

[42] See also the discussion in chapter 20 of miscalculations which lead to intelligence failures.

clues of a missile deployment, induced in part by the high priority the White House gave to relaxation of tensions with the
Soviet Union. According to this thesis, knowledge of Kennedy's
policy goal subtly discouraged intelligence specialists from giving more weight to discrepant information coming in that suggested a possible Soviet missile deployment. Though Mrs.
Wohlstetter does not employ the language of psychological
theory on behalf of her interpretation, it is nonetheless quite
consistent with cognitive dissonance theory.[43] Her study of
Pearl Harbor and other cases leads her to emphasize the pervasive influence of the dominant policy background on intelligence evaluation:

> When an official policy or hypothesis is laid down, it tends to ob-
> scure alternative hypotheses, and to lead to overemphasis of the data
> that support it, particularly in a situation of increasing tension, when
> it is important not to "rock the boat." [44]

This is an important generalization, and Mrs. Wohlstter's
explanation is indeed plausible. But in the absence of more
direct evidence than she is able to provide, it is not compelling.[45] Roger Hilsman has examined her hypothesis and rejected it, arguing at some length that "the intelligence community had been concerned about the possibility that the
Soviets might put missiles in Cuba from the beginning of the
arms build-up." [46] He indicates that many of the early reports of Soviet activity that have been alluded to as clues

---

[43] See Festinger, *Theory of Cognitive Dissonance.*

[44] R. Wohlstetter, "Cuba and Pearl Harbor," pp. 699, 701. A similar thesis is
reflected in Allison's *Essence of Decision.*

[45] Mrs. Wohlstetter's point, however, is part of a more comprehensive interpretation advanced in her article. Some other factors she mentions appear to be
more important than the general policy background in accounting for Washington's sluggishness and lack of receptivity to the possibility of a missile deployment. The other factors include: (1) technological and/or logistical surprise; (2)
inevitable physical delays in transmission and checking of intelligence reports;
(3) the "cry-wolf" phenomenon; (4) the human tendency, in which policy-
makers and intelligence specialists share, to see what one wants or expects to
see; (5) an incorrect general expectation as to the opponent's behavior patterns.

[46] Hilsman, *To Move a Nation,* p. 175.

whose significance was overlooked at the time were not yet available to the estimators when the NIE of September 19 was formulated. Far from discouraging sensitivity to new clues, Hilsman argues, the NIE "did warn that the military advantages of a successful deployment of missiles to Cuba would be so great that the intelligence operators should be particularly alert." [47]

An entirely different picture of the nature and impact of the U.S. policy background just before the Cuban crisis erupted has been advanced by revisionist historian David Horowitz. According to Horowitz, Kennedy was seeking a showdown with the Soviets (and not, as Wohlstetter has it, a relaxation of tensions). If the Horowitz thesis is correct, this policy background should have made administration officials not unreceptive to warning, as the Wohlstetter interpretation implies, but particularly alert to any clues of a missile deployment. In developing his thesis, Horowitz drew upon several articles by Cyrus Sulzberger in the *New York Times* (October 20, 22, 24, 1962; February 25, 1963). Horowitz argues that there was "an important dynamic element in the planning of U.S. policy." [48] The administration's strong action in the Cuban crisis was, for Horowitz, by no means merely a response to the military threat created by the missile deployment. Rather, he holds, citing Sulzberger, that some weeks before the Cuban confrontation, Washington had become convinced that the moment of truth over Berlin would arise later in the year and resolved to have a showdown with Russia at a time and place of its own choosing. Accordingly, Horowitz implies, when the Soviets were caught deploying missiles into Cuba, the Kennedy Administration deliberately overreacted, seizing upon it as "an opportune moment" to demonstrate its nuclear superiority and its willingness to risk war.[49]

The Horowitz thesis, published in 1965, would encounter severe difficulties if it attempted to take account of detailed ma-

[47] *Ibid.*, pp. 187–89.   [48] Horowitz, *Free World Colossus*, p. 388.
[49] *Ibid.*, pp. 388–90.

terials published since then on the near failure of U.S. intelligence and American policy-making before and during the missile crisis. His thesis correctly grasps some aspects of Kennedy's rationale for *responding* to the missiles as he did; but it oversimplifies and distorts matters by reading history backwards to conclude that Kennedy must have been planning to escalate the Cold War and seized upon the missile deployment for this purpose. (The structure of Horowitz's interpretation is not an unfamiliar one in revisionist writings; we have seen that a similar interpretation has been offered for the outbreak of the Korean War and, for that matter, for Pearl Harbor.)

DOMESTIC AND BUREAUCRATIC POLITICS

Both the Wohlstetter and Horowitz theses can be criticized for oversimplifying the policy background and for dealing with, at best, only one strand of a more complex policy environment. There was in fact considerable diversity of view within the government at the time regarding what U.S. policy toward the Soviet Union should be, both in general and on specific issues. It is difficult to establish conclusively the influence of an unsettled policy background of this kind on the perception of the developing Soviet military buildup in Cuba. However, there is considerable evidence that disagreement over U.S. policy toward Cuba and toward the growing Soviet influence in Cuba did set into motion the play of "bureaucratic politics" within the administration, in ways that affected the use and interpretation of available intelligence on a possible Soviet deployment of missiles into Cuba.

Thus, it may be presumed that intelligence about the Soviet military buildup in Cuba, based on refugee and agent reports, was being leaked in one way or another to critics of the administration's policy.[50] The sources from which Senator Keating received the reports of a missile deployment which he used

---

[50] Allison, *Essence of Decision*, p. 192, asserts that some members of the military and intelligence community who disagreed with the administration's position leaked intelligence to congressmen and the press.

to criticize the administration have never been disclosed. Whether Senator Keating and other critics obtained their information through direct leaks from administration sources, or indirectly from some of the same intelligence sources which supplied the administration with some of its "raw" refugee and/or agent reports it is not possible to say.

We noted earlier that top-level officials in the administration were mobilized to counter the impact on public opinion of alarmist charges being made by Senator Keating and other critics. For this purpose, administration officials drew on their own classified intelligence estimates. As a result, intelligence specialists who were monitoring and appraising available information on Soviet activities in Cuba were forced to operate in a highly charged political atmosphere. But what effect this had on their estimates is not clear.

The situation was further complicated by the fact that John McCone, Director of the CIA, as early as the spring of 1962 had indicated a suspicion that the Russians might install medium-range missiles in Cuba. The first intimation that Soviet ground-to-air defense missiles were reaching Cuba hardened McCone's suspicion and, on August 22, he suggested to President Kennedy and McNamara that the SAMs were being emplaced in order to hide and protect the introduction of longer-range offensive missiles.[51] What is not clear in available accounts of McCone's views is to what extent his suspicions achieved prescience and to what extent they were arrived at through hindsight, during the course of bureaucratic maneuvers that occurred after the event, to avoid or shift blame for the near failure of American intelligence. There may be some truth, in other words, to Roger Hilsman's contention that "no one knows how much doubt McCone really felt, for he often played the devil's advocate in arguing with his own estimators."[52] Nonetheless,

[51] According to Allison, "Kennedy heard this [McCone's interpretation of Soviet intentions] as what it was: the suspicion of a professional anti-Communist. McNamara seems to have feared that McCone's aggressiveness might push the Administration into unwarranted action." *Ibid.*, p. 150. On McCone's role, see also Krock, *Memoirs*, p. 378; and Weintal and Bartlett, *Facing the Brink*, p. 60.

[52] Hilsman, *To Move a Nation*, p. 173.

there are important discrepancies between Hilsman's account and other accounts concerning the seriousness of McCone's suspicion and the extent to which he pushed it, against other members of the intelligence community, in an effort to alert top-level policy-makers.[53]

One senses from available accounts of McCone's views and activities in this case a disturbing paradox: to the extent that the CIA director was playing devil's advocate, the very power and prestige of his position may have made it more difficult to secure an adequate assessment of his suspicions about Soviet intentions! The person filling the top-level intelligence position must indeed subject the judgments of estimators under him to independent, critical scrutiny before accepting them. Certainly he should also insure that alternative hypotheses—particularly unpopular ones—are adequately considered by well-qualified personnel. In this connection, he may have to encourage some of them to play the devil's advocate role, should it be necessary to do so in order to obtain a careful and sympathetic case for unpopular or low-probability hypotheses. But, it may be argued, so highly placed an intelligence official as the CIA Director should not attempt to play the devil's advocate role himself and to try to combine it with his other functions, with which it is likely to conflict. Rather, he should reserve his unique high-level position for evaluating the competing interpretations, including those produced by devil's advocates elsewhere within the organization.

[53] Hilsman reports (*Ibid.*, p. 173) that McCone was eventually persuaded by the more conservative (i.e., optimistic) interpretation advanced by intelligence appraisers in CIA who concluded that the Soviet Union would not go beyond deployment of air defense SAMs. But other sources (Abel, *Missile Crisis*, pp. 7–8, 12–13), evidently draw upon post-crisis interviews with McCone to report that the CIA Director waged a continuing struggle to have the NIE of September 19 reflect his greater concern about a possible missile deployment. From Cap Ferrat, where he was honeymooning, McCone is reported to have sent a series of telegrams to his deputy in CIA, General Marshal S. Carter, on September 7, 10, 13, 16, and 20. General Carter, however, did not distribute McCone's telegrams to the White House or elsewhere outside CIA. As Abel reports it, Carter did not do so because "He felt McCone had made plain his views before leaving Washington," and besides, McCone's hypothesis had been taken into account in preparing the NIE. *Missile Crisis*, pp. 12–13.

This point is reinforced by indications that McCone's effort to serve as devil's advocate did *not* produce an adequate treatment of the unpopular hypothesis that the Soviets might well be putting missiles into Cuba. The CIA Director must be credited with shrewd deductive reasoning in arguing his suspicions that air defense SAMs were being emplaced in Cuba primarily to hide and protect the later deployment of offensive missiles. But not being a specialist on Soviet behavior himself, he could not provide a plausible line of reasoning on the basis of which Soviet leaders might engage in such unusual behavior.

Moreover—a point to which we are inclined to give particular emphasis—McCone's personal espousal of a seemingly implausible hypothesis of Soviet intentions placed him in sharp competition with professional specialists on the Soviet Union. If a top-level intelligence official such as the CIA Director embraces a "wild" hypothesis and, because of his status in the government, is in a position to influence policy, it can indeed create special pressures on the professional specialists whom he outranks. In the present case, McCone's view of Soviet intentions—which in a sense he developed prematurely and in the absence of any evidence—may have served to mobilize Soviet specialists within the government on behalf of the conservative, more plausible view of Soviet intentions.[54]

Given the grave impact McCone's hypothesis could have had on U.S. policy and given the acute and growing domestic political controversy surrounding the issue of Cuba, it must have seemed all the more important to the professional estimators to counter his views and to provide top policy-makers in the government with more responsible estimates of the opponent's intentions. If this interpretation is correct, it illustrates the adverse effects political controversy and bureaucratic politics can have on the performance of the intelligence function.

Available accounts give no indication that McCone or anyone else went beyond his shrewd deductive hypothesis concerning the possible relationship between SAMs and medium-

[54] Abel remarks, without clarifying his sources, that "within the intelligence community, some professionals smiled indulgently at McCone's seemingly fantastic conception." *Missile Crisis*, pp. 7–8.

range missiles to construct a plausible account of how Soviet
leaders might come to regard the risks of a missile deployment
as calculable, controllable, and therefore acceptable. To develop this kind of plausible construction of Soviet risk calculations, McCone would have needed the help of specialists on Soviet behavior which, apparently, he did not have and may not
have attempted to obtain. Rather, by personally undertaking advocacy of the unpopular hypothesis, the CIA Director may have
inadvertently forced Soviet specialists within the administration
to combine in rebutting him and may have pushed them into
providing the "single best" guess of Soviet intentions rather
than several well-reasoned alternative interpretations.

U.S. MISUNDERSTANDING OF
THE SOVIET APPROACH
TO RISK CALCULATION

We have already discussed the general failure of the high-level
policy-makers in the Kennedy Administration to base their attempt to reinforce deterrence on an understanding of the peculiarly Soviet approach to risk calculation. Apparently, the same
failure occurred at the level of intelligence assessment and
analysis. Although in preceding years, U.S. intelligence agencies had gained a rather good general understanding of Soviet
foreign policy behavior, either they had not yet penetrated the
Soviet attitude on risks, or else they failed to apply their knowledge to the case at hand. Certainly, so far as can be told from
the available record, the assessment of the evolving Cuban situation during September and early October did not include any
awareness that the Soviets, while recognizing the fairly substantial *overall* risks implicit in a missile deployment, might regard
the more dangerous hazards as likely to appear later in probable
scenarios, after a sequence of intervening events that could be
controlled. That such a view of the missile deployment option
might reasonably be held in Moscow, and might lead to an acceptance of the option's risks, does not appear to be reflected in
U.S. intelligence assessments at the time.

Understandably, Western analysts as well as decision-makers have tended to assume that Soviet risk acceptance was similar to their own. Failing to appreciate the distinctive Soviet understanding of the logic of hazard—in some ways more sophisticated than the usual Western approach—they have tended to blur the important time factor in risk acceptance; they have tended to be disturbed by risks of high magnitude, even though these risks may be some steps removed in time; they have been disposed to give less attention and weight to the controllability of risks through manipulation of intervening events. As a result, Western leaders and analysts both have been inclined to make distorted judgments regarding Soviet intentions, either exaggerating in their own minds the Soviet willingness to incur major risks (as, for instance, in some of the Berlin crises) or underestimating the willingness of the Soviets to undertake certain options (like the Cuban missile deployment) in the mistaken belief that the Soviets would regard them as too hazardous.[55]

Distinguishing the approaches of different nations to risk acceptance is a kind of differentiation which has hardly been encouraged by traditional deterrence theory and practice, despite its importance—as the Cuban missile crisis shows.[56] Here again, we see American decision-makers willing to make a much more careful assessment of probable Soviet behavior in attempting to rescue the situation once deterrence has failed

[55] For a further development of these observations regarding the Soviet approach to calculation, see A. L. George, "The 'Operational Code': A Neglected Approach to the Study of Political Leaders and Decision-Making," *International Studies Quarterly*, 13, No. 2 (June 1969), 190–222.

[56] The general theory of deterrence assumes the same kind of rationality for all actors; it does not call attention to the important variation among actors who attempt to behave rationally in their approach to risk calculation and risk acceptance. Applications of deterrence strategy in real-life situations, however, must make this differentiation. The assumption that the opponent's approach to risk-calculation and risk-acceptance is the same as one's own will lead to possibly serious miscalculations of his intentions and to inadequate signaling of the credibility of one's commitment and resolution in reinforcement efforts. At the same time, however, to acquire reliable knowledge of an opponent's general orientation to risk-calculation and risk-acceptance, and to apply it effectively in the variety of situations that may arise, cannot be regarded as an easy task.

than in attempting to forestall its failure. In earlier crises, the Truman and Eisenhower Administrations had responded—as discussed in earlier case studies—with considerable caution to Soviet initiatives. Their cautious response was influenced by the peculiar image they held of Soviet leaders as being unpredictable and capable of impulsive behavior if "provoked" by American behavior in a crisis situation. In contrast, in the Cuban missile case Kennedy acted boldly in seizing the initiative and exerting severe pressure on Khrushchev. He did so on the basis of a quite different image of the opponent than that held by Truman and Eisenhower. As Robert Kennedy was to note, his brother's image of Khrushchev played a decisive role in determining the choice of response to the discovery of the missiles. "The President believed from the start," Robert Kennedy recalled, "that the Soviet Chairman was a rational, intelligent man who, if given sufficient time and shown determination, would alter his position." [57] It is interesting that Kennedy maintained this image of Khrushchev, which was not universally held in the West by those who had viewed with dismay the Soviet Premier's penchant for apparently uncontrollable outbursts.

Of a piece with Kennedy's view of Khrushchev's personality were his assumptions regarding the approach Soviet leaders take toward the management of international conflict. When at the outset of the crisis Kennedy and his advisers were considering what response to make to the missiles, the critical question they faced was whether Khrushchev could be induced to remove the missiles without direct application of force. Were the Soviet leaders committed irrevocably to the daring venture on which they had embarked? Had they already gone beyond the point of no return? Or were the Soviet leaders capable of "retreating," as the classical Bolshevik doctrine had enjoined, when faced with overwhelming danger? Soviet experts in Washington supported the latter theory, and Kennedy, too, shared this premise regarding the Soviet "operational code."

[57] Robert Kennedy, *Thirteen Days*, pp. 126–27.

He felt that Soviet leaders had miscalculated the risks of their action and that they were capable, at least in principle, of retreating. Such a premise, of course, bolstered the idea of a blockade coupled with a tightening of the screw and careful adherence to the requirements of crisis management. Were some other premise regarding Soviet behavior operative, it might well have favored an immediate air strike or, at the other extreme, an attempt at appeasement to buy Khrushchev's withdrawal of the missiles at a high price.

Aftermath: Deterrence since 1963

The Cuban missile crisis marked a turning point in the Cold War. The immediate consequences for Soviet-American relations were beneficial. As on earlier occasions in history when both sides in a tense crisis stepped back from the brink of war, a détente in U.S.-Soviet relations quickly followed. During the next ten months, Kennedy and Khrushchev cooperated to bring about the partial test-ban treaty. Policies that had dangerously exacerbated the earlier conflict were reexamined and modified. Contrary to all indications prior to the Cuban crisis, the Soviet government did not resume pressure on West Berlin; nor did Khrushchev's successors stir up this familiar battleground of the Cold War. Instead, negotiations pursued with patience and seriousness over a period of years finally resulted in 1972 in important agreements covering the status of West Berlin and the relationship between East and West Germany.

Perhaps of equal importance was the sobering effect the crisis had on Cold War uses of deterrence strategy and strategic power which, as we have emphasized, played an important role in the origins of the Cuban missile crisis. Thereafter, both sides substantially lowered their expectations regarding the extent to which deterrence and counter deterrence strategies could be used on behalf of foreign policy objectives. This was coupled, moreover, with a tacit mutual understanding that each side would have to place greater reliance on other means of diplomacy for controlling and mediating their conflicting interests. We consider these developments in greater detail in the concluding chapter of this book. Here, we should note that the use of deterrence strategy as an instrument of American foreign policy indeed did not end after the partial détente of 1963. In a number of crisis or precrisis situations since then, the United States has attempted to apply deterrence on behalf of a weaker ally or neutral state. It would be beyond the scope of both the present study and the resources available to attempt to give detailed case history treatment to these more recent instances. They can only be briefly noted here.

The United States, of course, has attempted and continues to project a general deterrence "blanket" over the state of Israel. While the precise nature of this commitment and the lengths to which the United States would go to protect Israel's survival have been left deliberately ambiguous, there is no doubt that a general effort to deter major attack on Israel has gone forward both in a consistent and oft-repeated declaratory policy and in action through the sale of advanced weapons, the exchange of intelligence information, etc. In addition, it has been reported that President Johnson delivered a specific deterrent threat to discourage Soviet intervention in the Six-Day War of 1967.

After the Soviet invasion of Czechoslovakia in 1968, the United States, in conjunction with NATO, appeared to make a somewhat ambiguous deterrence effort on behalf of Rumania and Yugoslavia, which seemed to be threatened at that time by large Soviet troop concentrations.

Following the election of Allende as President of Chile in 1970, the United States evidently indicated that it would not intervene so long as Soviet military bases did not appear in Chile. It is not clear whether this was intended as a deterrence effort and, indeed, whether Washington took seriously the possibility that Soviet military bases might be established in that country.

A clearer instance of the resort to deterrence policy is provided by the Nixon Administration's response to reports, beginning in September 1970, that a submarine base to service Soviet missile-carrying submarines was being built in Cuba. The administration issued warnings that such a development would be viewed with the "utmost seriousness" as a violation of the 1962 agreement between Kennedy and Khrushchev for removal of the missiles from Cuba.

Deterrence efforts of various kinds have also been made in connection with the war in Southeast Asia. Prior to the U.S. escalation in 1965, the threat of American air attacks appears to have been intended to deter Hanoi from stepping up its assistance to the Viet Cong. Similarly, it seems probable that soon after coming to office in 1969, President Nixon conveyed a threat to resume air attacks against North Vietnam in order to deter any new large-scale North Vietnamese action in the South.

During the India-Pakistan War of 1971, the administration has asserted, it was concerned about and attempted to deter an Indian attack upon *West* Pakistan. To this end it employed declaratory policy, diplomatic gestures at the United Nations and elsewhere, and especially the signal of diverting the aircraft carrier *Enterprise* into the Indian Ocean.

In these cases and perhaps others the United States may have begun to experience a foretaste of what deterrence policies will need to adjust themselves to in the 1970s and possibly beyond, which we take up in the last chapter.

Bibliography

Unusually detailed accounts of American policy-making leading to the confrontation over the missiles appear in publications by former members of the Kennedy Administration, particularly those by Hilsman, Schlesinger, and Sorensen. Elie Abel obtained important new material and details from interviews with members of the administration. Of the several congressional hearings that went into one or another aspect of the crisis, particularly valuable are the ones by Senator Stennis' Preparedness Investigating Subcommittee and the House DOD Appropriations Subcommittee. Chronologies and documents are provided by *The New York Times'* "Cuban Crisis: A Step-by-step Review," Larson, and (with valuable interpretations as well) Pachter.

Information on Soviet policy-making is, of course, much more limited. The full authencity of the memoir *Khrushchev Remembers* remains uncertain. Available data and interpretations are provided by Horelick, Horelick and Rush, Kolkowicz, Tatu, Ulam, Allison, Lipson, and Linden.

A number of detailed scholarly studies of the missile crisis have been published. Particularly useful for our purposes are those by Horelick, Horelick and Rush, Young, Roberta Wohlstetter, and the joint article by the Wohlstetters. The Allison study is not only rich in insights and alternative hypotheses but covers available sources with unusual thoroughness. The study by George, Hall, and Simon focuses on Kennedy's use of coercive diplomacy and crisis management; it also contains material on Kennedy's complex motivation that has been incorporated into the present study.

The secret correspondence during the crisis between Kennedy and Khrushchev was declassified by the State Department in 1973. Through the courtesy of Professor Barton Bernstein, Stanford University, we were able to see it before this book went to press. The correspondence does not add significant new details to the public record.

Major sources for the discussion of Cold War uses of deterrence and strategic threats and of the "missile gap" problem are Horelick and Rush, Hilsman, Quester, and Licklider.

Analysis of the near-failure of American intelligence draws on a number of sources. Suspicion that the U-2 flights over Cuba had not been scheduled in an optimal manner had arisen even before the crisis was over; Kenworthy, *New York Times*, November 3, 1962. The Stennis Committee examined the possibility of a "photography gap" in U-2 coverage of Cuba in early 1963 and rejected the charges as "unfounded." However, that report ignored altogether the critical question of the U-2 flight paths over Cuba between September 5 and October 24, noting merely that these flights "completed the coverage of those areas of Cuba which had been spotlighted as requiring early attention." Congress, Senate, *Interim Report*, pp. 3, 8–9. Yet, the "photography gap" of some 38 days in U-2 coverage of *western* Cuba had already been officially confirmed in early February 1963 by Defense Secretary McNamara's grudging admission of it during persistent cross examination by Congressmen Minshall and Ford. Congress, House, *Defense Appropriations*, esp. pp. 67–71 and 362–63, but also 25, 27–28, 45–6, 74. Writing in August 1963, Henry Pachter (*Collision Course*, p. 8) made no reference to a possible "photography gap" in U-2 coverage; but he offered indirect support for this thesis in vague hints by administration sources that in view of the emplacement of Soviet air defense missiles in Cuba, reconnaissance flights during September 1962 had been limited to "sideways approaches" and may not have utilized U-2 planes. In 1965 Sorensen (*Kennedy*, p. 672) remarked cryptically that U-2 incidents elsewhere in the world had led to a "high-level reexamination of that airplane's use" over Cuba "and some delay in flights."

These pieces were put together later in 1965 by Roberta Wohlstetter ("Cuba and Pearl Harbor"), who suggested that the administration's fear of losing a U-2 to Soviet air defense missiles may have led it to be cautious in scheduling U-2 flights over Cuba. But confirmation and adequate evaluation of this matter was not possible until additional disclosures concerning a change in policy governing U-2 flights were made by Elie Abel (*Missile Crisis,* 1966) and Roger Hilsman (*To Move a Nation,* 1967). Hilsman's earlier article on the Cuban crisis in 1964 had not disclosed the explanation for or consequences of the "photography gap." There was also no mention of this or, indeed, of the role of the U-2 in the intelligence effort in Knorr's article, "Failures in National Intelligence Estimates."

Allison's otherwise informative and incisive analysis fails to deal clearly with the effect of the photography gap on the near failure of U.S. intelligence in discovering the presence of missiles in Cuba. Instead, Allison gives misplaced emphasis in his explanation to the role of "the routines and procedures of the organizations that make up the U.S. intelligence community" and to the role of "overlapping bargaining games" among the suborganizations engaged in the intelligence effort. *Essence of Decision,* pp. 118–23, 187, 191–92. In his effort to emphasize the importance of two analytical models—the organizational process model and the bureaucratic politics model—of how foreign policy is made, Allison tends to impose these theories on the data, which distorts the explanation for the sluggishness and near failure of the U.S. intelligence effort. Thus, the high-level decision of September 10 to avoid direct overflights of western Cuba, which led to the photography gap, cannot be explained in terms of either the organizational process model or the bureaucratic politics model; it requires a different kind of explanation, which we attempt to provide in this chapter.

Abel, Elie. *The Missile Crisis.* Philadelphia, Lippincott, 1966.
Acheson, Dean. "Review of R. F. Kennedy's *Thirteen Days,*" *Esquire,* February 1969.
Allison, Graham T. *Essence of Decision.* Boston, Little, Brown, 1971.
Baldwin, Hanson W. "The Growing Risks of Bureaucratic Intelligence," *The Reporter,* August 15, 1963.

Brzezinski, Zbigniew. "How the Cold War Was Played," *Foreign Affairs*, 51, No. 1 (October 1972), 181–209.

Bundy, McGeorge. "The Presidency and the Peace," *Foreign Affairs*, XLII (April 1964).

Chayes, Abram, Thomas Ehrlich, and Andreas F. Lowenfeld. "The Cuban Missile Crisis," in *International Legal Process*. 2 vols. Boston, Little, Brown, 1969; Vol. II, pp. 1057–1149.

Crane, Robert D. "The Sino-Soviet Dispute on War and the Cuban Crisis," *Orbis*, VIII (Fall 1964), 537–49.

Daniel, James, and John G. Hubbell. *Strike in the West*. New York, Holt, Rinehart and Winston, 1963.

Eisenhower, Dwight D. *The White House Years: Waging Peace, 1956–1961*. Garden City, N.Y., Doubleday, 1965.

Festinger, Leon. *A Theory of Cognitive Dissonance*. Evanston, Row, Peterson, 1957.

Gerberding, William P. "International Law and the Cuban Missile Crisis," in *International Law and Political Crisis*, ed. Lawrence Scheinman and David Wilkinson. Boston, Little, Brown, 1968.

George, Alexander L., David K. Hall, and William E. Simons. *The Limits of Coercive Diplomacy*. Boston, Little, Brown, 1971.

Hermann, Charles F. *Crises in Foreign Policy*. Indianapolis, Bobbs-Merrill, 1969.

Hilsman, Roger. *To Move a Nation*. New York, Doubleday, 1967.

——. "The Cuban Crisis: How Close We Were to War," *Look*, 28 (August 25, 1964).

Holsti, Ole R., Richard A. Brody, and Robert C. North. "Measuring Affect and Action in International Reaction Models: Empirical Materials from the 1962 Cuban Crisis," *Journal of Peace Research* (1964), pp. 170–89.

Horelick, A. "The Cuban Missile Crisis: An Analysis of Soviet Calculations and Behavior," *World Politics*, XVI (April 1964).

——, and M. Rush. *Strategic Power and Soviet Foreign Policy*. Chicago, University of Chicago Press, 1965.

Horowitz, David. *The Free World Colossus*. New York, Hill and Wang, 1965.

Hyland, William, and Richard W. Shryock. *The Fall of Khrushchev*. New York, Funk & Wagnalls, 1968.

"Interview with President Kennedy," *Washington Post*, December 18, 1962.

Kahan, Jerome H., and Anne K. Long. "The Cuban Missile Crisis: A Study of Its Strategic Context," *Political Science Quarterly*, LXXXVII, No. 4 (December 1972).

Kateb, George. "Kennedy as Statesman," *Commentary*, June 1966.

Kaufmann, William W. *The McNamara Strategy*. New York, Harper & Row, 1964.

Kennedy, Robert F. *Thirteen Days*. New York, Norton, 1969.

Khrushchev Remembers. Introduction and notes by Edward Crankshaw. Boston, Little, Brown, 1970.

Knorr, Klaus. "Failures in National Intelligence Estimates: The Case of the Cuban Missiles," *World Politics*, XVI (April 1964), 455–67.

Knox, W. E. "Close-up of Khrushchev During a Crisis," *New York Times Magazine*, November 18, 1962.

Kolkowicz, Roman. "Conflicts in Soviet Party-Military Relations: 1962–1963." RAND RM-3760-PR. The RAND Corporation, August 1963.
——. *The Soviet Military and the Communist Party*. Princeton, Princeton University Press, 1967.
Krock, Arthur. *Memoirs*. New York, Funk & Wagnalls, 1968.
Larson, David L., ed. *The "Cuban Crisis" of 1962: Selected Documents and Chronology*. Boston, Houghton Mifflin, 1963.
Licklider, Roy E. "The Missile Gap Controversy," *Political Science Quarterly*, LXXXV, No. 4 (December 1970), 600–13.
Linden, Carl A. *Khrushchev and the Soviet Leadership, 1957–1964*. Baltimore, Johns Hopkins Press, 1966.
Lipson, Leon. "Castro on the Chessboard of the Cold War," in *Cuba and the U.S.*, ed. John Plank. Washington, D.C., Brookings Institution, 1967; pp. 178–99.
Mongar, Thomas M. "Personality and Decision-making: John F. Kennedy in Four Crisis Decisions," *Canadian Journal of Political Science*, II (1969), 200–25.
Pachter, Henry M. *Collision Course*. New York, Praeger, 1963.
Penkovskiy, Oleg. *The Penkovskiy Papers*. New York, Doubleday, 1965.
Quester, George H. *Nuclear Diplomacy: The First Twenty-Five Years*. New York, Dunellan, 1970.
Salinger, Pierre. *With Kennedy*. New York, Doubleday, 1966.
Schelling, Thomas C. *Arms and Influence*. New Haven, Yale University Press, 1966.
Schlesinger, Arthur. *A Thousand Days*. Boston, Houghton Mifflin, 1965.
Sidey, Hugh. *John F. Kennedy, President*. New York, Atheneum, 1963.
Sorensen, Theodore C. *Kennedy*. New York, Harper & Row, 1965.
——. *The Kennedy Legacy*. New York, Harper & Row, 1965.
——. *Decision-making in the White House*. New York, Columbia University Press, 1963.
"Special Cuba Briefing," U.S. Department of Defense, by Robert McNamara, February 6, 1963.
Steel, Ronald. "Endgame" (review of Robert F. Kennedy's *Thirteen Days*), *New York Review of Books*, March 13, 1969.
Stone, I. F. "The Brink" (review of Elie Abel's *The Missile Crisis*), *New York Review of Books*, April 14, 1966.
Sulzberger, C. L. Articles in *New York Times*, October 20, 22, and 24, 1962; February 25, 1963.
Tatu, Michael. *Power in the Kremlin*. New York, Viking, 1969.
Ulam, Adam. *Expansion and Coexistence*. New York, Praeger, 1968.
U.S. Congress, House Committee on Appropriations. *Hearings on Department of Defense Appropriations for 1964*, 88th Cong., 1st sess., Part I, 1963.
U.S. Congress, House Committee on Armed Services. *Hearings on Military Posture*, 88th Cong., 1st sess., 1963.
U.S. Congress, Senate Committee on Armed Services, Preparedness Investigating Subcommittee, *Interim Report on Cuban Military Build-up*, 88th Cong., 1st sess., 1963.
U.S. Department of Defense, "Special Cuba Briefing," by Robert McNamara. February 6, 1963.

de Vosjoli, Philippe Thyraud. *LAMIA.* Boston, Little, Brown, 1970.
Weintal, Edward, and Charles W. Bartlett. *Facing the Brink.* New York, Scribner's, 1967; chap. 4, "Challenge on the Doorstep."
Wohlstetter, Albert, and Roberta Wohlstetter. "Controlling the Risks in Cuba." Adelphi Paper No. 17. London, Institute of Strategic Studies, 1965.
Wohlstetter, Roberta. "Cuba and Pearl Harbor," *Foreign Affairs,* July 1965.
Wolfe, Thomas. *Soviet Strategy at the Crossroads.* Cambridge, Harvard University Press, 1964.
Young, Oran R. *The Politics of Force.* Princeton, Princeton University Press, 1968.

Part Three

Toward a Reformulation of Deterrence Theory

Chapter 16

The Role of Theory in Policy-Making

The Gap between Deterrence Theory and Deterrence Policy

MUCH OF PART ONE of this study revolved around the theme that the contemporary abstract, deductivistic theory of deterrence is inadequate for policy application, notwithstanding its having been offered in a normative-prescriptive mode. The eleven cases we have now examined indicate the kinds of complexities which arise when the United States makes actual deterrence attempts, complexities which in many respects are not addressed by the abstract theory of deterrence.

To be sure, deterrence theorists have always acknowledged that like any other theory theirs, too, simplifies reality. It does not suffice, however, to stop with such a caveat. In addition, there is an obligation, recognized by most deterrence theorists, to go further and identify those aspects of deterrence phenomena in real-life settings which may be critical for determining deterrence outcomes but which are not encompassed by the simplifying assumptions of the theory in its present form. This difficult task, all the more necessary since deterrence theory has offered guidelines for policy-making, has not been satisfactorily accomplished. At the same time, it must be recognized that prudent and successful application of deterrence strategy to real-life situations is highly problematic without a clear grasp of precisely those complexities which deterrence theory simplifies or ignores.

It is not surprising, therefore, that the simplifying assumptions of prescriptive deterrence theory should have seriously restricted its relevance and usefulness for foreign policy–making. The inability of deterrence theorists to make an adequate analysis of the gap between the assumptions of their theory and the complexities of deterrence behavior in real life has necessarily left that important task in the hands of policy-makers. Left to their own devices, American policy-makers have filled this gap as best they could in their own way, and the results have often been unfortunate. Moreover, deterrence *strategy*, as applied by policy-makers, bears only a loose resemblance to the primitive, abstract, only partly developed deterrence *theory*. Hence neither the successes nor the failures of deterrence strategy in American foreign policy can be attributed to the influence of formal deterrence theory, which has stopped well short of the level of detail required of a policy-relevant theory and therefore has had only modest influence.

As a prescriptive theory, deterrence theory remains incomplete and unsatisfactory. It has become increasingly clear that initial statements of the theory merely adumbrated a starting point and that the necessary development and refinement of the theory did not follow. (It is instructive to reflect on this experience and what it implies more broadly for the goal of developing policy-relevant theory for different aspects of international politics. We consider some of these questions in the Appendix.)

Let us briefly recall seven simplifying assumptions of abstract deterrence theory that were discussed in chapter 3:

Assumption 1: Each side in the deterrence situation is a unitary, purposive actor. (This assumption overlooks the fact that the policy behavior of governments is affected by the dynamics of organizational behavior and internal governmental politics.)

Assumption 2: The payoffs and choices of action by the actors in the deterrence situation can be deduced by assuming a single general "rationality."

Assumption 3: General deterrence theory can be useful to policy-makers, even though it does not define the scope or relevance of deterrence strategy as an instrument of foreign policy.

Assumption 4: The major threat to the defending power's interests lies in its opponents' capacity for launching military attacks.

Assumption 5: Deterrence commitments are always a simple "either-or" matter, i.e., either the defending power commits itself or it does not; if it does, then the commitment is strong, unequivocal, unqualified, and of indefinite duration.

Assumption 6: The deterring power can rely upon threats to persuade the opponent not to alter the status quo.

Assumption 7: The critical and only problematical task of deterrence strategy is to achieve credibility of commitment.

The assumptions of prescriptive deterrence theory have often had to be discarded or modified by the policy-maker in diagnosing specific situations. A few examples will suffice to indicate the poor or even misleading quality of formal deterrence theory for the situational diagnoses needed in policy-making. Against the second assumption just listed, we noted in Part Two the chronic difficulty American policy-makers experienced in trying to estimate how the opponent calculated the risks of his options. In all three Berlin cases, the Korean War, and the Cuban missile crisis, American policy-makers were surprised by the action the opponent took. In each case American officials had thought the opponent would not act as he did because such action would entail high risks. In fact, there is reason to believe that in each of these cases the opponent regarded his initiative as a low-risk strategy through which he was confident of controlling and avoiding unwanted risks of greater magnitude. It is evident that to make the diagnoses needed in assessing situations, the policy-maker cannot work on the assumption that all actors operate with the same kind of "rationality." Rather, the policy-maker needs more discriminating theoretical models of how particular opponents behave in conflict situations.

With respect to the third assumption, our case studies

suggest, to the contrary, that the scope and relevance of deterrence strategy for foreign policy needs to be strictly and carefully defined. Our case histories of the Eisenhower Doctrine for the Middle East and the Communist Chinese intervention in Korea both illustrate the risks of U.S. overreliance on deterrence strategy. The deterrence commitment embodied in the Eisenhower Doctrine paradoxically increased internal political instability in some of the Middle Eastern countries which it was designed to help. Our study of Chinese intervention in Korea emphasizes that deterrence strategy cannot be a reliable substitute for a sensible foreign policy or be used, as Truman and Acheson did in that case, to avoid the consequences of a dangerously provocative foreign policy error. Only a timely abandonment of the policy of trying to unify Korea by force could have reliably reduced the danger of war with Communist China by removing or substantially reducing its motivation to intervene.

More broadly, the American policy of containment during the Cold War suffered badly from a *failure to define limits to the scope and relevance of deterrence strategy.* While containment logically required some use of deterrence strategy, the need for selective, discriminating use of deterrence to uphold containment gave way to a rigid attempt to exclude loss of any territory, even the offshore islands lying a few miles off mainland China. The deformation of containment led to a proliferation of American deterrence commitments throughout the world and, as George Kennan was to complain, also to a "militarization" of containment. As we noted in our account of the Taiwan Strait crisis of 1954–1955, the American effort to extend containment from Europe to Asia invited serious new risks because of the different structure of the situation, which was dangerously fluid and not neatly structured, as Europe was, for a classical *defensive* application of deterrence strategy. Because the Chinese civil war remained unresolved, the American effort to employ deterrence strategy on behalf of the Nationalist regime on Taiwan resulted in a confusion of containment with "liberation," thereby increasing tensions and inviting crisis.

Finally, as our account of the origins of the Cuban missile crisis stressed, the risks and untoward consequences of too heavy a reliance by both sides on deterrence strategy and strategic power during the Cold War to achieve a broad range of foreign policy objectives contributed to bringing about the most dangerous confrontation of the two nuclear superpowers.

In contrast to the fifth assumption, regarding the "either-or" character of commitments, our case studies indicate that policy-makers need a much more complex understanding of the nature of commitments both in order to convey their own commitments more effectively and to diagnose better the commitments other actors are making. Commitment theory is taken up in more detail in chapter 19.

As for the sixth assumption, which concerns the central role of threats in deterrence strategy, we argue to the contrary that the policy-maker would be better served in the conduct of foreign policy by a broader influence theory. A variety of policy means should be considered for reducing, rechanneling, accommodating, deterring, or frustrating challenges to different kinds of interests, not just deterrent threats. The need for threatening sanctions cannot be properly judged by the policy-maker on the basis of a prescriptive theory that confines itself to indicating that such threats are likely to be necessary to deter encroachments on one's interests. A policy-maker who diagnoses conflict situations solely from the standpoint of how to make more effective use of threats will find that threats are often irrelevant or dysfunctional. This irrelevance of deterrence threats was evident in the Middle East crises of 1957–1958. Some of their harmful consequences are suggested by the Berlin crisis of 1961; after it was over President Kennedy wondered whether some of the moves he had taken to signal resolution had not aggravated the crisis by forcing Khrushchev to undertake similar moves.[1]

In certain situations, moreover, threats may be provocative. The threats the United States and its allies made in 1941 to

[1] Schlesinger, A *Thousand Days*, p. 347–48.

deter Japan from further encroachments against Asian countries were all too potent and credible to Japanese leaders. They decided they had no choice but to resort to a still more ambitious strategy and attack the United States. But the fact that deterrent threats against a highly motivated opponent are sometimes ineffectual or may boomerang does not permit us to conclude that deterrent threats will surely be more effective against a cautious opponent who confines himself to low-risk and controlled-risk options. In the Quemoy and the Cuban missile crises, threats did not deter the controlled low-risk strategies the opponents were engaged in.

A policy-maker who invariably relies upon threats to deter encroachments on his interests is likely in some situations to pay a high price for temporary deterrence successes which do not really remove the sources of the conflict. We called attention to this in our accounts of the Taiwan Strait and Quemoy crises of 1954–1955 and 1958. A deterrence success of this kind buys time for efforts to restructure the situation after the crisis subsides, in order to defuse its conflict potential. Failure to utilize a temporary deterrence success to alter the situation invites a repetition of the crisis in the future, perhaps under new circumstances in which resort to deterrence strategy may be even more costly and ineffectual.

Viewed from a broader perspective on international relations, therefore, controlled crises of the kind we have seen in Berlin and the Taiwan Strait often have a *catalytic* function for bringing about changes that are necessary if war is to be avoided in the longer run.[2] While deterrence may be necessary to avoid the dangers of "appeasement" under pressure, a deterrence success in such crises creates dangers of another kind if it encourages the defending power to ignore the need for utilizing other policy approaches in the ensuing noncrisis period to find more viable, mutually acceptable solutions to the conflict of interests.

[2] On the useful catalytic function of some international crises, see also the remarks of several contributors to Hermann's *International Crises*, pp. 19, 28, 34, and 270.

The Role of Theory in
Situational Analysis

It is evident from historical experience that there is need for a better theory of deterrence that might correct the kinds of flaws in policy-makers' applications of deterrence which we have just noted and which emerge in the case studies.

Perhaps the greatest need of policy-makers, which better theory could fill, is enhanced ability to diagnose specific situations that arise. The importance of such "situational analysis," as we shall call it, in policy-making is not well enough understood by those engaged in developing theories of international politics. Theory in this realm, whether it concern deterrence or other questions, can and should serve an important diagnostic function for policy-makers; but this fact is sometimes ignored in efforts to develop policy-relevant theories. And yet few would disagree with the observation that whenever possible in the conduct of foreign policy, correct diagnosis should precede prescription. We will address these general themes in greater detail in the Appendix. Let us consider now their implications for deterrence theory.

The policy-maker cannot operate effectively with an understanding merely of the general requirements of deterrence, which is what contemporary deterrence theory offers. Rather, the policy-maker must judge whether these general requirements are met or are likely to be met in particular situations at hand. Moreover, the policy-maker often has to develop a specific, discriminating diagnosis of the ways in which the general requirements of deterrence are or are not being met in deteriorating situations in order to decide whether and how deterrence strategy can be tailored more effectively to the solution of problems.

From this standpoint, it is evident that the abstract, deductivistic theory of deterrence we examined in Part One, despite its presentation in a normative-prescriptive mode, does not eliminate the necessity for situational analysis or act as a substitute for it. Nor does it give the policy-maker much assistance in doing the kind of situational analysis required when he is attempting to employ deterrence strategy.

Contemporary deterrence theory shares with many other theories in the field of international politics the fact that it has poor diagnostic power when applied to a single situation. There are several reasons for this. One is that those engaged in formulating these theories often do not attempt to develop a differentiated typology of situations in which the phenomenon in question—in this case, deterrence—manifests itself. Yet whether deterrence strategy would be a relevant policy, what its requirements would be, the likely costs and risks of using it, and the prospects for successful deterrence—the answers to all these questions, critical for policy-making, depend upon the characteristics of the situation. Deterrence theory attempts to be prescriptive, however, without recognizing the important variations among situations to which deterrence strategy may be applied or misapplied.

Second, scholars engaged in formulating deterrence theory have been insufficiently concerned with *explanatory,* as opposed to directly prescriptive, theory. As noted in chapters 3 and 4, deterrence theory was not developed to provide retrospective explanations for past events, and it has rarely been used for this purpose. But it is impossible for a theory to be useful in diagnosing present situations unless it is also capable of explaining past ones. The recent history of U.S. foreign policy, as we have seen at length in Part Two, provides many cases from which explanatory theory can be developed which, in turn, may then have diagnostic utility.

It should be noted that an explanatory theory will not *necessarily* have strong diagnostic power; whether or not it does depends on the focus and content that we choose to give the theory. To acquire strong diagnostic power of the kind needed for situational analysis, an explanatory theory must acquire a capability for *discriminating* explanations. That is, it must be capable of offering differentiated explanations of a variety of deterrence failures and, to the extent possible, for deterrence success as well. The emphasis on discriminating explanations is necessary because scholars interested in building theories often give priority to developing rather general explanatory hypotheses that will apply to a relatively large number of cases. In one sense, to be sure, these generalizations have considerable explanatory power: they call attention to the fact that the explanations for many cases contain a common component, even though they differ in other respects. But in another sense, more important for situational analysis, general explanatory hypotheses have low explanatory power, in that they ignore other components of the overall explanation for each case which vary from one case to another. Since that part of the explanation which differs from one case to another may be—indeed, usually is—more important for situational analysis, an explanatory theory that is composed largely of general explanatory hypotheses will have lower diagnostic power for situational analysis of the kind needed for policy-making.[3]

One example, admittedly a rather extreme one, will perhaps suffice to illustrate the difference between a general explanatory theory and one which has the capability for more discriminating explanations. Our example should also serve to demonstrate why the latter has greater policy relevance. Consider the familiar proposition: "War is the result of miscalculation." This is certainly a broad explanation that applies to many (though not all) cases. But its generality severely limits the value it has to the policy-maker for diagnosing emergent situations in which deterrence may fail as a result of miscalculation. Nor does this generalization provide anything more than the loosest kind of guidance as to what actions should be taken in a given situation to reduce the likelihood of miscalculation. A policy-oriented theory of deterrence, we feel, must move considerably beyond "first-order" generalizations such as "war is the result of miscalculation" if it is to be of practical value. At the very least, dif-

[3] Admittedly, the differentiated explanatory theory favored here can be achieved only at some cost in parsimony. But the level of parsimony that is desirable and acceptable in a theory cannot be determined in a vacuum; it obviously depends on the use to which one intends to put the theory. The policy use of deterrence theory requires a more complex, differentiated explanatory theory than has heretofore been available.

ferent kinds of miscalculations must be identified, and the conditions under which each kind tends to occur need to be specified. If successful, this kind of analysis leads to what may be called "second-order" generalizations about the role of different kinds of miscalculation in different kinds of deterrence failure. These second-order generalizations are what we will be seeking to extract from the case studies presented in Part Two.

One of the objectives of this study, therefore, is to develop a more detailed explanatory theory of deterrence outcomes. We deliberately put aside and reject the attempt to formulate a better version of the normative-prescriptive theory of deterrence.

In our view it is not the function of theory to attempt to provide policy-makers with high-confidence prescriptions for action in each and any contingency to which deterrence strategy may seem applicable.[4] We seek, rather, an explanatory theory that is policy-relevant *without* being prescriptive. Its policy relevance will flow from its ability to identify (1) variables that may affect the opponent's behavior in deterrence situations, over which the deterring power may or may not be able to exert influence; (2) variables that may affect the deterring power's own perceptions, evaluations, or behavior; (3) various difficulties that can arise in attempting to make effective use of a deterrence strategy and the circumstances that tend to generate these difficulties; (4) different patterns in which deterrence may partially or completely fail; and, perhaps most important, (5) the valid uses and the limitations of deterrence strategy as an instrument of foreign policy.

Constructing an Explanatory Theory of Deterrence

The statement that we seek an explanatory theory that can help provide *differentiated* explanations for deterrence out-

[4] For a further discussion of these views regarding the relation of theory to action see the Appendix; and also the Introduction to George, Hall, and Simons, *Limits of Coercive Diplomacy.*

comes may strike some readers as a concealed plea for purely historical explanation of each case. Our remarks may also be misinterpreted as constituting a tacit admission that the explanation for each deterrence outcome has to be highly idiosyncratic. We may be challenged, therefore, for asserting that explanatory theory can go beyond the level of broad general hypotheses. The objection may be raised that if, as we have stated, such general explanatory hypotheses are not very helpful to policy-makers, this simply reflects the complexity of deterrence problems in real life. To the extent that the regularities in deterrence behavior are less important than the variance from case to case, it will be argued, then the sober conclusion has to be drawn that situational analysis of the kind the policy-maker engages in must necessarily be conducted on a purely ad hoc basis. In other words, even an explanatory theory cannot be of much help.

It is premature and unnecessary to accept so bleak a conclusion. A more differentiated explanatory theory is still possible if we can formulate "contingent generalizations," that is, regularities that occur only under certain specific conditions. (These conditions will be discussed in a subsequent chapter.) Explanatory hypotheses of this kind are also of a general character, though they apply only to subsets of the deterrence phenomena that are suggested by the specified conditions. Put differently, we seek to identify several different *causal patterns* associated with variation in deterrence outcomes.

For this our approach to the development of explanatory theory must differ substantially from that utilized in the earlier statistical-correlational analysis of deterrence outcomes that was reviewed in chapter 4. The reasons that this earlier approach yielded disappointing results must be understood and taken into account in designing an alternative approach to the development of theory. Let us examine the basis of this alternative approach.

The earlier studies, of which Bruce Russett's "Calculus of Deterrence" is the best known, did not succeed in identifying adequately the *theoretically relevant variation in the dependent variable* (i.e., the deterrent outcome). They posited a simple distinction, or variation, between two general outcomes: "deterrence success" and "deterrence failure." There is reason to believe, however, that neither the subclass of deterrence "success" nor that of "failure" should be regarded as sufficiently homogeneous for theory-building purposes. To assume homogeneity, as Russett does, leads the investigator to lump together as instances of deterrence failure cases that may differ from one another in theoretically (and pragmatically) interesting ways. The separation of the dependent variable into only two subclasses, deterrence success and deterrence failure, has proven unproductive for the development of explanatory theory. The varied historical cases that qualify as instances of "deterrence failure" do not correlate well enough, Russett found, with many independent variables considered to be of theoretical relevance.

Given this discouraging experience, the investigator has two further options. One is to examine other theoretically interesting independent or intervening variables. The other is to try to describe the variance in the dependent variable in a more differentiated manner. We have pursued both these possibilities. Thus we have looked at a number of intervening variables associated with the initiator's decision-making calculations (which Russett chose to leave out altogether); and we have also developed a more differentiated way of describing the variance in "deterrence failure."

What we are suggesting, so far as deterrence failures are concerned, is that deterrence can fail for different reasons and in different ways. Few would disagree with this observation. The task remains of formulating what we think we know or suspect about deterrence failures more systematically into an explanatory theory. For this purpose we employ an inductive procedure in analyzing historical cases of deterrence failure. We treat each historical case as if it were a "deviant case," examining it to note in what ways it differed from (as well as resembled) other cases.[5] The "deviant case" treatment of historical ex-

[5] On the logic of deviant case analysis and the role it can play in the development of theory see, for example, Kendall and Wolf, "The Analysis of Deviant Cases in Communications Research."

amples of deterrence is more selective and more theoretically oriented than the traditional approach to intensive single case studies. Deviant case analysis focuses on independent and intervening variables presumed to be of general relevance. (And it differs from the traditional type of case study, again, in being linked with an inductive, abstracting procedure that is necessary in theory development.)

The inductive procedure employed is qualitative. It consists in abstracting out and formulating in more general terms elements of the particular explanation arrived at in a single case study. Doing this for many different cases yields a number of general causal patterns that are linked in turn to different types of deterrence failure. This qualitative inductive procedure is very similar to one explicated in recent years by other writers who have argued persuasively that the disappointingly small contribution which single case studies had made to theory-development in the past is finally giving way as new methods are developed to use comparative case studies for this purpose.[6]

The inductive procedure we have followed has yielded a typology of deterrence failures which will be reported in chapter 18. Each type of deterrence failure is linked with a somewhat different causal pattern. We should note the diagnostic value this kind of differentiated explanatory theory is likely to have for policy-making. Knowledge of the diffferent likely patterns of deterrence failure should sensitize the policy-maker to available situational clues so that he can make a more discriminating analysis of whether, how, and why deterrence may fail.

---

[6] See, for example, Sidney Verba's remarks about what he calls the "disciplined configurative approach," in which the investigator does not merely take note of the idiosyncratic aspects of the explanation for each case but formulates these aspects in terms of theoretically relevant variables and classes. As Verba puts it, "The 'unique historical event' cannot be ignored, but it must be considered as one of a class of such events even if it happened only once." "Some Dilemmas in Comparative Research," p. 114. See also Eckstein, "Case-Study and Theory in Macropolitics," unpublished. A revised version of this paper will appear in Greenstein and Polsby, *A Handbook of Political Science*, forthcoming.

The Problem of Identifying
Deterrence Success

A well-designed study of deterrence would include not only cases of deterrence failure but also instances where deterrence policy was successful. It is difficult, however, to identify cases of deterrence success reliably in the absence of better data on the policy calculations of potential initiators who were presumably deterred. Instances of apparently successful deterrence, as Bruce Russett noted,[7] may be spurious. The adversary in fact may not have harbored an intention to act and, hence, did not need to be deterred from doing so by the defending power. Even if the adversary wished to see a change in the status quo, he may have been dissuaded from initiating or seriously threatening military action by other considerations —i.e., not by the expected costs the defender might impose but rather by ideological, political, moral, or legal considerations; or by pragmatic considerations, such as a belief that scarce resources should be allocated to other national objectives. If any of these considerations were dominant in the initiator's decision-making, then it would be inappropriate and misleading to regard the absence of a challenge to deterrence as a valid instance of deterrence success. Conversely, if a deterrence policy is activated and no challenge is made to it, one cannot conclude that no challenge would have come in any case, and hence the deterrence effort was unncessary.

Because of the practical difficulty of identifying genuine deterrence successes, we have not attempted a systematic comparison between cases of deterrence success and deterrence failure.[8] However, inferences along these lines are possible in-

---

[7] Russett, "Calculus of Deterrence," p. 98.

[8] Such a comparison was indeed attempted by Russett in "Calculus of Deterrence"; but this study did not deal adequately with the problem of valid identification of genuine successes. It may be noted that Russett defined "deterrence success" as "an instance when an attack on the pawn is prevented *or repulsed* without conflict between the attacking forces and regular combat units of the major power 'defender' " (emphasis added; p. 98). This somewhat idio-

sofar as some of the historical cases studied may be regarded as instances of mixed outcomes—partly a deterrence success, with respect to certain options the initiators may have been deterred from using, and partly a deterrence failure, in view of the action the initiator did take. It should be noted, too, that the diagnosis of deterrence failures will be in terms of variables and conditions that are relevant also in deterrence success. The propositions that will be stated in the next chapter will identify the implications of these conditions for both deterrence success and deterrence failure. But, of course, since the implications for deterrence success rest on a more slender empirical base—because we have necessarily restricted the study largely to historical cases of deterrence failure—our explanatory theory can be asserted more confidently for understanding deterrence failure.

---

syncratic definition leads him to include a number of historical cases as deterrence successes that other investigators would regard as instances of deterrence failure or partial failure. Four of Russett's six cases of "deterrence success" are of this character: the Soviet blockade of Berlin, in which, according to Russett's definition, the U.S. successfully deterred (i.e., "repulsed)" the USSR; the Anglo-French attack on Egypt in 1956, which Russett regards as having been successfully deterred ("repulsed") by the USSR; the Chinese Communist artillery blockade of Quemoy in 1958, according to Russett successfully deterred by the United States; the U.S. Bay of Pigs fiasco in which, Russett asserts, the Soviet Union successfully deterred the United States.

We believe that understanding of deterrence processes and development of an explanatory theory of deterrence require a much stricter definition of "deterrence success" than Russett's. In all four cases, we think it is much more useful to regard the initiator's action challenging the status quo as a failure or at least partial failure of deterrence, even though stronger military options for changing the status quo available to the initiator were not employed.

In our judgment Russett confuses the successful outcome of a defender's response as deterrence begins to fail with the success or failure of his previous effort to deter the attack in the first place. To blur, as Russett does, the question of successful *defense* with the prior question of successful *deterrence* makes it impossible to employ inductive procedures to develop an explanatory theory of deterrence. (For other criticisms of Russett's article, see Fink, "More Calculations about Deterrence.)

Moreover, as the reader will recall, we include as examples of deterrence failure cases such as the Berlin blockade, in which the initiator avoids direct use of force, because such actions would force the defender to consider using force himself to maintain a threatened position. They also heighten tension and the probability of a major war, and hence are appropriately included as lesser deterrence failures.

Bibliography

Eckstein, Harry. "Case-Study and Theory in Macropolitics," in Fred I. Greenstein and Nelson Polsby, *A Handbook of Political Science* (forthcoming).

Fink, Clinton F. "More Calculations about Deterrence," *Journal of Conflict Resolution,* March 1965.

George, Alexander L., D. K. Hall and W. E. Simons. *The Limits of Coercive Diplomacy.* Boston, Little, Brown, 1971.

Hermann, Charles F., ed. *International Crises: Insights from Behavioral Research.* New York, Free Press, 1972.

Kendall, Patricia, and Katherine M. Wolf. "The Analysis of Deviant Cases in Communications Research," in *Communications Research, 1948–49,* ed. Paul F. Lazarsfeld and Frank Stanton. New York, Harper & Bros., 1949.

Russett, Bruce. "The Calculus of Deterrence," *Journal of Conflict Resolution,* VII, No. 2 (June 1963).

Schlesinger, Arthur M. *A Thousand Days.* Boston, Houghton Mifflin, 1965.

Verba, Sidney. "Some Dilemmas in Comparative Research," *World Politics,* October 1967.

Chapter 17

Initiation Theory and the Conditions
of Deterrence Outcomes

The Problem of Initiation
in Deterrence Theory

WE HAVE NOW SHOWN why we seek an explanatory theory of deterrence employing "conditional generalizations" regarding deterrence outcomes. One of our principal goals is the differentiation and identification of separate patterns of deterrence outcomes and the elucidation of the principal properties of each. We seek, in short, a typology of deterrence situations, which we believe can be of material policy relevance.

Logically, the most critical component of any such typology is, of course, the identification of the basic variables which are responsible for the existence of the different types—that is, the identification of the basic causal factors, or "conditions," that generate each type. In this chapter we introduce and examine these conditions; in the next, we demonstrate how they generate several different types of deterrence situation.

We start from the premise that the initiating and not the defending nation is the locus of the conditions we are looking for. We shall, in effect, take the initiator's behavior as the dependent variable. The reasons for this can be adduced either from the diagrammatic model of the deterrence process presented in chapter 4 or from the case studies of Part Two taken as a whole. It is the initiator's behavior that determines, in the immediate sense of the word, whether or not an attempt to change the status quo will be made and what means will be employed to that end. The defender's behavior, insofar as it influences the initiator and whether intended as deterrence or not, is to be regarded as an independent variable which, together with other variables, affects the initiator's behavior.

Accordingly, a critical component of our explanatory theory of deterrence will be what can be called "initiation theory"— i.e., theory about the conditions under which a potential initiator is likely to undertake different kinds of challenges to deterrence. We will, of course, select and abstract elements which we believe we can show on the basis of the case studies normally to be critical components in the initiator's decision-making process when a challenge to deterrence is being contemplated. In the interests of parsimony we shall focus on these, and not overburden the process of constructing explanatory theory by asking that it attempt to cover all aspects of the initiator's decision-making process.

POSTULATES OF INITIATION THEORY

Like any theory, initiation theory must be based on assumptions or postulates. We shall employ a single basic assumption and two corollaries. All three of these postulates are simple, demonstrably relevant, and empirically verifiable from the cases presented in this study or, we believe, from any case.

The basic assumption is a very elementary one: *Nations interested in changing the status quo normally have more than one option for doing so.* The relevance of this observation to the design of defenders' deterrence policies is self-evident. The defender's strategy must be made relevant to the *range* of alternative options possibly available to the initiator. A deterrence policy which discourages an opponent from employing some options but not others is incomplete and may not prevent a failure of deterrence. An opponent who is bent upon altering a given status quo may design around the viable aspects of the deterrence strategy that confronts him. That is, he may seek to formulate an option for challenging the status quo that takes advantage of loopholes, weaknesses, or uncertainties that he perceives in the deterrence strategy of the defending power.

Not only does the availability of multiple options to the initiator complicate the task of deterrence strategy for the defender, it makes possible a *mixed* deterrence outcome, part success and part failure. This is the case when the defender succeeds in deterring certain actions by the initiator but not others. Several of the cases in Part Two may perhaps be scored as having mixed outcomes of this kind. Thus in the Taiwan Straits crises of 1954–1955 and 1958 it is possible that the Chinese Communists were deterred from engaging in an all-out invasion of the offshore islands, but the deterrence strategy employed by the United States in those two situations did not succeed in deterring Peking's artillery action against the islands or the other measures it employed as part of a strategy of controlled pressure. Similarly, one might say that in the Berlin crises of 1958–1959 and 1961 U.S. deterrence strategy may have deterred the Soviets from imposing a blockade upon West Berlin. It did not, however, succeed in deterring the Soviets from threats to do so that were effective enough to draw the Western powers into negotiations on changing the status of West Berlin. Nor did the otherwise strong U.S. deterrence strategy vis-à-vis encroachments on West Berlin deter the Soviets from erecting the Berlin Wall in August 1961. Finally, whether or not the Eisenhower Doctrine was needed to deter the possibility of overt Soviet military actions in the Middle East, it was incapable of deterring Soviet economic and military assistance or covert activities.

A corollary to the principle of multiple options open to the initiator is that the effectiveness of each option, from his viewpoint, is likely to differ. If the initiator has three options for challenging the status quo (for instance, an all-out military attack, a limited military probe, and an indirect, politico-diplomatic approach), the probability that the defender's deterrence strategy will succeed in deterring him may vary considerably among the three. The initiator is likely to assign quite different utilities to his several options. That is, his estimate of the expected benefits, costs, and risks, and of the probabilities of success, may vary widely among the options. His perception of the impact of the defender's deterrence attempt may vary substantially from option to option.

A second corollary is that the initiator is likely to weigh and assess his various options on the basis of his estimate of their utilities, given the defender's apparent deterrence policy. That is, the initiator is capable of taking a *calculated risk* based on his assessment of the likelihood, nature, and acceptability of the defender's response to the particular option the initiator is contemplating.

Major Conditions
Affecting Deterrence Outcomes

The thrust of the basic postulate of multiple options on the part of the initiator and its corollaries is to draw attention to the potential complexity of the initiator's decision whether and how to challenge deterrence. Of course, one could identify an almost endless number of considerations that can enter into such decisions. But an explanatory theory that will have diagnostic power for policy-makers must strive to reduce the most significant considerations to a manageable number. On the basis of the case studies, we have identified two major and six minor conditions that normally have a strong "leverage" effect upon the initiator's decision, and hence upon the outcome of any deterrence challenge. The two major conditions will be discussed in some detail because of their intrinsic importance, and because they will become the basis of our typology of deterrence situations. We will treat the six minor conditions in less detail at the close of this chapter. After discussing each condition, we shall then state its implications for deterrence theory in the form of *propositions,* nine of which altogether will be presented in this chapter.

The two major conditions are: (1) the initiator's view of the exact nature of the defender's commitment, if any, on behalf of its ally or friend; and (2) the initiator's judgment of whether the risks of a particular option open to him can be calculated and/or controlled so as to make that option an acceptable risk.

These conditions, and the six minor ones to follow later, are variables in the initiator's decision-making process. The manner in which these variables change from case to case—the values they take on—is the principal subject of what we have called initiation theory.

THE FIRST CONDITION: THE INITIATOR'S VIEW OF THE DEFENDER'S COMMITMENT

It has been widely believed that wars involving the United States occurred in the past because an opponent came to believe that the United States was not committed to come to the defense of the country that was attacked and would not make a serious effort to defend it. This broad generalization, which we discussed earlier in another context, came into vogue after World War II as an explanation for the origin of that war as well as World War I. The "war is a result of miscalculation" thesis was powerfully reinforced by the Korean War. It was taken up by John Foster Dulles, among others, and he drew from it the practical lesson that major wars in the future might well be avoided if the United States made clear to potential aggressors in advance that it *was* committed to defend an ally against "aggression." Explicit commitments of this kind, according to this policy theory, would prevent the opponent from miscalculating, and hence war would be avoided.

A similar proposition was accepted somewhat uncritically in the normative-prescriptive deterrence theory we reviewed in

Part One. Accepting the premise that the defender's commitment was critical for deterrence, the theory moved quickly to
discussing the technical problem of achieving "credibility" for
the commitment in the eyes of the potential initiator. Deterrence theorists made little effort to subject to critical analysis
the "war is a result of miscalculation" thesis, which had entered
securely into the conventional wisdom on these matters. Most
deterrence theorists were probably aware of the fact that the
thesis did not apply to all cases of war initiation. In 1941, for example, the Japanese government was not deterred from moving
into southeast Asia by the deterrence commitment the United
States had made. Nor did the Japanese question the credibility
of the U.S. commitment. On the contrary, they regarded it as
quite credible! Frustrated by the American deterrence effort
and also feeling severely threatened by the simultaneous coercive diplomacy to which the United States was subjecting it, the
Japanese government was provoked into attacking the United
States rather than being deterred.[1]

While the Pearl Harbor case has often been singled out for
intelligent comment as an example of the risks of deterrence
strategy or as an example of the "irrationality" that governmental leaders (i.e., the Japanese) are capable of, its implications for the "war is a result of miscalculation" thesis have not
been adequately resolved. Some writers attempted to save the
thesis by stretching the notion of "miscalculation" to cover a
broader range of incorrect assumptions and calculations that
may lead a government to initiate war. The fact remains, however, that the Japanese initiation of war flatly contradicted the
theoretical assumption that a credible commitment by the defender is a necessary and sufficient condition for deterrence
success. From the standpoint of theory development, Pearl Harbor constitutes what in chapter 16 we called a "deviant case,"
but one whose potential value for developing a more differen-

[1] For a brief discussion of the origins of the Japanese attack against Pearl Harbor from the standpoint of the theory of coercive diplomacy, see George, Hall,
and Simons, *Limits of Coercive Diplomacy*, pp. 245–46.

tiated and more valid deterrence theory has not been utilized adequately by deterrence theorists.[2]

The generalization "war is the result of miscalculation" is at best a partial truth. Other historical cases besides Pearl Harbor fail to support the hypothesis that deterrence failures are the result of initiator's belief that a credible deterrence commitment is lacking. In many of the case studies presented in Part Two clear U.S. commitments did not prevent serious encroachments of various kinds. The history of the Cold War indicates that communist leaders indeed have always paid attention to whether an American commitment existed. But they have also subjected American commitments to close analysis to assess the implications for their own behavior. As our case studies indicate, communist leaders have tried to differentiate between U.S. deterrence commitments that were unequivocal and those that were uncertain or incompletely formulated. They have also differentiated between U.S. commitments that appeared to be firm and those that might turn out to be "soft" and unstable in the sense that they could be eroded when subjected to carefully chosen pressures. Finally, communist leaders have also shrewdly perceived that some American commitments, while firm and unequivocal, would be difficult to implement against the option with which they chose to challenge the status quo. Deterrence strategy often has difficulty in achieving comprehensive coverage against all the options available to the initiator. Some of the ways in which the status quo can be challenged are either very difficult for the defending power to deter or are, as we have suggested several times in this study, essentially nondeterrable.

Our examination of historical cases in Part Two indicated that, with few exceptions, communist leaders acted to alter the status quo on many occasions *even* in the face of a U.S. commitment. (The major exceptions were the North Korean attack on

[2] For an interesting and partially successful attempt to do so, see Russett, "Pearl Harbor"; see also John Mueller's discussion of the "rationality" of the Japanese decision to go to war in his *Deterrence, Numbers and History*.

South Korea, the Soviet intervention in Hungary, the Chinese Communist invasion of the Tachen Islands, the erection of the Berlin Wall.) On these occasions communist leaders chose their action on the basis of rationally calculated risks to suit the occasion. This was the case in the Berlin crises, the Chinese Communist intervention in Korea, the controlled pressures in the two Taiwan crises, indirect Chinese assistance to the Viet Minh in Indochina, and in the Soviet deployment of missiles into Cuba.

An American commitment per se, therefore, is clearly insufficient to prevent failure of deterrence. If the opponent has an option for challenging the status quo that seems to him likely to advance his interests at an acceptable cost-benefit ratio, deterrence can fail even in the presence of a credible U.S. commitment. And it can fail even though the opponent realizes that his initiative entails some risk of consequences that he considers unacceptable, if he believes he can avoid them by careful management of the crisis triggered by his action.[3]

We conclude, therefore, that empirical and explanatory deterrence theory must include among its important propositions the following:

PROPOSITION 1: The initiator's perception of defender's commitment may be a necessary condition for deterrence success but it is *not a sufficient* condition for deterrence success.

PROPOSITION 2: The initiator's perception of the defender's commitment, however, may severely constrain his choice of options.

These propositions indicate that the initiator's evaluation of the defender's commitment exercises a more decisive influence on *how* deterrence fails than on whether it fails.

[3] For more detailed attention to "commitments," see chapter 19.

THE SECOND CONDITION:
THE INITIATOR'S VIEW OF THE
CALCULABILITY OR CONTROLLABILITY OF HIS RISKS

We find this condition, on the other hand, to be more decisive than the first in accounting for *whether* deterrence succeeds or fails. In almost every historical case examined, we found evidence that the initiator tried to satisfy himself before acting that the risks of the particular option he chose could be calculated and, perhaps even more importantly, controlled by him so as to give his choice of action the character of a rationally calculated, acceptable risk.[4]

It must be acknowledged that evidence bearing on the risk calculations of communist leaders in the cases examined in Part Two is indirect and circumstantial for the most part; better historical materials on their decision-making are simply not available. While we hope the interpretations of the communist government's calculations offered in the case studies are at least plausible, it is possible that other investigators will argue that one or another initiative taken by the communist side during the Cold War entailed risks which the leaders of that government did not believe to be calculated or controllable.

Our theory by no means excludes the possibility of cases in which the initiator feels compelled to challenge the status quo, even though he cannot calculate the risks and assure himself that he can manage to avoid incurring large or catastrophic costs. One might be inclined to assume that this kind of challenge to deterrence could come about only when the initiator's motivation is extremely strong—when there is a quality of desperation in his need to change a situation which he finds intolerable.

The Japanese attack on Pearl Harbor comes to mind as a *possible* example of this kind of decision. A closer examination of the rich historical material available on the Japanese decision, however, does not entirely support this view. Bruce Rus-

---

[4] It goes without saying that the initiator's belief that this is so may reflect poor judgment or wishful thinking or may, for whatever reason, prove to be incorrect.

sett finds that Japanese decision-making leading to the attack on Pearl Harbor displayed the characteristics of a rationally considered and calculated decision.[5]

Evidently, we must distinguish in the Pearl Harbor case, and no doubt in others, between (1) a willingness to take what are calculated to be very high risks (which seems to have characterized Japanese leaders in this instance), and (2) a willingness to act when unable to calculate the risks. Regarding the second of these, it is possible that greater constraints on the initiator's willingness to act might develop if he were able to calculate the risks and to see more clearly that he could not control or avoid the worst of them. In this case a more effective deterrence strategy might make a difference, since it would not be clear whether the initiator's motivation was strong enough to override a specific estimate of high risks entailed. In contrast, when the decision to initiate reflects, as in the Pearl Harbor case, a willingness to *accept* very high risks, the initiator's motivation dominates the defender's effort to impose risks through his deterrence strategy.

Although we assert the critical importance of the second condition for deterrence failure, we do not claim that this is always true. The Cold War cases of deterrence failure or partial deterrence failure examined in Part Two do not permit complete confidence in this assertion, since almost all the communist initiatives in our sample were, after all, instances of what communist leaders believed to be relatively *low*-risk strategies. Either their motivation to change the status quo was not so strong or the time pressure they experienced for changing it was not so urgent as to lead them to initiate *high*-risk strategies. A possible exception to this is the Chinese Communist intervention in the Korean War. It would appear that in both respects—strength and urgency—Peking's motivation was sufficient to lead it to accept at least moderately high risks. Interpretations of Peking's behavior on this occasion differ. Some analysts argue that the Chinese knowingly took very high

[5] Russett, "Pearl Harbor," pp. 89–91, 100.

risks which, moreover, they were not at all confident of being able to control. However, the preponderance of scholarly opinion seems to agree that the Chinese leaders were attempting to some extent to calculate and control the worst risks of their intervention, thus suggesting that they wished to accept only moderately high risks. A third possibility exists. Those identifying with General MacArthur's viewpoint in the controversy that has developed over American policy in the Korean War argue that the Chinese intervened only because they had been assured, by inept or treasonous behavior on the American side, that the American reaction would be a mild one—i.e., that Peking pursued a low-risk strategy.

Another case in which communist motivation appears to have been unusually strong as well as urgent was, of course, the decision to erect the Berlin Wall in August 1961. However, there are indications that the risks were considered to be largely calculable and controllable. We are probably justified in regarding this as a calculated risk, a view that supports our observation of the great rarity of uncalculated, uncontrollable challenges to deterrence.

We conclude, therefore, that empirical and explanatory deterrence theory must include among its important propositions the following:

PROPOSITION 3: The initiator's belief that the risks of his action are calculable and that the unacceptable risks of it can be controlled and avoided is, with very few exceptions, a *necessary* (though not sufficient) condition for a decision to challenge deterrence, i.e., a deterrence failure.

PROPOSITION 4: The initiator's belief that the risks of options available to him are not calculable or controllable is usually a sufficient condition for deterrence success, with respect to *those options*.

If this latter belief applies to all the options available to him, then it is a condition sufficient for a complete deterrence success. (It is not a necessary condition, since deterrence can succeed for other reasons, such as when the initiator calculates the costs to be too high.) More frequently, however, the initiator may believe that certain options are incalculable or uncontrollable but that others are not. Accordingly:

PROPOSITION 5: The initiator's desire to be able to calculate and control the risks of any option he employs will constrain his choice among options.

Minor Conditions Affecting Deterrence Outcomes

In addition to the two major conditions regarding the initiator's perceptions of the range of the deterrent commitment and the calculability and controllability of his risks, there are six additional conditions which, though less critical, are quite important. In the interests of space we will simply present them here, with little discussion. They have received attention in the case studies and will be mentioned again in later chapters. These six "minor" conditions are variables that may favor or disfavor the success of a deterrence policy. Unlike the major conditions, they do not involve sufficiency or necessity.

The third condition. The initiator's perception of the adequacy and appropriateness of the defender's military capabilities. Just as the defender's commitments may be designed around, so may his capabilities, even if his commitments are more complete.

The fourth condition. The initiator's perception of the adequacy of the defender's motivation. Despite appropriate commitments and capabilities, the defender may be expected to be constrained in executing deterrence by vacillating will, or by domestic or allied political opinion.

PROPOSITION 6: Deterrence success will be favored but not insured by the belief of the initiator that the defender possesses (*a*) an adequate and appropriate spectrum of capabilities; [6] (*b*) sufficient motivation to employ them; and (*c*) probable freedom from impeding political constraints in the relevant time period.

PROPOSITION 7: Deterrence failure will be favored, but not insured, by the absence of any one of these three beliefs on the part of the initiator.

The fifth condition. The initiator's perception that only force or the threat of it can bring about the desired change. If the defender can supplement deterrence of coercive challenges with inducement to noncoercive initiatives in acceptable directions, the initiator may never launch politico-diplomatic or military offensives in the unacceptable directions.

PROPOSITION 8: Deterrence success will be favored, but not insured, by the defender's supplementing deterrence with appropriate inducement policies vis-à-vis the potential initiator.

The sixth condition. The initiator's willingness to accept compensation elsewhere. When deterrence in a particular local area is essential to the defender, he may be able to offer compensation in another area in return for the initiator's pledge not to challenge the deterrence.

PROPOSITION 9: Deterrence success will be favored, but not insured, by the defender's offering compensation elsewhere as a *quid pro quo* in return for a tacit or explicit agreement by the potential initiator not to challenge deterrence.

---

[6] It should be noted that this proposition challenges the conventional wisdom, which holds that successful deterrence is a function of the defender's possession of ample military capabilities and increased defensive options. In fact, paradoxically, improved capabilities for selective or graduated response by the defender may at times increase the likelihood that the initiator will challenge deterrence by a low-level move. This would follow if the initiator were led to believe that the defender would confine his initial response also to a low level, thus making it possible for the initiator to calculate and control the risks of his opening move. See Schelling, *Arms and Influence*, p. 44.

The seventh condition. The strength and nature of the initiator's motivation to change the status quo.

The eighth condition. The time pressure the initiator feels for achieving his desired change. The seventh and eighth conditions are likely to be outside the defender's control in many (but not necessarily all) cases, but the defender will want to include them in estimating the probability, nature, and timing of any expected challenges to deterrence.

The Significance of Initiation Theory

These nine propositions summarize initiation theory as it emerges in the present study. Initiation theory is different from, and richer than, the implicit notions about the initiator contained in abstract-deductivist deterrence theory. As discussed in chapter 3, that theory implicitly suggests that potential initiators challenge deterrence if they do not perceive a very visible "signal" or do not find the signal "credible." But empirical investigation does not suggest that communicating signals and making them credible are the most visible, urgent, or policy-significant factors influencing the behavior of potential initiators. They play a role in the nine propositions, but it is not a dominant one.

On the contrary, if a single factor must be chosen as dominant, our investigation suggests it should be not signaling or credibility but *the initiator's possession of multiple options.* It is because his options nearly always are multiple, not single, that most of the above propositions arise. Commitments and/or capabilities may have an insufficiently broad range to buttress deterrence; some of the initiator's options may have inherently controllable and calculable risks attached; and so forth. "The logic of the initiator's multiple options," furthermore, is a concept with diagnostic power for the policy-maker.

Bibliography

George, Alexander L., D. K. Hall, and W. E. Simons. *The Limits of Coercive Diplomacy*. Boston, Little, Brown, 1971.

Mueller, John. *Deterrence, Numbers and History*. Security Studies Project No. 12. Los Angeles, University of California at Los Angeles, 1968.

Russett, Bruce M. "Pearl Harbor: Deterrence Theory and Decision Theory." *Journal of Peace Research*, No. 2 (1967).

Schelling, Thomas C. *Arms and Influence*. New Haven, Yale University Press, 1966.

Chapter 18

Patterns of Deterrence Failure:
A Typology

Sources for a Typology

WE ARE NOW EQUIPPED with a list of the conditions that appear to be most critical in a potential initiator's decision to challenge deterrence. We also observe that these conditions very strongly influence his *choice* among the multiple options available to him. From the defender's viewpoint, these conditions are therefore major indicators of whether deterrence will succeed or fail; and if it is to fail, how it will fail. Many of the propositions developed in the last chapter deal with whether deterrence is likely to succeed or fail. But additional explanatory and diagnostic assistance to policy-makers can be made available by identifying common patterns of *how* deterrence fails.

In this chapter we identify some principal patterns of deterrence failure, labeled according to the type of initiative the initiator takes. These types of initiatives are determined by the type of calculated risk the initiator decides he can run, which in turn is determined largely by the various possible arrangements of the conditions we have already identified. Or, schematically:

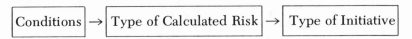

This diagram depicts the logical structure of our explanatory theory of how deterrence fails. The content of this theory is necessarily derived empirically by analyzing in these terms the historical material presented in Part Two. There we offered detailed explanations of the often complex origins of each crisis and the circumstances leading the initiator to challenge deterrence. We did not hesitate to include idiosyncratic, background, and contextual factors in each interpretation in order to achieve a reasonably comprehensive historical explanation of many aspects of deterrence operating in each case. Now, however, to develop an explanatory theory we must adopt a somewhat different procedure. We shall focus selectively only on those portions of the cases that relate to the theory structure depicted above. In each case, we shall abstract from the narrative of how deterrence failed, the conditions, type of calculated risk, and type of initiatives that led to that particular failure.

In developing these patterns, we did not expect to find as many as there are historical cases. It is true that in the qualitative approach to theory development followed in this study, each historical case was treated as if it were a possible deviant case from which a new causal pattern might be extracted. But we were prepared to find essentially the same causal pattern imbedded in the historical explanations of several cases. Moreover, the number of possible patterns is constrained by the relatively few "conditions" employed in the theory and the few variants of each condition that are postulated. The number of patterns depends in part on how detailed a typology of deterrence failures we choose to specify. Our preference is to develop as simple a typology and as parsimonious a theory as possible, so long as this does not reduce the validity or diagnostic power of the theory.

We have thus identified three basic patterns of deterrence failure. Most of the historical cases examined in Part Two, we shall note, can be subsumed under one of these three patterns.[1]

---

[1] If our detailed historical explanation of a case is incorrect and some other explanation is more plausible, that case of course will have to be reassigned to another basic pattern. However, the explanatory power of the theory as a whole

In some cases, however, the failure of deterrence passed through several phases, each of which fits a different pattern. The three patterns are generated by alternative configurations of the two major conditions identified in the previous chapter— the initiator's view of the exact nature of the defender's deterrence commitment, and the initiator's judgment of the calculability and controllability of his risks. The remaining, minor conditions either concern whether (as opposed to how) deterrence is challenged, or else generate variations in the three basic patterns.

Pattern One:
The Fait Accompli Attempt

The prototypical historical case for establishing this pattern is the North Korean attack on South Korea in June 1950. According to our interpretation, the initiator (whether North Korea alone, as some revisionist historians contend, or North Korea and the Soviet Union) believed that there was no commitment by the defending power (United States) to come to the military defense of South Korea. Given this view of defender's *non*military commitment, the type of initiative that recommended itself to the initiating side was a variant of what has

---

is not dependent upon the correctness of any of these historical explanations. Theory-building does not require that historical explanations of individual cases fulfill the historian's ideal of a "definitive" explanation, which in any case historians seldom achieve. Rather, it suffices for our theory-building enterprise that the historical explanations be plausible and consonant with the available historical data and relevant knowledge, and that alternative explanations of a plausible nature also be considered. If one had sufficient confidence in the design and implementation of laboratory-type deterrence games, they too could be used for theory-building purposes. While we have not made use of laboratory data of this kind for this study, the "synthetic history" so generated is in principle relevant and, indeed, sometimes indispensable for theory development. On the use of simulations for theory-building in international relations see Guetzkow, "Some Correspondences between Simulations and 'Realities,' " pp. 202–69.

Pattern One: The Fait Accompli Attempt *

Conditions	Type of Calculated Risk	Type of Deterrence Failure
Re No. 1: Initiator believes *no* commitment by defender exists	The best option is to make a maximum effort to achieve the objective quickly so as to deprive the defender of time and opportunity to reverse his policy of no commitment and to make an ad hoc decision to block initiator's action	A fait accompli
Re No. 2: Initiator believes risks of option he chooses are calculable and controllable		

*Cases: (1) North Korean attack; (2) Cuban missile deployment (Phase 1); (3) Soviet intervention in Hungary; (4) Chinese Communist invasion of Tachens (1955).

been called the "quick, decisive" military strategy.[2] The North Koreans mounted a substantial attack in the hope of overrunning the South Korean defenders and destroying the South Korean government as quickly as possible before the United States could organize an effective flow of military equipment to the South Koreans. .

The fait accompli strategy, it may be noted, *is* the most "rational" way to initiate an effort to change the status quo when the initiator believes that a strong potential defending power has written off the territory in question altogether or has made what appears to be a firm decision to limit his aid to military and economic assistance and diplomatic support. A maximum effort by the initiator to achieve his objective quickly confronts the potential defending power with a fait accompli, giving him little or no time to reconsider and reverse his policy of noninvolvement. From the standpoint of the initiator, the fait accompli strategy may well appear the least risky way in these circumstances to change the status quo.

[2] The alternative military strategies are: (1) the quick, decisive option; (2) coercive diplomacy; (3) war of attrition; (4) test of capabilities within restrictive ground rules. For discussion see George, Hall, and Simon, *The Limits of Coercive Diplomacy,* pp. 15–21.

The appeal and relevance of the North Koreans' fait accompli strategy are explicitly recognized in Khrushchev's account of the calculations behind Stalin's approval of the North Korean plan:

> I remember Stalin had his doubts. He was worried that the Americans would jump in, but we were inclined to think that if the war were fought swiftly—and Kim Il-sung was sure that it could be won swiftly—then intervention by the USA could be avoided.[3]

The third condition—the adequacy and appropriateness of the defender's capabilities—may reinforce or complicate the attractiveness of the fait accompli strategy for the initiator. In the North Korean case, it reinforced it; in the Cuban missile deployment case, on the other hand, it complicated the strategy and imposed additional requirements for its effective use. In the North Korean case, we noted that there was good reason for Soviet and North Korean leaders to believe it would be difficult for the American government, even if it reversed its policy of no military commitment to South Korea, to mobilize and deploy effective military forces into South Korea in time to block the North Koreans' fait accompli attempt. In other words, with respect to the second condition, the risks of the fait accompli option were so calculable that there needed to be no special concern about the ability to "control" undesired risks of a timely and effective American military intervention.

A variant of the fait accompli strategy can be seen in the Soviet deployment of medium and intermediate range missiles into Cuba. We find it useful to distinguish between two phases of Soviet decision-making in this case. (The second phase will be discussed under Pattern Three.) In the first phase, prior to President Kennedy's deterrent warnings in early September 1962, the Soviets may have judged that there was no U.S. commitment (or its equivalent) to prevent such weapons from being deployed to Cuba. Khrushchev and other leaders may have persuaded themselves that their justification for doing so was so in-

---

[3] *Khrushchev Remembers*, p. 368. The full authenticity of these reminiscences is uncertain.

contestable, given the fact that the United States had many times deployed elements of its strategic nuclear force to overseas bases near the Soviet Union. Soviet leaders might have assumed, as they later openly argued, that the rules of the game regarding such deployments must surely be the same for both sides. According to this interpretation, the Soviet leaders assumed—with good reason, they thought—that there was no tacit commitment on Kennedy's part to oppose such a deployment.

At the same time, however, the Soviet government knew that the large missile deployment it was contemplating was designed to achieve quite ambitious objectives at the expense of American interests. As Khrushchev concedes in his reminiscences, the Soviet objective in deploying the missiles was not merely to protect Cuba from a possible American invasion but also to equalize the balance of power. Since much would be at stake for the United States, it might decide not to observe the "rules" once it became aware of the missile deployment, its dimensions, and its implications. Moreover, in this case, in contrast to the North Korean one, the United States had ample capabilities for a quick and effective response to block the missile deployment, should it decide to do so. This consideration not only strengthened the rationale for a rapid missile deployment to confront the United States with a fait accompli, but it also argued for secrecy and deception.[4] In this case, therefore, the third condition, regarding capabilities, complicated the initiator's assessment of the utility of the option and imposed the additional requirement of secrecy as a precondition for its being accepted as a calculated, controlled risk.

Two other cases discussed in Part Two deserve brief mention here: the Soviet intervention in Hungary in 1956 and the Chinese Communist invasion of the Tachen Islands in January 1955. Strictly speaking, these two cases cannot be regarded as deterrence failures, since the United States did not attempt to

---

[4] As Khrushchev reportedly puts it, ". . . I had the idea of installing missiles with nuclear warheads in Cuba without letting the United States find out they were there until it was too late to do anything about them." *Khrushchev Remembers*, p. 493.

apply deterrence. In fact, its purpose was quite the opposite. In both cases the U.S. deliberately clarified matters for the initiator's risk calculations by a timely, authoritative communication that it had no commitment and was not attempting to employ deterrence strategy. These two cases could be regarded as variants of Pattern One in that the two conditions, type of calculation, and choice of initiation strategy in the two cases conform to those that characterize that pattern.

Pattern Two:
The Limited Probe

This pattern occurs when the initiator creates a controlled crisis in order to clarify the defender's commitments.

The prototypical cases for this pattern are probably the two crises in the Taiwan Strait. In the 1954–1955 crisis the controlled military pressure exerted in the Taiwan Strait obliged the Eisenhower Administration to clarify its commitment to various islands, which it did in different ways. The existing U.S. commitment to Taiwan and the Pescadores was reinforced and formalized in a treaty. The Tachen Islands were written off and the United States Navy helped evacuate Nationalist forces stationed there before they were taken over by Chinese Communist military forces. The offshore islands—the Quemoy and Matsu island groups—were given, on the face of it, a conditional U.S. commitment; that is, the United States would defend them if the President judged an attack on them to be part of an attack on Taiwan and the Pescadores. After obtaining this clarification of the U.S. commitments, the Chinese Communists invaded the Tachens (exemplifying Pattern One, as noted earlier) but made no attempt to expand their probe into stronger and more ambitious operations against the offshore islands or, of course, Taiwan itself. The Chinese Communist artillery shelling of the offshore islands was limited in nature and easily reversible. Chinese Communist leaders obviously believed the risks of their actions to be calculable and controllable.

Pattern Two: The Limited Probe *

Conditions	Type of Calculated Risk	Type of Deterrence Failure
Re No. 1: Initiator believes defender's commitment is uncertain	The best option is controlled application of limited force that will require defender to clarify the ambiguity of his commitment	A limited (reversible or expandable) probe
Re No. 2: Initiator believes risks of option he chooses are calculable and controllable		

* Cases: (1) Berlin blockade 1948 (Phase 1); (2) Taiwan Strait 1954–1955 (Phase 1); (3) Quemoy 1958 (Phase 1); (4) Berlin Wall 1961.

A similar statement can be made about the first phase of the Quemoy crisis in 1958. The initial purpose of the heavy artillery shelling of Quemoy was to find out whether the conditional commitment that Eisenhower had entered into in the earlier 1954–1955 crisis still applied or whether Washington was willing to stand aside and let the Chinese Communists attempt to wrest the offshore islands from the Nationalist defenders stationed there. Peking's initiative was very much a limited probe; it could be easily reversed or expanded, depending on how the United States clarified its commitment. The United States made it clear in early September that its earlier commitment still applied. Thereupon, the crisis entered into a second and different phase, which will be discussed later as exemplifying Pattern Three.

Since ample means were available to Washington for responding punitively, if it wished, to the Chinese Communist initiative in both Taiwan Strait crises, the third condition in our theory (regarding appropriate capabilities) is particularly relevant. Peking's awareness that the United States had potent options at its disposal served to reinforce its judgment that a limited, easily reversible probe was the best strategy in this complex and somewhat ambiguous deterrence situation. Rational assessment by Peking of the initiation strategies available to it clearly had to exclude resort to the fait accompli tactic that had appeared optimal in the North Korean case. Given Peking's uncertainty as to a U.S. commitment to defend the offshore islands, it would have been much too risky and imprudent to have launched an all-out attempt to grab them without first clarifying U.S. intentions through a limited, carefully controlled probe. The risks of the artillery shelling used for this purpose were more modest, more easily calculated, and certainly more controllable, since the shelling could easily be called off if the U.S. showed any signs of a military overreaction.

If the limited, reversible probe is ideally suited to occasions of this kind, it can be a poor choice for the initiator in other situations when, as in Korea in 1950, the defender is believed to have no commitment. In the latter circumstances, a cautious, slowly unfolding effort to alter the status quo has the disadvantage of giving the defender plenty of time and opportunity to make an ad hoc decision to reverse his no-commitment policy and to assemble and deploy the forces needed to intervene.

A variant of Pattern Two is the case of the Berlin Wall. While the Western powers had given various intimations that their commitment to West Berlin did not include opposition to the erection of a barrier between East and West Berlin, Soviet and East German leaders probably remained in some uncertainty as to how the Western powers would respond. The manner in which the Wall was erected suggests that initially the Soviets were proceeding on the basis of a limited, reversible probe rather than attempting a quick fait accompli. When the Allies indicated that, however much they deplored the erection of a Wall, they would not physically interfere or attempt to coerce the communist side to take it down, the East German regime proceeded to erect a more substantial barrier to replace the flimsy one first erected.

Much the same pattern appears in the initial phase of the Berlin Blockade in 1948, although the circumstances and the nature of the initiative were somewhat different. Certainly the initial, temporary "baby blockade" of early April seems to have been a cautious limited probe. (Indeed, Soviet interference with Allied access to the city on that occasion may not have been intended as a blockade.) Similarly, even the full blockade of all ground access to West Berlin that began in late June retained a flexible, reversible character which permitted the Soviets to clarify whether it would be challenged by the Western powers in a way that would pose undue risks. When it became clear that the Allied response would be a limited one and would exclude any dangerous form of escalation or resort to coercive diplomacy, the Soviet initiative entered a second phase which, as with the comparable aspects of the Cuban missile and Quemoy crises, is more appropriately discussed as an example of Pattern Three.

Pattern Three: Controlled Pressure

The prototypical examples of this pattern [5] are the Berlin crises of 1958 and 1961. In these and the other cases listed (see footnote to table), the initiator's view of the defender's commitment (condition 1) differs significantly from what it was in the other cases considered. Either at the outset of the crisis or after having clarified the defender's commitment through a limited probe, the initiating side regarded the deterrence commitment as *unequivocal*. (In Pattern One, the initiator's belief is that there is no commitment; in Pattern Two he believes that there is uncertainty or ambiguity regarding a commitment by the defender.) However, as we noted in chapter 17, the initiator's belief that the defender has made an unequivocal commitment does not always lead to a deterrence success for the defender. If strongly motivated and resourceful, the initiator may find an option that designs around the defender's commitment and his deterrence capabilities, and still satisfies the requirement of condition 2—namely, that the initiator must believe he has as his

[5] For a useful discussion of controlled pressure strategies, see Richardson, *Germany and the Atlantic Alliance*, pp. 245–63.

Pattern Three: Controlled Pressure *

Conditions	Type of Calculated Risk	Type of Deterrence Failure
Re No. 1: Initiator believes defender's commitment is unequivocal but "soft"	The best option is carefully applied pressure that attempts either (a) to convince defender that he will have great difficulty and incur unacceptable risks if he attempts to honor his commitments; or (b) to erode defender's commitment to the weak ally by undermining the ally's confidence in defender's ability and willingness to honor fully its commitment	Controlled pressure by various tactics, e.g., (a) blockade of defender's access to disputed territory; (b) diplomatic blackmail and counterdeterrence; (c) piecemeal restriction of defender's rights in and around disputed territory
Re No. 2: Initiator believes risks of option he chooses are calculable and controllable		

* Cases: (1) Berlin blockade (Phase 2); (2) Taiwan Strait (Phase 2); (3) Quemoy 1958 (Phase 2); (4) Berlin 1958; (5) Berlin 1961; (6) Cuban missile deployment (Phase 2).

disposal an option in which the risks are calculable and controllable.

For Pattern Three, therefore, conditions 3 and 4 become of particular collateral importance in determining whether deterrence will be challenged. Thus, deterrence is likely to fail first if the initiator believes that defender does not have effective options with which to respond to the particular strategy of controlled pressure the initiator expects to employ (condition 3); or second, if initiator believes that the defender may have usable options of this kind at his disposal but that there is a good chance of eroding defender's willingness and ability to use them (condition 4).

Let us review the Berlin crises of 1958–1959 and 1961 briefly from this standpoint. In contrast to the North Korean case (Pattern One) in which the initiating side believed there was no U.S. commitment, and in contrast also to the first phase of the two Taiwan Strait crises (Pattern Two) in which the initiator thought the U.S. commitment to the offshore islands was uncertain or ambiguous, the Soviets recognized in 1958 and again in 1961 the existence of an unequivocal, strong U.S. commitment on behalf of West Berlin. The commitment was not challenged by direct options at the disposal of the Soviet Union and its East German partner; presumably, the initiating side did not regard direct challenges as useful or relevant, or perhaps it was deterred from employing them in the belief that they were too risky. However, the Soviets believed that the U.S. commitment was potentially vulnerable to certain kinds of threats and pressures. The controlled pressure the Soviets and East Germans employed in these two crises was intended to erode the U.S. commitment and, in effect, to bypass it by forcing the West to negotiate a new status for West Berlin more acceptable to the communist side.

Thus, in designing its strategy for challenging deterrence the initiating side may take advantage of favorable asymmetries in the structure of the situation that can, perhaps, be turned to account by means of various controlled pressure tactics. In the Berlin crises the asymmetries that provided leverage for the Soviets included the isolated position of West Berlin, which lies deep in East Germany; latent disagreements among the Western powers regarding the value of maintaining their position intact in West Berlin and the level of risks that should be accepted; constraints of domestic public opinion on the policies and actions of the Western powers; and, of course, the fear that war might break out later if crisis interactions got out of hand.

When confronted by controlled pressure tactics, the defender's task of making deterrence effective can be severely complicated. It may be evident to everyone, the adversary included, that the defender will have great difficulty in "operationalizing" his strong, unequivocal commitment. Given the indirect and controlled pressure his commitment is subjected to, the defender's problem is not whether to resist a *military* encroachment. That has not yet occurred, though it may be threatened. Rather, the defender's problem is how to counter the initiator's *nonmilitary* encroachments by nonmilitary moves of his own; or, failing that, the defender faces the onerous decision of whether, when, where, and how to initiate use of force himself or other counterpressures (e.g., counterblockade, economic sanctions, other kinds of reprisals) that might weaken or put an end to the initiator's nonmilitary moves. Hence the importance of conditions 3 and 4.

Pattern Three can also be seen in "Phase 2" of several other crises. After clarifying and learning that a U.S. commitment did indeed exist in the Berlin blockade, Taiwan Strait, and Quemoy cases, the initiating side did *not* immediately call off its challenge. Rather, it converted its initial limited probe into a strategy of controlled pressure, having correctly observed that the commitment the defender signaled in response to the initial limited probe did not vitiate the initiator's ability to calculate and control the risks of a controlled pressure strategy. The comments we made about the dynamics of Pattern Three for the Berlin crises of 1958 and 1961 applies as well to Phase 2 of these other cases.

Some additional comment is required concerning the Cuban missile deployment. We have suggested that its initial phase prior to Kennedy's deterrence warnings of early September, can be subsumed under Pattern One. But after Kennedy issued his two public warnings, the Soviet government had an opportunity to reconsider the missile deployment, to alter in some way the strategy of seeking a covert fait accompli,[6] or to call it off altogether. Instead, it decided to continue and, if anything, to speed up measures to achieve operational readiness for its missiles as soon as possible. It could be, therefore, that Soviet leaders took Kennedy's warnings as indicating an unequivocal commitment but one that could be eroded and/or bypassed

---

[6] The alternative strategy of the limited probe type had been available to the Soviets at the outset. Thus, they could have introduced the missiles into Cuba more slowly and justified the action in order to accustom the United States to the idea. But to restructure the attempted covert fait accompli deployment into a limited probe was probably no longer possible at the time Kennedy issued his warnings. The covert missile deployment had already gone too far for the Soviets to switch to a limited probe effort to introduce the missiles openly into Cuba.

once a sufficient number of missiles became operational. Insofar as Kennedy's warning implied a threat to resort to force *immediately* upon discovery of missiles, the Soviets could and did regard his threat as lacking in credibility. In other words, the fait accompli strategy might still succeed; it continued to be acceptable as a calculated, controllable risk. Therefore, in the unusual circumstances of the Cuban missile deployment the logic of Pattern One could be replaced by the different logic of Pattern Three without any change in the way the Soviets were acting.

Idiosyncratic and Nondeterrable Cases

Three of the cases discussed in Part Two are not easily subsumed under any one of the three types of deterrence failure identified in this chapter. These idiosyncratic cases are the Chinese intervention in Korea, the Indochina crisis of 1953–1954, and the Middle East crises of 1957–1958. Cases of this kind are important and have been included in the study because they illustrate some of the limitations of deterrence theory and strategy.

While for some purposes the Chinese Communist intervention in the Korean War can be regarded as a failure of deterrence for the United States, the strong element of coercive diplomacy employed by Peking in this case makes it difficult for us to attempt to place it under one of these three patterns. As was suggested in the case study, the Chinese intervention developed in stages. Peking's objectives and its strategy for achieving them appear to have been shaped and reshaped on the basis of perceived feedback regarding the impact of preceding Chinese moves on American and United Nations policy and behavior. The initial Chinese effort to deter the United States from occupying North Korea having failed, Peking evidently resorted to coercive diplomacy to bring about a modification of U.S. policy and behavior. This strategy appears to have gone through several phases; at first, China used limited force in a relatively restrained manner to induce the United States to stop its advance well short of the Yalu River; then, when this failed, more extensive force was employed to evict U.S. forces from Korea. The American effort to deter Chinese intervention was complicated not only by the provocative U.S. policy of attempting to unify Korea but also by Washington's failure to interpret Chinese behavior as part of an effort at coercive diplomacy.

In the Indochina case of 1953–1954 the objective of U.S. deterrence strategy was to prevent a *major* Chinese Communist intervention on behalf of the Viet Minh. The paradox and dilemma that unexpectedly confronted the Eisenhower Administration in March 1954 was that the Viet Minh were about to defeat the French forces *without* benefit of a major Chinese intervention. The indirect military assistance Peking had provided the Viet Minh was indeed valuable and contributed to their success, but the nature of Peking's assistance was well below the level of the major intervention Dulles had been trying to deter by means of Massive Retaliation deterrent threats since mid-1953. This case illustrates, therefore, that deterrence strategy is much less likely to achieve the desired goals against nonmilitary options of the kind Peking employed on this occasion than against overt military actions.

Turning to the Middle East case, the crises that occurred in that area during 1957–1958 had their origins in developments for which deterrence strategy had little or no relevance. Crises of this kind fall outside of the scope of deterrence strategy; they are essentially nondeterrable events. Soviet economic and military aid to Middle Eastern states, especially Egypt and Syria, did circumvent the U.S. deterrence commitment embodied in the Eisenhower Doctrine. However, these Soviet activities were neither necessary nor sufficient causes of the crises that erupted in the area. Rather, as shown in our study of this case in Part Two, these crises were for the most part products of the internal stresses within the Jordanian, Syrian, and Lebanese societies.

Bibliography

George, Alexander L., D. K. Hall, and W. E. Simons. *The Limits of Coercive Diplomacy*. Boston, Little, Brown, 1971.

Guetzkow, Harold. "Some Correspondences between Simulations and 'Realities' in International Relations," in *New Approaches to International Relations*, ed. Morton A. Kaplan. New York, St. Martin's Press, 1968.

Khrushchev Remembers, with an introduction by Edward Crankshaw. Boston, Little, Brown, 1970.

Richardson, James L. *Germany and the Atlantic Alliance*. Cambridge, Harvard University Press, 1966.

Chapter 19

Commitment Theory

The Problem of Commitment in Deterrence Theory

IN DEVELOPING AN EXPLANATORY deterrence theory, we have focused up to this point on the initiator's behavior. We have identified the principal conditions that influence the initiator's decisions whether and how to challenge deterrence, and we have identified major patterns into which such challenges tend to fall. We now shift our attention to the defender's behavior, focusing in this chapter upon the phase of this behavior which precedes any challenge to deterrence, and in the next chapter upon the phase that follows a challenge.

The overall intellectual and practical problem of deterrence can be seen as dividing into three segments, illustrated in the diagram. Of these three segments or phases of the deterrence

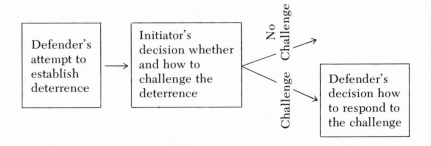

process, it is the first which has received the overwhelming preponderance of attention from theorists to date. Indeed, it is not much of an exaggeration to say that the other two segments of the deterrence problem, dealing with developments subsequent to the establishment of deterrence, have as yet received almost no systematic attention from theorists. These "subsequent" two phases of the overall deterrence phenomenon are, of course, receiving attention in this study, respectively in the preceding two, and the next, chapters.[1]

But we do wish to consider the first phase as well—the problem of the defender's attempt to establish deterrence. The central problem in this phase of the deterrence phenomenon is, of course, the successful communication to a potential initiator of an adequate deterrence commitment. This has been recognized by theorists, who, as discussed in chapter 3, have concentrated largely upon this aspect ("signaling") and upon "credibility" as presumptively the principal issues in designing an adequate commitment. In this chapter we want to suggest ways in which commitment theory can and should be expanded. However, those suggestions must be preceded by some additional critical attention to traditional commitment theory— not with the intent of censuring past efforts, but in order to demonstrate the need for explanatory, empirically based theory.

Three problematical aspects of traditional commitment theory have already been discussed in chapter 3. Abstract-deductivistic approaches to deterrence have tended to assume that commitments have a simple "either-or" character. One is committed or one is not. The resulting distortions are reinforced by the additional assumptions that each side in the deterrence equation is a unitary, purposive actor and that action choices and payoffs of the actors may be analyzed and calculated by means of a single standard of rationality.

There are three additional problematical aspects of traditional commitment theory which demand attention.

---

[1] The second of these three phases received attention first because we wished to begin our explanatory theory-building with the "dependent" variable.

THE EFFECT ON COMMITMENTS
OF BELIEFS ABOUT
THE INTERNATIONAL SYSTEM.

It is time and past time that commitment theory be removed from the very special historical context of the Cold War. During that period American policy-makers saw themselves in the throes of a bipolar, zero-sum conflict with the Soviet Union. It is important to note that the international system was perceived as not merely highly polarized and highly conflictful, but also as highly unstable. American policy-makers viewed the international situation as one in which a setback in one locale could have a profound destabilizing effect in others as well. The different parts of the international system were seen as tightly "coupled," so that perturbations in one locale, it was feared, could cause strong repercussions in other areas that might throw the rest of the international system (like a row of dominoes) into greater disequilibrium.[2]

Such beliefs had important implications for American foreign policy during the Cold War. They encouraged the United States to make commitments to many weaker countries and to resort to deterrence strategies in support of these commitments. The parallel belief that a setback to "international communism" in one area would increase the likelihood of setbacks in other areas tended to increase the value assigned by American policy-makers to maintaining noncommunist regimes in all peripheral areas. The conception of the American interest in preserving the "freedom" of weaker countries was thus inflated by the Cold War significance imputed to them and by a fear that any local setback might set the dominoes effect into motion.

This view of the international system, besides encouraging a proliferation of American commitments, tended (1) to increase

[2] The impact of such beliefs about the international system on foreign policy is incisively analyzed by Singer and Wildavsky in "A Third World Averaging Strategy."

the perceived importance of protecting countries in peripheral areas; (2) to homogenize rather than differentiating the commitments made to various countries, and (3) to encourage a belief in the "interdependence of commitments" i.e., the belief that failure of the United States to honor any one commitment effectively would weaken the credibility of all other American commitments and, hence "invite" further challenges.[3]

Especially noteworthy is the way the special historical context of the Cold War encouraged oversimplifications and distortions in the policy-maker's commitments that ran parallel to those to be found in the normative-prescriptive theory that was being formulated during the same period. Something more than mere coincidence is suggested here which, at the same time, stops well short of a direct causal relationship. What seems to have happened is that the special dynamics of international conflict during this era may have dulled the critical sensibilities of deterrence theorists and encouraged them to intuit that the simplifying assumptions of game-theory methodology on which they were basing deterrence theory were not so unrealistic or questionable. Thus normative-prescriptive theory was more historically bound than those who formulated it were aware of. Cold War "reality" made it appear less necessary to question and elaborate upon the simplifying assumptions of the theory.

THE AHISTORICAL CHARACTER
OF DETERRENCE THEORY

If deterrence theory was in fact historically bound in a manner unrecognized by most deterrence theorists, it suffered at the same time from being ahistorical. This paradox arises from the

---

[3] Several writers have discussed the fact that actors in an acute conflict relationship, such as the Cold War, are often impelled to stress the interdependence of their commitments as a bargaining tactic. Schelling, *Arms and Influence*, pp. 55–59; Jervis, "Aspects of Security and Bargaining"; Snyder, "Crisis Bargaining," p. 231. An incisive critical analysis of the faulty premises of attempting to use "interdependence of commitments" indiscriminately as a bargaining tactic is provided by Maxwell, "Rationality in Deterrence," p. 19.

fact that the state-of-the-world assumptions of deterrence theory remained largely implicit and were taken for granted. At the same time, the prescriptive content of the theory was formulated in general terms for actors who were assumed not to be imbedded in any particular historical configuration or, at least, not one subject to variation and change. Thus, the theory was being *presented* invalidly as general and above history, while simultaneously being *in fact* history-bound in a way that was both unnecessary and unappreciated.

Historical experience that contradicted the premises and propositions of deterrence theory was largely overlooked or set aside by its exponents. For example, history teaches that the commitments a nation makes on behalf of weaker countries are often inadequate to prevent encroachments on their independence and sovereignty. Treaty guarantees have always tended to be equivocal, uncertain instruments for deterring attempts to change the international status quo. In how many historical cases did major powers decide not to honor their pledges! [4] Nor is this at all surprising, since, as is well known to those having a familiarity with diplomatic history, commitments and "guarantees" are by no means all alike. They can and do vary in a number of critical respects, according to: (1) The nature of the threats to the weak ally which the defending power perceives and expects, i.e., the actions to be deterred; (2) The scope and magnitude of the defensive effort to which the defending power commits itself; (3) The circumstances and motives which occasion the defender's commitment. These may have little to do with deterrence per se, but they qualify the guarantee and/or provide a loophole for the guarantor. With respect to this last variable, we may cite the example of the Locarno Pact of 1925 which, according to A. J. P. Taylor, "rested on the assumption that the promises given in it would never have to be made

---

[4] Thus, Russett concludes his examination of the value of guarantees with the observation that "a small nation was as safe without an explicit guarantee as with one. . . . such guarantees existed in fewer instances of [deterrence] success (one in six) than in cases of failure (six of eleven)." "Calculus of Deterrence," p. 102.

good—otherwise the British Government would not have given them." [5]

Moreover, every student of diplomatic history—and, one has to add, the decision-maker in every country interested in changing the international status quo—knows that a nation's existing treaty commitments are no sure guide to its actions should deterrence be challenged. For one thing, treaty commitments often leave the *casus foederis* so vaguely defined as to permit an escape if one of the partners to the treaty, or the guaranteeing power, is so inclined. Second, even if a firm commitment is originally intended, a change in the protecting power's domestic situation or international position may alter the calculus of interest underlying its initial guarantee. Third, the value placed by the protecting power on maintaining the independence and territorial integrity of a weaker ally may decline (or increase) over a period of time. Fourth, the *expected costs and risks* of honoring a commitment may rise or fall with changes in the international balance of power. Fifth, a guaranteeing power may suffer a temporary or more indefinite decline in resources with which to meet its commitments. Sixth, while maintaining or even increasing its military resources, a power may nonetheless become "overcommitted" as a result of having added too many countries to the list of those it wishes to protect. Seventh, it may become temporarily overextended by virtue of using a relatively large proportion of its available resources to honor a particularly expensive and onerous commitment when deterrence has failed. Eighth and finally, commitments may vary with changes of administration and other changes in domestic politics.

In listing various circumstances under which commitments are ambiguous, unpredictable, and subject to change we have avoided suggesting that they invariably turn out to be weaker than when initially formulated. It must be recognized that commitments that are initially perfunctory, weak, or limited may become stronger as new developments increase the value at-

[5] Taylor, *English History, 1914–1945*, pp. 221–22.

tached to the independence of a weak ally by the protecting power. Such a strengthening of commitments can occur overnight. South Korea, for instance, increased in importance in the eyes of American policy-makers when it was unexpectedly attacked by North Korean forces in June 1950.[6]

For various reasons, therefore, commitments are highly context-dependent. We must add to this that the relevant context in which deterrence has to operate can change significantly, gradually or abruptly, expectedly or unexpectedly, weakening (or strengthening) deterrence thereby.

THE APOLITICAL CHARACTER OF DETERRENCE THEORY

Not only was normative-prescriptive deterrence theory presented as ahistorical, it was also regarded as apolitical. The political character of commitments was not altogether ignored by deterrence theorists, but it was dealt with in a primitive way that adversely affected the validity and relevance of the theory. The task of constructing an abstract deterrence theory was indeed facilitated by assuming that a deterrence commitment is dichotomous: a defending power commits itself or it does not, and if it does the commitment is unequivocal. In fact, however, commitments vary in strength and scope, depending upon judgments about interests, as just discussed.

Judgments of interests and the values placed on them are essentially national political matters, though they do have strategic and military aspects. As Stephen Maxwell, among others, has noted, there has been a tendency in deterrence theory to focus on the strategic dimension apart from its political context. Deterrence theorists have generally tended to avoid or to gloss over the complicating but fundamental role that the actors' perception of "interests" and of their relative values necessarily plays in deterrence interactions. As Maxwell puts it, "the iden-

[6] See in this connection May, "The Nature of Foreign Policy."

tification of an interest is more complicated than most nuclear strategists have supposed the identification of a 'commitment' to be. . . . the obvious conclusion to be drawn from the failure of a commitment is simply that the commitment did not represent an interest worth defending, at the level of violence and risk estimated to be necessary." [7]

Not only are judgments of interest and value essentially political rather than strategic, but judgments of this kind by the leaders of a nation are affected and shaped by political processes both operating within the governmental structure and impacting on it from the outside. The formulation of a commitment and, if deterrence fails, its implementation are subject to the play of conflicting interests, judgments, and pressures. In sharp contradiction to normative-prescriptive theory's assumption that a government's behavior in deterrence situations is the result of rational calculations made by a unitary actor, the members of the government and their constituencies can disagree on many components of deterrence policy: (1) the nature of the deterrence commitment and its value from the standpoint of the national interests perceived to be at stake; (2) the means to be employed on behalf of the deterrence commitment; (3) the level of costs and risks to accept in upholding the commitment; (4) how to evaluate different deterrence options; and (5) how best to signal credibility.

It was suggested earlier that deterrence commitments are not always fully formulated or consistently interpreted. This becomes more understandable in light of the political nature of judgments involved in a commitment and the political processes affecting such judgments.

[7] Maxwell, "Rationality in Deterrence," p. 18. An earlier writer concluded that guarantees have worked only when definite in character and limited in scope to areas where the guarantor had real interests. Headlam-Morley, *Studies in Diplomatic History*, pp. 105–92, cited by Rothstein, *Alliances and Small Powers*, p. 313. A critical analysis of alliance theory is provided in chapter 1 of Holsti, Hopmann, and Sullivan, *Unity and Disintegration in International Alliances*.

Commitment Theory:
The Role of Interests

An empirically based theory of commitment must cope with the complexities of the commitment decision. Once we abandon the oversimplified assumption that deterrence commitments are simple either-or phenomena, with the other problematical assumptions just discussed, we see that policy-makers need a much more complex understanding of the nature of commitments to formulate and project their own commitments more effectively and to diagnose the nature of those made by other actors in international politics.[8] This conclusion is amply justified by some of the historical experience reviewed in Part Two. There we saw, in clear contradiction of the "either-or" assumption, that the nature of the American commitment varied substantially from one case to another. Also, American policy-makers found it difficult on several occasions (i.e., during the Berlin blockade, the Korean War, the Taiwan Strait and Quemoy crises) to formulate their commitment or to clarify it on the basis of warning that deterrence might be about to fail. We noted, too, that even unequivocal, strong commitments, such as the American commitment to West Berlin in 1958, do not necessarily speak for themselves but can beneüt from a more careful definition of the complex interests which are and are not covered by the commitment. Dulles' effort to do so in the initial phase of the 1958 "deadline crisis" illustrates very well the necessity for both policy-makers and deterrence theorists to subject the notion of a general "commitment" to a more discriminating analysis in terms of the various interests and different values involved. Our case studies strongly indicate that

---

[8] Here and throughout the analysis we do not, of course, mean to imply that previous students of international relations have been unaware of these complications. Rather the primary point is that this generalized awareness has not found its way into systematic deterrence *theory* to date, or into the norms and prescriptions which deterrence theorists have offered.

the opponents, too, did not act on the basis of an assumption that American commitments are an either-or proposition.

The critical role of interests and their valuation greatly reduces the value to policy-makers of norms and prescriptions concerning credibility which are offered by deterrence theory. The fact of the matter is that the task of achieving credibility is secondary to *and dependent upon* the more fundamental questions regarding the nature and valuation of interests. Traditional commitment theory has tended to focus on those factors affecting the credibility of commitments and signals that are more readily subject to manipulation. Insufficient attention has been given to the less easily manipulated factor of interests on which credibility depends.[9]

As a result, theoretical writing and speculation on this subject suffers from its narrow focus on various *devices* one may employ for strengthening "one's commitment" or "reinforcing" the credibility of one's signals. Thus, it has been said (by Schelling, Russett, and others) that the defender can reinforce the credibility of its peacetime pledge to defend a weaker ally by taking actions that would increase the damage to its interests if it failed to honor the pledge. That is, the defender can deliberately increase what would be at stake for him, for example, by increasing his economic ties with the weak ally, by strengthening or dramatizing his friendly political relations, or by deliberately making the commitment to protect the ally a matter of prestige with his own electorate or with other allies. Such devices may indeed serve to enhance credibility and deterrence. But the adoption of such devices is not cost-free; and the prior question remains whether and to what extent a defending power wishes to commit itself to the defense of a weaker ally. This, in turn, requires a hard assessment of the value of doing so from the standpoint of the defending power's national interests, available resources, and other commitments.

The emphasis on devices for credibility and signaling is

[9] On this point see the discussion in Jervis, *Logic of Images*, chapter 3, "The Manipulation of Indices."

also unfortunate insofar as it implies—or permits the assumption—that deterrence can usually be made to succeed, and that success is largely a matter of learning to signal more effectively. This premise is not merely mistaken; it can be dangerous, in that it encourages a technocratic and mechanistic view of deterrence. Technical skill in signaling is indeed needed to make deterrence work, but it will not carry the day in cases where a policy of deterrence has been misapplied or stretched beyond what the national will can or should support.

What tends to be overlooked in traditional commitment theory is that effective deterrence and effective signaling require in the first instance that the interests of the United States be sufficiently engaged by what is at stake in the area or country in question. Commitments which rest on relatively weak national motivation are more likely to be challenged.[10] Technical proficiency in signaling commitment may not compensate in situations in which the motivation of the United States as the protecting power is weak relative to the opponent's strong desire to change the status quo at the expense of one of our weak allies.

It would be less necessary to stress the risks of overreliance on signaling were it not for the fact that policy-makers often experience considerable difficulty in trying to define the "national interests" at stake in a situation and to agree, even among themselves, upon the value to be placed on these interests both before making a commitment and before deciding to "honor" it when it is challenged. It is all too easy, therefore, for policy-makers to move prematurely to the task of signaling credibility before making a satisfactory analysis of the interests at stake for both sides. Instead of encouraging this tendency by emphasizing the critical importance of credibility and signaling to deterrence strategy, theorists would do better to caution that sophisticated opponents will judge credibility on the basis of a more fundamental analysis of the defender's interests. For this pur-

---

[10] This is not to say that commitments resting on strong national motivation will never be challenged!

pose, the opponent is likely to pay more attention to strategic, political, economic, and ideological factors determining the nature and magnitude of those interests than to rhetorical and other signaling devices the defending power may employ to enhance credibility.[11] In Robert Jervis' terms, that is, the opponent is more likely to be impressed by "indices" rather than by "signals."

The Initiator's Multiple Options and the Problem of "Tailoring" Signals

Several of the historical cases reviewed in Part Two called attention to the failure of the United States to signal its commitment and its resolution in ways that would influence the opponent's behavior in the desired way. In historical cases the inability of signaling to prevent deterrence from failing can be explained in a number of different ways, and it is not always possible for the historian to determine which explanation applies to a particular situation. One possibility is that the defender's efforts to signal a credible commitment were encumbered by some of the ambiguities and uncertainties associated with commitments which have just been discussed. Another possible explanation is that the opponent was simply not psy-

[11] Similar points are made by Stephen Maxwell: "In the real world . . . commitments cannot be signalled as unambiguously as the 'bridge-burning' and other analogies [employed by deterrence theorists] suggest. . . .
". . . the chief part of any assessment of the strength of a contestant's commitment to an objective must be a process of political evaluation focused on the value of the objective [to the deterring power]. . . .
"The political contours of the world are not so easily manipulated for strategic ends, as the language of nuclear strategists often suggests." "Rationality in Deterrence," pp. 18–19.
Several other writers have also attempted to find a basis for distinguishing among different types of commitments. See, for example, Weinstein, "The Concept of Commitment," and Sullivan, "Commitment and the Escalation of Conflicts."

chologically receptive even to well-designed, cogent signals on behalf of an unequivocal, strong commitment. Another possibility, however, is that the defender employed signals to convey his commitment that were overly general, incomplete, or misleading. It is this latter possibility which we will single out for closer attention there.

We noted earlier that when the initiator has multiple options for attempting to change the status quo (which is the usual case), the task of designing an effective deterrence strategy may not be easy for the defender. Under these circumstances the defender's task of signaling, too, becomes more difficult; the requirements for achieving credibility of commitment become more diverse, and perhaps also more specific. What will be credible and potent enough to deter Option A will not necessarily be credible and potent enough to deter Option C, or vice versa. Similarly, the task of deterring multiple, diverse options raises the question of the *relevance* of the deterrent threats made by the defending power. Threats that are relevant for deterring Option A may not be relevant for deterring Option C, and vice versa. In situations of this kind, the issue of the credibility and potency of deterrent threats cannot be separated from the issue of their relevance to the different options at the initiator's disposal. (This point recalls, of course, the critique of Dulles' Massive Retaliation threat.)

Several alternatives are available to the defending power when confronted by situations of this kind. One alternative is to formulate and communicate a broad, generalized deterrent threat which will try to cover all the options available to the initiator. At times, Massive Retaliation was intended as a generalized threat of this kind. This type of signaling strategy can be depicted as follows:

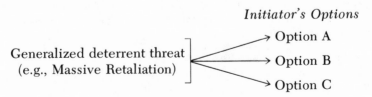

Initiator's Options

Generalized deterrent threat
(e.g., Massive Retaliation)
→ Option A
→ Option B
→ Option C

Massive Retaliation attempted to achieve generalized deterrence power according to a special rationale which, on occasion, John Foster Dulles articulated. It was his view (and his unjustified hope) that the *strength and certainty* of the U.S. commitment to act against encroachments against its allies was more important for preventing miscalculation by the opponent than the specification of means the United States threatened to employ in case an encroachment of some kind took place. Dulles hoped that lower-level options (for example, Options B and C in our hypothetical list) could be deterred by the threat of "Massive Retaliation" when coupled with this kind of firm U.S. commitment to an ally. The real meaning of Massive Retaliation in this context was not, as Dulles ineptly implied in his first use of this awesome slogan, a threat of initiating thermonuclear war as an immediate or even eventual response to a low-level attack. Rather, as Dulles managed to explain when clarifying what he meant, Massive Retaliation was a threat to escalate low-level conflicts if necessary. It was Dulles' way of serving notice upon opponents that the United States would not allow the opponent to choose the conditions of warfare which best suited him but would feel free to escalate such conflicts to levels of warfare at which U.S. capabilities would be more effective. As Dulles put it, the United States would respond "at places and with means of its own choosing." Beyond this, however, Massive Retaliation was deliberately vague, presumably in part to take advantage of the element of uncertainty it attempted to introduce into the initiator's calculations. Besides, Massive Retaliation was a *declaratory* policy; while it had implications for action, it by no means dictated the responses Eisenhower would make when deterrence failed. As a matter of fact, when crises occurred during his administration, Eisenhower's response was not at all of a Massive Retaliation type.[12]

---

[12] Dulles introduced the concept of Massive Retaliation in a speech before the Council on Foreign Relations on January 12, 1954. An important clarification was contained in a subsequent article, "Policy for Security and Peace." An influential critique was published by Kaufmann: "The Requirements of Deterrence."

Another signaling strategy when one is faced with an opponent who has multiple options is to formulate and communicate a number of specific threats which together provide comprehensive deterrence coverage. One hypothetical example (among many) of this type of focused, differentiated signaling strategy can be depicted as follows:

Initiator's Options

Threat of full-scale intervention ⟶ Option A

Threat of air and naval
intervention ⟶ Option B

Threat of increased military
and economic aid to weak ally ⟶ Option C

This signaling strategy corresponds roughly with the politico-military doctrine of Flexible Response introduced by the Kennedy Administration.

The problem of tailoring signals is more complicated, however, than is implied by this example. It is easy enough to state the effect which signaling should achieve—namely, to deter the opponent by influencing the risk and utility calculations he assigns to each of the options available to him. But it is far more difficult to specify those characteristics of signaling that will achieve the desired impact. The task of tailoring signals to achieve a credible commitment and to generate sufficiently persuasive threats is multidimensional. Perhaps the best way to express these dimensions is to refer to questions an initiator generally seeks to clarify before deciding whether and how to challenge deterrence:

(1) Which *options* by the initiator does the defender commit himself to oppose?
(2) What means will the defender employ initially if confronted by this, that, or another action by the initiator challenging the status quo?
(3) To what extent will the defender be prepared to go later if his initial response to his opponent's initiative does not suffice?

When the defender's signals do not clearly spell out his commitment in all these three respects, the opponent will be forced to infer what position the defender has privately taken or is likely to take on each. Self-interest requires the initiating side to clarify ambiguities it perceives in the signals directed toward it by the defender and to interpret other clues bearing on the defender's intentions. Even when the defender signals rather specific answers to these three questions, the initiator must still consider whether the defender is engaged in a complete or partial bluff, or misrepresents his intentions for other reasons.

It takes no great perspicacity on the part of the initiator to be aware of the possibility that the defender sometimes engages in calculated ambiguity when signaling a commitment. The more difficult problem the initiator faces is that of accounting for the reasons or strategy behind any particular instance of calculated ambiguity. The defender may resort to ambiguity to take advantage of the possibility that in certain (though not all) situations it might pay to keep the opponent guessing. But ambiguity may recommend itself for other reasons: the defender may not yet know how it would react to a failure of deterrence, or it may wish to avoid various penalties and costs associated with disclosing prematurely the details or strength of its commitment. Several of these considerations can be seen at work complicating the task of reinforcing deterrence in the summer of 1958 when U.S. policy-makers received warning that the Chinese Communists were about to initiate some kind of action against the offshore islands.

In this chapter we have commented critically on the tendency of earlier deterrence theory to oversimplify the nature of foreign policy commitments by treating them as "either-or" phenomena. We have argued that a more differentiated view of commitments is needed, one that regards them as based on interests that can vary greatly in magnitude of importance and, moreover, can change substantially over time. In the last chapter of the book we shall return to this alternative view of commitments as being highly variable and context-dependent in order to consider its implications for deterrence and a more flexible U.S. foreign policy.

Bibliography

Dulles, John Foster. "Policy for Security and Peace," *Foreign Affairs*, XXXII (April 1954).

Headley-Morley, Sir James. *Studies in Diplomatic History*. London, Metheun, 1930.

Holsti, Ole R., P. Terrence Hopmann, and John D. Sullivan. *Unity and Disintegration in International Alliances*. New York, Wiley, 1973.

Jervis, Robert, "Aspects of Security and Bargaining," in *Coercion*, ed. J. Roland Pennock and John W. Chapman. Chicago, Aldine, 1972.

——. *The Logic of Images in International Relations*. Princeton, Princeton University Press, 1970.

Kaufmann, William W. "The Requirements of Deterrence" in *Military Policy and National Security*, ed. W. Kaufmann. Princeton, Princeton University Press, 1959.

Maxwell, Stephen. "Rationality in Deterrence." Adelphi Paper, No. 50. London, Institute of Strategic Studies, August 1968.

May, Ernest. "The Nature of Foreign Policy: The Calculated versus the Axiomatic," *Daedalus*, Fall 1962.

Rothstein, Robert. *Alliances and Small Powers*. Boston, Little, Brown, 1972.

Russett, Bruce M., "Calculus of Deterrence," *Journal of Conflict Resolution*, VII, No. 2 (June 1963).

Schelling, Thomas C. *Arms and Influence*. New Haven, Yale University Press, 1966.

Singer, Max, and Aaron Wildavsky. "A Third World Averaging Strategy," in *U.S. Foreign Policy: Perspectives and Proposals for the 1970's*, ed. Paul Seabury and Aaron Wildavsky. New York, McGraw-Hill, 1969.

Snyder, Glenn H., "Crisis Bargaining," in *International Crises: Insights from Behavioral Research*, ed. Charles F. Hermann. New York, Free Press, 1972.

Sullivan, Michael P. "Commitment and the Escalation of Conflicts," *Western Political Quarterly*, XXV, No. 1 (March 1972).

Taylor, A. J. P. *English History, 1914–1945*. New York, Oxford University Press, 1965.

Weinstein, Franklin B. "The Concept of Commitment in International Relations," *Journal of Conflict Resolution*, 13, No. 1 (March 1969).

Chapter 20

Response Theory

The Problem of Response
in Deterrence Theory

WE HAVE NOW DISCUSSED the first segment of the overall deterrence problem, the defender's attempt to establish deterrence—commitment theory—and the second segment, the initiator's decision whether and how to challenge deterrence—initiation theory. It remains in this chapter to take up the third segment, the defender's decision how to respond to indications that the opponent may have decided to challenge deterrence—the problem of response to "warning" indicators.

A preliminary but vital point in "response theory" is that the defender dare not wait for a positive action by the initiator, or even for intelligence indications that one is forthcoming, to rethink his commitments. It is inherent in deterrence that its requirements and expected efficacy must be continually reassessed. The defender cannot know for certain whether his deterrence strategy is adequate for the present, and even greater uncertainty arises in judging whether it will remain adequate in the future. So long as deterrence is not openly challenged, the defender is inclined to assume that deterrence is working. But the impression that deterrence is successful may be illusory. The adversary may not wish to undertake an alteration in the status quo for reasons that have little or nothing to do with the deterrent threats to which he is exposed. An illusory deterrence success, of course, gives the defender false confirmation of the adequacy of his deterrence strategy. Even a genuine deterrence success, however, may provide misleading assurance that the deterrence measures employed will remain adequate in the future. Deterrence success is not necessarily stable over time. The conditions and factors which influence the adversary's behavior are subject to change.

The defender must also contend with the fact that the inadequacy of his deterrence measures can be known for certain only when deterrence fails. Thus there are important limits on the extent to which the defender can rely on feedback to assess the adequacy of his deterrence effort. Under these circumstances, the defender is necessarily dependent upon intelligence indications that his adversary is getting ready to challenge the status quo in order to evaluate and improve, if necessary, his deterrence posture.

Two types of intelligence warning of the adversary's intentions may be available for this purpose. "Strategic warning" comprises longer-range indications that the opponent may be preparing to act. "Tactical warning" includes more immediate indications that the adversary is about to act or has actually begun to act. Both types of warning may be "equivocal" with respect to *whether* the adversary is really preparing or is about to act, and/or "ambiguous" as to exactly *what* action the opponent will take and *when* he will act.

Warning of the opponent's forthcoming action is sometimes so meager or so highly inconclusive that it is difficult, even with the benefit of hindsight, to argue that the defender should have been alerted. Often, however, the available warning is much less equivocal. It can be plausibly argued that in such cases intelligence specialists and policy-makers could have been alerted had they not misperceived or misjudged the warning or had they been more responsive to its implications. Diagnosis of past intelligence failures and inadequate policy response to good intelligence, therefore, may indeed lead to improved performance in these respects. But it would be naïve, to mistake the remarkable clarity of hindsight in these matters as indicating that a similar level of foresight can also be achieved.

Response to Limited Probes and Controlled Pressure

In chapter 18 we identified three principal patterns by which initiators challenge deterrence. Pattern One, the "fait accompli attempt," by its nature requires the defender to respond to strategic or at least tactical warning, or to fashion a response *after* deterrence has failed decisively. (We observe in passing that traditional deterrence theory has tended implicitly to presume the presence of this pattern—on analogy from the problem of strategic deterrence and also perhaps on such analogies as the Japanese attack on Pearl Harbor. Hence that theory has tended to obscure the richer material for a response theory inherent in the other patterns.)

Pattern Two is the limited probe. A defining characteristic of this pattern, it will be recalled, is precisely that the initiator is attempting to test what the defender's response may be to a challenge of deterrence. The initiator hopes to obtain feedback that will enable him to control and manipulate the slowly developing crisis in one or another of the following ways:

(1) to perfect his calculation of the expected gains from his initiative and his judgment of the best means to employ;
(2) to condition the defender and the international public to acceptance of the forthcoming challenge;
(3) to gauge and control the risk that the defender may overreact to the initiative;
(4) to develop justification and public and international support for his action.

Under Pattern Two, therefore, the failure of deterrence in stages reflects the initiator's decision to proceed cautiously and purposefully. A rather intricate set of maneuvers and probings may precede final commitment to action.

Such was the case in the Quemoy crisis of 1958, where the initial purpose of the shelling was to probe the United States' response to a renewed challenge to the Chinese Nationalists. In this instance, the U.S. response could be and was a reaffirmation of its commitment. In other instances the probe-and-response process gives the defender a valuable opportunity to reassess his commitment. In the Taiwan Strait crisis of 1954–1955, the Chinese probe led the Eisenhower Administration to clarify and more sharply structure a previously somewhat "blanket," undifferentiated deterrence commitment. In other instances, of which the erection of the Berlin Wall in 1961 is an example, the probe-and-response process permits the defender to signal that he does *not* have a commitment to deter an an action by the initiator, or that the commitment is to prevent a gross and far-reaching action but not a minor one.

Whether the response takes the form of reaffirmation of the commitment, restructuring of it, or implicit affirmation that it does not exist or apply, the opportunity for a thoughtful response is the principal feature of Pattern Two, the limited probe, and a feature which the defender ignores at peril in his deterrence practice, or his theory.

Pattern Three is controlled pressure on the part of the initiator against the defender's deterrent posture. It differs from Pattern Two, among other ways, in that the initiator is not attempting to discover what the defender's real commitment is; rather, the initiator believes that he knows it, indeed that he knows it well enough to design around it and otherwise exploit weaknesses he believes it possesses.

In fashioning his response to the developing deterrence failure, the defender would most like to know just *what* weaknesses the initiator believes he has found in the defender's posture. Unfortunately, this is a peculiarly difficult kind of information to come by, except insofar as it emerges from the initiator's actions. The controlled pressure pattern, however, possesses a particular feature which aids the defender's task. Normally the controlled pressure pattern will only come up in a certain kind of situation, namely, one where the complexity of detail in the situation (and/or other factors) results in *ambiguity* and considerable *maneuvering room.* Or, putting it negatively: normally it is difficult for an initiator to design a controlled pressure strategy with acceptable risks and a reasonable hope of success in a situation whose intrinsic simplicity includes few factors that can be manipulated or otherwise employed in maneuvers.

These propositions are amply illustrated by the Berlin crises of 1958–1959 and 1961. The complexity of the Berlin situation and the ambiguity surrounding many of its details were ideal for the Soviets' application of a controlled pressure strategy. The fact that the defender knows (or should know) that the controlled pressure pattern possesses this particular feature gives him the only available assistance in fashioning his responses. For here is a situation where the most painstaking kind of analysis and contingency planning is likely to fully justify its costs. Pragmatic, hard-working policy-makers know that it is easy to oversell the virtues of sheer thought and analysis in foreign policy–making. But the study of situations that are particularly vulnerable to controlled pressure from a potential initiator is likely to be helpful. We noted in our analyses of the Berlin crises of 1958–1959 and 1961 the significance of inadequate contingency analysis on the part of the Western allies. (We believe the "gaming" of these situations, playing out the various contingencies, can be fruitful.)

In addition to attempting in this manner to cope with the particular properties of the controlled pressure pattern of deterrence situations, the defender also can often treat the initial pressuring moves by the initiator as if they were probes under Pattern Two, and reassess, restructure, and/or withdraw its original commitment.

Under both these patterns, the somewhat gradual and fluid quality of the challenge potentially offers the defender opportunities to fashion a flexible, creative response. If these opportunities are to be seized, however, the defender must be receptive to early indications of the coming challenge—"warning," broadly conceived—and retain sufficient flexibility to be able to respond imaginatively and constructively. In the remainder of this chapter we examine factors affecting these prerequisites of an adequate response.

Response Theory: the Problem of Receptivity to Warning

The value of available warning to the defending side is often quite limited. Various mechanisms imbedded in individual psychology, the dynamics of group behavior, the processes of organizational behavior, and the play of governmental politics may hamper the defending side's receptivity to and proper evaluation of warning indicators.

Laboratory studies of difficulties in perception of stimuli provide useful analogies to the problem of receptivity to warning indicators in deterrence situations. The results of these perception experiments hardly offer encouragement regarding the possibility of easy or complete solutions to this problem. As Joseph de Rivera notes, studies of a person's ability to recognize a stimulus that is imbedded in other stimuli have shown at least three factors to be important: [1]

(1) the signal-to-noise ratio (i.e., the strength of the signal relative to the strength of confusing background stimuli);
(2) the expectations of the observer; and
(3) the rewards and costs associated with recognizing the signal in question.

One might be inclined to assume that the stronger the signal and the less the background noise, the easier it should be to detect the signal. However, the task of signal detection both

---

[1] De Rivera, *Psychological Dimension of Foreign Policy*, p. 53. Robert Jervis provides a detailed summary of available findings regarding psychological obstacles to correct perception and evaluates their implications for foreign policy decision-making in his forthcoming study, *Perception and Mis-perception in International Relations*.

in the laboratory and in deterrence situations is far more complicated than this. The strength of a stimulus may be relatively easy to define, measure, and control in laboratory experiments that focus on relatively simple psychophysical auditory or visual stimuli. But the nature of the problem changes and the difficulty of recognition increases when we move from these perceptual experiments to the task of correctly recognizing indications of the opponent's intentions in a deterrence situation. Recognition of intention indicators (one can hardly speak of them as simple stimuli) requires complex cognitive interpretations. The process of interpretation is far more important for the correctness of the perception than the inherent strength or clarity of the stimuli.

In any case, de Rivera reports that even the results of simpler perceptual experiments indicate that "it is incorrect to think that a signal will be detected simply because it is strong relative to the background noise." [2] The second and third factors mentioned above can cancel out the effect of a signal's strength on the subject's ability to detect it. Thus, experiments on signal perception suggest that we shall have to pay particular attention to the importance of two factors for the observer's evaluation of warning indicators. These are his expectations, or "set," and the rewards and costs associated with his recognition of the correct stimulus. The importance of these factors is also evident in studies of intelligence failures, such as Roberta Wohlstetter's pioneering study of Pearl Harbor and some of the cases presented in Part Two.

Various psychological mechanisms imbedded in individual, small group, and organizational behavior may reduce receptivity to warning.[3] This is especially likely whenever in-

[2] De Rivera, *Psychological Dimension of Foreign Policy*, p. 56.

[3] Small group dynamics that may interfere with a realistic perception of external threats to the values of the group and disrupt its capacity for rational decision-making are emphasized and illustrated in Janis, *Victims of Groupthink*. Disruptive dynamics of organizational factors on decision-making are discussed by Wilensky, *Organizational Intelligence;* Downs, *Inside Bureaucracy;* and Allison, *Essence of Decision*. An effort to interrelate the individual, small group, and organizational dimensions of this problem is presented in George, "Adaptation to Stress in Political Decision Making."

telligence indicates that something may be about to happen that policy-makers would prefer not to happen or are not prepared to deal with. Not only the individual mind but organizations as well are capable of engaging in various stratagems for diluting or discrediting information that challenges the structure of existing expectations, preferences, habits, convenience, etc. Discrepant information of this kind is often required, in effect, to meet higher standards of evidence and to pass stricter tests to gain acceptance than new information that supports existing expectations and hypotheses. (Many but not all the reasons for this have been subsumed under "cognitive dissonance theory.") The equivalent of the scientist's null hypothesis is rarely available or welcomed in policy-making, and is seldom utilized effectively in analyzing the significance of a warning. As a result, it is relatively easy for intelligence specialists and policy-makers to discredit discrepant information or to interpret it in such a way as to save a preferred hypothesis or policy.

The third factor mentioned above—the reward-cost implications of correct signal detection—can play a particularly important role in reducing the policy-maker's receptivity to warning. To take available warning seriously may require policy-makers to make new decisions of a difficult or unpalatable character. There is a subtle feedback from the policy-maker's anticipation of the response he might have to make to warning that affects his receptivity to warning. Once policies have been made within the government, they usually acquire a momentum of their own and the support of vested interests. Decision-makers are often reluctant to reopen policy matters that were decided earlier only with great difficulty; to do so, they fear, will plunge the government once again into the crisis and turmoil of decision-making.

Something of this kind, we suggested earlier, accounted in part for the Truman Administration's pronounced lack of receptivity to warning of the North Korean military action against South Korea. Taking available warning seriously always carries the penalty of deciding what to do about it. In this case, it would have required Truman and Acheson to reconsider their earlier decision on where to draw the line in the Far East. A reversal of the existing policy of no military commitment to South Korea would have been politically inconceivable unless Truman and Acheson had also been willing to extend a new commitment to the Chinese Nationalist regime on Formosa.

As this case and others show, then, the policy background at the time warning becomes available may subtly erode the policy-maker's receptivity to it. Prior to the Korean War, defense planning for Asia had been geared to the contingency of general war in which, clearly, direct defense of South Korea made no sense from a military strategic standpoint. Both military and political planners operated without a clear image of the threat of limited war, and no contingency military plans had been made for dealing with the kind of situation that erupted in Korea. We also noted in Part Two the importance of the policy background later on in the Korean War in reducing the Truman Administration's receptivity to the rather clear threat of Chinese Communist intervention.

Similarly, for American policy-makers to have taken the possibility of a blockade of West Berlin seriously in the spring of 1948 would have required them to face up to extremely difficult, controversial policy problems that had not yet been solved. Seizing upon the available warning to "reinforce" deterrence would not have meant the reaffirmation of an existing commitment, since a commitment to West Berlin did not yet exist. Rather, a new decision would have had to be made whether to make such a firm commitment and to accept significant costs and risks in upholding it. Officials within the administration were badly divided over the wisdom of trying to defend the Western outpost that lay deep in Soviet-occupied East Germany. Under these circumstances, it was easier to believe that the Soviets would not undertake serious action against West Berlin than to decide beforehand what the American response should be to such an eventuality.

We conclude, therefore, that the difficulties of improving receptivity to warning and interpreting it correctly are deeply imbedded in stubborn dynamics of individual, small group, and organizational behavior. These difficulties will not lend themselves easily to corrective measures. Procedural and other efforts to improve recognition and utilization of warning can hope to meet with some success, but it would be dangerous to assume that the fundamental difficulties highlighted by the historical experience reviewed here can be fully or reliably eliminated.

Response Theory: the Uses of Warning

Contrary to an assumption that is often made, policy-makers do not need to acquire high-confidence interpretations of the adversary's intentions before undertaking sensible measures of one kind or another. Even ambiguous or equivocal warning that deterrence may fail may be usable in some way. As Roberta Wohlstetter has emphasized,

> The problem of warning . . . is inseparable from the problem of decision. We cannot guarantee foresight. But we can improve the chance of acting on signals in time to avert or moderate a disaster.[4]

At the very least, policy-makers can utilize unclear warning to step up the acquisition of information bearing on the opponent's intentions.

In addition, they can often take some action that fits the ambiguities of presently available information in order to reduce the risks that could arise from inaction in the face of danger. Thus, various measures might be taken to reduce vulnerability to one or more of the actions the adversary might initiate. Familiar in this regard is the principle of selective, graduated action to reduce the vulnerability of military forces and improve their combat readiness. Warning can also be used in various ways to reduce the political and diplomatic costs of an initiative by the opponent.

[4] Wohlstetter, "Cuba and Pearl Harbor," p. 707.

These two uses of warning are familiar enough. Less thought has been given to the other possible uses of warning. A third use was indicated in our analysis of the outbreak of the Korean War. American officials might have used the ambiguous warning of a possible North Korean attack to assess the expected damage to U.S. interests from such an action, to envisage the political and psychological pressures that would be brought to bear for American military intervention if the North Koreans invaded, and to review the relevance and adequacy of American contingency plans. In other words, even ambiguous warning can serve a useful purpose if it encourages policy-makers to undertake a rehearsal of the decision problem they will face in case deterrence does fail.

A fourth possible response to warning by the defender is to reinforce deterrence. It is tempting to add to prescriptive deterrence theory the suggestion that the defender should use available warning, even ambiguous warning, to engage in an ad hoc strengthening of deterrence in various ways: by alerting or deploying military forces, signaling strong commitment and resolution, making threats to induce the opponent to pull back, even at the last minute, from his potential challenge. But there are circumstances in which responding to warning in these ways is not desirable. First, efforts to reinforce deterrence in the pre-crisis period or in the early stages of a crisis may contribute to its escalation rather than its control. As in the Berlin crisis of 1961, the other side may feel obliged to match or counter the moves the defender makes in attempting to reinforce deterrence as the crisis develops. In situations of this kind, the defender's reinforcement of deterrence strategy may impel the opponent to make counterdeterrence threats of his own. While mutual escalation of threats does not necessarily increase the probability of overt conflict, it may preclude alternative ways of dealing with the conflict of interests through diplomacy, inducement strategies, and mutual accommodation.

Second, even successful reinforcement of deterrence may entail important costs. It may harden the defender's commitment and make it more difficult after the immediate crisis subsides to recapture the political and diplomatic flexibility that is needed to find a diplomatic solution to the problem. It becomes more difficult thereafter for the defending power to deal with the weak ally. Relevant in this respect is the gradual erosion of Washington's freedom of action vis-à-vis the Chinese National-ist regime after Truman extended presumably temporary pro-tection to Formosa following the North Korean invasion of South Korea. In successive crises in the Taiwan Strait in 1954–1955 and in 1958 the Eisenhower Administration felt it-self under considerable pressure to harden and extend its com-mitment. Moreover, deterrence success in the Taiwan Strait hardened U.S. policy on precisely those peripheral issues on which flexibility would have served overall American interests far better. The 1954–1955 crisis ended with the administration more firmly committed to the defense of the offshore islands than before, and less able to turn to a more flexible diplomatic posture in order to reduce the conflict potential in the Taiwan Strait.

Third, successful reinforcement of deterrence may inflate the ideological dimensions of the conflict. In the two Taiwan Strait crises Eisenhower and Dulles succumbed to the tempta-tion of drawing upon the awesome military force available to them to generate the threats needed to buttress a questionable application of deterrence strategy. As noted in our account of the 1958 crisis, the use of national power to enforce deterrence in situations of this kind invariably requires policy-makers to engage in rhetorical inflation of the national interests at stake. When leaders repeatedly resort to rhetorical inflation to justify their acceptance of the risk of war as part of upholding ques-tionable commitments, they can often end up believing their own rhetorical arguments about "monolithic international com-munism" and the danger of a "row-of-dominoes" effect from any local setback.

Fourth, reinforcement of deterrence may include the cost of disaffecting or alienating allies other than the one immedi-ately being protected. They may also have interests, but par-tially competing ones, in the threatened area. Or they may come to resent the reinforcement effort as absorbing attention and resources better devoted to themselves. It is certainly true, for instance, that U.S. efforts to reinforce deterrence in the Far East have often been received less than warmly by the NATO allies.

Finally, reinforcement of deterrence in a crisis may succeed in deterring the opponent, but at the cost of hardening his conviction that the defender is unresponsive to the legitimate interests that lie behind his effort to obtain a change in the situation. As a result, the initiator may resolve to prepare more effectively for the next round by acquiring additional military or other capabilities with which to neutralize the defender's deterrent threats. The Berlin crisis of 1961 offers an example of this kind of hidden, delayed cost that deterrence success may entail: Kennedy's success in thwarting Khrushchev's demands for a change in the status of West Berlin by invoking American strategic superiority in the autumn of 1961 undoubtedly contributed to the Soviet decision to place missiles in Cuba.

One theme of this study has been a doubt as to the wisdom of relying rigidly upon deterrence strategy when faced with pressures for changes in the international status quo. Receipt of warning that deterrence may fail provides the policy-maker not merely with an opportunity to reinforce deterrence but, we have emphasized, an even more important opportunity for *reviewing the commitment*. This, then, is the fifth of the possible responses the defender can make to receipt of warning that an opponent may be getting ready, or has begun in a careful, controlled way, to challenge deterrence.

After considering the extent to which important interests are at stake and estimating the expected costs of maintaining them under challenge, the defender may indeed decide to maintain or even harden his commitment. But he may also decide to redefine or clarify his commitment, to reduce it, or to abandon it altogether. In several crises examined in Part Two of this study the receipt of warning led American policy-makers to review their commitment. The review conducted by Eisenhower during the Taiwan Strait crisis of 1954–1955 resulted in three different decisions: the administration affirmed and formalized its existing commitment to defend Nationalist-held Formosa and the Pescadores; it added a new commitment to the offshore islands; it made it unequivocally clear that it would not defend the Tachen Islands. At an early stage in the Hungarian crisis of 1956 Eisenhower, fearing desperate and irrational behavior on the part of the Soviet leaders, thought it best to signal that the United States would not intervene. In the Berlin crisis of 1961 the Kennedy Administration conveyed a similar signal, though perhaps only indirectly, by making no effort to caution the Soviets and East Germans against erecting a wall between East and West Berlin.

In the Cuban missile crisis, on the other hand, Kennedy used the quite equivocal warning that was available to draw the line against a missile deployment. In the events leading to the Berlin blockade of 1948, warning was taken seriously enough by Washington to initiate a policy review, but disagreements among American officials prevented them from clarifying their commitment. In the Korean War case U.S. policy-makers appear to have made no use whatsoever of available warning, neither stepping up their intelligence effort nor reviewing their policy toward South Korea.

Warning can also have the useful function of encouraging policy-makers to define and differentiate the complex interests that lie behind a strong commitment made earlier, and to signal a willingness to negotiate on peripheral rather than on central interests. Thus in the Berlin 1958 case, Dulles responded to warning by indicating a limited and defined flexibility on secondary issues, thereby displaying a sophisticated appreciation of the limits of exclusive reliance on deterrence strategy.

Intelligence Failures
and the Problem of Surprise

We have reviewed some of the reasons why available warning of the adversary's intentions may be ignored, minimized, or misinterpreted and, as a result, the defending power will be taken by surprise by the opponent's initiative. The possibility of intelligence failures that result in surprise attack has preoccupied Americans, particularly since Pearl Harbor, and has given strong impetus to the development of deterrence theory and to the emphasis on deterrence strategy as an instrument of foreign policy.

Roberta Wohlstetter's studies of Pearl Harbor and the Cuban missile crisis have emphasized that a number of factors can contribute to intelligence failure and surprise. In both cases, she finds, the American intelligence failure can be traced to some element of technological or logistical surprise achieved by the opponent, delays in transmission or evaluation of intelligence, the "cry-wolf" phenomenon, expectations and preferences of American officials, the influence of the policy background,[5] successful deceptions by the opponent, the presence of confusing "noise," and inadequate appraisal of the opponent's risk calculations.

Some but not all of these eight factors identified by Mrs. Wohlstetter were present also in other cases of deterrence failure considered in Part Two. To her list of eight factors we would add four more: underestimation of the opponent's motivation; underestimation of the opponent's capabilities; the costs of responding to warning if it were taken seriously; and the influence of domestic and organizational politics within the executive branch. Some of these additional factors have already been mentioned in the preceding discussions of receptivity and response to warning. Here we shall comment on the important role the defender's general image of his opponent plays in efforts to assess the opponent's intentions. We do not regard the image of the opponent as a separate factor, but rather as a fundamental cognitive variable that underlies several of the twelve factors listed above.

[5] While Mrs. Wohlstetter's thesis regarding the importance of the policy background in the near failure of American intelligence in the Cuban missile crisis is plausible, our own interpretation of it in Part Two does not agree with this part of her thesis.

It is by now a truism that available intelligence bearing on the task of estimating an adversary's intentions rarely speaks for itself. This is so even in the extreme case when intelligence on the adversary's intentions is plentiful, consistent, and relatively free of noise. To interpret such indications properly requires hypotheses about the way in which that particular adversary— not any political actor—approaches political conflict. For this purpose the analyst needs a theory or model of that adversary's behavioral style and approach to calculating political action.

A single familiar historical example will suffice to illustrate that one's general image of the opponent plays a critical role in interpreting even so-called hard intelligence concerning his intentions. Prior to the Nazi attack on the Soviet Union in 1941, ample high-quality intelligence of Hitler's military dispositions and plans was available to Stalin. The Soviet leader, however, could not believe that Hitler would launch a surprise attack. Stalin's image of the Nazi leader's behavioral style encouraged him to believe that Hitler would first present demands and attempt to bargain before deciding whether he needed to resort to force. The menacing Nazi military buildup on the Soviet border, Stalin evidently believed, was intended to set the stage for serious negotiations and bargaining. Perhaps Stalin's defective image of Hitler's style of behavior resulted from too facile a generalization of the way in which Hitler had behaved in the past; perhaps it also reflected wishful thinking on Stalin's part or a tendency to attribute the same style of behavior to Hitler that he would have followed himself in such a matter. Whatever the explanation, it is clear that Stalin miscalculated Hitler's intentions not because hard intelligence was scanty or in itself equivocal, but rather because he did not think Hitler would behave in the way he did.[6]

More recent historical cases of U.S. policy examined in this study also indicate that the general image of the opponent held by intelligence specialists and policy-makers is often critical for correct assessments of an opponent's intentions. One's image of

[6] For an analysis of Stalin's miscalculation of Hitler's intentions, see Whaley, *Codeword Barbarossa.*

the opponent includes the understanding one has of his ideology, his "operational code," and his mode of calculating utility and assessing risks. One's image of an opponent affects one's interpretation of available intelligence, even when it is not inherently ambiguous on the opponent's intentions. An incorrect or defective model of the opponent's behavioral style can distort even reasonably good factual information on what he may be up to.

Miscalculation of the adversary's overall intention can arise from misjudging any component of his utility calculations. Moreover, an error as to one aspect of the opponent's calculus often encourages misjudgment of other components of it as well. For example, underestimation of the opponent's motivation can lead to an erroneous estimate of his risk acceptance in a given situation. Erroneous estimates of several components of his calculations can be mutually reinforcing. Some of these possibilities are illustrated by the U.S. miscalculation of Chinese Communist intentions in the Korean War. In the autumn of 1950 rather good intelligence was available for assessing the threat of Chinese Communist intervention. But it was rendered equivocal when filtered through the incorrect U.S. image of the Chinese Communist leaders. By failing to comprehend the ideology and complex motivational calculus of the Chinese Communists, U.S. leaders misread the Chinese Communist perception of the magnitude of what was at stake for them in Korea. Underestimation of the opponent's motivation, in turn, distorted the U.S. estimate of the way in which Chinese leaders were calculating risks and deciding what level of risk to accept.

Even a reasonably good model of an opponent's general style of behavior, however, does not insure correct interpretation of his intentions in any given situation. This is illustrated by the case of the Soviet missile deployment into Cuba, when U.S. analysts who had developed considerable knowledge of Soviet behavior were nonetheless taken by surprise. They erred not so much because they operated with an incorrect image of the Soviet leaders' general patterns of behavior or mode of calculating, but because they did not correctly envisage how Soviet

Causes of U.S. Intelligence Failures Leading to Surprise

(+ = factor played a role;   0 = no appreciable role;
? = uncertain, difficult to interpret)

	Pearl Harbor	Berlin Blockade	Korean War	Chinese Intervention	Berlin 1958	Cuban Missile Crisis
1. Technological or logistical surprise	+	0	0	+	0	+
2. Delays in transmission / evaluation of intelligence	+	0	0	0	0	+
3. "Cry-wolf" phenomenon (a) withholding or downgrading intelligence from higher-up or theater authorities	+	0	+	0	0	+
(b) Nonreceptivity of higher authorities to intelligence warnings of "cry-wolf" type	0	0	?	0	?	+
4. Expectancies and preferences	+	+	+	+	+	+

leaders perceived the situation at hand. Miscalculation of Soviet intentions in this case was not due, as in the case of the Chinese Communist intervention in Korea, to underestimation of the opponent's motivation. Rather, the failure to give credence to the possibility that the Soviets would deploy missiles into Cuba can be traced to a faulty assessment of Soviet risk calculations. American analysts erred in assuming that the Soviet leaders would regard a missile deployment as a high-risk strategy and,

	Pearl Harbor	Berlin Blockade	Korean War	Chinese Intervention	Berlin 1958	Cuban Missile Crisis
5. Influence of policy background	+	0	+	+	+	?
6. Successful deception	+	0	0	?	0	+
7. "Noise"	+	?	+	0	+	+
8. Underestimation of opponent's motivation	+	0	+	+	?	0
9. Underestimation of opponent's capabilities	+	0	+	+	0	+
10. Inadequate appraisal of opponent's risk calculations	+	+	+	+	+	+
11. Problem of response if warning is credited	?	+	+	+	0	?
12. Influence of domestic and organizational politics	+	+	+	+	0	+

therefore, would not undertake this option. In fact, however, Soviet leaders evidently convinced themselves that the missile deployment was a calculable, controllable low-risk strategy.

The inability of American officials to grasp fully the Soviet approach to risk calculation and risk acceptance was in fact a chronic problem in the Cold War. Earlier in 1948, despite considerable warning which included the "baby blockade" of April, American leaders were taken by surprise when the Soviets imposed a blockade on Allied ground access to West Berlin in late June. Most American officials had assumed that Soviet leaders would recognize that a move against West Berlin constituted a high-risk strategy, and hence would reject it as unacceptable.

VARIATION IN THE FACTORS
MAKING FOR
INTELLIGENCE FAILURE

It may be useful to note the presence or absence of the twelve contributing factors in some of the cases we have studied in which U.S. intelligence failure contributed to surprise. We have prepared a table that treats five of those cases: the Berlin blockade of 1948, Korea, the Chinese Communist intervention, the Berlin "deadline crisis" of 1958, and the Cuban missile crisis. We add to this the Pearl Harbor case, relying on Mrs. Wohlstetter's study for this purpose.

From this it is clear that not all the twelve factors that can contribute to intelligence failure are present in each case of surprise. Some factors will be absent in some cases, and furthermore, the relative weight that should be assigned to factors which are present will vary from one case to another and will be difficult to determine with precision. Of course, policymakers and intelligence specialists must constantly consider the possibility that any or all twelve of the factors may be operating in the problems they are facing at any given time.

Bibliography

Allison, Graham. *Essence of Decision*. Boston, Little, Brown, 1971.
De Rivera, Joseph. *The Psychological Dimension of Foreign Policy.*Columbus, Ohio, Merrill, 1968.
Downs, Anthony. *Inside Bureaucracy*. Boston, Little, Brown, 1967.
George, Alexander L. "Adaptation to Stress in Political Decision-making," in *Coping and Adaptation* ed. G. V. Coelho, D. A. Hamburg, and J. Adams. New York, Basic Books, 1974.
Janis, Irving L. *Victims of Groupthink*. Boston, Houghton Mifflin, 1972.
Jervis, Robert. *Perception and Mis-perception in International Relations*. Princeton, Princeton University Press, forthcoming.
Whaley, Barton. *Codeword Barbarossa*. Cambridge, Mass., MIT Press, 1973.
Wilensky, Harold L. *Organizational Intelligence*. New York, Basic Books, 1967.
Wohlstetter, Roberta. "Cuba and Pearl Harbor: Hindsight and Foresight," *Foreign Affairs*, 43, No. 4 (July 1965), 707.

Chapter 21

From Deterrence to Influence
in Theory and Practice

The Narrowness of
Deterrence Theory and Practice

IT MAY BE USEFUL to begin the final chapter of this study with a brief summary of what we have undertaken to do and what general findings and conclusions we have reached thus far. From the dual perspective of theory and practice, we have examined deterrence as it applies to crisis and limited-war situations—a rather different case from strategic deterrence. Some opinions to the contrary notwithstanding, policy-makers can indeed benefit, perhaps greatly, from theory about deterrence of this kind. Properly formulated, theory can assist in diagnosing emergent situations and in determining how best to apply a deterrence strategy. Perhaps more importantly, the diagnosis can, with the assistance of theory, determine whether a deterrence strategy is really applicable and desirable in any given situation.

We have discussed the special characteristics a theory must have to be relevant to policy and the problems the investigator encounters in attempting to develop more valid policy-relevant theory. (These matters are discussed from a more general perspective in the Appendix.) We have found that deterrence theory to date has been seriously deficient in the requirements for policy-relevance. It is in the nature of any theory that it must simplify some aspects of the reality it seeks to comprehend. But if policy use is to be made of a theory, those elements of the real-life phenomenon that were left out or oversimplified in the formulation of the theory must be identified, and their implications for the theory's content and its use by policy-makers must be noted. This is just what has not been done with deterrence theory. Reasoning deductively from decision theory, and especially from game theory, investigators have offered a relatively abstract theory of deterrence which has received little testing against historical reality. Moreover, this theory has been presented in the prescriptive mode—that is, as a guide for policy— despite the fact that it does not in actuality meet the requirements for policy-relevance.

In order to identify the existing theory more fully and to rectify some of its deficiencies, we have examined in detail some historical experiences with the use of deterrence in American foreign policy. By looking inductively at the problem of deterrence in concrete historical situations, we have been able to identify many factors that affect the uses and limitations of deterrence strategies in foreign policy—factors that were not taken into account properly, or at all, in previous formulations of deterrence theory. Using these case studies we have developed an explanatory—not primarily prescriptive—theory of the conditions under which deterrence succeeds or fails, becomes applicable or inapplicable. And we have analyzed important components of the deterrence process in chapters on initiation theory, commitment theory, and response theory.

We have not confined our critical appraisal to deterrence theory. Nor have we restricted our examination of American foreign policy to showing how systematic study of history can assist in developing a better theory of deterrence. We have also been critical of certain aspects of American foreign policy itself during the Cold War period. While this book is certainly not intended as a comprehensive or systematic study of American foreign policy in the years after World War II, we felt that the critical appraisal of deterrence theory that we were undertaking would benefit from, and in fact required, a critical stance toward the use of deterrence strategy in American foreign policy. The reason for this is a simple one: since deterrence is an instrument of foreign policy, its uses and limitations are very much affected by the nature of that foreign policy and by the sophistication and skill with which policy-makers use all instruments of policy, of which deterrence is but one, on behalf of national goals. Accordingly, in the case studies presented in Part Two we criticized different aspects of American foreign policy as it developed and was applied during these years, as these were relevant to questionable uses of deterrence strategy.

Rather than presenting a more detailed summary of our findings to this point, we will now focus attention on a fundamental shortcoming of both the theory and the practice of deterrence since World War II. Deterrence theorists have erred, we submit, in regarding deterrence as a separable, self-contained phenomenon about which a useful general prescriptive theory could be developed. The work of early theorists was flawed by the evident assumption that a viable theory of deterrence could be developed independently of a broader theory of inter-nation influence, one that would encompass the utility of positive incentives as well as threats of negative ones. American policy-makers erred in a similar manner by relying on deterrence strategy too heavily and making insufficient use of other means of influencing and controlling the conflict potential in their relations with other states. For understandable reasons the narrowness of this focus on deterrence was not readily apparent to policy-makers and scholars at the time. It seemed a necessary corrective to the earlier overreliance of the Western powers on more conciliatory diplomatic approaches to adversaries—first toward Hitler in the 1930s, then toward Stalin during the latter part of World War II and immediately thereafter. As a result of these events, "appeasement" fell into such disrepute as to discredit more generally the traditional reliance of classical diplomacy upon negotiation and conciliation for adjusting conflicting interests and for reconciling change in the international system with the requirements for stability.[1]

A major conclusion of this study, therefore, is that deterrence should be viewed not as a self-contained strategy, but as an integral part of a broader, multifaceted influence process. Concerning theory, what is needed is not merely a better deterrence theory per se but rather a broader theory which encompasses deterrence as one of a number of means that can be employed, separately or in some combination, to influence conflict processes and to control the conflict potential in interstate relations. Concerning practice, policy-makers need to recapture the perspective of classical diplomacy at its best, which emphasized flexible, discriminating use of a variety of means for influencing adversaries and avoiding conflict. Whether deterrent threats are necessary and useful in a particular historical situation cannot be judged either in theory or in practice on the basis of a prescriptive theory that narrowly confines itself to indicating how to make threats: threats that are credible and potent enough to force an opponent to conclude that it is not in his self-interest to encroach on the defender's interests.

These criticisms of the narrowness of deterrence theory and of the overreliance of American foreign policy on deterrence strategy apply, we maintain, even to the height of the Cold War. One of the limitations of deterrence theory noted repeatedly in different ways throughout this study is that it did not attempt to define the scope and relevance of deterrence strategy in American foreign policy. Throughout the years of the Cold War, therefore, deterrence theory offered no help (to say the least!) in curbing a tendency to globalize and rigidify the policy of containment; it offered no criteria for making selective, discriminating use of deterrence.

---

[1] On the historical setting of deterrence theory see, for example, Luard, "Conciliation and Deterrence," and Herz, "The Relevancy and Irrelevancy of Appeasement."

The Changing Context
of Deterrence

While some observers did perceive the need for a more balanced view of the role of deterrence in American foreign policy even during the height of the Cold War, since then such recognition has been forced upon foreign policy–makers by important changes in the international and domestic environment in the past decade.

A brief listing of these developments will suffice to remind us of the remarkable transformation that has taken place in the arena of world politics since about 1960: (1) the political and economic recovery of many nations from the dislocation of World War II; (2) the emergence of many new nations and their increasing ability to maintain their independence and to avoid becoming simply battlegrounds for the Cold War; (3) the passing of American strategic superiority and the achievement of strategic parity by the Soviet Union; (4) the increasing limits on American power and American ability to influence world developments unilaterally or in concert with allies (of this the Vietnam War is only the most obvious and tragic example); (5) the change in the nature of the communist challenge with the passing of Moscow's monolithic control of the international communist movement and the emergence of competing centers of communist doctrine, power, and practice; in particular, the development of a profound Sino-Soviet split; (6) the trend away from a rigid bipolar structure of the world system to a more fluid multipolar system; (7) the growing constraints on American resources available to support foreign policy and the strongly felt need of the American people to shift priorities to urgent domestic problems; (8) the increasing unwillingness of domestic opinion in the United States to support costly foreign policy commitments.

These important changes in the world environment have entered, however slowly, into the perceptions of leading architects of American foreign policy. That they have affected the formulation of the Nixon Doctrine has been explicitly acknowledged. As President Nixon put it on February 25, 1971, in his annual foreign policy report to Congress:

> The post-war order in international relations—the configuration of power that emerged from the Second World War—is gone. With it are gone the conditions which have determined the assumptions and practices of United States foreign policy since 1945.[2]

The Nixon Administration attempted to respond to widespread feelings within the country that American foreign policy had to move toward at least partial disengagement from the extensive commitments throughout the world that it accumulated during the Cold War. The policy of containment as it was applied during that era was considered obsolete. To be sure there remained a tendency to cling to some of the essentials of containment policy if not also its rhetoric, in the absence of a well-developed alternative concept. Thus, the Nixon Doctrine, which President Nixon announced shortly after coming to office, was an odd mixture of containment (though not referred to as such) and hints of a successor to that policy. Nixon foresaw the necessity for redefining American interests in Asia to make them more compatible with the legitimate interests of Communist China, for shrinking the American role in world politics more generally, and for fundamental changes in the international system. While he expressed a willingness to move in those directions, he also emphasized that the changes would have to be gradual and undertaken cautiously, not merely because they would be difficult to work out but also because efforts at more rapid change could be highly destabilizing for international peace. Thus, the 1971 report to Congress warned that "precipitate shrinking of the American role would not bring peace." [3]

The Nixon Doctrine, it is clear, was *not* a plan for the rapid liquidation of U.S. foreign policy commitments. The doctrine tacitly accepted the long-standing argument of critics of Ameri-

---

[2] Nixon, *U.S. Foreign Policy for the 1970's*, 1971, p. 3.   [3] *Ibid.*, p. 16.

can policy that the United States was overcommitted and had to redefine its commitments to reflect its more important and vital interests. But Nixon and his advisers were extremely sensitive to the dangers of drawing a new line which would make clear what the United States was and was not committed to defend. Clearly, they wished to avoid the risks associated with specific delimitation of a "defense perimeter" of the kind that Truman and Acheson formulated and announced in the winter of 1949–1950 which, many have felt, contributed to the outbreak of the Korean War. Accordingly, in statements of the Nixon Doctrine the administration took pains to emphasize that the administration would "respect the commitments we inherited— both because of their intrinsic merit, and because of the impact of sudden shifts on regional or world stability. To desert those who have come to depend on us would cause disruption and invite aggression." [4]

At the same time, while it rejected outright abandonment of any commitment, the Nixon Doctrine clearly signaled an intention to engage in a *more differentiated* assessment of U.S. interests in deciding *what means* to employ on behalf of each commitment. In this connection, the Nixon Doctrine deliberately rejected the notion of "either-or" commitments which, as we have noted in this study, was one of the more serious of the oversimplified assumptions of deterrence theory and also a persistent theme in U.S. deterrence strategy during the Cold War. Many of the critical observations and recommendations we made in the chapter on commitment theory are implicit in the Nixon Doctrine's carefully worded language regarding the need to move away from the rigid concept of a commitment which required, if challenged, as much American involvement as was necessary to "honor" it. [5]

[4] *Ibid.*, pp. 12–13.

[5] For example, Nixon's 1970 report to Congress on foreign policy distinguished between "commitments" and "interests" and emphasized the primacy of the latter in the conduct of foreign policy. In his press conference remarks introducing the report, President Nixon emphasized that the administration felt it necessary to reexamine commitments around the world "to see that they are consis-

The Nixon Administration also gave indications that it would like to recapture political flexibility and discretion with regard to whether and how the United States would honor various commitments under various contingencies. Statements of the Nixon Doctrine clearly indicated a general intention to limit the involvement of American forces if it became necessary to honor some commitments, though without indicating which allies the principle applied to. With regard to Asian allies, not only did the Nixon Doctrine weaken the commitment to an automatic military response. In addition, however cautiously and gradually, the administration undertook to withdraw U.S. military forces stationed on the territory of some of its Asian allies. It was not immediately apparent how far the administration would go in reversing the "forward strategy" in the Pacific. But, of course, if American forces which constituted "trip wires" and symbols of firm U.S. commitment were removed, then the basis for automatic U.S. response in case of attack on an ally would also be removed. At the same time, however, the capacity for a quick military response would presumably be retained by virtue of the strength of U.S. air and naval power in the Pacific.

In these and other respects, the Nixon Doctrine returned to certain, though by no means all, of the components of the Eisenhower Administration's defense policies in Asia. Noteworthy in this respect, as has been widely noted, was the Nixon Doctrine's attempt once again to place reliance on U.S. air and naval power and to shift primary responsibility for ground forces to the countries directly threatened.[6] Unlike the Eisenhower New Look, however, the Nixon Doctrine did not

---

tent with our interests." The report itself underscored this point: ". . . Our interests must shape our commitments, rather than the other way around." *New York Times*, February 19, 1970.

[6] Avoidance of another Vietnam is acknowledged to be an important objective behind the strategy of more limited U.S. military involvement in future local conflicts of this kind. In Vietnam, it may be recalled, the war was "Americanized" in 1965 by the introduction of large U.S. combat forces. Nixon's Vietnamization policy attempted to "de-Americanize" the war. It is clear that the Nixon Doctrine projects the Vietnamization policy into a more general strategy for the immediate future in Asia and elsewhere.

accompany its emphasis on air and naval power with a perceived need for and a willingness to use nuclear weapons in a variety of limited conflicts.[7] The vastly greater conventional military capabilities achieved by U.S. air and naval forces in the Pacific since the Eisenhower era made it unnecessary for the Nixon Administration to rely upon early tactical use of nuclear weapons in order to avoid defeat at the conventional level.

In these and other respects the Nixon Doctrine was not without important ambiguities.[8] Some of these ambiguities, certainly, were due to the fact that the doctrine addressed a multiple audience or, at least, had to take into account the fact that different interested audiences were listening. As Robert Johnson notes, the administration was very conscious of the fact that it spoke

> to both a domestic audience wishing for disengagement and an Asian audience, a part of which is worried about disengagement. Accordingly, the Administration has indicated that the need to maintain public support at home and confidence abroad are the two critical factors determining tactics of implementation of the Doctrine.[9]

Nonetheless, the fact remains that the Nixon Doctrine contained explicit and implicit disavowals of various premises and components of the earlier American Cold War policy and philosophy.[10]

[7] Rather, the Nixon Doctrine indicated a reduced role for nuclear weapons in Asian conflicts. American nuclear power was to provide a deterrent "shield" for friendly Asian countries who lacked nuclear weapons of their own—e.g., Japan, India, etc.— to safeguard them against nuclear blackmail by unfriendly nuclear powers—i.e., Communist China and the Soviet Union. As President Nixon put it in his 1971 statement on *U.S. Foreign Policy for the 1970's:* "Their concern would be magnified if we were to leave them defenseless against nuclear blackmail, or conventional aggression backed by nuclear power." P. 13.

[8] Thus, for example, the administration felt itself obliged to hedge and to blur its announced preference for limited U.S. involvement in future conflicts: "No President can guarantee that future conflicts will never involve American personnel—but in some theatres the threshhold of involvement will be raised and in some instances involvement will be much more unlikely." Nixon, *U.S. Foreign Policy for the 1970's*, 1971, p. 14.

[9] Johnson, "The Nixon Doctrine," p. 176.

[10] Charles Gati plausibly argues that the Nixon-Kissinger foreign policy is based on premises that bear a remarkable similarity to the early criticisms of contain-

Much had changed in this respect, of course, before Nixon came to office in 1969. The turning point in the Cold War was the Cuban missile crisis or, to place the emphasis more exactly, the willingness and ability of Kennedy and Khrushchev to move from that brink of catastrophe to a partial détente. From that time the fulcrum of American foreign policy began to shift away from the premises of the Cold War. Since then we have seen a growing willingness of successive presidents and their administrations to recognize that the acute phase of the Cold War is over, and that major changes in the international environment impose upon them a search for a new basis for American foreign policy.

In noting the decline of fundamental Cold War premises, let us recall that containment policy rested on a particular image of Soviet behavior as expansionist. It attributed to Soviet rulers a strong, almost compulsive desire to expand into any vacuum in order to enhance Soviet power and influence, and to bring the rest of the world under some kind and degree of Soviet control. The Soviet Union was seen as at the head of a monolithic international communist movement, either behind any challenge to the status quo or poised to exploit ruthlessly any takeover by a noncommunist reformist or revolutionary group. This "devil image" of the opponent, which attributed malevolence and ruthless efficiency to Soviet rulers, gave way gradually as experience showed that the Soviet Union was often quite cautious and unsuccessful in expanding its influence. Moreover, the rulers and peoples of many new countries proved themselves able to accept Soviet economic, military, and diplomatic support without losing their independence.

Following the Cuban missile crisis, Kennedy and Khrushchev moved quickly to a détente. What was significant in this development was that American leaders began to view the Soviet Union as a limited adversary rather than as a total enemy. Similarly, the nature of the conflict with the Soviet Union was now perceived in non-zero-sum terms rather than, as in the

---

ment offered by critics such as Walter Lippmann. See Gati's "What Containment Meant."

acute Cold War era, in terms of a zero-sum contest. This change was dramatically signaled in President Kennedy's eloquent American University address of June 10, 1963, when he called upon the American people to reexamine their views on the Cold War and warned his listeners "not to see only a distorted and desperate view of the other side, not to see conflicts as inevitable, accommodation as impossible and communication as nothing more than an exchange of threats. No government or social system is so evil that its people must be considered lacking in virtue." [11]

The significance of the limited détente in U.S.-Soviet relations lay in the tacit understanding of the two sides that they would henceforth attempt to separate and "de-couple" as much as possible the issues on which they disagreed.[12] Moreover, instead of attempting to resolve at one and the same time all the major outstanding conflicts between them, the two antagonists in effect agreed not to push and thus exacerbate their long-standing disagreements over Central and Eastern Europe, arms control inspection, Cuba, overseas U.S. bases, etc. Such issues, evidently deemed too difficult for early solution, were set aside for the time being; there was a tacit understanding that they would continue to disagree on these issues without reviving acute forms of Cold War vituperation and political warfare.

Whereas the Cold War had been dominated by a belief in the necessary indivisibility of issues, with everything somehow connected with everything else, the limited détente ushered in a mutual willingness to reach agreement on many single issues that could be separated from other, more important matters on which agreement would have been more difficult. A number of such agreements were quickly made—the partial test ban, the "hot line" agreement, cooperation on peaceful uses and exploration of space, etc. Other agreements, such as the nuclear nonproliferation treaty, followed more slowly.

[11] *New York Times*, June 11, 1973, p. 16.

[12] See Roger Fisher's discussion of "fractionating" conflict in his *International Conflict and Behavioral Science*, pp. 91–109.

Thus, it may be fairly said that the "era of negotiation" which President Nixon heralded on coming to office in 1969 had its roots in the limited détente which Kennedy and Khrushchev initiated in 1963.

Unfortunately, however, the acute Cold War version of containment policy persisted vis-à-vis Communist China and contributed to the embroilment of the United States in Vietnam. Finally, though, the slow movement toward a détente with Peking made significant progress during Nixon's first term. The rigidity of U.S. containment policy toward China, as toward Soviet Russia earlier, was now softened and replaced by a mutual, if cautious, desire to search for accommodation and conciliation, to emphasize areas of agreement, and to defer issues on which no agreement was possible in the near future. As with the Soviet Union some years before, the "devil image" of Communist China to which important American policy-makers had subscribed for twenty years was replaced by a new image of Peking as a limited adversary.

As a result of these developments in U.S. relations with both major communist powers, deterrence strategy has assumed a less prominent role in American foreign policy. Even though one must regard containment as continuing today in some of its essentials, despite a softening in rhetoric, U.S. policy-makers have come to rely less exclusively and less mechanically on deterrence threats to protect American interests abroad and to discourage encroachments upon allies.

In recent years there has been a much greater readiness in American foreign policy to employ negotiation and conciliation as a means of forestalling, if not fully and immediately resolving, potentially dangerous conflicts of interest with communist opponents. Recall that during the height of the Cold War, American policy-makers wished to defer negotiation of outstanding issues until they had achieved a "position of strength," as Dean Acheson put it in the early fifties; or else they fell back upon negotiations only under the pressure of an ongoing crisis, as Dulles felt it prudent to do during the Quemoy crisis of 1958 and the Berlin crisis of 1958–1959. In contrast, recent years have seen American policy-makers ready to make serious and patient use of negotiations in *precrisis* situations to prevent, if possible, a conflict of interests over a particular issue, such as Berlin, from developing once more into a dangerous crisis. By giving priority on a timely basis to a search for diplomatic solutions and accommodations, American policy-makers are tacitly downgrading the reliance earlier administrations placed upon deterrence strategy to prevent challenges to U.S. interests abroad and encroachments on allies.

Deterrence in Alternative American Foreign Policies of the Future

In the present, and in the probable near future, therefore, deterrence is playing and is likely to continue to play a less dominant role in U.S. foreign policy—a happy development, we believe, as previously policy depended too heavily upon deterrence efforts. But this is not to say (as some might be tempted to believe or hope) that deterrence will fade away entirely as an instrument of American foreign policy. It is much more likely that its place will be redefined but still quite significant in the post-Vietnam period. Some thought should be given to what that redefinition should consist of and how it might be arrived at.

Various alternative U.S. foreign policies are possibilities for the post-Vietnam period. Despite active attention to the options by the scholarly community, no consensus has yet emerged, or seems likely to shortly. And official statements by the administration have remained ambiguous on the subject, evidently reflecting not merely calculation but also genuine uncertainty. While a retrenchment from the forward strategy of the past and a dilution of commitments are clearly under way, the United States will surely stop well short of full-blown isolationism in its stance toward the rest of the world. This option is widely mentioned only as something which almost everyone rejects.

Short of this unpalatable extreme, however, there is a wide range of possible foreign policies of a post–Cold War variety. In a complex continuum of choices we might crystalize four nameable options, each with its implications for the theory and practice of deterrence.

1. "Mild and realistic isolationism" might imply a fairly thoroughgoing retrenchment of U.S. commitments to a "security minimum"—a firm defense of NATO, ANZUS, and the Americas and a nuclear guarantee to Japan. Otherwise, alterations in the status quo, excepting (presumably) those involving Israel, would tend not to be defined as challenges to the U.S. national interest. Comparatively little presidential attention would go to foreign affairs, and a comparatively low budget would be assigned to defense. Although his campaign statements were unclear, we take it that this is approximately the policy Senator George McGovern favored in 1972.

The implications of this type of foreign policy for U.S. deterrence strategy may not be as completely obvious as they might appear. While presumably for most areas of the world, deterrence would not be attempted seriously, a vigorous and declaratively firm deterrence effort *would* be required for those areas which remained under U.S. protection. This would be doubly true if the general pullback seemed to be inviting serious challenges designed to test its limits.

2. To some extent supplemental to rather than competitive with this mild isolationism might be a foreign policy emphasizing the "North-South" division of the world. Along with this option an activist program commanding considerable presidential attention and major resources would focus upon assistance to the less developed countries, and support for activities of the U.N. General Assembly and functional agencies. International stability would be sought through major development efforts rather than through politico-military means, with threats to the status quo managed through the U.N. as a "collective security" organ. Presumably, the U.S. would structure its security commitments, and hence its deterrence strategy, much as in the first option.

3. A "modified and updated containment" policy, probably called something else for domestic political reasons, would represent essentially a continuation of policies and assumptions that were applied to areas other than Southeast Asia in the latter part of the 1960s. Relatively large defense expenditures and a relatively strong foreign policy would buttress a containment line, somewhat ambiguously drawn (and perhaps excluding Taiwan). The amount of attention and effort allocated to the "containment problem" would decline only relatively slowly, as cautious additional progress toward détente was made with China and the Soviet Union.

Deterrence under this option would be relatively similar to U.S. deterrence strategy of the present and recent past. But there would be an increasing need for gradually less visible, more subtle applications of deterrence (both declaratively and, in the event of new East-West crises, in action), inasmuch as provocativeness would need to be minimized lest détente be jeopardized, even while some type of "containment" remained in force.

4. Growing attention is being given to the so-called balance-of-power option, modeled on international relations in nineteenth-century Europe, whereby five "great powers"—the United States, united Europe, the USSR, China, and Japan—would maneuver among themselves. This system would presume little of the rigidity that often arose from ideological or Cold War intentions and fears, and the great powers operating within it would place a premium on flexibility in their manipulations. Under such a system, deterrence would appear frequently, as a national tool, but in a somewhat different form than in the Cold War era. Rather than emphasizing the permanence and "blanket" character of the deterrence commitment, as Cold War policy-makers have tended to do, policy-makers operating in a balance-of-power system would need to emphasize the precise conditions applying to their commitments, usually including a time limit. Deterrence efforts in this system would need to be relatively short term, highly flexible, and well integrated with other national foreign policy tools. Deter-

rence would be employed often but more subtly than it was during much of the Cold War.

The first two options in this set would require, almost by definition, a more selective and more discriminating use of deterrence combined, no doubt, with more attention to positive incentives as means of influencing the behavior of other states. But options 3 or 4 (which may be more likely ones) or some mixture of the two would also require, albeit in somewhat different ways, more selective, careful, and differentiated use of deterrence strategies. Both these options would also require, again in somewhat different ways, increased attention to positive incentives as tools in foreign policy.

It is noteworthy that options 3 and 4, modified containment and balance of power, do not mix very readily, despite the fact that the apparent current trend in American foreign policy is to attempt to do just this. This is true in a number of respects, but we shall focus upon deterrence here. Under option 3 (modified continuing containment) the emphasis in both the declaratory and the action aspects of deterrence policy, despite some degree of retrenchment and the introduction of ambiguity, would have to be upon the stability and continuity of traditional commitments (and hence, traditional threats). But option 4, if it is to make sense, requires enormously greater flexibility. Shifting alignments, whereby any of the great powers may enter into limited alliances with any of the others for comparatively short periods, requires the abandonment of all or nearly all the traditional deterrence commitments and the adoption of only temporary new ones.

As we see it, therefore, *the problem of deterrence does not vanish* in the post-Vietnam era of U.S. foreign policy; rather it changes form, more or less drastically and in any of several ways. What seems safely predictable is that, *whatever* tack American foreign policy takes, its deterrence component will need to be applied more selectively, with more careful attention to the inherent limits as well as the potential benefits of deterrence, and where deterrence *is* adjudged necessary, with more thoughtful attention to its actual operational requirements.

In short, there is an increasing, not decreasing, need for the kind of differentiated analysis of deterrence problems which we have emphasized in this study.

From Deterrence to Inducement

The rapidly shifting context of U.S. foreign policy provides greater room—and a newly receptive audience—for analysis of the broader problem of "influence" among nations.

At its most general, of course, "influence" encompasses all or nearly all aspects of relations among nations, and its study is virtually coextensive with the entire discipline of international relations and with the entire conduct of foreign policy. But it is not to this level of generality that we urge attention. Rather, it is "influence" in the context of conflict reduction which, we believe, demands fresh study, especially for its applications to the post-Cold War world of the 1970s and beyond. In theory, there are major devices besides threats for reducing or preventing overt conflict. For example, a contingent promise may be more appropriate in some situations than a contingent threat.

All influence devices including deterrence may be thought of analytically as falling into two broad, not wholly distinct categories according to the time-horizon to which they apply. Devices other than deterrence are potentially available for dealing with short-term problems of crisis or with a threat of crisis. One such is appeasement in its original and honorable sense of giving the opponent his minimum, essential demands in the interests of peace. This device, perhaps now better termed "conciliation," is appropriate under two circumstances: (1) where there are grounds for believing that the opponent's objectives are in fact limited and can be satisfied at a reasonable cost; or (2) where one needs to appease a greedy opponent in order to buy time in order to prepare ways of dealing with him more effectively.

But when we turn to the *long-term* development of the international system we find greater reasons still for examining the entirety of inter-nation influence—including deterrence but not limited to it and indeed, deemphasizing it. It is in this respect that American foreign policy is likely to be particularly weak and in need of help from specialists in international relations. For, obviously, it is inadequate merely to deter unfavorable change; one must also create and/or guide change in favorable directions.

These two categories are not rigidly distinct. Strategies aimed at dealing with short-term problems in ways substituting for or supplementing deterrence can also be a part of one's longer-term plans. But the distinction is useful because in the two categories the policy-maker's roles and activities differ. In one case he begins with the immediate situation and searches for means to cope with it; while in the other he begins with a model or image of his desired future international reality and deductively reasons back from it toward the present, in order to devise appropriate strategies or means for pursuing the longer-range objectives. The latter task is the more difficult of the two, especially for the United States. Inevitably, the United States in important respects is a status quo power. Less inevitably, the United States also lacks, except in the vaguest terms, any vision of how it wishes world politics to develop over the long run.[13] The result is the widely observed "reactive" character of U.S. foreign policy, a tendency to do little until a challenge to the status quo arises, and then to deal with it as a threat. Deterrence is an influence policy peculiarly appropriate to these attitudes.

For this reason and doubtless others as well, deterrence has been singled out by American theorists and policy-makers for special attention, with other kinds of influence policies left in the hazy background. But appreciation of the importance of supplementing deterrence theory has been growing among specialists in international relations. Roger Fisher in his *International Conflict for Beginners* notes that "in this era of nuclear weapons and deterrence the Department of Defense has be-

[13] Stanley Hoffmann addresses himself to this in some detail in chapter 5, Part Three of *Gulliver's Troubles*.

come quite sophisticated about making threats [but] we have no comparable sophistication regarding the making of offers." And he believes that "this is an important way of exerting influence on which there has been far too little organized consideration."[14]

Probably many theorists would agree that the time is overripe for deterrence theory to be supplemented with what might be called "inducement theory," the two together forming an important ingredient of the broader inter-nation influence theory to which we have referred. Under the circumstances of the 1970s, and foreseeably the 1980s, not only must deterrence be comprehended and executed in more subtle ways than in the past, as discussed earlier in this chapter; but deterrence increasingly must be supplemented with inducement policies as well.

In beginning to examine the problems of inducement, it is important that analysts avoid repeating the errors committed earlier in the development of deterrence theory. Specifically, it does not seem productive to attempt to develop an abstract, deductive theory or model of inducement, derived from game theory, decision theory, or other sources. Aside from the difficulties inherent in such an effort, the resulting theory might be positively undesirable if it were offered as a prescriptive theory, as deterrence theory has been.[15] Rather, inducement should be approached in an empirical and inductive fashion, utilizing either qualitative methodologies like the focused-comparison method employed in the present work or quantitative methodologies when testable and relevant propositions are available. Despite the large literature on world politics since World War II, there exists hardly any significant study of this

[14] Fisher, *International Conflict for Beginners*, p. 106. Fisher carries the analysis of influence processes further in his most recent book, *Dear Israelis, Dear Arabs*.

[15] This is not to say that abstract hypothesizing might not be useful if it were pursued for its heuristic value for empirical inquiry. See, for example, Thomas Schelling's general remarks on the problems of "promises" in *The Strategy of Conflict* (Oxford, Oxford University Press paperback, 1960), pp. 43–46, 131–37, and 175–77.

particular aspect of national interactions in this period. The Cold War and post–Cold War period can provide numerous, and earlier diplomatic history many more, cases of both success and failure of inducement efforts.

The immediate goal of such empirical inquiries should be the building of historical-explanatory theory of the kind discussed in chapter 16—that is, theory which explains why inducement succeeded or failed in given cases or classes of cases. The general conclusions that emerge from these empirical inquiries will not necessarily have direct prescriptive value for the present problems of decision-makers, and should not automatically be so used. They are more likely to have relevance and real utility to policy-makers, however, if they can discriminate among separate varieties of cases, deriving differentiated or "conditional" conclusions. Such findings may assist decision-makers in diagnosing contemporary situations to which inducement may be applicable, suggest the uses and limitations of inducement strategies, illuminate some of the variables affecting one's own or the opponent's behavior, and indicate different ways in which inducement efforts can succeed or fail.

Research into the nature and problems of inducement will need to take cognizance of the fact that, while inducement is simpler than deterrence in some respects—for instance there is much less ambiguity about whether it has succeeded or failed in most specific cases—it is more complicated in other respects. One is its greater complexity as a *long-term* device. A deterrence policy may be extended indefinitely, but an inducement policy will usually require new initiatives periodically or it will fail. But even short-term inducement policies are likely to be more complex than similarly short-term deterrence policies. Let us consider some of the complexities of short-term inducement policies first before we return to the special difficulties that U.S. policy is likely to experience in attempting to employ inducements on behalf of longer-term goals.

One complication is that "positive influence," i.e., inducement, can either be pursued as a line of policy by itself, or it can be pursued in conjunction with "negative influence" policies such as deterrence or coercive diplomacy. It is useful to distinguish between "pure" and "mixed" influence strategies because the mechanisms involved and the patterns of success and failure are likely to be significantly different. A "mixed strategy" usually appears, if at all, in crisis and crisis-preventive diplomacy, and generally represents an effort to increase the probability of a favorable outcome by combining "carrots" with the "sticks." Historically, it has probably been more common to include an inducement factor in what is fundamentally a deterrent or coercive-diplomatic strategy than vice-versa.[16] Inclusion of an inducement factor in a deterrent strategy, for instance, will be intended to increase the opponent's incentives not to challenge deterrence. Rather than a simple threat of the form "if you do x, I shall do y to you," one attempts to strengthen or reinforce deterrence by adding to the threat a promise that "if on the other hand you do not do x, I shall do z for you." Explicitly or implicitly, indeed, the inclusion of an inducement factor is a relatively common means of attempting to cope with an anticipated challenge to deterrence. In the Berlin deadline crisis of 1958–1959, for example, Secretary Dulles's immediate reaction on receipt of warning that deterrence was about to fail was to suggest that the U.S. could approve a certain kind of East German control of the access routes. This could be viewed as an implicit inducement offer to the Soviets.[17]

A "pure" inducement strategy, however, will rarely appear

[16] That efforts at coercive diplomacy can and should often include an inducement factor is emphasized in A. L. George, D. K. Hall, and W. E. Simons, *The Limits of Coercive Diplomacy* (Boston, Little, Brown, 1971).

[17] We do not wish to pursue the problem of mixed strategies to deeper levels of analysis here. It may be worth noting, however, that the mixture can be sequential as well as simultaneous. For instance, a deterrence success which one fears may be only temporary could well be followed promptly by an inducement effort as an attempt to forestall a second challenge to the deterrence policy. We remarked earlier in this study on the failure of the Eisenhower Administration to do just this immediately following the largely successful maintenance of deterrence in the Taiwan Strait and Quemoy crises of 1954–1955 and 1958, and in the Berlin deadline crisis of 1958–1959. Note also the importance of a simultaneous "inducement" as a means of minimizing the costs to the opponent of accepting defeat of his challenge to deterrence.

in crisis or crisis-preventive diplomacy (at least as we have been using this term here). A pure inducement strategy which is *not* a piece of some general, long-term effort to alter the international system would seem to be relevant to two kinds of situations. First, if one anticipates that a potential adversary might be tempted to mount a challenge to some area under one's protection at some future date, then under some circumstances one might offer him inducements not to do so rather than mounting a deterrence effort. As against this crisis-preventive use, inducements can also be employed, of course, simply to get something one wants: "if you do *x* for me, I shall do *y* for you." This second use of inducement as part of a political *trade* involves an intended change in the status quo rather than a defense of it.

These two types of short-term inducement strategy are parallel to the essential distinction between deterrence and coercive diplomacy. The interrelationships are suggested in the table, which sets out a typology of short-term "influence policies." The middle "tier" of mixed strategies is regarded as a continuum within the typology, since the mixture involved can include any proportion from nearly pure deterrence to nearly pure inducement.

It is worth noting in this connection the manner in which the term "coupling" has changed in use in U.S. foreign policy

Typology of Short-term Influence Policies

Type of Influence Strategy:	*Objective:* Preservation of the status quo	*Objective:* Alteration in the status quo
Pure positive	Inducement to forestall crisis ↓	Inducement for political "trade" ↓
Mixed	Mixes of inducement and deterrence ↑	Mixes of inducement and coercive diplomacy ↑
Pure negative	Deterrence	Coercive diplomacy

in the last decade, from a meaning associated with "deterrence" in this typology (lower left) to one associated with "inducement for political 'trade' " (upper right). When "coupling" was a term in the taxonomy of containment, it referred to the presumed interlocking character of commitments to maintain the containment line. Every commitment was coupled to every other, on the presumption that the failure to honor any would jeopardize all. As part of the Nixon Doctrine, "coupling" has come to refer to the presumedly interlocking character of the various elements in the détente process. A relaxation of traditional hostilities in one region or in one topic area both presupposes and assists to some degree relaxation in others. "Coupling," in fact, may turn out to be at least as valid and useful in a long-term inducement process as it ever was in deterrence.

We have distinguished thus far between inducement as part of a long-term effort to alter the international system and inducement as a short-term strategy. In general, the Nixon Administration and its successors are likely to make much more effective use of the various inducements at their disposal for short-term objectives of foreign policy than for the longer-range goal of building a more viable international system. As many observers have noted, short-term objectives of foreign policy are typically more clearly defined and more salient to American foreign policy–makers than is their image of a desired international system in the more distant future.

The Task Ahead

It is particularly important, therefore, for American policy-makers to address themselves to the admittedly difficult task of defining more clearly the kind of preferred international system toward which to strive, and to map out interim objectives and steps toward that future goal. Writing in 1968, Henry Kissinger stated that "In the years ahead, the most profound challenge to American policy will be philosophical: to develop some concept of order in a world which is bipolar militarily but multipolar politically." The central task of American foreign policy, he added, is "to develop some concepts which will enable us to contribute to the emergence of a stable order." And, in concluding this essay, written before he became President Nixon's Special Assistant for National Security Affairs, Kissinger warned that the next administration "must found its claim not on pat technical answers to difficult issues; it must above all ask the right questions. It must recognize that, in the field of foreign policy, we will never be able to contribute to building a stable and creative world order unless we first form some conception of it." [18]

But it is precisely in this respect that little progress was made during the first five years of the Nixon Administration. What Nixon was moving *away* from—namely, the residue of the Cold War—is clearer than what he was moving *toward*. It is true that while maintaining all existing U.S. commitments, the administration also implied that a more fundamental change in American foreign policy was desirable and was to be expected at some later point. Indeed, the Nixon Doctrine itself has been portrayed explicitly as a transitional phase in the development of new international and regional structures of peace and stability.[19] But the outlines of this future system remain opaque indeed. Elliptical hints from time to time that the administration favors a pentapolar balance-of-power system for the future (involving the United States, the Soviet Union, Communist China, Japan, and Western Europe) do not offer assurance that it has carefully thought through either the desirability or the feasibility of such an international system.[20]

[18] The essay, "Central Issues of American Foreign Policy," appeared originally in *Agenda for the Nation* (Washington, D.C., The Brookings Institution, 1968). It was reprinted in Kissinger's *American Foreign Policy*. The quotations are from pp. 79, 91, and 97 of the latter publication.

[19] See, for example, the brief discussion, "Beyond the Nixon Doctrine," in *U.S. Foreign Policy for the 1970's*, 1971, pp. 92, 97–98.

[20] In a detailed analysis of the administration's apparent effort to revive a balance-of-power system, Stanley Hoffmann finds this concept neither feasible nor desirable: "Weighing the Balance of Power." Critical observations are also of-

As if responding to critics of his new balance-of-power concept, President Nixon took pains in his 1973 report to Congress to dissociate himself from some of the interpretations made of his earlier statements: "We seek a stable structure, not a classical balance of power." Continuing, he noted that "the classical concept of balance of power included continual maneuvering for marginal advantages over others. In the nuclear era this is both unrealistic and dangerous. It is unrealistic because when both sides possess such enormous power, small additional increments cannot be translated into tangible advantage, or even usable political strength. And it is dangerous because attempts to seek tactical gains might lead to confrontation which could be catastrophic." At the same time, however, "national security must rest upon a certain equilibrium between potential adversaries," and therefore, "a certain balance of power is inherent in any international system and has its place in the one we envision. But it is not the over-riding concept of our foreign policy." [21]

However desirable the longer-range goal of establishing and maintaining "a certain balance of power" may appear to be, it is likely to have an adverse influence on the handling of some important short-term foreign policy problems. A possible example of this was the administration's policy in the Bangladesh crisis, which may have inadvertently contributed to the India-Pakistan conflict of December 1971. Siding with China and Pakistan, the United States did not succeed in its efforts to "balance" India and Russia. As Stanley Hoffmann notes:

> Neither America nor China were ready to commit forces, and a verbal "tilting" toward Pakistan, aimed at safeguarding our rapprochement with Peking and at warning Moscow, merely underlined Moscow's successful exploitation of India's desire to

---

fered by Alastair Buchan, "A World Restored?" and Zbigniew Brzezinski, "The Balance of Power Delusion." Writing in 1968 Henry Kissinger himself noted that "many of the elements of stability which characterized the international system in the nineteenth century cannot be re-created in the modern age." ("Central Issues of American Foreign Policy," *American Foreign Policy*, p. 57).

[21] Nixon, *U.S. Foreign Policy in the 1970's*, 1973, p. 230.

dismantle Pakistan and strengthened unnecessarily the bonds between Moscow and Delhi.[22]

What the Bangladesh crisis suggested is that, if guided by a vague desire to act as if a balance-of-power system already exists or can somehow be wished into existence, the United States is likely to deal with short-term issues in which the vital interests of small powers are involved "as if these countries were merely pawns in a global balancing game." [23]

Whatever the contemporary meaning and value of "balance of power," it is hardly likely to make much of a contribution to a durable structure of peace without the further development and strengthening of institutions of international order. The challenge to U.S. foreign policy remains, therefore, one of finding a longer-term image of a desirable world order—a genuine international community—which will be acceptable domestically and which can enlist cooperation among the nations; and of finding *all* the mechanisms of inter-nation influence, emphatically including inducement strategies, that can take us to this goal.

[22] Hoffmann, "Weighing the Balance of Power," p. 630.   [23] *Ibid.*

Bibliography

Baldwin, David A. "Inter-Nation Influence Revisited," *Journal of Conflict Resolution*, 15, No. 4 (December 1971), 471–86.
——. "The Power of Positive Sanctions," *World Politics*, 24 (October 1971), 19–38.
Barnett, A. Doak. "The New Multipolar Balance in East Asia: Implications for United States Policy," *The Annals*, 390 (July 1970), 73–85.
Brenner, Michael. "The Problem of Innovation and the Nixon-Kissinger Foreign Policy," *International Studies Quarterly*, 17, No. 3 (September 1973), 255–94.
Brzezinski, Zbigniew. "The Balance of Power Delusion," *Foreign Policy*, No. 7 (Summer 1972), pp. 54–59.
Buchan, Alastair. "A World Restored?" *Foreign Affairs*, 50, No. 4 (July 1972), 644–59.
——. *Power and Equilibrium in the 1970's*. New York, Praeger, 1973.
Chace, James. "The Five-Power World of Richard Nixon," *New York Times Magazine*, February 20, 1972, pp. 14 ff.
——. *A World Elsewhere: The New American Foreign Policy*. New York, Scribner, 1973.
Fisher, Roger. *International Conflict for Beginners*. New York, Harper & Row, 1969.
——. *International Conflict and Behavioral Science*. New York, Basic Books, 1964.
——. *Dear Israelis, Dear Arabs: A Working Approach to Peace*. New York, Harper & Row, 1973.
Fulbright, J. William. "In Thrall to Fear," *The New Yorker*, January 8, 1972, pp. 47–62.
Galtung, Johann. "Two Approaches to Disarmament: the Legalist and the Structuralist," *Journal of Peace Research*, IV, No. 2 (1967), 161–95.
Gati, Charles. "What Containment Meant," *Foreign Policy*, No. 7 (September 1972), pp. 22–40.
Herz, John H. "The Relevancy and Irrelevancy of Appeasement," *Social Research*, 31, No. 3 (Autumn 1964), 296–320.
Hoffmann, Stanley. *Gulliver's Troubles*. New York, McGraw-Hill, 1968.
——. "Weighing the Balance of Power," *Foreign Affairs*, 50, No. 4 (July 1972), 618–43.
Hsiung, James C. "The 'New' Nixon Doctrine, Multilateral Balance, and the Future of International Relations in Asia." Paper presented at the 1972 an-

nual meeting of the American Political Science Association, Washington, D.C., September 5–9, 1972.

Iklé, Fred Charles. *Every War Must End.* New York, Columbia University Press, 1971; Epilogue, "Ending Wars before They Start," pp. 106–31.

Johnson, Robert H. "The Nixon Doctrine and the New Policy Environment," in *Indochina in Conflict: A Political Assessment,* ed. Joseph J. Zasloff and Alan E. Goodman. Lexington, Mass., Heath, 1972; pp. 175–200.

Kissinger, Henry A. *American Foreign Policy: Three Essays.* New York, Norton, 1969.

Laird, Melvin R. *Fiscal Year 1971, Defense Program and Budget.* February 20, 1970.

——. *Fiscal Year 1972–1976, Defense Program and the 1972 Defense Budget.* March 9, 1971.

Lewis, Flora. "Nixon Doctrine," *Atlantic,* November 1970.

Luard, Evan. "Conciliation and Deterrence," *World Politics,* XIX, No. 2 (January 1967), 167–89.

Mansfield, Mike. "Perspective on Asia: The New U.S. Doctrine and Southeast Asia." Report of Mike Mansfield to Foreign Relations Committee, September 1969. Washington, U.S. Government Printing Office, 1969.

Nixon, Richard M. "Asia after Vietnam," *Foreign Affairs,* 46 (October 1967), 111–25.

——. "Background Briefing for the Press," Guam, July 25, 1969.

——. *U.S. Foreign Policy for the 1970's: A New Strategy for Peace.* February 18, 1970. Washington, U.S. Government Printing Office, 1970.

——. *U.S. Foreign Policy for the 1970's: Building for Peace.* February 25, 1971. Washington, U.S. Government Printing Office, 1971.

——. *U.S. Foreign Policy for the 1970's: The Emerging Structure of Peace.* February 9, 1972. Washington, U.S. Government Printing Office, 1972.

——. *U.S. Foreign Policy for the 1970's: Shaping a Durable Peace,* May 3, 1973. Washington, U.S. Government Printing Office, 1973.

Pool, Ithiel de Sola. "Deterrence as an Influence Process," *Studies in Deterrence.* China Lake, California, U.S. Naval Ordnance Test Station, November 1965.

Ravenal, Earl C. "The Nixon Doctrine and Our Asian Commitments," *Foreign Affairs,* 49, No. 2 (January 1971), 201–17.

Rosenthal, Martin. "Deterrence Theory and the Nixon Doctrine." Seminar paper, Stanford University, 1972.

Singer, J. D. "Inter-nation Influence: A Formal Model," *American Political Science Review,* 57 (June 1963), 420–30.

Appendix

Theory for Policy in
International Relations

THE PURPOSE OF THIS APPENDIX is to provide the larger theoretical context and framework within which this study has proceeded. We have attempted to make clear in the main body of the text our methodology for our deterrence inquiry itself; but many of the assumptions upon which this methodology rests have gone unarticulated, deferred deliberately to this point. We prefer to isolate and state explicitly here our views upon the nature of the theory-action relationship as it appears in the context of international affairs—or, as it is now commonly called, the problem of "policy-relevant theory" or simply "policy science." Our examination of deterrence theory and practice is meant to be taken as, among other things, a demonstration of a particular approach to the problem of "theory for policy" which we favor,

A substantially expanded version of this Appendix by the authors appeared under the title "Theory for Policy in International Relations," in *Policy Sciences*, December 1973.

This Appendix elaborates and develops further some themes presented initially in other studies by the authors: the Introduction to *The Limits of Coercive Diplomacy* by Alexander L. George, David K. Hall, and William R. Simons (Boston, Little, Brown, 1971); chapter 4 of "Toward the Control of Escalation," by Richard Smoke (unpublished version, Ph.D. dissertation, MIT, December 1971); and "Problems in Strategic Theory and Diplomatic History: Bismarck's Non-Escalating Wars as a Case Instance," by Richard Smoke (unpublished paper delivered at the Western Political Science Association convention, April 1971).

and the intellectual basis for which we now attempt to explain and justify. Let us begin from the perspective of the theorist of international relations.

The Nature of Policy Science

Many years ago Walter Lippmann proposed an important tripartite distinction in the major varieties of possible theories in international affairs, a distinction which has since come to be widely accepted.[1] One kind of theory is *empirical theory*, which most scholars mean first and foremost when they speak generally of "theory" in international relations. Empirical theory attempts to explain processes and to identify causal factors and other regular correlations in the real world of relations among states. On the assumption that experience includes not only single, isolated events but also elements of regularity and patterns, empirical theory attempts to identify those regularities and patterns and to develop propositions, sometimes probabilistic in form, describing and/or explaining them. Although there is much disagreement regarding the appropriate concepts, objects of study, necessary degree of abstraction, etc., for it, all empirical theory aims at understanding the nature of international events. Its source of information is history—actual history or on occasion the "synthetic history" of simulations. An important element of its character is the absence of values. It is the ideal of the social scientist thinking *qua* social scientist.

A second variety is *normative theory*, which concerns itself

---

[1] Lippmann's tripartite distinction is described and elaborated upon by Kenneth W. Thompson in his essay "Toward a Theory of International Politics," *American Political Science Review*, XLIX, No. 3 (September 1955), 733–46. This essay is essentially a report of a conference attended by Lippmann and a number of other theorists. Stanley Hoffmann reprints Thompson's essay in his book, *Contemporary Theory in International Relations* (Englewood Cliffs, N.J., Prentice-Hall, 1960), and repeats the tripartite distinction approvingly in his surrounding essay. Here we employ Hoffmann's nomenclature for the three kinds of theories.

with the "ought" rather than the "is" of international affairs. This may take the form of reasoned critique or comment upon a given line of foreign policy or the proposal of a different line. On another level of abstraction, it may take the form of the identification of long-term goals (or even final goals) for the international system, and their attendant strategies. (Representative examples of the latter might include the more serious theories of "world federalism" and of "world peace through world law.") In any case, normative theory inescapably possesses some philosophical dimension; and invariably it is deeply concerned with values.

Finally, there is *policy science* in international relations. This kind of theory attempts to provide guidance for action to the decision-makers of nations, or at least to provide insights and aids for coping with specific problems of the present and expected future. Unlike nearly all empirical theory, the output of policy science is cast in relatively action-oriented terms that require few or no additional steps in "translation" to be directly comprehensible, and potentially usable, by decision-makers and the bureaucracy. Unlike nearly all, even narrowly targeted, normative theory, the output of policy science is focused less upon the "what" ("withdraw from Southeast Asia") than upon the "how" of policy.

Policy science has been accused of skipping over the problem of values,[2] but we believe that the accusation may partially misconstrue the nature of this kind of theory. Policy science, as we would define it, is itself value-free, although in a different sense from the value-freedom of empirical theory. The policy theorist, acting as such, accepts the values of the constitutionally authorized decision-makers of his nation and offers contingent advice: "if you want to accomplish x, do y in your policy." The policy objectives *initially* favored by the decision-maker, however, often do not adequately reflect the values to which he subscribes. In our view, the policy scien-

[2] Stanley Hoffmann, "Theory and International Relations," in *The State of War* (New York, Praeger, 1965), p. 15.

tist's functions include the important task of value clarification. When necessary, the policy analyst should indeed urge that the objectives of current or contemplated policy be redefined to make them more consistent with what he perceives to be the more final goals of decision-makers. However he does not assert his own "final" goals or values (except perhaps negatively by declining to assist in implementing certain policies).

This tripartite distinction among the varieties of possible international relations theory is a useful one, so long as it is kept in mind that few theories fit wholly into one one of these categories. If one is surveying the intellectual geography, a more useful way of arraying theories might be to envision these three ideal-types as the points of an equilateral triangle, where any or almost any actual, present-day theory is located somewhere on the "field" within the triangle. Nearly all theories contain, explicitly or implicitly, elements or aspects of all three; and from the viewpoint of the detached scholar, any of them can and should be assessed from all three viewpoints.[3]

But if one is examining not some particular theory but the shape of international relations theory as a whole, then it is striking that the distribution of extant theories is far from even around this triangular field. We would argue that policy science in international affairs is notably underdeveloped, compared to empirical theory, and even perhaps to normative theory. There is the theory of strategic deterrence, the strategic balance, and the management of the strategic arms race—which seems to have been a considerable success. There are a few others, some of which we will take up shortly. But the "policy sciences"

---

[3] The authors thus accept the view that it is impossible to construct theory which is *entirely* value-free, and that "empirical theory," while being predominantly or perhaps overwhelmingly so, will necessarily reflect some values, if only implicitly in the theorist's selection and formulation of what he considers to be significant problems. At the same time, we vigorously reject the notion, prevalent in some circles, that for this reason there are no useful distinctions to be drawn between more and less "value-laden" theories, or more and less "objective" ones. We view the role of values in theory, or as some philosophers term it, the problem of the relation between the "is" and the "ought," as much more complicated than this simplistic notion implies.

corner of the triangle is populated mainly with free-floating generalizations and isolated insights. The notable fact is that there is relatively little that integrates these, or presents them in ways that decision-makers can employ on an orderly basis. (This is the more striking when one considers the enormous growth within the last five years or so of the policy sciences generally, and of institutions devoted to policy analysis.)

We argue that the underdeveloped state of theory for policy results, in part, from some traditional misconstructions of the role which theory is called upon to play in the decision-makers' creation of policy. That role, we consider, defines intellectual requirements which may be unique to policy science (and for that reason, we believe policy science is indeed usefully viewed as a separate category of theory, as Lippmann suggests.) Following, then, the Aristotelian view that to find out what a theory should be and do, one needs to know first why one needs it or what use one will put it to, we begin with some observations on the role of theory in the decision-making process.[4]

The Policy-Makers' Needs

Consider the decision-maker who is faced with a relatively short-term but serious policy problem: for example, a Berlin crisis, an Indo-Pakistani war, or an upcoming conference on European security. What does the decision-maker already have in hand, and what does he see himself needing from the policy scientist? Typically, he already possesses a moderately large amount of information, with a good deal more readily available. Typically, he also is in possession of a set of goals, at least in the sense of visualized "desired outcomes"; specific policy objectives usually are another matter. And typically, he is (or very rapidly becomes) familiar with his repertoire of available tools

---

[4] This Appendix considers only roles which are the most directly relevant to most deterrence decisions. Certain other roles are identified and discussed in the expanded, *Policy Sciences,* version of this essay.

and resources for implementing any policy—which repertoire, in the short term, usually cannot be much expanded.

But the decision-maker typically is lacking or deficient in several other ingredients for which he may be expected to turn to the policy scientist. He needs help in sorting and comprehending his information; in understanding the connections between his desired outcome and the possible concrete policy objectives; and in making a selection from his repertoire of tools. Let us pause for a moment on these needs.

In many cases, and especially in crisis and near-crisis situations, the decision-maker will need assistance in comprehending *the meaning of the information* he possesses about the problem at hand. Although this information may be deficient in important respects, it is likely to be abundant (perhaps even overabundant) in other respects. In any event, the available facts rarely speak for themselves; they need to be interpreted. The nature of the situation facing him is a problem, not a "given," for the decision-maker. Do the available facts suggest that the situation is of one sort, or another sort? Is the Soviet ultimatum demanding the "normalization" of Berlin within six months a probe of the Western position, an attempt to erode it, or the opening gun in a determined assault? Is Saigon the losing capital in a civil war or the victim of external aggression it could not reasonably be expected to repel? Decision-makers need to identify what kind of situation they are facing. It is all but impossible for short-term problems to be taken truly *sui generis;* some amount of categorization, labeling, and comparison with past events is inevitable. And a misjudgment here can be serious. In short, decision-makers need help in diagnosing emergent situations.

The determination of what specific policy objectives could best lead to obtaining one's desired outcome and the selection among available policy tools are both *ends-means problems*—at different levels of generality and immediacy.[5] Decision-makers

[5] The distinction between these two levels of ends-means problems is very similar to Austin Ranney's distinction between "decisional outputs" and "policy outcomes"; *Political Science and Public Policy* (Chicago, Markham, 1968), p. 8.

may reasonably expect policy theory to assist them with these problems in matching means to the ends they seek. At its simplest, policy science may merely uncover logical or practical inconsistencies in the ends-means chain and suggest corrective action. More challenging is the identification of a new formula for arranging the means more efficiently or effectively. What mixture of deterrence policies, "compellence" or "coercive diplomacy" policies,[6] and inducement policies will be most likely to preserve the essential Western position in Berlin? Or, within the general policy objective of establishing deterrence in Berlin, what mixture of declaratory statements, private diplomatic messages, and signals such as force mobilization will best meet this objective? Because it needs to be emphasized that policy science serves goals selected by decision-makers, we choose to call this kind of contribution "contingent predictions": statements of the form "means x will best serve end y," or "if you do x the result will be y."

We conclude, then, that policy science can make its most significant contributions to decision-making for what we are terming "short-term problems" by assisting with the *diagnosis* of the problem and with *contingent predictions* regarding the ends-means calculi for it. This is not simply abstract speculation: examination of the U.S. decision-making process in the Cuban missile crisis, for example, reveals that top decision-makers turned to academic and other expert "policy scientists" for help mainly with three questions: What are the Soviet objectives in making this gamble? (diagnosis) Can the Soviets retreat or are they committed to keeping the missiles in Cuba? (diagnosis and contingent prediction both) What are the most likely

---

[6] "Compellence" is a term introduced by Thomas C. Schelling; see *Arms and Influence* (New Haven, Yale University Press, 1966), chapter 2. "Coercive diplomacy" is the preferred term of Alexander L. George, David K. Hall, and William R. Simons, in their work *The Limits of Coercive Diplomacy* (Boston, Little, Brown, 1971). Both terms refer to the use of threats of force to accomplish a "positive" end, requiring the opponent to do something, rather than the "negative" end, as in deterrence, of requiring him not to do something.

escalation scenarios if the U.S. takes certain offensive actions in Cuba? (contingent prediction) [7]

The importance of diagnosis and contingent prediction from policy science is not limited to crisis situations, but applies as well to other policy issues that fit within the category we are calling "short term." Stanley Hoffmann, for instance, provides as an example of policy science for international affairs the literature that flowered in the late 1950s on United States policy vis-à-vis its European partners. Here the policy goals involved fashioning a harmonious and more equal relationship with European powers who had passed out of the historical phase of recovery from the ravages of World War II and were beginning, particularly in the case of France, to assert a more independent attitude. The policy problem was not of the type we are terming "long-range": decision-makers were not contemplating any important reorientation of the U.S. role and posture in the world, nor any significant shift in the values underpinning that role and posture. But they needed to rethink what policies—executed over a period of up to several years—might serve their unchanged ends, and in doing so drew to some unknown degree upon "policy science" literature then being offered on the problem.[8] In this instance, the policy scientist's

---

[7] Accounts within the extensive literature on the Cuban missile crisis which emphasize the U.S. decision-making procedures include Roger Hilsman, *To Move a Nation* (New York, Doubleday, 1967) and "The Cuban Crisis: How Close We Were to War," *Look*, Vol. 28 (August 25, 1964); Arthur M. Schlesinger, *A Thousand Days* (Boston, Houghton Mifflin, 1965); Theodore C. Sorensen, *Kennedy* (New York, Harper & Row, 1965); Elie Abel, *The Missile Crisis* (Philadelphia, Lippincott, 1966); Robert F. Kennedy, *Thirteen Days* (New York, Norton, 1971 edition); Graham T. Allison, *Essence of Decision* (Boston, Little, Brown, 1971); and chapter 3 of George, Hall, and Simons, *The Limits of Coercive Diplomacy*.

The answer to whether the Soviets could retreat or were committed to keeping their missiles in Cuba involved both diagnosis and contingent prediction: it required judgment as to whether the Soviets, by doctrine and practice, could retreat *in general* (diagnosis) plus, on the premise of an affirmative answer to this, judgment about the best means of activating their capability for retreat in the specific circumstances then reigning (contingent prediction).

[8] Stanley Hoffmann, *The State of War* (New York, Praeger, 1965), pp. 10–11.

roles of "diagnosis" and "contingent prediction" may have been somewhat more melded together than they usually are in crisis situations, but they were still distinguishable. Contingent prediction about appropriate policy tools for dealing with DeGaulle, for instance, depended upon but followed diagnoses of how DeGaulle was behaving and why he was behaving that way.[9]

The examples of DeGaulle and the Soviets in Cuba suggest that one way in which policy scientists contribute to the decision-making process is by providing expert knowledge and understanding of specific foreign countries to policy-makers trying to cope with those countries' behavior. (This may be contrasted to understanding and theory about "processes" of interactions among nations; for instance, the arms race, the strategic balance, deterrence, escalation, coercive diplomacy, détente, alliance-formation, accommodation and conciliation, etc.) Indeed, Sovietologists and other national or area specialists have played perhaps the clearest role to date in contributing to decision-making, and perhaps have been the most widely and unreservedly accepted of the policy scientists in policy-making circles. In essence, such specialists supplement the expertise of the State Department's national desks, and of experts elsewhere in the bureaucracy and in the embassies abroad, by providing more scholarly, and wider and deeper historical, knowledge of the nation or area in question. They may also bring to bear formal models of the normal behavior of the subject nation or its

[9] As Hoffmann points out (*Ibid.*), it is true that some of this literature explicitly or implicitly included the theorists' valuation that a steady tightening of the U.S.-European relationship was desirable for its own sake over the long run. (There was also a certain amount of rhetoric to this effect from the Kennedy Administration, though very much less from its predecessor or successor administrations.) Nevertheless, the *policy problem* was perceived overwhelmingly as one of fashioning Atlantic relations in the immediate future as a response to "problems" created by changing conditions. The most influential "policy science" on the problem (such as Henry A. Kissinger's *The Necessity for Choice*, [New York, Harper & Row, 1961], chapter 4) accepted that perception of the issue. However, the instance illustrates that policy science for the short and long terms are rarely completely distinct.

leaders, such as the "operational code".[10] Although largely missing and/or underutilized in some instances—e.g., Vietnam in the early years—this kind of national or area specialization has certainly been of greater utility to date in diagnosis and contingent prediction than the kind of (extremely underdeveloped) policy science that focuses on inter-nation processes like deterrence, escalation, etc.

Consequences of the Lack of an Adequate Policy Science

The need of policy-makers for assistance in diagnosis and contingent prediction and their tendency to turn to the universe of theory for assistance should not be underestimated. In the absence of an adequate policy science to turn to, this need has led to two paradoxically related consequences, both unfortunate.

On the one hand, in the absence of sophisticated assistance in diagnosis and contingent prediction policy-makers tend to apply dangerously oversimplified and/or irrelevant generalizations to their present crisis or problem. As Ernest May discusses at length in *Lessons of History*, American (and other) decision-makers often employ misleading historical analogues, comparing a present problem with a past event in ways that oversimplify, at best, the new issues.[11] Comparing Vietnam to the

[10] See Alexander L. George, "The 'Operational Code': A Neglected Approach to the Study of Political Leaders and Decision-Making," *International Studies Quarterly*, June 1969. The "operational code" method was pioneered by Nathan Leites in his book *The Operational Code of the Politburo* (New York, McGraw-Hill, 1951), and elaborated in his *A Study of Bolshevism* (Glencoe, Ill., The Free Press, 1953).

[11] Ernest R. May, *Lessons of History* (London, Oxford University Press, 1973). A number of other writers have also called attention to the tendency of policy-makers to draw incorrect lessons from history or to misapply correct lessons to new cases; for instance, Robert Jervis, "How Decision-Makers Learn from History" (unpublished MS.). See also the Introduction to George, Hall, and Simons, *The Limits of Coercive Diplomacy*.

Malaysian or the Greek Civil War in ways that ignore the important differences is an obvious example. But the generalizations that are misapplied to present problems can also be, and often are, "theoretical" in nature as well. For instance, "undemocratic regimes launch aggressive wars," "if we appease the opponent now we shall have to fight a much larger war against him later," and "arms races lead inevitably to war," are three highly generalized theories or hypotheses which probably have been applied simplistically to short-term U.S. policy problems within the last few decades. Sometimes decision-makers will wed a misleading historical analogy to an oversimplified theoretical generalization to form a compound, and perhaps even more dangerously erroneous, "working theory." The domino theory, as applied to Southeast Asia, reflects both kinds of errors. One of the most important tasks of the policy scientist is to forestall the use of such oversimplified generalizations.

Yet those interested in policy science can seriously misapprehend how this kind of oversimplification by decision-makers is to be prevented; this brings us to the second unfortunate consequence of the present underdeveloped status of policy theory. Some inhabitants of the world of theory, aware of the dangers of oversimplified or irrelevant generalizations, have chosen to warn that theory *cannot* provide the kind of assistance that policy-makers are looking for. Consider an example: Richard Goodwin, a former policy adviser in the Kennedy and Johnson administrations, has suggested that Thomas Schelling's book *Arms and Influence* is "troubling" because it may tempt decision-makers to employ Schelling's theories in the actual development of policy.[12] Goodwin argues that historical events are *sui generis*, and therefore to try to deduce theory from generalizations from history, as he believes Schelling does, "almost guarantees error." There is no way for policy science to get around this, since to have theory at all one "cannot escape the necessity of drawing general conclusions from particular episodes." Furthermore, Goodwin believes that even if some sort

[12] Goodwin's review appears in *The New Yorker*, February 17, 1968.

of theoretical generalization were somehow derived, its relevance to any immediate policy problem could not be established, since in almost any situation decision-makers must act without knowing all the facts and the variables in the situation "are so numerous that they elude analysis." Goodwin's conclusion, clearly, amounts to the position that policy science for international affairs is impossible—not merely at present, but forever and in principle. This belief, sometimes heard in "softer," more ambiguous, or more reserved positions, appears to define a fairly widespread although probably declining school of thought on the question.

Yet we have just observed that decision-makers themselves feel the need for assistance in diagnosis and in contingent prediction so acutely that when they do not receive it they proceed to employ their own dangerously oversimplified generalizations. It is our conviction that this practice reflects a genuine and urgent "cognitive" need of decision-makers. The fashioners of policy are usually unwilling—indeed may often be unable— to cope with their problems in a wholly nonabstract, atheoretical, *sui generis*, ad hoc manner. Attempts to get them to do so are not merely unhelpful, but risk forcing them unwittingly back onto unexamined, potentially ill-founded, and perhaps only semiconscious generalizations. What is truly needed to prevent decision-makers from falling into the traps of oversimplified theory is not warnings such as Goodwin's that relevant theory is impossible, but the discovery of *what kinds* of relevant theory *may* be possible, identifying both the valid domain of theory and its undoubtedly serious limits.

For the school of thought typified by Goodwin appears to rest upon a mistaken image of the nature of policy science as something that does seek, or ought to seek, to provide decision-makers with detailed, precise, high-confidence prescriptions for action in any contingency, actually at hand or potential. If this is one's view of the scope and role of policy science in international affairs, then indeed this school is correct: such a thing is impossible—as, incidentally, many policy scientists, including Schelling, have noted.

But the choice is not between detailed, precise, high-confidence prescriptions for action and nothing. There are other possibilities, not in degree—we are not advocating undetailed, imprecise, low-confidence prescriptions for action!—but in kind. Policy science should not try to seize the role of offering "prescriptions for action" at all, but should accept other, more feasible, roles.[13] As noted earlier, it is our belief, that diagnosis and contingent prediction are two valid and feasible roles for policy science; neither is by any means the same as "prescription." (Indeed, decision-makers might quite reasonably be suspicious of any attempts by policy scientists to offer detailed prescriptions for action but be receptive to their diagnoses and contingent predictions.) Let us examine further how the decision-maker sees his need for assistance, and why this kind may be valid and feasible.

The "Policy Science" of the Policy-Maker

Policy-makers do not always abuse simple generalizations in seeking to diagnose and predict emerging situations. Rather, they often go beyond available generalizations to try to note, in addition, what is special about the case in hand. That is, they supplement available generalizations with ad hoc assessments of other relevent variables. We need more study of this practice of decision-makers, both for its own value (for political science) and for hints on how policy science can make itself more useful.

This practice apparently can take several different forms. It can consist of interpolating a plausible reconstruction of events intervening between other events which are known and understood. Available theory may seem to explain some portions of a sequence of events adequately, leaving gaps requiring ad hoc

[13] See also, for example, the useful discussion of the relationship between theory and practice in Robert L. Rothstein, *Planning, Prediction and Policy-Making in Foreign Affairs* (Boston, Little, Brown, 1972).

interpolation. (This method is reminiscent of the historian's process of providing a detailed recounting of events occurring between two situations which themselves seem plausibly accounted for by available generalizations.) [14] The decision-makers' practice can also consist of using a concrete theory or model about how a particular nation—say the opponent in a specific situation—is likely to behave, a theory or model which a decision-maker may have developed on the basis of personal experience or which may have been offered to him by policy science. Or, in making contingent predictions about the outcomes of his own policy decisions, he may employ a similar theory or model about how his own nation (his own bureaucratic structure, his own missions abroad, his own army) is likely to behave. Decision-makers sometimes search mentally for the presence or absence of one or more key variables, which presence or absence they have previously concluded is likely to have critical leverage upon the situation in some way.[15] Finally, policy-makers often seek to learn not only what is similar between the current situation and some past one (this amounts to a simple generalization), but also what is different between the current situation and one or more past ones which in *some* respects seem similar (this also amounts to an implicit generalization, of a different and slightly more complicated kind).

We observe, then, that decision-makers receive, in effect, one or more simple models of their problem, made up of selected facts and simple generalizations or analogies, from interests within the bureaucracy or from the "conventional wisdom."

[14] Carl Hempel argues that some historical events can be identified adequately with explanatory generalizations, but that others require an explanation that is "filled out" with a detailed reconstruction of what occurred. See his essay "The Function of General Laws in History" in *Readings in Philosophical Analysis,* ed. H. Feigl and W. Sellars (New York, Appleton-Century-Crofts, 1949).

[15] For instance, Dean Acheson was quite explicit about searching in situations he faced for the "missing ingredient"—that is, the element which, if provided by the United States, would materially alter developments. If no such element could be found, he would recommend against taking action. See David S. McLellan, "The 'Operational Code' Approach to the Study of Political Leaders: Dean Acheson's Philosophical and Instrumental Beliefs," *Canadian Journal of Political Science,* IV, No. 1 (March 1971), 63.

But the sophisticated decision-maker attempts to move beyond that simple model (and/or weigh competing simple models) by extending it in various directions to make it fit the situation more accurately and hence more diagnostically, and/or to make it generate contingent predictions of genuine utility. It is really for assistance in this process of *extending and enriching* the model he will use for decisions that the policy-maker turns to policy science. And it is to this process of extending and enriching the model—in useful ways, of course—that policy science should be much better prepared to contribute than it now is.

With this conceptualization of the role of policy science, we can begin to espy the appropriate relationships between policy science and the more traditional, better-developed "empirical theory" of international relations, upon which, we noted earlier, the policy scientist needs to draw to fulfill this role. We can usefully distinguish what might be termed, without prejudice, "passive" and "active" postures he might take in this process. In a very short period of time—days, weeks, or even a month or two—it is usually not possible for the policy scientist to do more than "passively" draw upon the present stock of knowledge and theory in the area of his expertise. In this posture, he can only acquaint himself with the simple models or model which decision-makers are employing (or as much of these as they will share), assess their validity in the light of his expertise, and assist the decision-makers in enlarging their diagnostic and predictive model to make it as appropriate as possible. The policy scientist may be very "active" indeed, in that even in this posture he should not simply answer the questions that decision-makers pose to him, but rather should examine their operating model critically. Of course, he should provide, as he can, diagnostic and predictive variables which the decision-makers already understand to be relative "unknowns"; but in addition, he should attempt to recheck the values which decision-makers have assigned to other variables and provide as he can additional variables which decision-makers may not have thought of.

"Adaptation" is a perfectly satisfactory term to describe how the policy scientist, in this posture, draws upon existing empirical theory in international relations to assist decision-makers with their problems in diagnosis and prediction. The policy scientist cannot, after all, expect to be either cleverer or more skillful at operating bureaucratic systems than the decision-makers; what legitimizes his participation in the decision-making process is his specialized knowledge of empirical theory (and/or of a particular nation's normal behavior), and his skill at adapting that knowledge rapidly and flexibly into the terms that are appropriate for the problem at hand. The use of policy scientists expert in escalation dynamics and in Soviet behavior at the time of the Cuban missile crisis is perhaps the paradigmatic example of this "passive" posture for policy scientists. The posture is a familiar one to all those engaged in policy science, and does not need to be dwelt on here.

But what do policy scientists in the sphere of international affairs do when they are not in this posture, advising on some immediate problem like a crisis? One thing they can do is cease to be policy scientists and take up academic research on the general and theoretical problems of empirical (or normative) theory. Research on these problems as they are traditionally conceived may or may not have much relevance to policy. Another thing they can do, which is currently popular, is to turn their gaze from the substantive to the "efficiency" aspects of policy science: e.g., cost-effectiveness and other approaches to resource allocation, or concern with efficiency in management and operating procedures. But such scholars can also work to increase the potential usefulness of the substantive theories and knowledge which make up their grocery bag of potential contributions to decision-making. In international affairs as a discipline, it is acceptable and common to refer to this kind of activity as "increasing the policy relevance" of what is nevertheless still "empirical" theory. (Under this view, presumably the individual is acting *qua* policy scientist only while studying efficiency questions or while actually engaged in "passively" adapting empirical theory to the immediate needs of an urgent policy problem.) For reasons to be stated momentarily, however, we prefer to take the view that research aimed directly at increasing the usefulness of theory to policy will generally have a somewhat different character from that of most "empirical theory," and therefore can and perhaps should be considered something else, i.e., policy science.

The policy scientist who is not engaged in immediate assistance in decision-making therefore has the option of doing policy science research on problems—which may even be fairly abstract, so long as they are of policy relevance. (For example, he might work on interaction "processes"—the arms race, deterrence, coercive diplomacy, etc.)" [16] We see this as an "active" posture for the policy scientist, in the sense that he is actively expanding the universe of theories, hypotheses, etc., directly applicable to policy issues, rather than passively transmitting whatever that universe contains at any particular moment into the decision-making circles. In this posture, the policy scientist clearly is doing something more complicated and more creative than simply adapting empirical theory to policy purposes.

One motivation for this kind of research could be the theorist's awareness of the severe inadequacies of contemporary empirical theory for the task of expanding and enriching the decision-makers' working model of a problem. Can we say more about the nature and sources of this inadequacy and about what the policy scientist can do toward remedying it? [17]

Comprehensive and Contingent Generalizations

We have already advanced the possibility that each of the three principal domains of international relations theory may

[16] "Policy science" as it is identified here is similar to what Davis B. Bobrow calls the "engineering analytic framework." See chapter 3 of his *International Relations: New Approaches* (New York, The Free Press, 1972).

[17] In the remainder of the discussion we exclude the kind of policy science involved in national or area studies such as Sovietology, preferring to focus on the more puzzling aspect of policy science: theory about "processes" such as arms control, deterrence, escalation control, etc. A clear distinction between "policy science" and "empirical science" in national and area studies is probably both impossible and unnecessary, anyway.

have its own intellectual or other "requirements" (and in that sense are indeed usefully seen as separate categories of theory). A fully adequate analysis of the differing requirements of empirical and policy theory would be a major undertaking and is not yet even in sight. But at this point we would suggest *one* significant difference which appears to play a key role in defining the mutual relationship of these two domains of theory.

Empirical theory, we would argue, is understood very widely to "require" the production of what we would term "comprehensive generalizations." By this we mean laws, rules, correlations, or other generalizations which attempt to identify and explain all or nearly all phenomena of any particular class. Examples might include "rules" as aggregated as the hoary "wars are the result of miscalculation" or generalizations as ostensibly policy-relevant as the principle that "deterrence depends upon the successful signaling of a credible commitment." (Comprehensive generalizations, as we shall point out, are to be contrasted with generalizations that identify and explain only a specific portion of the phenomena in any class.) Normally in constructing empirical theory, it is presumed that the more cases which can be found to which a generalization does *not* apply, the less useful and/or true it is. If there are too many, the generalization must be thrown out. This "decision rule" for the building of empirical theory seems to be quite pervasive, and to be accepted by qualitatively and quantitatively oriented theorists alike. A few examples may illustrate (though not prove) the pervasiveness of this desideratum.

The "realist theory" is a "classical" empirical theory in international affairs.[18] It defines the goal of states to be the pursuit of "interests" and of "power" needed to secure them. This theory has been elaborated in considerable, and in some respects widely convincing, detail. As developed to date, however, it has

---

[18] The "realist theory" has collected to itself a reasonable amount of literature. The core statements of the theory probably remain, however, Hans J. Morgenthau's works, *Politics among Nations: the Struggle for Power and Peace* (3d ed.; New York, Knopf, 1960), and "Another 'Great Debate': The National Interest of the United States," *American Political Science Review*, XLVI, No. 4 (December 1952).

not proven successful at identifying or explaining *which* interests or forms of power nations pursue under *which* particular circumstances.

Another kind of empirical theorizing constructs hypothetical models; examples include Morton Kaplan's "systems theory," [19] George Modelski's "theory of foreign policy," [20] and George Liska's "equilibrium theory." [21] Theories of this variety have in common the construction of an abstract world in which formally defined entities are allowed to make formally defined moves; logically compelling conclusions can be obtained. But questions of which moves real nations choose to make in what kinds of real-world situations are not touched by this kind of theory.

Another kind is the "correlational" variety exemplified by the "Correlates of War" and "Dimensionality of Nations" projects.[22] Such studies have the important strength of identifying factors correlating with important phenomena such as war, on a basis which is at once rigorous and empirical. But they have not yet been refined to the point of defining factors which correlate only under some (defined) circumstances with variables of policy relevance.

Another kind is the "decision-making approach" pioneered by Richard Snyder and his colleagues.[23] But as time has passed it has become clear that it is precisely an *approach*, not a theory; and that there are, in fact, *many* decision-making approaches, not one. (Some of these approaches have justifiably attracted the attention of theorists interested in policy, however,

[19] Morton Kaplan, *System and Process in International Politics* (New York, Wiley, 1957).

[20] George A. Modelski, *A Theory of Foreign Policy* (London, Pall Mall Press, 1962).

[21] George Liska, *International Equilibrium* (Cambridge, Harvard University Press, 1957).

[22] J. David Singer, "The 'Correlates of War' Project: Interim Report and Rationale," *World Politics*, XXIV, No. 2 (January 1972); R. J. Rummel, "Some Empirical Findings on Nations and Their Behavior," *World Politics*, XXI, No. 2 (January 1969).

[23] Richard Snyder, H. W. Bruck, and Burton Sapin, *Foreign-Policy Decision-Making* (New York, The Free Press, 1962).

since they can include variables of interest and relevance to decision-makers.)

Another kind of empirical theorizing picks out a particular process of interactions among nations, ostensibly on grounds of policy-relevance, but proceeds to study it mainly—again—in search of comprehensive generalizations. Almost certainly the most thoroughly examined such process is deterrence, on which quite a sizable literature has grown up over the last twenty years. But (as noted in chapter 3), this literature turns out to be derived to a quite striking degree deductively from decision- and game-theory postulates; and devoted very largely to the search for general rules about, for instance, "how to make one's deterrence commitment credible," rather than rules about, for instance, "when and when not to apply deterrence policies."

We would not push our argument to its logical extreme. After all, as noted at the outset, nearly all existing theories can be viewed as being "inside" the triangle, possessing normative and policy as well as empirical properties. But—as a generalization probably "comprehensive" enough to pass most tests of empirical theorists!—there appears to be a pervasive tendency for empirical theory in international affairs to search for and embrace conclusions that assertedly cover all or most cases in any given class. Such "comprehensive generalizations," to the extent they apply only to *some* rather than to nearly all cases, tend to be *rejected* on just that ground. Whether this is a necessary and/or desirable requirement of empirical theory we shall not debate here. It may be. Our point is that it is a requirement somewhat inimical to the needs of policy science.

If we are correct that decision-makers seek assistance from theory primarily for diagnosis and contingent prediction in coping with their short-term problems, then their needs cannot normally be met by comprehensive generalizations. Theoretical conclusions that are (or try to be) valid at all times and places, or even ones that are valid, say, of all post-Renaissance, or post-Napoleonic, or even postnuclear, cases, are of quite limited value to the policy-maker precisely because of their comprehensiveness. If they apply to all cases the policy-maker will or could experience, then they are a constant part of the background, like the speed of sound or the length of the day.

For purposes of diagnosis and contingent prediction in a short-term, current problem, decision-makers need—and *a fortiori* policy scientists need—theoretical conclusions of a more sophisticated order: conclusions that identify how relevant situational variables change and vary according to circumstances. We call conclusions of this kind "contingent generalizations": generalizations which may or may not be true, according to the contingency, and which specify the contingencies that "activate" or "validate" them. Generalizations such as those identifying when and when not to attempt to apply deterrence policies, or when and how to rescue or reinforce a failing or challenged deterrence posture might exemplify this kind of contingent generalization.

Contingent generalizations are by no means absent from what policy scientists traditionally have provided decision-makers. But they tend to be offered in an unsystematic and ad hoc—and hence only somewhat useful—fashion. Most knowledgable and experienced empirical theorists have a "sense" of when many of their generalizations apply and when they do not, and can offer advice in this vein, particularly when the decision-maker is clever enough to demand explicitly just this kind of assistance. But the lack of deliberate theoretical attention to contingent generalizations tends to give such advice a haphazard quality, and to make it far more dependent than is necessary or desirable on the "wisdom" of the individual theorist. (This is the basis of our remark at the outset that the "policy science" corner of the triangle of international affairs theory tends to be populated mainly by "free-floating generalizations and isolated insights.") Further and perhaps more dangerous: the widespread lack of deliberate attention to contingent generalizations has tended to obscure many points of direct policy importance—when and when not to expect a deterrence policy to be successful, for instance, or the preconditions required for launching a strategy of coercive diplomacy.[24]

[24] Eight such preconditions are identified in George, Hall, and Simons, *The Limits of Coercive Diplomacy*, chapter 5.

Another set of labels for the distinction in kinds of theoretical conclusions we are advancing might be "undifferentiated" versus "differentiated" generalizations. What decision-makers seek from policy science is *differentiated theory*—theory that discriminates among different cases and classes of cases to throw up variables of direct diagnostic and predictive significance. A policy-relevant theory of escalation control, for example, needs to differentiate among different classes of cases that arise, the differing populations of significant variables in the different classes, and the values of these variables that have implications or meaning for potential policy situations.[25]

Indeed, one could view decision-makers themselves as a genus of ad hoc, intuitive policy theorists who deal with differentiated generalizations. One could then argue that policy scientists should do systematically, carefully, and regularly what decision-makers do intuitively, hastily, and proximately. If so, policy science would do well to look closely at how decision-makers go about coping with their problems for insights into the logic of policy science itself. We listed earlier some of the ways decision-makers try to go beyond available simple generalizations to generate a richer and more useful model of their immediate problem. Here is the same list cast into more formal language:

(1) within the case, they differentiate between what seems to be and what seems not to be covered by available generalizations;

(2) they differentiate the behavior of particular nations from the general behavior of all nations in situations of the same kind (the particular nations receiving special attention being primarily the opponent and one's own);

(3) they differentiate what is distinctive in their own case compared with other, somewhat similar ones;

(4) they differentiate their own and similar cases from the general run of cases of the same basic kind; and

(5) they differentiate "key variables" thought to have a leverage effect from the totality of variables present.

[25] This approach to the problem of escalation control is attempted in Richard Smoke, *Controlling Escalation* (forthcoming).

The second item involves the function of national or area specialists, but the others primarily concern processes of interaction among nations. To a large degree these could be studied before the emergence of a particular problem, precisely because problems are not entirely *sui generis* but fall into families along various dimensions. (While any new problem will of course possess some features that can hardly be anticipated, many of its variables will be of kinds that can be isolated and differentiated in advance.)

The Utility Criterion for Contingent Generalizations

The objection may be raised that contingent generalizations of the kind being advocated there are too difficult and sophisticated a kind of theorizing for the present state of the art, and of our knowledge, to bear. This objection would have force if it were assumed that contingent generalizations, to be useful, would have to enjoy the same degree of validation and formal verification that is enjoyed by acceptable comprehensive generalizations in empirical theory. Such is not the case, however. This brings us to a *second* key difference between empirical theory and policy science.

Empirical theory rightly is greatly concerned with the task of validating its conclusions, and has developed moderately stiff tests for doing so, because this kind of theory fundamentally is concerned with discovering what is *true* about the international system. Policy science, however, is fundamentally concerned with what is relevant and *useful* to say about that system for decision-makers. What is true and what is useful are intimately connected, but they are not the same. Policy science is permitted to, indeed probably is required to, generate relevant conclusions for decision-makers, *even though* these may enjoy a lesser degree of verification. To enrich their simple models of problems, decision-makers can validly employ theoretical conclusions which are not "established" or widely accepted as generally true, because it is always possible to judge whether these general hypotheses are *at least true and relevant for the case at hand.* It should be clear that the "contingent generalizations" we have just discussed represent a kind of theory which is peculiarly appropriate to this standard of admissibility. Conversely, one of the reasons so much traditional empirical theory is so irrelevant to policy-makers is that its variables and generalizations have been selected with a view to meeting the tests of verification and validation rather than the tests of utility.

Policy scientists are not hereby relieved of *all* responsibility for the "truth content" of their generalizations, rules, and principles. But our reasoning does imply that the criteria of admissibility of generalizations into the domain of policy science are different from those of generalizations into empirical theory. What, in detail, the criteria of admissibility for policy science shall be doubtless will be worked out over a long time. Here we will confine ourselves to a single observation. The utility or applicability of any generalization to a particular policy problem can only be determined, of course, when that problem arises. In preparing theory for placement "on the shelf" until that time, however, a criterion of *plausibility* would seem appropriate as a "truth test" for many kinds of policy science generalization. If, for instance, one is interested in escalation dynamics at low levels of violence and even in mere threats of violence, and if in researching this as a policy scientist one is examining Cold War case studies, it does *not* seem necessary for *policy* theory to know, for instance, the Soviets' exact mix of motives in the Berlin area. One can derive conclusions of policy relevance from a plausible assumption about this (and more such conclusions, usually, from alternative plausible assumptions). What represents a plausible assumption, however, is not arbitrary. One criterion might be: an assumption is plausible for the purposes of policy science if it does not contradict established facts, and if some facts, at least, support it.

The Growing Appreciation
of Differentiated Theory

The contingent generalizations and differentiated theory being advocated here as important ingredients of policy science are not entirely new, of course. The problem of making orderly identifications of differences in particular cases or subclasses of cases from other cases in the same general category is one of growing interest in the behavioral sciences—for instance, in the field of comparative politics, where the traditional problem of reconciling "configurative" and "nomothetic" studies is a close analogue to the policy scientist's problem of finding or making generalizations that will be relevant for decision-makers. Sidney Verba has examined this problem, arriving at an approach similar to the one being advocated here:

> To be comparative, we are told, we must look for generalizations or covering laws that apply to all cases of a particular type. But where are the general laws? Generalizations fade when we look at particular cases. We add intervening variable after intervening variable. Since the cases are few in number, we end up with an explanation tailored to each case. The result begins to sound quite idiographic or configurative. . . . We shall get closer to [a] resolution if we realize that the dichotomy between the generalized law approach [i.e., comprehensive generalizations] and the configurative-idiographic approach [i.e., each case *sui generis*] is false. The patterns for which we try to account . . . are immensely complicated. . . . But the "unique" explanation of a particular case can rest on general hypotheses. What is needed, then, is a *disciplined* configurative approach. The approach could be described as multivariate analysis if the variables were more easily quantified and amenable to statistical treatment. . . .[26]

Recently, Harry Eckstein has distinguished "disciplined-configurative" studies from other varieties, such as "heuristic" and "plausibility probe" studies. Virtually suggesting our present argument for differentiated theory in *policy* science, he points

[26] Sidney Verba, "Some Dilemmas in Comparative Research," *World Politics*, XIX, No. 1 (October 1967), 111–27.

out that "disciplined- configurative study is related to theory as applied science is to pure science." [27]

There have been several studies to date within the field of international affairs that have tried various approaches to the generation of differentiated theory and contingent generalizations. In *The Politics of Force* [28] Oran Young formulates a small number of specific hypotheses and examines them in the context of a specific set of Cold War crises, attempting to account for variations in the outcomes. Lincoln Bloomfield and Amelia Leiss, in their *Controlling Small Wars*, [29] study fourteen post–World War II cases, employing thirteen general groups of factors encouraging the escalation or deescalation of conflict, attempting to explain variations in factors across cases that might be relevant to conflict-control. Ole Holsti's *Crisis, Escalation, and War* [30] compares two cases in particular (the outbreak of World War I and the Cuban missile crisis) and several others in lesser degree, with respect to psychological and decision-making factors in escalation. Alexander George, David Hall, and William Simons, in *The Limits of Coercive Diplomacy*, examine three recent cases in depth, attempting to uncover variables explaining the failure in one case and the differing degrees of success in the other two cases of a particular foreign policy technique.[31] All these efforts attempt to generate differentiated theory, employing moderately but not greatly divergent research methodologies. All are oriented toward the generation of policy-relevant theory.

All of them, however, are also of some utility in the con-

[27] Harry Eckstein, "Case Study and Theory in Macropolitics" (unpublished MS., July 1971). A revised version of this paper will appear in Fred I. Greenstein and Nelson Polsby, eds., *A Handbook of Political Science* (forthcoming).

[28] Oran Young, *The Politics of Force* (Princeton, Princeton University Press, 1968).

[29] Lincoln Bloomfield and Amelia Leiss, *Controlling Small Wars* (New York, Knopf, 1970).

[30] Ole Holsti, *Crisis, Escalation and War* (Montreal, McGill–Queen's University Press, 1972).

[31] George, Hall, and Simons, *Limits of Coercive Diplomacy*.

struction of empirical theory. Our last point on the relationship of policy science and empirical theory is to emphasize the *interactive* quality of the relationship. Variables thrown up by the kind of differentiated theory we have discussed here—or by other useful approaches to the problems of assisting decision-makers in diagnosis and contingent prediction—will inevitably be of interest as well to the purely abstract theorist who is interested in enriching his empirical explanations of international reality. For instance, as noted in chapter 21, an enlarged and enriched theory of "inter-nation influence" might emerge from policy scientists' research into different forms and patterns of deterrence phenomena, coercive diplomacy phenomena, and—where knowledge is now sorely lacking—inducement or conciliation phenomena. Even from a purely academic viewpoint, therefore, the policy scientist need not fear that intellectually he may be a "second class citizen." The results of his work will end up irrigating the fields of scholarly theory as well as the plots of policy-makers.[32]

What we are suggesting, in sum, is that the policy scientist can and should reproduce certain features from both the principal audiences or clients with whom he interacts. From the empirical theorists he can reproduce many specific research methods, as well as the general scientific procedure of examining phenomena systematically. But from decision-makers he can reproduce a good deal of the basic logic of the "decision model enrichment" process. Employing ingredients from these two worlds (but heuristically) he can maximize his value to the fashioners of policy, while launching an interactive dialogue with the empirical theorists that will redound to the benefit of policy and empirical theory alike.

[32] Bruce M. Russett discusses aspects of the problem of "differentiated theory" (although not calling it that), and focuses on appropriate research methodologies for it, in his essay "International Behavior Research: Case Studies and Cumulation," in Michael Haas and Henry S. Kariel, *Approaches to the Study of Political Science* (Scranton, Pa., Chandler, 1970).

Index

NOTE: This Index includes the names of authors referred to in the text or in footnotes and the names of books and articles referred to in the text. For other authors' names, please consult the chapter bibliographies.